A Cr...

of

English Literature

VOLUME I

DAVID DAICHES

A Critical History
of
English Literature

IN TWO VOLUMES

VOLUME I

Mandarin

A Mandarin Paperback
A CRITICAL HISTORY OF ENGLISH LITERATURE

First published in Great Britain 1960
by Martin Secker & Warburg Limited
Revised edition published 1969
This edition published 1994
by Mandarin Paperbacks
an imprint of Reed International Books Ltd
Michelin House, 81 Fulham Road, London SW3 6RB
and Auckland, Melbourne, Singapore and Toronto

Reprinted 1995, 1996

A CIP catalogue record for this title
is available from the British Library

ISBN 0 7493 1893 7

Printed and bound in Great Britain by
BPC Paperbacks Ltd
A member of
The British Printing Company Ltd

To my former students
on both sides of the Atlantic

però pur va ed andando ascolta

Preface

THIS IS AN AGE of specialist scholars, and for one man to attempt a complete history of English literature is now both rash and unusual. I cannot claim to be a specialist in all the periods on which I have written, nor, in spite of my best attempts, have I been able to keep abreast of all new developments in English studies. But I have been reading English literature continuously and closely ever since I began my studies at Edinburgh University in 1930, and I have long felt the urge to describe the whole scene as I see it. This, therefore, is one man's history of English literature; it is intended less as a work of reference than as a work of description, explanation, and critical interpretation. It is not meant to be looked up, but to be read. I have given myself generous space in dealing with major figures such as Shakespeare and Milton, without bothering whether, in strict terms of relative greatness, they deserve so much more than I have given to some other writers. Indeed, the chapters on Shakespeare and Milton can perhaps stand as independent critical studies, capable of being extracted from the rest of the *History* and read as short books on their own. Nevertheless, though the word "critical" in my title is important, I have tried never to lose sight of the fact that this is a history, not a series of separate critical studies, and the appropriate kinds of historical generalizations and the proper continuity of narrative have, I hope, been maintained throughout. I may sometimes have treated a minor writer who interests me particularly at greater length than he deserves, or rather briefly summarized something important and well known. But I have tried to see my subject steadily and see it whole; and I have tried to write interestingly, less as the impersonal scholar recording facts than as the interested reader sharing his knowledge and opinions.

On matters of pure scholarship I have, of course, often had to depend on the researches of others. On questions of emphasis and assessment I have done so as little as possible, although occasionally even the most conscientious critical historian must be content to take the word of a sympathetic expert about the value of an odd minor work to which he himself has never devoted a great deal of careful attention. Art is long and life is short, and one cannot always be wholly original in everything. I hope, however, that the pattern which a single mind imposes on this vast material will make my account more lively and suggestive than the conscientious composite works of reference by teams of experts, from which I have myself profited but which are not literary history in the sense that this book is intended to be.

I have been more liberal in quotation from the works under discussion than is usual for a literary historian; I have found that the critical side of the work demands this. I have been deliberately inconsistent in the texts of my quotations. As a rule I have modernized spelling and punctuation, though not in Middle English texts, which lose too much by such modernization. In sixteenth-, seventeenth-, and eighteenth-century texts I have retained the original spelling where it is important as giving a period flavor or indicating some historical aspects of the language or of literary convention; otherwise I have modernized it. My principle in this and other matters has been maximum ease of reading compatible with sound scholarship and intellectual responsibility.

DAVID DAICHES

Jesus College, Cambridge
February, 1960

Contents

VOLUME I

VOLUME II

CHAPTER ONE

Anglo-Saxon Literature

THE ANGLO-SAXON INVADERS, who came to Britain in the latter part of the fifth century A.D. and eventually established their kingdoms there, were the founders of what we can properly call English culture and English literature. They gave England its name, its language, and its links with "Germania," that great body of Teutonic peoples whose migrations disrupted the Roman Empire and utterly changed the face of Europe. Some four hundred years before they arrived in Britain, the Roman historian Tacitus had given his account of the Germanic peoples and how they looked to his civilized Roman eyes; and though we can see that Tacitus' *Germania* idealizes the barbarians in order to hold up the noble savage as an example to decadent Rome, we can nevertheless trace in his account something of the qualities of these people as they emerge out of the mists of history and legend at a later period. To the Romans, whose world they threatened and finally overcame, they were "barbarians," appearing out of nowhere to endanger, with their primitive vigor and alien ways of thought, both the political structure of the Empire and the ideological structure of Greco-Roman thought. After the Roman Empire had become Christianized, the contrast between barbarian and Roman was even more striking, for the former were heathen and their life and their society reflected heroic ideals far removed from Roman Christian theory or practice. Yet the history of much of Europe in the so-called "Dark Ages" is the story of the gradual fusion of these two ways of life and thought, the growing together of barbarian and Christian and the grounding of both in an appropriately modified phase of the Greco-Roman tradition.

Precisely who the invaders were whom we have for so long called "Anglo-Saxon" is not of primary importance to the student of literature. That they belonged to the group of Teutonic peoples to which we can appropriately give Tacitus' name of Germania is clear. According to Bede, writing his ecclesiastical history of England two hun-

3

dred years and more after their arrival, they came "from three very powerful nations of the Germans: that is, from the *Saxones, Angli,* and the *Iutae.*" We know something about the Saxons, who appear to have come from the low country south of Denmark and east of Holland, the modern Holstein. The Angles appear to have lived in modern Jutland and the neighboring islands before they appeared in Britain, while the Jutes, whose origin is the most obscure of the three, perhaps came from the country east of the lower Rhine and perhaps, though less probably (the apparent similarity of names not being the cogent argument it might appear to the modern ear), from Jutland. In Anglo-Saxon England there were Saxon kingdoms (in the south and southwest), Anglian kingdoms (in the east, north, and midlands), and the Jutish kingdom of Kent in the southeast. The cultural differences between the three groups are of comparatively little moment: their language was essentially the same, though with important dialectical differences; and they all considered themselves part of "Germania," that loosely associated group of peoples who included Goths, Burgundians, Lombards, and others, and who had a common set of heroes who might belong to any one of these.

Of the Romanized Britons whom the invading Anglo-Saxons pushed into western corners of England the historian of English literature has little to say. A Celtic people who had been taken into the Roman Empire, they were left to fend for themselves when the Romans, desperately trying to hold their empire together against barbarian invaders, withdrew from England in A.D. 410. A prey to the ruder Picts and Scots in the north, they soon found themselves more seriously threatened by the invaders from across the North Sea, to whom they were an alien people known as "Welsh," which was simply the Germanic peoples' name for foreigners who were not part of Germania. Only in Wales have these Cambro-Britons continuously preserved their language and their traditions; their contribution to specifically English literature is sporadic and oblique, and does not appear until long after the Anglo-Saxon period. If Arthur, who plays such an important part in Middle English romance, was really a historical Cambro-British character from this period—and we have no mention of him before the ninth century except for a passing remark by an early seventh-century Welsh poet that a certain warrior, while brave, "was not Arthur"—there is still no reason for considering his metamorphosis into a hero of medieval romance and a focus for a host of "Arthurian" stories as any part of a direct and continuous heritage from Celtic Britain into later times. It was not until the twelfth century, when English literature sought its inspiration from the French, that the Arthurian romances began to appear, and while it is true that it was an Englishman, Geoffrey of Monmouth, who first elaborated the Arthurian story (in his *Historia Regum Britanniae*) to provide rich material for these romances, the Anglo-French development of the material is very far removed from any Celtic origins. Whatever the origins of the Arthurian story, therefore, we are justified in beginning the history of English literature with the Anglo-Saxons.

Of surviving Anglo-Saxon literature, that which brings us most closely into contact with the Germanic origins of the invaders is the heroic poetry, which still bears traces not only of the pre-Christian heroic society of the continental Saxons and others, but also of that community of subject which linked these early English with the wider civilization of Germania. This is written in the language we know as Old English or Anglo-Saxon, which is essentially the English language in an earlier stage of its development, with inflections which have since disappeared, a relatively small vocabulary from which many words have since been lost (though some which are lost to standard English remain in altered form in Scots and in regional English dialects), and significant differences between, for example, the West Saxon dialect of the south and the Anglian dialect of Northumbria. The verse is alliterative and stressed, without rhyme, each line containing four stressed syllables and a varying number unstressed. There is a definite pause (caesura) between the two halves of each line, with two stresses in each half.

> We geascodon   Eormenrices
> wylfenne geþoht;   ahte wide folc
> Gotena rices;   þæt wæs grim cyning.
> Sæt secg monig   sorgum gebunden,
> wean on wenan,   wyscte geneahhe
> þæt þæs cynerices   ofercumen wære.

To the superficial eye this looks very far removed from modern English; and in a sense it is. (The letter þ—"thorn"—has the sound of "th.") But a literal translation helps to bring out its relation to modern English:

> We have learned of Eormanric's
> wolfish disposition; he held wide dominion
> in the realm of the Goths. That was a cruel king.
> Many a man sat bound in sorrows,
> anticipating woe, often wishing
> that his kingdom were overcome.

Some thirty thousand lines of Anglo-Saxon poetry have survived, nearly all of it contained in four manuscripts,[1] and we have no reason to believe that the older, nonreligious poetry that survives is more than a casually preserved fragment of what was written. Specifically religious poetry might be expected to have earned ecclesiastical care and preservation, but the heroic poetry which connects more directly with the Germanic origins of the Anglo-Saxons could not be expected to arouse any special ecclesiastical interest even when it had been superficially purged of its pagan feeling and in some degree Christianized in thought. The conversion of the English peoples began with the arrival of Augustine in Kent in 597; he had been sent by Gregory the Great with a band of monks in order to achieve this missionary task. But, though Æthelberht, king of Kent, was duly converted to Christianity and Augustine was soon able to establish the seat of his bishopric at Canterbury, the permanent establishment of Christianity throughout England proved a much lengthier task and one which required the active intervention of Celtic missionaries from Ireland and Scotland. Differences between the customs and practices of the Irish Church—which had remained somewhat isolated from Rome—and the Roman Church, which had sponsored Augustine's mission, made for certain difficulties between those English ecclesiastics who looked to Rome and those who looked to Iona and to Ireland, and these were not resolved until the Synod of Whitby in 663;[2] but it is sufficient for the historian of literature to note that the development of English Christianity was not continuous but sporadic for the first century and more, with certain notable setbacks such as the defeat and death of the Christian Edwin, king of Northumbria, at the hands of the pagan Penda, king of Mercia, in 632, which meant the disappearance of the Christian Church in Northumbria until its re-establishment by Aidan and his followers from Iona. If even the external ecclesiastical organization was thus unstable in the early centuries, it is not difficult to see how traces of pagan thought in varying kinds of relation to Christianity persisted for some time after the nominal conversion of the English.

[1] These are: (1) MS Cotton Vitellius A XV in the British Museum, which contains *Beowulf, Judith,* and three prose works. (2) The Junius Manuscript in the Bodleian Library, Oxford (MS Bodleian Junius 11), which contains *Genesis, Exodus, Daniel,* and *Christ and Satan.* (3) The Exeter Book, given by Bishop Leofric to Exeter Cathedral, containing *Christ, Juliana, The Wanderer, The Seafarer, Widsith, Deor,* and many other short pieces. (4) The Vercelli Book, preserved in the cathedral library at Vercelli, in northern Italy, which contains *Andreas, The Fates of the Apostles, Address of the Soul to the Body, The Dream of the Rood,* and *Elene.*

[2] Not 664, as is traditionally held. Bede dates it 664, but he begins his year in September, and as the Synod can be shown to have been held in late September or early October, this would mean 663 in our dating.

Unfortunately, though much is known in general about the mythology of the Germanic and the Norse peoples, we have very little definite information about the heathen background of Old English culture. Though we can draw analogies between what we know of Scandinavian heathendom and what we surmise of its Old English equivalent, the fact remains that the common origin of the two was already far in the past by the time we find the Anglo-Saxons in England. Old English place names give some indication of pre-Christian activity associated with certain localities in Anglo-Saxon England, but tell us nothing of the larger patterns of attitude and belief which are of the most relevance for a study of the literature. That Anglo-Saxon heroic poetry, even as we have it, is the product of a pagan heroic society and in social tone and general mood bears evidence of its origins, can hardly be disputed. But debate on the degree to which *Beowulf*, for example, has been modified by a relatively sophisticated Latin culture—not only by Christian sentiment but, as has been claimed, by a Virgilian tradition—cannot be resolved without knowledge of more details than it seems likely we shall ever possess about primitive Anglo-Saxon beliefs. On the whole, it would seem likely that *Beowulf* and such other remains of early English heroic poetry as survive are closer to their pagan origins in mood and purpose than is sometimes believed.

Though there are difficulties in placing the earliest extant Anglo-Saxon poetry in its cultural context, we can take some comfort from the knowledge that what has survived of Anglo-Saxon poetry, fragmentary though it is and an arbitrary sample though it may be, is of earlier date than any extant poetry of the other Germanic literatures —of Old High German or Old Norse, for example. Anglo-Saxon heroic poetry is the nearest we can get to the oral pagan literature of the Heroic Age of Germania. The stressed alliterative verse of Anglo-Saxon poetry is clearly the product of an oral court minstrelsy; it was intended to be recited by the *scop*, the itinerant minstrel who frequented the halls of kings and chiefs and sometimes found continuous service with one master. One of the earliest surviving Anglo-Saxon poems, *Widsith*, is the autobiographical record of such a scop. The poem as we have it is probably not homogeneous—some of the lines seem to be later interpolations—but the core of the work finely reflects the heroic attitude to the bard's function and gives us a fascinating glimpse of the Germanic world as it appeared to the imagination of the Anglo-Saxons. The text we have of the poem is in the Exeter Book, and is thus tenth-century and in the West Saxon dialect; the poem—which must have been originally composed in Northumbria—dates from the late seventh or early eighth century, though parts of it must be older even than that. Widsith, the "far wanderer," tells of his travels throughout the Germanic world and mentions the many rulers he has visited. Many of the characters he mentions figure in other poems—in *Beowulf*, for example, and in the fragmentary stories of Finn and Waldhere. The princes he claims to have visited cover virtually the whole Germanic world and their lifetimes extend over two hundred years. He was, he tells us, with Eormanric (the Gothic king who died about 370); "likewise I was in Italy with Ælfwine," he tells us elsewhere in the poem, and Ælfwine is Alboin, king of the Lombards, who died about 572 (and who is, incidentally, the latest character to be mentioned in any Germanic heroic poem). The poem thus cannot be true autobiography. It is, however, something much more interesting than that: it is a view of Germanic history and geography as it appeared to a Northumbrian bard of the seventh century drawing on the traditions of his people. What strikes us most forcibly is its catholicity: praise is meted out impartially to Huns, Goths, Burgundians, Franks, Danes, Swedes, Angles, Wends, Saxons, Langobards, and many others. "Ætla [Attila] ruled the Huns, Eormanric the Goths, Becca the Bannings, Gifica the Burgundians, . . . Theodric ruled the Franks, Thyle the Rondings, Breoca the Brondings, Billing the Wærnas. Oswine ruled the Eowan, and Gefwulf the Jutes, Fin Folcwalding the race of the Frisians. . . . Offa ruled Angel, Alewih the Danes; he was the most courageous of all these men, but he did not excel Offa in his mighty deeds." We are given here a bird's eye view of the subject matter of Germanic heroic poetry; and we are reminded that the heroes of that poetry were not regional or national but common to all Germania.

Widsith may be primitive stuff as poetry—indeed, the first catalogue of rulers in the poem is cast in the form of a very early type of genealogical verse and may well date from the beginning of the sixth century or even from before the coming of the Anglo-Saxons to Britain—but it is this very primitive quality which is of most interest. In its combination of historical memories and heroic traditions it shows us something of the historical foundations of heroic poetry and reminds us of the nature and extent of that wide world of Germania which the author of *Beowulf* was equally to take for granted as familiar to his audience and thus as suitable material for allusion and analogy. The whole world of barbarian wanderings and conquests—the world which collided with, in a sense destroyed, and in a sense was absorbed by, the Roman Empire—is here sketched out. And that world provides the orchestration, as it were, for *Beowulf*.

Beowulf holds a special position in Anglo-Saxon literature—indeed, in older Germanic literature as a whole—because it is the only complete extant epic of its kind in an ancient Germanic language. Nowhere else is a traditional theme handled in a long narrative poem against a background which reveals to us the culture and society of the Heroic Age of the Germanic peoples. Whether there were in fact other Anglo-Saxon epics, which have not survived, is a question which may well be debated forever; but the fact remains that *Beowulf* survives in a single manuscript, which was damaged by fire before it was ever studied or transcribed. If it is impossible to determine conclusively whether it was *the* Anglo-Saxon epic or simply *an* Anglo-Saxon epic (though it should be mentioned that modern opinion inclines to the belief that it was the only poem of its kind composed in Anglo-Saxon times), it can at least be said that it is a poem technically impressive in its handling of narrative verse, remarkably successful in rendering that combination of heroic idealism and somber fatalism which seems to have been part of the Germanic temper, yet structurally weak and providing insufficient unity of tone or organization to hold together effectively the two central episodes and the many digressions which make up the whole. Though the ultimate origin of the story is folklore (working, as folklore does, on history), and behind the poem probably lies a variety of popular lays, the poem as we have it is generally agreed to be the work of a single author writing in the first half of the eighth century, though a powerful case has been made out for its having been composed orally by a heathen considerably earlier, with the Christian references (of which there are about seventy) representing later revision or interpolations. Future scholars may well return to this latter view.

Beowulf falls into two main parts. The first deals with the visit of Beowulf, nephew of King Hygelac of the Geats (the Geats probably occupied what is now southern Sweden), to the court of King Hrothgar of Denmark. The aging Hrothgar had long been plagued by a man-eating monster, Grendel, who came regularly to the king's great hall of Heorot to prey on his warriors, and it was to slay the monster that Beowulf came to Denmark. He fights with and mortally wounds Grendel in Heorot, and when Grendel's mother comes to take revenge for the death of her son he follows her to her underwater home and after a desperate struggle slays her too. Beowulf and his companions then leave for home, laden with honors and presents from the Danish king. The second part takes place fifty years later, when Beowulf has long been king of the Geats. A dragon, guarding a hoard of treasure, has been disturbed, and has been going out to wreak slaughter throughout the land. Beowulf, to save his country from the dragon's ravages, undertakes to fight it, and though he succeeds in slaying it he is himself mortally wounded in the struggle. The poem ends with an account of Beowulf's funeral: his body is burned on an elaborate funeral pyre, amid the lamentations of his warriors.

There are historical elements in *Beowulf*, though they are seen through the folk memory and the folk imagination, in combination with a variety of marvelous legends. There are also numerous digressions and allusions which make it clear that the author is taking for granted among his readers (or auditors) knowledge of a whole body of stories concerning Germanic heroes. In the feast at Heorot celebrating Beowulf's victory over Grendel we are told how the minstrel recited the story of Hnæf's death at the hands of the sons of Finn and the subsequent vengeance taken on Finn by the Danes, whose leader Hnæf had been. Part of the minstrel's recital is given at considerable length in *Beowulf*, but it can have had little meaning to anyone without a knowledge of the whole story. We can in some degree reconstruct the sequence of events with the help of a fragmentary Anglo-Saxon lay, *The Fight at Finnsburh*, which appears to deal with other events in the same story, told on a different scale. Other stories are referred to in *Beowulf* more casually, and part of its interest lies in the thread of Germanic story that runs, through allusions, analogies, and references, through the poem. Though it is an Anglo-Saxon poem, composed in England, it harks back to the period of Germanic history before the Anglo-Saxon invasion and shows no bias toward English heroes. Geats, Danes, and Swedes occupy the foreground of the narrative, and emerging briefly from the background are a number of figures whom we also meet in Scandinavian tradition and in the poetry and legends of a variety of Teutonic peoples.

On the surface, *Beowulf* is a heroic poem, celebrating the exploits of a great warrior whose character and actions are held up as a model of aristocratic virtue. It reflects the ideals of that state of society we call the Heroic Age, and its resemblance to the *Odyssey* in this respect has often been noted. The grave courtesy with which men of rank are received and dismissed, the generosity of rulers and the loyalty of retainers, the thirst for fame through the achievement of deeds of courage and endurance, the solemn boasting of warriors before and after performance, the interest in genealogies and pride in a noble heredity—all these things are to be found in both poems. But *Beowulf* is also a record of marvels rather different in kind from those encountered by Ulysses in his adventures, and, further, its Anglo-Saxon gravity is reinforced by the introduction of Christian elements which do not, however, seriously weaken the pagan atmosphere of the poem, for they are concerned with large elemental facts such as God's creation and governance of the world and such Old Testament stories as that of Cain's murder of Abel. If the general atmosphere of *Beowulf* can be called seriously pagan, with the seriousness deepened and the pagan heroic ideal enlarged by Christian elements, it is certainly not uncivilized, though the civilization it reflects is primitive enough. There is a genuine ideal of nobility underlying its adventure stories.

It is the splendid gravity of the poem that falls most impressively on modern ears. Sometimes in a single line the poem conveys atmosphere and mood to perfection. We are given an account of Beowulf's reception at Heorot, and his confident words before his warriors lay themselves down to sleep. Then:

> Com on wanre niht
> scriðˢan sceadu-ȝenȝa. Sceotend swæfon,
> þa þæt horn-reced   healdan scoldon,
> ealle buton anum. . . .
>   Ða com of more   under mist-hleoþum
> Ȝrendel ȝonȝan,   Ȝodes yrre bær. . . .

> Came on the dark night
> gliding, the shadowy prowler. The warriors slept
> who were to hold the antlered hall,
> all but one. . . .
>   Then from the moor under the misty cliffs
> came Grendel marching; he bore God's anger. . . .

The tone is not uniform, but the poem is at its most effective in its moments of slow terror or suspense, and in its more elegiac moods. It has neither the larger epic conception of the *Odyssey* nor the fine polish of a "secondary" epic such as the *Aeneid*. But it is an impressive, if uneven, performance, carrying us successfully into the Anglo-Saxon heroic imagination, with its emphasis on solemn courtesy, generosity, fidelity, and sheer endurance. And underlying all is the sense of the shortness of life and the passing away of all things except the fame a man leaves behind.

There is little else surviving of Anglo-Saxon literature which makes direct contact with the older heroic view of life. *Deor*, an interesting poem of forty-two lines, is the complaint of a minstrel who, after years of service to his lord, has been supplanted by a rival, Heorrenda. He comforts himself by recounting the trials of Germanic

ˢ ð, like þ, has the sound of "th." D is the capital form of ð.

heroes, all of which were eventually overcome. After each reference to the troubles of some famous character there occurs the refrain

> Þæs ofereode,   þisses swa mæg.
> That was surmounted; so may this be.

We get fascinating glimpses of figures famous in Germanic legend—Weland the smith, Theodoric the Ostrogoth, Eormanric the Goth, and others—and of the troubles they suffered or caused; but the main interest of the poem lies in its combination of this kind of subject matter with a personal, elegiac note, not common in Anglo-Saxon poetry, though found even more intensely in *The Wanderer* and *The Seafarer,* to be discussed later.

Two fragments make up the remainder of what we have of older Anglo-Saxon heroic poetry, and the fact that both were discovered by accident illustrates the arbitrariness as well as the incompleteness of the extant body of Anglo-Saxon verse. The first is a fragment of fifty lines, incomplete both at the beginning and the end, dealing with the same Finn story which we hear of in *Beowulf.* It is part of a lay, and describes the attack on Hnæf's hall by the followers of Finn (the *Beowulf* passage being a paraphrase of a handling at much greater length of the same general subject, though there are difficulties in reconciling it with the fragment). The second fragment is part of an Anglo-Saxon treatment of the Waltharius story, a story well-known on the continent and preserved in its most complete form in the Latin epic of Waltharius by Ekkehard of St. Gall, who lived in the latter part of the tenth century. The Anglo-Saxon fragment—which, though earlier than Ekkehard's *Waltharius,* shows evidence of a Christian editing of which the Latin poem gives little sign—is generally known as *Waldhere:* it consists of two separate parts of about thirty lines each, and its chief interest is in offering further evidence of the popularity of stories of continental Germanic heroes among the Anglo-Saxons. The two leaves of manuscript which contain the fragmentary *Waldhere* were not discovered until 1860.

The Christianizing of the Anglo-Saxons had more far-reaching effects on their literature than the addition of Christian elements to heroic poems. By the eighth century the techniques of Anglo-Saxon heroic poetry were being applied to purely Christian themes, with the result that we have a substantial body of Anglo-Saxon religious poetry, representing a quite new development in English literature. Here we see the Anglo-Saxons breaking loose from their pagan origins and, instead of seeking subjects for their poetry in the heroic themes common to old Germania, turning to face the new world of Latin Christianity. It is Christianity that brought the Anglo-Saxons into touch with Christian Europe, and Christian Europe in turn had its contacts with the classical civilization of Greece and Rome. We must thus distinguish between that part of Anglo-Saxon literature which sought nourishment from "barbarian" Germanic traditions that had nothing to do with classical civilization and that part whose inspiration is Latin and which represents an English treatment of themes and attitudes common throughout Christendom and thus found all over Europe. The Christian literature of the early English shows them in touch with the new European civilization as well as with the ancient classical world. It also enabled Anglo-Saxon poets to work on biblical story and so connected them with the Hebrew imagination.

Religious poetry seems to have flourished in northern England—Northumbria—throughout the eighth century, though most of it has survived only in West Saxon transcriptions of the late tenth century. Bede, the great English ecclesiastical historian and scholar who lived from 673 to 735, tells in his *Ecclesiastical History of the English People* how in the monastery of the abbess Hilda at Whitby a lowly lay brother named Cædmon suddenly and miraculously received the gift of song and "at once began to sing in praise of God the Creator verses which he had never heard before." As the abbess Hilda died in 680, this puts the beginnings of Anglo-Saxon religious poetry before that date.

The only poem we have which is certainly by Cædmon is the nine-line poem quoted by Bede in his account of the poet's first inspiration. Bede wrote his *Ecclesiastical History* in Latin (though it was translated into Anglo-Saxon under King Alfred), but fortunately in one of the manuscripts of the work the original Northumbrian text of the poem has been preserved:

> Nu scylun hergan   hefænricæs Uard,
> Metudæs mæcti   end his modgidanc,
> uerc uuldurfadur,   sue he uundra gihuæs,
> eci Dryctin,   or astelidæ. . . .

> Now let us praise the guardian of Heaven's kingdom,
> The Creator's might and His purpose,
> The work of the Father of glory, as He of all wonders,
> Eternal Lord, established the beginning. . . .

(The difference between Northumbrian and West Saxon can be seen at a glance if we put beside the Northumbrian version, quoted above, the following later West Saxon version:

> Nu sculon herigean   heofonrices Weard,
> Meotodes meahte   ond his modgeþanc,

weorc wuldorfæder,   swa he wundra gehwæs,
ece Drihten   or onstealde. . . .)

This shows, clearly enough, the vocabulary of praise which the earlier scop had applied to his lord now being applied to God, and gives some indication of how the heroic style could be adapted to biblical subjects. Bede tells us that Cædmon went on to sing "about the creation of the world and the origin of mankind and the whole story of Genesis; about the exodus of Israel from Egypt and their entrance into the promised land; about many other stories from Holy Writ; about the incarnation, passion, and ascension into Heaven of the Lord; about the coming of the Holy Ghost and the teaching of the apostles." There are Anglo-Saxon poems on many of these subjects, and for a long time these were held to be Cædmon's. But the relative stiffness of the nine lines quoted by Bede seems to represent an earlier stage in the development of Anglo-Saxon religious poetry than that represented by such poems as *Genesis, Exodus,* and *Daniel,* which show greater variety and ease of movement (though it is true that nine lines do not give much basis for comparison), and the poems once attributed to Cædmon are now thought to be later in date though still regarded as belonging to the "Cædmonian school."

The Junius manuscript[4] contains four "Cædmonian" poems, of which the first three are based on Old Testament story. The first, and the longest, of these is *Genesis,* a poem of nearly three thousand lines which, after a brief preliminary account of Satan's rebellion, God's anger, His casting out of Satan and his crew, and His decision to "establish again the glorious creation . . . when His boastful foes had departed from heaven on high," goes on to narrate the substance of the first twenty-two chapters of Genesis. The manuscript is imperfect and there are several gaps in the text. There is also a remarkable interpolation of over six hundred lines, different in language and style from the body of the poem and clearly coming from another work. This interpolated passage (generally known as *Genesis B,* to distinguish it from the rest of the poem, known as *Genesis A*) deals with the temptation of Adam and Eve and their fall and, in considerable detail, with Satan's rebellion, which is so much more briefly dealt with in the introduction to *Genesis A.* The poetic vigor and dramatic detail of *Genesis B* is remarkable; the poem is a rudimentary *Paradise Lost* and, indeed, its finest passages can bear comparison with parts of Milton's epic. Satan's first speech ("Why should I toil? I need have no master; I can work as many wonders with my hands. . . . Why should I wait upon His favor, bow before Him with such homage? I can be God as well as He.") has tremendous if primi-

4 See above, p. 6, note 1.

tive verve, while his second and longer speech, made after he has been cast into Hell, has something of the true Miltonic ring:

> Ah, had I but the strength of my hands
> And could for one hour win out of here,
> For one winter hour, then I with this host—!
> But around me lie iron bonds,
> The fetter's chain rides on me . . .
> I look not to behold that light again which he thinks
>   long to enjoy.
> That happiness with his host of angels; we shall never gain
> Softening of Almighty God's anger. Let us take it from
>   the sons of men,
> That heavenly kingdom, now that we may not have it, lead
>   them to forsake his allegiance
> To transgress what he bade them with his word . . .

Satan's rhetoric in *Genesis B* is the primitive rhetoric of the heroic age compared with the subtler parliamentary rhetoric of Milton's Satan; but there is real poetic imagination at work here, an ability to give vigorous new life to a traditional character. The story of the fall of Satan is not, of course, in the biblical Genesis, but it had long been part of Christian tradition. The original author of *Genesis B* was not English, but wrote in Old Saxon on the continent; the Anglo-Saxon poem which we have is a translation of an Old Saxon original of which only portions have been found.

Genesis A, which is far the larger work, lacks the higher imaginative quality of *Genesis B*, but the versification shows a fine technical ease and the adaptation of the conventions of heroic poetry to biblical narrative is done with real skill. Its source is essentially Jerome's standard Latin translation of the Bible, known as the Vulgate, but the author has drawn also on patristic commentary and Christian legend. He must, therefore, have been a "clerk"—i.e., a churchman of some kind—for no one else could at that period have had the requisite education. It was probably written in Northumbria early in the eighth century. *Genesis B* cannot be earlier than its Old Saxon original, which dates from the ninth century. As the Junius manuscript, in which the poem is found, dates from the late tenth or early eleventh century, the poem as we have it in Anglo-Saxon must have been produced between the end of the ninth and the end of the tenth centuries.

The adaptation to religious verse of the style and conventions of heroic poetry is even more vividly demonstrated in the Anglo-Saxon *Exodus*. The scriptural narrative is followed less closely than in *Genesis A*. Moses emerges as the "glorious hero" leading a warlike

people to freedom and victory. The description of the drowning of
the Egyptian host in the Red Sea is done with great verve:

> . . . Streamas stodon,   storm up gewat
> heah to heofonum,   herewopa mæst;
> laðe cyrmdon,   lyft up geswearc,
> fægum stefnum;   flod blod gewod.
> Randbyrig wæron rofene,   rodor swipode
> meredeaða mæst.   Modige swulton,
> cyningas on corðre,   cyre swiðrode
> sæs æt ende. . . .

> . . . The seas reared up, the storm uprose
> High to the heavens, the great clamor of an army;
> The foe cried out (the air above grew dark)
> With doomed voices; blood spread through the waters.
> The wall of shields was pulled down; scourged the sky
> The greatest of water-deaths; brave men perished,
> Kings in their pride, their chance of return vanished
> At the sea's end. . . .

Linguistic evidence suggests that *Exodus* is the oldest of the
Anglo-Saxon biblical poems, and it perhaps dates from the beginning
of the eighth century.

Daniel is less interesting, with much less dramatic quality and a
more prosaic tone throughout. It is a paraphrase of the first five chapters of the biblical book of Daniel as it appears in the Vulgate, with
the apocryphal prayer of Azariah interpolated in the middle. The
interpolation seems to derive from a separate poem dating from the
middle or late ninth century; the main part of *Daniel* was probably
composed in Northumbria early in the eighth century.

In the same manuscript that contains the two *Genesis* poems,
Exodus and *Daniel,* there is found also an untitled religious poem
which is now generally called *Christ and Satan.* This shows an
Anglo-Saxon poet working not directly from biblical sources but
from a variety of Christian traditions. Here we get a picture of Satan
in Hell which represents him not as the defiant spirit of *Genesis B*
but as a lost soul lamenting bitterly his exclusion from the joys of
Heaven. He is given several speeches, each with considerable elegiac
eloquence; the author is clearly concerned to emphasize the difference between Heaven and Hell and the different results of following
Christ and following Satan. The latter part of the poem concentrates
on Christ, though at the very end, after an account of Satan's temptation of Christ in the wilderness, we return to Satan in his frustration.

Christ and Satan seems to have been influenced by the school of
Cynewulf, a poet who may have flourished early in the ninth century
and who is the first Anglo-Saxon poet to sign his work (by means of

runic letters woven into the poem). Four of Cynewulf's poems are extant, all showing a more self-conscious craftsmanship than is found in the Cædmonian poems and suggesting in style and structure the influence of classical models. The heroic strain, so successfully transplanted from the older poetry in such a poem as *Exodus*, is lacking in Cynewulf, and in its place we find a more meditative and contemplative tone. The four Anglo-Saxon Christian poems which have the name of Cynewulf worked into them in acrostic form are *Christ*, *Juliana*, *Elene*, and *The Fates of the Apostles*. All these poems possess both a high degree of literary craftsmanship and a note of mystical contemplation which sometimes rises to a high level of religious passion. The story of Christ as told in the poem of that title draws on a variety of ecclesiastical and patristic sources, but it handles its subject—the Advent, the Ascension, and the Last Judgment[5]—with an intensity all its own. The dialogue between Mary and Joseph in the first part, brief though it is, shows a real feeling for the dramatic situation, and is, besides, the earliest extant dramatic passage in English literature. *Juliana* is a more conventional work, a typical saint's life, following its Latin prose source without any significant deviation, while *Elene* is the story of the discovery of the true cross by St. Helena, mother of Constantine, told with a keen sense of the wonder of it all and a relish for the romantic suggestions of distant scenes and places. *The Fates of the Apostles* is a short poem of one hundred and twenty-two lines (and may be the concluding part of *Andreas*, which it follows in the manuscript: if so, then *Andreas*, too, is by Cynewulf, for *The Fates of the Apostles* contains the runic signature). The author is here meditating on the adventures of the various apostles after they dispersed to spread the Gospel, but its interest for the modern reader lies largely in the personal passages. Its opening shows an interesting mutation of the heroic into the personal elegiac strain: "Lo, weary of wandering, sad in spirit, I made this song, gathered it from far and wide, of how the bright and glorious heroes showed forth their courage."

With Cynewulf, Anglo-Saxon religious poetry moves beyond biblical paraphrase into the didactic, the devotional, and the mystical. These qualities are also exhibited by many of the religious poems which seem to have been written under his influence. The most remarkable of these is *The Dream of the Rood*, fragments of which are to be found inscribed in runic letters on the Ruthwell Cross in Dum-

[5] Some scholars maintain that only the second part, to which they give the title of *The Ascension* (or *Christ B*), is by Cynewulf, for only this part contains Cynewulf's name in runic characters. The other two parts they consider to be separate poems, giving one the title of *The Advent* (or *Nativity*, or *Christ A*) and the other the title of *Doomsday C* (or *Christ C*), grouping it together with two other poems on the Last Judgment which they call *Doomsday A* and *Doomsday B* respectively.

friesshire, Scotland (probably an early eighth century version, pre-Cynewulf), while the complete poem exists in the Vercelli Book, in a much later version (probaby late ninth century). The tone of the complete version as we have it suggests that the earlier version had been afterward adapted by a poet of the school of Cynewulf, perhaps even by Cynewulf himself. It is the oldest surviving English poem in the form of a dream or vision—a form which was later to be used for such a variety of purposes. The dreamer tells how he saw a vision of the bright cross, brilliantly adorned with gems, and goes on to tell the speech that he heard it utter. The speech of the cross, in which it tells of its origin in the forest, its removal to be made into a cross for "the Master of mankind," its horror at the role it had to play but its determination to stand fast because that was God's command, the suffering of "the young Hero" who ascends the cross resolutely in order to redeem mankind—all this is done in verse charged with a simple eloquence and sustaining a high note of religious passion and wonder. The speech ends with an exhortation to each soul to "seek through the cross the kingdom which is far from earth," and the poem then concludes with the dreamer's account of his own religious hopes. Other poems associated with the school of Cynewulf are *Andreas,* which tells of the adventures, sufferings, and evangelical successes of St. Andrew, with deliberate emphasis on the wonderful and the picturesque, and a perhaps excessive exploitation of the rhetorical devices of Anglo-Saxon poetry (the source of the poem is a Latin rendering of the apocryphal Greek *Acts of Andrew and Matthew*); two poems on the life of the English hermit St. Guthlac; *The Phoenix,* of which the first part, deriving from the Latin poem *De Ave Phoenice,* attributed to Lactantius, describes an earthly paradise in the East, the beauty of the phoenix, its flight to Syria after it has lived for a thousand years to build its nest, die, and be reborn, while the second half takes the phoenix as an allegory both of the life of the virtuous in this world and the next and as a symbol of Christ; and—following *The Phoenix* in the Exeter Book— a poem entitled *Physiologus* or *Bestiary* which belongs to the popular medieval literary form of beast allegories, where real or (more often) imaginary qualities of animals are given a moral application. *Physiologus,* which derives ultimately from a Greek original, is incomplete, and deals with the panther, the whale and, incompletely, the partridge. It has the same lushness of descriptive style that is found in *The Phoenix,* and its natural history is equally fabulous. The whale is given the charming name of Fastitocalon—a corruption of Aspidochelone, originally applied to the turtle.

Finally, there falls to be mentioned among significant Anglo-Saxon religious poems the fragmentary *Judith*, of which only the concluding sections survive, in the same manuscript that contains *Beowulf*. The poem is a version of the Vulgate text of the apocryphal book of Judith, and the extant portion tells in vigorous and rapidly moving verse of Judith's beheading of the drunken Holofernes after his confident feasting, her rallying of the Hebrews to attack the Assyrians, the consternation of the Assyrians on discovering Holofernes' headless body, the rout of the Assyrians by the Hebrews, and Judith's triumph and praise to God. *Judith* possesses a fierce energy in describing the death of Holofernes and the defeat of the Assyrians, a note of positive jubilation, which is quite different from anything in the older heroic poetry. In fluidity of movement the verse form shows itself to be fairly late, and the poem may date from the end of the ninth century or possibly even later.

Though some of the Anglo-Saxon religious poems, especially some of those by Cynewulf and his school, express a personal devotional feeling, none of them can be said to be really lyrical in character or to have been written primarily for the purpose of exploring personal emotion. Neither the heroic nor the religious poetry of the Anglo-Saxon tends toward the lyric, and though a note of somber elegy is sometimes struck, it is rarely developed for its own sake. There is, however, a group of Anglo-Saxon poems in which a mood of lyrical elegy predominates, and these stand somewhat apart from the poetry we have already discussed. Of these *The Wanderer* and *The Seafarer* are the most similar to each other. *The Wanderer* is the lament of a solitary man who had once been happy in the service of a loved lord but who now, long after his lord's death and the passing away of that earlier time of happiness and friendship, has become a wanderer journeying the paths of exile across the icy sea. The poem ends with some conventional moralizing, but the main part of the elegy is an impressive lament for departed joys, done with a plangent tone of reminiscence and an effective use of the *ubi sunt?* theme—"where are the snows of yesteryear?"—that was to become such a favorite in medieval literature. *The Seafarer*, which has the same melancholy tone, the same mingling of regret and self-pity, is the monologue of an old sailor who recalls the loneliness and hardships of a life at sea while at the same time aware of its fascination. Some critics take it to be a dialogue, in which the old sailor urges the hardships of the seafaring life against the arguments of an eager young man anxious to take to the sea and attracted by the difficulties, and the poem can indeed be read in this way; but the fluctuating moods of the poem seem more impressive if taken as the alternation of weariness and fascination in the same person. Whichever way we read it, however, it is the elegiac element that stands out from among the sometimes obscure sequence of moods, which ends, like *The Wanderer*, with a conventional religious sentiment. The date of both these poems is uncertain: they may be almost as old as *Beowulf*. Both are found in the Exeter Book.

Another poem in the Exeter Book, which is generally given the title of *The Wife's Lament*, can also be considered as belonging to this group of elegiac monologues. It is difficult to follow the precise situation the speaker is describing, but apparently the wife has been separated from her husband and forced to dwell in a cave in the forest by the plottings of his kinsmen. In spite of the comparative obscurity of the situation, the central emotion comes through strongly, and the note of personal passion—the love and longing for the absent husband, the curse on the enemy responsible for her present plight—rings out with remarkable clarity. Similar in many ways to this poem is *The Husband's Message*. Here the speaker is the piece of wood on which the letter is carved: it first tells the wife its own life story and then goes on to speak the message now carved on it. The husband reminds the wife of her earlier vows, tells her that he has been driven from her by a feud, and bids her join him across the sea. *Wulf and Eadwacer* is another dramatic monologue, existing only in a fragment of nineteen lines in the Exeter Book, which, for all the obscurity of the situation described, expresses an intense romantic passion in a way quite uncharacteristic of Anglo-Saxon poetry as it has come down to us. Wulf is the woman's outlawed lover and Eadwacer her hated husband, or at least the man with whom, against her will, she is forced to live. The passionate cry of

> Wulf, min Wulf, wena me þine
> seoce gedydon, þine seldcymas
> murnende mod, nales meteliste—

> Wulf, my Wulf, my longings for thee
> Have made me sick, thy rare visits,
> It was my sorrowful heart, not want of food—

might be Iseult calling for Tristan as conceived by some nineteenth-century romantic poet. *The Wife's Lament, The Husband's Message,* and *Wulf and Eadwacer* represent all we have of Anglo-Saxon love poetry. They have not been tampered with by clerics anxious to give a moral and religious twist to the end, but have survived in all the intensity of their original utterance. How many poems in a similar style may have been lost it is impossible to tell, nor is it easy to see for what kind of an audience this kind of poetry was written. We know to what taste the Anglo-Saxon heroic poet catered, and we can understand the appeal of the religious poetry of the age; but these passionate renderings of personal emotion, devoid of either heroic atmosphere or religious teaching, must have appealed to a taste one is not accustomed to thinking of as at all prevalent in the Anglo-Saxon period of English culture.

There is one other interesting Anglo-Saxon poem with an elegiac tone; it is a description of a ruined city (perhaps Bath) in about fifty lines, found in the Exeter Book. It is a sad picture of desolation and decay set against an account of the earlier prosperity of the place, and, though the text is imperfect, the sense of passionate regret at the passing away of what was once lively and beautiful is conveyed with impressive eloquence. No clerical improver has tagged a religious moral on to it (or, if he has, it has not survived in the incomplete version which alone is extant) and the mood is somberly fatalistic. *The Ruin* is not incompatible in feeling with much of *Beowulf*, which has its own stern sense of fate, and we can see from it how in Anglo-Saxon poetry one kind of elegiac mood was the reverse of the medal whose obverse was heroic.

The Exeter book contains nearly a hundred Anglo-Saxon riddles, some of which seem to have been translated from Latin originals composed in England by clerics of the seventh and eighth century and some derived from the fourth- to fifth-century Latin writer Symphosius. This form of literary amusement has little appeal for the modern reader, though many of *The Riddles*—which are in regular Anglo-Saxon verse form—show considerable literary skill, particularly in descriptive passages. Their chief interest today lies in the incidental glimpses they give us of the daily life of Anglo-Saxon England and the folk beliefs of the time. Similarly, the so-called "Gnomic Verses," some of which are also in the Exeter Book, and some in a British Museum manuscript, with their generalizations about morals and experience and the properties of objects encountered in daily living, are of interest to the social historian as the only group of existing Anglo-Saxon poems which are not on the whole aristocratic in origin; they reflect the manners and opinions of the peasantry of the period.

Toward the end of the Anglo-Saxon period the old heroic note, so long unheard, re-emerges finely in two poems dealing with contemporary history. *The Battle of Brunanburh* appears in the *Anglo-Saxon Chronicle* under the date 937: it celebrates the victory of

Æthelstan of Wessex and Eadmund, his brother, against the combined forces of Olaf the Norseman, Constantine, king of Scots, and the Britons of Strathclyde. There is an important difference, however, between the heroic tone of this poem and that of the older Anglo-Saxon poetry. In the older heroic poetry, emphasis was laid on the individual hero, and his national origins were of little importance—he was one of the heroes of Germania and as such claimed the admiration of all the Germanic peoples without any national prejudice. But *The Battle of Brunanburh* shows strong patriotic sentiment. The victory is regarded as a victory of the English forces against Norse, Scots, and Welsh enemies, and though the heroism of Æthelstan and Eadmund is celebrated, the two princes appear not as heroes in their own right so much as champions of their nation. The *Battle of Maldon* appears in the *Anglo-Saxon Chronicle* under the date 991. It deals in the older epic manner with one of the many clashes between English and Danes that resulted from the latter's attacks on England, which culminated in the conquest of the country by Cnut (Canute) in 1012. The older heroic poems did not, of course, deal with historical events that had only just occurred, nor, as we have noted, did they show any trace of national patriotic feeling. Yet *The Battle of Maldon* is remarkably similar in spirit to the older heroic poetry. It is the story of a disastrous English defeat: Byrhtnoth, ealdorman of Essex, who led the English forces, fought and died in a recklessly courageous attempt to stem the Danes. The poem contains nine speeches, mostly of exhortation and encouragement to the English forces, delivered by seven different speakers; many of the English warriors are mentioned by name (though not one of the Danes is so singled out); the passionate loyalty of retainers to their chief is eloquently presented; and the tone of desperate courage against hopeless odds becomes more and more intense as the poem proceeds, to culminate after the death of Byrhtnoth in the final words of his old retainer Byrhtwold:

> Hige sceal þe heardra,   heorte þe cenre,
> mod sceal þe mare,   þe ure mægen lytlað.
> Her lið ure ealdor   eall forheawen,
> god on greote;   a mæg gnornian
> seðe nu fram þis wigplegan   wendan þenceð.
> Ic eom frod feores;   fram ic ne wille,
> ac ic me be healfe   minum hlaforde,
> be swa leofan men,   licgan þence.

> Thought shall be the harder, heart the keener,
> Courage shall be the more, as our might lessens.

> Here lies our lord, all hewn down,
> The good man in the dust; ever may he lament
> Who now from this war-play thinks to turn.
> I am old in years; from here I will not go,
> But I by the side of my lord,
> By the man so dear, purpose to lie.

And, in this high strain, Anglo-Saxon heroic poetry comes to an end.

The Anglo-Saxon invaders of Britain brought with them their own poetry, but there is no evidence of their having possessed any literary prose tradition. The development of Old English prose does not therefore go back to earlier Germanic origins, as the poetry does: it takes place wholly in England, and largely as a result of the Christianization of England. It is not surprising that prose developed later than poetry: that is the normal thing in the history of any literature, for the primal urge to artistic expression is bound to be poetic, while the proper maturing of the more utilitarian prose medium of communication follows the emergence of later political and cultural needs. With the Germanic peoples, the delay in the development of prose was emphasized by their contact with the old and mature Greco-Roman civilization, which supplied clerks ready to act as secretaries to their leaders and a sophisticated Greek or Latin prose more than capable of making any formal communications or keeping any legal or historical records which might be required. For the celebration of their own heroes and the perpetuation of their own legends, a native poetry was necessary and indeed inevitable, but the need for prose was only felt by barbarian chieftains after they had come into contact and had been deeply affected by the civilization they threatened; and that civilization could easily supply the need of which it made them aware.

There were exceptions to this generalization, but there can be little doubt that it applies to the Anglo-Saxons, or that English prose begins in the reign of King Alfred in an attempt by the King and his associates to bring within range of the people the most significant aspects of earlier thought. Latin was, of course, the language of the Christian Church, and an essential tool in clerical education; perhaps if England had been geographically closer to Rome, Latin might have stifled a native prose altogether, just as its prestige and availability had earlier hampered the development of a formal native prose among many of the Germanic peoples. But, as one of the most perceptive historians of early English prose has put it, "when Gregory the Great sent his missionaries to England, Latin civilization reached a land which was so remote from Rome that Latin could influence the native language without depressing it,"[6] and when the laws of Kent were amended to introduce new Christian notions, the new clauses were written not in Latin but in English.

King Alfred of Wessex, known in political history for his achievement in stemming the Danish conquest of England, the acceptance of his overlordship by—in the words of the *Anglo-Saxon Chronicle*—"all the English people except those who were under the power of the Danes" and the consequent advance of the peoples of the various Anglo-Saxon kingdoms toward an awareness of their political unity as Englishmen, and for his remarkable combination of the statesman, the military strategist, and the patriot, is even more important in the history of English education and the history of English literature. Throughout a reign troubled by military problems of desperate urgency, not all of which had been resolved by the time of his death in 899, he yet found the time and the energy to meditate on the means of bringing the fruits of Western culture to "all the free-born young men of England" and to see those means in large measure achieved. In his preface to his translation of the *Cura Pastoralis (Pastoral Care)* of Pope Gregory the Great he tells of his concern at the dearth of scholars in England at the time of his accession to the throne (in 871) and at the destruction of churches and books by the Danes, and his wonder why earlier English scholars had not translated any of those books into the vernacular; then he immediately proceeds to answer the last question by saying that those earlier scholars can never have supposed that a knowledge of the original languages should have declined to such a degree. But he realized that Christian culture had its roots in Hebrew, Greek, and Latin sources, and that if these were to be made available to the people an ambitious program of translation into the vernacular would have to be undertaken. "When I remembered how Latin learning has already decayed throughout England, though many can read English writing, I began, among many other varied and manifold cares of this kingdom, to translate into English the book which is called in Latin *Pastoralis* and in English 'Hierde-boc' (herd's book, i.e., shepherd's book, pastoral)."

Alfred's program of translation did not include direct translations from the original sources of Christian culture, but concentrated on later Latin works in which, as he believed, much of the ancient wisdom was distilled. Thus Gregory's *Cura Pastoralis*, a work describing the duties and responsibilities of a bishop which had come to be

[6] R. W. Chambers, "The Continuity of English Prose," in *Harpsfield's Life of Sir Thomas More,* edited by Elsie Vaughan Hitchcock and R. W. Chambers, London, 1932. Page lix.

regarded as a manual of a parish priest's duties, came first on his list: he must have been attracted by Gregory's emphasis on the bishop's duty to teach the laity. Alfred was especially concerned with the training of teachers—who would all, of course, be clerics, and whose teaching would be religious—as his choice of this work indicates. All the free-born English youth should be able to read English, and those who wished to proceed to the priesthood would, after learning English, go on to Latin. English was necessary as a first step both for priest and layman.

The translation of the *Cura Pastoralis* was done by Alfred with the assistance of scholars who explained the meaning to him "sometimes word by word, sometimes sense by sense"; for Alfred was late in learning Latin and depended on a number of helpers of whom seven are known to us by name. It is on the whole a literal rendering, but it flows easily and there is little indication of the forcing of one language into the idiom of another such as we might expect in a pioneer translation. Alfred's next work was a translation of the *Historiae adversum Paganos* of the fifth-century Latin writer Paulus Orosius, a work written under the influence of St. Augustine in order to prove that the introduction of Christianity had not made the world worse than it had been before. Orosius chronicles the calamities of mankind from the Fall of man to the fall of Rome with an equal disregard for historical accuracy and literary grace, and it is a pity that this shoddy production was the only world history available to Alfred. Fortunately, Alfred treated his original rather freely, adding his own illustrations and omitting much propaganda; more important, he added two entirely new narratives, one told him by Ohthere, a Norwegian who had explored from his home within the Arctic Circle, sailing round the North Cape as far as the White Sea, the other told him by a voyager named Wulfstan who had sailed the Baltic from Schleswig to the mouth of the Vistula. These lively accounts of foreign lands and peoples, together with Alfred's additions to Orosius drawn from his own knowledge and experience, give this translation its present value. The voyages of Ohthere and Wulfstan are justly celebrated as among the high spots of Anglo-Saxon prose, and the prose is certainly Alfred's own.

The translation of Bede's *Historia Ecclesiastica* (*Ecclesiastical History of the English People*) associated with Alfred's name is a literal rendering of the Latin, perhaps not done by Alfred himself though certainly inspired by him. Alfred's two final translations were of more philosophical works. That of the *De Consolatione Philosophiae* (*The Consolation of Philosophy*) of Boethius, a Roman philosopher and statesman of the late fifth and early sixth centuries, made avail-

able in Anglo-Saxon one of the most popular philosophical works of
the Dark and Middle Ages, later translated by Chaucer. It deals (in
the form of a dialogue between the author and Philosophy) with the
fundamental problems of God's government of the world, the nature
of true happiness, good and evil, and the question of God's fore-
knowledge of man's free will; though there is no specific reference
to Christianity anywhere in the work and the general tone of the
work derives from Greek and Roman ethical thought rather than
from Christian teaching, its high idealism and, in particular, its
reconciliation of God's perfection with the apparently imperfect
state of His world, appealed to Christian thought. To the eighteenth-century Gibbon "such topics of consolation, so obvious, so
vague, or so abstruse, are ineffectual to subdue the feelings of human nature," but the medieval mind found them more helpful. Alfred in his later years had left history and geography to meditate on
profounder philosophical themes, and the work of Boethius—written
in prison while the author was awaiting execution—had a particular
appeal to a man and to an age familiar with sudden reversals of fortune and anxious to find a wider and a calmer perspective from
which to contemplate human vicissitudes. Alfred's last work was a
book of "Blossoms" derived for the most part from the *Soliloquies* of
St. Augustine but with freely interspersed original comments and
illustrations. In his preface Alfred compares himself in his literary
endeavors to a man collecting wood in a vast forest which contains
plenty of materials for all kinds of building. The analogy is apt
enough, and expressed in a fine piece of Anglo-Saxon prose: it can
serve as a summing up of Alfred's literary purposes.

Alfred's Laws, though of great importance to the political historian must, like the laws of other Anglo-Saxon kings and like Anglo-
Saxon charters and similar nonliterary prose works, remain outside
the purview of the historian of literature, even though they, like the
charters, have considerable interest for the student of the development of English prose. The Laws, however, are prefaced by a translation of chapters 20 to 23 of Exodus, which tell of the giving of the
law to Moses (including the Ten Commandments and other civil and
criminal laws), followed by the passage from the fifteenth chapter
of Acts describing the enactment of the council of Jerusalem and the
relation of the Mosaic law to the new dispensation, which represent
the earliest extant English biblical translations except for some
literal renderings of the Psalms. Bede (who died in 735) was said to
have translated the Gospel of St. John from Latin into English, and
probably did translate the first six chapters, but the work has not
survived.

It was probably in King Alfred's time that the great *Anglo-Saxon Chronicle* was begun, a series of annals which commence with an outline of English history from Julius Caesar's invasion to the middle of the fifth century and continues (in one of its seven manuscripts) to 1154. The different manuscripts, each of which was kept and continued at a different locality, diverge considerably after the beginning of the tenth century, often including material of especial local interest. The *Chronicle* includes some fine examples of prose narrative, one of the most notable being the story of Cynewulf and Cyneheard, occurring under the surprisingly early date of 755, which shows that at least one English writer of the middle of the eighth century had at his command a prose style comparable to that of the Icelandic prose sagas. The continuity of English prose from the Old English (or Anglo-Saxon) period to the Middle English period is demonstrated by the *Chronicle* more clearly than anywhere else, and its different manuscripts are of prime importance for the student of the English language. The level is far from consistent, dropping considerably in the middle of the tenth century (which is surprising, for that was a period of stability and prosperity) and flaring up into some vivid descriptions at the end of the tenth and the beginning of the eleventh centuries, when the second great wave of Danish invasions was tearing the country apart. The manuscript known as *D* gives a full and lively picture of the relations between England and Scandinavia in the reign of Edward the Confessor (1043–66) and a most important account of the Norman invasion and subsequent events, while another manuscript, *C*, which ends in 1066, gives a vivid account of the conflicts with the Danes in the reign of Ethelred the Unready (978–1016). The latest entry is in a manuscript that was continued at Peterborough; it is for the year 1154. By this time the English language had developed from the stage we call Anglo-Saxon or Old English into Middle English. By this time, too, as a result of the Norman Conquest and what followed, English as a literary language seemed about to disappear and English historical prose appeared to have come to an end. Until well into the fourteenth century, English, replaced at court by Norman French since 1066, seemed to be dwindling away into the rustic speech of a handful of "uplandish men." But, as we shall see, the tradition did not wholly dry up; it was to emerge again triumphant three hundred years after the Conquest; the English language eventually conquered the language of the Norman conquerors, and English prose rose to new life in the fifteenth century.

Alfred and the writers who kept up the *Anglo-Saxon Chronicle* were not the only writers of Anglo-Saxon prose. Alfred's associates were also responsible for translations, and we know that Bishop Wærferth of Worcester translated the *Dialogues* of Gregory the Great. The most notable of all Anglo-Saxon writers was Ælfric, abbot of Eynsham, the great English scholar of the Benedictine reformation of the tenth century, whose sermons in the vernacular (the first two series known as the *Catholic Homilies—Homiliae Cath-olicae*—and the third as *Lives of the Saints—Passiones Sanctum*— though their subject matter is not as clearly distinguished as these titles would suggest) with their careful balance and prose rhythm display a fine virtuosity. Ælfric also produced a somewhat abbre-viated version in Anglo-Saxon of the first seven books of the Old Testament (the *Heptateuch*) done with sufficient skill to enable us to call him the first English Bible translator to have gone a consider-able way toward achieving an appropriate literary prose style for biblical translation. Beside the carefully balanced sentences of Æl-fric we can set the more fiery eloquence of his contemporary, Wulf-stan, Archbishop of York from 1002 to 1023. His famous *Sermon to the English*, entitled in the manuscript *Sermo Lupi ad Anglos*, was delivered in 1014: in it Wulfstan paints a vivid picture of the horrors brought about by the Danish invasions—a picture of wrongdoing, betrayal, violence, crop failures, civil war, treachery, murder, im-morality of every kind—and uses it as a means of hammering home to his audience the necessity of amendment if they are to avoid hell-fire and earn "the glory and the joy that God has prepared for those that do His will on earth." A desperate sense of the imminence of doomsday pervades the whole sermon, from the opening statement that "this world is in haste and approaches its end" to the powerful "God help us!" of the conclusion. Wulfstan's prose, though he, like Ælfric, uses alliteration and antithesis, gives an impression of breath-less passion, of eloquence breaking out through its own force, which is markedly different from Ælfric's finely chiseled urbanity.

The ravages of the Danes at the end of the ninth century had wrought havoc with the organization of the English church and, while Alfred's translations represented a remarkable attempt to im-prove the state of education, it was not until the middle and latter part of the tenth century that a real revival of religious learning took place in England. That revival was the work of the great churchman Dunstan who, after a life devoted to monastic reform, was translated to the See of Canterbury in 960; of Oswald of Worcester and Æthel-wold of Winchester, who carried further the monastic revival begun by Dunstan; of Æthelwold's pupil Ælfric, who led the literary move-ment; and of Archbishop Wulfstan, Ælfric's friend for whom he wrote some of his famous "Pastoral Letters." If Ælfric and Wulfstan extended the range of effective Anglo-Saxon prose, it was not because they or any ecclesiastic of the time were primarily interested in vernacular literature, but rather because the vitality of the movement of which they were a part carried over into this field. To a tenth-century cleric, Latin was the language of learning and of literature, and concessions to the unlearned in the form of translations were achievements of minor importance. The main thing was to keep up the standard of Latin scholarship among the clergy. The most popular of Ælfric's works with the modern reader is a set of simple Latin dialogues (the *Colloquy*) intended to teach Latin to boys in a monastic school. These dialogues (between the teacher and a monk, the teacher and a plowman, the teacher and a shepherd, the teacher and a fisherman, etc.) interest us today because of the lively glimpses they give us of the daily life of the time; but for Ælfric they were means to a very important end.

Ælfric's *Colloquy* reminds us that with the triumph of Christianity all culture was ecclesiastical culture and all ecclesiastical culture was based on Latin. The Latin literature of the Anglo-Saxon period is much greater in bulk than that written in the vernacular, and the history of Anglo-Saxon learning is more extensive and in many ways more remarkable than the history of Anglo-Saxon literature. The story of the conversion of England and the development of its ecclesiastical institutions from the landing of Augustine in Kent in 597 through the Synod of Whitby to the tenth-century reformation, which includes the story of English Latin culture, the art of illuminating manuscripts and of handwriting—and, indeed, all the other arts, including architecture—is a rich and noble one. It would include the names of Aldhelm, "perhaps the most learned man of his day in Europe"; of Boniface, who lacked Aldhelm's over-elaboration of style but whose Latin writings have their own individual power and charm; of Benedict Biscop of Northumbria, who founded the two famous Benedictine monasteries of Wearmouth and Jarrow; and of Bede (673–735), Biscop's great pupil, who spent his life as a monk at Jarrow and is one of the really great scholars of England and of Europe, author of numerous works of Biblical interpretation, history, biography, and science; of Alcuin of York (735–804) who ended his career as adviser to Charlemagne and head of his palace school, thus playing an important part in the European cultural movement known as the Carolingian Renaissance; as well as of the tenth-century writers who have been already discussed. It would include the story of the relations between scholars who looked to Ireland and those who looked to Rome, and the special contributions of each, and it would tell of the part played by English churchmen as missionaries in Frisia and Germany and Scandinavia. All this is important, because it emphasizes the role of the clerics in carrying on the cultural tradition in this period. Yet it is not strictly a part of the history of English literature. Literature as such, even in Latin, did not yet play the central part in embodying and transmitting the cultural tradition that it was to do later, particularly from the Renaissance on. The man of culture belonged first of all to the church, and the impressive claims of secular literature had not yet begun to be asserted.

CHAPTER TWO

The Development of Middle English Prose and Verse

THE NORMAN CONQUEST of England in 1066 provides one of those convenient landmarks for the historian, whether political, social, or cultural, that divide up his subject almost too neatly. The temptation to take 1066 as the dividing line between the old Anglo-Saxon England and the new Anglo-Norman England is indeed difficult to resist, and of course it should not be altogether resisted. The Norman Conquest imposed a French-speaking ruling caste on England, with the result that Anglo-French developed as the literary language of the highest social classes and Anglo-Saxon (now rapidly developing into that stage of the English language known as Middle English) was for a period relegated to the lower classes. English, which remained the language of the vast majority of the people, eventually won out over French, and by the beginning of the fourteenth century its victory was clearly evident, but its re-establishment as a polite literary language after the period of Anglo-French ascendancy did not mean that it was starting altogether anew, without awareness of its Anglo-Saxon roots. The English which finally ousted French as the language of the literature of England was a language changed in many important respects—it had lost the Anglo-Saxon inflections and had greatly enriched its vocabulary from French—but it had not wholly lost touch with its traditions, and there is a greater continuity between Anglo-Saxon and Middle English literature than the casual reader of both might imagine. It is true that in English poetry the rhymed verse of French soon replaced the Anglo-Saxon alliterative tradition, though there was a remarkable revival of alliterative verse in the fourteenth century. And the English tradition in prose, which, after the achievements of the Alfredian translators and the homiletic tradition of Ælfric and Wulfstan, was much more

31

advanced than anything in French prose, did not prevent French influence from making verse the medium of much Middle English historical and miscellaneous writing for which prose would have been (and, in the Anglo-Saxon period, was) the appropriate vehicle. Yet, though French influence brought rhyme instead of alliteration to English poetry and restricted the range of English prose, and though the French language affected both the vocabulary and the pronunciation of English, Middle English literature—English literature between the early twelfth and the late fifteenth centuries—is in many important respects the heir of its Anglo-Saxon ancestry, and the elements which distinguish it most sharply from Anglo-Saxon literature are those which might well have flowed into it in the normal course of international cultural influence. The influence of French literary methods and French literary attitudes was felt all over Europe, and would have been felt in England even if there had been no Norman Conquest. We are entering the period of French cultural domination of Europe, which is a much more significant phenomenon—even for English literature—than William the Conqueror's victory in 1066.

But if the long-term development of English literature was less affected by the Norman Conquest than might at first sight be imagined, there can be no doubt that the immediate effect of the Conquest was to disrupt the course of English[1] literature considerably. The position with regard to language was enough to ensure that. Even though modern scholars tend to regard as exaggerated the older view which held that French was the regular language of the upper classes for more than two and a half centuries after the Conquest, and stress the evidence that points to the use or at least the knowledge of English among the upper classes outside the immediate circle of the Court, the fact remains that for over two centuries the literature produced under courtly or aristocratic patronage was French both in tone and in language, while literature in English was either rough and popular (much of it oral, and so lost), or simply didactic, written by the lower clergy with the object of instructing the common people in biblical story and the duties required by their

[1] I am using the term "English" to refer to the whole field of literature discussed in this book, as I regard the Anglo-Saxon phase as an integral part of the English literary tradition. The logical term to use for Anglo-Saxon for anyone with this point of view would be "Old English," which gives us the neat tripartite division of the English language into Old English, Middle English, and Modern English, the common word "English" emphasizing the continuity. Many modern scholars do this, yet "Anglo-Saxon" remains the older-established and better-known term, and it seems pedantic to refer, for example, to the well-known *Anglo-Saxon Chronicle* as the *Old English Chronicle*, as is sometimes now done.

religion. The immediate form in which Anglo-Saxon alliterative verse survived was less technically subtle, more simply accentual, than the stricter form of the Anglo-Saxon period: it probably represented a popular oral tradition which was less likely to be affected by the displacement of polite English literature by French, and it was certainly a kind of verse which was more susceptible to the influence of the French rhymed couplet, toward which it moved. One might, indeed, distinguish two lines of development of the old Anglo-Saxon alliterative verse. One moves via this popular tradition toward the rhymed couplets of the French, the long alliterative line breaking into two, acquiring rhyme, and becoming metrically regular. The other somehow made contact with the purer and stricter alliterative tradition and emerged in the so-called "Alliterative Revival" of the fourteenth century, which produced, in western and northern parts of the country where national English feeling had remained strongest, some of the most interesting works in the whole of Middle English literature.

But if some aspects of the Anglo-Saxon verse tradition lingered on, the same cannot be said for the heroic note of Anglo-Saxon poetry. The Norman Conquest was itself the last of those many movements, migrations, invasions, and expeditions, which had ended the Roman Empire and brought a new Europe into being; by the beginning of the twelfth century this new Europe had defined its relation to the Roman past, had established itself as a Christian civilization, and had become sufficiently stable culturally to form its own norms of politeness both in life and in letters. The heroic age was gone, and new kinds of courtly sophistication replaced the heroic ideal in manners. There are, of course, links between the new Europe and the old, and we can trace the movement from the *chansons de geste*, with their sterner note of heroic endeavor—they include the verse tales of Charlemagne and his peers—to the Arthurian romances, with their stress on courtly behavior and new ideals of love and sentiment. Of these romances, more hereafter; at the moment we note merely that the old heroic note was dying away throughout Europe, because the new Europe of the Middle Ages was not a heroic society in the strict historical sense but a feudal society with its own conventions of service, honor, and obligation, its own kind of literary patronage, and its own social conditions breeding its own view of the relation between the sexes. The Norman Conquest did not bring this feudal organization to England; it had been developing in late Anglo-Saxon times; but it certainly hastened the process and, what is more important to the literary historian, it brought England more immediately into contact with continental civilization and especially with the new flowering of French culture which was to change the pattern of all medieval European literatures. Again, we must not imagine that Anglo-Saxon England had been isolated from the continent, and that it was not until 1066 that relations between England and the continent developed. There were in fact powerful Norman influences working in England in the generation before the Conquest, and the Anglo-Saxon kingdoms, at the height of their prosperity, had many and significant European contacts. But the Norman Conquest brought a more immediate, a more active, and a more continuous relationship with the continent, and, by imposing a French-speaking ruling caste on England, brought the achievements of the new French culture more rapidly and more forcibly to the attention of Englishmen.

The story of English literature during the two centuries and a half after the Norman Conquest is the story of what the late seventeenth-century critics were to call, with reference to the achievement of their own poets, "the refinement of our numbers." Forced back to its more popular elements, English literature soon began to rise again slowly in the social scale, gradually acquiring an ease, a skill, and a polish which would enable it to hold its own with French. The full and triumphant achievement of this new ease and skill and polish—in the work of Chaucer—coincides in date with the final re-establishment of English as the universal national language, the speech, both written and spoken, of both Court and people. It was a very different language now from that of *Beowulf* or of Ælfric, having come under many influences in addition to undergoing those changes in pronunciation and word structure which any language undergoes with the passing of time. But it was the legitimate descendant of its Anglo-Saxon parent. The reader of English literature of this period is struck by the number of different Middle English dialects: it was not until toward the end of the Middle English period that the East Midland dialect became more or less the standard literary language. The reason for the number of Middle English literary dialects was that, as a result of the Conquest, Wessex lost its political and cultural importance, and its dialect, West Saxon, which had established its supremacy as the literary language, therefore similarly lost its prestige. With the Court and aristocratic circles using French, there was no force making for the supremacy of any one Middle English dialect over the others, so writers in English used the language of their own region. These regional dialects of Middle English were the descendants of their Anglo-Saxon ancestors: the Northumbrian dialect of Anglo-Saxon split up into Scots and Northern English; Mercian developed into East Midland and West Midland; West Saxon divided into the Southwestern and Central-Southern dialects; and Kentish became the basis of the dialects of the Southeast. Where there is no central standard of polite usage, a language will always split up into regional dialects, which is of course why a popular literature, developing independently of polite standards, will tend to use the language of its own region, as in American folk song to this day. This also explains why, for example, Scots, originally a branch of Northumbrian English and later, as a result of its use by the Middle Scots poets, a fully developed literary language in its own right, split up into regional dialects after the Middle Ages, when, as a result of increasing association with England, Scotland more and more adopted standard English as its literary language and thus lost its standard for polite Scots. Just as the eclipse of Wessex and the loss of the standardizing power of its language produced by the Norman Conquest and the emergence of French as the courtly language led Middle English to relapse into a series of dialects even as a written language, so the union of the crowns of England and Scotland in 1603 and the union of the parliaments of the two countries in 1707 made English the standard polite language of Scotland and split Scots up into the series of local dialects which it has remained until our own time, when the movement of contemporary poets to create a synthetic Scots literary language is at last trying to reverse this trend.

As French receded, even among the upper classes, and English moved slowly up in the social scale, the possibility of a new standard form of literary English grew steadily, until, by the end of the Middle English period, the dialect of London, now the dominant city of England, reigned supreme. The London dialect had originally been a Southern dialect, with its characteristics largely Southeastern, but by Chaucer's time it had become mainly East Midland in character, with the result that standard modern English derives from East Midland and not, as any one looking at the English literary scene about the year 1050 might have predicted, West Saxon.

The loss of Normandy by the English in 1204, and royal decrees in both England and France in 1224 making it illegal for any one to hold land in both countries, must have helped to make the descendants of the Normans in England consider themselves bound purely to England and encouraged the growth among them of the English language. Besides, it must be remembered that the Norman Conquest did not represent—as did the invasions of the Saxons and the

Danes—a national migration. The army brought to England by William, Duke of Normandy, consisted of no more than about six thousand men, and some of these were mercenaries who returned across the Channel after the subjugation of England was completed in 1070. William gave English estates to his followers and made them into a small ruling class which replaced the Anglo-Saxon nobility, but underneath, English life went on very much as usual. It is true that Henry II (1154–1189), the first of the Plantagenet kings, possessed vast realms in France, extending from the Channel to the Pyrenees (having inherited Normandy and Maine from his mother, and Anjou and Touraine from his father, and acquiring Poitou, Guienne, and Gascony by his marriage to Eleanor of Aquitaine, and Brittany through his son Geoffrey, who married Constance, heiress of that province), and throughout the late Middle English period English kings regarded themselves as the rightful kings of France (a claim which produced the Hundred Years War, which began in 1338[2]). But, though this intimate contact with France kept the influence of French culture very much alive in England, it could not prevent the steady rise of the English language until it became again, in the fourteenth century, the polite as well as the popular language of England; for the masses of Englishmen had spoken English all along.

The classic document on the rehabilitation of English in educated circles is a paragraph in John of Trevisa's translation of the *Polychronicon* of Ralph Higden. Higden, writing about 1350, had stated that ever since the Normans came to England Englishmen had been forced to leave their native language and do everything in French, and that the children of gentlemen were taught to speak French from infancy. Trevisa, translating Higden's work from the Latin in 1385, adds his own comment on Higden's statement:

Þys manere was moche y-vsed tofore þe furste moreyn, and ys seþthe somdel ychaunged. For Iohan Cornwal, a mayster of gramere, chayngede þe lore in gramerscole and construccion of Frensch into Englysch; and Richard Pencrych lurnede þat manere techyng of hym, and oþer men of Pencrych, so þat now, þe 3er of oure Lord a þousand þre hondred foure score and fyue, of þe secunde kyng Richard after þe Conquest nyne, in all þe gramerscoles of Engelond children leueþ Frensch, and construeþ and lurneþ an Englysch . . .

---

[2] In spite of some impressive victories over the French, such as Crecy and Poitiers (1346 and 1356 respectively), the English never established their claim for any length of time; even Henry V, who after his victory at Agincourt in 1415 and his triumphant entry into Paris had himself named the heir to the French throne, never lived to be King of France, and in the following reign, that of Henry VI, the revival of French national feeling resulted in the driving out of the English. By 1453, when the Hundred Years War (which had been far from continuous since 1338) came to an end, the only French possession left to the English was the port of Calais.

This was the general custom before the first plague [the Black Death of 1349], but things have changed now. For John Cornwall, a school teacher, changed the method of teaching in school and made his pupils translate from French into English; and Richard Pencrych learned that way of teaching from him, as did other men of Pencrych, so that now, 1385 A.D., the ninth year of the reign of King Richard II, in all the grammar schools of England children have abandoned French and translate and do their lessons in English.

This sets the date of the change from French to English as the means of instruction in schools fairly precisely, and when we realize that formal educational methods are always conservative and are slow to reflect public opinion, we can see why the social and cultural rehabilitation of English can be said to have been achieved in the first half of the fourteenth century. English was introduced into the law courts in 1362,[3] and English was used for the first time in the opening of parliament in 1363; the work of Chaucer came in the immediately following decades. By this time, too, Anglo-French—the development of Norman French in England—was giving way in England to Parisian French, the standard French of France, which indicated that its knowledge was a polite accomplishment rather than a native endowment.

Besides French and English there was Latin, the learned language of Christian civilization. Latin had also, of course, been the learned language in Anglo-Saxon times, and it was only the dearth of good Latinists in England that led to the use of Anglo-Saxon in serious didactic literature (we saw earlier how King Alfred's program of translation was caused by his fear that Latin had declined throughout the country). This illustrates very clearly how ignorance—of a kind—can encourage the growth of a vernacular literature, a not uncommon phenomenon in the history of culture. Anglo-Saxon literary prose was among the best developed in Europe, and far more advanced than French prose; but had the Danish invasions not produced a decay of Latin learning, it would never have developed as it did. The ecclesiastical reforms introduced into England by the Normans restored Latin as the language of serious didactic works and thus did grave harm to the tradition of English literary prose—though, as we shall see, the tradition did survive, to re-emerge impressively later.

With the Latin literature of medieval England we are not concerned in this history, though no one who wishes to understand the

[3] At least, an Act of Parliament of that year ordered that all pleas should be conducted in English; but in fact French remained the language of the law courts for much longer.

literary culture of the Middle Ages can ignore it. Latin was not only the language of theological and didactic works; it was also the language of science, philosophy, history, and a great deal of poetry. Latin was also used for all official documents, and was the legal language of Norman England until it was replaced by Anglo-French in the thirteenth century. (Anglo-French remained the official legal language of England until 1731.) Perhaps the most interesting Latin prose works produced in England in the early Middle English period were the histories. Such Anglo-Latin historians as William of Malmesbury, whose histories of England show both learning and a critical judgment, and Matthew Paris, the greatest of the twelfth-century English historians, are of more interest to students of historiography than to those concerned primarily with literature, but the *Historia Regum Britanniae* of Geoffrey of Monmouth, written in the third decade of the twelfth century, provided a mine of material which was later to be fruitfully employed by poets and romancers. Geoffrey was a Welshman, and drew on old British traditions, including the Welsh historians Gildas and Nennius. He gives us a picture of the Anglo-Saxon invasions seen through the eyes of the retreating Britons, and his pages are filled with figures which were to become famous in imaginative literature. Here we first find the stories of Lear and Cymbeline and Gorboduc, and here, most important of all, we get the first full-dress story of the exploits of King Arthur. It is Arthur himself, rather than his knights, who keeps the center of the picture: we hear nothing yet of Lancelot or Tristan; but we have Uther Pendragon and Merlin; we have the treachery of Arthur's nephew Mordred and the disloyalty of Guanhumara (Guinevere), and we have the final bearing of the mortally wounded Arthur to Avalon. Arthur is a great hero to Geoffrey, rather than a great symbolic figure in the background, as he was later to become, and the knights by whom he is surrounded are loyal feudal retainers rather than epitomes of courtly virtues. Geoffrey has Arthur successful in · war against enemies both at home and abroad, until, rejecting Rome's demand for tribute, he sets out to conquer Rome itself. But the disloyalty of Mordred and of Guinevere recalls him, and so the story goes to the last great battle and the journey to Avalon. Here is the outline of the story that so much later medieval literature was to use as a grand backcloth for innumerable individual incidents.

The *De Nugis Curialium* ("Courtiers' Trifles") of Walter Map is another twelfth-century Latin work likely to interest the reader of medieval English literature, though for very different reasons from those which lead him to Geoffrey of Monmouth. It is a lively collection of the most miscellaneous material, loosely organized in the form of a satire on contemporary abuses. It contains anecdotes, folk tales, pieces of invective, witty observations, amusing stories, and similar entertaining matter, and its existence is a reminder that medieval Latin was not the language only of solemn works. Walter Map was long credited with many of those lively Latin lyrics—satirical, amorous, irreverent, bacchanalian, and sometimes indecent—which belong to the medieval Goliardic tradition, the tradition of the wandering scholars, the rollicking secular protest against official Christendom's focusing on the next world. How many of these poems, if any, Map himself wrote is not known; but Goliardic poetry, with its secular moods and its frequent metrical skill, represents a chapter of European poetry of the greatest interest to anyone concerned with any of the European literatures. The movement from classical Latin quantitative verse to the rhymed accentual Latin verse of medieval hymns and of these Goliardic poems represents a major shift in the nature of the European ear for poetry, one might almost say, and it can be studied more happily than elsewhere in the fascinating literature of the wandering scholars. The clear voice of the disinterested lyrist comes to us from the Middle Ages more often than we realize in the Latin words of some impoverished but singing scholar:

> Musa venit carmine,
> dulce modulamine:
> pariter cantemus . . .
>
> The Muse comes with song,
> with sweet harmony.
> Let us sing, too.

There was also an important Anglo-French literature in England in the twelfth and thirteenth centuries. Much of it is religious and didactic—and we must never forget that by far the largest number of medieval works in any language are religious and didactic—of which only a few have any strictly literary interest, among them the allegorical poem *Le Chasteau d'Amour* by the brilliant and learned Robert Grosseteste, bishop of Lincoln, where praise of the Virgin and many aspects of Christian theology are presented through an elaborate allegory of a castle and its defenders. The lively and metrically interesting *Voyage of St. Brendan,* with its rich collection of marvelous adventures, is another Anglo-French poem of some literary interest today. There are also many Anglo-French chroniclers, among whom by far the most significant for the reader of English literature is Wace, whose translation of Geoffrey of Monmouth's *Historia Regum Britanniae,* in the middle of the twelfth century, represented an important stage in the transmission of the Arthurian legend. Wace's *Roman de Brut,* as his work is generally called, is more than a simple translation of Geoffrey of Monmouth; he also includes Arthurian stories from other sources, and is the first actually to mention the Round Table, though his references to it seem to indicate that it was already known to his readers. The *Roman de Brut* consists of fifteen thousand lines of verse, done with vivacity and a feeling for dramatic incident that strike the imagination more forcibly than the straightforward historical narrative of Geoffrey of Monmouth. It is with the translation of Wace's *Roman de Brut* by Layamon early in the thirteenth century that the Arthurian story first appears in English.

Works in French written in England during this period also include a number of romances, verse stories written purely for entertainment, and some shorter verse narratives, generally based on folklore and often dealing with the supernatural, to which the name Breton *lais* has long been given. The *lai* is of Celtic origin, and seems to have derived both from Welsh and Breton sources. (Brittany, it will be remembered, was settled by fugitives from Britain after the Anglo-Saxon invasions, so that the Bretons were very closely akin, both in speech and in traditions, to the Britons of Wales and Cornwall; they spoke almost the same Celtic tongue and cherished alike the Arthurian and other Celtic British legends.) The best known author of *lais* was Marie de France, who was apparently born in France but wrote in England and dedicated her *Lais* to King Henry II. Of the romances we shall speak in greater detail later; they represent one of the most important branches of medieval secular literature and require separate treatment.

Anglo-French literature, whether written in that form of French which, since King John's loss of Normandy in 1204, had been developing in its own way in England, or written in England in the French of Paris, was part of the wider stream of French literature which, partly because of the Norman Conquest but more fundamentally because of the extraordinary efflorescence of French literature in the twelfth century, swept into English literature in the Middle English period and moved it far away from the Anglo-Saxon heroic mold. We shall have to look more closely, therefore, at French literature and the techniques, attitudes, and subject matter which it introduced.

But what, meantime, was happening to the native Anglo-Saxon tradition? In poetry, there is little extant to show precisely what was happening in the late eleventh and early twelfth centuries. We have some fragments of religious and didactic poetry which are sufficient to indicate that the Anglo-Saxon alliterative line was continued, though in a looser and more popular form. The *Worcester Fragments* (so called because they consist of the remnants of a manuscript which had been cut up and pasted together to make the covers of a book in the library of Worcester Cathedral) preserve, in addition to portions of Ælfric's *Grammar* (in West Saxon), a short poem lamenting that the people are no longer taught in English, as they used to be in Anglo-Saxon times by the great Anglo-Saxon saints and scholars, but are left in ignorance by foreign teachers, so that both teachers and people are damned together.

> Nu is þeo leore forleten and þet folc is forloren.
> Nu beoþ oþre leoden þeo læraþ ure folc,
> And feole of þen lorþeines losiæþ and þet folc forþ mid.

> Now is this teaching abandoned and the people is lost.
> Now it is men of other languages that teach our people,
> And many of the teachers are damned and the people as well.

The language here is early Middle English, and probably represents a late twelfth century scribe (about 1180) transcribing into his own West Midland dialect a poem originally written in West Saxon soon after the Conquest. The language is, indeed, transitional between Anglo-Saxon and Middle English and is nearer to the language of Ælfric than to that of Chaucer. The verse form is still the Anglo-Saxon alliterative line, though looser than in classical Anglo-Saxon poetry. But neither this poem nor the fragmentary *Debate between the Body and the Soul* which follows it is of any general literary interest: their interest lies in their illustration of the development of the language and of the verse forms of the Anglo-Saxons in the twelfth century. The development can be traced further in much religious and didactic literature (including paraphrases of parts of the Bible), though there is little else that is so close to the Anglo-Saxon tradition. We soon begin to see the increasing influence of French models, an influence particularly noticeable where, as often happened, the Middle English work was itself a translation from the French.

A startling break with any tradition is the curious *Orrmulum*, written probably about the year 1200 by an Augustinian canon named Orm or Ormin. Orm's intention was to translate into English verse the Gospels that were read in the Mass during the whole year, but the verse he used employed neither the rhyme of the French nor

Anglo-Saxon alliteration, depending simply and wholly on strict syllabic regularity. It can be best illustrated by quoting the opening line:

> Þiss boc iss nemmnedd Orrmulum forrpi patt Ormm itt wrohhtë
> This book is called Orrmulum, because Orm made it.

This is the first of the ten thousand extant lines of the poem (fortunately, only about one-eighth of the whole survives), and each of the other lines is of exactly the same length, each has precisely the same metrical pattern, with fifteen syllables and a "feminine" ending, and there is nothing to vary the intolerable monotony. Orm's spelling is also original: it is a phonetic spelling, with a double consonant after every short vowel except when the vowel is in an open syllable. Whatever his reason for doing this (and it has been much debated) he produced a very odd-looking text, interesting to philologists but of more than usual tedium to the general reader. Orm's meter is not in itself unusual—if we divide his line into two we get the standard ballad measure:

> He turned his face unto the wall,
>   And death was with him dealing:
> "Adieu, adieu, my dear friends all,
>   And be kind to Barbara Allan."

Wordsworth was partial to it:

> And hark! how blithe the throstle sings!
> He, too, is no mean preacher:
> Come forth into the light of things,
> Let Nature be your Teacher.

But Wordsworth and the ballad writers at least had the variety of rhyme, and none of them ran to ten thousand lines.

Orm might have done better to accept the French rhyming fashion, which was now beginning to come into Middle English religious and didactic verse. The four-hundred line *Poema Morale* or *Moral Poem* is a late twelfth-century versified sermon written in the same meter as the *Orrmulum*, but with more flexibility and employing rhyme. Though hardly the most exciting of poems, the *Poema Morale* has a certain vigor and some signs of personal feeling that are wholly lacking in the *Orrmulum*. It deals with the usual medieval religious commonplaces—lost opportunities in this life, the Last Judgment, the horrors of Hell, the joys of Heaven, the call to repentance—but the note of earnest conviction which comes through saves it from being the purely mechanical rehearsal of commonplaces.

Once the Middle English writers had learned rhyme, nothing could stop them, and a didactic writer or long-winded romancer given his head in a clippety-clop meter was very hard to stop. Octosyllabic couplets could go on for ever:

> Men yhernes rimes for to here,
> And romans red on maneres sere,
> Of Allsaunder þe conquerour;
> Of Iuly Cesae þe emparour;
> O Grece and Troy the strang strijf;
> Þere many thosand lesis their lijf;
> O Brut that bern bald of hand,
> Þe first conquerour of Ingland;
> O Kyng Arthour þat was so rike,
> Quam none in hys time was like,
> O ferlys þat hys knythes fel,
> Þat aunters sere I here of tell,
> Als Wawan, Cai and oþer stabell,
> For to were þe ronde tabell;
> How Charles kyng and Rauland faght,
> Wit sarazins wald þai na saght;
> O Tristrem and hys leif Ysote,
> How he for here be-com a sote,
> O Ioneck and of Ysambrase,
> O Ydoine and of Amadase. . . .

This is the opening of the *Cursor Mundi*, an enormous poem of some thirty thousand lines which deals with all the important incidents of both Old and New Testament story and a great variety of moral and religious topics. The poem, which dates from the last quarter of the thirteenth century, is encyclopedic in scope, and is carried along through its varied subject matter by its author's determined and not unskillful rhyming. It is a good introduction to the medieval view of world history and of much else, and serves to remind us once again of the didactic purpose of so much medieval writing.

With properly varied rhymes and metrical skill—which took a long time to develop—the Middle English poet was able to achieve something far removed from anything possible to his Anglo-Saxon predecessor, and even the most stereotyped religious subject could be made fresh and moving with the proper lilt and the proper imagery. One of the earliest successful religious poems in Middle English is the twelfth-century *Love Rune* by Thomas of Hales. It urges the vanity and transience of earthly love and advocates instead the love

of Christ. The traditional theme of *ubi sunt qui ante nos fuere?*—
where are those who lived before us?—rings out with a new confidence:

> Hwer is Paris and Heleyne
> Þat weren so bryht and feyre on bleo [face],
> Amadis and Ideyne,
> Tristram, Yseude and alle þeo,
> Ector, wiþ his scarpe meyne,
> And Cesar, riche of wordes feo [wealth]?
> Heo beoþ iglyden vt of þe reyne [world]
> So þe schef is of þe cleo. [As the sheaf is from the hillside
> *or* As the sheaf is (cut) by the reaping-hook.]

This sounds the true note of medieval plangency, a note sounded
first (as far as the Middle Ages knew) by the late fifth- and early
sixth-century Roman philosopher Boethius, one of the most popular
writers in the Middle Ages, translated both by King Alfred and by
Chaucer. Boethius had asked:

> Ubi nunc fidelis ossa Fabricii manent,
> quid Brutus aut rigidus Cato?

> Where now lie the bones of the faithful Fabricius,
> What now is Brutus or upright Cato?

King Alfred, in his rendering, substitutes for the remote classical
character figures nearer home, and asks, "Where are now the bones
of the famous and wise smith Wayland, and who knows where they
be? . . ."

A late thirteenth-century English lyrist asked the same question:

> Were be they þat biforen us weren, [that were before us]
> Houndes ladden and havekes beren, [led hounds and carried hawks]
> And hadden feld and wode? [field and forest]

And a century later, in France, Villon was to ask:

> Dictes moy où, n'en quel pays,
> Est Flora, la belle Rommaine;
> Archipiada, ne Thaïs,
> Qui fut sa cousine germaine;
> Echo, parlant quant bruyt on maine
> Dessus rivière ou sus estan,
> Qui beaulté ot trop plus qu'humaine?
> —Mais où sont les neiges d'antan?

A sense of transience of earthly life pressed hard on the Middle Ages, and medieval writers developed their own kind of cadence for its expression. It is equally far removed from Æschylus' stern sense of fate, from the chastened melancholy of Sophocles, and from the civilized, almost self-indulgent sadness of Virgil; nor has it anything of the thoughtful introspection of Matthew Arnold's "Dover Beach." It is perhaps a simpler note than any of these, and it comes impressively into medieval literature only after the development of rhyme and meter had made it possible for medieval poets to express it with that special kind of lyric lilt. Anglo-Saxon alliterative verse was an effective medium for the older heroic poetry; but new kinds of sensibility demanded a lighter and more flexible mode of expression. The new rhyme and meter that the French brought to Europe meant, as we have said, a change in the European ear, but that corresponded to a deeper change—a change in European sensibility.

The octosyllabic couplet, which English learned from French, is not always, even in the early Middle English period, handled by determined and long-winded didactic writers; apart from its use in romances, it is found in a variety of works. One of the earliest appearances of this verse form in English is one of the most successful —in the vivacious *The Owl and the Nightingale*, written probably around 1200, the first example in English of the *débat*, the contest in verse between two or more speakers. The verse debate had become a literary convention in both Latin and French, and could serve a great many different purposes. In *The Owl and the Nightingale* the two birds, who pursue their altercation with great spirit and with all the legal tricks of a twelfth-century lawsuit, presumably stand allegorically for two ways of life, the monastic and the secular, or for two kinds of poetry, the didactic and the amorous. The nightingale is the more sympathetic character to modern readers, but, though the conflict is unresolved by the end of the poem, the owl would appear to have won on points. But whatever the allegorical intention, it is clear that the author delighted in the dramatic quality of the poem and that his main interest lay in giving life and spirit to a conventional form. The narrative is handled with an accomplished ease, and the dialogue succeeds in painting with great vividness not only the characters of the two speakers (the respectable owl and the hedonistic nightingale) but also aspects of the daily life of the period.

But these exceptional instances of accomplished early Middle English poems must not be allowed to obscure the fact that the recovery of an English poetic style after the Norman Conquest was a

slow business, and was not generally accomplished until the fourteenth century. There were individual successful poems before the
fourteenth century, but no great English poet. The substitution of
rhyme and meter for the Anglo-Saxon alliterative verse was not the
result of a revolution in taste and attitude, such as some literary historians have seen in the Romantic Movement; it was a slow process
of imitation of and adaptation from the French, with the English
language itself continually growing in vocabulary and in flexibility
until it reached the point where it could handle the new verse form
with confidence and variety. Without the French element in Middle
English vocabulary, the possibilities for rhyme would have been very
restricted.

Some of the early Middle English poems we have quoted above
will show how the native Anglo-Saxon tradition gave way to the new
rhyming fashion; but the alliterative tradition was not altogether
dead. We can see it; in its more popular form, in Layamon's *Brut*, a
metrical history of Britain based on Wace's *Roman de Brut* and
written some time in the late twelfth century. Layamon's verse lacks
the careful parallelism of Anglo-Saxon verse as well as such Anglo-
Saxon poetic devices as the "kenning," and his lines have become
purely accentual in rhythm, but he uses alliteration and no rhyme.
More impressive testimony to the survival and even development of
the Anglo-Saxon alliterative tradition is the group of accomplished
alliterative poems which suddenly appear in the fourteenth century.
These include romances, religious poems, and satirical and allegorical works. In the last group is the well-known *Piers Plowman*, to be
discussed later, and among the romances is the remarkable *Sir
Gawain and the Green Knight*, one of the most brilliant of all Middle
English allegorical tales of adventure and of the marvelous, written
in alliterative blank verse each paragraph of which concludes with
four short lines having alternate rhyme. Among the religious poems
of the so-called "Alliterative Revival" are three which are found in
the same manuscript as *Sir Gawain;* they are *Patience, Purity,* and
Pearl, of which the first is a homily on the virtues of patience illustrated by an effective recounting of the story of Jonah, and the last
is both an elegy on the poet's dead daughter and an allegory of Christian faith, one of the most interesting and skillful religious poems of
the Middle Ages.

In prose, it is easier to trace the continuity of the Anglo-Saxon
tradition. Its variety and liveliness had made Anglo-Saxon prose
remarkable among European literatures of the period: translations,
homilies, and didactic, devotional, and informative works of many

kinds were to be found in prose, while in the *Anglo-Saxon Chronicle* a tradition of historical prose was maintained for centuries. Copying of Anglo-Saxon prose works went on assiduously in monasteries after the Conquest, and the *Chronicle* was continued: the last entry was made in the Peterborough Chronicle in the middle of the twelfth century, after a gap caused probably by the confusions of King Stephen's reign, and it is between the language of this final scribe and that of his predecessor who brought the narrative up to 1132 that scholars have drawn the necessarily somewhat arbitrary line between Anglo-Saxon (Old English) and Middle English. This was the end of the Anglo-Saxon tradition of historical prose, and England now loses its lead in the development of vernacular historical writing. The Norman clerics who took over the local and national administrative positions in England after the Conquest introduced Latin as the language of official communication and historical record, and English historical prose did not emerge again until the time of the Tudors. At the same time French influence was leading English writers to turn to rhymed verse rather than prose for historical and other kinds of writing which had been prose in Anglo-Saxon times, while the increase of dialectical differences in Middle English helped to make a standard literary prose impossible. As far as English historical prose was concerned, then—as with such other arts as manuscript illumination, metal work, and jewelry—the Norman Conquest put the clock back.

In homiletic and devotional prose, however, the tradition was not lost; in spite of handicaps, the work of instructing the people in the vernacular went on after the Conquest. Here the fall from supremacy of the West Saxon literary language in favor of different local dialects was less significant, for instruction of the common people could in any case be most effectively done in their own dialect. Thus the Anglo-Saxon homiletic tradition—carrying on the work of Ælfric with modernizing of and additions to his sermons—continued to flourish, and English religious prose prospered side by side with the new French verse renderings of similar literature. This was especially true in the west of England; in the southeast French seems to have predominated even in this field early in the thirteenth century, but the mass of homiletic literature in the West Midland dialect of this period carried English religious prose safely through the danger period to provide continuity with the prose of Tudor times. The fact that Wulfstan, bishop of Worcester, retained his see after the Conquest until his death in 1095 must have helped to encourage this vernacular prose tradition in the west; it is significant that after his death his biography was written in English by Coleman, a Worcester monk.

The sermons, translations, saints' lives, and other devotional and didactic works in which this prose tradition manifests itself are of little literary interest, though they are of importance to the philologist and to the historian of thought and society. The earliest writings of this kind after the Conquest are those known as the *Katherine Group*, and include the lives of three virgin saints, Katherine, Margaret, and Juliana, a treatise pointing out the discomforts of marriage and the advantages of virginity, and a prose homily in which Wit, the informed master, and Will, the foolish mistress, appear struggling (amid a great number of allegorical figures) for control of the soul. These works are written in a conscious literary prose, with use (especially in the three saints' lives) of alliteration and deliberate rhythmic effects. They were addressed to a female audience, as was the *Ancren Riwle*, a manual of instruction intended for three young girls who had decided to become anchoresses. In addition to the usual devotional and didactic material, the *Ancren Riwle* contains much lively incidental material by way of illustration, and the author's use of proverb, anecdote, character sketch, and realistic detail, as well as his numerous references to matters of daily life—domestic affairs, farming, travel, sport, among other aspects—makes the work an important and interesting historical document as well as providing it with a human interest which the modern reader appreciates so much more than the conventional didactic element. It was written probably about 1200 in the West Midland dialect, and its influence and popularity were enormous. Its influence on the religious prose of the thirteenth and fourteenth centuries was largely instrumental in ensuring the transmission of the prose tradition of the Anglo-Saxon homilies to such writers as Richard Rolle of Hampole, the fourteenth-century mystical and devotional writer, and his follower Walter Hilton. Rolle is important both for the movement of devotional piety, with its ascetic bias and lyrical development of personal feeling in religious matters, which he founded, and for the clarity and cogency of his prose (which is in the northern dialect of Yorkshire). There is a modern ring to Rolle's prose style, partly because he tends to reduce the inflections as in modern English, but more significantly because of the simple directness of his word order. His rhymed verse is technically less distinguished. Of Rolle's followers, Walter Hilton (who died in 1396) is the most interesting, and his prose work *The Scale of Perfection*, which debates the respective claims of the active and the contemplative life, is another important document in the history of English prose style. How unreadable fourteenth-century religious treatises could be when devoid of any personal inspiration or stylistic grace can be seen in Michael of Northgate's *Ayenbyte of Inwyt* (*Prick of Conscience*) a translation of a thirteenth-century didactic work done with an infuriating mechanical dullness, not even accurately, and not always intelligibly. (This is the work whose title haunts Stephen Dedalus in Joyce's *Ulysses*, symbolizing his feeling of guilt with reference to his mother.) Its importance has been magnified by philologists, to whom it is a great treasure, for it is written in the pure Kentish dialect of Canterbury and its date is known precisely, a note at the end of the manuscript making clear that it was finished on October 27, 1340.

Contemporary with Walter Hilton is John Wyclif, a very different figure from any member of the Rolle group, for Rolle was a contemplative mystic by temperament and sought to withdraw from the world, while Wyclif, controversialist, philosopher, politician, and reformer, was with his followers responsible not only for attacks on some important claims and practices of the Church but also for the first complete translation of the Bible into English. The Wyclif Bible was certainly not all translated by Wyclif; but it was done under his inspiration. Nicholas of Hereford seems to have done part of the earlier of the two versions (finished between 1382 and 1384) and John Purvey the later (finished soon after 1388). The translation is done from the Latin text of the Vulgate and it has little grace or life, though the later version is better in this respect than the earlier. The Wyclifite versions have neither the strength nor the idiomatic flow of Rolle's prose, and scholars today are inclined to put Rolle and Hilton far above Wyclif, both among those responsible for the continuity of English prose from Anglo-Saxon to modern times and as pioneers of English prose style. They helped to keep a standard of English prose alive until the late fifteenth century, when the increasing use of English prose in both secular and religious writing meant that the danger was over, and henceforth the development of English prose, however uneven, was part of the natural progress of the language and its literature.

One of the most striking differences between Middle English and Anglo-Saxon literature lies in the realm of verse narrative. The replacement of the older heroic poetry by the verse romance marks a significant change in taste and sensibility. Heroic poetry is sterner in mood, more realistic in treatment, and claims to deal with the exploits of heroes who have had some real place in history; the romance is more frankly escapist and the marvelous is introduced for its own sake. Fighting in heroic poetry is a grim affair, engaged in for some specific purpose, and even the most valiant hero is liable to lose if he fights against heavy odds; in the romance, characters fight on principle, as it were, or as a matter of fashion, often without any specific object; the outcome depends more on the character of the fighter than on the odds against which he is fighting, and the whole thing is done ritualistically, as a stylized sport rather than a desperate necessity. The transition between heroic poetry and medieval romance can be seen in the French *chansons de geste*, of which the *Chanson de Roland* is the best known example. These poems are really short heroic epics, and it is not improbable that similar poems, dealing with Germanic heroes, existed in Anglo-Saxon England: perhaps *The Battle of Brunanburh* and *The Battle of Maldon* are lone survivors of this sort of thing. But the *chansons de geste* are also early romances as well as late heroic poems, for they already show something of the interest in idealized character and in purely imaginative elaboration which was to be the mark of the fully developed romance. This transitional kind of poetry flourished in France from the ninth to the twelfth centuries.

These heroic tales of action, the *chansons de geste*, were mostly produced in northern France; it was from the south, especially Provence, that the new elements of sentiment and courtly love came to produce a wholly new kind of romantic story. Provence had already developed, in the lyric poetry of the troubadours, a remarkable new literary form. The rise of Provençal language and literature in the tenth and eleventh centuries represents one of the most profound—and still one of the most mysterious—movements in European culture. In the tenth century the Provençal dialect—French in its southern form, the *langue d'oc*—began to prevail over others as the literary language of southern Europe. This was one of the results of the breakdown of Latin under the influence of the languages of the barbarians, and the process was fraught with the most far-reaching consequences. About 1100 a host of Provençal poets arose with remarkable suddenness, producing sophisticated love lyrics different in both tone and technique from anything hitherto known in Europe. The meter was regular and syllabic, and rhyme was used. The transition from classical Latin quantitative metrics to rhymed verse can be traced in late Latin hymns; it is one of the most fascinating stories in literary history; but it is no direct part of the history of English literature. The point that chiefly concerns the historian of English literature in dealing with the Middle English period is that English literature, like most of the

MIDDLE ENGLISH PROSE AND VERSE 51

European literatures at this time, was in the French cultural orbit and that therefore what French literature had become by this time is directly relevant to any account of what was happening in English.

One might distinguish between the narrative romance of action, unaffected by the courtly and sentimental ideals of the south, and the romance as it was modified by the new Provençal sophistication. The former, the product of the *trouvères* (northern equivalent of the troubadours, professional minstrels who went around entertaining in the halls of the great houses), was written in the northern dialect of France, or *langue d'oil*, and, as we have seen, bore some resemblance to the earlier heroic poetry. Influenced by the southern love lyric, it bred the characteristic medieval form of literary entertainment, the romance in which loyalty to one's king is no greater force than loyalty to one's lady; where both love and war are ritualized by elaborate techniques of service; where the devoted knight overcomes fabulous obstacles by virtue of the strictness of his honor and the strength of his passion. We shall discuss later the ideal of courtly love which so affected the tone of medieval romance and indeed had an incalculable effect on all subsequent love literature; let us first look at the subject matter of these works.

The late twelfth-century *trouvère* Jean Bodel, in an often quoted couplet, divided the subject matter of medieval romance into three categories, the "Matter of France," the "Matter of Britain," and the "Matter of Rome the Great." The first of these groups was the earliest to be developed; it deals with the activities of Charlemagne and his knights, and its tone is nearer that of heroic poetry; it finds its greatest expression in the *Chanson de Roland,* which tells a desperate story of a courageous fight against hopeless odds, ending with the hero's death. As the cycle grew, the interest turned more and more away from the character of Charlemagne to concentrate on the exploits of individual members of the group of warriors that surrounded him, just as in the Arthurian cycle of romance the interest shifted from Arthur to his knights. The driving moral force behind the earlier romances of the "Matter of France" cycle is the sense of Christendom pushing back the infidel Saracen invaders of Europe, and it has been suggested that these romances were encouraged or even produced by monks of the monasteries on the pilgrim routes who thought in this way to identify their founder with one of Charlemagne's heroes and so attract patronage. Other romances in this group are concerned with the struggle of individual heroes against the Emperor's tyranny, or indeed with any kind of adventure which in the process of time became attached to the name of Charlemagne or one of his heroes. The "Matter of Britain" is concerned with the Arthurian stories, which we have seen beginning in Geoffrey of Monmouth and Layamon's *Brut*. But both Geoffrey and Layamon conceived themselves to be writing history, not romance; the Arthurian romances derive rather from the French Arthurian legends which were common long before Geoffrey wrote his history. The stories of a historical Romano-British or Cambro-British leader of his people against the Anglo-Saxon invaders may well have been handed down in Wales to be carried thence to Brittany by Welshmen who emigrated there in the ninth century, and it was from the Breton legends rather than from the English chroniclers that most of the later Arthurian romances seem to have sprung. These romances, dealing with the adventures of individual knights of the Round Table, are far removed in tone from the *Chanson de Roland:* they have lost the old heroic note completely and treat with extraordinary elaboration the practice and ideals of courtly love. The "Matter of Rome the Great" represented another great popular kind of subject matter—the ancient classical world, as seen through medieval eyes. This is not the world of Homer or of Pericles or of Virgil, but a curiously medievalized ancient world derived from sources and traditions far removed from what we would today consider the mainstream of classical culture. The story of Troy, which so haunted the medieval imagination, they got not from Homer but from the fourth-century Latin writer Dictys Cretensis (Dictys of Crete) and the somewhat later Dares Phrygius (Dares of Phrygia), who claimed to have been actually at the siege and told the story as eyewitnesses, Dictys on the Grecian side and Dares on the Trojan. If the *Aeneid* was the original source of the Troy story as the Middle Ages knew it,[4] it was the work of Dictys and Dares which developed the tradition, to be worked up in the late twelfth-century French romance, the *Roman de Troie* by Benoit de Saint Maure. A century after the *Roman de Troie,* came the *Historia Destructionis Troiae* by Guido delle Colonne, a full Latin version of the same material. The major figure in the development of the medieval Troy tradition is Benoit de Saint Maure, whose work first brings the material together to make it accessible to later medieval story; here we get not only a

---

[4] Virgil was known in the Middle Ages, though popularly as a "wizard" rather than a great poet. The *Aeneid* was made the basis of a French romance, the *Roman d'Eneas*. But the Troy story, as the Middle Ages knew it, was Benoit's, not Virgil's. Virgil's Dido, like the Medea of Ovid's *Metamorphoses* and other heroines from Ovid's *Heroides,* were treated as basic romantic love stories by the medieval courtly love poets.

full treatment of the Trojan war which is to be the standard medieval way of looking at it, but also the story of Troilus and Cressida, to be used so effectively by later English writers.

The "Matter of Rome" included not only stories of the siege of Troy, but other stories of the ancient world, of Thebes, of Alexander the Great, and of Julius Caesar among others. The medieval view of the civilization of Greece and Rome can be clearly seen in the "Matter of Rome" romances. Greece, of course, was more remote, and was seen less as a period of history than a group of legends concerning Greek historical and mythological figures who were conceived of as feudal lords with their retainers: we can see this very clearly in Chaucer's Knight's Tale. As far as the Trojan war was concerned, medieval Europe was on the side of Troy; indeed, many countries of Western Europe traced their origins from Trojan ancestors. Rome (also founded by a Trojan) was closer to them: its language was the international learned language of their day; its organization had enabled Christianity to establish itself throughout Europe once the Emperor himself had been converted; its roads and aqueducts were often still in use and still admired. It was the Roman Empire, not the earlier Republic, that the Middle Ages admired: Dante put Brutus and Cassius,[5] who conspired against the potential founder of the empire, in the lowest circle of Hell; for the Roman Empire was the divinely ordained machinery through which Christianity would come to Europe, and the term "Holy Roman Empire," in spite of the fact that the political entity so designated may have been neither holy nor Roman nor an empire, had real meaning to medieval minds in terms of historical continuity between the Christian and the Roman world. Yet with all this there was no real historical knowledge or historical perspective, no sense at all of different stages and kinds of civilization, no ability to conceive a radically different political or economic organization than their own. "Duke" Theseus, even to Chaucer, was essentially a medieval feudal lord. The medieval mind playing with the fragments of a lost classical civilization is a fascinating aspect of the history of culture.

The French romances dealing with the "Matter of Britain" and the "Matter of Rome" combined adventure and sentiment, the latter deriving from the elaborate conventions of courtly love which began in the love lyrics of Provence. The idea of courtly love proved to be one of the most far-reaching and one of the most revolutionary in

[5] With the revival of interest in the Stoic tradition in the Renaissance, it was the Republic rather than the Empire that was admired. Contrast Shakespeare's attitude to Brutus with Dante's, and note also Milton's attitude to Roman history.

the history of European sensibility; it spread rapidly throughout Europe, penetrating both lyrical and narrative literature from the Mediterranean to the North Sea, wherever the spirit of the Romance literatures touched. Hitherto, love between the sexes had been regarded simply as physical passion, or as a form of affection (but lower than that between man and man), or as a kind of madness, or as a combination of any of these three elements. In the poetry of the troubadours a new conception of love first appears. Love is service, like that of a slave to his master except that it is not based on outside compulsion. The knight serves the lady of his choice, suffers any and every kind of indignity for her sake, thinks only of her, commends himself to her when he goes into battle, and in referring to her uses language that is scarcely, if at all, distinguishable from that used in religious poems with reference to the Virgin Mary (and indeed there is a clear reciprocal influence between the cult of the Virgin Mary and the courtly love tradition). The slightest favor the lady chooses to bestow upon her servant is sufficient reward for the greatest hardship he may undergo for her sake. He is her humble vassal, and she is his liege lady. He must be loyal to her for life, however she may treat him. However desperate he is, however hopeless of winning his lady's favor, however he may sigh and moan because of unrequited love, he must never think of ceasing to be the servant of her whom he has originally chosen, for it is better to be in love than to have no liege lady to serve. Love is, as it were, its own reward, and though a more concrete reward is desired and sometimes obtained, the lover must not swerve in his allegiance if it does not come. This is not a relation between husband and wife: indeed, throughout most of this literature it is taken as a matter of course that a husband cannot be the lover of his own wife. That is a role to be taken by someone else. The courtly love tradition implies, in fact, an idealization of adultery, and if modern romantic love is automatically linked to marriage that is because the sixteenth- and seventeenth-century poets deliberately grafted the idea of courtly love onto the domestic ideal of married happiness. The concept of falling in love, wooing, and marrying, which has been one of the staple themes of fiction for two centuries, represents a modification of the medieval courtly love tradition while deriving from that tradition. In medieval courtly love, when a poet offers love to a lady he does not bother about her husband at all: his real rival is anyone who seeks to be a lover of the lady in the same way as himself. The lover's conduct must conform at all points to a strict code of honor: in addition to the service of his lady he must dedicate himself to the cause of women in a general sense, always ready to defend them, always prepared to succor damsels in distress. The rules of knightly behavior were carefully defined, and involved many subtle points of conduct: by these rules every lover was bound. There were, in theory if not in practice, "Courts of Love," which adjudicated on subtle points of honor and the proper conduct in love affairs.

The origins of this influential new conception of love between the sexes must be sought partly in social conditions, partly in the way in which such Latin writers on love as Ovid were interpreted in the Middle Ages, partly in a religious attitude which shifted attention from woman as Eve, the origin of all our human woes, to woman as the Virgin Mary, the pattern of ideal maidenhood. One must remember that feudal civilization (especially on the continent, where central government was generally less effective than in England) tended to resolve itself into separate islands of social life, the lord of the manor living with his lady in a little nucleus of civilization of which he was the guardian. Among his retainers and hangers-on there would be a great variety of male types who, while far above the land-tilling peasantry who supported the whole group by their labor outside the walls of the castle or manor, were nevertheless inferior to the lord of the manor and his lady: adventurers, landless knights, squires, pages, would look up to their master and mistress as their feudal superiors. The lady would become the source and arbiter of courtesy within the community, superior in rank to all except the lord himself, and, if he were away at the Crusades or on some other adventure, superior to all without exception. Thus service and courtesy were her rights anyway, and if any of the men of the community were to love her, the love would have to be expressed in a context of service and courtesy. Perhaps the genealogy of the courtly poet also throws some light on the ideals of humility and service so bound up with the new romantic attitude. Before the real troubadour poetry began, it was the common practice for the lord to have about him for his personal entertainment minstrels, *jongleurs,* at first merely primitive mummers or acrobats. When the new Provençal poetry began to develop, these humble entertainers— who were socially among the lowest of the castle servants—often took on the function of court poet, ceasing to be mere *jongleurs* and becoming troubadours. And though the troubadours rapidly rose in the social scale until they included in their number many of the lords themselves, it is not fantastic to see in the stress on service in courtly love poetry some trace of the humble position of the original troubadours, who were merely glorified clowns. Marriage, of course, would be out of the question between the lady and either the trouba- dour or one of her husband's male followers. An even more cogent reason for courtly love remaining outside marriage was that in feudal times marriage was so bound up with the inheritance and transmis- sion of property that questions of love could not be allowed to enter into it. Lordship of land being the very basis of the system, anything connected with the disposal or acquisition of estates was a purely business matter into which sentiment must not intrude. Nor was the teaching of medieval religion calculated to drive the new conception of love into legal channels. Romantic passion in the relation between the sexes was not regarded by religion as a virtue under any circumstances, and there was no encouragement by the Church to graft the new feeling onto any conventional view of domestic happiness. From every point of view the difference be- tween courtly love and the relations between man and wife was emphasized. The lady was mistress (in a literal sense) but never wife, and often had to be courted secretly (this explains much that is otherwise puzzling in the relations between Troilus and Criseyde in Chaucer's poem). The courtly lover did not even *wish* to marry his lady, though he sought a consummation of his love outside mar- riage. Marriage, the idea often seems to have been, would spoil everything. It was only later that the romantic ideal of love was linked with marriage and the passion was regarded as virtuous provided that it had marriage in view.

It is clear, therefore, that this conception of courtly love that swept over Europe and penetrated its literature was one that origi- nated among the aristocracy and had little relation to the everyday lives of humbler men and women. It was, at its simplest, a conven- tionalization of the attitude of the high-placed feudal servant to his lord's wife, and if the lord himself was away at the Crusades there was all the more scope for the courtly lover. How far this attitude was a mere convention and how far it had a realistic basis is very difficult to say. Sometimes the whole business was nothing but a polite game, but we know that life often imitates art and the emotional pattern laid down in a literary convention is often spon- taneously followed in real experience. There must have been some- thing real behind it all. Of course to some the convention was just an opportunity to discourse subtly on the psychology of love, and it is to be noted that the psychological treatment of romantic love, so common in European literature, begins with the medieval allego- ries of courtly love.

This, then, was the kind of sentiment with which the medieval French romances surrounded their action. Such romances were produced in England as well as in France, for, as we have seen, French was the language of the English upper class from the Conquest until the fourteenth century, and during this period the "polite" literature of England was French, either imported or domestically produced. The translations of French romances into English give us an interesting indication of the difference in social polish between the audience for works in the French language in England and that for works written in English. The English translators were adapting a sophisticated, sentimental French literature for a much less sophisticated audience, who were more interested in the story than in the refined speculations about love and honor so characteristic of the courtly love tradition. The French romances combined sentiment with adventure; the English translators as a rule left out the sentiment and stuck to the adventure. The English romances were thus on the whole shorter, cruder, and more of a straight "story" than the French. Such a popular French romancer as the twelfth-century Chrétien de Troyes, who specialized in what a later age was to call "the language of the heart," in the psychology of courtly love, never achieved the popularity among the English that he had in France and Germany. The one English romance known to have been translated from Chrétien is the early fifteenth century *Ywain and Gawain* (a characteristic "Matter of Britain" story, telling of the adventures of a knight called Ywain who marries the widow of a conquered foe, is separated from her, and after many valorous deeds becomes reunited with her; with Gawain serving as a foil to Ywain and the figure of Arthur presiding dimly in the background). This was condensed from the much longer *Ywain, ou le Chevalier au Lion* of Chrétien; the long speeches, designed to illustrate the psychology of the speaker and the courtly conventions under which both thought and action develops, are cut in the translation. Those in England who were courtly and sophisticated enough to appreciate the finer points of courtesy and psychology, expected their literature to be in French: the English translations were for their ruder compatriots.

We must see these English romances against the larger European background to understand what they really were. The "Matter of France," with its echoes of the conflict between Christian and Saracen in Europe, attracting to itself and to its presiding figure Charlemagne folk legends and miscellaneous tales of adventure, providing one great focus for the medieval imagination; the "Matter of Britain," deriving originally from Celtic traditions of Arthur in Wales and Strathclyde and Cornwall and Brittany, providing a mold into which new notions of courtesy and honor could be poured, a strange symbolic fusion of Christian ideals, feudal convention, erotic fashion, and a deep underlying sense of change and fate; the "Matter of Rome," showing how the ancient classical world came by devious ways into the medieval imagination, with its sense of a lost world of heroes, the doom of Troy, the pathos of Dido, the grandeur of Alexander, the dignity of Theseus—to see all this, to understand the materials with which the medieval romancer worked, is to get closer to the minds of medieval people than any political or philosophical history could take us. The English romancer was part of this world of medieval romance, and if he often abbreviated and simplified his French originals because he was writing for a less courtly audience (and it is audience rather than readers, for these romances would as a rule be read or recited aloud to a group), this does not mean that he thought of himself as in any way living in a different world than that of fellow romancers, either in France or in England, who wrote in French. It is perhaps misleading to look at surviving English romance and conclude that that gives a representative picture of what the English produced in that field during the Middle Ages. There is little really interesting "Matter of France" material surviving in English, for example, but we know that the Charlemagne cycle was popular in England, for one of the earliest of the surviving manuscripts of the *Chanson de Roland* (and the best) was written in England, and there are references in contemporary literature to the popularity of these romances. The oldest surviving English romance dealing with "Matter of France" is the dull *Otuel*, dating from the first half of the fourteenth century; it is one of those deriving from a French group dealing with Roland's warfare against the Saracens and deals with a duel fought between Roland and the Saracen Otuel. The subject was popular and was treated more than once in English romance. More popular still was the story of Firumbras, Saracen king of Alexandria, and the combat between him and Roland; the late fourteenth-century *Sir Firumbras* is one of a number dealing with this material. Most interesting of the relatively few surviving English Charlemagne romances is the northern *Raif Coilyear*, written in Scotland and possessing a distinct Scottish background. This romance is a late example of its kind, composed in the last quarter of the fifteenth century and extant in a unique printed version of 1572. It is written in the popular thirteen-line stanza, of which the first nine lines are long, with anything from five to seven stresses, and the last four are shorter with three or four stresses. The versification is rough, jogging along with little polish, but the story has humor and vivacity and immense gusto. The story is a widespread folk tale which has been grafted on to the Charlemagne background: it tells of how Charlemagne seeks shelter in the forest hut of a collier, who entertains him rudely but lavishly without being aware of his identity; meeting him later at the palace, the collier learns who his guest was and is knighted by him.

The surviving English "Matter of Britain" romances are a more varied and more interesting lot, and at least three of them—the alliterative *Morte Arthure;* the romance entitled *Le Morte Arthure* which deals with the Maid of Ascolot, the discovery of the love of Lancelot and Guinevere, the combat between Lancelot and Arthur, and the passing of Arthur; and *Sir Gawain and the Green Knight*—having impressive qualities as literature, especially the last, which is one of the great literary productions of the Middle Ages. The ramifications of the Arthur story, with the development of its different phases, is the subject for a book in itself; all we can note here is that the romances can be grouped into those that deal with the whole story of Arthur's life (of which the alliterative *Morte Arthure* is easily the finest); those concerned with Arthur's youth, which is involved with the character of Merlin (e.g., *Arthur and Merlin*); those that deal with Gawain, who is the true hero of Middle English Arthurian romance, the only one to become the hero of a whole cycle of romances, eleven in all, of which *Sir Gawain and the Green Knight* is the most remarkable and *Golagrus and Gawain* and *Ywain and Gawain* are able and interesting; those that deal with Lancelot, never as popular a figure in the English romances as in the French, where he is the hero of an immense and widely popular prose romance, though he is the hero of the admirable late fourteenth-century English romance *Le Morte Arthure;* those that deal with the Holy Grail, an aspect of the Arthur story not much handled in English before Malory, though *Joseph of Arimathie,* one of the two English romances which do handle it, is historically interesting as being one of the earliest alliterative poems in Middle English; and the Perceval legend, a popular and widespread folk tale which became grafted on to the Arthurian story in the twelfth century, represented in English by a single romance, *Sir Percyvelle of Galles,* though more fully treated by the French romancers who developed him from a type of the simple innocent to the ideal and perfect knight who eventually attains the Grail (it is this Perceval who is Wagner's Parsifal). Finally, there is the story of Tristram, or Tristan, which in later times became perhaps the most popular of all the

Arthurian stories. The love of Tristram and Isoude (Iseult) is older in its origins than that of Lancelot and Guinevere and is another of those independent stories which eventually became associated with the Arthurian cycle; it is represented in English by a single northern romance, *Sir Tristram*, written at the end of the thirteenth century.

Of the origins of the stories of the different knights, Gawain, Lancelot, Tristram, and others, much has been written, and there has been much discussion, too, about the obscure origins and complicated development of the Grail legend; but we must pass these matters by and concentrate on the literature as we have it. And the Arthurian romance literature in English is remarkable enough. Its greatest document, as we have remarked, is *Sir Gawain and the Green Knight*, one of four notable poems written in the Northwest Midland dialect in the late fourteenth century and presumably by the same author.[6] The 2,530 lines of this poem are arranged in stanzas of unequal length, each of which contains a number of long alliterative lines followed by five short lines rhyming alternately (*ababa*), the first having one stress and the remaining four having each three. There is real technical accomplishment in the handling of this difficult stanza; the author also has great skill in setting a scene and a lyrical feeling in showing the movement of the seasons reflected in the changing face of nature. The story opens with the appearance at Arthur's court of the strange and menacing Green Knight, who asks for a volunteer from among the Knights of the Round Table to strike him a blow with the heavy axe he would provide, on the understanding that a year and a day later the knight would come and receive a similar blow from him. The knights are amazed and silent, and Arthur himself is driven to volunteer, but Gawain, model of courtesy, nobility, and courage, steps in and gives the blow. He strikes off the Green Knight's head, but the Knight simply picks his head up and rides off, telling Gawain to keep his bargain and appear at the Green Chapel a year and a day later to suffer a similar blow. A year passes, and we see the earth changing from winter to spring, then to summer, then to autumn, with angry winds and leaves falling from the tree, and finally to winter again. In the New Year Gawain sets out to look for the Green Chapel. On the way he seeks shelter at a castle and is handsomely entertained there by the lord and lady. Each morning the lord goes off to hunt, and his hunting is described with lively detail; Gawain stays in the castle, and is tempted by the lady who wants him to make love to her. He has a difficult time retaining his perfect courtesy and at the

[6] See p. 46.

same time repulsing her advances; but he goes no further than allowing her to kiss him. Gawain and the lord have promised to exchange with each other whatever they gain during the day, and in accordance with this bargain the lord gives Gawain the animals he has killed in the hunt and Gawain gives the lord the kisses. But on the last day the lady presses Gawain to accept a memento of her, and he accepts a green girdle which she says will give him invulnerability, which he will require in his encounter with the Green Knight. He says nothing of this girdle to the lord. Then Gawain leaves to find the Green Chapel, which turns out to be a grassy mound nearby. He meets the Green Knight, who strikes him with his huge axe, but deflects the blow as Gawain flinches. He taunts Gawain for flinching, and Gawain replies that he will not flinch again. He strikes a second time, Gawain remaining steady, but again he turns away the blow. The third time the axe lands, but only wounds Gawain slightly on one side of the neck. Gawain now says that he has fulfilled his bargain and demands a chance at a fair fight, but the Green Knight good-naturedly laughs at his ferocity and reveals himself as the lord of the castle; the slight wound on Gawain's neck is for the girdle which he took from his lady in order to preserve his life. Gawain, humiliated, admits his weakness and reproaches himself bitterly, but the Green Knight absolves him and tells him to keep the girdle. On his return to Arthur's court Gawain tells the whole story, not as a heroic exploit but as an example of moral failure, and Arthur comforts him and all the knights agree to wear a green belt for Gawain's sake.

The story clearly has deep roots in folklore and is capable of many kinds of allegorical interpretation. But it interests the reader today for the grace and liveliness with which the narrative is presented, for the technical skill of the versification, for the simple moving way in which the ideal of courage and courtesy is illustrated in Gawain's behavior, for the charm and conviction of Gawain's conversation with the lady and the genial humor of the Green Knight's last conversation with Gawain, for the brilliant detail of the hunting scenes, and above all for the feeling for nature and the movement of the seasons, embodied perhaps best of all in the description of the chill winter morning when Gawain leaves the castle to keep his appointment at the Green Chapel. It is a civilized and sophisticated work, and it shows what an unusually accomplished English romancer could make out of one of the Arthurian stories when the particular tradition represented by that story had reached just the proper stage. A story of marvels is interpreted in the light of a high ideal of physical and moral courage. The Gawain we see here is the true heroic Gawain, before he was ousted from his supremacy by Lancelot, who in later Arthurian romance completely replaced Gawain (even in England, where Gawain remained the great hero longer than in France) as the central heroic figure of the Arthurian cycle. The Gawain of Malory, as of Tennyson, is no longer the model of virtue, courtesy, and courage but an altogether debased figure. *Sir Gawain and the Green Knight* splendidly preserves the older, heroic Gawain, and does so in a typical Arthurian context, with Arthur presiding over his knights at Camelot at Christmas time and the spotlight on the individual adventure of one of them. In it the English romance achieves full literary stature. Elements from Anglo-Saxon, Norman, and French combine in a remarkable way: apparently the Anglo-Saxon alliterative tradition survived in modified form in the north, while the Arthurian legends were centered in the West, so a Northwestern poet, as the author of *Sir Gawain* appears to have been, was in a good position for uniting Anglo-Saxon and Celtic traditions. The vigor of the Anglo-Saxon, the polish of the French, and the magical folk strain of the Celtic combine successfully in the poem. Only Chaucer among medieval poets could achieve this kind of synthesis.

Jean Bodel's third category, the "Matter of Rome the Great," must be stretched to include a very miscellaneous collection of stories. There are lives of Alexander in both verse and prose, poems on the siege of Troy (of which the fourteenth-century West Midland alliterative poem, *The Gest Historiale of the Destruction of Troy* is the liveliest), verse accounts of the destruction of Jerusalem, and of course Chaucer's Knight's Tale. Apart from the last of these, which is a special case, an elaborate and polished verse narrative by a master, these romances are more important for the light they throw on the medieval imagination than for any special literary achievement. More important for English literature was a fourth category of which Jean Bodel says nothing, for it is peculiarly English. This is a group of romances drawing their material from English history; stories of these English heroes must have come down orally, and eventually reached the Anglo-French romancers who turned them into French verse narratives. Only after they had been rendered in French did they appear in English, sometimes as translations and sometimes as renderings of the version currently popular in England. (Evidently the English romancers did not feel that a popular oral tradition about an English hero was worth the dignity of being turned into a written romance unless it had already attracted the

Anglo-French romancers: this seems to be the only explanation of the fact that, English though these stories are in origin and subject, only those of them which have French originals or parallels appear in English romance.) On the analogy of Jean Bodel's classification, the subject matter of these romances has been called the "Matter of England," and this is a convenient enough term. That part of the "Matter of England" which achieved permanence in written romance must have represented but a small portion of the oral legends celebrating popular English heroes such as Athelstan, Offa, Earl Godwin, Eadric the Wild, and Hereward the Wake: we know of these oral traditions because they are referred to by the historians William of Malmsbury and Henry of Huntingdon.

Some of the most popular of the "Matter of England" subjects dealt with in English romance seem to derive from traditions associated with the Viking raids on England. *King Horn*, the earliest of the extant romances in the English group, tells the story of Horn, son of the king of Sudene, who after his father's death at the hands of pirates is set adrift and comes ashore at Westerness, where Rimenhild the king's daughter falls in love with him. Horn, after living with the king's household, eventually departs to prove his knighthood and returns after destroying a pirate crew. King Aylmar of Westerness finds Horn and his daughter embracing, and banishes Horn, who goes to Ireland where he does knightly deeds. He returns in disguise to Westerness in time to prevent Rimenhild's marriage to another prince, and, after further complications which almost duplicate earlier parts of the story, Horn slays his rival, regains his father's kingdom, and makes Rimenhild his queen. The poem is interesting for its meter; it is in short rhyming couplets which perhaps show the old alliterative line giving way before French influence or may be more directly related to contemporary French and Anglo-French verse. The short rhyming lines give the story rapidity of movement, and a certain declamatory tone which indicates that it was intended to be spoken. The audience envisaged is clearly a simple one; the tale is essentially naïve, with the interest deriving wholly from the sequence of incidents and the shifts in the fortunes of the protagonists. *King Horn* is a good example of the way in which the English romancers left out the courtly elements of the French; the love element is not dwelt on, and the emphasis is on action and adventure. The story trots on from incident to incident:

> He fond bi þe stronde,
> Ariued on his londe,
> Schipes fiftene,

Wiþ sarazins kene.
He axede what isoȝte
Oþer to londe broȝte.
A Payn hit of herde
And hym wel sone answarede,
"Þi lond folk we schulle slon
And alle at Crist luue vpon,
And þe selue riȝt anon;
Ne schaltu todai henne gon."

This simple movement of verse narrative is a pretty fair sample of the way the ordinary folk of thirteenth-century England liked to have their stories told. The story itself, with its folk elements of the returned exile and the reuniting of lovers, shows how a legend originally deriving from history can be overlaid by folk material to become an unsophisticated romance. There is also an early fourteenth-century North Midland version of the story in twelve-line stanzas, known as *Horn Childe*, and there are several ballad versions.

Another "Matter of England" romance which apparently derives from events of the Viking period but which also has been overlaid with much folk material (indeed, the central plot is a common folk tale which, as so often happens, became attached to a particular hero late in its history) is *Havelok the Dane*, one of the most successful of the simple tales of adventure in Middle English verse narrative. The story opens with the death of King Athelwold and the appointment of Earl Godrich as guardian of his infant daughter Goldeboru; but Godrich seizes power himself and imprisons Goldeboru. Then we are taken to Denmark, where Earl Goddard plays a similar role to that of Godrich. Having been appointed guardian of the children of King Birkebayn, Havelok and his two sisters, Goddard takes over the kingdom himself, kills the daughters, and hands Havelok over to Grim the fisherman with orders that he is to be drowned. But Grim, made aware by a supernatural sign of Havelok's royal birth, saves Havelok, and with his wife takes him and his own five children to England, where he founds the town of Grimsby. Havelok eventually takes a job as scullion to Earl Godrich's cook, and impresses everybody by his beauty, physique, and skill at games and in arms. Godrich, thinking that Havelok is "some churl's son and no more," plans to marry him to Goldeboru, and thus confirm his own possession of the throne. He forces the reluctant pair to marry, and they return to Grimsby, where Goldeboru learns from a mysterious light issuing from Havelok's mouth that he is really of noble blood and, at the same time, an angel's voice announces Havelok's royal parentage and glorious future: this cheers her immensely and at once puts the relation between the pair on a proper footing. Further adventures bring them to Denmark where Havelok destroys Goddard and regains his ancestral throne before returning to England to make an end of Godrich and gain the English crown as well.

The story moves along in rapid octosyllabic couplets: like *King Horn* it concentrates on the physical adventures and plays down the love interest. The scenes describing Havelok's activities as a scullion have a lively realism, and there are accounts of popular sports and a sense of the ordinary people of England at work which give this romance a special interest and vitality. A brief quotation may give some indication of the speed and vigor of the narrative: this is from the section describing Havelok's life as a scullion:

> Þet oþer day he kepte ok   [second   kept watch for also]
> Swiþe yerne þe erles kok,   [very eagerly]
> Til þat he saw him onþe brigge,
> And bi him mani fishes ligge.   [lying]
> Þe erles mete havede he bouht
> Of Cornwaile, and kalde oft: [called]
> 'Bermen, bermen, hider swiþe!'   [quickly]
> Havelok it herde, and was ful bliþe
> Þat he herde 'bermen' calle;
> Alle made he hem dun falle   [them]
> Þat in his gate yeden and stode   [way went stood]
> Wel sixtene laddes gode. . . .

In addition to the romances of these four "matters," there are a number of miscellaneous romances dealing with independent subjects. The mid-thirteenth-century *Floris and Blancheflour* is a pleasing rendering in rhymed couplets of a popular legend of eastern origin. It is a story of love triumphant, with Floris following his Blancheflour to the harem of the Emir of Babylon, who in the end is so moved by the tribulations of the lovers that he forgives them and has them married. The plot is one of many that came into Europe from the East through the Crusades bringing a special kind of imagination with them. The thirteenth century, when Welsh, Norman, and Anglo-Saxon traditions mingled in England, when Bretons and French influenced each other's storytelling, when mental traffic between east and west had been stimulated by the Crusades and by the journeys of merchants and scholars and pilgrims who took advantage of the relatively long period of internal peace in Western Europe, was a great century of literary cross-fertilization. *Floris and Blancheflour* is a product of such cross-fertilization, and brings a refreshing change from the constant fighting and courtly love-making of the typical romance and from the treatment of the Saracens as conventional infidels which we get in most of the "Matter of France" romances—for Floris is a Saracen (though he becomes a Christian in the end), Blancheflour is the daughter of a French widow carried off to Spain by a Saracen king, Floris' father, and the whole setting of the romance is Saracen. Another of the unclassified medieval romances is the fresh and charming *Sir Orfeo*, which shows a different kind of cross-fertilization: here the classical story of Orpheus and Eurydice has been treated as a Breton *lai* and in the process has been changed into a light-hearted fairy story far removed in tone from the stern Greek myth of Hades. *Sir Orfeo* was probably translated from a French original in the South or South Midlands of England soon after 1300. The story trips along in four-stressed rhyming couplets, simple without being dull, naïve in tone but with the incidents well manipulated and the story well constructed. The setting is medieval, of course, with nothing Greek about it: it is a minstrel tale of a rescue from fairyland through the power of music; Sir Orfeo regains his Dame Herodis—there is nothing about his not looking back—and the story ends happily. W. P. Ker has said of *Sir Orfeo* that "one may refer to it as a standard, to show what can be done in the medieval art of narrative, with the simplest elements and smallest amount of decoration."

There are other unclassifiable Middle English romances on a great variety of themes, some dealing with the patience and constancy of an abused woman, some dealing with stock courtly situations, some combining history and folklore in one way or another. The four-teenth-century *Ipomadon* is an especially interesting example of those dealing with stock courtly situations: a translation of an Anglo-French romance, it provides all the standard material of the typical French romantic story—the noble knight falling in love with a lady he has never seen, the faithful service, the analysis of emotion, the tournaments, disguises, all the physical and psychological goings-on that the medieval audience so delighted in; and the English transla-tor has cut less of the passages of sentiment than he usually did. There are two verse versions and one in prose; the earlier of the two verse renderings is by far the better, though unlike the later, it sub-stitutes for the French rhyming couplets one of the favorite and most wearisome of the English romancer's stanzas—the twelve-line stanza with *rime couée* or tail rhyme, whose monotony Chaucer illustrated (in a six-line stanza of exactly the same kind) in his parody of *Sir Thopas:*

Yborn he was in fer contree,
In Flaundres, al biyonde the see,
At Poperyng, in the place.
His fader was a man ful free,
And lord he was of that contree,
As it was Goddes grace.

The verse forms of the English romances are not always the happiest for narrative; they vary from short rhyming couplets to the complicated stanza of *Sir Gawain and the Green Knight*. There was clearly a lot of experiment in versification going on among the English romancers. They were learning how to rhyme in English in the French manner and trying out different kinds of stanzas. The simple, lively trot of *Havelok* or *Sir Orfeo* represents favorably the level of metrical competence in couplets. Sometimes the handling of stanzas is reasonably adroit, but the stanza itself is not suitable for narrative verse. And all the time Middle English verse is learning to become as supple and assured and polished as the French: with Chaucer it more than achieves this.

Middle English Literature: Fabliau, Lyric, Dream Allegory, Ballad

THE COURTLY French romance, as we have seen, drew its ideals partly from feudal notions of service and honor, sometimes (as in many of the Arthurian stories) oddly combined with more specifically Christian virtues; and when it was rendered into English much of the courtliness was lost and interest centered on the physical adventures. Not all medieval French narrative was "polite," however; from France also came a type of short narrative poem, realistic, humorous, often coarse, known as the *fabliau*, and *fabliau* and romance existed side by side. The *fabliau* is associated with the new middle classes who slowly grew in importance as the feudal system developed only to decay. If romance begins in France as the entertainment of a feudal aristocracy, *fabliau* is the product of the class which was eventually to destroy feudalism. The development of a money economy out of a natural economy, hastened both by the commutation of different kinds of feudal service to money-payments and the growth of towns with their trading communities, gradually took away the very basis of the feudal system by encouraging the growth of a class which had no place in it. This new class, town dwellers who carried on commercial activity of one kind or another, traders and artisans who no longer lived on the land but who obtained their food and their raw materials by selling to the peasants the goods they manufactured, were less impressed by courtly notions of love and honor than the more conservative feudal landowners; realistic, iconoclastic, priding themselves on knowing life as it really is and on refusing to look at it through the rose-colored spectacles of sentimental idealists, they sponsored a boisterous, satirical kind of narrative which was, as it were, the antitype of the idealizing vision of courtly knight or pious churchman.

This middle-class challenge of the knightly ideal was but one phase of a significant movement in the history of European culture. The heroic age, reflected in Germanic epic, had given way to the feudal age, with its own concept of the hero; when a more commercial civilization develops, the whole possibility of heroism in the modern world is re-examined. We are approaching Don Quixote, the knightly hero as fool, and Don Quixote, who though a fool is also in an oblique way admirable, is a sign on the road which in England comes at last to Robinson Crusoe, the hero as prudential merchant who, even when cast away on a desert island, spends his time recreating as best he can the urban business world he left behind him. When prudence and self-interest become the chief motive power of the hero, a reaction sets in, led by those who deplore the loss of the "crowded hour of glorious life." Prudential morality is examined ironically (as in Fielding or Thackeray) or is reluctantly conceded to be a condition of progress by a novelist such as Scott who in his best novels weighs the competing claims of commercial progress and heroic tradition, of Baillie Nicol Jarvie and Rob Roy, to conclude that while the future lies with the former the latter is more attractive and its loss a bitter price to pay for material advancement. The fate of the hero in English literature will emerge more clearly in subsequent pages of this history; here we pause to remark only that the *fabliau* represents the first real challenge in European literature to the notion of heroic idealism as a way of life, and that challenge can be traced in its influential course from Cervantes to Evelyn Waugh.

Fabliaux are found in France in the twelfth and thirteenth centuries but are rare in England before 1400; they apparently originated in Northern France. There are many types: some are indecent stories of town life whose only point is their indecency; others are humorous, satiric tales of intrigue; others again, like the *Roman de Renart* cycle, are animal stories, also generally humorous and satiric in tone. Some are made into awful warnings or otherwise turned into *exempla*, "examples," for the use of preachers; the *Gesta Romanorum*, of which we have an early fifteenth-century English version, is a collection of such *exempla*, moralized tales for the enlivening of sermons (such as Chaucer's Pardoner's Tale). In Middle English literature, strangely enough, there are very few individual *fabliaux*, though French literature abounds in them. The only English *fabliau* that has survived by itself is *Dame Sirith*, a low tale of how a merchant's wife is persuaded by a trick to allow a clerk to make love to her in her husband's absence. Yet reference to (and warnings against) such stories in contemporary religious literature make it clear that they were common in medieval England; presumably, however, being a popular rather than a courtly form of literature, they were not often written down. The clergy would have had no interest in them, except in their moralized form, and the clergy were the guardians of the written word throughout the Middle Ages. We do find the *fabliau*, however, in Chaucer, who puts stories of this kind into the mouths of the Merchant, the Miller, the Reeve, the Shipman, and the Summoner in his *Canterbury Tales*.

Another popular medieval literary form—indeed, a popular form in most ages and civilizations—is the fable, which came to the Middle Ages from both Greek and Indian sources. The fable is a short story in which animals, acting more or less as human beings, behave in such a way as to illustrate a simple moral. Beast tales represent a very widespread kind of popular literature, and the fable develops out of the beast tale in much the same way as the *exemplum* develops out of the *fabliau*. In spite of the popularity of the fable in medieval England, especially in the twelfth and thirteenth centuries, no Middle English collection of fables exists. Books of fables in French and Latin survive, but there are only a handful of extant English fables from before Chaucer, and each of these is found as part of a longer work (two, "The Owl and the Falcon" and "The Fox and the Cat," in *The Owl and the Nightingale*). Beast tales were also adapted for satirical purposes: by having animals act as men it was easy to satirize human follies and vices, the presentation of men as animals being itself an implicit criticism of man's claim to superiority over the brutes. These stories about animals varied considerably in tone: some are substantially *fabliaux* with the characters animals instead of men, others are more purely satires, others again are simply entertaining stories about the cunning or resourcefulness or misadventures of animals.

A whole cycle of the beast stories developed, with Reynard the Fox as the principal hero (or villain); one of the most popular of these collections was the French *Roman de Renart*, of which no Middle English translation (if it was made) has survived. Indeed, there are only three Middle English extant representatives of that cycle of animal tales sometimes called the "beast epic," and these are *The Fox and the Wolf*, the sofar unpublished *Fox and Geese*, and Chaucer's *Nun's Priest's Tale*, though it seems fairly certain that there were other such stories which have not survived. The coarse, satirical tone of so many of these animal stories cannot have made them welcome in monastic libraries, the true custodians of literature in the Middle Ages. *The Fox and the Wolf* is a lively, humorous tale in rhymed octosyllabic couplets, with spirited dialogue, shrewd characterization and a general lightness of touch: the story appears to have been translated from the French; it is in the *Roman de Renart* and was told again in the *Fables* of the fifteenth-century Scottish poet Robert Henryson.

A rather different kind of interest in animals shows itself in the medieval bestiary, a literary form which probably originated in Egypt in the second century A.D. and comes from the Greek through the Latin into medieval literature. The bestiary is a series of accounts of animals, of their qualities and of the legends associated with them, with a moral application made at the end; first there is the description, then the "significacio" or moral meaning. In the Middle English Bestiary, the lion, eagle, adder, ant, hart, fox, spider, mermaid, elephant, turtledove, panther, and dove are dealt with in seven hundred rather crude rhyming lines of varying length. The work is of little interest as literature, but it provides an interesting window onto the medieval mind, with its mixture of pseudoscientific description, wonder, and moralizing, and it provided a storehouse of animal lore which continued to be used in literature long after the bestiary was forgotten.

More congenial to the modern mind, and more readily appreciated by the modern reader, is Middle English lyrical poetry, much of which reaches across the ages with a freshness and directness that sometimes positively startle:

> Fowler in þe frith,
> Þe fisses in þe flod,
> And I mon waxe wod.   [must grow mad]
> Mulch sorw I walke with
> For beste of bon and blod.

This passionate stanza survives in a manuscript with its musical annotation, reminding us that so much early lyric poetry, like the ballads, was meant to be sung. The tone of Middle English lyrics, even when it is one of sorrow or complaint as in the poem just quoted, is far removed from the more meditative elegiac strain of these few Anglo-Saxon poems which can perhaps be called lyrical—*The Wanderer* or *The Seafarer*, for example. Whether the Anglo-Saxons had any body of short lyrical poems is doubtful; none has survived at any rate. And when we realize how accidental has been the preservation of those secular Middle English lyrics which we have—often scribbled by a bored clerk on the margin or a blank leaf of a manuscript

dealing with some quite different subject—we can see how dangerous
it is to generalize from extant Middle English literature. On a blank
leaf of a manuscript in the Bodleian Library, Oxford, some one
noted down a tantalizing little rhyme, to be worked up by W. B.
Yeats many centuries later:

> Icham of Irlaunde,
> Ant of the holy londe
> Of Irlande.
> Gode sire, pray ich þe,
> For of saynte charite,
> Come ant daunce wyt me
> In Irlaunde.

And on the same blank page we find another fragment:

> Maiden in the mor lay,
> In the mor lay,
> Seuenyst fulle, seuenist fulle,
> Maiden in the mor lay,
> In the mor lay,
> Seuenistes fulle ant a day.
>
> Welle was hire mete;
> Wat was hire mete?
> Þe primerole ant the,—
> Þe primerole ant the,—
> Welle was hire mete;
> Wat was hire mete?—
> The primerole ant the violet. . . .

Much of the Middle English secular lyric that we have consists of
casually preserved scraps.

There is no extant English lyric poetry from before the twelfth
century. The first record that we have of a Middle English lyric is
found in the *Historia Eliensis* of the twelfth-century chronicler
Thomas of Ely, who tells us that when Canute (died 1035) was rowing near the Isle of Ely he heard the monks singing and, pleased with
their singing, he himself composed a song in English of which the
Chronicler gives the first four lines:

> Merie sungen the Munekes binnen Ely.
> Tha Cnut ching reu ther by.
> Roweth cnites noer the land.
> And here we thes Muneches sæng.
>
> Merrily sang the monks of Ely
> When King Canute rowed thereby.

"Row, knights, near the land
And hear we the singing of these monks."

The chronicler adds that this and "other verses which follow are to this day sung publicly in dances and remembered in proverbs." This proves at least that there was a song of this kind known in the twelfth century and regarded then as a *carole* (a song with a refrain sung by a chain of dancers, with a leader singing the stanzas and the whole group joining in the refrain), though it does not prove that Canute was in fact the first English lyrist. Whether the *carole* existed in Anglo-Saxon England we cannot tell; it was certainly popular in England soon after the Conquest, presumably as a result of French influence. Giraldus Cambrensis, writing his *Gemma Ecclesiastica* (a series of saints' lives) at the end of the twelfth century, tells the story of a company of dancers singing and dancing all night in a churchyard in Worcestershire with the result that the following morning the priest, unable to get the refrain of their song out of his head, intoned at Mass not *Dominus vobiscum* but "*Swete lemman, dhin are*" ("Sweet mistress, have mercy").

The *carole* comes at the end of a long tradition of development which cannot be certainly traced, even in French literature. Its ancestry may well include pre-Christian seasonal celebrations, communal work songs sung to the rhythms of spinning or threshing or rowing among other activities, or the danced folk song arising from pure play and recreation. Its movement from folk art to the professional craftsmanship of the minstrel brought with it not only sophistication of technique but some significant shifts in attitude—for example, folk love poetry tends to give the woman's view, while the love lyrics of the *trouvères* present the courtly love attitude of the man languishing for love of the woman. What begins as a spontaneous accompaniment to work or play, largely feminine in inspiration (for the women would do most of the work for which rhythmic singing was a suitable accompaniment, as in the Hebridean wauking songs today), develops into the careful product of a conscious art predominantly masculine in origin and point of view.

We get our first glimpse of written French poetry when this process has just been completed. The new development is recent enough for it still to bear marks of its origin (the woman's point of view for example, being preserved in that species of *chanson d'aventure* where the *trouvère* reports what he has overheard a woman singing), yet the process of sophistication is sufficiently far advanced for the new ideas of courtly love to provide most of the conventions. The courtly love lyric from Provence traveled northward through France to reach England at last and influence English poetry. This French influence intermingled with that of Latin hymns, which were written in that accentual Latin verse which derived orginally from popular songs and soldier songs of Rome. The goliardic poems of the "wandering scholars" show clearly how these influences could come together as well as how the technique of rhymed accentual Latin verse influenced both French and English versification.

As so often in medieval literature, we can see the whole picture more clearly in France than in England. There, in addition to the sophisticated lyric of courtly love, we find varieties of lyric of a more popular kind representing a development halfway between the folk song and the fully professional composition. There is the *chanson d'aventure*, where the poet tells of what happened to him when he went abroad one morning; there is the *aube*, song of lovers parting at dawn; the *chanson de mal mariée* gives a woman's complaint against married life overheard by the poet (another example of the older folk point of view—the woman's—surviving in these more popular though no longer folk lyrics); the *chanson de carole*, dance song with refrain, both popular and courtly varieties; and other kinds. The more popular kinds of poetry cannot always be sharply distinguished from the more courtly, but different layers of sophistication can be traced.

It is not until well into the thirteenth century that we find any significant number of English lyrics, though their quality makes it clear that the tradition of lyrical poetry in English had by this time been well established and confirms other evidence that much has been lost. The well-known "Sumer is icumen in" is found in a manuscript of about 1240, together with a fairly elaborate musical setting: the refrain indicates the *carole* ancestry of the poem, while the theme was a common one in medieval Europe:

> Sumer is icumen in,
> Lhude sing cuccu!
> Growe sed and blowe med
> And spring þe wde nu.
> Sing cuccu! . . .

The hailing of spring is often—as in the French lyric—the prelude to the description of the woes of the lover whose mistress is cold to him, but the welcome of spring for its own sake is also an important theme, an expression of genuine excitement at the return of the growing season after the bleak medieval winter without adequate heat or light or food. Joy in spring was no mere convention in the Middle Ages, when men had not yet learned to make themselves an artificial summer indoors or found a way of feeding cattle adequately during the winter. Darkness, cold, isolation, a diet at best of salt meat—these were the accompaniments of the medieval winter, and we must bear them in mind when we read such poems as:

> Lenten ys come wiþ loue to toune,
> Wiþ blosmen and wiþ briddes roune,
>   Þat al þis blisse bryngeþ.
> Dayeseȝes in þis dales,
> Notes suete of nyhtegales,
>   Vch foul song singeþ.
> Þe þrestelcoc him þreteþ oo,
> Away is huere wynter wo,
>   When wonderoue springeþ.
> Þis foules singeþ ferly fele,   [wondrous many]
> Ant wlyteþ on huere wynter wele,   [warble]
>   Þat al þe wode ryngeþ.

This joyful hail to spring is found in the great Harleian Manuscript 2253 in the British Museum, in which much of the best extant Middle English lyric poetry has been preserved. The manuscript was probably written at Leominster and dates from the first quarter of the fourteenth century. It contains a fine variety of lyrical poems. The nightingale, spring, and love make their usual conjunction in one typical poem:

> When the nyhtegale singes the wodes waxen grene,
> Lef and gras and blosme springes in Averil, I wene,
> And love is to myn herte gone with one spere so kene, . . .

Or a similar theme treated with greater metrical dexterity:

> Between March and Averil,
>   When spray beginneth to spring,
> The little fowl hath their wil
>   On their lud to sing.   [in their own language?]
> I live in love-longing
> For semlokest of alle thing;   [fairest]
> He may me blisse bringe—
>   Icham in her baundoun.   [I am at her disposal]
>
> (Refrain)
>
> An hendy hap ichabbe yhent;   [gracious got]
> Ichot from heaven it is me sent;   [I know]
> From alle wymmen my love is lent
>   And light on Alysoun.

Another of the Harleian poems has the refrain:

> Blow, northerne wynd,
> sent thou me my suetyng!

> blow, northerne wynd,
> blou! blou! blou!

A rather unexpected poem is a swinging, humorous lyric addressed to the man in the moon, the only one of its kind among surviving medieval lyrical poetry.

The political lyric was another medieval form, written chiefly in Latin or French in England before the fourteenth century. When it does appear in English it clearly owes the usual debt to Latin hymns and French lyrics as far as versification goes, but its inspiration is, naturally, purely native. The only political poem in English which has survived in complete form (it also is in Harley 2253) is the "Song of Lewes," a mocking poem addressed by the triumphant followers of Simon de Montfort after the battle of Lewes (1264) to Richard, Earl of Cornwall, the king's brother, who is regarded as a trickster responsible for misleading Edward, the king's son; it has a narrative basis, with the catchy refrain:

> Richard, thah thou be ever trichard,   [trickster]
> Tricchen shalt thou nevermore!   [deceive]

In the fourteenth century, popular interest in social and political matters is reflected in an increasing number of political songs and poems, of which perhaps the most impressive, and certainly the briefest, is the grim little couplet summing up the year 1390–91 and explaining more eloquently than any historian why men turned against Richard II:

> The ax was sharpe, the stokke was harde,
> In the xiiii yere of Kyng Richarde.

We know, too, the couplet which the radical priest John Ball used in preaching his equalitarian doctrine at the time of the Peasants' Revolt in 1381:

> When Adam dalf, and Eve span,   [delved (dug)]
> Who was then the gentleman?

The fourteenth century also produced the patriotic versifier Laurence Minot, who illustrated the growing national feeling of England in his political poems attacking the French and the Scots and celebrating English victories over them. Secular literature is expanding its scope, reflecting an increasing number of aspects of the life and thought of the time. Between the purely conventional courtly love lyrics and the simple and heartfelt political pieces can be found every stage of sophistication; the fourteenth-century lyric has become capable of handling a relatively wide range of subjects with varying degrees of stylization and polish. Spring and love are still the dominant themes—and with the sweep of the Petrarchan tradition over Europe is to be confirmed as a dominant theme for another three hundred years—among secular lyrics, but there is also "occasional" poetry, springing from particular events or situations.

But of course the commonest theme among surviving Middle English lyrics—especially among those of the earlier Middle English period—is religious, for religious poems would be most likely to have been transcribed and preserved in an age when clerics were in charge of both activities. The relation between the Middle English religious lyric and the medieval Latin hymn can be seen most clearly in those "macaronic" poems where Latin and English are used together.

> Of on that is so fayr and briȝt
> *velud maris stella,*
> Briȝter than the dayis liȝt,
> *parens et puella,*
> Ic crie to the, thu se to me,
> Leuedy, preye thi sone for me,
> *tam pia,*
> That ic mote come to the,
> *Maria.*

Sometimes the words of an actual hymn are worked into a macaronic poem:

> *Ave maris stella,*
> The sterre on the see,
> *Dei mater alma,*
> Blessed mot sche be!
> *Atque semper virgo,*
> Pray thy sone for me.
> *Felix celi porta,*
> That I may come to thee.

But secular themes and techniques soon begin to influence religious poetry, and the folk tradition, too, is employed for religious themes, as in many Christmas carols and in songs of Mary and the holy child:

> This endris night I saw a sight,   [other]
> A maid a cradell kepe,
> And ever she song and said among
> 'Lullay, my child, and slepe.'

The medieval religious lyric ranges from the simply moral to the devotional and even mystical, and between these extremes we can find many kinds of use of religious material, including the merely

descriptive and anecdotal. In later phases of English literature we
distinguish between the religious poem (as we get it, say, in John
Donne or George Herbert) and the hymn (such as those of Isaac
Watts), the former being a personal handling of religious experience
so as to produce a complex and highly individual lyrical poem while
the latter, intended for the singing of a congregation, reflects a communal emotion and is both less complex and less individual. Something of the same distinction may be drawn in the Middle English
religious lyric, though by no means so definitely. The picture is complicated by the continuous clerical attempt to turn secular emotion
into religious, an attempt which was part of the Church's perpetual
warfare against "songis of lecherie, of batailis and of lesyngis." Some
time in the fourteenth century, Bishop Richard de Ledrede composed Latin songs for the minor clergy of his cathedral "ne guttura
eorum et ora deo sanctificata polluantur cantilenis teatralibus turpi-
bus et secularibus" ("so that they should not pollute their throats
and mouths, sanctified to God, with disgraceful and secular minstrel
songs") and they were set to the tunes of well-known secular lyrics.
The most extreme case of the deliberate adaptation of secular poetry
to religious purposes is the Scottish *Gude and Godlie Ballatis* of the
mid-sixteenth century, in which even such an unpromising poem as
"John come kiss me now" is given a religious meaning by having
John represent man and the wooer God: though these are Protestant
poems, with a strong anti-Papal bias, they represent in an extreme
form something that was happening right through the Middle Ages.
Clearly something similar has happened to this poem:

> The shepard upon a hill he satt;
>   He had on him his tabard and his hat,   [short coat]
> His tarbox, his pipe, and his flagat;   [flagon]
> His name was called Joly Joly Wat,
>   For he was a gud herdes boy.
>   Ut hoy!
>   For in his pipe he made so much joy.
>
> The shepherd upon a hill was laid;
> His dog to his girdell was taid;
> He had not slept but a litill braid,   [time]
> But 'Gloria in excelsis' was to him said.
>   Ut hoy!
>   For in his pipe he made so much joy. . . .

Sometimes, elements from Christian story are treated in a dramatic
fashion which reminds one of the ballads, as in the famous thirteenth-century *Judas*, which some have seen as the earliest extant
English ballad:

... In him com ur Lord gon, as is postles seten at mete:
"Wou sitte ye, postles, ant wi nule ye ete?

Wou sitte ye, postles, ant wi nule ye ete?
Ic am iboust ant isold today for oure mete."

Up stod him Iudas: "Lord, am I that?
I nas never o the stude ther me The evel spec."   [place]

Dramatic in a more subdued way is the Crucifixion dialogue preserved in MS Harley 2253:

> "Stond wel, moder, under rode,
> Byholt thy sone with glade mode,
>   Blythe moder myht thou be!"
> "Sone, hou shulde Y blithe stonde?
> Y se thin fet, Y se thin honde
>   Nayled to the harde tre." ...

The note of simple devotion is effectively sounded in some of the lyrics on the Virgin:

> I sing of a mayden
>   that is makeles   [peerless]
> King of all kynges
>   to here sone che ches.   [chose]
>
> He cam also stylle
>   ther his moder was,
> As dew in Aprylle
>   that fallyt on the gras.
>
> He cam also stylle
>   to his moderes bowr,
> As dew in Aprylle
>   that fallyt on the flour. ...

Lyrics in praise of Mary, or describing her sorrows, or invoking her, are common in the fourteenth century; carols in the modern sense of Christmas carols range from pagan celebrations of the holly and the ivy and the boar's head to awed celebrations of the Nativity; there are religious poems where a secular *chanson d'aventure* has been adapted to a religious context, as in one with the Latin refrain, "Quia amore langueo"; there is occasionally a deft treatment of the theme of original sin and the Christian scheme of redemption, as in this remarkable little piece:

> Adam lay i-bowndyn,
>   bowndyn in a bond,
> Fowre thowsand wynter

> thowt he not to long;
> And al was for an appil,
>   an appil that he tok,
> As clerkis fyndyn wretyn
>   in here book,
> Ne hadde the appil take ben,
>   the appil taken ben,
> Ne hadde never our lady
>   a ben hevene qwen.
> Blyssid be the tyme
>   that appil take was,
> Therfore we mown syngyn
>   *Deo gracias.*

This is a skillfully compact account of what modern critics call "the paradox of the fortunate fall," rendered in terms of lyric simplicity, very different in tone but similar in general idea to the view Milton expresses in *Paradise Lost*, where Adam, after hearing of the Christian plan of redemption from Michael, exclaims:

> O goodness infinite, goodness immense!
> That all this good of evil shall produce,
> And evil turn to good; . . .

In the medieval religious lyric Christian themes mingle in many different ways with themes deriving from a variety of other traditions; there are, as in the secular lyric, varying degrees of sophistication, of technical accomplishment, and individual sensibility. These lyrics illustrate, sometimes with startling clarity, some of the ways in which religion entered men's imagination in the Middle Ages. Sometimes, in coalescing with pre-Christian material which reached back into a dimly remembered world of symbolism, a poem can achieve an unexpected effect, as in the Corpus Christi poem found in an early sixteenth-century manuscript commonplace book in the library of Balliol College, Oxford:

> He bare hym up, he bare hym down,
> He bare hym into an orchard brown.
>
> In that orchard there was a hall,
> That was hanged with purpill and pall.
>
> And in that hall ther was a bede,
> Hit was hanged with gold so rede.
>
> And in that bed ther lythe a knyght,
> His wounde bledying day and nyght.

By that bedes side ther kneleth a may,
And she wepeth both night and day.

And by that beddes side ther stondeth a ston,
Corpus Christi written thereon.

This is essentially a folk song, of which, interestingly enough, versions have been found in modern times in the oral traditions of both Britain and America; its meaning went far deeper than either the compiler of the Balliol manuscript or the modern folk singer could have known. The central symbolism of the poem appears to derive from the Grail legend: Joseph of Arimathea bore Christ's blood, which he had collected in the Grail, to Avalon ("He bare hym up"); the wounded knight is the Maimed Knight, the keeper of the Grail, whose hall is the Castle of the Grail; and so on. Behind this lies a pre-Christian symbolism. The whole poem is based on the same set of symbolic meanings which T. S. Eliot employed in *The Waste Land*. Thus the medieval poet, mingling themes of different origins and at different levels, was often working with richer materials than he guessed. The Christian tradition, as mediated through sermons, Church worship, and the pictures on stained-glass windows; the classical world, obliquely reflected through late Latin writers and a mass of legends and traditions; memories, folk notions, and fragments of pre-Christian paganism changed in strange ways in the process of oral transmission—these helped to condition the mind and the imagination of the Middle English poet and to give unexpected overtones of meaning to his poetry.

If the medieval writer sometimes dealt with materials of whose symbolic significance he was unaware, he also dealt often in conscious and deliberate allegory whose meaning he knew perfectly well. Indeed, as has often been pointed out, the medieval mind worked naturally in allegory in a way that we seem to have lost, and produced a body of allegorical writing which is of central importance in European literature. The origins of the medieval allegorical mode are complex. Allegorical interpretation of parts of Scripture had already a long history in both Jewish and Christian biblical commentary; late Latin poetry tended to use the old Roman gods as personifications of abstract qualities and psychological situations; and the new introspective tendency that Christianity encouraged induced men to objectify their mental and spiritual struggles by personifying their desires and aims, the appetites and qualities that produced them. By the time courtly love appears on the scene the allegorical mode is ready to be its medium, and so at length we have the allegorical romance, the most artificial and in many respects the most influential and tenacious of the different kinds of literature produced in the Middle Ages. Of the three major kinds of literature we consider in this and the previous chapter—the narrative romance, the lyric, and the allegorical romance—the allegorical romance was the last to appear, and the only one which underwent no development from popular to sophisticated. This was essentially a "polite" literature from the beginning: or, if it was not very "polite" in its earliest, germinal stages, it was at least learned.

The most noteworthy allegorical romance of the Middle Ages, the most elaborate specimen of its kind and the most influential on subsequent literature, for which it proved an inexhaustible quarry, is the *Roman de la Rose,* of which the first part (over four thousand lines in short couplets) was composed by Guillaume de Lorris about 1227, and the second, over twenty-two thousand lines, was written by Jean de Meun in the years 1268-77. Guillaume de Lorris' share represents the true allegory of courtly love, where the new psychology of love-making is treated with great subtlety and effectiveness. Qualities of the heroine, such as shame, fear, kindliness, courtesy, etc., are personified, and the hero's encounter with the lady in her different moods—in some of which she encourages and in others of which she repels his suit—is described as an attempt to obtain the "rose" (standing for the lady's love) which is enclosed within a hedge in a garden which is the scene of the action. In his attempt, the hero is aided by such personified qualities as the heroine's natural kindliness and courtesy (*bialacoil,* "fair welcome") and hindered by, for example, fear and shame. The whole background of the story is courtly life, a life of leisure and good breeding, where there is nothing to do but dance and sing and make love.

The story as Guillaume de Lorris planned it is unfinished, and the conclusion written by Jean de Meun about forty years later is quite different in aim and nature. Jean's bulky work is quite formless beside the well-constructed earlier portion, and it shows little ability to handle the allegorical method with effectiveness. The allegory in the first part is done with real skill and finesse; but Jean is a clumsier and more realistic writer, and the fine allegorical fabric of Guillaume de Lorris comes to pieces in his hands. His purpose is not to tell a subtle love story so much as to produce a piece of work which is at once didactic, philosophic, satiric, scientific, religious, and lots of other things besides. There is a strong satiric strain in his writing which is quite absent from the earlier part of the poem: Jean sometimes gives the impression that he is utterly contemptuous of the courtly love tradition and takes every opportunity to leave the story and digress at inordinate length on philosophic, satiric, or mythological subjects.

We see in his attitude something of the temper of the rising class of realistic writers which the new bourgeois element was producing at this time. Polite, courtly literature is no longer sufficient to satisfy the reading (or listening) public, even with the alternative of simple narrative romances of wonder and marvelous action. There is growing up a taste for something different both from the sentimental, sophisticated love story and the simple tale of derring-do. Jean de Meun is still working within the courtly tradition, but he is out of sympathy with it. He has more learning and philosophy, more of a serious didactic purpose, than the typical *fabliau* writer shows; yet in many ways he has something of the same temper and illustrates the same movement from a courtly to a bourgeois tradition.

The influence of the *Roman de la Rose*, especially of the first part, was enormous. The poem was translated all over Europe, and its characters and conventions are to be met with again and again throughout later literature. In England it was translated, at least in part, by Chaucer. The scene at the beginning of the *Roman de la Rose* is a riverbank outside a walled garden, and the hero enters the garden through a wicket gate: this scene becomes a stock property in later medieval literature. The story is told by the narrator in the form of a dream, from which he awakes at the conclusion, and this dream form is copied by later writers. The story opens on a May morning, with the birds singing and nature looking her best. The May morning, the wandering into the country, the falling asleep and dreaming, the garden—these are the characteristic features of this type of literature, known as the dream allegory. The dream allegory is literature produced for a leisured audience, an upper-class audience cut off from the simple routines of labor that formed so important a part of the life of the peasant and the yeoman and cut off likewise from many of the oral folk traditions that simpler folk perpetuated in their daily work. Even more than the sophisticated French narrative romance of courtly love, the dream allegory represented a literature of self-conscious sensibility. The influence of the *Roman de la Rose* is relatively late in coming into English literature: it is seen in Chaucer and in the poets that follow him.

The dream allegory is sometimes used for very different purposes from those which either of the authors of the *Roman de la Rose* had in mind. The late fourteenth-century poem *The Pearl*, an elegy in some twelve hundred lines arranged in groups of twelve-line stanzas, is cast in the form of a dream: the poet falls asleep in an arbor on an August (not the usual May) morning and has the dream which forms the substance of the poem. *The Pearl* has little else in common with the *Roman de la Rose*, however. Using both rhyme and alliteration, it is the product of that alliterative revival (or survival) which produced also *Sir Gawain and the Green Knight, Patience,* and *Cleanness*; because, in addition, all four poems are of the same date and are in the same West Midland dialect, they are sometimes assigned to the same author, though this is mere conjecture. In mood, tone, and emotional effect *The Pearl* stands alone. The poet is lamenting the loss of a little girl, who died before she was two years old. Looking in vain for his "precious pearl without a spot," he falls asleep and in a marvelous dream finds himself in a land of great beauty with a bright river running by. He cannot cross the river, but sees on the other side, where the country is even more beautiful, a shining maiden dressed in white with ornaments of pearl. She is the lost child, and he is speechless with wonder and fear. She speaks to him, however, and explains her position in the New Jerusalem. The poet attempts to cross the river to be with her, but she warns him that this cannot yet be: since Adam's fall the river can only be crossed in death. He grieves at this, but is told to be patient and resign himself to God's will and mercy. She then tells him much about the means of salvation, answering his questions in detail, and finally he sees her in a procession of virgin brides of Christ, led by the Lamb. In an ecstasy of joy and longing the poet again attempts to cross the river to be with this glorious vision, but he awakes to find himself again in the arbor, sad yet resigned to the will of God. The poet shows real dexterity in handling a difficult rhyme scheme and in arranging a complex pattern in the poem as a whole; but the most arresting quality is the richness of color and the profusion of imagery, combined with a wide emotional range which enables him to domicile theology in elegy and sometimes in wonder. *The Pearl* stands alone in Middle English religious poetry for its sustained emotional quality and technical mastery of versification. *Patience* and *Cleanness* (i.e., purity), which discuss these moral virtues and illustrate them by re-telling appropriate biblical stories, are technically accomplished but lack the special kind of sensibility which makes *The Pearl* so impressive.

All this while, the English language was being exercised, developing its literary potentialities, and English writers were learning to handle their tongue with cunning and flexibility. With Chaucer, the rehabilitation of English as a literary language seems to be complete: here is a master who can handle it in verse as the ablest French poets handled their language. But before we leave the great army of anonymous medieval writers to dwell on the first great known poet of Middle English, something must be said about another kind of anonymous literature which was to have such a great effect on English writing centuries later—the ballad. The ballads, which are orally transmitted narrative poems dealing either with themes common to international folk song or with themes derived from the romances, or with popular class heroes, or with historical or semihistorical events, date, in most of the versions which we now have, from the sixteenth and seventeenth centuries and later; but there can be no doubt that the ballad flourished in the late Middle Ages, even though, being still at this stage a purely oral literature, it was not likely to be written down and so has not survived in its earlier forms. Oral transmission is the very essence of balladry; whatever the origin of the ballad—and the older view that it was the spontaneous communal creation of "the folk" is not now maintained in its primal simplicity —their original life was that of sung poems which were sometimes improved and sometimes corrupted by generations of singers. Nevertheless, the great majority of the ballads which we have are not medieval, and some of them deal with specific historical events which took place in the sixteenth century and later. The Robin Hood ballads date from long after the period to which they are supposed to refer and have little if any historical basis: Robin Hood is a yeoman hero, the hero of a class, not a historical figure: there is evidence of the existence of "rymes of Robin Hood" in the fourteenth century, but of the Robin Hood ballads that we have, two are of the fifteenth century and the others are known only in sixteenth-century texts. We have, in fact, not more than a total of fourteen ballads surviving in manuscripts or printed texts earlier than 1600. In the seventeenth century, broadsides and songbooks make many more available. From the mid-eighteenth century onward, interest in the recording and collecting of ballads proceeds apace, but the early collectors freely altered and "improved" the texts which they got from oral recitation or written sources. The dating of ballads is therefore not easy: we can say in general that ballads were known in the fourteenth century and popular in the fifteenth, while the sixteenth and early seventeenth century was the period productive of most of the ballads of which we have record. The ballad, indeed, is not so primitive a literary form as used to be thought: it is far removed from the heroic epic, which celebrates a hero of the whole race; it is the product of a settled group and deals with the affairs of that group. There is no trace of the ballad anywhere in Europe until after the great migrations had long been completed, and if we look at the ballad picture in Germany, France, Spain, and Scandinavia as well as Britain, we can see that the ballad, as a rule, develops in the late Middle Ages.

Some of the most impressive ballads deal with folk themes common to many nations; these generally deal with a single situation involving revenge or jealousy or a return from the grave or simply the finality of loss. "Lamkin" is a good example of the first, "The Twa Sisters." of the second, "The Wife of Usher's Well" of the third, and "The Unquiet Grave" with its plaintive opening—

> The wind doth blow today, my love,
>   And a few small drops of rain;
> I never had but one true-love,
>   In cold grave she was lain—

of the fourth. Or the ballad might create an atmosphere of violence or tragedy or horror for its own sake, as in the well-known "Lord Randal" and "Edward," or deal with deception, betrayed lovers, or the testing of love. Some deal with the supernatural, with transformations and witchcraft and the intrusion into human affairs of the world of faery: in "Tam Lin," for example, the hero has been carried off by the fairies and is redeemed when the heroine, following his instructions, holds him fast throughout a series of terrifying transformations (this old folk theme is found in the *Odyssey,* when Menelaus gets information from Proteus, the old man of the sea, by holding fast to him throughout his many transformations). Another important category of ballads deals with historical events, either real events in national history or recollections of local events which have often been modified by some folk theme. "The Battle of Otterburn" and "Chevy Chase" represent the former and "Sir Patrick Spens," the latter.

The ballads are often thought of as peculiarly Scottish, because the enthusiasm of Scottish collectors gathered so many Scottish examples; but, in fact, they have been found in all parts of England as well as elsewhere in Europe. (The popularity of Scott's *Minstrelsy of the Scottish Border* accounts similarly for the belief that most Scottish ballads come from the Borders: the majority, in fact, come from Aberdeenshire.) Some of the best extant ballads deal with events in Scottish history, real or imagined, but what makes them ballads is the treatment rather than the provenance. The ballads are narrative poems which, completely suppressing the personality of the narrator, tell a story dramatically by moving—often without any specific indication of the transition—from one incident to the next:

> The king sits in Dunfermline toun,
>   Drinking the blood-red wine:
> O whare will I get a guid sailor
>   To sail this ship of mine?

> Up and spak an eldern knicht,
> Sat at the king's right knee:
> "Sir Patrick Spens is the best sailor
> That sails upon the sea."
>
> The king has written a braid letter,
> And signed it with his hand,
> And sent it to Sir Patrick Spens
> Was walking on the sand. . . .

In these last two lines the sudden shift to a picture of Sir Patrick Spens walking on the sand—comparable, as Mr. M. J. C. Hodgart has pointed out, to the motion picture technique of "montage"—is characteristic of the ballad method. In the dialogue in "Lord Randal" and "Edward" the lack of background explanation enhances immeasurably the dramatic effect.

Other devices used in the ballads to increase dramatic effect include "incremental repetition," that is, the repetition of one line from the preceding stanza with an addition leading closer to the climax:

> In and come her father dear,
> Canny cam he stepping in;
> Says, "Haud your tongue, my dochter dear,
> What need ye mak sic heavy mene? [moan]
>
> "Haud your tongue, my dochter dear,
> Let all your mourning be;
> I'll carry the dead corpse to the clay,
> And I'll come back and comfort thee."

The repetition of the questions in "Lord Randal" shows the same sort of thing worked up to an extraordinary pitch of tension. Repetitions often have something of an incantatory effect in the ballads:

> They hadna been a week from her,
> A week but barely ane,
> When word came back to the carline wife
> That her three sons were gane.
>
> They hadna been a week from her,
> A week but barely three,
> When word came to the carline wife
> That her sons she'd never see.

The stanza is generally the simple "ballad meter" of alternate four- and three-stressed lines, though sometimes (as in "Lord Randal") all the lines are four-stressed: the music of the ballads, where it is known, is a better guide to the stresses than some of the printed texts. Many of the extant ballads are pretty rough affairs, others have been unduly refined by such collectors as Bishop Percy or Scott; but ballads are by nature subject to change, and there is no point in being puritanically censorious either about popular corruptions or literary polishing—both fates are part of the destiny of the ballad. The uncanny power of the best of them remains something to wonder at; the mixture of simplicity and cunning, of elementary verse form and mastery of some subtle effects of rhythm and expression, is of a kind we rarely get in "art" poetry. And, like some of the lyrics we discussed earlier, only more continuously and arrestingly, they can make contact with deep-seated folk themes with quiet power. The second stanza of "The Wife of Usher's Well" is a good example of this controlled suggestiveness:

> It fell about the Martinmass,
>   When nights are lang and mirk,
> The carlin wife's three sons came hame,
>   And their hats were o the birk.

> It neither grew in syke nor ditch,   [stream]
>   Nor yet in ony sheugh;   [trench]
> But at the gates o Paradise,
>   That birk grew fair eneugh.

It is not enough to explain the *frisson* that the reader gets from that simple statement about the birk to say that it is an oblique way of saying that the returned sons were in fact dead, or to explain the magical or other significance of the birk (the earliest of English trees to come out in full spring green): the touch of quiet horror derives from the balladist's having made contact with some deep stratum of human fear. The ballad at its best can do this with extraordinary effect. Though its development belongs to the later Middle Ages and not earlier, it is the last literary species to draw nourishment from what might be called the anthropological past: it was this element in it that stirred the imagination of later poets such as Coleridge (not Wordsworth, who looked to the printed broadside ballad, a much cruder affair) and so helped to fertilize Romantic and later poetry.

CHAPTER FOUR

Chaucer, Gower,
Piers Plowman

GEOFFREY CHAUCER, who was born in the early 1340's and died in 1400, marks the brilliant culmination of Middle English literature. He had the metrical craftsmanship to handle English with a subtlety, a flexibility, and a polish which made it at once the equal, as a literary language, of French or Italian; he had the European consciousness, too, to enable him to render in English the dominant themes and attitudes of European literature and at the same time the English national consciousness to allow him to present the English scene as it had never been presented before. He had the relaxed, quizzical attitude that let him contemplate the varieties of human nature with a combination of sympathy, irony, and amusement, together with the good fortune to have opportunities of knowing men in all ranks of society; he was trained in the courtly life, the diplomatic life, and the urban life of affairs; his visits to France and Italy on Government service gave him an opportunity of coming into direct contact with French and Italian men of letters and enriching his knowledge of the literature of those countries. He was, in fact, fitted by both natural genius and the circumstances of his life to become the most technically accomplished, the most widely ranging, and the most universally appealing of medieval English writers, and indeed one of the most skillful and attractive of English writers of any period. With Chaucer, the English language and English literature grew up. The gradual process of recovery and refinement which the English language had been undergoing since it emerged after the Conquest in rough popular renderings of French romances was now complete. It was a happy accident that the man who had the technical brilliance in the metrical handling of language also had the breadth of view, the knowledge, the interests, the experience of life, and largeness of sympathy to enable him, in the latter part of his poetic career, to embody his great secular vision of his fellow men in brilliant literary form. He used the intellectual and imaginative resources of the Middle Ages, not, as Dante did, to present a great concrete embodiment of the moral and theological universe in which medieval man lived, but to bring alive, with vividness and cunning, the psychological and social world of his time, which turns out to be also the world of our own and every other time.

Chaucer—to whom, it must be remembered, French was a language as familiar as English—early absorbed the courtly love tradition as represented by the somewhat overstylized French poets of his own time. He knew and drew on the poetry of Guillaume de Machaut, Jean Froissart, and Eustace Deschamps, and he was thoroughly familiar with (and, at least in part, translated) the *Romance of the Rose,* the source of so much fourteenth-century French poetry and especially of Machaut's sophisticated exercises in the conventions of courtly love. The dream allegory had by now become the standard method of entering into a poem. The waking dream, where the sleeper wanders into a garden on a May morning, gay with blossoming flowers and the singing of birds, and there encounters the characters who tell him their love affairs or lament their misfortunes in love or act out their story, derives from the *Romance of the Rose,* but is now treated with a sophistication, a formal manipulation of standard properties, with heraldic colors and shapes and a highly wrought surface finish, of which neither the fresh vision of Guillaume de Lorris nor the encyclopedic and more cynical mind of Jean de Meun was capable. Guillaume's brightly pictured characters dancing in the garden and Jean's learned misogynistic digressions mingle in Chaucer's early poetry, presented in narrative frameworks and with picturesque detail which owe a considerable amount to Machaut and others. But the debt is simply an indication that Chaucer is working in a European tradition. As he developed, he was to draw on more and more aspects of that tradition and to make a more and more specifically English use of it. His visits to Italy in 1372–73 and in 1378, brought him into contact with the work of Dante, Boccaccio, and Petrarch, and this widened and deepened his literary resources and encouraged him to seek wider fields than the formal garden of Guillaume de Lorris. And all the time his career as courtier, man of affairs, and civil servant (for Chaucer was a bourgeois with courtly connections and thus had the freedom of at least two social worlds) brought him into contact with people of all ranks and professions to provide increasing opportunities for his clear-eyed observation of his fellow men.

Chaucer was thus brought up on the Rose tradition and on later French developments of it before moving to the deeper seriousness of Italian poetry. The ritual dance of an idealized courtly life, with its emphasis on "gentilesse" and "franchise" (nobility and generosity of character), gives way to larger concern with the fundamentals of human character and behavior and this, in turn, moves into contemplation (both delighted and ironical) of the foibles, vanities, absurdities, pretensions, villainies, the color, vitality, and exuberance, the everyday virtues and vices, of men as he knew them. But it would be a gross simplification of Chaucer's literary career to trace it merely from an imitative formalism through a greater seriousness and flexibility to subtle and realistic psychological observation, conventionally symbolized by reference to his "French," "Italian," and "English" periods. From an early stage he was free of a wider world of books than is suggested by any of these categories. What the Middle Ages knew of the classical world—its history, its mythology, its literature —Chaucer knew; what it knew of astronomy, astrology, medicine, theology, philosophy, he knew as well as a layman could; and it is not the least testimony to his genius that his poetry gives us the richest picture in English of how the ancient world of Greece and Rome appeared to the medieval imagination, its curiously transmuted image mingling with patristic thought, scholastic categories, and popular beliefs to produce an attitude to man and the world which is still an important part of the Western tradition. If the *Romance of the Rose* and the poetry of Machaut and Froissart and Deschamps were important to him, so were Virgil's *Aeneid*, Ovid's *Heroides* and *Metamorphoses*, Lucan's *Pharsalia*, Statius' *Thebaid*, Boethius' *De Consolatione Philosophiae* (which he translated), Macrobius' commentary on the *Somnium Scipionis* of Cicero, the Troy stories of Dares Phrygius and Dictys Cretensis and of later writers, Pope Innocent III's *De Contemptu Mundi* (which he apparently also translated), and much patristic literature, to say nothing of the Vulgate, the Latin liturgy of the Church, vast numbers of medieval romances, and a miscellaneous assortment of medieval scientific, religious, historical, and entertaining works. This assorted reading blended in his mind, as it did in the minds of his contemporaries, to produce a world of the imagination in which "Pluto and his queene, Proserpina, and al hire fayerye" can meet in a walled garden made by a merchant—a garden

> So fair . . .
> That he that wroot the Romance of the Rose
> Ne koude of it the beautes wel devyse—

and quote to each other "Jhesus, filius Syrak" (author of Ecclesiasticus) and "this Jew, this Salmon" (i.e., King Solomon). Classical myth transposed into the key of medieval folklore and seen against a background of biblical story and in an ethical context which includes the courtly notion of "gentilesse," Christian ideals of virtue, and a robust acceptance of human weakness and absurdity in the *fabliau* tradition—this is typical of Chaucer and of the civilization for which he spoke. In this sense Chaucer is fourteenth century, and his work gives us a vivid insight into the fourteenth-century world; but in his art he transcended the bounds of his time, so that he illuminates his background rather than allows his background (if we have learned it) to illuminate him. We need make no historical allowances for Chaucer at all, for he fully justifies his picture of the world by the literary uses to which he puts it. He is perhaps the first English poet known by name for whom this claim can be made unreservedly.

Chaucer's first narrative poem, *The Book of the Duchess*, is in the dream allegory convention and draws considerably on Machaut. It was written at the end of 1369 on the death of Blanche, Duchess of Lancaster, to celebrate the dead woman and console the bereaved Duke: in a dream the poet sees "a man in blak" in a wood, who tells him of his courtship of his beautiful lady and ends by revealing that his present mourning is for her death. This ingenious adaptation of the dream allegory for the twin purposes of eulogy and elegy is already straining out of its conventional framework: the interest lies less in the celebration of the dead duchess than in the life given to the poem by the current of psychological curiosity that runs through it. The octosyllabic couplets move easily enough, though without the combination of control and variety that characterizes Chaucer's maturer verse, and they begin by presenting a picture of the poet suffering from insomnia, reading the story of Ceyx and Alcione (in Ovid) to while away his sleepless night. He tells the story, with speed and economy, lingering only on an occasional detail that will add vividness, as when Juno's messenger comes to Morpheus, the god of sleep:

> This messenger com fleynge faste
> And cried, "O, ho! awake anoon!"
> Hit was for noght; there herde hym non.
> "Awake!" quod he, "whoo ys lyth there?"
> And blew his horn ryght in here eere,
> And cried "Awaketh!" wonder hye.

Having told the story, he goes on to describe how he settled down to sleep, hoping that "thilke Morpheus, /Or hys goddesse, dame Juno / Or som wight elles, I ne roghte who" would send him sleep, and offering Morpheus a feather bed "Yif he wol make me slepe a lyte."

He finally falls asleep, and dreams that he wakes to find himself in bed on a May morning with the birds singing sweetly. The windows of his room attract his attention:

> For holly al the story of Troye
> Was in the glasynge ywroght thus,
> Of Ector and of kyng Priamus,
> Of Achilles and Lamedon,
> And eke of Medea and of Jason,
> Of Paris, Eleyne, and of Lavyne.
> And alle the walles with colours fyne
> Were peynted, both text and glose,
> Of al the Romaunce of the Rose.

This is the world in which the poem moves. The poet goes outside, into a wood, and finds a hunt in progress. On inquiring from a huntsman who is hunting here, he is told:

> "Syr, th'emperour Octovyen,"

an answer which seems somehow appropriate in the trancelike atmosphere of the dream, with its stylized, heraldic scenery. The hunt is forgotten when the poet comes upon the black knight, whose lamentations leave the poet rather stupidly puzzled as to their cause. Chaucer—and this was to be a frequent device with him—makes himself out to be somewhat obtuse, and even when the knight goes on to a description of his courtship of his lady he does not realize that it is the loss of the lady that now causes his grief. After the account of his wooing and winning his love, done with a grave and formal beauty in spite of its use of the conventional courtly love properties, the poet asks where the lady is now, and the knight falls into lamentation again. Still the poet is puzzled.

> "Allas, sir, how? what may that be?"
> "She ys ded!" "Nay!" "Yis, be my trouthe!"
> "Is that youre los? Be God, hyt ys routhe!"

At this moment the hunt returns, the nearby castle bell strikes twelve, and the poet awakes to find the book with the story of Ceyx and Alcione by his side. Chaucer has succeeded in infusing some slight element of psychological and dramatic liveliness into this formal, visionary elegy. But the world of the poem is trancelike and its forms and colors heraldic.

With *The House of Fame*, which is probably Chaucer's next work, we move out of the world of trance, though the framework is still the dream. The influence of Dante's *Divina Commedia* is clear in the second and third of the three parts, but the mood of the poem is far from Dantesque. Book I opens with a discussion of dreams (a subject on which Chaucer was much given to speculation) and proceeds to describe a dream in which he found himself in a temple of glass— "Hyt was of Venus redely, /The temple"—on whose walls was engraved the story of the *Aeneid*, with special emphasis (as always in the medieval treatment of the *Aeneid*) on the Dido episode, which Chaucer tells in a hundred and forty lines; this leads him to give a conventional list of faithless lovers (Ovidian in origin) before continuing the story up to Aeneas' marriage with Lavinia. The incidents are presented as a series of pictures, introduced by the formula "Tho saugh I" ("Then saw I"). Coming out of the temple doors he sees a golden eagle shining in the sky. At the opening of Book II the eagle, having descended, seizes the poet in its claws and bears him aloft. With this, the mood of the poem changes from the visionary to the lively, humorous and colloquial. The poet describes his fright, the eagle's reassuring words and subsequent conversation. The eagle explains to Chaucer that he is taking him to the House of Fame, for the poet is a dull fellow who knows nothing of his neighbors. There he will learn of love tidings and of all the jealousies, fears, and hypocrisies of men. The eagle lectures the unhappy man (whom he addresses familiarly as "Geffrey") on acoustics, explaining how all speech eventually reaches the House of Fame, and prides himself on his ability to explain difficult scientific matters simply to an ignorant man. The poet replies in placatory monosyllables. Nothing can stop the flow of the eagle's didactic talk, which continues until he lands the poet on the steep slope below the House of Fame. Book III, beginning with an invocation to "God of science and of lyght" imitated from Book I of Dante's *Paradiso*, goes on to describe the poet's difficult ascent to the House of Fame, which was situated on a high rock of clear ice. The names of many famous people were engraved on this rock, but some letters of every name had melted away. On the other side he saw names of famous persons of antiquity, and they were still as fresh as ever. The castle itself is made of beryl stone, and Chaucer's account of what he saw there is a crowded collection of deliberately incongruous detail, presented with an air of naïve wonder. In the hall he saw statues of Josephus, Statius, Homer, Dares Phrygius, Dictys Critensis, Guido della Colonne, Geoffrey of Monmouth, Virgil, Ovid ("Venus clerk"), Lucan, Claudian (who wrote the *De Raptu Proserpinae*), among others; and then a large company of people swarmed in, beseeching the Goddess of Fame to grant them her favor:

> And somme of hem she graunted sone,
> And somme she werned wel and faire,
> And some she graunted the contraire
> Of her axyng outterly.
> But thus I seye yow, trewely,
> What her cause was, y nyste.   [I know not]

Another group ask for good fame and get the reverse; a third ask for it and receive it; a fourth group of well-doers do not wish for fame, and receive the oblivion they seek; a fifth group with a similar request receive immortal fame; a sixth group, of idlers, seek the good fame of active heroes and receive it; a seventh, in a similar position, are refused it; a group of people guilty of treachery ask for good fame and are denied it; finally, a group of cheerful and self-satisfied evildoers ask for fame as evildoers, which is granted them. All this is done with sounding of trumpets, crying of heralds, and much lively ceremonial. Chaucer, though he is still in the world of medieval dream allegory, is beginning to enjoy himself in a new way.

After Fame has disposed of the final group, a man turns to the poet and asks:

> Frend, what is thy name?
> Artow come hider to han fame?

Chaucer hastily disclaims any such intention, and says he is there to learn some new tidings. The man takes him out of the House of Fame to the House of Rumor, a building of twigs more strangely wrought than the famous Labyrinth built by Daedalus. This cagelike building, full of holes to let the sound out, seethes with the noise of rumors of all kinds. As the poet wonders at the strange place, he sees his eagle perched on a stone nearby—

> And I gan streghte to hym gon,
> And seyde thus: "Y preye the
> That thou a while abide me,
> For Goddis love, and lete me seen
> What wondres in this place been . . ."
>   "Petre! that is myn entente,"
> Quod he to me.

"Precisely why I am here," in fact, and the eagle takes him up to a window, where he hears people reporting gossip to each other. Each man tells his neighbor, and so the tidings grow and spread until they go out by the holes in the house, to come to Fame, who determines their future duration. The poem ends abruptly, unfinished, with the poet's discerning a man who

> seemed for to be
> A man of gret auctorite.

With these words the poem ends. Presumably, the man of great authority was to announce some important tidings, which may or may not have been the nominal *raison d'être* of the poem.

A strange mélange of a poem. The dream and the allegorical figures belong to a hackneyed enough convention, but the poem strikes notes that had not before been struck in English. The conversation of the eagle in Book II, with its quizzical humor, the poet laughing both at himself and at the loquacious and self-important bird, and some of the detail of action and conversation in the crowded Book III, let a fresh wind into the medieval garden of poetry. Echoes of Dante add occasional overtones of high seriousness, but the comic tone predominates, even though the poet touches now and again on some of the most profound of human problems. The versification has a sureness and flexibility that *The Book of the Duchess* lacks, while the handling of dialogue would itself justify the claim that *The House of Fame* is one of the important transitional poems in English, pointing forward to far-reaching developments in the presentation of character and conversation in fiction:

> With that this egle gan to crye,   [began]
> "Lat be," quod he, "thy fantasye!
> Wilt thou lere of sterres aught?"   [learn]
> "Nay, certeynly," quod y, "ryght naught."
> "And why?" "For y am now to old."
> "Elles I wolde the have told,"
> Quod he, "the sterres names, lo,
> And al the hevenes sygnes therto,
> And which they ben."   "No fors," quod y.
> "Yis, pardee!" quod he; "wostow why? . . ."

The Parliament of Fowls is probably Chaucer's next major poem. It, too, is in the dream convention, but elements from both Dante and Boccaccio now enrich the style and the content. The verse form is the seven-line stanza (rhyming *ababbcc*), known as "rhyme royal" because of its later use by James I of Scotland in his *King's Quair* (if James I really was the author), and Chaucer handles it with a poise and a liquid flow of language that is something new in Middle English:

> The lyf so short, the craft so long to lerne,
> Th'assay so hard, so sharp and conquerynge.
> The dredful joye, alwey that slit so yerne:
> Al this mene I by Love, that my felynge

> Astonyeth with his wonderful werkynge
> So sore iwis, that when I on hym thynke,
> Nat wot I wel wher that I flete or synke.

He goes on to say—and this is typical of Chaucer's combination of gravity with irony—that he himself knows love not from experience but from books. He had been reading, he says, the *Somnium Scipionis* (as interpreted by Macrobius), which he proceeds to summarize, after a comment on the significance of old books which gives us a vivid insight into Chaucer's attitude toward his reading:

> For out of olde feldes, as men seyth,
> Cometh al this newe corn from yer to yere,
> And out of olde bokes, in good feyth,
> Cometh al this newe science that men lere.

Old books and personal observation—"experience" and "auctoritee" to use Chaucer's terms—are the two sources of knowledge and understanding, and for Chaucer character was largely determined by the use an individual makes of each. For the Wife of Bath, experience was to be enough—

> Experience, though noon auctoritee
> Were in this world, is right ynough for me;

enough at least to tell her all she needed to know about marriage, though the lady was not averse to reinforcing her conclusions with copious reference to authorities. In Chaucer's own literary career the relation between literary sources and personal observation keeps shifting. It is not that he moves from the former to the latter—no writer moves simply from literature to life, however much more simply derivative his earlier work may be than his later—but he finds more original and richer ways of combining the two elements and allowing each to illuminate the other. Like *The House of Fame, The Parliament of Fowls* imposes the author's personality on conventional material. A graver utterance from Dante and picturesque descriptions from Boccaccio's *Teseide* (which he was to draw on more extensively in the Knight's Tale) are part of the new literary materials he assimilates in the *Parliament*, which in its narrative outline and its theme are wholly conventional.

After reading the *Somnium Scipionis*, the poet goes to bed, as daylight is failing:

> The day gan faylen, and the derke nyght,
> That reveth bestes from here besynesse,
> Berafte me my bok for lak of lyght . . .

This echoes Dante's

> Lo giorno se n'andava, a l'aere bruno
> toglieva li animai che sono in terra
> dalle fatiche loro,

and there are several other such echoes throughout the poem. They are all subdued to the mood of the poem, and the mood itself is deftly modulated through several different keys. Sleep produces its dream in which, after a Dantesque journey with Scipio Africanus as his guide ("Can not I seyn if that the cause were /For I hadde red of Affrican byforn, /That made me to mete [dream] that he stod there"), he comes to a garden by a river, with the usual birds singing, and the usual allegorical characters disporting themselves. Cupid, Pleasaunce, Curteysie, Delyt, Gentilesse, Beute, Youthe, Flaterye, Desyr, and others. It is yet another picture of the ubiquitous garden of the Rose tradition, but described freshly enough for all that. He sees the temple of Venus, too, with its appropriate characters, and comes at last to a beautiful soft green place, where the goddess Nature, on a hill of flowers, was presiding over a great congress of birds. This was Saint Valentine's Day, and the birds had assembled to choose their mates in accordance with Nature's rule. Three noble eagles claim the hand of the beautiful formel eagle perched on the goddess's wrist, and each of the three (in descending order of rank) claims the formel eagle as his bride in proper courtly-love terms. Then the mass of birds take up the debate: many of them have little patience with the niceties of courtly love, the goose in particular laughing at the notion of constancy to a beloved who does not love in return—

> But she wol love hym, lat hym love another.

The sparrow hawk in turn scorns the goose's vulgar attitude. "Lo, here a parfit resoun of a goos!" he exclaims contemptuously. The turtledove defends constancy, and the argument grows into a magnificent hubbub until Nature silences them all and gives her verdict, that after waiting a year the formel eagle should make her choice. Then the birds sing a roundel for Saint Valentine's Day, "to don to Nature honour and plesaunce" before flying away, and the poet wakes.

The Parliament of Fowls is thus a poem in celebration of Saint Valentine's Day, using the convention of the dream allegory and the demande d'amour. It may also have been prompted by some specific royal courtship, and scholars have spilt much ink in debating which one. But any contemporary reference is irrelevant to the true significance of the poem, which is a deftly handled "occasional" piece, showing Chaucer's growing mastery of his medium, his ability to impose his own tone on conventional material. The mood shifts easily from one of quiet gravity through an occasional flash of irony to a lively and humorous realism, to end on a note of happy celebration.

Troilus and Criseyde, written probably in the middle 1380's, is a major work in which the full genius of Chaucer as metrical technician, as storyteller, and as student of human character is triumphantly displayed. It is in a sense the first real novel in English: it tells a love story with a delicacy of psychological awareness, a brilliant handling of detail, a firm sense of structure, and a mastery of controlled digression. The verse—which is the rhyme royal stanza again—adapts itself easily to the changing demands of the narrative, and in its liquid flow seems to increase the sense of fate and inevitability which hangs over the action throughout. Its immediate source is Boccaccio's *Il Filostrato,* but, while taking the main action and many specific incidents from Boccaccio, he expands the simple, highly-colored, fast-moving Italian story of love and betrayal into a multidimensional work, subtler in psychology, more varied in detail, and richer in moral overtones. Behind the *Filostrato* lies the curious and characteristically medieval transmutation of a couple of minor Homeric characters, who originally have no connection with each other at all, into the familiar story of Troilus' love for Cressida, his winning of her, and her eventual desertion of him for the Greek Diomede. Homer's Briseis and Chryseis were Trojan captives whose disposal helped to produce the wrath of Achilles. Dares Phrygius—whose importance for the medieval view of the Troy story we have noted—gives brief character sketches of Troilus, Diomede, and Briseis, but does not bring them together in a story. Benoit de Sainte-Maure's *Roman de Troie* makes Briseida the daughter of Calchas, the Trojan seer who deserted to the Greeks on foreseeing their ultimate victory, and makes Troilus in love with her, but the only part of the story he dwells on is the winning of her love by Diomede after she has been sent to join her father among the Greeks. Guido della Colonne in his *Historia Trojana* follows Benoit. Briseis and Chryseis eventually coalesce as Criseida (later Cressida), and Boccaccio is the first to tell the story of Troilus and Cressida now so familiar. Boccaccio dedicates his poem to the lady whom he loves and who has left him, as a memorial "of your worth and of my sadness," and it has a personal, lyrical, youthful tone throughout. He first introduces Pandarus, whom he makes the brother of Criseida and contemporary of Troilus, a young man who brings his sister and his friend together out of his friendship for the latter. Chaucer's Pandare is Boccaccio's Pandaro in function but not in character or behavior: he is Criseyde's uncle as well as Troilus' friend, evidently an older man, much given to quoting proverbs and precedents: a shrewd, good-natured, worldly-wise, affectionate man who shows infinite resource in bringing the lovers together but who is helpless in the face of the final tragedy. Chaucer's Troilus is the parfit, gentil knight, not substantially different from Boccaccio's Troilo. But Chaucer's Criseyde is drawn with a psychological subtlety that makes her into a wholly new character: she is the first truly complex heroine in post-classical European literature.

This development of a story which grew up within the framework of the Troy story throws interesting light not only on the medieval perspective on the classical world but also on Chaucer's methods and on the way in which his imagination worked. The Middle Ages had not the sense of literary property that we now have, and there was nothing improper in Chaucer's taking Boccaccio's story as a basis for his own—he had done that sort of thing before and was to do it again. On that story Chaucer brought to bear both "experience" and "auctoritee," his own knowledge of human nature, and his wide reading. The conception of the wheel of fortune, ever turning so that the individual is now up, now down, and the whole problem of fate and free will as discussed by Boethius, pervade the poem. Boethius is more than once paraphrased at length; Dante, Petrarch, and Ovid are drawn on for lines or images or situations; indeed, a whole world of reading is domiciled in the richly textured narrative. And Chaucer's own insight and humor and irony and sympathy play over all.

The Trojan war is the background. A medievalized Troy is presented to us in varied detail, with the classical properties somehow made to fit a medieval way of life; sallies out from the city walls against the besieging Greeks are daily occurrences, a constant opportunity for the performance of knightly deeds. We see Troilus first, the gay young knight scornful of love, and then Criseyde, the demure young widow, standing in the temple at a religious festival in her black habit. Troilus sees her there and is suddenly smitten— he has fallen in love in church, as it were. Criseyde is the very perfection of womanhood:

> She nas nat with the leste of hire stature,
> But alle hire lymes so wel answerynge
> Weren to wommanhood, that creature
> Was nevere lasse mannyssh in semynge.
> And ek the pure wise of hire mevynge

> Shewed wel that men myght in hire gesse
> Honour, estat, and wommanly noblesse.
>
> To Troilus right wonder wel with alle
> Gan for to like hire mevynge and hire chere,
> Which somdel deignous was, for she let falle
> Hire look a lite aside in swich manere,
> Ascaunces, "What! may I nat stonden here?" . . .

Troilus at once feels all the woes of the courtly lover. He automatically assumes that his beloved is unattainable, infinitely superior to him in every way. The cheerful, bustling, proverb-quoting Pandare finds him lamenting in bed, and after much vivid talk—it is remarkable how Chaucer can give the very accent of conversation in verse—gets his secret from him. When it turns out that Troilus is in love, and with Pandare's niece, Pandare has no doubt that all can be managed. This is courtly love, and it must be secret and outside marriage, free from scandal and the breath of wicked tongues (the contradiction at the heart of the courtly love notion, that love is supremely honorable yet the lady's reputation is injured if it be known, comes out clearly in the poem). More is involved than the winning of Criseyde's love: she must first be brought to lay aside her fears for her reputation and be reassured that everything can be done with discretion.

Those fears are particularly strong in Criseyde's case, for she is in a difficult position as well as fearful by nature. Her father is a traitor who has deserted to the other side, and she therefore must be especially careful in her behavior. Pandare has his work cut out. Meanwhile Troilus, reassured by Pandare, rouses himself and performs deeds of great valor against the Greeks. For courtly love ennobles the character and makes the heart more brave and generous:

> For he bicom the frendlieste wighte,
> The gentilest, and ek the mooste fre,
> The thriftiest and oon the beste knyght,
> That in his tyme was or myghte be.
> Dede were his japes and his cruelte,
> His heighe port and his manere estraunge,
> And ecch of tho gan for a very chaunge.

Book II opens on a note of hope. Echoing the opening of the *Purgatorio,* Chaucer begins:

> Owt of thise blake wawes for to saylle,
> O wynd, o wynd, the weder gynneth clere; . . .

This book is taken up with the maneuverings of Pandare. He visits his niece and, after a bantering conversation to put her in a good mood, he begins to warm up to his news, eventually rousing her to such a pitch of suspense that she can hardly wait to hear it. He then tells her of Troilus' love, saying that he asks only that she take pity on the young man and be nice to him, else he will die of love. And if Troilus dies, Pandare will die too. She reacts unfavorably at first. She is afraid of scandal. She is afraid of losing her independent way of life as a widow. She is afraid, it appears, of committing herself to any such relationship because it will mean adventuring out of her accustomed and comfortable single existence. But she is interested and, in spite of herself, excited. "Kan he wel speke of love?" she eventually asks her uncle, who then "a litel gan to smyle," for he knew the first round was won. And when Troilus, fresh from a victorious encounter with the Greeks, rides by her window amid the cheers of the crowd, she looks out and sees his handsome and knightly figure and his modest bearing

> And leet it so softe in hire herte synke,
> That to hireself she seyde, "Who yaf me drynke?"

But the siege is far from over. With a subtle combination of real reluctance and concern for appearances, both of which cover a genuine excitement about Troilus, she concedes little at first, and has to have her defenses broken down one by one. The story of this breaking down—too long to be satisfactorily summarized—is a brilliant piece of psychological fiction. The question of the genuineness of Criseyde's reluctance can still arouse heated argument among the critics, which is sufficient testimony to Chaucer's skill in character drawing. Criseyde is, in fact, the first character in English literature whose character is argued over as though she were a real person. First she is persuaded to receive—and to answer—a letter from Troilus. Then Pandare, by an ingenious device, brings them together briefly, but long enough to allow Troilus to offer and Criseyde to accept him with the ambiguous proviso "myn honour sauf." Finally, Pandare invites Criseyde to dinner when rain is expected; the heavy rain prevents her from going home and he gives her a bed in his house. Of course Troilus is there—he is supposed to have arrived suddenly, out of his wits because he has heard that Criseyde has been having an affair with someone else. Pandare brings Troilus to Criseyde's bedside and he explains his fears; she reproaches him for them so violently that he faints; Pandare heaves him into Criseyde's bed and after further maneuvering leaves him to be restored by Criseyde. Criseyde is now caught—or is it Troilus?

Pandare is gone, taking the candle with him, with the remark that it isn't good for sick folks' eyes. And Criseyde—when Troilus calls on her to yield at last, she answers passionately in his arms:

> Ne hadde I er now, my swete herte deere,
> Ben yold, ywis, I were now nought heere!

And a night of passion follows, described by Chaucer vividly but not coarsely. His account of the lovers' wonder in each other is done with a fine psychological realism. The morning follows, and the *aubade*, the song of lovers reluctantly parting at dawn. Thus Troilus and Criseyde become lovers, and continue to love secretly and happily until Fortune's wheel turns again.

This brings us to the beginning of Book IV, which tells of the exchange of prisoners and the decision to send Criseyde to her father, in the Greek camp, in return for Antenor. The distress of the lovers, Troilus' bitter speculations on fate, their final night together with their railings on fate and vows of eternal constancy take up most of the book. Troilus proposes that they steal away together, but Criseyde dismisses the plan as dangerous and impracticable. She fears scandal. She promises that she will contrive to get back to Troy on the tenth day after her departure. But of course she does not come, and the fifth book moves from Troilus to Criseyde showing the state of mind of each. Criseyde is led to the Greek camp by Diomede, handsome, self-confident, unscrupulous, an experienced lady's man. He lays siege to her at once, and she, fearful among strangers, glad to have his protection to fall back on, unable to face the dangers of the return to Troy, and taking the line of least resistance, accepts him as her lover. In Troy the line of least resistance had been to remain in her single wedded state; in the Greek camp, friendless and bewildered, acceptance of Diomede is the easy way. For all her good qualities, she was "slydynge of corage"; she lacked will power. She repulses Diomede's first attempt with a "not yet," which already shows that the game is up. And when she yielded to him she said to herself pathetically:

> But syn I se ther is no bettre way,
> And that to late is now for me to rewe,
> To Diomede algate I wol be trwe.

As for Chaucer:

> Ne me ne list this sely womman chyde
> Forther than the storye wol devyse.
> Hire name, allas! is punysshed so wide,
> That for hire gilt it ought ynough suffise.

> And if I myghte excuse hire anywise,
> For she so sory was for hire untrouthe,
> I wis, I wolde excuse hire yet for routhe.

Troilus waits for her return in vain. The picture of him waiting day after day, until dusk, at the city gates, making excuses for her delay, thinking he sees her in the distance only to find that it is "a fare-carte" (traveling cart), is one of the most poignant and perfectly wrought things in English literature. At last he writes, and receives a loving but suspiciously evasive answer; and finally he finds on a cloak taken from Diomede in fight the brooch that he himself had given to Criseyde, and he knows for certain what he had for some time suspected. With nothing to live for he becomes bold and cruel in battle, and is eventually slain by Achilles. The poem concludes with a picture of Troilus' spirit looking down from above at this tiny world, and laughing at the shabby human scene with its distracting emotions.

> Swych fyn hath, lo, this Troilus for love!   [such end]
> Swych fyn hath all his grete worthynesse! . . .
> Swych fyn hath false worldes brotelnesse! . . .

The end of the poem is religious, an appeal from human love to divine love, with a sonorous devotional stanza from the *Paradiso* to conclude.

The literary greatness and historical significance of *Troilus and Criseyde* lie in the way Chaucer has presented and enriched the narrative. It has more dimensions than anything that had hitherto appeared in English. Some of the most important effects are lost in a summary—the touches of humorous realism in the conversation of Pandare, particularly in his talk with his niece; the flashes of amused or ironic perception; the subtle discernment of character in all its phases; the moral and philosophical overtones; the adroit use of his reading to achieve these overtones; and the flow and flexibility of the steadily moving verse. The English prose novel was well advanced before anything comparable was to appear in English literature.

In *The Legend of Good Women* Chaucer returns to the love-vision for his framework. This unfinished work is a somewhat tiresome collection of accounts of loving and faithful women—including Cleopatra, Medea, Lucrece, Ariadne, Philomela, and others—which Chaucer explains was required of him as a penance by the god of love for having written heresies against love's law, and particularly for having drawn the character of a faithless woman in *Troilus and Criseyde*. The legends themselves, constructed on the analogy of that common medieval form, the legendary or collection of saints' lives, seem to have been written without any great enthusiasm, and there is nothing in them approaching the art of the *Troilus*. But the prologue to *The Legend of Good Women*—which exists in two interestingly different versions—has a charm and liveliness that the body of the work lacks. It opens with a sprightly discussion of the relation between book knowledge and experience:

> A thousand tymes have I herd men telle
> That ther ys joy in hevene and peyne in helle,
> And I accorde wel that it ys so;
> But, natheles, yet wot I wel also
> That ther nis noon dwellyng in this contree,
> That eyther hath in hevene or helle ybe,
> Ne may of hit noon other weyes witen,
> But as he hath herd seyd, or founde it writen; . . .

We must trust old books in matters of which nobody has direct experience; the poet himself reverences them

> So hertely, that ther is game noon
> That fro my bokes maketh me to goon,
> But yt be seldom on the holyday,
> Save, certeynly, whan that the month of May
> Is comen, and that I here the foules synge,
> And that the floures gynnen for to sprynge,
> Farewel my bok, and my devocioun!

And then Chaucer turns to a description of the conventional May morning of the Rose tradition; but it is done with a freshness and a sprightly charm that raises it far above most of the hundreds of other such descriptions in medieval literature. This freshness and sense of personal delight in the world of growing things which we find in the prologue is all the more remarkable when we consider that not only is the setting conventional, but the theme which he goes on to elaborate—the worship of the daisy—is itself bound up with a literary fashion of his time and the passage celebrating the daisy is based on a poem by Deschamps. By his choice of images, by the limpid flow of the couplets, by his cunning distribution of pauses and emphasis, Chaucer gives new life and conviction to this traditional material. The appearance in the meadow of the god of love and his queen Alceste occurs in the dream which he has after falling asleep in the open. The god reproaches him for his heresies against love, Alceste defends him and seeks to soften her lord's anger, and the result is that he is given the penance of writing the stories of faithful women betrayed by false men. The task, however, was one which Chaucer's genius had outgrown.

He must have been already thinking of the plan of *The Canterbury Tales*, that magnificent unfinished *opus* in which he finally drew the various strands of his genius together. What more perfect wedding of "auctoritee" and "experience," of books and life, than a collection of true-to-life pilgrims drawn from every class of contemporary Englishman who, to while away the hours of journeying, tell tales drawn from whatever literary or folk source seems most appropriate to the individual character? Some of the tales had been written before the plan to link them through the pilgrimage device had been thought of: the Second Nun's Tale, for example (the legend of Saint Cecilia) is early, as are the "tragedies" used in the Monk's Tale, and the Knight's Tale, a reworking of Boccaccio's *Teseide* probably done about the same time as the *Troilus*. The *General Prologue*, which establishes the characters and sets the scene, probably dates from the late 1380's; and the whole scheme—two stories from each pilgrim on the outward journey, and two each again on the return—was far from complete when Chaucer died. But the real purpose of the scheme was to give Chaucer the opportunity of welding his observation of men with his literary knowledge, and that purpose could be achieved without the completion of the total plan. The scheme was thus not so much a literary form in itself as a device for giving new life to other literary forms.

A group of linked tales told by different people was not unknown in earlier medieval literature, and scholars have come up with various parallels, of which perhaps the closest is the *Novelle* of Giovanni Sercambi, where the setting is also a pilgrimage, though the author himself (one of the pilgrims) tells all the tales. It is doubtful whether Chaucer knew Boccaccio's *Decameron*. But Chaucer's work is unique in its individualizing of the narrators and in the whole sense of the contemporary social scene which he brings to the reader. He brings together at the Tabard Inn at Southwark representatives of every class in the England of his day (except, it should be noted, the very highest and the very lowest; there is no one higher than the Knight or lower than the Plowman, who was a tenant farmer and not a tied laborer). Each pilgrim is at once a fully realized individual and a representative of his class or his profession. They are on holiday, not at their daily labors, so that they are more relaxed and self-revealing than they would otherwise be. Further, only on a pilgrimage could such a heterogeneous collection of people of different social status be brought together. The characters move between the inn and the shrine, the two places where different classes are likely to mingle. But their daily lives, their normal habits of thinking, their prejudices, professional bias, most familiar ideas, and personal idiosyncrasies come out in their conversation and their behavior. They are more than a framework: their conduct affects and is affected by the telling of the tales.

The *Prologue*, which describes them one by one, takes up the details that would strike the eye of a fellow traveler. There is a deliberately contrived disorder in the way in which the facts about each character are brought to our attention. For example, he describes the Cook's skill in boiling, roasting, grilling, and frying, then remarks

> But greet harm was it, as it thoughte me,
> That on his shyne a mormal hadde he.   [growth]
> For blankmanger, that made he with the beste.

The afterthought about the "blankmanger" (an elaborate creamed dish) gives an air of absolute naturalness to the description, and this air of innocent observation—the author as fellow pilgrim naïvely noting what he sees or learns about the others in the casual order which occurs to him—can be put to most effective ironic uses when Chaucer so desires. It is worth noting, too, how more than once he begins a new description on the second line of a couplet. Thus the first line of the Shipman's description follows immediately on the last line of the description of the Cook:

> . . . For blankmanger, that made he with the beste.
> A Shipman was ther, wonynge fer by weste;
> For aught I woot, he was of Dertemouthe. . . .

This again gives an air of naturalness and spontaneity. A good example of both these devices is in the description of the Monk, followed by that of the Friar. The account of the Monk concludes:

> Now certainly he was a fair prelaat;
> He was nat pale as a forpyned goost.
> A fat swan loved he best of any roost.
> His palfrey was as broun as is a berye.
> A Frere ther was, a wantowne and a merye, . . .

The color of the Monk's horse comes in casually at the end of his description, as though the author had just noticed it, and then the Friar is introduced in the same couplet.

Chaucer's naïveté as observer is assumed for purposes of irony. Nothing could be more perfectly done than the description of the Prioress: it is mere innocent observation, it seems, until we discover

that the details add up to an amused picture of a nun whose real
interest in life was to affect genteel behavior:

> Ther was also a Nonne, a Prioresse,
> That of her smylyng was ful symple and coy;
> Hire gretteste ooth was but by Seinte Loy;
> And she was cleped madame Eglentyne.
> Ful weel she soong the service dyvyne,
> Entuned in hir nose ful semely,
> And Frenssh she spak ful faire and fetisly,
> After the scole of Stratford atte Bowe,
> For Frenssh of Parys was to hire unknowe.
> At mete wel ytaught was she with alle;
> She leet no morsel from hir lippes falle,
> Ne wette hir fyngres in hir sauce depe;
> Wel koude she carie a morsel and wel kepe
> That no drope ne fille upon hire brest.
> In curteisie was set ful muchel hir lest.
> Hir over-lippe wyped she so clene
> That in hir coppe ther was no ferthyng sene
> Of grece, when she dronken hadde hir draughte.
> Ful semely after hir mete she raughte. . . .

Only the Knight, the poor Parson, and the Plowman are treated
without any touch of irony at all, as almost ideal figures, and it is
significant that they are all something like anachronisms by Chaucer's time. The Knight represents the highest ideals of chivalry and
courtesy; the poor Parson's genuinely Christian behavior is implicitly
contrasted with that of the other representatives of the church; and
the Plowman, honest, hardworking, goodhearted, would be hard to
find in the age of the Peasants' Revolt and the Statute of Laborers.
These perhaps nostalgic portraits represent Chaucer's oblique comment on the troubles of his time, which he never overtly discusses.
It is worth remembering—what would not be guessed from a study
of Chaucer's writings—that the period in which he lived was a time
of rapid change and even of confusion. The growing tendency for
the commutation of labor service for money-payment combined with
the results of the Black Death to cause the decay of villeinage and to
increase the independence of the laborers, who, left small in number
by the ravages of the plague, were able to set their own price on their
labor. In vain the governing class tried to stop the rise in laborers'
wages by statutes of laborers. The clock could not be put back, and
the results of the Black Death in depopulating the countryside put
the laborers in an extremely favorable position. Villeins slipped away
from the land to which they were legally bound, to offer their services to the highest bidder. With harvests rotting for lack of workers,
landowners were forced to pay in wages what was asked. In addition

to the unrest produced by this problem, there were many other causes for general dissatisfaction in the last years of Edward III's reign and the beginning of Richard II's. England was being governed by a selfish and corrupt clique; France was slipping away from her control and her supremacy at sea being steadily destroyed; the glory of Crecy and Poiters had departed and—worst of all—the country was being taxed almost out of existence in a vain endeavor to win back the lost power and glory. English commerce depended largely on the maintenance of English sea-power, and the revival of French might by land and sea was more than a military question. Amid this general discontent the Peasants' Revolt broke out in 1381. Change was in the air, and to a contemporary it might well have seemed to be decay. Chivalry had become a farce. Every kind of magnificence was to be seen in the state of the small minority who wielded the power, while disease and misery prevailed throughout the countryside. The State had grown lopsided. When the Black Prince took Limoges in 1370 he massacred all the citizens, including hundreds of women and children, yet he treated the few knights who were in the town with exaggerated kindness and courtesy. In 1377 the Black Prince died, but the spirit exemplified in his action of 1370 prevailed now more than ever. The practice of knighthood had degenerated into a stupid pageantry: the old order was breaking up, with all the usual symptoms produced by the working of unrecognized forces. And in the Church, too, corruption was reaping an unpleasant harvest. Wyclif was a portentous symbol, and the connection of the priest John Ball with the rebellious peasants, however much Wyclif may have disapproved, was no accident.

Against such a background the characters of the Knight, the Parson, and the Plowman seem like nostalgic idealizations, and perhaps Chaucer meant them as such. For the rest, he takes men as he finds them, obtaining that kind of amusement in the ironic yet sym-. pathetic observation of his fellows which yields itself only to the artist's vision. The social and economic background, with its confusions and upheavals, is transmuted through human character into individual examples of self-interest or rascality, portrayed with that relish for human behavior and human weakness that we find so often in Shakespeare. But we must not, as some critics have tended to do, play down Chaucer's irony. A high proportion of his pilgrims are rascals, and Chaucer knows that they are. Nor can we ignore his clear attack on corruption in the Church, though here again the attack is done obliquely through the presentation of individual characters. The Monk and the Friar and the Summoner are amusing enough characters as Chaucer describes them, but the behavior of the latter two, brilliantly presented and magnificently comic though it is, is the behavior of petty blackguards, while the Pardoner, perhaps Chaucer's greatest masterpiece of character drawing, implies a whole world of moral hypocrisy. Chaucer's point of view is secular throughout—in spite of evidence of his genuine religious feeling and of the famous "Retraction" which follows the Parson's Tale in the manuscripts—and he is intrigued rather than shocked by the weaknesses of human nature. But irony always has moral implications, and Chaucer in *The Canterbury Tales* was not an ironist for nothing.

Attempts have been made to identify some of the pilgrims with historical characters, but even if this could be done it adds nothing to our view of Chaucer's achievement. He gives us a collection of individuals who also represent the different social and professional strata of the England of his day. The Church, with its many representatives (for the Church was the dominant profession in the Middle Ages); the Knight and his son the Squire representing the upper classes (but not the high aristocracy); the Merchant represents the well-to-do middle classes, and the five members of trade guilds, also middle class; the Franklin, a nonaristocratic landowner; the Yeoman, independent but lower down in the social scale; professional men such as the Sergeant of the Law and the Doctor of Physic; executive or managerial characters such as the Manciple (who purchased provisions for an inn of court) and the Reeve (assistant manager of an estate); and so on down to the Plowman. Almost all have more characteristics than their representative capacities demand. The tales they tell, and the incidents in which they become involved, are for the most part suited to both their occupations and their characters, though Chaucer did not have time to fit all the tales to suitable tellers. These tales together give an almost complete conspectus of medieval literary forms, including the courtly romance (Knight's Tale), the *fabliau* (Miller's and Reeve's Tales), the Breton lay (Franklin's Tale), the saint's legend (the Second Nun's and Prioress' Tales), the preacher's *exemplum* (Pardoner's Tale), the beast fable (Nun's Priest's Tale), the sermon (Parson's Tale), and so on.

The Knight's Tale is a shorter and more rapidly moving version of Boccaccio's *Teseide*, one of the stories quarried by the Middle Ages out of the material about Thebes found in Statius' *Thebaid* and the *Roman de Thèbes*. In this tale of Palamon and Arcite and their joint love for Emily, Chaucer's narrative art is seen working with supreme efficiency. The rhymed decasyllabic couplets move smoothly and flexibly forward; incident is handled with vigor and vividness; highly colored picturesque details are brought in to provide appropriate pauses in the narrative; an undertone of gravity is properly subdued to the surface polish of the tale; glimpses of irony peep out occasionally to lighten a potentially tragic incident; and, altogether, the world of the chivalric romance lives here with a brightness and a charm rarely found in other examples of the species. The characters are not highly individualized, for the world of chivalric action and courtly love does not demand such individualization; but everybody has the characteristics necessary to take him through his assigned part with dignity and spirit. The Knight's Tale has not the depth or the modernity of the *Troilus:* it is a formal and graceful exercise in a medieval mode, perfectly executed.

The formal courtesy and gravity of the ending of the Knight's Tale—

> Thus endeth Palamon and Emelye;
> And God save al this faire compaignye!—

is followed by the drunken Miller's insistence on telling his tale next. This is Chaucer at his liveliest and most characteristic:

> Our Hooste saugh that he was dronke of ale,
> And seyde, "Abyd, Robyn, my leeve brother;
> Som bettre man shal telle us first another.
> Abyd, and lat us werken thriftily."
> "By Goddes soule," quod he, "that wol nat I;
> For I wol speke, or elles go my wey."
> Oure Hooste answerde, "Tel on, a devil wey!
> Thou art a fool; thy wit is overcome."
> "Now herkneth," quod the Millere, "alle and some.
> But first I make a protestacioun
> That I am dronke, I knowe it by my soun;
> And therfore if that I mysspeke or seye,
> Wyte it the ale of Southwerk, I you preye.
> For I wol telle a legende and a lyf
> Both of a carpenter and of his wyf,
> How that a clerk hath set the wrightes cappe."

The Reeve (whose duties apparently also involved carpentering) took offence, and protested violently at the Miller's "lewed dronken harlotrye:"

> It is a synne and eek a greet folye
> To apeyren any man, or hym defame,   [injure]
> And eek to bryngen wyves in swich fame.
> Thou mayst ynogh of others thynges seyn."

But the Miller persists, and tells his coarse and rollicking *fabliau* about a credulous carpenter and his pretty wife, who cuckolded him with an ingenious and personable young clerk. The company laugh,

and "Osewold the Reeve" who "was of carpenteris craft" felt somewhat annoyed. He could requite the Miller with a bawdy story of
"bleryng of a proud milleres ye," but he is getting old, and his days
of play are over. With a sudden yet wholly appropriate change of
mood Chaucer has the Reeve burst into an eloquent self-pitying
account of his growing old, using the images appropriate to his
daily work:

> . . . For sikerly, whan I was bore, anon
> Deeth drough the tappe of lyf and leet it gon;
> And ever sithe hath so the tappe yronne
> Til that almoost al empty is the tonne. . . .

But he finds the energy to requite the Miller with another coarse tale
of the *fabliau* variety, of how a crooked miller had his wife and
daughter seduced by a couple of Cambridge students. His conclusion
shows his satisfaction:

> And God, that sitteth heighe in magestee,
> Save al this compaignye, grete and smale!
> Thus have I quyt the Millere in my tale.

The Reeve's tale sends the Cook into roars of laughter, and he begins
a tale of his own, evidently in similar vein, as far as we can tell from
the sixty lines of it that alone are extant.

The Man of Law's Tale comes in the manuscripts after the unfinished Cook's Tale, preceded by "the wordes of the Hoost to the
compaignye" and followed by further talk: it is clearly a separate
fragment of the whole work. This tale is in quite different vein from
that of the Miller's or the Reeve's. Told in rhyme royal, it is a symbolic story of the manifold misfortunes of Constance, daughter of a
Roman Emperor, and her final delivery from woe after a series of
tribulations sufficient (as in the case of patient Griselda of the Clerk's
Tale) to drive most people out of their minds. The whole thing has
the dream quality of so much medieval pseudo-history (its source is
Nicholas Trivet's *Anglo-Norman Chronicle*), and may well be an
earlier work. The characters are figures in a tapestry, and while the
tale has a certain formal beauty it lacks complexity and life.

Another fragment contains the Wife of Bath's Prologue and Tale,
the Friar's Tale, and the Summoner's Tale. The Wife of Bath's Prologue is one of the high points of *The Canterbury Tales*. The character creates herself as she talks, strong-willed, opinionated, highly
sexed, frank, humorous, and masterful. Her account of her five husbands, her defense of human frailty and arguments against chastity
as a practicable ideal, the gusto and vigor and uninhibited relish of

her talk, present a character at once highly individualized and the first of a type that has had many successors in English fiction. In spite of her appeal to "experience" rather than "auctoritee," she can quote authorities with the best. For the antifeminist arguments which the Wife puts into the mouth of one of her former husbands, as well as for aspects of the Wife's own character, Chaucer drew on a great variety of sources, including the second part of *The Romance of the Rose*, Deschamps' *Miroir de Mariage*, Jerome's *Epistola Adversus Jovinianum* and Walter Map's *Epistola Valerii ad Rufinum de non Ducenda Uxore* (*Valerius' Letter to Rufinus about not Marrying a Wife*): seldom has such a variety of material—which includes the most important antifeminist literature known to the Middle Ages —been so perfectly welded into a splendid original character portrait.

The Wife of Bath is concerned not only to defend the active use of sex in marriage—

> I wol bistowe the flour of al myn age
> In the actes and in fruyt of mariage—

but also to insist that married happiness is only possible if the husband yields the "maistrye" to the wife, and her tale, based on a story found in both literary and folk tradition, is designed to prove her point. It is the story of the "loathly lady" who turns out to be young and beautiful when the husband, whom she has acquired by doing him a service which he has promised to repay in any way she asks, promises to put himself under her "wise governance." The tale, told in decasyllabic couplets, combines magic with touches of shrewd realism, and a tone of romantic delicacy emerges at the end. This is perfectly in character, for the Wife of Bath believed in love and romance, though on her own terms.

The Wife of Bath's Tale is the first of a series of stories which deal with the question of "maistrye" in marriage. The theme is not pursued immediately, for the Friar and the Summoner, who have been spoiling for a quarrel since they interrupted the Wife of Bath's autobiographical discourse with mutually offensive remarks, proceed to tell their stories at each other's expense as soon as the Wife's tale has been concluded. Both stories are little masterpieces and show a brilliant handling of detail. The Friar tells of a rascally Summoner who meets the devil in the disguise of a yeoman and whose dishonest behavior finally puts him into the devil's power, so that he is carried off to Hell. The Summoner replies with a coarse story of a grasping Friar whose rapacity lands him in a comically humiliating situation. The picture given in this tale of the Friar's visit to a sick man, his hypocritical words of comfort and advice, his infuriatingly patronizing sententiousness, is one of the finest pieces of realistic etching Chaucer ever did. The dramatic exchanges between the Friar and the Summoner before and between the tales provide a setting and a "human interest" that make the whole episode a work of art in itself.

The Clerk's Tale, which begins another fragment, takes up the marriage question again. He tells of patient Griselda, a tapestry tale like the Man of Law's, presented in rhyme royal, based (as the Clerk acknowledges) on a Latin story by Petrarch, which is itself a rendering of a story from Boccaccio's *Decameron*. This picture of wifely meekness and obedience carried to an outrageous extreme is too much for Chaucer himself, who intervenes at the end with his own comment:

> Grisilde is deed, and eek hire pacience,
> And bothe atones buried in Ytaille;
> For which I crie in open audience,
> No wedded man so hardy be t'assaille
> His wyves pacience in trust to fynde
> Grisildis, for in certein he shal faille.
>
> O noble wyves, ful of heigh prudence,
> Lat noon humylitee youre tonge naille,
> Ne lat no clerk have cause or diligence
> To write of yow a storie of swich mervaille
> As of Grisildis pacient and kynde. . . .

The Merchant follows with the story of January and May—of an old husband and a young wife, who hoodwinks him with her young lover. A curious but effective mixture of antifeminist satire and magic, the story, told in decasyllabic couplets, makes skillful use of a great variety of literary sources. The Merchant's Tale ends this fragment, and another fragment begins with the Squire's Tale, an unfinished story of wonder and romance, set in "Sarray, in the land of Tartarye." It has the naïve enjoyment of wonders appropriate to the young squire, and its *Arabian Nights* atmosphere still has a certain appeal. Milton referred to it in his "L'Allegro" as the

> half told
> Story of Cambuscan bold.

The Franklin's Tale, which follows in this fragment, continues the marriage debate. It is a gentle and charming tale of a loving wife who, through no fault of her own, becomes involved in a promise to yield herself to another lover. Her husband, recognizing that promises must be kept, advises his wife, in tears, that she must fulfill her promise. The young man, when the lady presents herself to him and tells him in bitter grief that she is prepared to go through with it, releases her from her promise, and he in turn, who is indebted to a learned man for the means of having the lady put in his power, is released from payment of the large sum which he was to be charged for the service. Courtesy and "franchise" prevail, and "maistrye" gives way to "gentilesse." This is the final answer to the problem of who is to have the "maistrye" in marriage:

> Love wol nat been constreyned by maistrye.
> Whan maistrie comth, the God of Love anon
> Beteth his wynges, and farewel, he is gon!

The husband, the lover, and the "clerk" in the end all vie with each other in courteous and "free" behavior, and the Franklin concludes by asking his audience: "Which was the mooste fre, as thynketh yow?"

Another fragment begins with the Physician's Tale, the doleful story of Appius and Virginia, in which the daughter is killed by her father rather than be yielded to the lust of a corrupt judge. It is probably an earlier story of Chaucer and does not read like his maturer work. The Host is upset by the story and—thinking he knows his man—turns to the Pardoner for a merry tale:

> ". . . Thou beel amy, thou Pardoner," he sayde,
> "Telle us some myrthe or japes right anon."

The Pardoner demands a drink first, and then—somewhat the worse for liquor, for he has had more than one drink of "corny ale" that day—he begins. What he says constitutes perhaps the most brilliant single passage in all of Chaucer's work. Somewhat affronted by the Host's assumption that he is capable only of "a myrie tale," he begins by telling his audience of his skill and virtuosity as a Pardoner. But he is so anxious to display his cleverness (and his natural caution has been dissipated by drink) that he reveals himself as an unscrupulous trickster who uses false relics and every kind of dishonest cunning to wring money out of even the poorest people. He tells how he preaches, how he blackmails the congregation into giving him money, how he impresses, bullies, frightens, and overwhelms his hearers. It is a picture of extraordinary virtuosity, whose motive is wholly evil. Having thus vindicated his cleverness at the expense of his character he proceeds to his story—which is not a merry tale, but another example of his professional skill, an *exemplum*, a story with a moral to move and impress his hearers. His tale of the three rioters who set out to find Death and find him unknowingly in a heap of treasure—for sole possession of which each treacherously kills the others—is perfectly done. Beginning with overt moralizing, which rises to an eloquent attack on drunkenness, he proceeds to paint a vivid picture of the riotous, blasphemous, and avaricious young men at the tavern. The story then moves with somber speed to its violent conclusion. It is a professional performance of the very highest quality. Having completed the story, the Pardoner, either led by the momentum of his own eloquence or deceiving himself into believing that his eloquence and narrative skill have effaced the effect of his earlier self-revelation, offers to sell the company pardons:

> Paraventure ther may fallen oon or two
> Doun of his hors, and breke his nekke atwo.
> Looke which a seuretee is it to you alle
> That I am in youre fellaweshipe yfalle,
> That I may assoille yow, bothe moore and lasse,
> Whan that the soule shal fro the body passe.
> I rede that oure Hoost heere shal bigynne,
> For he is moost envoluped in synne.
> Com forth, sire Hoost, and offre first anon,
> And thou shalt kisse the relikes everychon,
> Ye, for a grote! Unbokele anon thy purs.

This invitation to kiss (for a fee) relics which he has already confessed are pigs' bones naturally outrages the Host, who replies with eloquent coarseness. The professional virtuosity of his tale clearly was not enough to pull the wool over the eyes of a tough-minded character like Harry Bailly. The Pardoner is enraged by his reply to his suggestion, and the Knight has to intervene to restore order.

Another fragment begins with the Shipman's Tale, an amusing *fabliau* with a folk source: there is some evidence that it was originally intended for the Wife of Bath and was transferred to the Shipman after Chaucer had decided to give the Wife another story instead. It is another tale of the wife and her lover fooling the husband. The Prioress' Tale, which follows, is a "miracle of our Lady," the story of little Saint Hugh of Lincoln murdered by "cursed Jewes" for singing a hymn to the Virgin as he walked through the Jews' quarter. It would of course be unrealistic and anachronistic to imagine that Chaucer or any of his contemporaries would have seen the fantastic and cruel libel perpetrated by such a story: there were no Jews in England in Chaucer's day, and they were known to Englishmen of the time solely in terms of anti-Semitic folklore. If we forget the implications, the story has a naïve charm which reflects something of the character of its teller. It is told in rhyme royal, and represents one of Chaucer's most assured handlings of this stanza.

The Host then turns to Chaucer himself,

> And sayde thus, "What man artow?" quod he;
> "Thou lookest as thou woldest fynde an hare,
> For evere upon the ground I see thee stare. . . ."

"Cheer up," says the Host to the timid and humble Chaucer of "elvyssh contenaunce,"

> "Tells us a tale of myrthe and that anon."
> "Hooste," quod I, "ne beth nat yvele apayd,
> For oother tale certes kan I noon,
> But of a rym I lerned longe agoon."

So the author of *The Canterbury Tales*, representing himself as the least skilled of all the narrators (this kind of humor was characteristic of him: we remember his respectful monosyllables before the eagle in *The House of Fame*), embarks on "Sir Thopas," that brilliant parody of the metrical romance. In the steady plod of the meter, in the mechanical piling up of detail, in the long catalogues of objects, in the language, situation, and tone, "Sir Thopas" burlesques all the main characteristics of run-of-the-mill popular romance in English verse. We have quoted from it in Chapter 2, but two more stanzas, illustrating the catalogue of the knight's physical attributes, will give some idea of the burlesque element:

> Sire Thopas wax a doghty swayn;
> Whit was his face as a payndemayn,
>   His lippes red as rose;
> His rode is lyk scarlet in grayn,
> And I yow telle in good certayn,
>   He hadde a semely nose.
>
> His heer, his berd was lyk saffroun,
> That to his girdel raughte adoun;
>   His shoon of cordewane.
> Of Brugges were his hosen broun,
> His robe was of syklatoun,
>   That coste many a jane.

The Host shuts him up after some thirty stanzas:

> "Namoore of this, for Goddes dignitee,"
> Quod oure Hooste, "for thou makest me
> So wery of thy verray lewednesse
> That, also wisly God my soule blesse,
> Myne eres aken of thy drasty speche.
> Now swich a rym the devel I biteche!
> This may wel be rym dogerel," quod he.

Chaucer then offers to tell "a litel thyng in prose," which turns out to be the long, tedious moralizing tale of *Melibee*, translated from the French. Whether Chaucer meant this to sound as it does to modern ears is not quite clear: he may not have been aware of how lacking in artistry his prose was compared to his verse. At any rate, the Host approved of the tale, and expressed the wish that his wife had the patience advocated and practiced by Melibeus' wife Prudence. The Host then calls on the Monk to tell a tale, assuming—as he had done with the Pardoner—that this secular-minded cleric will tell something lively. He addresses the Monk in a tone of cheerful agreement with his assumed opinion that clerical celibacy was a bad thing. But the Monk's professional dignity is offended, and he tells a series of tragedies—"De Casibus Virorum Illustrium." "Tragedy" to the medieval mind was a story of reversal of fortune from high to low. As the Monk says:

> Tragedie is to seyn a certeyn storie,
> As olde bookes maken us memorie,
> Of hym that stood in greet prosperitee,
> And is yfallen out of heigh degree
> Into myserie, and endeth wrecchedly.

This is presumably an earlier work of Chaucer's. It tells, in eight-lined stanzas rhyming *ababbcbc*, of the falls of Lucifer, Adam, Samson, Hercules, "Nabugodonosor," Balthasar, Cenobia, Pedro, king of Castille, Peter, king of Cyprus, Bernabo Visconti, Ugolino (see Dante's *Inferno*, Canto XXIII, which was presumably Chaucer's source), Nero, Holofernes, Antiochus, Alexander, Julius Caesar, and Croesus, before he is interrupted by the Knight, who can stand no more of these dreary stories:

> "Hoo!" quod the Knyght, "good sire, namoore of this!
> That ye han seyd is right ynough, ywis,
> And muchel moore; for litel hevynesse
> Is right ynough to muche folk, I gesse.

And the Host agrees fervently:

> "Sire Monk, namoore of this, so God yow blesse!
> Youre tale anoyeth al this compaignye."

He asks the Monk for a story of hunting, but the Monk replies sullenly that he doesn't want to play. The Nun's Priest is now called upon.

The Nun's Priest's Tale of Chauntecleer and Pertelote is perhaps the best known of all Chaucer's works, and justly so, for it represents Chaucer at absolutely the top of his form. The quiet, realistic opening describing the poor widow and her way of life, the account of the cock and the hen with its superb satire on human marital relationships, the use of learning in the discussion of the causes and meaning of dreams with the deftly drawn differences of approach between Chauntecleer and Pertelote, the ironic effect achieved by the application of human psychology to the behavior of the birds—all this has been discussed and praised often enough. Drawing on material from the medieval beast epic and on medieval notions of medicine, astrology, and psychology, Chaucer has produced a story so aerated with wit, so cunningly wrought at all points, so artfully blended of mockery and sympathy, of irony and understanding, that the traditional nature of the materials is lost sight of in the brilliant finish of the performance. But there is much of medieval thought and attitude in the tale, which in fact makes one of the handiest windows onto the Middle Ages for anybody who wishes to enter directly into that world. Yet the story is permanently modern, kept alive by artistry, wit, and insight into human (presented as animal) weakness.

Another fragment begins with the Second Nun's Prologue and Tale. These are conventional religious performances, probably written by Chaucer considerably earlier. The Prologue contains an invocation to the Virgin Mary, drawing on a variety of sources including the *Paradiso* and several Latin hymns, and the tale itself is an account in rhyme royal of the life and martyrdom of Saint Cecilia. The company are then enlivened by the appearance of a Canon and his Yeoman, who join them after hard riding. The Canon is an alchemist, and the Yeoman tells the company something of his master's methods for tricking people out of their money, which so enrages and shames the Canon that he rides off again. The Yeoman then tells his tale, which differs from all the others in that it is represented as something in which he was recently involved. It is the story of an elaborate plot on his master's part to obtain money fraudulently from credulous people who imagined that his alchemy could obtain riches for them. The theme was common enough in Chaucer's time, but it is told here with an immediacy and a freshness that correspond perfectly to the situation out of which it is made to arise.

Another fragment contains the Manciple's Prologue and Tale. The Prologue contains a lively quarrel between the Manciple and the Cook, the latter of whom is drunk. The Manciple's brief tale is of the telltale crow who tells the husband of his wife's infidelity: it was a story common in one form or another throughout Europe and the Orient. Finally, there is in another fragment the Parson's Prologue and Tale, which follows directly after the Manciple's Tale, for it begins with a reference to its having just ended. The Host asks the Parson for a story, and the Parson replies that he will tell no story but a sermon.

> Why sholde I sowen draf out of my fest,
> Whan I may sowen whete, if that me lest? . . .
> But trysteth wel, I am a Southren man,
> I kan nat geeste 'rum, ram, ruf,' by lettre,
> Ne, God woot, rym holde I but litel bettre; . . .

He does not hold with the alliterative poetry of the North, or with rhyme. He will tell his tale in prose, "to knytte up al this feeste, and make an ende." He then delivers a long sermon on penitence, which includes a treatise on the seven deadly sins. The prose is somewhat featureless, and the work is more interesting to students of medieval preaching than to the literary critic. After it, in all the manuscripts which contain the complete tale, is Chaucer's "Retraction," a conventionally pious renunciation of his works "of worldly vanitees," including the *Troilus, The House of Fame, The Legend of Good Women, The Parliament of Fowls,* and those of *The Canterbury Tales* "that sownen into synne." Neo-orthodoxy hails this as a commendable turning from this world to eternity, but it is difficult to be satisfied with a point of view which so blithely renounces what has made a man immortal.

The conclusion is self-evident. With Chaucer, the English language and English literature grew at a bound to full maturity. No other Middle English writer has his skill, his range, his complexity, his large humane outlook. Unfortunately, the English language (as Chaucer foresaw in a stanza at the end of *Troilus and Criseyde*) was still in the process of rapid change, and major shifts in pronunciation and accentuation were to occur in the following century and a half. This meant that Chaucer's achievement in establishing English as a fully developed literary language could not be adequately exploited by his immediate successors. It was not long before readers were unable to scan him properly. This fact helps to emphasize Chaucer's loneliness. His followers lack both his technical brilliance and his breadth of vision, leaving him the one undisputed master in medieval English literature. Not until Shakespeare is there an English writer with Chaucer's combination of technique and insight and his ability to put each at the service of the other, and Shakespeare's genius, which was the greater, ran in different channels. But no other English narrative poet is his equal.

The large canvas on which *The Canterbury Tales* are painted, the varied view of humanity in action which Chaucer gives us, were later to become characteristic qualities of English literature, represented in both the drama and, later, the novel. The often quoted phrase of Dryden's, "Here is God's plenty," referring to *The Canterbury Tales*, can be applied to much in Shakespeare, Fielding, and Dickens, to name only a few. However much attention is paid to the principal character or characters in the foreground, English dramatists and novelists have had a fondness for filling in the background with a large range of characters diminishing in subtlety, but not in life, the further in the background they are. Men tend to be seen against the colorful pattern of a stratified society rather than only in intimate relation with the select few in contact with whom their destiny is determined. This is not, of course, always true, and less true of tragedies than of other kinds of work (compare *Othello* with *Henry IV*, for example or Jonson's *Bartholomew Fair* with his *Sejanus*), but on the whole the crowded canvas, with the characters shading off from fully realized individuals to types and oddities, seems to be a preference of the English literary genius. Chaucer, however, does not go in for Jonsonian "humours" (though he knows and uses the psychological theory behind them) or Dickensian eccentrics. His vision, if ironic, is central; his tone, if often comic, is never merely funny; and each of his characters represents some essential truth about men.

If Chaucer's work helped to make the East Midland dialect of Middle English into the English literary language, we are reminded by the work of his contemporary, John Gower (died 1408), who wrote in French and in Latin as well as in English, that the claims of the other two languages were still strong. French, however, was rapidly giving way to English, and it is significant that of his three major works—*Miroir de l'Homme*, *Vox Clamantis*, and *Confessio Amantis*—the first is in French (in its Anglo-Norman variety) and the last, written toward the end of his career with Chaucer's example before him, is in English. Gower's reputation has been eclipsed by Chaucer's, but he was popular in his own day and was still read by the Elizabethans. He is a more typical representative of his age and class than Chaucer could claim to be: conservative, moralistic, drawing with considerable technical skill but without any great originality of perception or liveliness of imagination on the traditional materials that were available to him. His long French poem is a manual of sins and sinners, a detailed and gloomy account of the prevalence of vice springing from man's corrupt nature. Repentance is, of course, the remedy. The *Vox Clamantis*, a dream allegory in Latin, deals with the Peasants' Revolt of 1381, giving a savagely gloomy picture of violence and disorder and of the general corruption of the age. The *Confessio Amantis* is a collection of tales in English octosyllabic couplets linked by a not very helpful framework. The poet announces, with a certain reluctance, that he will leave morality for love, for readers prefer the latter. He then describes the conventional May morning, with himself going out into a wood and meeting Venus, the Queen of Love, who advises him to make his confession to Genius, her priest. Genius considers it necessary to discuss the seven deadly sins, with the numerous sub-sins in each category, and he proceeds to illustrate each one by a story; it is these stories which make up the main material of the poem. The relation between the story and the sin it is meant to illustrate is often forced and sometimes preposterous, and it would have been better if Gower had rid himself altogether of this cumbrous machinery. But the tales themselves are told with a quiet skill. Gower lacks altogether Chaucer's vivacity and humor: he tends to be merely fluent. Here, for example, is part of his description of the cave of sleep from his tale of Ceyx and Alcione (which Chaucer told in *The Book of the Duchess*):

> Under an hell there is a cave,   [hill]
> Which of the sonne mai noght have,
> So that noman mai knowe ariht
> The point between the dai and nyht:
> Ther is no fyr, there is no sparke,
> Ther is no dore, which mai charke,   [creak]
> Whereof an yhe scholde unschette,   [an eye should open]
> So that inward there is no lette. . . .

The stories are interspersed with digressions on a great variety of subjects. His views are always the conventional views of his age. There is no originality in his imagination or in his ideas. The constant moralizing wearies, and though many of the tales hold the interest, the smooth flow of over thirty thousand lines becomes infinitely tiresome. "Moral Gower," as Chaucer called him in the dedication of the *Troilus*, is one of the most interesting examples in medieval English literature of verse craftsmanship without genius; he is an excellent mirror of his age; he is more disturbed by the upheavals in contemporary society than Chaucer ever shows himself to be; but he is a dull fellow, lacking the true spark, and we cannot read him for any length of time without making historical allowances.

Moral in a more passionate and personal way and more deeply concerned with the religious, social, and economic problems of his time is the author of *Piers Plowman*, an impressive allegorical poem (or series of related poems) written in the old alliterative meter in the latter part of the fourteenth century. The author is traditionally taken to be William Langland, and he certainly refers to himself as Will in the poem; but the attribution is uncertain, and in any case it is possible that the later two of the three main versions of the poem which exist represent revisions and alterations by one or more other writers. The Prologue describes how the author fell asleep on a May morning on the Malvern Hills and saw in a dream "a faire felde ful of folke," with ploughmen, wasters, hermits, merchants, jesters, beggars, pilgrims, and friars, each going about his business; the list closes with a pardoner with his papal bulls offering to "assoil" the people, and neglectful priests deserting their flocks for an easy life in London. A king appears, and an angelic voice admonishes him in Latin to follow justice and mercy; then—with that dream logic where one scene suddenly transforms itself into another—we find a group of rats and mice deciding to put a bell on the cat so that they can have warning of his approach, then finding none of them willing to tie the bell on to the cat, and finally being warned that that is not how to handle the problem of a dangerous ruler. The Prologue ends with another crowded picture of the social scene, with barons, burgesses, tradesmen, and artisans of different kinds, laborers, and innkeepers crying "Hot pies!" at the doors of their taverns.

We can see at once that this is a new use of the dream allegory. The gentle movement of the traditional variety of love vision, generally told in rhymed couplets, has here given way to the more vigorous rhythms of the older alliterative line, obviously handled by someone who had long been familiar with it. There is a rapidity and a bustling quality about the verse, a sense of men at work, that is not easily paralleled in medieval English literature:

> A faire felde ful of folks   fonde I there bytwene,
> Of alle maner of men   the mene and the riche,
> Worchying and wandryng   as the worlde asketh.
> Some putten hem to the plow   pleyed ful selde,
> In settyng and in sowyng   swonken ful harde,
> And wonnen that wastours   with glotonys destruyeth.
>   And some putten hem to pruyde   aparailed hem thereafter,
> In contenaunce of clothyng   comen disgised.
>   In prayers and in penance   putten hem manye,
> Al for loue of ower lorde   lyueden ful streyte,
> In hope forto haue   heueneriche blisse. . . .
>   There preched a Pardonere   as he a prest were,
> Broughte forth a bulle   with bishopes seles,
> And seid that hym-self myghte   assoilen hem alle
> Of falshed of fastyng   of vowes ybroken.

The vision then develops into an allegorical interpretation of life. The first "passus" (the name given to the divisions of the poem) introduced Holy Church, a fair lady who expounds the way of salvation to the dreamer. In the second, Lady Mede (reward, bribery) appears, richly dressed, and is to be married to Falsehood; but Theology objects and the various characters proceed to London to have the matter decided by the King. The King threatens punishment to Falsehood and the other figures surrounding Lady Mede (Flattery, Guile), who run off and leave Mede alone to face the court. In the third passus, Mede tries her tricks on the justices. She confesses to a friar and is shriven, and makes a good impression by promising to pay for new windows in a church (which leads the author to utter a warning against those who hope to attain heaven by having their names engraved as benefactors on church windows: that is not the way to salvation). She recommends the acceptance of bribes to mayors and justices. The King is fooled, and proposes a marriage between Mede and Conscience, but Conscience objects and delivers a formidable indictment of the lady. Some lively argument follows, in the course of which Conscience gives an eloquent account of a time coming when

> Shal na more Mede   be maistre, as she is nouthe,   [now]
> Ac love and lowenesse   and lewte togederes,   [loyalty]
> Thise shal be maistres on molde   treuthe to save.   [earth]

Passus IV develops the argument, with Wit, Wisdom, Peace, Reason, and Wrong taking part: the King is convinced by Reason in the end, and asks him to stay with him always.

In Passus V the poet awakes briefly, then falls asleep again "and thanne saw I moche more." He sees the same field full of folk, and describes first Reason preaching to the people that recent plagues and tempests were punishment for sin. The Seven Deadly Sins hear Reason's call to repentance, and are moved to repent. This introduces one of the liveliest and most interesting sections of the poem. Pride, Luxury, Envy, Wrath, Avarice, Gluttony, and Sloth, each personified, give accounts of themselves before their repentance, and some of these accounts, taken together with the author's description, amount to brilliantly drawn portraits. There is of course no more individualization than is necessary to make the particular vice clear and to illuminate the behavior which it implies, but within these limits the character drawing is vivid and skillful. The most appealing is the picture of Gluttony in the tavern, where he stops on his way to church. The interior of a medieval tavern is described with Hogarthian realism: Gluttony's fellow drinkers are not personifications, but real people:

> Cesse the souteresse   sat on the benche,   [female shoemaker]
> Watte the warner   and hys wyf bothe,
> Tymme the tynkere   and tweyne of his prentis,
> Hikke the hakeneyman   and hughe the nedeler,
> Clarice of cokkeslane   and the clerke of the cherche,
> Dawe the dykere   and a dozeine other. . . .   [ditcher]

The level of the allegory is not consistent. Gluttony is a gluttonous person, who does not repent until he has made himself drunk and awakes two days later with a hangover. Sloth appears to be a self-indulgent and lazy priest who prefers to read "rymes of Robyn hood" to performing his priestly duties.

The repentant company then determine to journey in search of Truth, but they do not know the way. It is at this point that Piers Plowman first appears on the scene. The company have vainly inquired of a returned pilgrim if he knows where a saint called Truth is to be found. Then

> "Peter!" quod a plowman   and put forth his hed,
> "I knowe hym as kyndely   as clerke doth his bokes;
> Conscience and kynde witte   kenned me to his place."
>   [kynde = natural]

Piers takes over the moral leadership of the company and tells them the way to Truth in Bunyanesque allegorical geography. This passus ends with a pardoner deciding that he cannot go without his papal bulls and letters of indulgence, and a common woman telling Piers simply that she will follow him.

Passus VI continues the story. Piers says he will act as guide to the company after he has ploughed his half-acre. He gives further moral advice to the company, in particular to a knight, who recognizes his duty to protect the church and the common people. Piers directs everybody to hard work, and those who shirk are disciplined by Hunger. A discussion of labor, wages, and similar economic factors, which illustrates the author's conservative view of such matters (he is looking back to an ideal stability before the present discontents) concludes this passus. In Passus VII, Truth sends Piers a pardon intended for all (though lawyers and merchants are eligible only with reservations), and a priest argues against its validity. The priest says that he can find no pardon there, but only a statement that those who do well shall find salvation and those who do evil shall not. The ensuing argument awakens the dreamer, and the passus concludes with the poet's passionate remarks on the superiority of good works to indulgences and papal bulls as means of pardon.

The remainder of *Piers Plowman*—most of it existing only in the two later versions—contains the vision of Dowel (Do Well), Dobet (Do Better), and Dobest. It is difficult to follow the somewhat rambling course of the prologues and ten passus of this extension of the poem; the author seems to be allowing his moral views and his religious emotion to deflect the poem at any point, and lively contemporary references, grand moments of religious passion, and flat didactic passages jostle each other. The author does not seem to have been able to subdue his material to an adequate literary form. But the main design is nevertheless visible. Underlying all the digressions, outbursts, symbolic incidents, moral indignation, prophecies, preaching, and visions is the notion of the quest, the search for the good life, for salvation, for truth, and for God. This search can be conducted on different levels and described from different points of view, and almost anything that men can do or think or feel or imagine is relevant to it. As the poem proceeds and the lives of Dowel, Dobet, and Dobest unfold with all the digressions and excursions, we get a picture of the fight against evil carried on simultaneously on different planes: the fight for the spirit against the dead letter, the fight against corruption in the Church, the fight against false religion. Faith, hope, and charity constitute the way; they follow from one another, culminating in charity, as Dobet follows Dowel to culminate in Dobest. The account of Dowel concludes with a triumphant description of the victory of Life over Death, of Light over Darkness, the meeting of Truth and Mercy, of Peace and Righteousness, with Christ's descent into Hell and his victory over Satan. The poet wakes to hear the joyous pealing of Easter bells. But in the ensuing account of Dobest we see Antichrist taking control after Christ's departure, and a sad picture of corruption and decay on the earth succeeds. Piers Plowman now reappears, as a symbol of Christ himself, of God *quasi homo* and of God's grace vouchsafed to all men. With a picture of a hard fought *psychomachia*, the vices pressing the virtues hard, and with Conscience finally rousing himself to seek in pilgrimage for Piers Plowman in his new symbolic meaning, the dream concludes, and the poet awakes in tears.

Though it lacks artistic unity and the author shows only sporadic control over his material, *Piers Plowman* is a remarkable work, with its alternation of bitter satire and tenderness, of vivid description of contemporary life and the stringing together of Latin tags, of social realism and religious vision. And the handling of the alliterative line is always easy and confident. There is none of Chaucer's relish of the human scene as a human scene, nor of his joy in his verbal artistry; *Piers Plowman* is the work of a religious idealist who is genuinely distressed by the social and moral condition of England and who is endeavoring to create a large and cumulative vision of what is wrong and where we must look for improvement. If the two later versions represent the work of other writers, then it seems clear that the original author succeeded in creating a tradition, a vehicle for carrying both a satirical and a religious content, which was exploited by those similarly troubled. There is something of the popular imagination as well as of the individual vision in *Piers Plowman;* even in its most visionary moments it is never private; the author is always thinking of the people, and in Piers himself he creates a symbol who eventually united the ideal of the common man with the ideal of God made man. Like Chaucer, the author of *Piers Plowman* made use of traditional material, and they both draw on the facts of contemporary society: but what different pictures they present! The difference is one of attitude, both personal and social, and it is a salutary check to hasty generalizations about the spirit of an age to consider that the same age produced *Piers Plowman* and *The Canterbury Tales.*

CHAPTER FIVE

The End of the Middle Ages

THE ENGLISH LITERARY SCENE after the death of Chaucer is not inspiring. The fifteenth century, though it saw a significant increase in lay literacy and marked an important stage in the rise of the middle class, suffered from the confusions and demoralization of the long reign of Henry VI and of the Wars of the Roses which followed it. Significant new forces were indeed working in the national culture; the victory of English over French was now clear and complete, a new class of readers was slowly developing, the new movement of Humanism was beginning to awaken English interest, and social and economic changes were bringing about the transformation of the feudal system into a freer society based on a money economy; but it was some time before these changes were reflected in any important new movement of the mind or the spirit. At the beginning of the fifteenth century it was clear that none of Chaucer's followers had his technical brilliance, his imagination, or his understanding of men, and there was none who could combine the courtly and the bourgeois tradition as Chaucer had done. Fifteenth-century courtly poetry sometimes uses the old modes with a certain freshness: *The Flower and the Leaf,* long wrongly attributed to Chaucer, uses traditional material with charm, giving a new twist to the handling of tapestry figures of allegorical significance by having the narrator a woman and by having the two opposing sets of characters (worshipers of the flower and of the leaf, the idle and the faithful) treat each other with gentle friendliness; and other works of the "Chaucer Apocrypha" have their own appeal, though none is as fresh as *The Flower and the Leaf. The Cuckoo and the Nightingale* is a *débat* using familiar properties; *La Belle Dame sans Merci* (which gave Keats a title) has a lover pleading in vain with a lady whose matter-of-fact indifference to his love almost breaks out of the whole courtly love tradition; *The Assembly of Ladies* tells in heavy allegorical detail of pleadings before the Lady Loyalty. We see here a tradition working itself out.

Thomas Hoccleve and John Lydgate are the best known of
Chaucer's followers in England; their lives overlapped Chaucer's,
and Hoccleve apparently knew the master personally, yet they seem
to belong to a different age. Hoccleve wrote less than Lydgate, but
he is the more interesting, for, though there is little to choose between the two on grounds of poetic merit (or lack of it), there are
realistic and autobiographical touches in Hoccleve's work that help
to enliven it for us. He was a minor civil servant, a connoisseur of
London night life and a tavern hunter, perpetually in need of money,
seeking noble patrons and writing them begging verse letters. His
Mâle Règle tells the story of his misspent life and ends with an appeal to the Lord Treasurer to pay him his overdue pension. There are
some fairly vivid touches:

> Wher was a gretter maister eek than y
> Or bet aqueyntid at Westmynstre yate
> Among the taverneres namely   [especially]
> And cookes? Whan I cam, eerly or late,
> I pynchid nat at hem in myn acate,   [purchasing]
> Wherfore I was the welcomer algate
> And for a verray gentil man yholde.

And there is the well-known line

> Excesse at borde hath leyd his knyf with me.

His longer works are mechanical and tedious. They include many
translations, among them the *Regement of Princes*, compiled from
a variety of sources. His religious and didactic works have little
value as literature, though they seem to reflect a genuine piety, for
all his love of taverns. Technically, his verse is extraordinarily un-
accomplished: he is content if he produces the requisite number of
syllables in the line, paying no attention to how they are stressed
(while Lydgate, on the other hand, is happy if he has the requisite
number of stresses and does not seem to care how many or what
kind of unstressed syllables he has). He had a genuine admiration for
Chaucer, and introduced into the *Regement of Princes* stanzas in
praise of him:

> O mayster deer and fadir reverent,
> My mayster Chaucer flour of eloquence,
> Mirrour of fructuous endendement,
> O universel fader in science . . .

Elsewhere he hails him as

> The firste foundere of oure faire langage.

Chaucer, it is clear, became a legend soon after his death; but this does not mean that any of his English admirers had the ability to follow in his footsteps.

Lydgate is almost universally written off as a bore, and though he has occasional felicitous touches there is little reason to disagree with this verdict. Unlike Hoccleve, Lydgate led a cloistered life as a monk, mostly at Bury St. Edmunds, and though this did not prevent him from managing to see a good deal of men and affairs—and certainly did not prevent him from reading widely, for the library at the Benedictine Abbey at Bury was one of the best-stocked in England— he had nothing of Chaucer's gift of turning both his reading and his experience to lively account in his own writing. Over one hundred forty-five thousand lines of his verse survive, including the mammoth *Fall of Princes* (from a French prose version of Boccaccio's *De Casibus Illustrium Virorum*), the almost equally lengthy *Troy-Book* (from Giudo delle Colonne's *Historia Troiana*), several lives of saints (done for different patrons), several translations from the French, and many miscellaneous shorter poems, both secular and religious in subject. There is a deadening lameness in his versification, together with a syntactical looseness, which makes the reading of his longer didactic works a severe penance. Lydgate's were the routine didactic interests of the unadventurous spirits of his time, and we can at least console ourselves with the thought that his work illustrates the early fifteenth-century English mind. He contributed something, too, both to the themes of English literature and to the vocabulary of English. His *Fall of Princes* is the first full-dress collection of "tragedies" (in the medieval sense of stories of falls from high to low estate) of the many that were to influence English thought and literature up to Shakespeare's *Richard III*. His *Dance Macabre* introduced to England (from the French) a theme of great significance in medieval thought and art of the period: Death the leveller, who addresses in turn all classes of men, Pope, Emperor, cardinal, king, and so on down the scale to laborer, friar, child, clerk, and hermit, points the grim moral of a common mortality which is found so often stressed in the fifteenth century. Lydgate added many new words to the English vocabulary, though he rarely employed them with much sensitivity or poetic force; they are mostly polysyllabic words from Latin or French, such as "inexcusable," "credulity," "tolerance," and "adolescence." But what the reader is most conscious of is his frequent use of tag phrases— "sothly to telle," "ther nis namor to say," "as to myn intent," "yiff I shal not lye," et cetera.

Lydgate is at his best in his shorter poems, and in those where the demands of the narrative compel him to some liveliness of detail (and it might be added that his feeling for small children has been noted in his favor). A good example is his tale, "The Churl and the Bird," rendered from the French. The churl has caught the bird and put it in "a praty litel cage"; the bird speaks:

> . . . And though my cage forged were of gold
> And the penacles of byral and cristal,
> I remembre a proverbe said of olde
> Who lesith his fredome in faith he lesith al,
> For I had lever upon a branche smal
> Merely to sing amonge the wodes grene
> Thenne in a cage of silver bright and shene.
>
> Songe and prison han noon accordaunce;
> Trowest thou I wol synge in prisoun?
> Songe procedith of ioye and of pleasaunce
> And prison causith deth and distructioun . . .

But even emotion seeks, in Lydgate, to express itself in didactic or proverbial form.

The professions of literary incompetence made by so many of these fifteenth-century poets represent doubtless a mere fashion; but they spoke more truly than they knew. Among the little surviving verse of Benedict Burgh is a short poem of compliment to Lydgate which begins in this common self-deprecatory vein:

> Nat dremyd I in the mownt of Pernaso,
> ne dranke I nevar at Pegases welle,
> the pale Pirus saw I never also
> ne wist I never where the muses dwelle . . .

John Walton, whose translation of Boethius into English verse shows better metrical control than most of his fifteenth-century contemporaries, begins his prologue in similar strain:

> Insuffishaunce of cunnyng & of wyt,
> Defaut of langage & of eloquence,
> This work fro me schuld have withholden yit . . .

The anonymous author of *The Court of Sapience* (he may have been Stephen Hawes), a long allegorical, didactic poem in two parts, the first dealing with the dispute between Mercy, Peace, Righteousness, and Truth concerning the fate of man and the second a conducted tour of medieval learning, varies the formula somewhat and speaks in livelier accents. He asks Clio to "forge my tonge to glad myn audytours," professing his own deficiencies:

> I knowe my self moost naked in al artes,
> My comune vulgare eke moost interupte,
> And I conversaunte & borne in the partes
> Wher my natyf langage is moost corrupt,
> And wyth most sondry tonges myxt & rupte . .

The Court of Sapience dates from about 1470: it is more vigorous in expression and competent in metrics than anything by Lydgate, but in theme it represents the uninspired development of the allegorical didactic tradition.

It seems as though the simple story romance, so popular with an earlier generation of Englishmen, had been pushed out by allegory and didacticism. And, with the decay of feudalism and the slow but steady rise of a realistic and iconoclastic bourgeoisie, there was no new source of idealism to revivify the increasingly uninspired and conventional didactic allegory. But by a fruitful coincidence, the last flare-up of chivalry in the courts of Europe, a last Indian summer of knightly ideals in the earlier manner, occurred at the same time that printing came in. Caxton, who had been in Burgundy witnessing this revival at the French-speaking court of the Duke of Burgundy, brought with him (from the Low Countries) the art of printing on his return to England. The revival of interest in the chivalric story romance which accompanied chivalry's final fling was just in time to take advantage of Caxton's imported art; which accounts for the fact that some of the first works printed in England were chivalric stories of the older kind. This revival of interest in romance, though influential, was brief; it was killed in the sixteenth century partly by the new movement of Humanism, which in England in its early phase took a narrow view of romantic tales and, with Roger Ascham, protested against idle stories of chivalry, and partly by the growing bourgeois taste for a more realistic, picaresque kind of story.

The attenuated courtly tradition; satirical, topical, and political verse of little literary merit but of considerable historical interest; didactic, moralistic, and religious writing: these were the three main categories of fifteenth-century English literature, and the third is the largest. The religious lyric, following the types discussed in Chapter 3, flourished during the period: indeed, most of what has been said of the fourteenth-century lyric applies to the fifteenth century also, though new themes and attitudes begin to make their appearance as the century advanced, and will be discussed later.

That the fifteenth century was a period of transition in England is obvious enough to the political and economic historian. The Wars of the Roses, where the nobility destroyed each other and the middle class rose steadily; William Caxton's introduction of printing into

England (Caxton's translation of Raoul de Fevre's *Le Receuil des Histoires de Troye*, printed by him as *Recuyel of the Histories of Troye* at Bruges in 1474, was the first printed book published in English, and his return to London in 1475 was followed by his printing in 1477 of *Dictes and Sayings of the Philosophers*, the first book printed in England); the gradual impact on English thought of the Humanism of the Renaissance; the establishment of the Tudor monarchy in 1485—these are obvious and significant marks of change. In the literature of the period, however, we see for the most part simply the progressive exhaustion of earlier medieval modes. Yet much that appears at first sight merely to exhibit this exhaustion can be seen on a closer view to be influenced in some degree by new ways of thinking. Stephen Hawes' allegorical romance, *The Pastime of Pleasure*, dedicated to Henry VII in 1506, continues the lame versification and the mechanical allegorizing of Lydgate, with even less notion of the true nature of allegory than his immediate predecessors:

> The light of truoth, I lacke cunnyng to cloke,
> To drawe a curtayne, I dare not to presume
> Nor hyde my matter, with a misty smoke
> My rudenes cunnyng, dothe so sore consume
> Yet as I may, I shall blowe out a fume
> To hyde my mynde, underneth a fable
> By covert coloure, well and probable.

It is a curious view indeed that the function of allegory is to obscure truth. Yet this "smokey," didactic, allegorical romance, telling (in first person narrative) of the pursuit and eventual attainment by the hero, Graunde Amour, of La Bell Pucell shows some interesting new features. The hero, encouraged by Fame (a lady) and accompanied by Governaunce and Grace (two greyhounds), receives an elaborate education in the Tower of Doctrine before engaging on the knightly adventures which culminate in his marriage to La Bell Pucell. Here we have the union of the active life and the contemplative life, which had hitherto been sharply distinguished in medieval thought, following St. Augustine's influential statement in *The City of God* that "the study of wisdom is either concerning action or contemplation, and thence assumes two several names, active and contemplative, the active consisting in the practice of morality in one's life, and the contemplative in penetrating into the abstruse causes of nature, and the nature of divinity." The knight and the clerk are united in Graunde Amour, representing a new ideal of lay education; further, the hero's love for La Bell Pucell is chaste and Christian and leads to marriage—something quite impossible in the earlier courtly love tradition. The interest—one might say the obsession—with education is characteristic of the age; the combination of the didactic romance with the romance of knightly adventure in a context of education looks forward to Spenser's *Faerie Queene*. And at the end, after the hero has married and lived happily ever after, he addresses the reader from the grave in the one memorable stanza of the poem:

> O mortall folk, you may beholde and se
> How I lye here, somtyme a myghty knyght.
> The ende of Joye and all prosperite
> Is dethe at last through his course and myght;
> After the day there cometh the derke nyght,
> For though the day be never so longe
> At last the belles ryngeth to evensonge.

The Seven Deadly Sins, and Fame, Time, and Eternity, all play their part in the final pageant, which shows a certain grandeur of conception in spite of the technical inadequacy of the verse.

How dismal—to the point of being positively comic—the verse can become is illustrated by the following passage, describing the hero's education in grammar at the hands of Dame Doctrine:

> . . . To whom she answered, right gently agayne,
> Saiyng alwaye, that a nowne substantyve
> Might stande without helpe of an adjectyve.
>
> The latyne worde, whiche that is referred
> Unto a thing, whiche is substantiall
> For a nowne substantive is well averred,
> And with a gender is declinall.
> So all the eyght partes in generall
> Are latyn wordes, annexed proprelye
> To every speache, for to speake formally.

This intolerable doggerel is representative of a whole area of late medieval English didactic verse. Yet not only does *The Pastime of Pleasure* have its moments of perception and even of eloquence; it is also a work of considerable historical importance in that it illustrates an attitude toward love, education, and the relation of the active to the contemplative life which foreshadows both the courtesy books of the Renaissance and the use of romance made by Spenser. Hawes saw himself, however, as a follower rather than as a pioneer, and he mentions Gower, Chaucer, and Lydgate (in that order) as his masters, listing the major works of the latter two. He seems utterly unaware of Chaucer's superiority to the other two, and Lydgate is especially praised for his eloquence:

> O master Lydgate, the most dulcet spryng
> Of famous rethoryke, wyth ballade royall,
> The chefe originall of my learnyng,
> What vayleth it, on you for to call
> Me for to ayde, nowe in especiall,
> Sythen your bodye is now wrapte in chest.
> I pray God to give your soule good rest.

Hawes' other allegorical-didactic romance, *The Example of Virtue*, is shorter and less interesting, and few other late medieval exercises in this mode have any special appeal. William Nevill's *Castell of Pleasure* (1518) is worth mentioning only because its printer, Robert Copland, himself (like Caxton) a translator and dabbler in letters, introduces a dialogue between the printer and the author at the beginning of the poem, and because, in its mechanical use of the allegorical formulas, it sinks to probably record depths of dullness. Nowhere is the popular medieval *ubi sunt* theme handled so flatly:

> Where is Tully, whiche had pryncypalyte
> Over all oratours in parfyte rethoryke?
> Where be all the foure doctours of dyvynyte?
> Where is Arystotyll for all his phylosophy & logyke?

Alexander Barclay (*ca.* 1475–1552) is a transitional figure of some importance. His *Ship of Fools* (1509) provided a new metaphor for English satire. It is a rendering of the *Narrenschiff* of the German Sebastian Brant through the Latin translation of Locher, a Swiss, but Barclay's own comments expand the poem to many times the length of his original. Satire, of course, was not unknown in the earlier Middle Ages; the *fabliau* tradition, as we have seen, is largely satirical, and Jean de Meun, Chaucer, and Langland have each his own satirical vein. The conception of the important people of the world as a collection of fools—courtiers, ecclesiastics, scholars, and merchants alike—seems to have become popular in the later Middle Ages, and Brant's idea of putting them all in a boat sailing off to Narragonia gave a new liveliness to the whole conception. It is a development of the older handling of the seven deadly sins, and the shift of attention from moral evil to intellectual folly is significant of a new temper in European civilization. *The Ship of Fools* looks forward to Erasmus' *Praise of Folly* as much as it looks backward to the theme of the seven deadly sins. Its interest is more in the contemporary social scene than with moral types, and this again marks an important development. Barclay's rhyme royal stanzas are pedestrian enough in movement, but the self-characterization of the representatives of different kinds of folly provides some vivid glimpses of the society of the time. Satire, so long directed against ecclesiastical abuses, is beginning to turn to wider themes, including life at Court (increasingly important with the establishment of the new national state with its centralized monarchy) and intellectual fashions. The satiric stream widens and deepens after Barclay, with Skelton's *Bowge of Court* and *Speak, Parrot* concentrating on the contemporary scene. The changes which Renaissance Court life and the first effects of Renaissance Humanism brought with them stimulated conservative minds to angry satire, and while the attack on folly is itself a Humanist theme, attacks on Humanism as well as on other novelties are made by angry conservatives. Indeed, angry conservatives have always produced the greatest satire, from Aristophanes to Swift, and while neither Barclay nor Skelton can be regarded as a great satirist they do share the great satirist's sense of outrage at what contemporary man is making of himself.

The pastoral also becomes at this time a vehicle for satire in English; it comes to replace the dream as the commonest kind of machinery for satirical as well as many other purposes. Barclay produced five eclogues, three translated (with many expansions) from the *Miserae Curialium* of Pope Pius II (Aeneas Sylvius Piccolomini) and two from the late fifteenth- and early sixteenth-century Italian poet, Baptista Mantuanus, known as Mantuan in England where he was much admired for his Latin pastorals in the sixteenth and seventeenth centuries. Thus a new breath from classical literature comes, though indirectly, into English literature, the first of very many such. The use of the pastoral for satire of Court life, urban life, ecclesiastical corruption, and other abuses of the time, as well as to discuss literary questions, established itself early in the Renaissance; Barclay is the first English writer to use a device, already common in Italy, which was to be developed significantly by succeeding generations of English poets, notably by Spenser in his *Shepherd's Calendar*. And as *The Shepherd's Calendar*, as we shall see, is in some sense both the manifesto and the first-fruits of the "new" English poetry, the pastoral tradition is clearly of prime importance in English literature; we shall have to look at it more closely later.

John Skelton (ca. 1460–1529) is the most interesting and original of all the transitional poets who, while considering themselves in the tradition of Chaucer, Gower, and Lydgate, are in fact Janus-faced, looking both toward the medieval past and to the Renaissance future. As a satirist, Skelton attacks the abuses of courtly life, new fashions in thought, religion and behavior, personal enemies, Scots, and aspects of the contemporary scene which he found annoying. *The Bowge of Court* is a satire of Court life in the traditional rhyme royal stanza, combining traditional medieval allegorical figures with the ship of fools device, the characters being sometimes allegorical personages and sometimes lively representatives of the contemporary scene. Less traditional in form and content is *Speak, Parrot,* a bubbling satirical piece mostly in rhyme royal but with some parts in other meters; the poet speaks through the bird in a characteristic mixture of bitterness and clowning. But *Colin Clout* and *Why come ye not to Court* represent his most characteristic and original satirical vein. The verse here is that short two-beat line which has become known as "Skeltonics"; the poems move with breathless abandon from point to point, highly personal in tone, deliberately discursive in progression, mingling fierce abuse, clowning humor, and bitter irony. Latin tags and even whole passages in rhymed Latin couplets, echoes or parodies of the Church liturgy or of the arguments of the schoolmen, are sprinkled freely among the wild and whirling verses. The life, the abandon, the high spirits, the reckless vitality of these pieces make them utterly unlike anything that English literature had yet produced. In *The Book of Philip Sparrow* he uses a similar technique to lament the loss of a young girl's pet sparrow: the lament is put into the mouth of the girl, and ends with Skelton's own tribute to the girl's charm and beauty. Its parody of the Office for the Dead and other aspects of the Latin liturgy of the Church is done with a cheerful recklessness reminiscent of the goliardic literature of the Middle Ages. The verse itself is crudely accentual—whether it derives from the breakup of a longer line or from medieval Latin poetry or from another source cannot be precisely determined—but it moves with extraordinary speed and vigor:

> Sometyme he wolde gaspe
> Whan he sawe a waspe;
> A fly or a gnat,
> He wolde flye at that
> And prytely he wold pant
> Whan he saw an ant;
> Lorde, how he wolde pry
> After the butterfly!
> Lorde, how he wolde hop
> After the gressop!
> And whan I sayd, Phyp, Phyp,
> Than he wold lepe and skyp,
> And take me by the lyp.
> Alas, it wyll me slo,
> That Phillyp is gone me fro!
>   *Si in-i-qui-ta-tes,*
> Alas, I was evyll at ease!
>   *De pro-fun-dis cla-ma-vi,*
> Whan I sawe my sparrowe dye!

The color and life of Skelton's most characteristic verse is perhaps best seen in *The Tunning*[1] *of Elinor Rumming*, a remarkable description of an alewife and the goings-on in her alehouse:

> Come who so wyll
> To Elynour on the hyll,
> Wyth, Fyll the cup, fyll,
> And syt there by styll,
> Erly and late:
> Thyther cometh Kate,
> Cysly, and Sare,
> With theyr legges bare,
> And also theyr fete
> Hardely full unswete;
> Wyth theyr heles dagged,
> Theyr kyrtelles all to-iagged,
> Theyr smockes all to-ragged,
> Wyth tytters and tatters,
> Brynge dysshes and platters,
> Wyth all theyr myght runnynge
> To Elynour Rummynge,
> To have of her tunnynge:
> She leneth them of the same,
> And thus begynneth the game.

His *Garland of Laurel* is an elaborate set piece in praise of himself: Fame and Pallas discuss his qualifications; Gower, Chaucer, and Lydgate hail him; a group of noble ladies make a laurel wreath with which to crown him. The incidental lyrics addressed to these ladies are in a new vein of lyrical tenderness, notably that addressed to Margery Wentworth:

> With margerain jentyll,
>   The flowre of goodlyhede,
> Enbrowdred the mantill
>   Is of your maydenhede . . .

Magnificence is a morality play with allegorical characters, showing how Magnificence is deceived and undone by vices, conquered by Adversity, and finally redeemed by Goodhope and Perseverance. It is aimed at Wolsey, but also has its general application.

Skelton moved in a Humanist atmosphere without fully realizing it; his attire was conservative in intention but in fact revolutionary n unconscious implication. His fiercely individual temperament, the

[1] Tunning: putting of beer into casks.

vigor which he infused into his rough accentual verse, his ambiguous relation with the courts of Henry VII and Henry VIII, his attacks both on Church abuses and on radical reformers like Wyclif and Luther, his bitter feuds with so many of his contemporaries, his strange mixtures of anger and tenderness, of self-conceit and moral indignation, of prophetic elevation and low abuse, show a highly individual temperament coping in a strongly individual way with some of the bewildering crosscurrents in the civilization of his day. His lively and unpolished verse and his violently personal manner attracted English poets in the 1920's and 1930's who were looking for a style in which to express similar reactions, and Pope's verdict of "beastly Skelton" has in recent times been enthusiastically reversed.

Meanwhile, the revival of interest in feudal ideals which, paradoxically but understandably, accompanied the final decay of feudalism in England, produced in the prose Arthurian tales of Sir Thomas Malory the greatest of all its monuments. Malory, who appears to have been a mid-fifteenth-century knight of lawless behavior who wrote his stories in prison, turned, first the English alliterative romance known as *Morte Arthure*, and then a variety of French romances about Arthur's knights, into a series of tales of Arthur and his knights in which the ideals of practical chivalry replaced the sentimental and doctrinal elements which figure so prominently in his French sources. He cut his way through the tangle of complexly interwoven tales, fitted together in pieces like a Chinese puzzle, with which his originals so often presented him, and, to use Caxton's term, "reduced" his material to a coherent group of related stories in which incidents followed each other with less interruption and the emphasis was on action and motive rather than on sentiment or doctrine. Caxton published the work in 1485, giving it a false unity by applying the title of the last group of stories—"The Morte Arthure Saunz Gwerdon"—to the whole collection. The discovery in 1934 of the Winchester MS of Malory's stories makes it clear that "Le Morte Darthur" is Caxton's title for the whole, not Malory's. Malory's work is in eight tales or groups of tales, each group originally written separately as an independent work, except for the sixth and seventh, which are explicitly linked in Malory's colophon to the sixth. The first (though apparently the second in order of writing) is the comprehensive "Tale of King Arthur"; it begins with the death of Uther Pendragon and Arthur's accession, and tells of Arthur's victorious wars against rebels and hostile neighbors, the stories of Balin, Gawain, Torre and Pellynor, much about Merlin, the plottings of

Morgan le Fay, Arthur's half sister, and a group of adventures engaged in by Gawain, Ywain, and Marhalt. The second group, "The Tale of the Noble King Arthur that was Emperour Himself through the Dignity of his Hands," was apparently the first to be written and derives from the alliterative *Morte Arthure:* it tells of Arthur's struggle against the claims of Rome, the battle between Arthur and Lucius, Arthur's triumph and coronation as Emperor in Rome. The third, "The Noble Tale of Sir Launcelot du Lake," turns for its hero from Arthur to Sir Lancelot, who appears here, not as the lover of Guinevere, but as an active and gallant knight who proceeds from adventure to adventure before returning to King Arthur's court, where the knights whom he has overcome testify to his prowess. "The Tale of Sir Gareth of Orkney" follows; it is a characteristic story, from an unknown French source, of a questing knight who champions a scornful lady, Lynet, who later comes to admire him, but too late to prevent his marrying her sister Lyonesse. "The Book of Sir Tristram de Lyones" is the fifth; it is a simplified and "reduced" version of the French prose *Romance of Tristan*, with the Grail material omitted, the love of Tristram (Tristan) and Isode (Isolde) treated with emotional gusts and with no sense of doom, Tristram's adventures and achievements as a Knight of the Round Table emphasized, and the lovers left at the end happily in Joyous Gard. Even so, Malory's "Book of Sir Tristram" is far from being a single tale; it is made up of many separate adventures, and is divided into seventeen parts—easily the longest of Malory's seven books. "The Tale of the Sankgreal" is Malory's fifth book; it is translated from the French *Queste del Saint Graal*, but emphasizes what might be called chivalric humanism as the underlying ethical pattern, at the expense of the religious. Lancelot is less the repentant sinner of the French original than the former hero of the Round Table whose chivalric ideals are never made to appear as basically inimical to the truly religious life. Malory plays down the basic dichotomy between Carbonec and Camelot, so important in the *Queste*, though of course something of it does come through from his original. "The Book of Sir Launcelot and Queen Guinevere" is partly based on the French *Mort Artu*, the final branch of the prose Arthurian Cycle. This goes together with the final book, "The Most Piteous Tale of the Morte Arthur Saunz Gwerdon" (based partly on the *Mort Artu* and partly on the English stanzaic *Morte Arthur*), and the two books again show Malory's characteristic minimizing of the religious in favor of the chivalric moral. Lancelot loves both his mistress and his king; these two chivalric loyalties are incompatible, and in the end they destroy him. It is not the clash between courtly love and heavenly love so much as the clash between courtly love and feudal loyalty that interests Malory. Here, indeed, the sense of doom rises; Lancelot becomes involved in battle against those he loves; and in the end, with the Round Table destroyed, Arthur "hurt to the death" in the final battle in which the treacherous Mordred is slain, and Guinevere retired to a nunnery, Lancelot decides to forsake the world too, out of love and despair rather than from a religious impulse. Guinevere dies repentant; Lancelot follows soon after, and Sir Ector speaks his obituary:

"A, Launcelot!" he sayd, "thou were hede of al Crysten knyghtes! And now I dare say," sayd syr Ector, "thou sir Launcelot, there thou lyest, that thou were never matched of erthely knyghtes hande. And thou were the curtest knyght that ever bare shelde! And thou were the truest frende to thy lover that ever bestrade hors, and thou were the trewest lover of a synful man that ever loved woman, and thou were the kyndest man that ever strake wyth swerde. And thou were the godelyest persone that ever cam amonge prees of knyghtes, and thou was the mekest man and the jentyllest that ever ete in halle amonge ladyes, and thou were the sternest knyght to thy mortal foo that ever put spere in the reeste."

It ends in desolation, with no comfort but memory of knightly deeds once done.

Malory's prose style, which moves with a simple cogency always perfectly adapted to the narrative line which he is developing, is not easily placed in the history of English prose. He is outside the tradition of English devotional prose which continues from Anglo-Saxon times to the Tudor and Elizabethan translations of the Bible. He begins by capturing something of the rhythms, and using some of the alliterative devices, of Middle English alliterative verse as represented by the verse romance *Morte Arthure;* he simplifies, tightens up, adds weight and precision and, at the same time, a conversational flow. He learns as he writes, and the later books show a fine ease in dialogue together with a dignity and eloquence which derive at least in part from the heroic element in the *Morte Arthure.* The flow is simple enough, marked by such conjunctions as "and," "for," "but," "then," and "therefore." The underlying rhythms provide a quiet emotional ground swell to the narrative; the dialogue is lively and often captures the individual quality of a character; the accounts of action rise and fall with a restrained epic movement which has quiet gravity without magniloquence. The result of it all is an impressive summing up of the "Matter of Britain" as seen through the perspective of the Indian summer of the Age of Chivalry; excessive sentiment, the pure devotional note, and over-abundant narrative complication are equally pruned away, and Malory gives us the

Arthurian stories set to an uncomplicated chivalric morality. But the epic note does not really belong to these nostalgic stories of a lost way of life; the defects of the code are manifest in the actions which are based on it, and in the end the heroic key is modulated into elegy.

It is paradoxical that William Caxton, who brought the art of printing to England, should have been so interested in chivalry and old romance. But the late fifteenth and early sixteenth century was a transitional period in which all sorts of paradoxical things were likely to happen. The work of Barclay and Hawes showed both old medieval modes and new Humanist influences. Humanism itself was one element in that complex movement we call the Renaissance, a movement whose reality has recently been questioned but which certainly was real, though its manifestations were not as sudden nor its causes as simple as was once thought. The world of medieval Christendom, set against the militant Moslem world, which bounded it on the south and east, had a significant religious and cultural uniformity; its intellectual and imaginative boundaries were limited, the scholar moving within the limits of "Latinitas," the philosopher and the scientist working deductively on truths taken from authority, the poet rendering his vision of past and present through notions of order and significance common to the whole of medieval Europe. The Holy Roman Empire, we know, was never more than an ideal, but the ideal represented a view of history and of society that lay behind most of the superficially differing attitudes which intelligent men in the Middle Ages expressed. The shift from the view of the Roman Empire as divinely ordained machinery for the Christianizing of the Western world to a view of the pagan culture of Greece and Rome as something more civilized, more splendid, more fully illustrative of what man can make of himself by cultivation of the arts and sciences than any subsequent phase of history, represented a real revolution in thought. And while it would be wrong to see this shift as simply the rapid result of the fall of Constantinople to the Turks in 1453, with the consequent emigration of Greek-speaking Christians from the Eastern Empire to Italy—for it was a slow process that had been going on since long before 1453—it would be ridiculous to assert that because the movement was gradual it did not take place. The writing of history is impossible without making generalizations, and it is impossible to make generalizations unless one deliberately cultivates the proper perspective. A cause is known as a cause by its effect; if looked at by itself it is simply an isolated phenomenon, and if looked at with reference to preceding events it becomes itself an effect. History is continuous; "movements" are arbitrary categories of the historian; but significant changes do occur, attitudes do alter radically, the old order does give place to the new. And the Renaissance is not a fiction of the historian's imagination.

Medieval Christendom established itself in the chaos that followed the collapse of the Roman Empire; it took over what it could from the Roman world, compromised where it had to with both old pagan and new barbarian, and achieved a synthesis in which the thought and institutions of the classical world played a certain limited part. Humanism, that movement which represented the desire to recover the purest ideals of Greek and Latin expression and to assimilate the most civilized aspects of classical thought, was essentially an attempt to get behind the medieval synthesis, to approach the original sources of classical culture directly, not through the medium of clerical "Latinitas." Italy had known this movement since the fourteenth century, and long before it reached England it had exerted its influence on Italian literature. North of the Alps the Humanist movement became more directly involved in religious and moral questions. The ambitious and ubiquitous machinery of the medieval Church was ceasing to function effectively; satire of clerical abuses, amusedly ironical in Chaucer, soon swelled to an angry and bitter chorus, and this in turn encouraged the *avant garde* to turn to the secular thought of the classical world for guidance and enlightenment. That secular thought, touched with the moral earnestness of Christian protest against abuses of Christian institutions, produced a school of Christian Humanists which was to include reformers who remained within the Roman Catholic fold as well as Protestants It must be remembered, too, that the "New Learning," as it was often called in the sixteenth century, encouraged the study of Hebrew as well as of Latin and Greek, and that the great German Humanist Reuchlin was even more important for the development of Hebrew studies in Europe than the great Dutch Humanist Erasmus was for the study of Greek. Hebrew and Greek, the languages of the Old and New Testaments respectively, were essential tools in any new approach to the Bible. If pre-Protestant reforming thought demanded vernacular Bible translation, it was the new scholarship of the Humanists that eventually made that translation possible from the original sources. Thus Humanism in spite of itself was drawn into new religious movements.

We have already noted the changes in the economic bases of society that were bringing about the end of feudalism. In the towns, a new upper class of merchants and professional men joined hands with the landowners in the country, where a prospering "gentry" were enclosing common land in the interests of sheep farming, to the distress of the peasants who were thus deprived of the opportunity of tilling the soil and forced to roam the countryside in search of work. Individualism asserted itself in economic as in other areas. The political genius of Henry VII, whose accession to the throne in 1485 after his victory over Richard III brought to an end the Wars of the Roses and ushered in the new Tudor despotism, enabled him to win the loyalty of merchant, professional man, gentry, and nobility alike and so to maintain a political stability in the country of which it was in desperate need, and at his death to leave a secure throne to his son. Henry VII thought of himself as a medieval monarch, re-establishing a medieval monarchy, and did not see the implications of his own reign. He was no friend to Humanists. But with the accession of Henry VIII in 1509, the Humanists in England had their chance, and the early years of his reign were years of promise and excitement for English culture. The scene changed in the latter part of Henry's reign, when Henry's insistence on divorce from Catherine of Aragon, his break with Rome, his suppression of the monasteries and the consequent destruction of so many English art treasures, and his assumption of the supreme headship of the English Church lost him the approval of such a moderate Catholic Humanist as Sir Thomas More, whose execution for high treason in 1535 marks the end of Henry's alliance with the most attractive elements of contemporary Humanism and arrested the Humanist movement in England for a generation. More, scholar, statesman, diplomat, political theorist (the ideal commonwealth described in his Latin work *Utopia* represents a Humanist rather than a Christian conception of the state), and patron of the arts, represented all that was best in the new ideal of culture. His piety led him to seek to purify, rather than radically to reorganize, the Church, and he remained devoted to papal supremacy; like Erasmus, he wished to remove corruption without changing theological doctrine or ecclesiastical structure, but unlike the Dutch Humanist he became involved in practical affairs to his own undoing. He remains the glory and the tragedy of Henry VIII's reign.

The "New Learning" had made itself felt in England as early as the fifteenth century, but these early manifestations left no permanent mark. John Tiptoft, Earl of Worcester, William Grey (later Bishop of Ely), John Free of Balliol College, Oxford, and John Gunthorpe (later Dean of Wells) all visited Italy in the latter part of the fifteenth century and returned with Latin manuscripts which they left to Oxford college libraries. But it was not until the introduction of Greek learning into England that a more permanent enthusiasm for classical scholarship was aroused. Thomas Linacre, William

Grocyn (who returned from Italy in 1490 to teach Greek at Oxford), and William Latimer, put Greek studies on a firm footing at Oxford, while at Cambridge the teaching of Greek by Erasmus from 1510 to 1513 gave a great impetus to Greek studies. John Colet, who had studied in Paris and Italy and was a friend of Erasmus, lectured on the New Testament at Oxford at the turn of the century and in 1510, then Dean of St. Paul's, endowed the Cathedral school of St. Paul's to bring the "New Learning" into secondary education. Richard Croke, who had studied Greek at Oxford with Grocyn and then studied at Paris and lectured at several continental universities, returned to Cambridge in 1518, where, the following year, he was appointed reader in Greek. He was succeeded by Sir Thomas Smith, and in 1540, when five new regius chairs were founded by Henry, Smith got that of civil law, while Sir John Cheke became professor of Greek. Cheke (hailed by Milton in one of his sonnets as having "taught Cambridge and King Edward Greek") later became tutor to the young King Edward VI: he did more than any other single person to make Greek studies popular in England.

The history of scholarship becomes important for the history of literature at this time because the new classical scholarship meant the establishment of direct contact with the achievements of classical culture and this in turn meant not only new ideals in literary style but new concepts of civilization and a sense that the Middle Ages had represented a vast deflection of progress of the arts and sciences off their true course. Further, the recovery of Greek science—which was one of the great achievements of Humanism, far too little realized—meant that Renaissance science could begin where Greek science had left off. Astronomy, physics, and medicine profited by this renewed contact with Greek thought: the scientific discoveries of the sixteenth and seventeenth centuries were made possible by the work of the fifteenth-century Humanists. In the Middle Ages, Greek science (and, indeed, much Greek philosophy) was only available in fragmentary and often distorted form through Latin translations from the Arabic, for the Moslem world were earlier heirs of Greek thought; now it became freely and directly available. No wonder that Renaissance thinkers came to regard the Middle Ages simply as an obstacle standing between them and the pure knowledge of the classical world. The ages of "Gothic superstition," which was all the seventeenth and, still more, the early and middle eighteenth century could see in the Middle Ages, were so regarded because they blocked the light of classical culture.

But this survey has taken us well beyond the transitional period. In the next chapter we shall examine, in some detail, the new movement and its consequences for literature.

CHAPTER SIX

The Early Tudor Scene

THE HISTORIAN of sixteenth-century English culture is liable to find himself devoting all his space to charting the different ways in which that vast complex of movements which we call the Renaissance affected men's minds and imaginations. But in a history of literature one must resist the temptation to dwell at too great length on the intellectual background, important and fascinating though it is, and let the works of literature tell their own story. We have already said something of the new interest displayed by the Humanists in the cultural monuments of Greece and Rome. Humanism had many aspects: the scholarly, concerned with the recovery or reconstitution of accurate texts of the classics; the stylistic, concerned with classical rhetoric and literary criticism and their application to an improved vernacular literature; the ethical, concerned with the highest ideals of Greek and Roman thought (which could be combined with or modified by Christian teaching); and what might be called the positively secular, the replacement of a theocentric universe by one based on man and his potentialities, the acceptance of human life and human values as of permanent significance if ordered and controlled by a sense of proportion, interpreted in the light of the best thought of antiquity, and enriched and illuminated by the arts. It would be difficult to find a writer who was influenced by all these aspects of Humanism simultaneously; many of the most active Humanists were pedantic and narrow in their view of classical "purity" and in their exaltation of Ciceronian Latin; but the sixteenth-century French essayist Montaigne—secular-minded, but not antireligious; curious about and tolerant of human foibles and attitudes; continually fascinated by the problems posed both by his own psychological and physical self and by the external world—could perhaps be taken as a typical representative of the humanist attitude in the broadest sense of that term. It was an attitude which found no such single typical representative in England, yet the attitude was

influential in England; it was in the air, and people were touched
by it and had to reckon with it.

The influence of the new geographical discoveries on men's imaginations (though it developed later than one might have expected) is
one of the more obvious points to be noted. Spenser can speak for
that when, justifying in the prologue to the second book of *The
Faerie Queene* his setting the scene in "that happy land of Faery,"
he observes:

> But let that man with better sense advise,
> That of the world least part to us is read:
> And daily how through hardy enterprise,
> Many great regions are discoveréd,
> Which to late age were never mentionéd.
> Who ever heard of th' Indian Peru?
> Or who in venturous vessel measuréd
> The Amazon's huge river now found true?
> O. fruitfulest Virginia who did ever view?
>
> Yet all these were, when no man did them know;
> Yet have from wisest ages hidden been:
> And later times things more unknown shall show. . . .

And John Donne addresses his mistress with

> O my America! my new-found-land, . . .
> How blest am I in thus discovering thee!

It was Donne, too, who, in often-quoted lines, expressed the effect
on many men's minds of the new astronomy:

> And new philosophy calls all in doubt,
> The element of fire is quite put out;
> The sun is lost, and th' earth, and no man's wit
> Can well direct him where to look for it.

The new astronomy was made necessary by the navigational needs
of the voyagers; and the voyagers themselves began by seeking for
a new route to the spices of the East after the land route had been
blocked by the fall of Constantinople; and spices were necessary in
order to preserve the cattle killed in the winter; and the cattle were
killed in the winter because no winter cattle-feed was yet known.
So the complex chain of cause and effect keeps on expanding.
Further, the new astronomy depended on the work of the Humanists.
The notion that the earth is a planet revolving round the sun had
been put forward by the Greek astronomer Aristarchus of Samos in
the third century B.C., and Copernicus was first led to consider such

a view by reading in a work attributed to Plutarch that the Pythagoreans had taught it. The editing and translating (into Latin) of Greek scientific works provides the bridge between Humanism and science in the Renaissance.

New geographical, astronomical, philosophical, and religious notions boil up and mingle in the most diverse ways throughout the sixteenth and seventeenth centuries. The new concept of the national state was helping to alter the medieval view of Christendom. On the accession of Henry VIII in 1509, the Court became the center of fashion and culture, and after the suppression of the monasteries the great country houses, which were so often built with their wealth and even from their ruins, took over the patronage of the arts. With the art of printing flourishing, books proliferated and reached an ever wider public. Religious and political questions were debated in multitudes of polemical pamphlets, so that it might be said that printing made the new ideas socially important at a speed unprecedented in earlier history. The religious controversies that raged throughout Europe were hastened and exacerbated by the printing press. Other new ideas reached less far down the social scale. The new ideal of the gentleman, combining the alternative medieval choices of the life of action and the life of contemplation, was reflected in the Italian "courtesy books" (of which the most influential, Castiglione's *Il Cortegiano*, was translated by Sir Thomas Hoby in 1561) and other works of education that appeared all over Europe to teach—in the words of Milton's pamphlet on education—"all the arts, both public and private, of peace and war." The Baconian view of the function of knowledge as "the relief of man's estate," as control over nature rather than abstract metaphysical insight, was even more limited in its influence, but it was nevertheless part of the intellectual climate. And with the establishment of Queen Elizabeth's court, with its *mystique* of the Virgin Queen, its patriotic self-confidence culminating in 1588 with the defeat of the Spanish Armada, and the growing sense of pride in the vernacular and its potentialities, the scene was set for a remarkable efflorescence of national culture.

All this, of course, is to simplify. The literary pattern to be set against this background can be traced more adequately if we go back and inquire about the state of poetry in the reign of Henry VIII. George Puttenham, the Elizabethan critic whose *Art of English Poesie* appeared in 1589, tells us in that work that in the latter part of Henry VIII's reign (1509–47) "sprang up a new company of courtly makers [poets], of whom Sir Thomas Wyatt the elder and Henry Earl of Surrey were the two chieftains, who having travelled into Italy and there tasted the sweet and stately measures and style of the Italian poesie as novices newly crept out of the schools of Dante, Ariosto and Petrarch, they greatly polished our rude and homely manner of vulgar poesie from that it had been before, and for that cause may justly be said the first reformers of our English metre and style." Wyatt (also spelled Wyat and Wiat) was the older of the two, living from 1503 to 1542, and in one sense it can be said that with him modern English poetry begins. He and the "courtly makers" who followed him exercised the language by translating from foreign models and experimenting with a great variety of lyric measures, to restore to English metrics the combination of flexibility and regularity which they had lost in the century following Chaucer, a century during which the rapid shift from that stage of the language we call Middle English to the stage we call Modern English had wrought havoc with the polished and controlled Chaucerian line. They were thus essentially craftsmen, treating a conventional subject matter over and over again in their attempts to hammer out a disciplined yet flexible poetic style. They borrowed, imitated, and translated from Italian and French poets as well as from one another, and had they not done so their ultimate achievement would have been less. They circulated their work in manuscript (publication during the poet's lifetime was not at this time common) and engaged in mutual encouragement and criticism. In 1557 (after the death of both Wyatt and Surrey) the printer Richard Tottel put out a collection of poetry by the "courtly makers" with the title *Songes and Sonnettes, written by the ryght honorable Lorde Henry Haward late Earle of Surrey, and other*, generally known as *Tottel's Miscellany*, which was a somewhat belated manifesto of the new poetry. Many more collections of songs and poems followed in Queen Elizabeth's reign (1558–1603), bearing such attractive titles as *The Paradise of Dainty Devices, A Gorgeous Gallery of Gallant Inventions, A Handful of Pleasant Delights, A Banquet of Dainty Conceits, The Arbor of Amorous Devices, England's Helicon*, and *England's Parnassus*. Many of the poems in these collections are little more than exercises; some are over-ingenious, some crude and mechanical; but by and large they demonstrate the immense success with which the earlier poets of the century had flexed the muscles of the English language to make it suitable for graceful poetic expression.

Some of Wyatt's most interesting—though not his most successful —poems are his sonnets. Like Chaucer, he had been sent on diplomatic missions abroad, and had visited Italy among other countries, to come (as so many poets in Italy and France had already done) under the spell of the fourteenth-century Italian poet, Francesco Petrarca (Petrarch), the great master of the sonnet of idealized love. The sonnet, one of the most popular verse forms not only of Elizabethan literature in England but of Renaissance European literature as a whole, developed first in Italy in the twelfth century before passing into France and then into England. Wyatt, facing the problem of restoring gravity and cogency of utterance to English verse after a period of linguistic change during which pronunciation had altered and metrical patterns had gone to pieces, turned to the Italian sonnet for help. Here was a highly conventional verse form, a form which demanded discipline and craftsmanship on the poet's part, a form which challenged the poet to mold his thought with wit and aptness to the precise shape of those fourteen balanced lines.

The sonnet was not simply a stanza of fourteen lines with a certain rhyme scheme: the lines were deftly balanced, the links and pauses between them creating a movement which, in most Italian sonnets, was in four parts—two of four lines each (*quatrains*) and two of three lines each (*tercets*). There were other ways of balancing the sonnet—such as Shakespeare's; he balanced it on a final couplet of rhyming lines—but the pattern most common in Italy employed two quatrains with a single pair of rhymes, *a b b a, a b b a,* the first and fourth rhyming and the two middle lines rhyming (as in Tennyson's *In Memoriam*), followed by two tercets in any one of a variety of arrangements—*c d c, c d c;* or *c d c, d c d; c d e, c d e;* or other groupings. In such a scheme the four parts of the sonnet really resolve themselves into two, the first consisting of two pairs of four lines (the *octave*) and the second of two pairs of three lines (the *sestet*). There were many other ways of patterning the fourteen lines, but the pattern just described was that most frequently used by Petrarch, whose sonnets celebrating his ideal love of Laura were immensely influential and represent the most important single influence on later love sonnets throughout Europe.

There are periods in the history of any literature when what poets need most is a formal convention which will enable them to study the demands of the medium quite objectively, with a craftsman's eye, and prevent them from merely splashing about in language that has not been tempered to meet the precise curve of the meaning. The sonnet form met this need for English poets in the sixteenth century, and Wyatt's sonnets represent one of the most interesting movements toward metrical discipline to be found in English literary history. Wyatt's problem was to handle the ten-syllabled iambic line with gravity in the individual line and at the same time to achieve a significant unity in the poem as a whole. The metrical tradition established by Chaucer had lost its usefulness because of changes in the language. While these changes (which brought with them a certain flexibility in accentuation during a transitional period) made it possible for Wyatt to experiment freely and effectively in numerous short-line stanzas where the sustained gravity of regular metrical utterance throughout a series of long lines was not required, they seriously handicapped him in writing the heavier kind of line demanded by the sonnet. As a result, his sonnets are less good than his lighter lyrics: he is not always quite sure where the accent falls in a given word, nor is he always able to keep before the reader's ear the basic swell of the metrical design, so necessary in this kind of formal utterance. In the lighter lyrical measures he was also helped by the rhythm of lute music.

It was not only the sonnet form that later poets got from Petrarch; the whole nature of the relation between the poet and his beloved became conventionalized in terms of an idealized courtly-love attitude which Petrarch manifested toward Laura in his love sonnets. This notion of the lover as the humble servant of the often cruel fair, wounded by a glance of her eye, tempest-tossed in seas of despair when his love is rejected, changing in mood according to the presence or absence of his beloved, is derived from the medieval view of courtly love which we have discussed in an earlier chapter. Petrarch moved this courtly love to a high, ideal plane of his own, and subsequent sonneteers for the most part kept it there. The Petrarchan sonnet thus provided the English poet with both a conventional form and conventional sentiments. (It should be added that innumerable Italian and French sonneteers after Petrarch had helped to conventionalize both form and content by the time the English sonneteers began writing.)

The difficulties Wyatt found in handling the iambic pentameter line in the sonnet can be illustrated by the opening line of the following sonnet (from Petrarch):

> Ever myn happe is slack and slo in commyng,
>> Desir encresing, myn hope uncertain,
>> That leve it or wayt it doeth me like pain,
> And Tigre-like, as swift it is in parting.

Wyatt's own spelling has been retained, because to modernize it is often to prejudge the question of pronunciation. The third line here has ten syllables but in no other way resembles an iambic pentameter line. "Uncertain" in the second line is accented on the final syllable; the verbal "-ing" ending is apparently accented at the end of the first and fourth lines. Wyatt's rhyming of verbal endings such as "-ing" and "-eth" and noun endings such as "-ness" and "-aunce" is a common habit, and shows much awkwardness. In a line such as

> Which holdeth the divine parte of nature

it is uncertain whether "nature" is accented on the first syllable, as it certainly was by Shakespeare's time, or on the second syllable, as Chaucer pronounced it. The rhyming of "nature" with "master" hardly helps us to decide. Or the opening of another sonnet from Petrarch—

> The longe love, that in my thought doeth harbar—

shows how far from the iambic beat Wyatt could get. Or is this line meant to be scanned as an iambic pentameter? One is tempted to scan it

> The lónge lóve, that in my thóught dœth hárbar

with perhaps the "e" of "longe" pronounced. But did Wyatt mean

> The lóng love, thát in mý thought dóth harbár?

Or something between these two? Either way, "doeth" is a monosyllable, though it is apparently disyllabic in other poems. The rhyming of "harbar" with "baner" (banner) leaves the accentuation of both words still in doubt. And what are we to make of such a quatrain as this (from the same sonnet)?

> She that me lerneth to love and suffre,
> And willes that my trust and lustes negligence
> Be rayned by reson, shame and reverence,
> With his hardines taketh displeasur.

"Reason" is apparently pronounced like the modern "reason," not like the Chaucerian "resóun," though no doubt Wyatt could pronounce it in the Chaucerian way if it suited the line. "Displeasur" is accented on the second syllable, one assumes, rhyming (if it can be called a rhyme) with "suffre," yet it might just as easily be pronounced with the accent on the final syllable. The pronunciation of English was changing even as Wyatt wrote. At the end of the remarkable poem beginning "They fle from me that sometyme did me seke" occur the lines:

> But syns that I so kyndely ame served,
> I would fain knowe what she hath deserved.

This scans regularly if we pronounce the "e" in "kyndely" and (which Wyatt surely did not do) in "knowe." But Tottel, printing the poem in 1557, emended these lines to

> But, since that I unkindly so am served:
> How like you this, what hath she now deserved?

This is neat and regular. But more than metrical changes have taken place. In the twenty or thirty years since Wyatt wrote, not only had it become impossible to pronounce "kyndely" as three syllables, it had also become impossible to construe "so kyndely" in the sense that Wyatt had intended, meaning "in such a fashion," and Tottel had to change it to "unkindly," thus giving a quite different force to the line. Sometimes we find in Wyatt remarkable effects of metrical subtlety achieved through cunning irregularity: but we can never be sure whether the irregularity really is the product of cunning or whether the effect was not intended—or whether, indeed, Wyatt scanned the passage as we do.

These difficulties, which are so apparent when Wyatt wrote the iambic pentameter line, seem to have largely disappeared when he wrote in lighter lyric meters, with (presumably) the help of musical accompaniment. There is nothing tentative or awkward about this (one can safely modernize the spelling now):

> Forget not yet the tried intent
> Of such a truth as I have meant,
> My great travail, so gladly spent,
>   Forget not yet.
>
> Forget not yet when first began
> The weary life ye know, since whan
> The suit, the service none tell can,
>   Forget not yet. . . .
>
> Forget not yet, forget not this,
> How long ago hath been, and is,
> The mind that never meant amiss,
>   Forget not yet.
>
> Forget not, then, thine own approved,
> The which so long hath thee so loved,
> Whose steadfast faith yet never moved,
>   Forget not this.

The same serene control can be seen in such lyrics as "Marvel no more" and "My lute, awake!"

> My lute, awake! perform the last
> Labour that thou and I shall waste,

> And end that I have now begun;
>   For when this song is sung and past,
>   My lute be still, for I have done. . . .

The refrain seems to help Wyatt, and his best songs are those
balanced on the concluding short-line refrain, "forget not yet,"
"Blame not my lute," "Say nay, say nay!" Yet these poems do not
represent any startling new development in the English lyric: their
verse-forms and rhyme-schemes are often to be found in medieval
Latin poetry and in Middle English lyrical poetry too. The Middle
English lyrical tradition flows directly into the Tudor song tradition,
and the reader who comes from fourteenth- and fifteenth-century
lyrics to the songs of Wyatt is conscious of no break. A fifteenth-
century manuscript, for example, has the following poem:

> Wimmen beth bothe goud and schene,   [schene: beautiful]
>   On handës, fete, and facë clene;
> Wimmen may no beter bene.
>   Witnesse on Marie.
>
> Wimmen beth gentel on her tour;
>   A wimman bare oure Saviour;
> Of all this world wimman is flour.
>   Witnesse on Marie. . . .

This is the exact stanza form of "Forget not yet." The lively movement and metrical assurance of "The Nutbrown Maid" (first printed
about 1502) shows all the virtuosity of later Tudor poetry; its internal rhyming is handled with great artfulness:

> Be it right, or wrong, these men among
>   On women do complaine,
> Afferming this, how that it is
>   A labour spent in vaine,
> To love them wele, for never a dele
>   They lofe a man againe;
> For let a man do what he can,
>   Ther favour to attaine,
> Yet if a newe to them pursue,
>   Ther furst trew lover than
> Laboureth for nought, and from her thought
>   He is a banisshed man. . . .

This spirited dialogue between "Squire" and "Puella" runs on for
thirty lively stanzas, each concluding with the phrase "banisshed
man." It seems clear that the sung lyric was not affected by the
changes in the language that seems to have caused the iambic
decasyllabic line to disintegrate. "Skeltonics" may represent a delib-

erate abandonment of metrical polish in favor of a rough, if effective, accentual measure, but while Skelton wrote, anonymous singers were keeping a smoother kind of verse alive so that it could be transmitted to later generations.

Wyatt's most perfect poems are not, then, his most original in form. In subject matter, he is as a rule even less original, content to appear in the conventional guise as the hopeless lover of a cruel mistress. Yet every now and again he handles the heavier line with a force and splendor that mark him as a pioneering original poet of extraordinary strength. Only a complete poem can illustrate this:

> They flee from me that sometime did me seek,
> With naked foot stalking in my chamber.
> I have seen them gentle, tame and meek,
> That now are wild, and do not remember
> That sometime they have put themselves in danger
> To take bread at my hand; and now they range,
> Busily seeking with a continual change.
>
> Thanked be fortune it hath been otherwise,
> Twenty times better; but once in special,
> In thin array, after a pleasant guise,
> When her loose gown from her shoulders did fall,
> And she me caught in her arms long and small,
> Therewith all sweetely did me kiss,
> And softly said, "Dear heart, how like you this?"
>
> It was no dream; I lay broad waking:
> But all is turned, thorough my gentleness,
> Into a strange fashion of forsaking;
> And I have leave to go, of her goodness,
> And she also to use newfangleness.
> But since that I so kindely am served,
> I would fain know what she hath deserved.[1]

The variations from the regular iambic line here are strangely moving, and the whole poem has the air of having caught, and rendered into impressive art, the very essence of an emotional situation. Wyatt occasionally does this even in those sonnets where the handling of the meter seems to be a hit-or-miss affair. Surrey never achieves the strength and subtlety of Wyatt at his best. Wyatt's three "satires," though derived from Horace (two) and the Italian poet Alamanni (one), have a freshness and a conversational tone which please in a different way. The first begins

[1] From this point on, now that we are in the period of "modern" English, the spelling of quotations is modernized except when the original spelling is necessary for reasons of meter or of poetic suggestiveness.

> Mine own John Poins, since ye delight to know
> The cause why that homeward I me draw,
> And flee the press or courts where so they go,
> Rather than to live thrall, under the awe
> Of lordly looks, wrappid within my cloak, . . .

and the second

> My mother's maids, when they did sew and spin
> They sang sometimes a song of the field mouse, . . .

His version of the seven penitential Psalms (deriving from Aretino's prose paraphrase) has its impressive moments; the prologues are in *ottava rima* and the psalms themselves in *terza rima,* both of which forms Wyatt handles with some skill, though unevenly. But on the whole Wyatt's Psalms can be classed among the Tudor exercisings of the vernacular. His most consistently good poems are his song lyrics; his few really remarkable pioneering poems in heavier meters flash out from a mass of uncertainly handled traditional material. And even where his sonnets are not successful, they do represent the first English attempt of the age at this verse form.

Henry Howard, Earl of Surrey, the only one of the "courtly makers" whose name appeared on Tottel's title page, was some fourteen years younger than Wyatt, whose poetic disciple he was. His execution in 1547, when he was barely thirty, on a trumped up charge of treason, put an end to one of the most spirited and promising careers of the time: Surrey was born into one of the noblest families of England and educated, at both the English and French courts, in a consciously aristocratic tradition. Like Wyatt, he was sensitive to the literary fashions that had invaded much of Europe from Italy, and like him he endeavored to exercise and enlarge the English poetic tongue in translations and adaptations from Italian and Latin and in variations on conventional themes. The first thirty-six poems in *Tottel's Miscellany* are by Surrey, and four more are included later in the book. The difference between Wyatt and Surrey can be summed up in a phrase: Surrey has less strength and more polish. He is more consistently successful than Wyatt in fitting the metrical accent to the normal accentuation of the word and stress of the spoken language, but he lacks Wyatt's moving and surprising touches. Wyatt is a greater poet, wielding a less perfect instrument, Surrey is the competent and graceful craftsman; his sonnets run with greater metrical smoothness than Wyatt's. The metrical control is clear in the following:

The soote season that bud and bloom forth brings
With green hath clad the hill and eke the vale,
The nightingale with feathers new she sings,
The turtle to her make hath told her tale: [make : mate]
Summer is come, for every spray now springs,
The hart hath hung his old head on the pale,
The buck in brake his winter coat he flings,
The fishes float with new repairéd scale,
The adder all her slough away she slings,
The swift swallow pursueth the flies smale,   [smale : small]
The busy bee her honey now she mings,   [mings : mingles]
Winter is worn that was the flowers' bale.
And thus I see among these pleasant things
Each care decays, and yet my sorrow springs.

This is a rendering of a sonnet of Petrarch's:

Zefiro torna, e 'l bel tempo rimena, . . .

but Surrey's nature imagery is livelier and more English than Petrarch's finely stylized picture, and, unlike Petrarch, he prolongs the
description of spring for twelve lines, to turn suddenly on a final
couplet. This handling of the sonnet form with the lines rhyming
abab abab abab aa is unusual in having only two rhymes, but its
grouping of three quatrains and a final couplet is characteristic of
Surrey and was to become a mark of the English form of the sonnet.
Surrey also uses the forms *abab abab abab cc, abba cddc effe gg*, and
abab cdcd efef gg. This last is the "Shakespearean" form, and Surrey
seems to have settled on it as the most convenient. It relieves the
poet from the necessity of running the same rhymes right through
(which is easier in Italian than in English) and so gives him more
freedom. Wyatt, like Petrarch, preferred five rhymes to the "Shakespearean" seven; he, too, ended his sonnets with a couplet, the
majority of them being in the form *abba abba cddc ee*.

Much of Surrey's verse handles the traditional Petrarchan theme
of love. More interesting are his autobiographical pieces, such as the
poem, in alternately rhyming iambic pentameter lines, which he
wrote on his temporary imprisonment in Windsor in 1545. The poet
is remembering his happy boyhood at Windsor with the king's
illegitimate son, the Duke of Richmond:

So cruel prison how could betide, alas,
As proud Windsor? Where I in lust and joy
With a king's son my childish years did pass
In greater feast than Priam's sons of Troy;

> Where each sweet place returns a taste full sour:
> The large green courts where we were wont to hove
> With eyes cast up into the maidens' tower,
> And easy sighs, such as folk draw in love;
> The stately seats, the ladies bright of hue,
> The dances short, long tales of great delight;
> With words and looks that tigers could but rue,
> Where each of us did plead the other's right; . . .

Among the verse forms with which Surrey experimented was the so-called "Poulter's Measure," a curious jog-trot which became very popular in the sixteenth century: it consists of lines of twelve and fourteen syllables alternating:

> Such wayward ways hath love, that most part in discord,
> Our wills do stand, whereby our hearts but seldom doth accord.
> Deceit is his delight, and to beguile and mock
> The simple hearts which he doth strike with froward, divers stroke.
> He causeth hearts to rage with golden burning dart,
> And doth allay with leaden cold again the tother's heart. . . .

Surrey was partial to this measure, and rendered passages from Ecclesiastes and some of the Psalms in it. These renderings—which are adaptations, infused often with personal feeling—have their own kind of eloquence. He used *terza rima*, sometimes in pentameter lines and once in octosyllables, and a variety of short stanzas. He could be didactic, moralistic, reminiscent, satirical, and epigrammatic as well as conventionally amorous. All in all, Surrey was an accomplished versifier whose responsiveness to the cultural movements of his time, together with his aristocratic idealism of mind, his quickness of wit, and his technical curiosity about his craft enabled him on occasion to write poetry of grace and eloquence. And to write English poetry of grace and eloquence in the first half of the sixteenth century was a historically important achievement, and one which had great influence on the subsequent course of English poetry.

Perhaps the most obvious pioneering achievement of Surrey was his use of blank verse in his translation of the second and fourth books of Virgil's *Aeneid*. This translation was apparently suggested to him by an Italian version of book four which appeared in 1534, and by the Italian version of the first six books which appeared in 1540: he presumably thought of blank verse as his mediun because that was the English equivalent of his Italian models. Surrey was also influenced by the important translation of the *Aeneid* (in rhymed couplets) by Gavin Douglas, the late fifteenth- and early sixteenth-century Scottish poet. Surrey's translation, published by Tottel as a separate book in 1557, has been praised for its speed and vigor, but the end-stopped lines soon prove wearisome and the verse on the whole has a wooden quality. Here is clearly a case where the historical importance outweighs the intrinsic worth.

The only other author named in Tottel is Nicholas Grimald: after thirty-six poems by Surrey and ninety-one by Wyatt, Tottel prints forty by Grimald, in a variety of styles and on a variety of subjects. The first is a love poem in Poulter's Measure:

> What sweet relief the showers to thirsty plants we see,
> What dear delight the blooms to bees, my true love is to me. . . .

There are other love poems in iambic pentameter couplets, poems of compliments in seven-foot iambic couplets, poems translated from the Latin of the sixteenth-century French Calvinist theologian Theodore Beza, as well as from other sources, some of which are in blank verse and some brief epigrams. Grimald's poems are followed by ninety-four attributed to "uncertain authors," among whom Thomas, Lord Vaux, has been identified, though most of Vaux' identifiable work appeared in a larger miscellany, *The Paradise of Dainty Devices*, 1576. Other authors who have been probably or certainly identified are: J. Canand, Sir John Cheke, William Gray, John Harington, John Heywood, Thomas Norton, Sir Anthony St. Leger, and an unknown D. Sand. Oddly enough, among the poems by uncertain authors is included a short lyric by Chaucer (beginning, as Tottel prints it, "Flee from the prese and dwell with sothfastnes") probably taken from one of the sixteenth-century editions printed by William Thynne. Sir Thomas Bryan and Thomas Churchyard are among the poets whose names have been associated with *Tottel's Miscellany* but whose poems have not been identified. These uncertain authors play variations on the themes set by Wyatt and Surrey. There are love poems, elegies, moralizing poems, poems of compliment, and poems of proverbial philosophy. The verse forms include couplets, both octosyllabic and decasyllabic, iambic hexameters, *ottava rima*, a variety of stanza forms, and nine sonnets. There are no outstanding poems in this section, which is interesting only as an exercising ground for Tudor poetry.

Tottel's aim is indicated in his introductory note to the reader which begins: "That to have well written, yea and in small parcels, deserveth great praise, the works of divers Latins, Italians, and other, do prove sufficiently. That our tongue is able in that kind to do as praiseworthy as the rest, the honorable style of the noble Earl of Surrey, and the weightiness of the deepwitted Sir Thomas

Wyatt the Elder's verse, with several graces in sundry good English writers, do show abundantly . . ." The work was published, as Tottel goes on to say, "to the honor of the English tongue and for profit of the studious of English eloquence." National pride in the vernacular, and the desire to improve it to the point where it could compete with or surpass Italian or even approach the classical tongues of ancient Greece and Rome, were important motives in sixteenth-century English poetry, which helped to form the ambitions of Spenser and, later still, of Milton. Indeed, the words with which in 1627 the young Milton broke off from a Latin vacation exercise to dedicate himself to writing poetry in English could fittingly speak for these Tudor experimenters:

> Hail native Language, that by sinews weak
> Didst move my first endeavouring tongue to speak,
> And mad'st imperfect words with childish trips,
> Half unpronounc't, slide through my infant lips,
> Driving dumb silence from the portal door,
> Where he had mutely sat two years before:
> Here I salute thee. . . .

Tottel's Miscellany went into nine editions between 1557 and 1587, later editions introducing new poems. This is sufficient evidence of the popularity of the "courtly makers," while the miscellanies that followed Tottel's (of which *The Paradise of Dainty Devices*, 1576, was the most popular) testified equally to the interest in the handling of the various lyric and other measures with which the poets of the time experimented. There was no real progress in the latter part of Henry VIII's reign and in the short reigns of his successors, Edward VI and Mary, but the versifying went on, with a great deal of mechanical jingling and much use of the jog-trot Poulter's Measure. Metrical regularity, once achieved, was apt to fall into the wearisome cadence of repetitious and inflexible arithmetical correctness. Of individual poets who were writing in the mid-sixteenth century, Thomas Churchyard (ca. 1520–1604) and George Gascoigne (ca. 1525–77), deserve mention. Churchyard, who began writing in the reign of Edward VI (1547–53) if not of Henry VIII, produced a great many poems in the styles of the day, most of them little more than mechanical exercises, but there is an occasional happy lyric in his collection called *Churchyard's Chips* (1575). Churchyard's longevity and versatility won him some reputation by the end of the century: Spenser referred to him in 1591 as "old Palemon . . . that sung so long until quite hoarse he grew." Gascoigne is a more interesting poet. His play *The Supposes*, acted at Gray's Inn in 1566, was a prose translation of a comedy by

Ariosto and is the earliest extant comedy in English prose, and his blank verse tragedy *Jocasta*, translated from the Italian of Ludovico Dolce's *Giocasta*, with the collaboration of Francis Kinwelmersh, was also presented in 1566. (Dolce's play was an adaptation of the *Phoenissae* of Euripides.) His blank verse satire *The Steel Glass* (1576) presents a picture of the failures of the different orders of society with that medieval sense of hierarchy and function in society which was carried undimmed into the Renaissance: the versification is dogged rather than effective, but it provided further exercise for the developing English form of blank verse, which Gascoigne at least uses rather more flexibly than Surrey. Among his varied other work are *Certain Notes of Instruction Concerning the Making of Verse or Rhyme in English* (1575), a pioneer critical essay on English prosody, primitive enough but showing remarkable good sense; moralistic prose pamphlets; a collection of meditative poems, or elegies; and a number of attractive lyrics of which the best known (either because or in spite of most readers' lack of awareness of its sexual theme) is "Gascoigne's Lullaby":

> Sing lullaby, as women do,
> Wherewith they bring their babes to rest,
> And lullaby can I sing too
> As womanly as can the best.
> With lullaby they still the child,
> And if I be not much beguiled,
> Full many wanton babes have I
> Which must be stilled with lullaby. . . .

The *Epitaphs, Epigrams, Songs and Sonnets* (1567) of George Turberville contains some pieces of genuine lyrical grace, and if his translations from Ovid and Mantuan are of less interest as poetry they at least show him helping to exercise the language by translation. George Whetstone (ca. 1544–87), a friend of Gascoigne's and usually coupled with Churchyard, wrote a considerable amount of miscellaneous verse in the styles of the time, but is remembered chiefly for his unacted play in two parts, *Promos and Cassandra*, in crude enough verse which, together with a prose version of the same story, provided the plot for Shakespeare's *Measure for Measure*. Finally, we must mention Edward de Vere, Earl of Oxford (1550–1604), whose poems in *The Paradise of Dainty Devices* and in other Elizabethan collections show the earlier Tudor lyrical tradition carried successfully into Elizabethan court poetry: contemporaries placed him at the head of the courtly poets of his day, but to the retrospective eye of the historian he seems rather to constitute a bridge between Tottel's courtly makers and such Elizabethan poet-courtiers as Sidney, Ralegh, and Fulke Greville, who are discussed in a later chapter.

The most ambitious single poetic achievement of the mid-sixteenth century was not, however, the work of those who "wrote well in small parcels." It was *A Mirror for Magistrates*, a composite didactic work intended originally as a continuation of Lydgate's *Falls of Princes* (itself derived from Boccaccio's *De Casibus Virorum Illustrium*). The printer J. Wayland suggested such a sequel to William Baldwin, who had already turned the biblical Song of Songs into English verse and written a prose *Treatise of Moral Philosophy*. Baldwin sought collaborators, and between them they produced seven new stories from English history, in the form of imaginary monologues spoken by the ghosts of eminent men who had suffered drastic reversals of fortune. These seven stories, originally published as a supplement to an edition of *The Falls of Princes*, were expanded to nineteen and published separately in 1559. Later editions included new stories and other changes, the most notable addition to the edition of 1563 being Thomas Sackville's "Complaint of Henry Duke of Buckingham" preceded by an "Induction" which remains the best known part of the *Mirror*. Thomas Churchyard's "Shore's Wife" also appeared in the 1563 edition. Other editions appeared in 1578 and 1587. Besides Baldwin, Sackville and Churchyard, the authors (who have not all been identified) included George Ferrers, Thomas Chaloner, Thomas Phaer (who translated the *Aeneid*), John Dolman, and Francis Seager.

A Mirror for Magistrates contains monologues written in rhyme with varying degrees of metrical facility and different kinds of rhythmic movement, from the impressive elegiac cadences of Sackville's "Induction" to reminiscences of the old alliterative measure and various kinds of jog-trot. The poetic quality of much of the work is low indeed, but Sackville possesses a Virgilian gravity and handles imagery with a fine original power, and Churchyard effectively introduces the note of passion in his account of Jane Shore. The stories are linked by prose discussions among the authors, in which they exchange views about the significance of the stories they tell, the ethical and political ideas underlying them, and the most effective ways of presenting them, thus showing themselves concerned both with the technical problems of their craft and with the intellectual currents of their time. For *A Mirror for Magistrates* is not merely a series of medieval "tragedies" after Lydgate, even though it was begun as a sequel to Lydgate, who remained popular in the sixteenth century. It embodies the Renaissance interest in the didactic aspect of history, in a study of the past as the proper education of a prince, teaching him by example what to follow and what to avoid. The authors are concerned with the nature of order and of justice, with the reasons for human suffering, with the ways in which divine retribution overtakes human crimes, and with cause and effect in human affairs. They are concerned with the proper behavior of a prince and the proper relation between ruler and ruled. In taking characters from English history from the time of Richard II to that of Henry VIII and making them speak of their fortunes, the authors were seeking to project the moral and educational meaning of history. The notion of history as the great teacher was common in the Renaissance and is to be found again and again in sixteenth-century European literature. And the idea of selected episodes of history constituting a mirror in which the consequences of good and bad government can be seen, for the proper instruction of those who govern, was a commonplace in Elizabethan England. The title *A Mirror for Magistrates* emphasizes the political didacticism of the work; and this concern with political didacticism arose from the concern of the age with the whole question of the education of the prince as well as from the specifically English interest in the moral of the Wars of the Roses and the possibilities of maintaining a unified and stable government without reverting to the bad old days, still vividly in men's minds, of civil war. Queen Elizabeth's being unmarried and thus having no direct heir increased English preoccupation with the problem of government, succession, and order. Writers of the age looked to history and biography to help them show, as in a mirror, the truth about human affairs with special reference to the relationship between power and virtue and between crime and suffering. *A Mirror for Magistrates* thus reinterpreted the medieval concept of the wheel of fortune and unpredictable fate to show the political and ethical background of those spectacular falls from high estate which the Middle Ages saw as "tragedy." The Tudor historians from whom Shakespeare drew the material for his history plays shared, in differing degrees (Edward Hall had it much more than Raphael Holinshed), this Renaissance view of the educational function of history: the most eloquent expression of this view in English is to be found in Sir Walter Ralegh's preface to his *History of the World* (1614).

In moralizing history, the Renaissance made it more amenable not only to treatment by philosophers but also to handling by poets and dramatists. An understanding of the true relation of history to politics and morality will help a prince to govern wisely and a subject to realize his duty; but when we begin to look for the working out of historical laws on the fate of individuals we are brought into the realm of psychology, and in the triple conjunction of politics, morality, and psychology the dramatist can find unlimited scope. Shakespeare's *Coriolanus*, no less than his *Richard III* and *Henry IV*, was the fruit of that conjunction.

CHAPTER SEVEN

Spenser and His Time

Looking back on the poetry of the sixteenth century with the historian's perspective, we can see clearly enough that the endeavor to establish English as a poetic language at least the equal of Italian and French prompted much of the experimentation and exercising that went on in Tudor verse. It is true that among the production of poets between Wyatt and Spenser we do find some accomplished lyrics and an occasional success in longer and graver kinds of verse; but an air of uncertainty still hung over everything, and the poet who could turn out a deft song at one moment might very well fall, on another occasion, into the crudest jog-trot or the most wooden kind of labored regularity. England awaited the poet who could pull together the diverse elements that had been operating in Tudor verse; who could profit by Renaissance Latinists, by Italian and French developments in the vernacular, by new ideas about the function and prestige of the poet, by classical example, by new currents in religious and philosophical thought, as well as by the exercising of the English language that had been going on; who could at the same time look back to Chaucer and, while absorbing and benefiting from all the new currents, re-establish contact with the great medieval master of English verse; and who would be simultaneously Elizabethan and European, drawing inspiration both from the national excitement of his own time and country and from the larger movements of the mind and the imagination which were agitating the whole of Western civilization Classical, medieval, and Humanist; inspired equally by the new Puritan idealism and by the reawakened interest in Platonic thought; moved both by the new Protestant gravity and by the Catholic sense of the unity of Western culture; supreme craftsman with a great synthesizing imagination—such was the poet the times now required if the full riches of Elizabethan England were to find adequate expression in poetry. The greatest genius that Eng-

165

land produced at this—and at any—time did not turn directly to this synthesizing task but used all this material with careless brilliance in the dramatic exploration of the relation between the moral and emotional aspects of man: Shakespeare was not the New Poet the Elizabethans were looking for; his genius was too large and too unself-conscious for him to see himself as contributing to any specific historical end. It was Edmund Spenser (1552–99) who saw himself, as he was seen by his contemporaries, in the role of the New Poet who was to draw the threads together and mark both a culmination and a new beginning in English poetry. Spenser was the great synthesizer for whom English nondramatic poetry was waiting.

The publication of *The Shepherd's Calendar* in 1579 marked Spenser's formal entry as the New Poet. An unpretentious and uneven work to modern eyes, not much read today except by specialists and students, *The Shepherd's Calendar* is the perfect example of a work of greater historical importance than of permanent and intrinsic poetic interest. The title, in Spenser's (or his printer's) spelling is worth recording: "The Shepheardes Calendar, Conteyning twelve Aeglogues proportionable to the Twelve monethes. Entitled to the Noble and Vertuous Gentleman most worthy of all titles both of learning and chevalrie M. Philip Sidney." The eclogue, or pastoral dialogue (spelled "aeglogue" by Spenser and many of his contemporaries because of a false derivation from the Greek word for goatherd) has its origin in Sicilian folk song and comes first into literature in the work of Theocritus, Bion, and Moschus, Greek Sicilian poets of the third century B.C. It was a form widely used in the Renaissance, deriving more often from the eclogues of Virgil than directly from the Greek pastoralists. By the time Spenser was writing there were eclogues in Italian and French as well as in Renaissance Latin, and pastoral poetry (i.e., poetry dealing with shepherds, or ideal shepherds) was established as an accepted poetic form, ranking below epic or heroic poetry, which was at the top of the poetic ladder in Renaissance criticism, and below tragedy, but laudable nevertheless and especially appropriate for a poet beginning his poetic career. Virgil had started with eclogues and moved on at last to his great epic: the proper course for an ambitious new poet was clear. Not only was the pastoral well established in Renaissance poetry by Spenser's time; it had also been frequently used in an allegorical manner for moral and satirical purposes. Pastoral allegory was thus an established note. Almost any aspect of human life could be presented through the elemental activities of shepherds. Rural work has always been an obvious prototype of all human endeavor, being, as it were, the primal human activity. And the work of the shepherd is not only an obvious example of rustic labor; it also includes the element of guardianship, which makes it easy to discuss either political rulers or spiritual leaders in pastoral terms. The elemental background of pastoral activity also makes pastoral poetry an appropriate vehicle for the presentation of the more elemental human emotions, such as love or grief. The Renaissance poets, excited at the potentialities of the literary use of the pastoral, exploited it to the point of exhaustion, with the result that it is now regarded as one of the most faded of literary forms. But for Spenser it was a richly promising medium, and an obvious one for a manifesto of the new poetry.

Linking his eclogues together in a calendar, Spenser found a happy way of combining unity with diversity, as well as of combining the simple and rustic with the elaborate and sophisticated. By varying the degree to which his shepherds were allegorical, he could vary the tone from the naïvely pastoral to the elaborately formal. And by making his shepherds compete in singing matches, in a formula that goes back to the Greek pastoralists, he was enabled to introduce into his pastoral framework a diversity of lyrical poems in different styles. The poet who influenced him most in his allegorical use of the pastoral was the fifteenth-century Italian, Baptista Spanuoli, known in literature as Mantuanus or Mantuan, whose ten Latin eclogues on moral and religious themes were used as a schoolbook throughout Europe. But Spenser also knew Theocritus and Bion (and there were Latin and French versions, if he needed help with the original), the Latin eclogues of Petrarch, Boccaccio, and Iacopo Sannazaro, and the two French eclogues of Clement Marot, which he imitated in his November and December poems. In short, Spenser was working confidently in a European tradition, both classical and Humanist.

Spenser sent *The Shepherd's Calendar* into the world with an introduction and commentary by "E. K.," who was probably Edward Kirke, who had been a fellow student of Spenser's at Cambridge, and who certainly had been briefed carefully by Spenser about his intentions in producing the poem. One is reminded of Stuart Gilbert's commentary on James Joyce's *Ulysses*, which was also an explanation of a new kind of work by someone who had had the benefit of talks with the author about its meaning and purpose. E. K. could make claims for Spenser that the poet was too modest to make himself but which nevertheless must have fairly represented Spenser's own view of his function and ambitions. E. K.'s introduction, addressed to Spenser's friend, the scholar and man of letters Gabriel Harvey, makes all the points necessary to emphasize the importance of the work. He begins with a quotation (or rather, misquotation) from Chaucer, and links Spenser both with Chaucer and with Virgil. He goes on to refer to Spenser's "wittiness in devising, his pithiness in uttering, his complaints of love so lovely, his discourses of pleasure so pleasantly, his pastoral rudeness, his moral wiseness, his due observing of decorum everywhere, in personages, in seasons, in matter, in speech, and generally in all seemly simplicity of handling his matter and framing his words: the which of many things which in him be strange, I know will seem the strangest, the words themselves being so ancient, the knitting of them so short and intricate, and the whole period and compass of speech so delightsome for the roundness and so grave for the strangeness." The emphasis on decorum is significant: decorum meant propriety and fitness of tone and diction and verse form, the suiting of the style to the matter, the deliberate avoidance of anything disproportionate or incongruous. It was an important Renaissance esthetic ideal, and in showing himself concerned with it Spenser is not only exhibiting a debt to the critical thought of his age but also showing his awareness of a prime need of English poetry at this time. Decorum was conspicuously lacking in the majority of the earlier Tudor poets. Biblical paraphrase in Poulter's Measure, for example, such as we find more than once in *Tottel's Miscellany*, is a clear violation of decorum:

> Knock and it shall be heard, but ask and given it is,
> And all that like to keep this course of mercy shall not miss.
> For when I call to mind how the one wandering sheep
> Did bring more joy with his return than all the flock did keep,
> It yields full hope and trust my strayed and wandering ghost
> Shall be received and held more dear than those were never lost.

Spenser put an end to this sort of thing. E. K. refers with contempt to the Tudor versifiers as "the rakehelly rout of our ragged rhymers (for so themselves use to hunt the letter [i.e., practice alliteration]) which without learning boast, without judgment jangle, without reason, rage and foam, as if some instinct of poetical spirit had newly ravished them above the meanness of common capacity." That is poetry without decorum, which Milton was later to call "the chief masterpiece to be observed."

E. K. praises Spenser for preserving the continuity of English poetry by using a certain number of older words, and using them appropriately. Spenser, he says, "hath laboured to restore, as to their rightful heritage, such good and natural English words as have been long time out of use and almost clean disherited." Pride in the vernacular comes out strongly in E. K.'s remarks on the English language and its potentialities. He praises Spenser both for his choice of words and for his "knitting of sentences, . . . and for all the compass of the speech," which he calls "round without roughness and learned without hardness." He classes him with the great classical and Renaissance poets, suggesting that *The Shepherd's Calendar* is the pioneer work of a new English poet worthy to be ranked with them: "So [i.e., in eclogues] flew Theocritus, as you may perceive he was all ready full fledged. So flew Virgil, as not yet well feeling his wings. So flew Mantuan, as being not full somd.[1] So Petrarch. So Boccaccio. So Marot, Sanazarus, and also divers other excellent both Italian and French poets, whose footing this author everywhere followeth, yet so as few, but they be well scented, can trace him out. So finally flieth this our new Poet, as a bird, whose principals be scarce grown out, but yet as that in time shall be able to keep wing with the best."

Though the modern reader may feel a certain anticlimax in coming from this enthusiastic preface to the poems themselves, he cannot fail, if he comes to *The Shepherd's Calendar* from earlier Tudor poetry, to be struck by the control and the assurance of Spenser's verse. In the January eclogue, the shepherd Colin Clout, who is Spenser himself (the name comes from an anticlerical satire of Skelton's), is complaining of his unrequited love for Rosalind. Spenser thus adapts a Petrarchan mood to a pastoral setting. The stanza has six lines, rhymed *ababcc:*

> A shepherd's boy (no better do him call)
> When winter's wasteful spite was almost spent
> All in a sunshine day, as did befall,
> Led forth his flock, that had been long ypent.
> So faint they woxe, and feeble in the fold,
> That now unnethes their feet could them uphold.
>
> All as the sheep, such was the shepherd's look,
> For pale and wan he was (alas the while);
> May seem he loved, or else some care he took;
> Well couth he tune his pipe and frame his style.
> Then to a hill his fainting flock he led,
> And thus him plained, the while his sheep there fed.
>
> "Ye gods of love, that pity lovers' pain
> (If any gods the pain of lovers pity),

1 Full somd: a falconer's term, meaning full fledged.

> Look from above, where you in joys remain,
> And bow your ears unto my doleful ditty.
> And Pan, thou shepherds' God, that once didst love,
> Pity the pains that thou thyself didst prove. . . ."

We see here the deliberate archaisms that Spenser was to experiment with much more before he settled on the diction for *The Faerie Queene*. Spenser is trying to combine rusticity with formality. The February eclogue, which tells the story of the oak and the briar, is written in a rougher accentual measure, which Spenser seems to have considered a genuine English verse-form and one suitable for the handling of more deliberately rustic themes. Whether this looser meter represents how Spenser and his contemporaries read Chaucer, not understanding the pronunciation of the final *e*, or whether Spenser was trying to do something resembling what Coleridge did in *Christabel*, is not clear; but it *is* clear that Spenser used this accentual verse deliberately, as a style appropriate to the subject of this eclogue. He used it again in the May and September eclogues. The March eclogue gives the dialogue of two shepherds in the old romance stanza that Chaucer had used so mockingly in *Sir Thopas*: Thomalin tells Willy how he saw Cupid in a bush, and they exchanged shots, but the naturalistic pastoral setting makes the incident sound rather incongruous: we expect a grouse or a partridge rather than "the little god." The April eclogue, after an introductory dialogue between Thenot and Hobbinol in flexible decasyllabic quatrains, introduces a formal song in praise of Elizabeth. The verse form, though perhaps suggested by Ronsard and his group, la Pléiade, is an interesting original experiment:

> Ye dainty nymphs, that in this blessed brook
>   do bathe your breast,
> Forsake your watery bowers and hither look,
>   at my request;
> And eke you virgins that on Parnasse dwell,
> Whence floweth Helicon, the learned well,
>   Help me to blaze
>   Her worthy praise
> Which in her sex doth all excell.

There is a careful chiming of vowels through the song (which has thirteen stanzas) and cunning variations of *tempo*, foreshadowing Spenser's later achievements in sound and movement.

The May eclogue is a dialogue between two shepherds in which, through the obvious pastoral disguise, Spenser attacks idle, deceitful, and worldly High Church clergy, whose fondness for elaborate ritual offended Spenser's Protestant idealism. June brings another complaint, in an eight-line stanza rhyming *ababbaba*. Colin complains not only of his lack of success in love, but of his lack of success in his poetry and his generally unsettled condition. The slow-moving verse rises and falls in a fine plangent cadence. The July eclogue is another Protestant satire, made, as E. K.'s "argument" tells us, "in the honour and commendation of good shepherds, and to the shame and dispraise of proud and ambitious pastors." The proud shepherd, Morrell (probably denoting John Elmer, the High Church bishop of London), argues with the humble and conscientious Thomalin, who concludes by praising Algrin (i.e., Edmund Grindal, Archbishop of Canterbury and Puritan sympathizer) as the type of the good shepherd. The verse form is alternately rhyming eight-syllabled and six-syllabled lines, handled with ease and assurance.

August gives a singing match, with a charming roundelay by Perigot and Willy followed by a much more formal *sestina* by Cuddie. The roundelay is fresh and artfully artless:

Perigot:	It fell upon a holy eve,
Willy:	hey ho holiday,
Per.	When holy fathers wont to shrieve,
Wil.	now ginneth this roundelay.
Per.	Sitting upon a hill so high,
Wil.	hey ho the high hill,
Per.	The while my flock did feed thereby,
Wil.	the while the shepherd self did spill,
Per.	I saw the bouncing Bellibone,
Wil.	hey ho bonibell,
Per.	Tripping over the dale alone,
Wil.	she can trip it very well. . . .

This draws on the popular tradition, but embodies more skill than may be at first apparent. The chiming repetitions and modifications of Willy's lines are handled with effective variety. The *sestina*, an elaborate verse-form from Petrarch, is a slow moving six-line stanza, with each stanza using the same words to end the lines, but in a different order. It opens:

> Ye wasteful woods, bear witness of my woe
> Wherein my plaints did oftentimes resound;
> Ye careless birds are privy to my cries,
> Which in your songs were wont to make a part.

> Thou pleasant spring hast lulled me oft asleep
> Whose streams my trickling tears did oft augment.

The lines of the second stanza end, respectively, with "augment," "woes," "resound," "cries," "part," "sleep." Those of the third stanza end "sleep," "augment," "woe," "resound," "cries," "part." Those of the fourth, with "apart," "sleep," "augment," "woe," "sound," "cries." And so on. Elaborate though this is, it is less elaborate than the Petrarchan *sestina*. Spenser is here performing a deliberate *tour de force:* it is Colin's (i.e., Spenser's) poem that Cuddie recites, and Perigot provides the applause afterward:

> O Colin, Colin, the shepherds' joy,
> How I admire each turning of thy verse. . . .

The September eclogue is a dialogue between Hobbinol and Diggon Davie. The latter is "a shepherd, that in hope of more gain drove his sheep into a far country. The abuses whereof, and loose living of Popish prelates, by occasion of Hobbinol's demand, he discourseth at large." Spenser takes many suggestions here from Mantuan, but the Protestant content is his own.

The October eclogue is in many ways the most important of all, for it voices, for the first time in English, the high Renaissance ideal of poetry. "In Cuddie is set out the perfect pattern of a poet," runs the argument, and though the presentation of this perfect pattern is accompanied by Cuddie's complaints that the age of great poetry is dead, the exhortations of his friend Piers sound the louder note. The argument reads like a summary of Sidney's "Defence of Poetry." Cuddie

. . . complaineth of the contempt of poetry, and the causes thereof; specially having been in all ages, and even amongst the most barbarous, always of singular account and honour, and being indeed so worthy and commendable an art; or rather no art, but a divine gift and heavenly instinct not to be gotten by labour and learning, but adorned with both; and poured into the wit by a certain ἐνθουσιασμὸς and celestial inspiration, as the author hereof else where at large discourseth . . .

The verse has a gravity suited to the subject:

> Abandon then the base and viler clown,
> Lift up thyself out of the lowly dust,
> And sing of bloody Mars, of wars, of jousts.
> Turn thee to those that wield the awful crown,
> To doubted knights whose woundless armour rusts,   [doubted:
> And helms unbruiséd waxen daily brown.   redoubted]

> There may thy Muse display her fluttering wing,
> And stretch herself at large from East to West; . . .

And again, Piers breaks out on hearing Cuddie lament the present decline of poetry:

> O peerless poesie, where is then thy place?
> If nor in Princes palace thou do sit
> (And yet is Prince's palace the most fit)
> Ne breast of baser birth doth thee embrace.
> Then make thee wings of thine aspiring wit,
> And, whence thou camest, fly back to heaven apace.

The strain of lament here is conventional; the note of faith in poetry's high destiny rings out clearly above it.

The November eclogue is a lament for "the death of some maiden of great blood, whom he calleth Dido." It is based on a similar poem by Marot. The lament is introduced as a song sung for pleasure rather than an expression of personal grief: the eclogue opens with Thenot asking Colin:

> Colin my dear, when shall it please thee sing,
> As thou were wont, songs of some jovisance?

And Colin replies that a joyful song is not seasonable in "sad Winter," when the "mournful Muse" is more appropriate. Like the poem in praise of Elizabeth in the April eclogue, the lament which Colin proceeds to sing is an exercise in the handling of vowel music and variations in *tempo*:

> Why do we longer live (ah, why live we so long?)
> Whose better days death hath shut up in woe?
> The fairest flower our girlond all among
> Is faded quite and into dust ygoe.
> Sing now, ye shepherds' daughters, sing no moe
>   The songs that Colin made you in her praise,
>   But into weeping turn your wanton lays,
>   O heavy hearse.
> Now is time to die.   Nay, time was long ygoe,
>   O careful verse.   [careful: sorrowful]

The short lines "O heavy hearse" and "O careful verse" are repeated as a refrain at the end of each stanza.

The December eclogue is an imitation of Marot's *Eclogue au*

Roy, in which the poet looks back over his poetic career. It is suited to the time of the year, the poet reviewing the change from the springtime of his days to the present time:

> So now my year draws to his latter term,
> My spring is spent, my summer burnt up quite.
> My harvest hastes to stir up winter stern,
> And bids him claim with rigorous rage his right.
> So now he storms with many a sturdy stour,
> So now his blustring blast each coast doth scour.

So ends this varied collection of eclogues in which Spenser tried out his genius and presented himself to the public as England's New Poet. Technically, they are of the very greatest interest: the thirteen different verse forms which Spenser includes in the twelve eclogues (two of them new to English verse and five Spenser's own invention) show what English verse craftsmanship was capable of in 1579, and they also point forward to later developments. But besides their importance for the craft of English verse, they are important for drawing together traditions from the golden age of medieval English poetry, from the Latin and Greek classics, and from the Renaissance literature of Italy and France, and domiciling them happily in English poetry, where they were to remain for three centuries. We see here, too, Spenser's Protestant idealism, something of his neo-Platonic philosophy, and his high claims for poetry. All of these elements were to combine later more richly and subtly in *The Faerie Queene*.

It is appropriate, and not merely a matter of historical convenience, to see all Spenser's earlier work in the perspective provided by *The Faerie Queene*, which is the culmination toward which Spenser was always moving and the great synthesis of themes and influences which the Elizabethan age had been awaiting. Spenser was well fitted, both by temperament and education, to absorb and to handle creatively the moral and intellectual currents of his time. At the Merchant Taylors' school, then presided over by Richard Mulcaster, a scholar with all the Renaissance enthusiasm for education and for the new ideal of the perfect gentleman, and at Cambridge, where he formed a lasting friendship with the scholar and critic Gabriel Harvey, who was both Puritan and Humanist, he came into contact with the kind of scholarship and enthusiasms to which his own high idealism responded immediately. Spenser's combination of Italian neo-Platonism with English Protestantism, his imaginative handling of his own very considerable scholarship, his responsiveness to the challenge and excitement of his age, reflect the interaction of his education and environment with his temperament. He was never the complete courtier, for place-seeking at Elizabeth's court was hardly in accordance with his own concept of the perfect Christian gentleman, and besides, his Puritanism led him to oppose aspects of Elizabeth's compromise between the extremes of Protestantism and Catholicism; his failure to secure a higher government position than that of a civil servant in Ireland, where he spent most of his life from 1580 until his death in 1599, or a more substantial governmental recognition of his claims than a pension of fifty pounds a year, is not surprising. But he became a friend and admirer of Sir Philip Sidney, whom, together with so many of his contemporaries, he regarded as the beau ideal of knighthood and courtesy, and was an active participant in the most significant literary discussions of his time. And much of his "occasional" writing deals, either directly or indirectly, with the contemporary scene. Indeed, he never withdrew from contemporary religious and political controversies into an unreal world of the imagination: he was always concerned with the problems of his day, as well as with broader issues, and *The Faerie Queene* itself is an allegorical commentary on the religious, political, and social scene as well as a more general poetic exploration of the nature of virtue.

Spenser's confident entry as the New Poet with *The Shepherd's Calendar* was not immediately followed up by anything spectacular. The first three books of *The Faerie Queene* were not published until 1590, and books four to six appeared in 1596, but in the interval he had written a variety of other verse of varying degrees of high seriousness. A volume of minor poems appeared in 1591, entitled *Complaints: Containing sundry small Poems of the World's Vanity*. This contains "The Ruins of Time," an elegiac poem written in slow-moving rhyme royal: its structure is borrowed from du Bellay's "Antiquités de Rome," and its theme combines the general medieval *ubi sunt* motif with reflections on the deaths of the Earl of Leicester, Sir Philip Sidney, and Sir Francis Walsingham: there is also the notion that poetry can confer immortality. "The Ruins of Time" is an uneven poem, which shows signs of having been put together in haste; but the verse is never out of control, and there are passages of richly musical elegy. "The Tears of the Muses" is the second of the *Complaints:* written in a stanza rhyming *ababcc*, it is more satirical than elegiac in tone and laments the decay of the arts and other abuses of the time in a rather mechanical manner. Each of the nine Muses speaks her complaint, and the whole apparatus is somewhat old-fashioned for a New Poet: it probably represents fairly early work. More interesting is the third poem in the collection,

"Virgil's Gnat," a lively rendering in *ottava rima* of the Latin *"Culex,"* an epyllion or little epic attributed to Virgil. But by far the most interesting poem in the book is "Mother Hubbard's Tale," a skillful and spirited satire on contemporary affairs in the form of a beast fable. Chaucerian in tone, with the rhymed couplets moving in a deliberately conversational cadence, this vigorous attack on abuses in economic, ecclesiastical, court, and government affairs, shows what Spenser could do when he kept his eye sharply on the contemporary English scene. Here is a very different poet from the author of *The Faerie Queene:*

> But if thee list unto the Court to throng,
> And there to hunt after the hopéd prey,
> Then must thou thee dispose another way.
> For there thou needs must learn to laugh, to lie,
> To face, to forge, to scoff, to company,
> To crouch, to please, to be a beetle stock
> Of thy great master's will, to scorn or mock;
> So may'st thou chance mock out a Benefice,
> Unless thou canst one conjure by device,
> Or cast a figure for a bishopric,
> And if one could, it were but a school-trick.

This links the accents of Chaucer with those found in the satires of Dryden and Pope.

The *Complaints* volume also contains some translations from Marot and du Bellay of no great interest in themselves, and the charming and sprightly "Muiopotomos, or The Fate of the Butterfly," a mock-heroic account in *ottava rima* of the capture and destruction of a beautiful butterfly by a baleful spider: it may or not have an allegorical meaning. The same year, Spenser published *Daphnaida: An Elegy upon the Death of the Noble and Virtuous Douglas Howard, Daughter and Heir of Henry Lord Howard, Viscount Byndon, and Wife of Arthur Gorges, Esquire,* a formal piece in a stanza which chimes interestingly in a rhyme scheme *ababcbc.* The model appears to have been Chaucer's *Book of the Duchess,* but Spenser's style is more rhetorical and his verse more highly wrought. *Colin Clout's Come Home Again,* published in 1595, is one of the freshest, most personal, and most attractive of Spenser's occasional poems. It tells, through a simple and easily penetrated pastoral allegory, of Sir Walter Ralegh's visit to Spenser in Ireland and Spenser's subsequent visit to London with Ralegh; there he was graciously received by Queen Elizabeth, but realized that court life was not for him, and he returned to Ireland. The poem is decasyllabic quatrains with alternating rhymes; occasionally the rhymes are repeated or otherwise linked in successive quatrains, with a highly musical effect. The ease and flow of the style, the combination of the autobiographical and the formal, the wholly successful mixture of the pastoral with the courtly, the rustic with the artificial, constitute one of Spenser's happiest attempts at synthesis.

The premature death of Sir Philip Sidney at the battle of Zutphen in 1586 called forth the usual spate of elegies, and Spenser's contribution was a pastoral elegy entitled "Astrophel," an uninspired performance in stanzas rhyming *ababcc*, modeled on Bion's lament for Adonis. That the death of so cherished a friend should have inspired such a highly conventional piece of work is an interesting commentary on the place of convention in Elizabethan art, while the fact that the poem is dedicated to Sidney's widow while referring in some detail to Sidney's love for "Stella," traditionally identified with Penelope Devereux, Lady Rich, who did not return Sidney's love, poses a problem in the relation between art and life that the modern mind finds hard to solve. The problem reminds us of how purely formal the notion as well as the handling of courtly love could be in Elizabethan times (and presumably earlier) and warns us against interpreting Spenser's allegorizing habit too naïvely.

A more interesting example of Spenser's handling of a convention of his time is provided by his *Amoretti*, love sonnets in the Petrarchan mode so dear to the Elizabethans. To what extent these sonnets celebrate his love for Elizabeth Boyle, his marriage to whom he celebrated in his "Epithalamion," is an unprofitable question: they tell the story of the poet's wooing of a mistress who at first rebuffed him, then relented and returned his love, and finally, as a result of some unhappy incident, turned against him again. If the "Epithalamion" represents the true end of this story, then we must suppose that the lady changed her mind yet again, and permanently this time. But again we must remember the place of the sonnet sequence in Elizabethan poetry and the place of convention in Elizabethan art. Spenser's sonnets may well have been a graceful Petrarchan exercise with a constantly shifting relationship to his personal experience. Just as in *The Faerie Queene* the allegory keeps shifting in perspective, as it were, at one point logically worked out in every detail and in another yielding to the psychological realism of the characters who are given emotions and actions beyond their allegorical role, so in other phases of his work Spenser was in the habit of varying the relation of his art to his life. A sonnet sequence was a formal handling of language which tested the skill and craftsmanship of the poet, and it was to be appreciated for the poetic life kindled within it, not for its autobiographical revelations. "Sincerity" in art does not mean autobiographical accuracy, but a full and subtle exploitation of the artist's medium so that the poem creates as it moves its own world of experience. That world, of course, does have reference to and does illuminate the real world of human experience, but not necessarily through a direct projection of the poet's autobiography. We should bear these obvious points in mind when we read the Elizabethan sonnet sequences, whether Spenser's, Sidney's, Daniel's, Drayton's, or Shakespeare's.

The eighty-nine sonnets that make up the *Amoretti* move with a limpid flow and show a remarkably consistent level of craftsmanship, though they never rise to some overwhelming moment like Drayton's famous "Since there's no help, come let us kiss and part," Sidney's "Leave me, O love which reachest but to dust," or some of Shakespeare's. There are, naturally, many echoes of Petrarch, and some of Tasso, Ronsard, Desportes, and others. The usual, though not invariable, rhyme-scheme is *ababbcbccdcdee*, with the first twelve lines deftly linked by rhyme and movement and separated from the final couplet. The best known of the sonnets of the *Amoretti* is a fair sample of the controlled flow Spenser achieves in these poems:

> One day I wrote her name upon the strand,
> But came the waves and washéd it away:
> Again I wrote it with a second hand,
> But came the tide and made my pains his prey.
> Vain man, said she, that dost in vain assay
> A mortal thing so to immortalize,
> For I myself shall like to this decay,
> And eke my name be wipéd out likewise.
> Not so, (quoth I) let baser things devise
> To die in dust, but you shall live by fame;
> My verse your virtues rare shall eternize,
> And in the heavens write your glorious name.
> Where, whenas death shall all the world subdue,
> Our love shall live, and later life renew.

The "Epithalamion" is an altogether more remarkable piece of work, and one of Spenser's highest achievements. This celebration of his own wedding (which took place in Ireland, probably in 1594) roused all Spenser's genius for enriching and transfiguring bare fact by poetic imagination and by the appropriate use of imagery and of rhythms. Convention and personal feeling here find their perfect meeting, and it is testimony to the way in which the whole tradition of European poetry had become part of Spenser's very personality that he should exploit that tradition most fully, most happily, and most originally when he came to express one of the supreme moments of his own life. The elaborate verse paragraph derives from the Italian *canzone,* but the handling of the melody, the use of the refrain, the adaptation of a lyrical poem to a narrative structure, the blending of descriptive details with the celebratory mood, the mingling of elements from Catullus, from Chaucer's *Parliament of Fowls,* from Irish setting, English folklore, and from classical tradition, shows original poetic genius in control of its richly diversified materials to a degree that English poetry had not yet seen. The architectonic quality both of the individual stanza and of the poem as a whole is remarkable, and the chiming refrain subtly varied yet sufficiently the same to bind the poem together with its incantatory repetition is something to marvel at. Here is the New Poetry reaching to heights of complex lyrical expression that were not before possible in English.

The narrative basis is simply the story of the wedding day: first the poet's announcement of his subject, then an account of the preparation for the wedding and the bidding of the guests, then a summons to the nymphs of the local woods, streams, and mountains to bring garlands for the bride and sing her praise, then dawn and the awakening of the bride. With the bride's appearance the verse takes on a new richness and a new excitement: her progress is described in language that echoes the Psalms:

> Lo where she comes along with portly pace,
> Like Phoebe from her chamber of the East,
> Arising forth to run her mighty race,
> Clad all in white, that 'seems a virgin best.
> So well it her beseems that ye would ween
> Some angel she had been.
> Her long loose yellow locks like golden wire,
> Sprinkled with pearl, and pearling flowers atween,
> Do like a golden mantle her attire,
> And, being crownéd with a girland green,
> Seem like some maiden Queen.
> Her modest eyes, abashéd to behold
> So many gazers as on her do stare,
> Upon the lowly ground affixéd are.
> Ne dare lift up her countenance too bold,
> But blush to hear her praises sung so loud,
> So far from being proud.
> Nathless do ye still loud her praises sing,
> That all the woods may answer and your echo ring.

The bride's beauty, both physical and spiritual, is now praised, and by this time the wedding procession has reached the church, and the bride enters to the sound of the organ:

> Open the temple gates unto my love,
> Open them wide that she may enter in, . . .

There follow the ceremony, the homecoming, the poet longing for the end of day—

> Ah! when will this long weary day have end,
> And lend me leave to come unto my love?
> How slowly do the hours their numbers spend!
> How slowly does sad Time his feathers move!
> Haste thee, O fairest planet, to thy home,
> Within the Western foam. . . .

The bride's attendants are dismissed, night descends, and the poet invokes peace and blessing on his bride. The moon rises and looks in at the window, and she too is invoked to bless the marriage; Juno and Genius are asked to grant the blessing of fruitfulness, and the poem ends on a note of calm yet eloquent benediction, with a seven-line coda in which the poet commends his song to his love.

This is poetic celebration carried as far as it can go: it is Spenser at the very height of its genius. Only quotation of the whole poem could demonstrate to those who are not familiar with it its extraordinary artistry, for each part gains immensely by contributing to the total movement. Not quite so rich, but equally brilliant in imagery and movement, is the "Prothalamion," a wedding poem written for the double wedding of Lady Elizabeth and Lady Catherine Somerset, daughters of the Earl of Worcester, to Henry Guilford and William Petre in 1596. Here again we have the massive and musical stanza with its concluding refrain ("Sweet Thames, run softly, till I end my song"), the adroitly varied line lengths, the movement from a hushed picture of early morning by the Thames to the ceremonious entry of the two swans who symbolize the two bridegrooms. The "Prothalamion" is more deliberately stylized than the "Epithalamion"; it has a tapestry quality, an almost heraldic tone; yet the personal note is effectively blended with this, and the poet himself is the vividly presented observer of the ceremonious scene. The benediction pronounced on the swans by one of the nymphs has a grave stateliness unsurpassed in English poetry:

> Ye gentle birds, the world's fair ornament,
> And heaven's glory, whom this happy hour

Doth lead unto your lovers' blissful bower,
Joy may you have and gentle heart's content
Of your love's couplement;
And let fair Venus, that is queen of love,
With her heart-quelling son upon you smile,
Whose smile, they say, hath virtue to remove
All love's dislike, and friendship's faulty guile
For ever to assoil.
Let endless peace your steadfast hearts accord,
And blessèd plenty wait upon your board,
And let your bed with pleasures chaste abound,
That fruitful issue may to you afford,
Which may your foes confound,
And make your joys redound,
Upon your bridal day, which is not long:
　Sweet Thames, run softly, till I end my song.

In 1596 Spenser published his *Four Hymns,* the first two, in honor
of Love and of Beauty, being early works, and the latter two, in
honor of Heavenly Love and of Heavenly Beauty, being written
much later. These hymns have been a favorite study of those interested in the influence of Platonism on Spenser, for they reflect that
influence more explicitly and consistently than any other of his
shorter poems; they are not otherwise of any great interest, for, while
displaying Spenser's usual control over his medium and rising occasionally to a fine rhetorical eloquence, they do not exhibit any new
powers or outstanding poetic qualities. The renewed interest in Plato
during the Renaissance is a commonplace of intellectual history;
Spenser had met it at Cambridge and he had met it, too, in the works
of the Italian neo-Platonists, in Giordano Bruno's treatise on love,
Degli Heroici Furori, in Marsilio Ficino's Latin translation of Plato,
his treatise on Plato's doctrine of immortality, and his commentary
on Plato's *Symposium,* in Castiglione's essay on the perfect courtier,
Il Cortegiano, translated into English by Sir Thomas Hoby in 1561,
and in many other works. The Platonic doctrine that one ascends
from a specific embodiment of beauty to a contemplation of the idea
of beauty as an end in itself, this idea being divine and its contemplation being a religious activity, was elaborated by the Italian
Platonists in a variety of ways. It was also often grafted on to the
medieval notion of courtly love to which at first sight it appears so
antithetical (for no medieval courtly lover would have considered it
proper to move from contemplation of his mistress's beauty to contemplation of beauty in others and then of beauty in the abstract).
Medieval courtly love, Platonism, and Christianity were blended in

many interesting ways by Renaissance writers, and Spenser's combination of Protestant idealism, Platonism, and native amorousness represented his own version of a synthesis common enough in his day.

In the "Hymn in Honour of Love" Spenser takes numerous ideas from the *Symposium*, the *Phaedrus*, and from the Italian neo-Platonists to present an account of the importance and significance of love, its loftiness and exalting capacity, the difference between true love and mere lust, and the necessarily long and arduous road to the enjoyment of true love. Similarly, in the "Hymn in Honour of Beauty" he celebrates true beauty, which is more than surface appearance, but the physical reflection of something much more profound and universal. In the former poem he declares:

> For Love is lord of truth and loyalty,
> Lifting himself out of the lowly dust
> On golden plumes up to the purest sky
> Above the reach of loathly, sinful lust
> Whose base affect through cowardly distrust
> Of his weak wings dare not to heaven fly,
> But like a moldwarp in the earth doth lie.

And in the latter:

> So every spirit, as it is most pure,
> And hath in it the more of heavenly light,
> So it the fairer body doth procure
> To habit in, and it more fairly dight
> With cheerful grace and amiable sight.
> For of the soul the body form doth take:
> For soul is form and doth the body make.

Beside this we might put the following passage from Hoby's translation of Castiglione:

I say that beauty cometh of God and is like a circle, the goodness whereof is the centre. And therefore, as there can be no circle without a centre, no more can beauty be without goodness. Whereupon doth very seldom an ill soul dwell in a beautiful body. And therefore is the outward beauty a true sign of the inward goodness, and in bodies this comeliness is imprinted more or less, as it were, for a mark of the soul, whereby she is outwardly known: as in trees, in which the beauty of the buds giveth a testimony of the goodness of the fruit.

In the hymns of Heavenly Love and Heavenly Beauty, Spenser implicitly repudiates the Platonic notion of the ladder, expresses regret for his earlier celebrations of earthly love and beauty, and speaks in a specifically Christian manner of divine love made manifest by the career on earth of Christ, and of the beauty and wisdom of God which infinitely transcends anything visible on earth. Calvin's *Institutes* and the Hebrew Wisdom literature are influences here alongside more obvious Christian sources and the Italian neo-Platonists, and the tone is far from Platonic in spite of Platonic echoes. These poems illustrate how literary and intellectual fashions affected Spenser's style and subject matter, but Spenser's genius was not for explicitly philosophical poetry, and the hymns are of more interest to the student of Renaissance thought than to the historian of English poetry.

Of Spenser's toying with the idea of writing English verse in classical quantitative measure instead of in traditional English metrical forms, all that need be said is that this interest in the possibilities of writing classical verse in English was an inevitable part of Humanist enthusiasm for the classics and for imitating the achievements of classical literature; Spenser's letters to Gabriel Harvey show the two writers exchanging views and experiments which had no effect on Spenser's poetic achievement. The suspicion of rhyme as a barbarous nonclassical invention was another phase of the same Humanist attitude, which had more fruitful results than the interest in classical measures for it led to blank verse and, in particular, led Milton to choose blank verse for his *Paradise Lost*. But Spenser needed rhyme, which he handled more richly and musically than any other English poet, and his classicizing was a brief and transient phase of his poetic career.

All Spenser's earlier poetry is in a sense but preparation and exercise for his unfinished epic, *The Faerie Queene*, one of the few great inclusive attempts made by an English poet to bring together in one rich pattern all the various strands of civilization with which he was acquainted. Drawing on the medieval allegorical tradition in both its secular and religious forms, on medieval romance, classical epic, Aristotelian ethics, Plato and Italian neo-Platonism, Renaissance Humanism, Protestant idealism, Malory, the Italian epic, English history, geography and folklore, Elizabethan patriotism and political thought, and almost every current of European thought and expression and convention which had reached the sixteenth century, he constructed his comprehensive poetic vision of *la condition humaine* as it was, in a context of ideal suggestion of what it should be. His immediate model was Ariosto's *Orlando Furioso*, which, as he told Gabriel Harvey, he hoped to "overgo," though his tone is quite different from Ariosto's and he lacks the Italian's comic exuberance and astonishing fertility of lively invention. The Italian epic provided the mold into which he could pour his serious and complex vision:

the vision itself was Spenser's own, for all his use of older traditions. Spenser wrote a letter to Sir Walter Ralegh (prefixed to the edition of 1590) "expounding his whole intention in the course of this work," in which he declared that "the general end . . . of all the book is to fashion a gentleman or noble person in virtuous and gentle discipline." He pointed out that he had learned from Homer, Virgil, Ariosto, and Tasso, "by example of which excellent Poets I labour to portray in Arthur, before he was King, the image of a brave knight, perfected in the twelve private moral virtues, as Aristotle hath devised, the which is the purpose of these first twelve books, which if I find to be well accepted, I may be perhaps encouraged to frame the other part of politic virtues in his person, after that he came to the king." The letter continued:

In that Faery Queen I mean glory in my general intention, but in my particular I conceive the most excellent and glorious person of our soveraine the Queen, and her kingdom in Faery land. And yet in some places else I do otherwise shadow her. For considering she beareth two persons, the one of a most royal Queen or Empress, the other of a most virtuous and beautiful Lady, this latter part in some places I do express in Belphoebe, . . . So in the person of Prince Arthur I set forth magnificence [the Aristotelian *megalopsychia*, *magnanimitas*, greatness of soul] in particular, which virtue for that (according to Aristotle and the rest) it is the perfection of all the rest, and containeth in it them all, therefore in the whole course I mention the deeds of Arthur applicable to that virtue which I write of in that book. But of the xii other virtues I make xii other knights the patrons, for the more variety of the history. Of which these three books [i.e., the first three books, published in 1590] contain three, the first of the knight of the Redcross, in whom I express Holiness; the second of Sir Guyon, in whom I set forth Temperance; the third of Britomartis, a lady knight, in whom I picture Chastity.

He goes on to explain that he begins *in medias res* in proper epic fashion, and since only three books are here presented he had better explain what has happened before the events there narrated (an explanation which he intended, again in proper epic fashion, to unfold in a suitable retrospect in a later book). "The beginning . . . of my history, if it were to be told by an Historiographer, should be the twelfth book, which is the last, where I devise that the Faery Queen kept her annual feast xii days, upon which xii several days the occasions of the xii several adventures happened, which being undertaken by xii several knights are in these xii books severally handled and discoursed." And he goes on to give a brief account of how the adventures of the Redcross Knight, of Sir Guyon, and of Britomart first started. And "many other adventures are intermeddled, but rather as accidents than intendments."

Of the total plan of twenty-four books, Spenser only completed six. The first three were published in 1590, and books four, five, and six in 1596. In 1609, ten years after Spenser's death, a folio edition was published containing the first six books and a fragment of book VII entitled "Two Cantos of Mutability." *The Faerie Queene* is thus very far from complete; a mere fragment of an epic. And in a work of such complex design incompleteness is bound to present difficulties of understanding and interpretation. Nevertheless, the work as we have it is noble and impressive, more than long enough to enable us to assess its quality and significance—long enough, indeed, to have frightened off generations of readers who have been content to judge the work by brief extracts or merely by reputation. It remains one of the great poems of the English language; but its greatness is of a rather special kind.

The notion that *The Faerie Queene* consists of an endless series of pictorial stanzas, each slow moving and musical, with an optional allegorical significance which all readers since Spenser's time have preferred to ignore, is still common enough to require correcting. The surface of the epic consists, as Professor C. S. Lewis has well put it, of "interlocked stories of chivalrous adventure in a world of marvels," and it is this surface which it shares with the Italian epic. The background is an indeterminate world of plains, woods, castles, dens, islands, and shores, a deliberate dream world through which we watch the characters move—

> And forth they pass, with pleasure forward led, . . .

> So forth they passed, and all the way they spent
> Discoursing of her dreadful late distress, . . .

> So forth he fared, as now befell, on foot, . . .

> So forth they pass, a well consorted pair, . . .

> So forth they rowéd, and that Ferryman
> With his stiff oars did brush the sea so strong, . . .

> So as they travelled, lo they gan espy
> An arméd knight toward them gallop fast, . . .

> Thus as she her recomforted, she spied
> Where far away one all in armour bright
> With hasty gallop towards her did ride; . . .

We watch, as it were in a trance, as characters approach and recede across this magic landscape. The very opening of the first canto of Book I strikes the note of observed adventure:

> A Gentle Knight was pricking on the plain,
> Y-clad in mighty arms and silver shield,

> Wherein old dints of deep wounds did remain,
> The cruel marks of many a bloody field;
> Yet arms till that time never did he wield.
> His angry steed did chide his foaming bit,
> As much disdaining to the curb to yield.
> Full jolly knight he seemed, and fair did sit,
> As one for knightly jousts and fierce encounters fit.

Yet the poem is not a sequence of pictorial scenes, each with its moral and religious and political allegorical significance. The shifts in tone and tempo, the range from homely realism to liturgical solemnity or spiritual exaltation, the deliberate alterations in perspective and in levels of probability, and above all the flexibility of the allegory which mutates from simple personification to oblique suggestion in accordance with the needs of the narrative, the interest of the characters and the degree to which the poet is approaching or moving away from a climactic moment in the unfolding of his complex ethico-religious meaning—all this gives the poem variety and liveliness and prevents that aimless drowsiness which somehow so many people have come to associate with Spenser. Thus in Book I the Redcross Knight, who is Holiness, accompanied by Una, who is Truth, becomes involved in a series of adventures which suggest (at a variety of levels) how man's pursuit of holiness can be hindered by error, hypocrisy, false devotion, and so on. At the same time the Redcross Knight is also Everyman, facing the ordinary temptations of this world, and needing the help of Grace (Prince Arthur) as well as Truth in order to lead the good life and attain holiness. The Redcross Knight both represents a quality (holiness) and represents man in search of that quality. (Spenser is also talking about religious conditions in England, putting the Protestant against the Catholic view of the good life, and bringing in many contemporary references. But this is unimportant.) The adventures, as well as having meaning on these levels, also have their own interest and their own ethical suggestiveness, just as the incidental characters may or may not have human qualities which enrich the story psychologically and ethically as well as their more formal allegorical significance, which again may vary in its degree of literalness. The monster Error, which the Redcross Knight slays, is described as "most loathsome, filthy, foul and full of vile disdain," prolific of her poisonous young, and, in the midst of the fight, vomiting forth books and papers together with lumps of foul flesh and "loathly frogs and toads." The description is vigorous, skillful, and thoroughly "Spenserian" in the popular sense; the allegory is simple to the point of childishness. Then Spenser goes on to describe how the knight was harassed by the monster's "cursed spawn":

The same so sore annoyéd has the knight,
That wellnigh chokéd with the deadly stink
His forces fail, he can no longer fight.
Whose courage when the fiend perceived to shrink
She pouréd forth out of her hellish sink
Her fruitful curséd spawn of serpents small,
Deforméd monsters, foul and black as ink,
Which swarming all about his legs did crawl,
And him encumbered sore, but could not hurt at all.

This is vigorous and effective; both the literal and the allegorical meanings are perfectly clear. But the next stanza changes the tone:

As gentle Shepherd in sweet eventide
When ruddy Phoebus gins to welk in west,   [welk: fade]
High on an hill, his flock to viewen wide,
Marks which do bite their hasty supper best,
A cloud of cumbrous gnats do him molest,
All striving to infix their feeble stings,
That from their noyance he nowhere can rest,
But with his clownish hands their tender wings
He brusheth oft, and oft doth mar their murmurings.

The background of pastoral life introduced here in the simile is reminiscent of some of Milton's similes in *Paradise Lost*, where he provides relief from the acrid atmosphere of hell by a simile which invokes one of the simpler and more elemental activities of men in the fields or on the sea. The sudden and brief metamorphosis of the Redcross Knight battling with a cursed spawn of serpents into a shepherd brushing off the innocent but annoying gnats brings in a more normal human world and establishes, as it were, a middle term between the world of chivalric action on the one hand and the world of ethical and religious ideals on the other. Because it is introduced as a simile it does not interrupt or spoil the force of the incident; but it humanizes it, and reminds us of the everyday world in which our ethical problems are to be encountered and solved.

This is a fairly obvious example of a shift in tone in *The Faerie Queene*. Spenser can shift through a much wider range of tones. Still confining ourselves to Book I, we can pick out in a short space a great variety of kinds of expression. There is the note of romantic adventure pure and simple:

At length they chanced to meet upon their way
An aged Sire, in long black weeds yclad.

There is the pastoral:

> A little lowly Hermitage it was,
> Down in a dale, hard by a forest's side.

There is the popular satirical:

> He told of Saints and Popes, and evermore
> He strewed an *Ave Mary* after and before.

There is the mythological-romantic:

> There Tethys his wet bed
> Doth ever wash, and Cynthia still doth steep
> In silver dew his ever-drooping head,
> While sad Night over him her mantle black doth spread.

There is the homely proverbial:

> A dram of sweet is worth a pound of sour.

There is the moralizing, religious note:

> Ay me, how many perils do enfold
> The righteous man, to make him daily fall!
> Were not, that heavenly grace doth him uphold,
> And steadfast truth acquit him out of all.

There is the poetic-proverbial (but it is worth remembering that these lines are spoken to entrap the Redcross Knight into despair and suicide):

> Sleep after toil, port after stormy seas,
> Ease after war, death after life does greatly please.

There is the lofty chivalric:

> O goodly golden chain, wherewith yfere
> The virtues linkéd are in lovely wise,
> And noble minds of yore allied were
> In brave pursuit of chivalrous emprise.

Perhaps the most effective display of Spenser's range is found toward the end of Book I, when he is describing the Redcross Knight's slaying of the dragon:

> So down he fell, and forth his life did breathe,
> That vanished into smoke and cloudës swift;
> So down he fell, that th'earth him underneath
> Did groan, as feeble so great load to lift;
> So down he fell, as an huge rocky clift,

> Whose false foundation waves have washed away,
> With dreadful poise is from the mainland rift
> And, rolling down, great Neptune doth dismay.
> So down he fell, and like an heaped mountain lay.

This is formal and stylized. But after this comes:

> And after, all the rascal many ran,
> Heapéd together in rude rabblement,
> To see the face of that victorious man,
> Whom all admiréd, as from heaven sent,
> And gazed upon with gaping wonderment.
> But when they came where that dead Dragon lay,
> Stretched on the ground in monstrous large extent,
> The sight with idle fear did them dismay,
> Ne durst approach him nigh, to touch, or once assay.

> Some feared and fled; some feared and well it feigned.
> One that would wiser seem than all the rest
> Warned him not touch, for yet perhaps remained
> Some longering life within his hollow breast,
> Or in his womb might lurk some hidden nest
> Of many Dragonets, his fruitful seed.
> Another said that in his eyes did rest
> Yet sparkling fire, and bad thereof take heed;
> Another said, he saw him move his eyes indeed.

> One mother, when as her foolhardy child
> Did come too near and with his talons play,
> Half dead through fear her little babe reviled
> And to her gossips gan in counsel say:
> "How can I tell but that his talons may
> Yet scratch my son or rend his tender hand?"
> So diversly themselves in vain they fray,
> While some, more bold, to measure him nigh stand
> To prove how many acres he did spread of land.

This is shrewd comic realism, very different indeed from Spenser's high romantic strain. One could multiply examples of Spenser's different styles indefinitely. The sudden questioning with which he opens the eighth canto of Book II, for example, startles by its difference from what has gone before:

> And is there care in heaven? And is there love
> In heavenly spirits to these creatures base,
> That may compassion of their evils move?
> There is: else much more wretched were the case
> Of men, than beasts.

In the same canto we also get the following:

> Horribly then he gan to rage and rail,
> Cursing his gods and himself damning deep:
> Als when his brother saw the red blood rail
> Adown so fast, and all his armour steep,
> For very felness loud he gan to weep,
> And said: "Catiff, curse on thy cruel hand
> That twice hath sped; yet shall it not thee keep
> From the third brunt of this my fatal brand:
> Lo, where the dreadful Death behind thy back doth stand."

Book II is concerned with the adventures of Sir Guyon, who represents Temperance, and at the same time represents Everyman tempted from health of soul and body by various kinds of excess and disease. The allegory weaves in and out of the story easily and effectively, with images of health in man and in nature opposing images of illness and perversion. The House of Temperance, "in which doth sober Alma dwell," represents the human body ruled by the soul, and its defense of the health of both against the besiegers has a clear enough allegorical meaning. The various kinds of smoldering passion which threaten bodily and spiritual health are magnificently embodied in such characters as Furor, Strife, Pyrocles, and Atin (some representing the forces that incite to rage and similar passions, others exhibiting the result of such incitement on human behavior and attitude—as always, the allegory works easily on several different levels). But bodily and spiritual health is more subtly threatened by false pleasures than by anger and grief—

> A harder lesson, to learn continence
> In joyous pleasure than in grievous pain,
> For sweetness doth allure the weaker sense
> So strongly, that uneathes it can refrain   [uneathes: scarcely]
> From that which feeble nature covets fain;
> But grief and wrath, that be her enemies,
> And foes of life she better can restrain—

and the latter part of the book deals with these subtler temptations. The temptation of Mammon is a magnificent set piece, and the final victory of temperance over her foes, followed by the destruction of the Bower of Bliss, which represents nature corrupted by the misuse of art, enables Spenser to pull out all the stops.

Book II illustrates clearly the way in which Spenser combines his Christian ideals with his neo-Platonism and his humanism. Nature itself is good, and even Phaedria, the laughing girl with the boat who represents frivolous mirth, is not evil but merely empty; growth, nurture, fertility, satisfying and fruitful sexual activity, temperance, health, and virtue are on one side, and opposed to them are every kind of distorting passion, excess, corruption, disease, perversion, and prurience. There is a Greek as well as a Christian ideal at work here, though how far Spenser is successful in combining them into a consistent Christian humanism is perhaps doubtful, as it is with Milton also. Book III, dealing with Britomart, who represents chastity, and Book IV, ostensibly dealing with Cambel and Telamond (representing male friendship) but in fact developing the general theme of love and its different varieties and continuing the stories of Britomart, Amoret, Scudamour, Florimel, and the other characters who embody or suggest the varieties of real love and their relation to false love, reach out into a complex suggestiveness. Spenser's chastity is not virginity but lawful wedded love, which is contrasted with adulterous courtly love represented by Malecasta and Busirane. The development of the story of the allegory in these two books is rich and fascinating: Spenser is combining views from Plato's *Symposium* with elements from the courtly-love tradition and from a variety of other sources to create an ideal of true love against which he sets the barren, demoralizing, perverse, enslaving love of the courtly romances. He splits the courtly-love ideal in half, dismissing its fruitless afflictions and self-pityings but retaining its high passion, and associates the half he retains with Christian marriage. The characters here operate at several different levels, and it is profitless to try to pin down the precise resemblances and differences of significance between, say, Britomart, Amoret, Belphoebe, and Florimel. What is required here is for the reader to surrender himself to the story; if he does this, he will find the picture of the varieties of true love in man and nature opposed to love's perversion building itself up cumulatively as the adventures and descriptions unfold. The two books are rich in set descriptive pieces which teem with moral and psychological suggestions.

Book V is more restricted in theme: it deals with Sir Artegal, who represents Justice, and the political allegory here more than once comes to the foreground, to the distress of the modern reader, who neither agrees with the Elizabethan concept of justice nor retains any interest in the political problems of Spenser's Europe. The sense of the importance of order, both in nature and in human society, and the necessity of everything and every one knowing his proper place and performing his proper function, is strong throughout the book. Spenser provides the clue to the Elizabethan view of the vice which

Marlowe made central in *Tamburlaine* and with which Shakespeare, too, was fascinated:

> O sacred hunger of ambitious minds
> And impotent desire of men to reign,
> Whom neither dread of God, that devils binds,
> Nor laws of men, that common weals contain,
> Nor bands of nature, that wild beasts restrain,
> Can keep from outrage and from doing wrong,
> Where they may hope a kingdom to obtain.
> No faith so firm, no trust can be so strong,
> No love so lasting then, that may enduren long.

The hero of Book VI is Sir Calidore, representing Courtesy, and in this charmingly varied section of *The Faerie Queene* Spenser explores the concept of "gentilesse" as developed in the Renaissance by such writers as Castiglione. Everything is here, from Christian humility to gentlemanly good manners, from pastoral simplicity to knightly honor, and the various threats to the ideal of true courtesy, from brutality to over-sophistication, are also presented. The meaning here emerges from the behavior of the characters rather than through formal allegory; the characters tend more to illustrate than to represent or suggest the qualities they stand for as they do in the other books. The pace is fairly slow, and the writing both assured and relaxed. The two Cantos of Mutability present, with an impressive combination of masquelike pageantry and rich philosophic reflection, a discussion of the relation between change and order, between the principle of alteration and decay and the principle of Nature, the ever renewing heart of things. A debate between Mutability and Nature concludes the cantos, and the poet's reflections on its meaning proceed for only two stanzas before the poem as we have it comes to an end. It is clear only that Spenser is concerned to find the relation between time (over which Mutability rules) and eternity, where "all things firmly stay."

At intervals throughout *The Faerie Queene*, related in a variety of ways to the action, Spenser strikes the patriotic note. English and Welsh history and geography, genealogies going back to Brut, the Trojan founder of the British race, and the mythology of the English countryside presented with a proper sense of what is appropriate to different regions, punctuate the adventures of the various knights and ladies. For all its setting in Faeryland, for all the romantic vagueness of its topography and the immense variety of European sources that lie behind it, *The Faerie Queene* is an essentially English poem, and Spenser exhibits his pride in his country and in his Queen through a host of devices and allusions. *The Faerie Queene* is an English Christian Humanist epic.

The stanza which Spenser invented for his epic, with its carefully chiming rhyme-scheme and concluding alexandrine, is capable of a great variety of effects, and the popular notion that it is less suited for narrative verse than for static pictorial description is not borne out by the way it actually operates in the poem. Spenser does indeed excel in certain kinds of set descriptive piece, but he can vary the speed and movement of the stanza to produce contemplative, discursive, dreamlike, exclamatory, formal, colloquial, satirical, and other styles and moods. His use of deliberately antique word forms, Chaucerian and pseudo-Chaucerian, is largely for purposes of stylization appropriate to a heroic poem, but he can also use older words to give a homely, proverbial effect. Altogether, *The Faerie Queene* is a poem of extraordinary richness and diversity, a remarkable synthesis of Elizabethan culture whose total effect cannot be properly judged because the work was left unfinished but whose quality and splendor can nevertheless be easily discerned. Yet the synthesis was a personal one: the union of chivalric, patriotic, Christian, and Platonic, of medieval and Protestant, of courtly love and Christian marriage, of Italian romance and medieval allegory, of pageantry and philosophy, of shrewd observation and high imagination, was not something that could be handed on unchanged to future poets. The English poets of the period who imitated Spenser imitated only one aspect of his multiple work—his allegory or his topographical patriotic poetry or his pastoralism—and there were more who turned away from him than who followed him. Ben Jonson was right in a sense when he told Drummond of Hawthornden that "Spenser writ no language." It was no imitable language; there was no further road along that way—the way of the allegorical heroic poem deriving its form from the Italian epic—in English literature. Yet Spenser's place in the English poetic tradition is indisputable: he was the first modern poet to exploit the full poetic resources of the English language; he had the highest ambitions for poetry while at the same time retaining a freshness of approach characteristic of the more casual and "occasional" singer. He inspired both Milton and Keats, in very different ways: to the former he was "sage and serious Spenser," England's first epic poet, while to the latter he stood for enchantment and high romance. And to Wordsworth (who considered Spenser—with Chaucer, Shakespeare, and Milton—as an example to be studied and, if possible, equaled) he was

> Sweet Spenser, moving through his clouded heaven
> With the moon's beauty and the moon's soft pace.

"The poets' poet" he has been called: but this does not mean (as is sometimes thought) that his work represents the quintessence of poetic lushness, but rather that, combining so many strands and occupying such a central position in the history of the English poetic tongue, he has continued to arouse the professional interest of other poets. *The Faerie Queene* may be a blind alley in English literary history: but its author remains a figure of the utmost importance to all interested in the poetic handling of the English language and the technique of English verse.

Spenser dedicated *The Shepherd's Calendar* to "the noble and virtuous gentleman most worthy of all titles both of learning and chivalry," Sir Philip Sidney, and addressed his explanatory letter about *The Faerie Queene* to Sir Walter Ralegh. Each of these figures was in his way representative of his time. Sidney (1554–86), whose brief life of thirty-two years ended in a scene of characteristic gallantry after he had been fatally wounded in a minor battle before the city of Zutphen, came as near to achieving the Renaissance ideal of the gentleman as any Englishman ever did; scholar, poet, critic, diplomat, and courtier, he was at once a man of affairs and a high idealist, regarded in his own lifetime as the epitome of knighthood. Ralegh (ca. 1552–1618), less simply attractive in character, shared with Sidney the varied gifts of the Renaissance courtier: his life was more tempestuous than Sidney's, with greater changes of fortune; he had a vigorous mind, in touch with the most advanced thought and thinkers of his day, a restless and active temperament, and real poetic skill.

None of Sidney's work was published during his lifetime, though much of it circulated in manuscript. In 1591, his sonnet-sequence *Astrophel and Stella* appeared. Nine years earlier, the publication of *Hekatompathia, or a Passionate Century of Love* by Thomas Watson, a friend of Sidney's and of other men of letters in the 1580's, attracted new attention to the Petrarchan sonnet and helped to set the fashion for sequences of love sonnets. But only one original sonnet of Watson's in this volume was a poem of fourteen lines of the kind to which we now restrict the term "sonnet": Watson called it a "quatorzain." Further, Sidney's sonnets may well have been written and circulated in manuscript before Watson's collection appeared. At any rate, Sidney had the wider influence and wrote the better poems, and can be said to be largely responsible for the spate of sonnet-sequences that followed the publication of *Astrophel and Stella*. Fulke Greville's *Caelica* (written about 1580 but not published until 1638), Samuel Daniel's *Delia* (1592), Michael Drayton's *Idea's Mirror* (1594), Spenser's *Amoretti* (1595), and Shakespeare's sonnets, which, though not published until 1609, were probably written in the 1590's, are among the more important sonnet-sequences which followed Sidney's, and there were many more by lesser writers, including Henry Constable (*Diana*, 1592), Thomas Lodge (*Phillis*, 1593), Barnaby Barnes (*Parthenophe and Parthenophil*, 1593), and Giles Fletcher (*Licia*, 1593).

Petrarch's sonnets to Laura were, of course, the ultimate inspiration of all these sonnet-sequences, but Ronsard, du Bellay, and other French and Italian poets were also drawn on, often freely. Many of these late Elizabethan and early Jacobean sonnet-sequences are of more interest to the student of literary fashion than to the critic or reader of poetry, and they raise some interesting questions concerning the place of convention in art. A series of sonnets addressed to a single lady, expressing and reflecting on the developing relationship between the poet and his love, can tell a complex and even a dramatic love story, which is what we sometimes get. The story does not have to be literal autobiography, and questions of "sincerity" in this simple sense of the word are hardly relevant. Nevertheless, the best of these sonnets can project a psychological situation with power and originality, in spite of the often routine "conceits" which had become so much a part of the Petrarchan tradition. Of the English Petrarchan sonneteers it can be said, as Johnson said of the "metaphysical" poets of the seventeenth century, that "to write on their plan it was at least necessary to read and think." Indeed, the "conceit" of the Petrarchan sonneteer is not basically different from that of the metaphysical poet—each developing analogies with ingenious logic and subtle wit and making such analogies emblems of an emotional state. But whereas the metaphysical poet combined colloquial vigor and a devastating emotional integrity with their ingenuities, the Petrarchan sonneteer remained on the whole more formal, more rhetorical, and more "sugared."

Sidney's Stella was Penelope Devereux, betrothed to Sidney in her youth; for some reason the engagement was later broken off, and she became the wife of Lord Rich, while Sidney himself married Frances Walsingham in 1583. The 108 sonnets and eleven songs which make up the *Astrophel and Stella* series provide a record of his hopeless love for Stella in terms which combine traditional Petrarchan "conceits" with considerable individuality of expression and feeling. Many of the sonnets read like mere exercises, distinguished only by ingenuity, but a handful stand out as among the finest examples of their kind which the age produced. Sidney himself claimed complete originality both of feeling and expression—

"Fool," said my Muse to me, "look in thy heart and write."

But even in repudiating the conventional language of the sonneteer
he is likely to use that language, exclaiming

> Let dainty wits cry on the sisters nine
> That, bravely masked, their fancies may be told,

or

> I never drank of Aganippe well,
> Nor ever did in shade of Tempe sit.

The best are also the best known. "With how sad steps, O moon, thou
climb'st the skies" is a beautifully modulated sonnet, opening softly
on a note of slow plaintiveness and changing with deliberate abrupt-
ness in the third line as the poet moves from melancholy to bitterness. In "Come sleep! O sleep, the certain knot of peace," an invocation to sleep is deftly turned at the end into a love poem to Stella.
In "Having this day my horse, my hand, my lance," he turns a Petrarchan compliment neatly in a context of chivalry. In "Stella oft
sees the very face of woe," the sonnet winds cunningly to its startling
last line:

> I am not I; pity the tale of me.

Some with admirable openings fall away into pallid ingenuities;
others are well sustained and artfully modulated. Sidney does not
always use the same sonnet form, rhyming sometimes *abba* and
sometimes (but less often) *abab*. His commonest rhyme-scheme is
abba, abba, cdcdee. He almost always ends on a couplet, on which
the poem is often balanced. Some of the songs have a splendid immediacy, notably the fourth song, "Only joy, now here you are,"
where Astrophel, alone with Stella in her house with every one else
in bed and all silent, pleads with her to

> Take me to thee, and thee to me,

and she replies, at the end of each plea,

> No, no, no, no, my dear, let be.

The hushed atmosphere, the passion of the speaker and the lady's
responding love subdued by virtue are admirably captured in a poem
that breaks through the Petrarchan love convention to give us a sudden glimpse of forbidden love in dramatic action.

Sidney's best known sonnet is probably the great repudiation of
human love in favor of divine, "Leave me, O love which reachest but
to dust." This forms no part of the *Astrophel and Stella* series, and is
found among a group of twenty-seven poems from Sidney's manu-

scripts which is included in the 1598 edition of *The Countess of Pembroke's Arcadia* under the title "Certain Sonnets." There are also sonnets and other verses sprinkled throughout the *Arcadia*.

Arcadia, written to amuse his sister, the Countess of Pembroke, is a prose romance interspersed with verses, an odd work to modern eyes, yet in its own way very typical of its age as well as of its author. The original version, known as the *Old Arcadia*, was written in the later 1570's and was not printed until 1926. Sidney revised his original version, adding much new material and altering his method of presentation, but he did not live to complete the revision. The fragmentary revised version was published in 1590, and in 1593 the Countess of Pembroke brought out a text consisting of the new version as far as it went, with the story completed according to the text of the original version. This composite version, though it has long been the accepted one, is obviously a makeshift and is less satisfactory as a literary work than either the *Old Arcadia* or the incomplete revision.

Old Arcadia is a pastoral love story, with a political background, based on Greek romance, that Alexandrian form of literature which dealt episodically with Mediterranean adventure, and regularly included disguises, capture by pirates, infants lost and recovered many years later, mistaken identity, and true love winning in the end. It tells the story of Basilius, king of Arcadia, who retires to rural irresponsibility with his wife and his two daughters, Pamela and Philoclea. Two visiting princes visit Arcadia, and each falls in love with one of the daughters, one disguising himself as a shepherd and the other as an Amazon in order to gain access to Basilius' family. The pursuit of the girls by the disguised lovers is complicated by a variety of circumstances (including the fact that Basilius and his wife both fall in love with the Amazon prince, the former thinking him to be female, the latter penetrating his disguise). The kingdom of Arcadia meanwhile gets into difficulties, and everything is finally disentangled and put in order by Euarchus, model king of Macedonia and father of one of the princes. This involves his condemning both princes for the supposed murder of Basilius, but this misunderstanding is finally cleared up and everything ends happily. The pastoral element in the story is real rather than symbolic: shepherds are introduced because Basilius and his family have retired into the country and are liable to come into contact with shepherds. The shepherds do not stand for ecclesiastical or political or other kinds of character, as they so often do in Renaissance pastoral. The political background of the work is straightforward: Basilius has fallen into culpable weakness, while Euarchus represents the ideal ruler. Against the political background the themes of love (between the princes and the princesses) and friendship (between the two princes and between the two princesses) are worked out with typical Renaissance high idealism and a good deal of equally typical Renaissance subtlety. Though from one point of view a "vain amatorious poem" as Milton called it in a fit of pique after having long known and profited from it, it is also, as Milton conceded, "a book in that kind full of worth and wit" with a serious moral both ethical and political. Ideal love, ideal friendship, and the ideal ruler are, directly and indirectly, discussed, suggested, and embodied.

The revised *Arcadia* introduces considerable complications into the plot and provides Basilius with a wicked sister-in-law, Cecropia, who corrupts her son Amphialus. Cecropia's activities in persecuting Pamela, Philoclea, and one of the princes gives Sidney an excellent opportunity to demonstrate virtue triumphantly resisting every kind of temptation, religion overcoming atheism, true love conquering the cruelest inducements to unfaithfulness, and constancy, fidelity, fortitude, and patience prevailing over every kind of evil persuasion and physical compulsion. The ethical and didactic element is thus considerably heightened in the revised version, and the relatively simple romance of the *Old Arcadia* is overlaid with so much new and more serious matter that the whole character of the work is altered, to become in scope and intention parallel to *The Faerie Queene*. The revised *Arcadia* is a noble work in the fullest sense of the term. Like Spenser's epic, it had as its "general end" the fashioning of "a gentleman or noble person in virtuous and gentle discipline"; both are the work of Protestant Humanists, combining Christian, Platonic, and Renaissance ideals.

The style of the *Arcadia* is highly "conceited," full of elaborate analogies, balanced parenthetical asides, pathetic fallacies, symmetrically answering clauses, and other devices of an immature prose entering suddenly into the world of conscious literary artifice. It has its moments of idyllic simplicity and stylized pastoral charm, and even passages of ironical humor and amused parody, but, on the whole, Sidney's prose in the *Arcadia* (in both versions, but especially in the revised) is a variety of that elaborate rhetorical prose which the Elizabethans often employed in an endeavor to bring the level of their prose artfulness and sophistication up to that of their poetry. John Lyly's *Euphues, The Anatomy of Wit* (1578) and its sequel, *Euphues and his England* (1580), had similarly tried to embellish English prose style. Lyly takes his hero Euphues through a series of adventures and experiences which involve debates on such standard Renaissance themes as youth and age, love and friendship, and other matters of interest to young gentlemen in search of amusement, education, and the idea of the good life. "Euphuism," as Lyly's prose style has since been called, differs in many fundamental respects from the style of Sidney's *Arcadia*, but there is a similarity of intention. Lyly's almost fantastic skill in arranging his sentences in antithetically balanced clauses (with both words and phrases answering to each other); his constant and ingenious parallelisms; his endless plays on words; his mathematically worked out alliteration and cross-alliteration; his comparisons and similes involving mythology and, more often, natural history (parodied by Falstaff in his speech in his own defense, *Henry IV Pt. I*, II, iv: "for though the camomile, the more it is trodden on the faster it grows, so youth, the more it is wasted the sooner it wears"); his frequent introduction of proverbs; and numerous other devices drawn from Renaissance rhetoricians—in these excessive efforts he wearies the reader and demonstrates clearly that Elizabethan prose had not yet grown up. Sidney is less consistent, less extreme, and less mechanical in his use of artifice.

Sidney's other important work is his *Defence of Poesie*, written in the early 1580's and first published in 1595 (in two editions, the other being entitled *An Apologie for Poetrie*). Here, with an ease of manner and grace of style, he answers the Puritan objections to imaginative literature in a series of arguments drawn largely from the Italian Humanist critics. The tone of the essay is that of a gentleman's conversation, and he works easily into his subject, with deliberate *sprezzatura* or nonchalance, by way of a casual discussion of horsemanship. Elizabethan criticism at this time was concerned mostly with practical matters of rhetoric and versification or with attack on or defense of the social influence of the theater. Sidney's is the first attempt in English of any significance to draw together the arguments about the nature, function, possibilities, and future of poetry into a unified critical discussion. Echoes of Aristotle and Horace as filtered through the Italian Renaissance critics can be found throughout the essay, but the tone and the spirit of the discussion are Sidney's own. The antiquity of poetry and its early civilizing function are stressed; the poet is a maker, a creator, who makes "things either better than Nature bringeth forth, or quite anew forms such as never were in Nature." Nature's "world is brasen, the Poets only deliver a golden." By creating a better world than the real world, and by presenting that world in such a persuasive and delightful manner that the reader is "moved" by it to try to embody this ideal world in his own living, poetry proves itself a better moral teacher than either philosophy (which lays down the precepts but does not move the reader to carry them out) or history (which is tied to the fact and can only tell what happened, and what happened is often most unedifying and not likely to lead the reader to virtue). The liveliness of the images which the poets create is contrasted with the dullness of historians and philosophers, and by this insistence on the poet's ability to captivate and move, Sidney provides himself with a theory of form and style. It is not enough for the poet to create a golden world: he must present that golden world in such a way that the reader believes it as he reads and is pleased and moved by it. From this point on he is free to discuss matters of form and style as achieving different degrees of conviction and "moving" in the reader. He goes on to discuss the different species of poetry and their several "excellences," before proceeding to a general account of the objections to poetry, which are dealt with easily enough on the principles he has laid down, with some amusing ironic characterization of the objectors. The essay concludes with an inquiry into the present state of poetry which shows Sidney unexpectedly cautious and precedent-ridden in his practical criticism. But it must be remembered that the essay was written just before the great flowering of Elizabethan literature in Spenser and Shakespeare.

Sir Walter Ralegh was an even more versatile character than Sidney—explorer, navigator, and chemist as well as soldier, courtier, politician, and historian. His poetical work is unequal and fragmentary, much of it remaining in manuscript until centuries after his death. Some of his poems appeared in Elizabethan miscellanies, but it seems certain that more were by him than were ascribed to him there. He has a notable sonnet on Spenser's *Faerie Queene,* in which he tells how Petrarch and Homer were overcome by the arrival of the Fairy Queen; but for the most part his poems lack the fashionable "conceits" of the time and have a masculine vigor of their own. His long *Cynthia* survives only in part in a first draft. It represents the Ocean addressing Cynthia (Queen Elizabeth); it is in alternately rhyming quatrains which lack smoothness but which often possess a rugged forcefulness not easily matched in the period. Some of his moralizing lyrics have a studied simplicity which must be the product of deliberate control:

> Go, soul, the body's guest,
> Upon a thankless arrant.
> Fear not to touch the best;

> The truth shall be thy warrant.
> Go, since I needs must die,
> And give the world the lie. . . .

This is the first stanza of a thirteen-stanza poem, "The Lie," in which every stanza except the last ends with "Give the world the lie." A similar studied simplicity is seen in:

> Give me my scallop-shell of quiet,
> My staff of faith to walk upon,
> My scrip of joy, immortal diet,
> My bottle of salvation,
> My gown of glory, hope's true gage,
> And thus I'll take my pilgrimage. . . .

One has the feeling that Ralegh, like the seventeenth-century Scottish poet the Earl of Montrose (who, like Ralegh, was a soldier and courtier who met death by execution), achieved poetry by sheer strength of character.

Another of Sidney's friends, who had been at school with him and traveled abroad with him, was Fulke Greville, Lord Brooke (1554–1628), courtier, poet, dramatist, Calvinist, Stoic, man of action. If Spenser and Sidney were able to resolve some of the conflicting currents of Renaissance thought, Greville tended to hold them separately in his mind, living in several worlds at once. His poetry and his plays (which followed the stricter Senecan form in protest at what he considered the looseness and triviality of contemporary dramatic practice) reflect a divided mind:

> Oh wearisome condition of humanity!
> Born under one law, to another bound;
> Vainly begot, and yet forbidden vanity;
> Created sick, commanded to be sound.
> What meaneth Nature by these diverse laws,
> Passion and Reason, self-division's cause?

This outburst, from the Chorus of Priests which concludes his play *Mustapha,* is typical of Greville in its sense of conflict. He has not Spenser's confident Platonic idealism, which can surround Christian and Humanist thought with a halo of philosophic optimism and enable him to work out a practical ideal of virtue which combines gentlemanliness with assurance of salvation. Indeed, Spenser's ability to combine notions of gentlemanliness with those of Christian faith and practice, typical though it was of a certain phase of Renaissance thought, looks somewhat odd to modern eyes, and Greville's eyes were surprisingly modern. The unworldly Christian life may be the way to ultimate salvation, and divine Grace the only means by which man can be enabled to lead that life; but life on earth as we know it has its own problems and standards, and if we are to live in the world we must concern ourselves with them. This seems to have been Greville's attitude, and he is thus one of the first figures in English literature for whom the "new philosophy" not only "called all in doubt" but suggested the kind of problem by which Aldous Huxley was tormented in his early novels. (It is significant that Huxley quotes Greville as the epigraph to *Point Counter Point*.) "I know the world and believe in God," Greville once wrote; but he did not know how to reconcile that knowledge with that belief. In practical political affairs he was Machiavellian; in personal ethical matters he was a Stoic; in religious thought he was a Calvinist.

Greville's poetry has thus a somber intellectual quality. His sonnet-sequence *Caelica* contains some powerful and striking poems, none more so than the opening one (which is not a strict sonnet, but a poem of three six-line stanzas):

> Love, the delight of all well-thinking minds;
> Delight, the fruit of virtue dearly loved;
> Virtue, the highest good that reason finds;
> Reason, the fire wherein men's thoughts be proved;
>   Are from one world by Nature's power bereft,
>   And in one creature, for her glory, left.

Or the remarkable Sonnet XXII (again, not a true sonnet):

> I with whose colors Myra drest her head,
> I that wore posies of her own hand making,
> I that mine own name in the chimneys read
> By Myra finely wrought ere I was waking:
>   Must I look on, in hope time coming may
>   With change bring back my turn again to play?
>
> I that on Sunday at the Church-stile found
> A garland sweet, with true-love knots in flowers,
> Which I to wear about mine arm was bound,
> That each of us might know that all was ours:
>   Must I now lead an idle life in wishes?
>   And follow Cupid for his loaves and fishes? . . .
>
> Was it for this that I might Myra see
> Washing the water with her beauties, white?
> Yet would she never write her love to me;
> *Thinks wit of change while thoughts are in delight?*
>   Mad girls must safely love, as they may leave:
>   *No man may print a kiss: lines may deceive.*

The indignant "I's" with which this poem opens, the contrast between simple rustic love and sophisticated betrayal, and the mingling of anger with reflection, give it an impressive immediacy.

Greville's verse treatises (of humane learning, upon fame and honor, and of wars) deal in strenuous though sometimes pedestrian verse with human weakness and pride, while his Senecan verse plays, *Mustapha* and *Alaham*, present the political implications of the human dilemma, the former dealing with imperial power abused, the second with royal weakness exploited. The verse of these plays is often rough and crabbed, and the thought is not adequately put at the service of character in action: the plays are commentaries on human affairs rather than the vivid and lively presentation of stories symbolic of human destiny. They have their magnificent moments, a piece of sad and thoughtful rhetoric or set recital of cogently phrased *sententiae*.

Meanwhile, miscellanies in songbooks poured from the presses, and Elizabethan lyrics of all kinds, fresh and faded, light and heavy, formal and gay, were printed in numerous collections throughout the latter part of the sixteenth and the early seventeenth centuries. It is the contents of these collections that has given the term "Elizabethan lyric" the connotation which it has so long had, and led us—rightly—to think of the middle and latter Elizabethan period as a great age of lyric and song. The improvement in the maturity and confidence of Elizabethan poetry between the poets represented in *Tottel's Miscellany* and the last decade of the century can be seen in the collection entitled *The Phoenix Nest* (1593), compiled by a certain R. S. *The Passionate Pilgrim*, put out by the printer William Jaggard in 1599 as "by W. Shakespeare," is actually a miscellany, with poems by a variety of authors. *England's Parnassus*, *Belvedere*, and *England's Helicon* all appeared in 1600; the last of these is one of the finest anthologies of English poetry ever produced, and contains poems by most of the poets of the middle and latter sixteenth century, including Sidney, Spenser, Drayton, Lodge, Peele, and Shakespeare. It includes poems from older miscellanies (including two from *Tottel*), songs from the madrigal books (a new fashion) and songbooks, and work by poets otherwise little known. The last of the Elizabethan anthologies was *A Poetical Rhapsody* (1602), a large and interesting collection whose second edition (1608) adds hitherto unprinted poems by Sir John Davies, Ralegh, and others, which might well have been lost if they had not been here published from manuscript.

Of the other Elizabethan sonnet-sequences, it can only be said that many of them show considerable skill in the handling of the

convention, but only occasionally does one of these poets rise to
the level of a memorable poem. Compliment, lament, hope, despair,
expressed with every variety of Petrarchan conceit and later development of such conceit, are the commonest themes. We hear Giles
Fletcher addressing his Licia:

> When as her lute is tuned to her voice,
> The air grows proud for honor of that sound,

or Barnaby Barnes complimenting Parthenophe:

> Mistress, behold in this true-speaking glass
> Thy beauty's graces, of all women rarest,

or William Percy complaining of his Coelia:

> Judged by my goddess' doom to endless pain,
> Lo! here I ope my sorrow's passion,

or William Smith's shepherd addressing his Chloris:

> Whole Showers of tears to Chloris I will pour
> As true oblations of my sincere love,

or Alexander Craig sighing for Pandora:

> Go you, O winds that blow from north to south,
> Convey my secret sighs unto my sweet.
> Deliver them from mine unto her mouth,
> And make my commendations till we meet. . . .

And so it goes. Sometimes a new note is struck. Some of the poems
in Barnaby Barnes' *Divine Century of Spiritual Sonnets* are lively
and interesting, with a certain freshness of imagery.

Daniel's sonnets to Delia show a uniformly high level of smoothness and flexibility, and occasionally rise to something more, as in:

> When men shall find thy flower, thy glory, pass,
> And thou, with careful brow sitting alone,
> Receivéd hast this message from thy glass,
> That tells the truth and says that all is gone. . . .

—a variation on a theme of Ronsard's which Yeats was also to use.
and Drayton's *Idea* contains, among many splendid and brilliantly
phrased sonnets, one of the most memorable that the age produced:

> Since there's no help, come let us kiss and part—
> Nay, I have done: you get no more of me;
> And I am glad, yea, glad with all my heart,

That thus so cleanly I myself can free.
Shake hands for ever, cancel all our vows,
But when we meet at any time again,
Be it not seen in either of our brows
That we one jot of former love retain.
Now at the last gasp of love's latest breath,
When, his pulse failing, Passion speechless lies,
When Faith is kneeling by his bed of death,
And Innocence is closing up his eyes,—
> Now, if thou wouldst, when all have given him over,
> From death to life thou might'st him yet recover!

Of Shakespeare's sonnets, perhaps all that need be said is that they are not so obviously or immensely superior to other good Elizabethan sonnets as his plays are to those of his contemporaries and successors, but they *are* superior, and represent a most remarkable achievement; in the unfolding of a dramatic story, in the apt mingling of thought and passion, in the turning of the Petrarchan conceits ironically back on themselves to produce a whole new area of expression, in the bittersweet exploration by means of imagery of the mutations of passion, in the careful balancing of the sonnet on the concluding couplet, which often rings out like a sardonic epigram, and in the sheer mastery of phrase, these sonnets reveal a degree of poetic maturity and subtlety which none of his contemporary sonneteers possessed. At the same time, it should be noted that Shakespeare chose the simplest possible sonnet scheme (*abab, cdcd, efef, gg*) and did not, as both Sidney and Milton in their own ways did, enlarge the potentialities of the sonnet form.

Christopher Marlowe, who is of course better known for his plays and receives fuller discussion in the following chapter, deserves mention among the Elizabethan poets if only for his popular "Passionate Shepherd to His Love" (beginning "Come live with me and be my love"), which appeared in *England's Helicon* and his remarkable narrative poem, *Hero and Leander*. The richness and magnificent flow of this unfinished eight-hundred-word poem, the luxuriant facility with which the story unfolds, is typical of one aspect of Elizabethan poetry. It is too much, really; this easy (or easy-sounding) eloquence requires a more astringent touch to subtilize and mature it; but it is wonderful in its way, and a remarkable technical achievement. The unfinished poem was completed by George Chapman in his more sober and less sensual style, but with considerable power and subtlety. *Hero and Leander* appears to have set a fashion for love stories based on classical mythology. Lodge's *Glaucus and Scylla* (1592), Shakespeare's *Venus and Adonis* (1593), Drayton's *Endimion and Phoebe* (1594), and Marston's *Metamorphosis of Pygmalion's Image* (1598) are later examples of this form. Shakespeare's scintillating exercise in amorous narrative has all of Marlowe's sensuality but has, too, an intellectual quality in its images and "conceits" which provides a greater stiffening than Marlowe's verse possesses. It is a brilliant exercise; and the same can be said of Shakespeare's other narrative poem, *The Rape of Lucrece* (1594), in which he demonstrated that virtue assailed and overcome by lust is as amenable to such treatment as love triumphant.

The emulation of foreign models, which in some degree lay behind these English renderings of classical story (Marlowe's *Hero and Leander* professes to be a paraphrase of a poem by Musaeus), runs right through Elizabethan literature and is responsible for those numerous Tudor and Elizabethan translations, both in prose and in verse, in which the literary language was exercised. Sir Thomas North's translation of Plutarch's *Lives* (1579) made them available to Shakespeare; William Painter's *Palace of Pleasure* (1566, 1567), a rich and varied collection of stories from classical, Italian, and French sources, provided abundant material for the Elizabethan dramatists, and numerous other translations from Latin and from Italian put more and more of the wisdom of the classical world and of Renaissance Humanism within the reach of the literate but unlearned Englishman. Of verse translations, Arthur Golding's rendering in "fourteeners" of Ovid's *Metamorphoses* has at least the merit of fluency, and he brought Ovid's compendium of classical mythology to many who might not otherwise have had access to it. Shakespeare knew Golding's Ovid. Thomas Phaer's *Aeneid* (1583) was also in fourteeners, as was Chapman's *Iliad*, a vigorous and swinging version much more Elizabethan than Homeric in tone. These long lines soon become monotonous, however vigorously handled, and for his translation of the *Odyssey*, Chapman employed rhymed iambic pentameter couplets. Sir John Harington's translation of Ariosto's *Orlando Furioso* (1591), in an *ababbcc* stanza, has verve and flexibility and sometimes achieves an almost Byronic tone; Edward Fairfax's rendering of Tasso's *Gerusalemme Liberata* (*Godfrey of Bulloigne*, 1600), in the same stanza that Harington had used for Ariosto, is a conscientious but on the whole pedestrian performance, though praised by Dryden for the "harmony of its numbers." These are but samples; Elizabethan translations, though not always achieving high literary merit in their own right, both helped to exercise the language and to make available to Elizabethan drama and to Elizabethans in general the riches of classical history and story, of Italian epic, and continental Humanist thought. To read them helps us—no less than an appreciation of such things as the secular pageantry which in large measure replaced medieval church ritual in Elizabethan life—to understand more fully the range and the sources of the Elizabethan imagination.

CHAPTER EIGHT

Drama from the

Miracle Plays to Marlowe

THE MAIN GLORY of English literature in the late sixteenth and early seventeenth century was its poetic drama. English drama before the sixteenth century is of mainly academic and historical interest, though there are occasional plays which possess charm and liveliness. But the early history of English drama, however uninteresting to the literary critic, is of the first importance as illustrating how the instinct for dramatic representation finds its outlets; in addition, it tells us a great deal about the workings of the popular imagination, and it throws some light on the themes and conventions of later drama. The details of the story are not always clear—our picture of the development of medieval drama is dependent on records which are far from complete—but enough material survives to enable us to see the outlines as well as a few remarkable details.

The ultimate origins of all drama are the concern of the anthropologist rather than of the literary historian. Drama and religious ritual seem to have been bound up with each other in the earlier stages of all civilizations; folk celebrations, ritual miming of such elemental themes as death and resurrection, seasonal festivals with appropriate symbolic actions—these lie in the background (sometimes far in the background) of all drama, though a sophisticated literary tradition may go far to obliterate their traces. So far as we can write the history of English drama, it begins with the elaboration of the ecclesiastical liturgy in mutually answering dialogues. Of the other sources—pre-Christian seasonal festivals, St. George and Robin Hood plays, Maypole dances, and similiar folk activities—we can say little more than that they undoubtedly existed. Nor can we establish any continuity between the origins of European drama in the early Middle Ages and the drama of Greece and Rome, which had already run its course by the time the Christian era began and only influenced vernacular European drama after the Renaissance had directed new attention to the literature of the ancient world. The early Church fathers saw Roman acted drama in its last immoral and degenerate phase and understandably condemned it; and even this decadent theater disappeared, with so much else, under the impact of the barbarian invasions of the sixth century. Strolling minstrels and other varieties of itinerant entertainments perhaps preserved for a time some of the traditions of the last phase of the Roman theater, but they eventually became absorbed in the miscellaneous repertory of the profession long before it contributed anything to the vitality of the acting of miracle and morality plays.

The ritual of the Christian Church, with its two great festivals of Christmas and Easter and its celebration of the significant points in Christ's career from birth to resurrection, was itself inherently dramatic. Indeed, the Christian year commemorated more than the career of the founder of Christianity, looking before it to the Annunciation and beyond it to the Ascension. The ceremonies with which these events were commemorated lent themselves naturally to dramatization; from simple antiphonal chanting between priest and choir or two sections of the choir to more elaborate acting out of a scene between two characters or sets of characters was but a step. These "tropes," or dramatic elaborations of part of the liturgy, represent the beginnings of medieval drama. We have a record of an "Easter trope" dating from the early tenth century: this is a Latin dialogue between the three Marys and the Angel at the tomb of Christ, introduced before the introit of the Easter Mass. "Quem quaeritis in sepulchro, Christicolae?" ("Whom do you seek in the sepulcher, Christians?") the Angel asks, and the women reply that they seek the crucified Jesus. "Non est hic," replies the Angel; "surrexit sicut praedixerat; ite, nuntiate quia surrexit de sepulchro." ("He is not here; he has arisen as he said he would; go and announce that he has arisen from the sepulcher.") Bishop Etholwold of Winchester describes the *Quem quaeritis* trope in his *Regularis Concordia* (written about 970) as a dialogue between one sitting holding a palm branch by the sepulcher and three others who enter with censers in their hands, as if seeking something. Later, the trope received additions and elaborations, with more characters added. Other simple plays representing other phases of the life of Christ followed the same model. A play bringing the shepherd to the crib of the infant was introduced at Christmas. An Epiphany play introduced the three kings and a mechanical star. A Passion play developed but, surprisingly enough, not (as far as we know) until the thirteenth century. The liturgy, biblical story, and other varieties of Christian literature contribute to the development of other simple plays with characters from both the New Testament and the Old.

The trope thus grew into the liturgical drama, which was fully developed in the twelfth century. So far they were in Latin, as the liturgy was, but as they increased in popularity and indeed tended to overshadow the original devotional ritual of the feast-days, vernacular elements began to appear. At the same time the elaboration of the plays made it difficult to confine the performance to the choir where, like their liturgical sources, they had originally been spoken, and the performance therefore extended down the nave, using appropriate parts of the church building as rudimentary properties. Finally, it moved out of the church altogether, first into the churchyard and then into the marketplace or a convenient meadow. Once outside the church, the vernacular ousted Latin and the story element moved away from the liturgy to make free use of the whole range of sacred history from the Creation to the Last Judgment. Liturgical drama, acted within the church as embellishment of ecclesiastical ritual, thus gave way to plays in English, performed in the open and completely divorced from the liturgy though still religious in subject-matter. These are known as "miracle plays." It is at this stage that elements from minstrel performances and older folk festivals begin to come in and provide new vitality for a drama whose primary function is now quite simply entertainment.

It is impossible to document adequately the transition from liturgical drama to miracle play, but we have three fragmentary Anglo-Norman miracle plays dating from the twelfth century and we know that in 1244 Robert Grosseteste, Bishop of Lincoln, ordered his archdeacons to stamp out the performance of miracle plays by clerks and that some sixty years later William of Wadington, in his *Manuel des Pechiez*, distinguished between plays about Christ's burial and Resurrection acted modestly as part of the Church service, which he approved, and miracle plays, which he denounced as sinful folly. Miracle plays must have developed rapidly in the thirteenth century; there are records of cycles of miracle plays in many regions of England during the fourteenth and fifteenth centuries and well into the sixteenth.

These cycles of plays were developed by extending the themes of liturgical drama both backward and forward, to include the

Creation, the Fall, and early Old Testament story at one end and Doomsday at the other. Once out of doors, the presentation of plays could not be indifferent to the seasons; so that they were no longer acted at the different church festivals. The establishment of the feast of Corpus Christi (falling in May or June) in 1264, confirmed in 1311, provided a suitable day for the acting of miracle plays, though some cities preferred Whitsun. Corpus Christi Day was suitable not only because of the time of the year when it fell but also because, being a processional observance with the Host carried about and displayed at various stations, it proved naturally hospitable to dramatic performances, which were generally given on wagons (known as "pageants")—stages on wheels which went from one station to another. Each "pageant" presented a different scene of the cycle, and the wagons followed each other, repeating their scenes at successive stations. With the plays no longer associated with ecclesiastical ritual, their organizing and financing passed into lay hands. It was the trade guilds—important in so many ways in the social and economic life of the Middle Ages—that took over the sponsoring of the plays (which were probably written by some local cleric). Each guild would make itself responsible for a wagon with its scene, which involved considerable effort and expense. Though a wagon stage could not be more than primitive by modern standards, considerable ingenuity was shown in the arrangement of the superstructure and of the stage properties.

Almost complete cycles of miracle plays survive from Chester, York, and Wakefield; two plays from the Coventry cycle survive, in late and corrupt texts; and we have also a Noah play from Newcastle, a play on the creation of Eve and the expulsion from the Garden of Eden from Norwich, and an Abraham and Isaac play (dealing with the sacrifice of Isaac) which has been preserved at Brome Manor in Norfolk. There is also a cycle of forty-two plays generally known as *Ludus Coventriae*, though they have nothing to do with Coventry, which seems from its dialect to have come from a town in East Anglia. All this represents but a small fragment of the large number of cycles of miracle plays produced by the trade guilds of the different towns of England, but what remains is sufficient to give us some idea of what these plays were like.

The Chester cycle contains twenty-five plays, beginning with the Fall of Lucifer and ending with Doomsday: it includes plays dealing with the Creation, the Fall, Noah, Cain and Abel, Abraham and Isaac, Balaam and Balak (with Balaam's ass); a group on the life of Christ beginning with the Annunciation and ending with the Ascension, and including a Nativity, a shepherds' play (*Pastores*), a Slaughter of the Innocents, a Raising of Lazarus, a play dealing with a number of events from the entry into Jerusalem to the conspiracy of Judas, a Last Supper and Betrayal, a Passion play, a Harrowing of Hell, and a Resurrection play with the *Quem quaeritis*. The plays are written in an eight-line stanza with *rime couée*, derived from the Romances (the shorter fourth and eight lines rhyming with each other, and lines one to three and four to seven rhyming). The development of the dialogue and action is naïve enough, with the story presented in simple outline. There are a few realistic touches, but they are slight compared with what some later miracle plays do with such characters as Noah's wife, Balaam's ass, and the midwives at the Nativity. The York plays are probably later; forty-eight survive out of an original cycle of fifty-four. Four groups have been distinguished within the cycle. Eighteen plays seem to be earlier than the others; they are fairly crude and simply didactic in tone; twelve of them are written in a twelve-line stanza divided into an octave and a quatrain, and the other six in four or eight-line stanzas. These earlier and less interesting plays include an Adam and Eve, a Building of the Ark, an Abraham and Isaac, Exodus, Annunciation, *Pastores*, Three Kings, Christ disputing with the Doctors (*Doctores*), Lazarus, Last Supper, Passion, Pentecost, Assumption, and Last Judgment, though this last may belong to a later group. A second group, by an author distinguished by his metrical skill—the verse is clearly differentiated from that of the other plays in the York cycle and shows the influence of the alliterative revival—includes some revisions of plays in the earlier group as well as new plays. In this group belong the Fall of Lucifer, the Death of Christ, the Death of the Virgin, the Resurrection, and others. The revisions and new work of this metrically skilled author apparently date from the very early fifteenth century, and to the same period belongs the work of a third York author or authors, who introduced elements of realistic humor into the plays dealing with Noah and with the Shepherds. Finally, a little later than these, there is the work of an author who had a more powerful dramatic sense than any of the others: he apparently revised the Passion play, where his hand is clearly discernible in the heightened tension, and he handled also the Conspiracy of Judas, the Agony in the Garden, the Betrayal, and the Condemnation. This writer has a real feeling for character (he has a fine portrait of Pilate, for example), though his metrics are confused and he has a tendency to splutter.

The Wakefield cycle contains thirty-two plays (sometimes known as the Towneley Plays because the manuscript was once owned by the Towneley family). These deal with the usual themes, though there are some gaps. The literary merit of the Wakefield plays is higher than that of any of the other cycles which have survived. The stanzas are handled with some assurance, there is an occasional note of real poetry, and in five of the plays there is a lively ironic humor and realistic characterization that show a sense of comedy and of satire to a degree unparalleled in any other existing miracle plays. Among these plays are a Noah and two shepherd plays (the *Prima Pastorum* and the *Secunda Pastorum*). The story of Noah is treated as broad realistic comedy, with Noah's wife portrayed as a talkative shrew who refuses to enter the ark. In the shepherd plays there is much talk of the oppression of rustic laborers by rich landlords and sharp, realistic painting of the lives of the poor. The *Secunda Pastorum* includes a lively comic episode which is an irreverent anticipation of the actual Nativity: Mak steals a sheep and brings it home to his wife, who puts it in a cradle so that it will appear to be a new-born baby. When the shepherds come in, looking for the stolen sheep, they find nothing but two empty platters and a baby in its cradle. They leave, but one of them returns to give the baby a sixpence. He bends over the baby to kiss him and—"What the devil is this? He has a long snout." Mak's fraud is discovered, and the three shepherds toss him in a sheet, and then leave. Then they hear an angel singing of the divine birth, and they go to the stable to find the infant Jesus. The language throughout is full of verve, and the story is presented against a sharply etched background of fifteenth-century rural life. The "Wakefield Master," as the anonymous author of the five outstanding Wakefield plays has been called, is the first English writer of realistic comedy. His main inspiration was clearly the realistic *fabliau* and his own observation rather than the Bible or the liturgy.

Revisions and additions make the text of the *Ludus Coventriae* as we have it somewhat confusing; the literary interest of the plays is confined to some short passages of lyrical or dramatic vitality. More interesting is the Brome Manor Abraham and Isaac, which, in spite of its doggerel verse, has more than the simple pathos of some other versions of the story: the characters of father and son, with the former's anguish of mind and the latter's childish trustfulness, are presented with some force. The two surviving Coventry plays are fragments of a New Testament cycle; a series of revisions has left the text in a state of metrical chaos. The Newcastle Noah, dealing with the building of the ark, has its moments of liveliness, though nothing as humorous as the Wakefield or even the York Noahs. Other surviving miracle plays include one dealing with the conversion of Saint Paul and one on Saint Mary Magdalen.

While the miracle plays were still in their heyday, another medieval dramatic form emerged, a form which has more direct links with Elizabethan drama. This is the morality play, which differs from the miracle play in that it does not deal with biblical or pseudo-biblical story but with personified abstractions of virtues and vices, who struggle for man's soul. The *psychomachia*, the battle for the soul, was a common enough medieval theme and intimately bound up with the whole development of medieval allegory. The allegorical habit of mind was so dominant in the Middle Ages that it is hardly surprising to see it emerging in the drama. The morality play handles the subjects that were most popular among medieval preachers and draws considerably on contemporary homiletic technique. The theme of the seven deadly sins was a commonplace of medieval art and literature as well as of the pulpit, and the notion of Mercy and Peace pleading before God for man's soul against Truth and Righteousness, which developed in the twelfth century, also played its part. There are references to morality plays in the fourteenth century (the earliest is to a "Pater Noster" play, which was apparently a treatment of the conflict between the seven deadly sins and the seven cardinal virtues), but the fifteenth century seems to be the period of its full development. A theme almost as common as the struggle of virtues and vices over man's soul is the "Dance of Death," also a common medieval motif, which treats of Death, God's messenger, coming to summon all, high and low alike: it is a dramatic rendering of the *ubi sunt* theme which figures so largely in the literature of the Middle Ages. In the earliest extant morality play, known as *The Pride of Life*, a king, *Rex vivus*, boasts of his power and freedom of action, refuses advice to think of his latter end, and disports himself with Mirth. A bishop reproves him, but the king dismisses him with abuse and sends Mirth to proclaim defiance of Death. This is as far as the existing fragmentary text goes, but we know from the prologue that at the end Death claims the king and his soul goes to the Devil, to be redeemed finally by the prayers of Our Lady.

The earliest complete extant morality play is *The Castle of Perseverance*, written probably about 1425, a relatively elaborate affair with thirty-four characters: the theme is the fight between Mankind's Good Angel and his supporters and his Bad Angel supported by the Seven Deadly Sins, and the action takes Man (*Humanum Genus*) from his birth to the Day of Judgment. *Mundus* (the world) claims Man's first allegiance, with Folly and Lust acting as Man's servants. The struggle goes this way and that; and at the end of the first part the Good Angel, aided by Shrift and Penitence, rescues Man from the Vices and lodges him in the Castle of Perseverance, which is then besieged by the Vices. At first the Virtues are victorious, but Covetyse seduces man afterward, and finally Death comes for him, and he has to leave all his worldly goods behind. Mercy, Peace, Truth, and Righteousness, the Four Daughters of God, dispute over Man's salvation before God's throne, and the play ends with God's reminder that "king, kaiser, knight and champion, Pope, patriarch, priest and prelate" must all answer at the great Judgment. An extant diagram shows that the play was staged in a ring in the center of which was a "castle" and round it five "scaffolds" for *Deus, Caro* (the flesh), *Mundus*, Belial, and Covetyse.

The Castle of Perseverance is one of three plays found in the Macro MS; of the other two, dating from the mid-fifteenth century, one has no title in the text, but is generally known as *Wisdom*, and the other is *Mankind*. In the former, the five Wits (i.e., senses), together with Mind, Will, and Understanding, are attacked by Lucifer in the guise of a worldly gallant. Lucifer convinces Mind, Will, and Understanding of the advantages of the worldly life, and a great number of personified vices are introduced to show them in their evil conduct—Mind led into sins of violence and oppression, Understanding to dishonesty, and Will to sensuality, all of which are represented by dances, in which the appropriate vices take part. After further developments, Mind, Understanding, and Will, together with the five Wits and Anima (the soul), are brought to repentance by Wisdom: the regeneration of Anima concludes the play. *Mankind* shows the hero, Mankind, urged to good works by Mercy and tempted into vice by Mischief and a group of representatives of the worldly life. The latter characters engage in coarse language and horseplay, and the play as a whole is characterized by the mingling of coarse comic elements with the serious morality. In the end Mankind is saved by Merey, who speaks the epilogue. Both the plays are in stanzaic verse.

The best known and in many ways the most appealing of surviving fifteenth-century morality plays is *Everyman*. Here the action is developed with a simple dignity and the personified abstractions play their part with forceful dramatic logic. Everyman is summoned by Death to a long journey from which there is no return. Unprepared, and unable to gain a respite, he looks for friends to accompany him, but neither Fellowship nor Goods nor Kindred will go; Good Deeds is willing to act as guide and companion, but Everyman's sins have rendered her too weak to stand. She recommends him to her sister Knowledge, who leads Everyman to Confession, and after he has done penance Good Deeds grows strong enough to accompany him, together with Strength, Discretion, Five Wits, and Beauty. But as the time comes for Everyman to creep into his grave, all the companions except Good Deeds decline to go with him. Knowledge stands by to report the outcome while Everyman enters the grave with Good Deeds. An angel announces the entry of Everyman's soul "into the heavenly sphere," and a "Doctor" concludes by pointing the moral. The play appears to have some relation to the Dutch morality play, *Elckerlijk*, and may be a translation of it. The verse form is naïve rhymed couplets, often effective in their very naïveté.

Toward the end of the fifteenth century there developed a type of morality play which dealt in the same allegorical way with general moral problems, though with more pronounced realistic and comic elements. This kind of play is known as the Interlude, though that name is also given to some much earlier secular moralities, such as the fragmentary thirteenth-century *Interludium de Clerico et Puella*, which is based on the *fabliau* of Dame Siriz, and the equally fragmentary *Dux Moraud* which preserves the speeches of the title character in a strange story of incest, murder, and repentance. These earlier "interludes" are perhaps not to be regarded as morality plays at all, but as dramatized versions of *fabliaux*. But the later kind of interlude, the secular morality play, develops its comic and realistic side and by the sixteenth century comes to include scenes far removed from the theme and atmosphere of the medieval morality. It is perhaps simplest to use the term *interlude*, whatever its origins and varying earlier uses—the term perhaps originally denoted a playlet performed between the courses of a banquet—as it is now employed by literary historians to denote those plays which mark the transition from medieval religious drama to Tudor secular drama. It is difficult to document that transition adequately, because so many of the texts have not survived. But there does seem to have been a continuous dramatic tradition, with the simple native drama absorbing foreign influences to become more secular and more sophisticated. Particularly significant is the development of the character known as "the Vice" from that of a diabolic tempter to a purely comic figure.

In Henry Medwall's *Fulgens and Lucres*, at the very end of the fifteenth century, we have the earliest extant purely secular play in English. Medwall had already written a morality play, *Nature*, of a more sophisticated kind than earlier moralities, and the transition from that kind of play to one with a "romantic" love interest must have seemed less significant at the time than it appears to later historians. Medwall was one of a group of early Tudor playwrights associated with the household of Cardinal Morton and thus with Sir Thomas More, who was known for his interest in amateur dramatics when he was a page in Morton's household. Medwall was at one time the Cardinal's chaplain. John Rastell (ca. 1470–1536) who printed *Fulgens and Lucres* and wrote plays himself, married More's sister, while John Heywood (ca. 1497–ca. 1580), the most important dramatist of the group, married their daughter, More's niece. The More-Heywood group of Tudor dramatists thus spanned two generations; its work bridges medieval and Elizabethan drama.

Fulgens and Lucres derives from a Latin short story by the Italian humanist Bonaccorso, which tells how Lucretia, daughter of the Roman senator Fulgentius, is wooed by a rich and worldly aristocrat and by a poor but virtuous man. She refers them to her father, who puts the choice between the two suitors up to the Senate, before whom each of the suitors pleads his cause. The story had already been translated into English by John Tiptoft, Earl of Worcester, and in turning it into a play Medwall very properly takes the decision away from the Senate and gives it to the girl (whom he calls Lucres). She chooses the poor but virtuous suitor. There is thus a morality element in the story, though it is not stressed. Medwall made a more significant change than this: he added a comic subplot, in which the servants of the two suitors are rivals for the love of Lucres's maid. This subplot parallels the main story on a lower and comic level, and is thus an early example of a tradition of mingling serious with comic scenes in English drama that was to become characteristic of the Elizabethan play and reach its highest point of development in Shakespeare. In his epilogue Medwall explains that his purpose was both to edify and to amuse. The verse form of the play varies between rhyme royal and, in the comic scenes, a shorter-lined stanza.

John Rastell's interlude, *The Nature of the Four Elements*, published anonymously early in the sixteenth century, is what might be called a Humanist morality play: various allegorical characters instruct Humanity in the new science and geography, with interesting reference to recent geographical discoveries. There are the usual low-life scenes with the Vices. Another Humanist morality play is John Redford's *Wit and Science*, dating probably from the 1530's. Wit, a student, seeks to marry Science, daughter of Reason and Experience, and before doing so must conquer the giant Tediousness and make a pilgrimage to Mount Parnassus. His adventures with these and other allegorical characters, good and bad, illustrate the ideals and difficulties of education as conceived by Redford. This emphasis on education (as distinct from salvation) clearly distinguished the Humanist interlude from its medieval predecessor. We have reached the age of secular plays written by schoolmasters and other educated laymen for purposes of entertaining and instruction.

John Heywood's interludes were often written as part of an evening's entertainment at a nobleman's house, and the emphasis is more on amusement than instruction. *Witty and Witless* and *The Play of Love* are lively debates between types; *The Play of the Weather* is an amusing presentation of how Jupiter sends round Merry-Report to find out what weather people want, and each person asked, because of his different occupation and interests, wants a different kind of weather (e.g., the water miller wants plenty of rain and no wind, the wind miller wants wind and less rain, the hunting gentlemen wants it "dry and not misty, the wind calm and still," and the schoolboy wants snow to make snowballs). Jupiter's decision is to leave things as they are, and everyone will get his share of his favorite weather. The moral here is slight, but it is there, reminding us of the older morality out of which the brief and lively Tudor interlude grew. In *The Play Called the Four PP*, a palmer, a pardoner, apothecary (quack doctor), and a pedlar introduce themselves, quarrel, and eventually agree that three of them should hold a lying competition with the pedlar as judge. The apothecary tells a bawdy tale of a marvelous cure, and the pardoner then tells in vivid detail how he visited Hell to find a neighbor, one Margery Corson; Lucifer and his comrades are only too glad to get rid of the woman, who is an insufferable shrew, and asks the pardoner to see to it (as he can in the course of his profession) that no more women come to Hell. The palmer, calmly accepting the detailed account of the visit to Hell, merely remarks that he fails to understand the part about women being shrewish and difficult, for he has never seen or known "any one woman out of patience." This thundering lie at once wins the competition. *A Merry Play between Johan Johan the husband, Tyb his wife, and Sir Johan the Priest* is on the ancient theme of the meek husband, the shrewish and unfaithful wife, and the wife's lover, a priest. The whole play is pure farce, knock-about domestic comedy, with no pretence at edification. Heywood's art thus matures into something resembling the modern music-hall or vaudeville sketch; drawing on a great variety of sources, both native and foreign, for his plots, he produced amusing dramatic anecdotes. The plots are rudimentary; he showed no sign of being able to contrive a sustained piece of dramatic structure; even his best pieces must thus be called sketches rather than comedies.

The shift of interest from salvation to education, which has already been noted as marking a distinction between the medieval morality play and the Tudor interlude, was accompanied by a parallel shift from religion to politics. And when religion *is* treated, it is treated in the spirit of controversy produced by the Reformation and the great debate about the true form of Christianity which raged throughout the Tudor period and later. Such controversial or propagandist morality plays inevitably abandoned the large universal moral and religious themes of the older moralities and were liable to make the vices into representatives of a degenerate Catholicism. John Bale (1495–1563) wrote a number of Protestant propagandist plays, one of them, *King Johan,* being at the same time a history play (of sorts): its hero is King John, who is treated as a Christian hero who defied the Pope in the interests of an independent Bible-reading England. Abstractions and historical figures are curiously mingled in *King Johan.* The situation is confused by the fact that the play survives only in a much revised form, but the movement to and fro between an historical and allegorical treatment of the characters seems to be an integral part of the play's method. Thus Usurped Power, Sedition, Dissimulation, Commonalty, Nobility, Clergy, and Civil Order are characters, some of whom at times become historical figures (Usurped Power, for example, being the Pope and Dissimulation Archbishop Stephen Langton). This play can in a sense be called the first English history play, but it is history treated in a very special way, and *King Johan* is thus not to be taken as an early example of the Elizabethan chronicle history play, which will be considered later. Bale's other plays include three on biblical themes in the manner of the miracle plays and one using allegorical figures in the morality tradition: all are strongly Protestant in tone.

The ethico-political theme preceded Reformation controversy in English drama. Skelton's *Magnificence* (ca. 1515), aimed at Cardinal Wolsey, shows the rise, fall, and final repentance of a worldly prince who is seduced and in the end redeemed by allegorical figures representing different virtues and vices. Though it ends on a conventional religious note, its main lesson is not that of the medieval moralities but rather the Aristotelian virtue of measure, or moderation—a Humanist rather than a Christian virtue. The treatment of ethical and political themes is closely bound up with the Renaissance interest in education, particularly the education of princes, and in Skelton's *Magnificence* and Bale's *King Johan* we can see the tendency to present such subjects through the lives of individuals which is reflected in such a work as the *Mirror for Magistrates*. But once dramatic interest is focused on an individual, whether as an awful warning or as an example of the fall of princes, the possibilities of more exciting and more profound exploration of human fate are likely to suggest themselves, and in the end we arrive at new conceptions of both comedy and tragedy. The political, ethical, and religious moralities of the early Tudor period, insofar as they led on occasion from allegorical personification of virtues and vices to the presentation of the fate of a single historical character, do represent, however faintly, a movement toward greater dramatic maturity.

But the movement is not one of simple chronological development. Allegorical, biblical, and historical morality plays existed side by side in the middle of the sixteenth century. *Respublica*, perhaps by Nicholas Udall, was first performed in 1553; it mingles the older kind of religion with new political themes. A decade later, plays which handled biblical stories from a Protestant propagandist point of view (under the influence of Bale) seem to have been popular. At the same time classical influences were making themselves felt, providing new themes and a new sense of structure. Nicholas Udall, at one time headmaster of Eton and at the end of his life headmaster of Westminster, wrote *Ralph Roister Doister* about 1553, taking its theme from the *Miles Gloriosus* of the Roman playwright Plautus, thus bringing the braggart soldier for the first time into English drama. Roister Doister is the braggart who courts Dame Custance, a lady of some fortune already engaged to Gawin Goodluck. His servant Matthew Merrygreek is both the "parasite" of Latin comedy and the Vice of the morality plays. (The Vice in the moralities had long since developed into a clowning practical joker.) Roister Doister's fatuous courtship, continually prompted but never really helped by Merrygreek, ends with his defeat at the hands of Dame Custance and her lively maids. Everything ends happily, with reconciliation all round. The plot is simple enough, but it does include a complication and a resolution and thus shows a firmer grasp on structure than had yet been displayed in an English comedy. *Gammer Gurton's Needle* was written by "Mr. S.," probably William Stevenson of Christ's College, Cambridge, a few years later, and produced at the College. Here again Plautine themes and characters are domiciled in a comedy of English rural life. The plot is crude: it concerns Gammer Gurton's loss of her needle, out of which a variety of complications develop until the needle is accidentally discovered sticking in the seat of Hodge's breeches (Hodge is Gammer

Gurton's farm servant). But the construction, in five acts, is ingenious and effective and the low-life comedy genuinely amusing. Diccon the Bedlam, the central comic figure of the play, again combines medieval Vice and classical parasite, but he is a thoroughly English character for all that. The verse form is primitive—rhyming "fourteeners"—but the accent of conversation gets through with remarkable vitality. Verse was still the regular medium for English plays, often doggerel yet also often surprisingly lively. It was not until George Gascoigne produced his play *Supposes* at Gray's Inn in 1566 that prose made its appearance in English drama. Gascoigne's play is another comedy adapted from a foreign source, this time from the Italian, Ariosto's *Gli Suppositi*, though Ariosto himself was indebted to Plautus. The plot concerns a student and his faithful and ingenious servant managing by disguise and intrigue to outwit the older generation so that the student finally gets his girl; before the witty confusions produced by the behavior of the hero and his servant are finally cleared up, there is such a muddle of suppositions and countersuppositions on all sides that the play almost explodes in a riot of misunderstanding. This is a much more sophisticated piece of work than *Ralph Roister Doister* or *Gammer Gurton's Needle:* its Italianate subtleties and its extraordinary plays on words are far removed from the bluff humors of English rustic comedy or domestic farce. Gascoigne's play reminds us that the native popular tradition of English drama was now to be modified both by classical influences and by the tastes of more sophisticated audiences at the Inns of Court, the universities, the country houses of noble patrons, and the Court of Queen Elizabeth. *Supposes* is the first of a series of witty Italianate comedies in English which includes Shakespeare's *Taming of the Shrew* (which draws on Gascoigne for its subplot), *The Two Gentlemen of Verona*, and *Much Ado about Nothing*, in which the *genre* reaches its climax.

We have already noted how Humanist influence showed itself in the educational and ethical interests of the Tudor interludes, and we have noticed, too, the domesticating of themes from Plautus in English comedy. It was inevitable that Humanist interest in the Latin and Greek classics should also produce a new kind of English tragedy. There were no tragedies, of course, among either the miracle or the morality plays; indeed, there was nothing that could be called tragedy in English drama before the classical influence made itself felt. The favorite classical writer of tragedies among English Humanists was not Sophocles or Euripides but Seneca, the Stoic Roman, whose nine tragedies, never meant to be acted, adapted the old Greek myths to produce violent yet somber treatments of murder, cruelty, and lust. (They were translated into English by Jasper Heywood and others in the mid-sixteenth century.) Written in a polished yet monotonous verse, Seneca's tragedies combine powerful rhetoric, Stoic moralizing, and horror; the emotional crises are punctuated by epigrams; the characters are not subtly drawn but are carried along by the violence of their emotions: altogether they present a strange mixture of sophistication and crudeness (suggesting the rather exhibitionist work of a bright young man), and were certainly no happy model for a young drama moving at last toward some concept of tragedy.

But Senecan tragedy was, in its own way, ordered and concentrated. English attempts to handle classical themes in the native way can be seen in Richard Edwards' *Damon and Pythias* (played in 1564) which handles the famous story of friendship with an extraordinary combination of fooling and moralizing. John Pickering's *New Interlude of Vice Containing the History of Horestes* (printed in 1567), tells the story of Orestes' revenge on his mother and Aegisthus ("Egestus") with a remarkable mixture of military violence ("make your battle lively," says a direction to the players), allegorical action with the Vice acting as both clown and tempter, and realistic English characters. A similar combination is found in *Apius and Virginia* by "R.B." (printed in 1575 and described on the title page as "a new tragical comedy") and in Thomas Preston's *Cambises* (ca. 1570), which is described as "a lamentable tragedy, mixed full of pleasant mirth." These are typical of a group of plays produced in the 1560's and 1570's and still popular in Shakespeare's day. The lumbering "fourteeners," with their padding and repetitive rhetoric, were mocked by Shakespeare both in the play given by Bottom and his companions in *A Midsummer Night's Dream* and in Falstaff's "for I must speak in passion, and I will do it in King Cambyses' vein" in *Henry IV, Part I*.

Sir Philip Sidney, in his *Defence of Poesie*, objected strenuously to this sort of thing, and approved only the Senecan tragedy *Gorboduc*, by Thomas Sackville and Thomas Norton, produced both at Inner Temple and before the Queen at Whitehall in 1561–62. "Our tragedies and comedies (not without cause cried out against), observing rules neither of honest civility nor of skilful poetry, excepting *Gorboduc*, . . . which notwithstanding, as it is full of stately speeches and well sounding phrases, climbing to the height of Seneca his style and as full of notable morality which it doth most delightfully teach." And again, after complaining that the English plays move freely from place to place and jump long periods of time, he continues: "But besides these gross absurdities, how all their

plays be neither right tragedies nor right comedies, mingling
kings and clowns, not because the matter so carryeth it, but thrust
in clowns by head and shoulders to play a part in majestical matters,
with neither decency nor discretion. So as neither the admiration and
commiseration, nor the right sportfulness, is by their mongrel tragicomedy obtained." Sidney was not merely pedantically defending
the "unities" of time and place and action on which the Renaissance
Italian critics had so insisted (deriving the notion of unity of action
from Aristotle's *Poetics* and expanding it to insist that plays should
represent action as taking place in a single locality and during a
single day); he was voicing a very natural exasperation with the
complete lawlessness of native English drama. Shakespeare was to
discipline this in his own way, and show the potentialities of the
native tradition; but Sidney, writing in the early 1580's, could only
hail the dreary Senecan *Gorboduc* as a herald of better things.

Gorboduc (also known as *Ferrex and Porrex*) is a tale of a divided
kingdom, civil war, and the awful consequences of split authority in a
state, which takes its plot from that mythical region of early English
history which the Tudor chroniclers regarded as fact and which Spenser occasionally used in *The Faerie Queene* and Shakespeare drew on
in *King Lear*. It is divided into five acts: it follows the classical manner
in avoiding violence on the stage; and it is written in a wooden blank
verse. It is sententious, rhetorical, and supremely dull. Though
historically important as the first English play in blank verse and as
an attempt at a purely "regular" form of tragedy which proved to
have no real future in England, it is a play which nobody today
would read for pleasure. There were imitations of *Gorboduc*, including *Jocasta*, by Gascoigne and Francis Kinwelmersh, presented
at Gray's Inn in 1566, and *Gismond of Salern* (later revised as
Tancred and Gismund), with a plot from the *Decameron*, which was
first written in rhymed verse and then rewritten "according to the
decorum of these days" in blank verse by Robert Wilmot. They too
are "regular" and sententious and dull. The fashion remained popular
for some time among certain "highbrow" groups, but no major
dramatist ever wrote this kind of neoclassic play in Elizabethan
England and, however the literary scene may have looked to Sidney
in 1580, English drama was not to go that way.

From church to churchyard to "stations" in the town; from ecclesiastical auspices to those of town guilds; from amateur clerical
authorship to professional authorship and professional acting—this
was the progress of English drama from the early medieval period to
Tudor times. At the same time the schools, the Inns of Court, the
universities, houses of noblemen, and the Queen's Court provided

opportunities for more sophisticated or more learned plays than were possible in the more public entertainments given by itinerant players in town innyards or on village greens. Nicholas Udall was a schoolmaster who wrote plays for his boys to act; and it was common enough in schools which had come under Humanist influence to have the boys act Plautus or Terence in Latin as part of their education. *Gorboduc, Jocasta,* and *Gismond of Salern* were first presented at Inns of Court. Latin comedies, derived largely from the Italian, were popular at Cambridge in the 1580's. It was at Cambridge, too, that *Gammer Gurton's Needle* was first acted, and that university also produced at the turn of the century a series of academic comedies about scholars, their way of life, and their prospects. Meanwhile, Oxford was producing Senecan tragedies in Latin.

As, with the progress of the sixteenth century, drama became more abundant and more various, professionalization developed both among authors and among actors. Some groups of actors were independent companies plying their trade where they could and doing so for their own profit. Others were servants of some wealthy nobleman and were under his protection. In 1583, Queen Elizabeth's Master of the Revels decided to form a company of players for the direct service of the Queen, and accordingly picked a number from among the companies attached to different noblemen—the Earls of Sussex, of Leicester, and of Oxford, among others—to form the Queen's men. This was perhaps a move on the part of the Court to defeat the claims of the Corporation of the City of London to control plays and players in the area under their jurisdiction. The Corporation shared some of the Puritan objections to the acted drama, and in addition, consisting as it did of employers of labor in the City, it objected to employees and apprentices being seduced by plays from their work. The opposition between the City and the stage had been developing steadily in the 1570's. In 1576, James Burbage, leader of the Earl of Leicester's men, had erected the first permanent theater (called simply the Theatre) on a field near Shoreditch, outside the City boundaries and so beyond the control of the Lord Mayor and Corporation. The Corporation kept restricting and even forbidding plays, but, with the Court on the players' side, they fought a losing battle. Other permanent theaters soon followed the Theatre—the Curtain, also in Shoreditch, in 1577, one at Newington Butts about 1580, the Rose, on the south bank of the Thames, about 1588, the Swan in Southwark about 1595, and the Globe in 1598. These theaters were built by companies of players who had begun as itinerant "vagabonds" but who were all now servants, theoretically at least, of noblemen, wearing their livery and free of the legal penalties of vagabondage. The structure of the theaters derived from the innyards which had served as their predecessors. They were round or octagonal, with the pit (or yard) open to the sky. Tiers of covered galleries ran round the yard, except for the section occupied by the stage, which was a large platform jutting well out into the yard and divided into an outer stage and an inner stage behind, which could be curtained off. Above the inner stage was the "upper stage," a gallery over which, supported by columns on the main stage, a thatched roof projected. Though costumes were often elaborate, properties were few and scenery in the modern sense nonexistent: the whole burden fell on speech and action. This platform stage of the Elizabethans must be clearly distinguished from the later picture-frame stage with its scenes "realistically" localized by means of a painted backcloth as well as from the more elaborate modern attempts to build up a complete illusion of physical realism on the stage. The Elizabethan stage was in essence a platform which could symbolically represent any place: it was up to the dramatist to create the proper illusion by his language. Often it was not necessary for the scene to be precisely localized at all. There were no actresses: boys took women's parts.

These were the public theaters; in addition there were "private" theaters, distinguished from the others by being roofed and by somewhat more complicated interior arrangements. They also charged rather more. The private theaters were originally used by child actors, drawn from the choirs of St. Paul's and the Chapel Royal. The first private theater was the Blackfriars, opened in 1576 for the children of the Chapel Royal, and we find it a few years later used by boy actors from other choirs as well (and in 1609-10 by Shakespeare's company). These boys, who were highly trained professionals, acted in more scholarly plays in the Humanist tradition with somewhat more elaborate staging than was employed in the public theaters. At times, they became serious rivals to the adult companies, as Shakespeare's reference in *Hamlet* to "an aery of children, little eyases, that cry out on the top of question, and are most tyrannically clapped for 't" makes clear.

There was thus the public theater, which produced popular plays appealing to all tastes; the private theater, where players, often boys, put on more sophisticated pieces for a more sophisticated audience; and the Court itself, as well as the halls of individual noblemen, where many kinds of entertainments, including plays, were produced to celebrate such occasions as visits by foreign notables, weddings, coronations, royal and other distinguished marriages, and visits by the Queen to different cities or country houses. The Court—which had had a permanent Master of the Revels since 1545—also put on entertainments at such festive seasons as Christmas, New Year, Twelfth Night, and Shrovetide, and could call on professional or semiprofessional companies attached to the royal household. The Master of the Children of the Chapel Royal had his carefully trained children available (Richard Edwards held this office, and his *Damon and Pithias* was played before the Queen by the Children of the Chapel), and the children of the choir school of St. Paul's (to be distinguished from the Grammar School also associated with the Cathedral) also performed at Court as well as joining the Children of the Chapel for public performances at the Blackfriars theater. As we have seen, the Queen's men were formed in 1583. These, and the companies in the service of noblemen, were available for Court and other private festivities and at the same time gave professional performances in the public theater.

The growing popularity and diversity of the drama, its secularization, and the growth of a class of writers and scholars who had no desire to be in holy orders (as the medieval scholar was bound to be) combined to produce a new literary phenomenon—the secular professional playwright. The group of writers known as the "University Wits," young men who had graduated at Oxford or Cambridge with no patrons to sponsor their literary activities and no desire to enter the Church, were the first to exploit this situation. They turned to playwriting to make a living, and in doing so they made Elizabethan popular drama more literary and in some respects more dramatic. Not all of them turned to the public theater: in writing plays for the Children of the Chapel to present at Court or at Blackfriars there was always the chance of attracting royal attention or achieving a noble patron. The University Wits thus had an important influence both on the public and the private theater; they wrote both roaring popular successes and sophisticated confections for connoisseurs. It could perhaps be claimed that they were the first to associate English drama permanently with *literature*. There is no necessary connection between plays and literature, and both in public and private entertainments the emphasis had often been as much on the action or the rant or (in Court performance) the splendor of the sheer *show* as on the dramatic effectiveness of the language itself. The University Wits, educated, ambitious, and opportunistic, often reckless bohemians in their personal lives but always professional men of letters, set the course for later Elizabethan and Jacobean drama and, in particular, paved the way for Shakespeare. The group consists of

John Lyly, Robert Greene, George Peele, Thomas Lodge, Thomas Kyd, Thomas Nashe, and Christopher Marlowe.

Lyly, who was born about 1554 and died in 1606, turned to drama after his success with *Euphues*, adapting his courtly artificial prose to the stage to produce a new kind of court comedy. It was for the Children of St. Paul's that most of his plays were written, to be performed at Court before the Queen. His intricately balanced and stylized prose is not the most suitable medium for dramatic dialogue, but it did at least impose some order on dramatic speech, even if his tendency to interrupt the action by cunningly wrought monologues is less agreeable to modern taste than it apparently was to that of those who saw the first Court performances; and in any case a move toward a polished prose, however overmannered, was an improvement over the doggerel "fourteeners" of his predecessors. The wit and grace of the prose of Shakespeare's "middle" comedies owe much to Lyly. For his plots, Lyly turned to Greek legend, but he did not simply dramatize well-known classical myths; he used characters and themes from mythology in a wholly original way. *A most excellent Comedy of Alexander, Campaspe, and Diogenes* (as the title page of the 1584 edition calls it) introduces characters from Greek history; its theme is the rivalry in love between Alexander the Great and the painter Apelles for the Theban captive Campaspe, and it is handled with a mixture of mythology and sentiment. Mythology is more pronounced in *Sapho and Phao*, *Endimion*, and *Midas*, which interweave more realistic subplots (in which Lyly shows that he could write a more vigorous, colloquial prose when he wanted to) with the main mythological theme, and in which also, perhaps, allegorical references to contemporary affairs are to be traced by the initiated. *Gallathea*, *Love's Metamorphosis*, and *The Woman in the Moon* are pastoral plays. The first is laid in Lincolnshire, the second in Arcadia, and the third in Utopia, but in fact the scene is the same in all three—a pastoral dreamland against which allegorical and mythological action concerning nymphs, swains, soldiers, monsters, goddesses, and a variety of human lovers and supernatural characters is played out. *The Woman in the Moon* is Lyly's only play in blank verse, and it is more satirical in tone than any of his others. *Mother Bombie* (if it is Lyly's) stands apart from his other plays: this is a comedy in the tradition of Plautus and Terence, where scapegrace young men and their ingenious servants outwit their more prudential elders in bringing their love affairs to a successful conclusion. The mythological and pastoral plays include some charming lyrics, which are not, however, certainly by Lyly, since they are first included in a posthumous edition of his "court comedies" in 1632. The phrase that comes to mind with reference to Lyly's plays is "faded charm." They are unequal; the subplots are not always effectively tied up with the main story; the euphuistic prose is often tedious; but there is a delicate imagination at work here, a sense of form, and a new conception of comedy, all of which held rich promise for later Elizabethan drama.

George Peele (ca. 1558–ca. 1596) began his career as a dramatist with a courtly mythological pastoral play in the same vein as many of Lyly's. This was *The Arraignment of Paris,* played by the Children of the Chapel before the Queen in the early 1580's. Peele takes the familiar story of the judgment of Paris, handling the love of Paris and Oenone and Paris's subsequent faithlessness with a smooth lyrical grace. The love of Colin for his hardhearted Thestylis provides a subplot, with rustic characters (whose names are derived from Spenser's *Shepherd's Calendar*) introduced to provide a more realistic level of action. Paris is summoned before the Council of the Gods, at the instance of Pallas and Juno, to be accused of partiality in his judgment. He defends himself in vigorous blank verse, and in the end Diana awards the disputed golden apple to

> a gracious nymph
> That honours Dian for her chastity,
> And likes the labours well of Phoebe's groves;
> The place Elizium hight, and of the place
> Her name that governs there Eliza is.

And so the play is turned into a compliment to Queen Elizabeth. It is written in a variety of verse forms, including "fourteeners" and blank verse, and includes some fine singing lyrics, notably the duet sung by Paris and Oenone, "Fair and fair, and twice so fair," which is sadly echoed later in Oenone's lament for her desertion by Paris. Peele's *Old Wives' Tale* is a play of wicked enchantment and true love which begins as a story told by Madge, wife of Clunch the blacksmith, to three gay fellows who have lost their way in the wood and whom she is entertaining at her cottage; but soon after she begins to tell the story the characters appear to act it out, so that Madge's story becomes the play. The introductory scene is in vigorous colloquial prose; the main part of the play is partly in a more mannered prose and partly in blank verse. Though the whole has a quaint charm, the different elements of which it is composed are too loosely connected to produce a satisfactory drama. *The Battle of Alcazar* is a crude piece of bombast, and *Edward I* a loosely linked, episodic treatment of history. *The love of King David and Fair Bethsabe* dramatizes the biblical story of David's love for

Bathsheba and Absalom's rebellion in richly ornamented and slow moving blank verse. Peele was a poet of skill and charm, who experimented with drama in order to further his career. He had little theatrical sense or gift for dramatic structure, but he had facility and versatility and his flowing lyricism brought something new to Elizabethan drama.

Robert Greene (ca. 1558–92), a prolific and versatile bohemian, is better known for his graphic autobiographical prose than for his plays, but he, too, turned to the drama as a source of livelihood. Greene himself tells in *A Groatsworth of Wit* how he came to write for the stage. Once, sitting by a hedge lamenting his misfortunes and poor prospects, he was overheard by a player who told him he required the services of a scholar to write plays, "for which you will be well paid if you take the pains." To which proposal he agreed, thinking it best "in respect of his present necessity to try his wit." The result was a group of plays characterized by a craftsmanlike plotting, a skillful mixture of a realistic native background and an atmosphere of romance, and an ability to portray a heroine who is both charming as a personality, attractive as a woman, and convincing as a human being. *The Honorable History of Friar Bacon and Friar Bungay* deals with Bacon's proof of his magical powers (which he ultimately renounces) before King Henry III and the Emperor of Germany and combines with this not only some colloquial humor but also a love idyll between Margaret, the fair maid of Fressingfield, and Lacy, Earl of Lincoln. The two plots are neatly fitted together; the action moves between Margaret's Suffolk, Friar Bacon's cell in Oxford, and the Court, with a simple fluidity that the platform stage, with its lack of scenery, made possible; the dialogue, mostly in workmanlike blank verse but occasionally in lively prose, carries the story along vigorously, in spite of some moments of unnecessary classical ornamentation in the love speeches. *The Scottish History of James the Fourth* is not, as its title might suggest, a history play, but a serious comedy derived from a story by the Italian Giraldi Cinthio. The play opens with a rather unusual piece of machinery: it is presented before Oberon, King of Fairies, by Bohan, a Scot, to prove his cynical view that the world is no place for a wise man to live in. The main story concerns King James' love for Ida, daughter of the Countess of Arran, and the evil (including countenancing an attempt on the life of his queen) into which this leads him. But Ida's steadfast discouragement of her royal wooer and Queen Dorothea's constancy to her erring husband (she is driven from court disguised as a page and wounded by a hired assassin) bring the story to a happy ending at last.

Dorothea combines the patience of Griselda with something of the self-reliance as well as the constancy of Shakespeare's Viola and Imogen, and the play, though slow moving, has some charming and some tenderly pathetic moments. Greene's other plays are less interesting (though *George a Green, or The Pinner of Wakefield,* which may well be Greene's but cannot be certainly attributed to him, shows many of his best qualities), *Orlando Furioso* (based on Ariosto) and *Alphonsus, King of Arragon* showing the influence, not very happily, of Marlowe's *Tamburlaine.* Unlike Lyly but like Kyd and Marlowe, Greene wrote for the public stage and aimed at popular success rather than Court favor. Like Lyly, he taught Shakespeare something about comedy, his plays being the first English examples of the *genre* to which critics have given the name "romantic comedy" —a *genre* of which Shakespeare's *Twelfth Night* and *As You Like It* represent the highest development.

Thomas Lodge (ca. 1557–1625) is much less important as a contributor to the development of the drama. His most interesting work is his euphuistic prose romance, *Rosalynde,* the source of Shakespeare's *As You Like It.* He wrote a considerable amount of miscellaneous prose and some accomplished sonnets, and collaborated with Greene in *A Looking Glass for London and England,* a moral play about a vicious tyrant called to repentance. His one certainly known wholly original play is *The Wounds of Civil War,* "lively set forth in the true tragedy of Marius and Scilla." This treatment of the civil war between Marius and Sulla is interesting as an early dramatic handling of Roman history, but on the whole it is a confused performance, despite some Marlovian moments. Thomas Nashe (1567–1601) had a hand in some plays by more than one author (collaboration being a not uncommon practice at this period), but the only complete extant play of his is *Summer's Last Will and Testament,* an allegorical play about the seasons which mixes satire with courtly compliment; it has incidental songs and some lively moments, in spite of a general weakness in both plot and character drawing. Nashe's most important work is his picaresque tale, *The Unfortunate Traveller,* which is discussed in Chapter 13.

If Greene founded what has been called "romantic comedy," Thomas Kyd (1558–94) was an even greater popular success as the founder of what might be called "romantic tragedy." Mingling the themes of love, conspiracy, murder, and revenge, Kyd found a way of adapting some of the main elements of Senecan tragedy to roaring melodrama. *The Spanish Tragedy,* probably first produced in the early 1580's, is the first, and in its own melodramatic way the most

powerful, of the series of revenge plays which so captured the Elizabethan and the Jacobean imagination. It opens with a prologue, in
which the ghost of Andrea, a Spanish nobleman slain in battle against
Portugal by the Portuguese Prince Balthazar, tells how Proserpine
in Hades has promised him revenge against his slayer, and Revenge,
a spirit who accompanies him, confirms that he will see vengeance
duly executed on Balthazar. But in fact, though revenge is a main
theme of the play, it is only incidentally Andrea's revenge, and the
prologue is somewhat misleading. As the plot unfolds, we find Bell-
imperia, daughter of the Duke of Castile and beloved of the dead
Andrea, being comforted by Horatio, son of Hieronimo, marshal of
Spain, and Andrea's faithful friend during his lifetime. But Lorenzo,
Bell-imperia's sister, and Balthazar, the Portuguese Prince now an
honorable prisoner in Spain, become suspicious of the growing affection between Horatio and Bell-imperia. Balthazar is himself in
love with Bell-imperia, and later it emerges that the new treaty of
friendship between Spain and Portugal calls for the marriage of the
two. Lorenzo, with the assistance of Balthazar, murders Horatio in
an arbor where he is making love to Bell-imperia. Hieronimo, driven
distracted by the death of his son, whom he discovers hanging dead
in the arbor after Bell-imperia's cries have summoned him from his
bed, plans his revenge with a mixture of madness and cunning (there
is a blending of real and feigned madness here which Shakespeare
was to use in *Hamlet*). He eventually achieves his revenge by arranging a play as part of the festivities celebrating the reconciliation
between Spain and Portugal: the play is a tragedy in which Hieronimo, acting the part of a Turkish pasha, slays Erastus, knight of
Rhodes (played by Lorenzo) to enable his friend the Turkish emperor (played by Balthazar) to possess Erastus' beautiful wife (played
by Bell-imperia). The wife then slays the emperor and stabs herself.
Hieronimo and Bell-imperia arrange that the killing shall be in
earnest, and thus Lorenzo and Balthazar are slain before the ad-
miring eyes of the King of Spain, the Duke of Castile, and the Vice-
roy of Portugal, who think it is all a show. Bell-imperia also really
slays herself, though Hieronimo had not intended that. Hieronimo
then gloats over his revenge, and when seized and told he will be
forced to tell the details of his crime, he bites off his tongue and
spits it on to the stage, to make sure that he will not talk. They then
say that he will be tortured until he writes the truth, but he defeats
them by calling for a knife on the pretense of mending his pen: with
it he stabs the Duke of Castile and then himself. Several minor

characters are also killed in the course of the play: the total list is
happily recited by the ghost by way of epilogue:

> Ay, now my hopes have end in their effects,
> When blood and sorrow finish my desires:
> Horatio murdered in his father's bower;
> Vild Serberine by Pedringano slain;
> False Pedringano hang'd by quaint device;
> Fair Isabella by herself misdone;
> Prince Balthazar by Bell-imperia stabb'd;
> The Duke of Castile and his wicked son
> Both done to death by old Hieronimo;
> My Bell-imperia fall'n as Dido fell,
> And good Hieronimo slain by himself:
> Ay, these were spectacles to please my soul! . . .

But a summary of the plot gives little idea of the power of the
play. Violence is everywhere, passion and intrigue work themselves
out in every kind of horror and cruel cunning. The blank verse
mingles exclamatory rhetoric with morbid sententiousness. After the
witty love play in the dialogue between Bell-imperia and Horatio in
the arbor—

> Bel.   If I be Venus, thou must needs be Mars;
>   And where Mars reigneth there must needs be wars.
> Hor.   Then thus begin our wars: put forth thy hand,
>   That it may combat with my ruder hand.
> Bel.   Set forth thy foot to try the push of mine.
> Hor.   But first my looks shall combat against thine.
> Bel.   Then guard thyself: I dart this kiss at thee. . . .—

we get the sudden intrusion of the murderers, the dispatching of
Horatio, Bell-imperia's outcry, Lorenzo's callous, "Come, stop her
mouth; away with her," and then the sudden entry of the aroused
Hieronimo:

> What outcries pluck me from my naked bed,
> And chill my throbbing heart with trembling fear,
> Which never danger yet could daunt before?
> Who calls Hieronimo? Speak, here I am.
> I did not slumber; therefore 'twas no dream,
> And here within this garden did she cry,
> And in this garden must I rescue her.—
> But stay, what murd'rous spectacle is this?
> A man hang'd up and all the murderers gone!
> And in my bower, to lay the guilt on me!

This place was made for pleasure, not for death.
>   *He cuts him down.*
Those garments that he wears I oft have seen—
Alas, it is Horatio, my sweet son!
O no, but he that whilom was my son!
O, was it thou that call'dst me from my bed?
O speak, if any spark of life remain:
I am thy father; who hath slain my son?
What savage monster, not of human kind,
Hath here been glutted with thy harmless blood,
And left thy bloody corpse dishonoured here,
For me, amidst these dark and deathful shades,
To drown thee with an ocean of my tears? . . .

In spite of the long rhetorical outbursts, the speed of the action is tremendous, event following on event with the grimmest kind of irony. The characterization in the play is crude to the point of nonexistence; the characters have passions and nothing else; but their passions do carry them on, making them dissemble and hate and go frantic as well as love and murder. *The Spanish Tragedy* was immensely "good theater"; it was one of the great successes of the Elizabethan public stage, and was continually being revived. Shakespeare of course knew it as a popular theatrical piece, and took many devices from it. Indeed, it might almost be said that *The Spanish Tragedy* is the great property-room of Elizabethan tragic devices: the revenge theme, the play within a play, the madness real and feigned, the Machiavellian master of malicious plotting who begins with Lorenzo and culminates in Iago. Time and time again later Elizabethan plays use or refer to something in *The Spanish Tragedy*. When, in *A Midsummer Night's Dream*, the bewitched Titania awakes and hears Bottom singing, she exclaims:

> What angel wakes me from my flowery bed?

—which is surely a deliberate parody of Hieronimo's

> What outcries pluck me from my naked bed?

It is supposed that Kyd wrote a *Hamlet* (which has not survived), on which Shakespeare based his *Hamlet;* but even without this presumed lost play of Kyd's we can see his kind of sensational melodrama lies behind the infinitely subtler and profounder Shakespearean tragedy. *The Spanish Tragedy* was sensational stuff all right, Senecan though it was in some respects (though not in its having violent physical action on the stage). But it was tragedy of a sort—

the first truly popular tragedy of the English stage, and one of the most influential.

Two other tragedies, both at one time or another wrongly ascribed to Shakespeare, date from this period. One is *Locrine*, a Senecan treatment of a story from legendary British history: it deals with Locrine, son of Brutus and King of Britain, his wife Gwendolen, and his paramour the fair Estrelda. As Spenser told the story, in Book II of *The Faerie Queene:*

> . . . He lov'd fair Lady Estrild, lewdly lov'd,
>   Whose wanton pleasures him too much did please,
>   That quite his heart from Gwendolen remov'd,
> From Gwendolen his wife, though always faithful prov'd.

Gwendolen seeks revenge in battle, and prevails. In the end, Estrelda and her daughter Sabrina are drowned in a river.

> Which of her name now *Severn* men do call:
>   Such was the end, that to disloyal love did fall.

Spenser's brief telling of the story and Milton's introduction of Sabrina in *Comus* testify to the popularity of the theme. As handled by the anonymous author, the tragedy shows the Senecan style adapted for the public theater with less theatrical liveliness than Kyd succeeded in introducing into *The Spanish Tragedy* but with similar machinery. Much more interesting as a play than *Locrine* is another anonymous tragedy, *Arden of Feversham*, the first example of what has been called Elizabethan domestic tragedy. It deals with a real-life murder, which had occurred in 1551 and was recorded by Holinshed in his *Chronicles of England, Ireland and Scotland* (1578). Thomas Arden of Feversham, a prosperous gentleman, has a wife Alice who has become enamored of a low-born and ill-bred fellow named Mosbie. To enjoy Mosbie's sole love she plots, with him, to murder her husband. While her motive is infatuation, his is desire for wealth. The story is presented with remarkable psychological realism, concentrating on the changing passions and doubts and fears of the principal characters with an insight into character that *The Spanish Tragedy*, for all its theatrical brilliance, never displays (though the play has been attributed to Kyd and to Kyd and Marlowe jointly). The atmosphere of Elizabethan middle-class life is vividly presented: this is no story of Spanish noblemen or Italian intrigue, but a grimly convincing account of domestic crime. In spite of some crudities of sentiment and expression, *Arden of Feversham* is an impressive play which anticipates many later developments in Elizabethan and Jacobean tragedy.

English tragedy had not yet, however, found a blank verse eloquent and musical enough to add the effect of poetic conviction to that of rhetorical excitement. Nor had it yet turned to themes that came truly home to the Elizabethan imagination. In the hands of Christopher Marlowe (1564–93) it advanced spectacularly toward the achievement of these two goals. Marlowe, the most striking personality and the most impressive dramatist among the University Wits, stormed his way into popular favor with *Tamburlaine the Great*, a play in two parts probably first produced in the winter of 1587–88 when the author was still in his early twenties. This flamboyant story of the conquering Scythian shepherd, presented in a richly declamatory blank verse abounding in colorful images of power and violence, brought a new kind of life to the English theater. Marlowe's prologue indicates his own notion of what he was doing:

> From jigging veins of riming mother wits,
> And such conceits as clownage keeps in pay,
> We'll lead you to the stately tent of war,
> Where you shall hear the Scythian Tamburlaine
> Threat'ning the world with high astounding terms. . . .

The presentation of a man slaughtering his way to world mastery, convinced of his own invincibility and drunk with a sense of his own conquering mission, might soon have become tedious if Marlowe had not found a form of blank verse whose sounding lines echoed sonorously across the stage and kept the play continuously at an emotional fever pitch. This is a study of lust for power and military achievement gloried in almost esthetically for its own sake: it requires—and receives—"a great and thundring speech." All the excitement of new geographical discoveries, all the richly luxurious implications which oriental splendor has held for the occidental imagination ever since the temperate Greeks faced the extravagant Persians or the restrained self-indulgence of Horace repudiated the "Persicos apparatus," all the new glory of Elizabethan poetic utterance, the Renaissance feeling for *virtù*, the fascination with what man can achieve along a single line of endeavor if he sets his mind and heart to it with sufficient fervor and lyrical enthusiasm; the interest in pride, in lust for power, in man as master of his own destiny, challenging and vying with the gods—"How noble in reason! How infinite in faculties! In form and moving how express and admirable! In action how like an angel! In apprehension how like a god!"—and imagining that by an effort of the will he can control Fortune's wheel—all this is in *Tamburlaine*, a play which ignores moral considerations to exhibit the impressiveness of boundless ambition coupled with determination and self-confidence that similarly know no limits.

We find in *Tamburlaine*, even in the speech of the minor characters, that resounding use of exotic place names which Shakespeare was to develop in *Antony and Cleopatra* and which Milton was to turn to his own rather different purposes in *Paradise Lost*. The characters conquered by Tamburlaine are themselves first built up in magnificence so that Tamburlaine's achievement in overcoming them and assuming their power and titles can be seen as greater still. When Cosroe supplants his brother as King of Persia he is hailed thus by his followers:

> We here do crown thee Monarch of the East,
> Emperor of Asia and of Persea,
> Great Lord of Medea and Armenia:
> Duke of Africa and Albania,
> Mesopotamia and of Parthia,
> East India and the late discovered Isles,
> Chief Lord of all the wide vast Euxine sea,
> And of the ever raging Caspian Lake:
> Long live Cosroe mighty Emperor.

Images of power and multitude combine in Bassoe's description of the power of Bajazeth, Emperor of the Turks, another powerful ruler to be subdued by Tamburlaine:

> My lord, the great Commander of the world,
> Besides fifteen contributory kings,
> Hath now in arms ten thousand Janisaries,
> Mounted on lusty Mauritanian steeds,
> Brought to the war by men of Tripoly.

Orcanes, "king of Natolia," planning an already doomed expedition against Tamburlaine with the most powerful allies he can muster, admits that

> Slavonians, Almains, Rutters, Muffes, and Danes
> Fear not Orcanes, but great Tamburlaine,
> Nor he but Fortune that hath made him great.
> We have revolted Grecians, Albanees,
> Cicilians, Jews, Arabians, Turks, and Moors,
> Illirians, Thracians, and Bythinians,
> Enough to swallow forceless Sigismond
> Yet scarce enough t' encounter Tamburlaine.
> He brings a world of people to the field,
> From Scythia to the Oriental Plage
> Of India, where raging Lantchidol
> Beats on the regions with his boisterous blows,
> That never sea-man yet discovered:

> All Asia is in arms with Tamburlaine,
> Even from the midst of fiery Cancer's Tropic,
> To Amazonia under Capricorn,
> And thence as far as Aechipellago;
> All Afric is in arms with Tamburlaine. . . .

This, of course, is overdoing it, and there is no doubt that the young
Marlowe does work his tricks to excess; but they are tricks that
Shakespeare was to learn from:

> He hath assembled
> Bocchus, the king of Lybia; Archelaus,
> Of Cappadocia; the Thracian king, Adallas;
> King Malchus of Arabia; King of Pont;
> Herod of Jewry; Mithradates, king
> Of Comagene; Polemon and Amyntas,
> The kings of Mede and Lycaonia, with a
> More larger list of sceptres.

So Shakespeare gives the Roman view of the enormity of Antony's
defection in "giving his empire up to a whore" and making common
cause with strange and sinister barbaric powers. Milton was to use
such geographical imagery in his own fashion:

> A multitude, like which the populous North
> Pour'd never from her frozen loins, to pass
> Rhene or the Danaw, when her barbarous Sons
> Came like a Deluge on the South, and spread
> Beneath Gibraltar to the Lybian sands.

Or, with the overtones more purely literary:

> For never since created man,
> Met such imbodied force, as nam'd with these
> Could merit more than that small infantry
> Warr'd on by Cranes: though all the Giant brood
> Phlegra with th' Heroic Race were join'd
> That fought at Thebes and Ilium, on each side
> Mixt with auxiliar Gods; and what resounds
> In Fable or Romance of Uther's Son
> Begirt with British and Armoric Knights;
> And all who since, Baptiz'd or Infidel
> Jousted in Aspramont or Montalban,
> Damasco, or Marocco, or Trebisond,
> When Charlemain with all his Peerage fell
> By Fontarabbia.

Geography, history, and romance came together in the Elizabethan
and seventeenth-century poetic mind, with powerful effect.

The intoxication with power is perhaps the main theme of *Tamburlaine,* and images of power abound in the play.

> Is it not brave to be a King, Techelles? . . .
> Is it not passing brave to be a King,
> And ride in triumph through Persepolis?

But "the thirst of reign and sweetness of a crown" do not represent a desire for any attainable object; nor does Tamburlaine show much interest in the fruits of power once he has attained it. His is the Faustian urge, the urge to reach beyond the limits of mortality, and though his ambition manifests itself in military conquest and often in outrageous cruelty and is not, like that of Dr. Faustus, intellectual in its primary impetus, there are moments when he sees its purely symbolic nature:

> Our souls, whose faculties can comprehend
> The wondrous architecture of the world,
> And measure every wand'ring planet's course,
> Still climbing after knowledge infinite,
> And always moving as the restless spheres,
> Will us to wear ourselves and never rest
> Until we reach the ripest fruit of all,
> That perfect bliss and sole felicity,
> The sweet fruition of an earthly crown.

Tamburlaine's conquests have no material objective in view: they are, one might almost say, metaphysical in inspiration. His love for Zenocrate does not project any serious dramatic conflict in the play —like that between love and honor which Dryden made out of *Antony and Cleopatra*—but is presented in order that the claims of beauty should be sounded in the same eloquent style that celebrates military power and conquest. But the scenes which must have struck the Elizabethan audience with most force are those where the imagery of power is projected in concrete situations: Bajazeth, the Emperor of the Turks, and his wife kept like beasts in a cage and taunted to desperation by Tamburlaine for the amusement of himself and Zenocrate; Tamburlaine using Bajazeth as his footstool as he climbs on to his chair; or, in the second part, Tamburlaine with his chariot drawn by conquered kings—"Tamburlaine drawn in his chariot by Trebizon and Soria with bittes in their mouthes, reines in his left hand, in his right hand a whip, with which he scourgeth them," as the picturesque stage direction of the early editions has it. Bajazeth finally dashes his brains out against the cage, and his wife, seeing what he has done, follows his example after a fine exhibition of Elizabethan frenzy. The early spelling gives its flavor more fully:

O Baiazet, O Turk, O Emperor, give him his liquor? Not I, bring milk and fire, and my blood I bring him againe, teare me in peeces, give me the words with a ball of wildefire upon it. Downe with him, downe with him. Goe to my child, away, away, away. Ah, save that Infant, save him, save him. I, even I speake to her, the Sun was downe. Streamers white, Red, Blacke, here, here, here. Fling the meat in his face. Tamburlaine, Tamburlaine, Let the souldiers be buried. Hell, death, Tamburlaine, Hell, make ready my Coch, my chaire, my jewels, I come, I come, I come.

She runs against the Cage and braines her selfe.

This is, indeed, crude sensationalism—though we recognize in it the pattern of many wild and whirling words to be spoken by later Elizabethan and Jacobean dramatic characters—but it is done with an immense gusto which is worlds apart from the stiffness of earlier academic plays. And again and again the language raises the physical violence into some symbolic quintessence of dominion, as when Tamburlaine addresses the conquered kings who draw his chariot:

Holla, ye pampered jades of Asia:
What, can ye draw but twenty miles a day,
And have so proud a chariot at your heels
And such a coachman as great Tamburlaine?

Tamburlaine is the perfect illustration of the view maintained by Hobbes in his *Leviathan:* "I put for a general inclination of all mankind, a perpetual and restless desire of power after power, that ceaseth only in death." In Tamburlaine's case this perpetual and restless desire for power after power does literally cease only in death: even "the death of his Lady and Love fair Zenocrate," which occurs in Part II, does not deflect him from his course, though it moves him to passionate speech. Part II has greater variety than Part I, for not only does it contain the death of Zenocrate, which effectively though temporarily interrupts the by this time somewhat monotonous run of Tamburlaine's victories, but it is in general rather more diversified than the earlier part, where the interest lies solely in Tamburlaine's triumphant career and the resounding verse in which he and others express themselves. The only moment in the first part when the hero is forced by events into some kind of introspection comes when he realizes that his love for Zenocrate must lead him to spare the life of her father, the Soldan of Egypt:

> There angels in their crystal armours fight
> A doubtful battle with my tempted thoughts
> For Egypt's freedom and the Soldan's life,
> His life that so consumes Zenocrate. . . .
> What is beauty saith my sufferings then?
> If all the pens that ever poets held
> Had fed the feeling of their masters' thoughts,
> And every sweetness that inspir'd their hearts,
> Their minds, and muses on admired themes:
> If all the heavenly quintessence they still
> From their immortal flowers of poesy,
> Wherein as in a mirror we perceive
> The highest reaches of a human wit—
> If these had made one poem's period
> And all combined in beauty's worthiness,
> Yet should there hover in their restless heads
> One thought, one grace, one wonder at the least,
> Which into words no virtue can digest.

In *Tamburlaine* "Marlowe's mighty line" first comes into Elizabethan drama: its successor, *The Tragical History of Doctor Faustus* (probably completed in the winter of 1588–89) is not as consistently declamatory in its verse, if only because its hero is less the confident extrovert than a man who seeks a more purely intellectual empire. The Faustus myth reaches more profoundly into tragic aspects of the human situation than the more purely spectacular story of Tamburlaine. Doctor Faustus is a Tamburlaine on the intellectual level; his ambition is for ultimate knowledge; and if knowledge for him means power, the same can be said in some degree of the view implicit in the whole Baconian tradition, that the function of knowledge is control rather than mere insight and the scientist works for "the relief of man's estate." But Faustus is not merely a man who seeks the practical fruits of knowledge: his inordinate thirst for ultimate understanding has something splendidly disinterested about it, and if he sells his soul to the Devil in exchange for forbidden knowledge there is an element of the heroic in the transaction which would be lacking if all he was seeking was the perfect washing machine. Tamburlaine operates outside the sphere of moral values, but Faustus comes up against them in their most elemental state, symbolizing in his own behavior the story of the Fall of Man through eating of the tree of knowledge. If he had had a less aspiring mind he would have been a better man: less imaginative, less interesting, and less daring, he would also have been more virtuous. Here we have the germ of a truly tragic situation—*corruptio optimi pessima*, the corruption of the best becomes the worst—and we can almost see a pointing forward toward the great tragic heroes of Shakespeare who are led to self-destruction by the implication of their own virtues.

Like *Tamburlaine, Doctor Faustus* is full of the spirit of Renaissance ambition and *virtù*, but there is also a specifically Christian background, and the pact with the Devil with its resultant damnation effectively sets against the Renaissance zeal for limitless understanding the popular Christian notion of a forbidden knowledge, all the dark ideas of witchcraft and black magic, which had haunted the mind of Europe for centuries. Faustus retains many elements of the old morality plays; he has a Good Angel to exhort him to repentance and amendment as well as an Evil Angel to urge him on to damnation; and he is not irrevocably damned until he has succumbed to the final temptation of despair and given up all hope of the possibility of his repentance.

Tamburlaine and Faustus—and this is true of nearly all of Marlowe's heroes—are lonely souls; they have no real confidants, and they play a lone hand. And just as Tamburlaine began life as a Scythian shepherd, so Faustus was born of "parents base of stock" and rises by his own endeavors and his own brilliance. We first see him when he has run through all available human knowledge but remains dissatisfied and eager for more:

> O, what a world of profit and delight
> Is promised to the studious artisan!
> All things that move between the quiet poles
> Shall be at my command: emperors and kings
> Are but obeyed in their several provinces,
> Nor can they raise the wind or rend the clouds.
> But his dominion that exceeds in this
> Stretcheth as far as does the mind of man.

And so he turns to magic and forbidden knowledge.

There is rich dramatic irony when Faustus, having conjured up Mephistopheles, finds him "pliant" and "full of obedience and humility," and even more so when Mephistopheles has the truth about his real condition forced out of him and Faustus laughs at him for being superstitious and lacking "manly fortitude." Self-confidence has made him fatuous, and he signs his compact with Mephistopheles—gaining twenty-four years of knowledge and power and a life of "full voluptuousness"—with a braggart light-heartedness:

> Had I as many souls as there be stars,
> I'd give them all for Mephistophilis.

But the actual signing of the compact is delayed, while the suspense is maintained by keeping alive the possibility of Faustus' repentance.

And even when Faustus has signed the deed in his own blood, all is not yet irrevocably lost; it is only before the final climax, when he gives up hope, exclaiming, "But Faustus' offence can ne'er be pardoned: the serpent that tempted Eve may be saved, but not Faustus," that the end becomes inevitable.

Marlowe's real difficulty comes when he has to illustrate the kind of knowledge Faustus has obtained by his compact with Mephistopheles and to present the kind of life he is now able to lead. True, there are textual confusions which make it doubtful that we have the play exactly as Marlowe wrote it, but even so it is clear that Marlowe was at a loss to illustrate superhuman knowledge and power in concrete dramatic situations. Milton, faced with the problem of putting divine wisdom into the mouth of God Almighty, solves it with simple confidence by making God say what Milton had already been maintaining for some time; Bernard Shaw, presenting in *Back to Methusaleh* his Ancients who have achieved a wisdom beyond anything yet available to man, puts into their mouths the views that Shaw had long been arguing; but Milton and Shaw stand alone in English literature in their confidence that their own ideas represented ultimate understanding. Marlowe has to fall back on petty conjuring tricks only rarely punctuated with splendid poetic passages in which he suggests the atmosphere of Faustus' present way of life. Of these the most celebrated and the most successful is his speech to Helen of Troy, when she (or her appearance) has been conjured forth:

> Was this the face that launched a thousand ships
> And burned the topless towers of Ilium?
> Sweet Helen, make me immortal with a kiss:
> Her lips suck forth my soul, see where it flies.
> Come, Helen, come, give me my soul again.
> Here will I dwell, for heaven be in these lips,
> And all is dross that is not Helena. . . .
> O thou art fairer than the evening air
> Clad in the beauty of a thousand stars;
> Brighter art thou than flaming Jupiter
> When he appeared to hapless Semele,
> More lovely than the monarch of the sky
> In wanton Arethusa's azured arms,
> And none but thou shalt be my paramour.

But time is always moving on, and we are never allowed to forget that Faustus has only twenty-four years before the Devil comes to claim his own. The periodic urges to repentance by symbolic figures become more desperate, and after he has sunk into the final sin of despair, the terrible end blazes forth in a magnificent poetic passage which properly places more emphasis on Faustus' state of mind than on the details of what is to become of him when he is damned:

> Ah, Faustus
> Now hast thou but one bare hour to live,
> And then thou must be damned perpetually.
> Stand still you ever moving spheres of heaven
> That time may cease, and midnight never come;
> Fair Nature's eye, rise, rise again, and make
> Perpetual day, or let this hour be but
> A year, a month, a week, a natural day.
> That Faustus may repent and save his soul.
> *O lente, lente currite noctis equi:*
> The stars move still, time runs, the clock will strike,
> The devil will come, and Faustus must be damned.
> O I'll leap up to God: who pulls me down?
> See see where Christ's blood streams in the firmament.
> One drop would save my soul, half a drop, ah my Christ!
> Ah rend not my heart for naming of my Christ,
> Yet will I call on him: O spare me Lucifer!
> Where is it now? 'tis gone. And see where God
> Stretcheth out his arm, and bends his ireful brows.
> Mountains and hill, come, come, and fall on me,
> And hide me from the heavy wrath of God.
> No, no.
> Then will I headlong run into the earth:
> Earth gapes. O no, it will not harbour me.
> You stars that reigned at my nativity,
> Whose influence hath allotted death and hell,
> Now draw up Faustus like a foggy mist,
> Into the entrails of yon lab'ring cloud,
> That when you vomit forth into the air
> My limbs may issue from your smoky mouths,
> So that my soul may but ascend to heaven.
> Ah, half the hour is past: *The watch strikes.*
> 'Twill all be past anon.
> O God,
> If thou wilt not have mercy on my soul,
> Yet for Christ's sake, whose blood hath ransomed me,
> Impose some end to my incessant pain.
> Let Faustus live in hell a thousand years,
> A hundred thousand, and at last be saved.
> O no end is limited to damned souls,
> Why wert not thou a creature wanting soul? . . .

> Curst be the parents that engendered me:
> No Faustus, curse thyself, curse Lucifer,
> That hath deprived thee of the joys of heaven.
>
> *The clock striketh twelve.*
>
> O it strikes, it strikes: now body turn to air,
> Or Lucifer will bear thee quick to hell.
>
> *Thunder and lightning.*
>
> O soul, be changed into little water drops,
> And fall into the Ocean, ne'er be found.
> My God, my God, looke not so fierce on me.
>
> *Enter divels.*
>
> Adders and Serpents, let me breath a while:
> Ugly hell gape not, come not, Lucifer,
> I'll burn my books,—ah, Mephistophilis!

This passionate, highly charged blank verse, rich in a compelling imagery that searches the emotional condition of the speaker at each moment, is as far as dramatic verse was to go before Shakespeare. It is still end-stopped, with the pauses falling regularly at the end of each line, but there is more flexibility than in the declamatory speeches of Tamburlaine, and the shifts in tempo correspond to the rise and fall in the emotion far more effectively than in any of the *Tamburlaine* passages, where the emotion ran more evenly and the speeches were far more set recitations. Nevertheless, even in *Doctor Faustus* Marlowe can achieve effective dramatic verse only in great moments of crisis. He is the dramatist of the passionate moment, and has not yet mastered the subtler art of expressing poetically, dramatically, and continuously the general run of the play's action. The art of using dramatic verse with fine poetic effectiveness in moments of low emotional tension in a play was not to be adequately developed in English before Shakespeare, and not even by him until the middle of his career.

Of Marlowe's other plays, *The Jew of Malta* (ca. 1590?) is a dramatic presentation of a "Machiavellian" man, full of greed and cunning, who will stop at nothing to attain his ends. But the ambition of Barrabas, the Jew of Malta, lacks the central drive of either Tamburlaine or Faustus, and the play, though it has some effective moments of grim irony lacking in any of Marlowe's other works, falls apart into a series of uneven episodes. *Edward the Second* (1591?), though the main interest still concentrates on a central character—this time a study of weakness rather than of strength: Edward II is the sentimental weakling betrayed and done to death by the forces of ambition and cruelty—spreads the emphasis over a number of personalities and moves less in purple passages than the other plays. Marlowe is gaining a greater control over his dramatic material, and is moving toward a new subtlety in character portrayal; he is interested both in Edward's weakness and in "the proud corrupters of the light-brained king." As a work of sustained dramatic invention this is the best of Marlowe's plays. The scene in which Edward is murdered shows Marlowe dealing for the first time in the pathetic: the play as a whole moves between violence and pathos. For further advance in this direction we have to wait until Shakespeare's *Richard II*.

Marlowe has yet other plays, but nothing he produced in the later part of his brief life—nothing, indeed, after *Tamburlaine* and *Doctor Faustus*—had the impact on the contemporary dramatic world of his first two. It is these two plays that reveal Marlowe's characteristic splendor, and if his early death by violence in 1593 cut short a career which might, if spared to develop, have rivaled Shakespeare's, it can still be said that his dramatic debut was one of the most remarkable in English literary history, and one which has left a lasting impression. He remains a living and not an academic figure, even to the most casual student of Elizabethan literature.

CHAPTER NINE

Shakespeare

WILLIAM SHAKESPEARE (1564–1616) doubtless saw himself as merely another professional man of the theater who moved almost casually from play acting to play writing. And indeed he was very much a man of his time, a man of the Elizabethan theater, who learned to exploit brilliantly the stagecraft, the acting, and the public taste of his day. It happens very rarely in the history of literature that a craftsman who has acquired perfect control of his medium and a masterly ease in handling the techniques and conventions of his day is also a universal genius of the highest order, combining with his technical proficiency a unique ability to render experience in poetic language and an uncanny intuitive understanding of human psychology. Man of the theater, poet, and expert in the human passions, Shakespeare has appealed equally to those who admire the art with which he renders a story in terms of the acted drama or the insight with which he presents states of mind and complexities of attitude or the unsurpassed brilliance he shows in giving conviction and a new dimension to the utterances of his characters through the poetic speech he puts in their mouths. It is a remarkable combination of qualities. Shakespeare has been praised for his "knowledge of the human heart," for his superb poetry, for his esthetic cunning in his disposition of the action, for his theatrical skill, and for his ability to create living worlds of people while himself remaining (as James Joyce's Stephen Dedalus said of the artist) "like the God of creation, within or behind or beyond or above his handiwork, invisible, refined out of existence, indifferent, paring his fingernails." Yet this was no poetic genius descending on the theater from above, but a working dramatist who found himself in catering for the public theater of his day. Unquestionably the greatest poetic dramatist of Europe, he was also Marlowe's successor, the heir to a tradition of playwriting which we saw developing in the preceding chapter. His contemporaries saw him as one dramatist among others

—a good one, and a popular one, but no transcendent genius who left all others far behind—and to the end of his active life he showed no reluctance to collaborate with other playwrights.

It was the eighteenth century—contrary to the popular view that this was a period of grudging admiration of Shakespeare as too way-ward a genius to be of the very highest order—which first recognized Shakespeare's pre-eminence, and ever since Rowe's edition of 1709, editors, scholars, critics, biographers, and later bibliographers, psychologists, and many other varieties of inquirers have been building up a body of knowledge and of ideas about the plays (little enough about Shakespeare the man, whose biography has many blank passages) which cannot possibly be even summarized in a short history of literature. Shakespeare's apparent indifference to the publication of his plays, his preoccupation with their performance rather than their production as books, meant that no authoritative "works" supervised by the author ever passed through the press. Texts of sixteen of the plays were printed individually in quarto editions in Shakespeare's lifetime, sometimes from the author's "foul papers," with inevitable errors. Some were corrupt and pirated editions, so that we have "bad" as well as "good" quartos, and the best were casual enough publications in which the author had no hand. For eighteen of Shakespeare's plays we have only texts published after his death (sometimes apparently from his own heavily corrected original drafts), notably in the First Folio, the first collected edition, edited by Heminge and Condell in 1623; for four we have only the Folio text and that of a corrupt quarto; for others we have both quarto and First Folio texts, sometimes more than one of the former, with variations among them which raise the question: Which represents what Shakespeare wrote? Into such problems the general literary historian cannot enter, nor can he pause to discuss the evidence on which scholars have come to arrange Shakespeare's plays in some sort of chronological order. Reference to a given play in a work of known date and reference in a play to an event of known date can help to determine the date of composition, and of course the publication of a quarto edition of a play gives a date before which it must have been written. Having constructed a skeleton chronology of the plays in this way, we can note shifts in style and technique and, very cautiously, draw some conclusions about the way in which Shakespeare's art developed which can then be applied to deciding the approximate date of other plays. Generations of scholars have worked on this problem; the literary historian can only accept such of their conclusions as seem most convincing, while relying for Shakespeare's text on the findings of those textual editors whose work seems soundest (though, except in the "bad quartos," the textual errors of even the worst printed plays are not serious enough to effect any major distortion). As for Shakespeare's relations with his company, and the fortunes of the companies of which he was such an important member (from 1594, the Lord Chamberlain's men, who became the King's men after 1603), that belongs to the history of the English theater rather than to English literary history, and can be only mentioned here as representing the conditions under which Shakespeare's genius operated.

Shakespeare's earliest identifiable plays, his prentice work, show him interested in a variety of Elizabethan dramatic traditions. The three *Henry VI* plays (ca. 1590–92) show him developing the chronicle play on English history which was already a popular variety of drama by the time he came on the scene. *Titus Andronicus* (ca. 1593) shows him—if it *is* by Shakespeare—exploiting the popular taste for blood-and-thunder Senecan drama as Kyd had done. *The Comedy of Errors* (ca. 1590) takes its plot from the *Menaechmi* of Plautus and exploits the comic possibilities of two pairs of indistinguishable twins, complicating the intrigue by some of the devices standard in Roman comedy and untying the various knots with reasonable skill at the conclusion. *Richard III* (ca. 1592–93) shows Shakespeare following Marlowe's footsteps and building a tragedy around a central villain. *The Taming of the Shrew* (with a problematical relationship to a play entitled *The Taming of A Shrew*, first printed in 1594, which *may* be a "bad quarto" of Shakespeare's play) shows him combining a certain amount of knock-about humor with a romantic love element in a kind of play which has been called "low romantic comedy," to distinguish it from the "high romantic comedy" of such plays as *Twelfth Night*. Of these early plays, only *The Comedy of Errors*, with its Roman affinities, was not written for the public theater. The others show a beginning dramatist trying his hand successively at the different kinds of play that were already popular on the public stage. Robert Greene's attack on Shakespeare, in a pamphlet written on his deathbed, as "an upstart crow beautified with our feathers" seems to indicate that here was a player who had the effrontery to try writing plays as well as acting them—the reference is apparently to the second and third parts of *Henry VI*. As a player, Shakespeare was in an excellent position to judge public taste.

Into the complicated problems of the relation between these early plays and other plays, which in some cases can be regarded as either sources or corrupt versions of Shakespeare's, we cannot here enter, except to note that recent scholarship restores to Shakespeare much that earlier scholars had taken away from him. But a working dramatist interested in providing actable plays for his company would have had no compunction in revising or rewriting other people's plays; such activity was regarded as perfectly ethical, and there is no doubt that Shakespeare used other people's material when he found it serviceable or when he had to get something together in a hurry. This is truer of the beginning of his career than of Shakespeare in his maturity; once his own genius found itself it took complete control and so reworked any alien material that it emerges as thoroughly and uniquely Shakespearean. The view that Shakespeare only wrote bits and pieces of his own plays is as completely false as the equally exploded view of him as the illiterate rustic from Stratford. Further, it represents a complete misunderstanding of the nature of a work of literary art. Shakespeare in almost every instance derived his plots from somebody else's work, but that is no more to his discredit than the Greek dramatists' use of popular myths is to theirs. It is by the shaping of the material and its bodying forth in language that a crude tale can be made into a profound work of art. A study of Shakespeare's sources, in Italian *novelle* or English chronicles or in other plays, only emphasizes the remarkable power of his "shaping spirit of imagination."

If Shakespeare had written nothing more than the early plays enumerated above, he would still be an interesting dramatist, and *Richard III* in particular would receive respectful attention as a remarkable dramatic presentation of the rise and fall of a villain-hero who succeeds by wit and cunning, by Machiavellian policies (as the Elizabethans understood them) and Renaissance *virtù*, and at the same time as a contribution to the Elizabethan conception of English history emerging from the horrors of the Wars of the Roses and the climactic evil of Richard III's reign to the glories of Tudor peace and unity. Modern interest in Tudor historians has led to an emphasis, perhaps an overemphasis, on Shakespeare's concern to present English history, in his history plays, as an ordered sequence of events beginning with the deposition of Richard II, the last medieval king in the true original succession. The sequence proceeds through "the unquiet time of Henry IV" (as the chronicler Hall calls it) to the temporary glories of Henry V's military achievements in France before nemesis strikes the Lancastrians in the latter part of Henry VI's reign; civil war shatters the peace and unity of England until the reign of Richard III finally unites all that is decent in the country against this monstrous tyrant, with the result that Henry Tudor wins at the battle of Bosworth in 1485, unites the "two noble houses," and, representing both the ancient Celtic line and the English line, begins a new and glorious epoch in history. It is true that the Tudor historians—Polydore Vergil, Edward Hall, Raphael Holinshed, among others—built up something like this picture between them (in Hall it is especially clear); it is true also that the Elizabethans regarded history as a "mirror for magistrates," and saw lessons in the deposition of Richard II, the military virtues of Henry V, the Wars of the Roses, and the accession of the Tudors which they felt could be usefully applied to contemporary politics. It is true, too, that there is some evidence that in his gallery of English kings Shakespeare was seeking to indicate, directly or indirectly, his view of the ideal king, and that Henry V's education as Prince Hal, his acquaintance with all strata of life and his final refusal of the opposite extremes of riot (Falstaff) and vainglory (Percy) to choose justice and true kingship, as presented in the *Henry IV* plays, show a morality play element which cannot be ignored. And it is convenient to arrange Shakespeare's history plays (with *King John* standing somewhat outside the group) into two groups of four, with the three parts of *Henry VI* and *Richard III* in one group, and *Richard II*, the two parts of *Henry IV* and *Henry V* in the other; the first group giving the second part of the epic story—civil war and tyranny followed by Tudor regeneration—and the second giving the original causes of it all with Henry V's stay of execution of nemesis by his personal virtue as the good king. But to look at the plays this way is to miss much— if not most—of what makes them interesting as plays, and to impose on the subtlety and complexity of Shakespeare's art a schoolroom patterning which sacrifices several levels of meaning to pedagogic convenience. Richard III is not merely an evil monster who by representing the culmination of tyranny and horror forces England to find herself in rebellion against him. He is, in his way, a hero as well as a villain; his psychology is far from simple; the stylized rhetoric in which he and other characters often express themselves is a way of exploring paradoxes of character as well as presenting simplified historical truths. As Dr. Johnson said of Shakespeare, "his story requires Romans or kings, but he thinks only on men." The character and behavior of Shakespeare's kings illuminate aspects of the human situation as well as displaying the Tudor view of history, and it is the former function that is the more important.

Shakespeare at no period in his career wrote only one variety of play, so that any attempt to discuss his works chronologically cannot treat the plays in kindred groups, nor, conversely, can a discussion of the plays by types keep to a chronological line. One gets a clearer picture of his achievement by sacrificing, in some degree, chronology to a more logical grouping. *The Two Gentlemen of Verona* (ca. 1594) is the first of a series of romantic comedies which includes *Love's Labour's Lost* (1594)—though with some qualifications—and *A Mid-*

summer Night's Dream (ca. 1596), *The Merchant of Venice* (1596–97), *Much Ado about Nothing* (ca. 1598–99), *As You Like It* (1599–1600), and *Twelfth Night* (1599–1600). The *Two Gentlemen* is clearly experimental: Shakespeare cannot yet handle with assurance the different elements (deriving from Lyly and Greene as well as from the Spanish pastoral romance *Diana Enamorada* by Jorge de Montemajor and from Italian comedy) which he blends with such extraordinary skill in *Twelfth Night. Heroine* disguised as a boy; a story of love and intrigue with a low comedy subplot; talkative clowns; neat pairing of characters; intermittent verbal fireworks; male friendship versus heterosexual love—these are some of the elements in the play which we meet again in later plays, more effectively handled. The *Two Gentlemen* has a sprightly stiffness which shows a gift for comedy, however slightly developed, but it lacks the stylized brilliance of *Love's Labour's Lost*, which is immature in a different way—it is an admirable example of a relatively immature kind of art rather than an imperfect example of something more ambitious.

Love's Labour's Lost was first published in a quarto volume in 1598, described on the title page as "a pleasant conceited comedy . . . presented before her Highness this last Christmas. Newly corrected and augmented by W. Shakespeare." It is a stylized and courtly play, of which the 1598 text apparently represents a corrected version to replace a lost "bad" quarto; it was probably originally written and later augmented for specific private performances. The play shows that Shakespeare was aiming not only at popular successes in the public theater but also at something more sophisticated, appealing to the witty and the educated. How Shakespeare acquired his intimate knowledge of Elizabethan courtly wit and his friendship with members of the nobility we may only surmise: we know that his *Venus and Adonis* (1593) and *Rape of Lucrece* (1594) were dedicated to the Earl of Southampton, the first respectfully, the second in language suggesting deep personal affection, and there is other evidence of his having made friends in the highest social circles. He was familiar by this time with both popular humor, courtly wit, and current intellectual fashions, and he could imitate or satirize any of these. *Love's Labour's Lost*, with its action resembling one of the entertainments offered to Queen Elizabeth by noblemen whom she visited on her "progresses," its many topical allusions, its delicate satire of romantic idealism on the one hand and pedantic affectation on the other, its echoing notes of love and melancholy, of royal grace, male vanity, and rustic reality, its combination of wit combats, formal speeches, and singing lyricism, its balance and precision and ballet-like movement, is clearly designed for a highly educated taste. The plot is rudimentary—indeed, the play can hardly be said to have a plot at all. Ferdinand, king of Navarre, and his three lords, Biron (or Berowne), Longaville, and Dumain, resolve together to spend three years in study and contemplation, turning the court into "a little Academe, Still and contemplative in living art." In that period they will see no woman, and eat and sleep sparingly. The arrival of a diplomatic mission from France, consisting of the Princess and her three ladies, Rosaline, Maria, and Katherine, destroys their resolution. The four men fall in love with the four ladies, who tease them with witty mockeries. Finally, news of the death of the Princess' father, the King of France, puts an end to this mocking sport. The ladies explain that they had received the gentlemen's protestations of love as "pleasant jest and courtesy, as bombast and as lining to the time," but now that they realize that they are meant in sober earnest, they propose to put these conceited and exuberant young men on trial for a year, after which they will reconsider their refusal.

The pairs of lovers, particularly the self-opinionated Biron and the witty Rosaline, are the first of a Shakespearean line of which better known representatives are Beatrice and Benedick in *Much Ado about Nothing*. But wit combats between the suitor and his beloved are far from constituting the main texture of *Love's Labour's Lost*. The minor characters—the pompous and fantastical Armado and his page Moth; the curate Sir Nathaniel, "a foolish mild man, an honest man, look you, and soon dashed"; Holofernes, the pedantic schoolmaster; Dull, the stupid constable; Costard, the clownish rustic— not only develop in their dialogue a constant stream of ironic criticism of contemporary manners and fashions by means of parody, but also act out within the play a countermovement to the formal motions of the principal characters. The minor characters put on, for the entertainment of the principal characters, the Masque of the Nine Worthies, with Armado as Hector, Costard as Pompey, Sir Nathaniel as Alexander, Moth as Hercules, and Holofernes as Judas Maccabeus. The actors are mercilessly mocked by their noble audience, but somehow Shakespeare contrives that the noble mockers lose, and the ignoble mocked gain, dignity in the end. Armado, boastful and grandiloquent though he is, and ludicrous though his rhymed speech as Hector sounds and is meant to sound, remains patient and courteous under the cruelest mocking. "The sweet war-man is dead and rotten; sweet chucks, beat not the bones of the buried; when he breathed, he was a man. But I will forward with my device. Sweet royalty, bestow on me the sense of hearing." And when he is mockingly asked to strip for combat, he excuses himself with the unexpected and quietly genuine remark: "The naked truth of it is, I have no shirt. I go woolward for penance." Similarly, when Holofernes is mocked off the stage by the noble lords, his retreating cry, "This is not generous, not gentle, not humble," contains both dignity and truth. The battle of the sexes ceases before the battle of the social classes, and the nobility join in mocking the pretensions and inadequacies of their inferiors. But the mockers are themselves mocked by Shakespeare. And the players—after an interruption when the messenger brings news of the death of the King of France and the main action is then concluded—return to conclude their pageant with a simple presentation of the Winter and Spring, singing two charming and simple songs ("When daisies pied" and "When icicles hang by the wall"), each representing one of these two seasons. On that simple lyrical note the play ends.

Love's Labour's Lost owes something to Lyly, something to the Italian *Commedia dell' Arte* with its conventional character types and improvised plots, something to the shows and pageants so frequent in Elizabethan courtly and country-house life. But it is far more than a combination of derivative elements. Its extravagant verbal play, set exercises in wit, and many topical allusions have helped to make it relatively unpopular among general readers, particularly in the nineteenth century. But more recent criticism and dramatic production have helped to show the kind of stylization which is the play's medium, so that it is now produced—most successfully—with something of the formality of a Mozart opera and the grace of movement of ballet. It was never the most popular of Shakespeare's plays, and nobody would claim for it the profundity and brilliance of the work of Shakespeare's maturity. But it was (except perhaps for *Richard III*) Shakespeare's first important and successful original play. It is significant that he began by writing for the popular taste of the public theater and achieved his first technical success (as it might be called) in writing for private performance: his greatest work was to combine both kinds of appeal and profit from both kinds of experience.

But it was the public theater which claimed Shakespeare's chief attention throughout his career. Only three of his plays—*Love's Labour's Lost, A Midsummer Night's Dream,* and *The Tempest*—were written originally for private performance.[1] *A Midsummer Night's Dream* was first written to be performed as part of a wedding festivity before being adapted for the public theater (or perhaps vice versa): it lacks the somewhat self-conscious wit of *Love's Labour's*

[1] Whether *Troilus and Cressida* was originally written for a private performance is still a matter of conjecture, and scholars have argued for and against the view.

Lost and shows Shakespeare moving toward an ideal of "romantic comedy" in which the fortunes of love and the humors of character are skillfully blended. The play is lyrical in tone and masquelike in movement. It lacks the graver undertones that are audible in Shakespeare's later comedies: it is a dream, a jest, a presentation of the comic irresponsibility of young love whose variations are lightheartedly attributed to the mischief-making (half deliberate, half accidental) of Puck. There are several strands, the marriage of Theseus and Hippolyta providing the background or the enclosing brackets which contain the play. In the foreground are the two pairs of lovers, the women constant, the men changing their affections as the magic herb "love in idleness" bids them. In the background is the fairy world, centering on Oberon and Titania and their quarrel, which involves (though they do not know it) the human lovers. Puck moves between the human and the fairy world, and it is interesting that the only human being in the play who comes into direct contact with that world is not any member of Theseus' court or one of the lovers, but Bottom the weaver. The incongruity of bringing the grossest element in the human world into contact with the gossamer world of fairy is exploited by Shakespeare with delicate brilliance. Bottom and his companions, thoroughly English figures for all their classical setting (just as the fairy element comes from English folklore, even though Titania's name is from Ovid and Oberon's from the medieval romance *Huon of Bordeaux*), show Shakespeare bringing a new dimension into English dramatic humor. Bottom is far from being the conventional clown of the sixteenth-century stage, though he doubtless derives from him: he is an affectionately mocking study of a kind of character who flourishes in every society, given precise and convincing localization and individualization. The way in which the love plot, the fairy plot, and the activities of Bottom and his fellows are brought together by means of the Theseus-Hippolyta background shows Shakespeare at ease in his dramatic technique in a new way. The "tedious brief scene of young Pyramus and his love Thisby" is at the same time a hilariously funny parody of the cruder kinds of drama still popular in Shakespeare's day, a vehicle for further developing Bottom's character, and a means of establishing the relation of the different social groups to each other. Theseus himself is a paternal figure, the benevolent ruler who governs with justice and humanity:

> I will hear that play:
> For never anything can be amiss,
> When simpleness and duty tender it.

But the vagaries of love are beyond even his beneficent control. The concluding benediction on the newly married couple for whose wedding the play was written is sung by the fairies; and the last word of all is Puck's. Thoroughly successful, thoroughly charming, delicate, happy, lyrical, *A Midsummer Night's Dream* shows Shakespeare the easy master of a new kind of comedy.

The Merchant of Venice (1596–97), *Much Ado about Nothing* (1598–99), *As You Like It* (1599–1600), and *Twelfth Night* (1600–01) show Shakespeare developing his variety of romantic comedy with increasing technical brilliance and new ways of counterpointing poetry humor. Though these plays have common features—the lively and witty heroines, the carefully placed moments of poetic hush, the delicate and happy treatment of love, the undertones of melancholy or prevented disaster, the element of fairy tale or folklore—each has its distinctive atmosphere and unique pattern. In *The Merchant of Venice* Shakespeare sets himself the almost impossible task of combining the fairy tale plot of the caskets, in which Bassanio figures as the lucky adventurer who wins the girl by a sort of predestinate good fortune, with a story of male friendship in true Renaissance vein (Bassanio and Antonio) and, more significantly, with the story of Shylock and the pound of flesh, a theme of larger dimensions and greater dramatic possibilities than the other strands in the play. For the story of the pound of flesh and the incident of the rings, Shakespeare drew (as he so often did) on an Italian short story or *novella;* in creating Shylock he was probably thinking of Marlowe's *Jew of Malta* as well as contemporary prejudice and the unhappy case of Roderigo Lopez, the Queen's Portuguese-Jewish physician. But he treats everything in his own way, and the result is an original and remarkable play on which Shakespeare's genius carried him beyond the limits of this kind of drama. In the casket plot and the Bassanio-Portia relationship, as well as the character and behavior of Shylock's daughter Jessica, we are in the realm of fairy tale, where characters act in a simple symbolic way and the moral and psychological implications of their behavior are not investigated. In a fully realized moral world, Bassanio would appear as a selfish adventurer and Jessica as a cruel and heartless daughter. But in the enchanted air of Belmont (and though much of the action takes place in Venice, it is Belmont that provides the golden fairy tale atmosphere) we see human beings only in a simple symbolic relationship, with good luck implying worthiness, movement from the Jewish to the Christian orbit seen always as good, and young love justifying all. Shakespeare, however, seeks to combine this world not only with a world of pure comedy, which can go with it perfectly safely, but with a world of moral and psychological realism. The result is—or perhaps this is the cause, not the effect, for it is likely that Shylock grew in his hands beyond his intention—that the character of Shylock is not simply that of a stylized villain, the alien devil who is bad because he does not accept the religion and the social standards of his environment, but a figure of power and dignity whose speeches and behavior, for all his conventional villainy, almost redeem him into tragedy. Even when we make allowances for the Elizabethan state of mind on these matters, and even though we realize that Shylock must not be played as a sympathetic and tragic figure, it is impossible not to feel that the fully realized moral world to which Shylock belongs challenges and even in a sense destroys the simple enchantment of Belmont. For a non-Christian girl to leave her ancestral faith and her family to join her Christian lover is wholly admirable according to the tradition of medieval romance and popular thought; but Shakespeare brings in a new dimension when he shows us Shylock's anguish, and indeed the whole fierce reality of Shylock's character produces a new level of probability in the play on which Bassanio and Jessica and even Portia have a much less real existence. The gap between the fairy tale and the real world shows in the play. Shakespeare tries to cover it up by sheer poetry. The simple beauty of Portia's speech when she gives herself to Bassanio mediates somewhat between the two worlds and brings her nearer the real one, while the famous scene between Lorenzo and Jessica at the beginning of Act V dissolves all disparities in music and moonlight. Portia's and Nerissa's tricks with the rings, childish though the whole incident is, help to mitigate in retrospect the realities of the great court scene, where Portia's speech on mercy rings out with (to modern ears) ironic overtones challenging the Christian attitude to Shylock as well as Shylock's attitude to his victim. *The Merchant of Venice* is a complex play whose different elements do not really belong to the same world. It is held together by moments of poetry as well as by Shakespeare's theatrical skill—for it is good theater throughout. Considered as a dramatic poem rather than as a play to be acted, it can, however, be seen to possess a unity in the pattern of imagery that suggests further meanings: the world of Antonio and Bassanio becomes almost a mirror-image of Shylock's world which in turn is a distorted but recognizable version—and so a deep criticism—of the Christian society about him.

In Shakespeare's next three "romantic comedies"—*Much Ado about Nothing, As You Like It,* and *Twelfth Night*—this form of Elizabethan drama reaches its golden perfection. Like *The Merchant of Venice, Much Ado* combines two plots, one of which has tragic overtones. In the wit combats between Beatrice and Benedick, Shakespeare brings to a more richly human level, and anchors more profoundly in human experience, a dramatic device with which he had earlier sported in a more distinctly formal manner. In the Claudio-Hero story, where the bridegroom is deluded by the wicked Don John into believing in his innocent bride's criminal wantonness and so denounces her at the altar, Shakespeare (taking his plot, as so often, from an Italian *novella*) provides a context in which the merry world of witty attitudinizing is shaken into a deeper reality. There is not here, as in *The Merchant of Venice*, a gap between a world of romantic magic and one of grim reality: the plots not only interlock neatly but also reinforce each other emotionally. Beatrice and Benedick, man-hater and misogynist tricked by friends into believing that each loves the other, discover their real mutual love in the shadow of Hero's tragedy, and the modulation of tone here between the tragic and the romantic is achieved with remarkable art. But Shakespeare keeps the tragic overtones muted by contriving that the forces of evil are already in the process of being discovered and exposed even before the terrible accusation against Hero at the altar, and we know that it is a matter of time before justice is done and Hero is vindicated. The elimination of potential tragedy by the exposure of evil—not too rapidly, but quickly enough to prevent irreparable harm being done—is achieved by the introduction of a third strand into the play, the comic-realistic strand represented by Dogberry and Verges, the officers of the watch who accidentally stumble across the villains and proceed, in their slow-witted and comically clumsy manner, to examine them. This third strand is pure English in inspiration, deriving from Shakespeare's own experience and observation of native character, and it is the first fully developed example of his genius in handling this kind of comedy. Don John's henchmen, and so the truth about Don John's villainy, are safe in the hands of these bumbling public servants from a relatively early point in the play; that the ultimate exposure should be delayed until potential tragedy has sealed the love of Beatrice and Benedick, and that at the same time this delay should be achieved by richly comic means, constitute a striking example of Shakespeare's mastery both of dramatic structure and of modulation of tone.

Of *As You Like It* (whose plot derives from Thomas Lodge's prose pastoral romance, *Rosalynde*) and *Twelfth Night* (the basic idea of whose plot derives ultimately from Greek comedy, via Plautus and sixteenth-century Italian comedy) there is little left to be said by the literary historian. The most popular of Shakespeare's comedies, they represent the ripest fruits of his imagination in its happy golden phase, the perfection of romantic comedy in English. Of the two, *As You Like It* is the lighter in tone, its moral pattern simpler, its happy solution of problems of love and politics in the carefree atmosphere of the greenwood achieved with careless ease. Rosalind, disguised as a boy in the greenwood, teasing her lover in the happy confidence that she is loved by him without having yet to declare her own love, is perhaps the most attractive of all Shakespeare's pert and resourceful young heroines. The exiled duke, "fleeting the time carelessly as they did in the golden world" in the forest of Arden, which is a deliberate mixture of a conventional romantic forest (the Arden of the original story was the Ardennes in France) and the Arden of his native Warwickshire; the melancholy Jacques, commenting on affairs with exhibitionist melancholy, Shakespeare's amused portrait of the traveling intellectual returned to sneer at everything at home; Touchstone, the clown, a new type of character for Shakespeare, and the first of a series which culminates in the Fool of *King Lear;* Touchstone and Audrey representing love between the sexes in its simplest physical aspect, contrasted with the romantic love between Rosalind and Orlando as well as with the exaggerated pastoral passion of Silvius for the scornful Phebe; these and other characters circle round Rosalind, who, once she has arrived in Arden, remains the center of the play. The dialogue is as much in prose as in poetry: the former is a far cry from Lodge's euphuistic prose, though it is in some degree based on it; it is light and sparkling and has the speed of talk as well as the form of art. The poetry has a lyrical clarity with overtones of gravity, shifting in tempo in accordance with the mood and character of the speaker. And the songs—"Under the greenwood tree," "Blow, blow, thou winter wind," "It was a lover and his lass" —echo through the play with a grave sweetness. The concluding wedding masque is perhaps more to the Elizabethans' taste than to ours, and the perfunctory solution of all remaining difficulties at the end not wholly acceptable even in terms of the level of probability set up by the play. It can be argued, too, that a note almost of mawkishness, of schoolgirl romanticism, occasionally comes to the surface, but this is a minority view and it represents a criticism of the theme rather than of the treatment. As a lyrical comedy of romantic love in a simple moral context whose basic pattern derives from folklore or at least from popular imagination working on a literary tradition, *As You Like It* stands supreme.

Twelfth Night, or What you Will (the first title indicates when it was first performed and the second, Shakespeare's cheerful carelessness about titles), uses similar elements to those found in *As You Like It,* but in different proportion, and with a somewhat more adult tone. The texture is richer, the overtones subtler. The comic elements enrich and comment on the romantic elements, and the romantic attitude itself is gently mocked at the same time it is glorified. The result is a play which presents an attitude to life through the combination of romantic and comic elements into a unity essentially lyrical in nature. Shipwreck, disguises and misunderstandings, romantic love, friendship, boisterous mirth, wit, trickery, self-deception, and above all and throughout all *music*—the songs, the references to music in the verse, the instrumental music off stage—music with a faintly melancholy tone underlying the whole play: these themes and devices Shakespeare welds together in what is perhaps the most perfect of all his comedies. If the light playing on *As You Like It* is that of the morning sun, the sun in *Twelfth Night* is now mellower and later, afternoon sunshine with a hint of sunset in its quality. From its opening, with the sad-sweet, self-indulgent music of the Duke's speech, "If music be the food of love, play on," to the Clown's concluding song, "When that I was a little tiny boy, With hey, ho, the wind and the rain," with its sense of wistful futility, the play moves through different phases of the romantic-comic combination to create a world in which passion, adventure, melancholy, and folly coexist and help to define each other. The comic scenes are rich in appreciative sense of human absurdity. There is no finer fool in literature than Sir Andrew Aguecheek, and the dialogue between him and Sir Toby Belch is splendid in its cheerful folly. It is significant, too, that it is against the background of this comic dialogue that Feste the clown sings what is perhaps the most haunting of all Shakespeare's songs, "O mistress mine, where are you roaming?" with its philosophy of comedy present in the second stanza:

> What is love? 'Tis not hereafter.
> Present mirth hath present laughter. . . .

The gulled Malvolio, "sick of self-love," is presented for our comic disapproval; the love-sick duke is loved by his own page, a girl in disguise, whose love for her master redeems him from sentimentalist into true lover; Viola, the shipwrecked, the resourceful, the disguised, steers her course as best she can, and in the process keeps the plot moving, until the happy ending can be worked out; the lady Olivia, like the Duke, is turned by events from self-indulgent emotion into a truer emotional life. And always we have the feeling that the comedy is balanced on a razor-edge: this world of afternoon sunlight is ringed round with traps and dangers, and eventually the dark will come anyway. Danger, misadventure, self-delusion, self-indulgence, misunderstanding, and the constant rise and fall of the human passions and appetites, all work out here to a happy ending, except for the mocked Malvolio. It is appropriate that they should; it is this kind of world and this kind of play; but in the distance we hear the sadder notes underlying the romantic—

> What is love? 'Tis not hereafter.
> Present mirth hath present laughter;
> What's to come is still unsure.
> In delay there lies no plenty;
> Then come kiss me, sweet and twenty,
> Youth's a stuff will not endure.

The golden moment passed, and Shakespeare was not to write this kind of play again.

Parallel with his development of romantic comedy, Shakespeare was maturing his handling of the history play. The three Henry VI plays, with which he opened his career, are of interest to those concerned with Shakespeare's attitude to English history as well as to those numerous scholars who have been attracted by the bibliographical and other problems which they raise. Uneven and sometimes crude both in dramatic movement and verse technique, they have their "Shakespearean" moments and show Shakespeare seeking a way from the episodic chronicle play to a more dramatic and more fully integrated handling of historical material. In *Richard III* he solves the problem of form by concentrating on the central character, a Marlovian villain redeemed from mechanical badness by his wit and energy; Richard projects his own character by the thoughtful rhetoric of his speech and the Machiavellian virtuosity of his actions, and the element of heroism which he acquires in his final defeat is kept from raising any moral difficulties by the passionate picture of the victorious Richmond, founder of England's Tudor dynasty, as the savior of his country. *Richard II* (1595–96) is a more complex and interesting play, deliberately ritualistic—even sacramental—in tone to suggest the Elizabethan view of the Middle Ages. The deposition of the last of England's medieval kings—for Shakespeare clearly thought of Henry IV as "modern," belonging to Shakespeare's own world, and his succession the result of personal ambition rather than divine right—had long acquired an aura of mystery and pathos in the minds of those who looked back to it, and Shakespeare deliberately set out to render that aura dramatically, providing both adequate psychological explanation and impressive poetic expression. Richard himself, petulant, childish, emotionally self-indulgent, incapable of asserting his authority over factious nobles but brooding and poetizing over his royal status once he is on the point of losing it, is the most complex character that Shakespeare had so far created, and the way he manipulates the audience's sympathy (first against, then in favor of Richard) shows remarkable dramatic cunning. Richard was the Lord's anointed, the last English king to rule in virtue of his direct and undisputed descent from William the Conqueror. His deposition was in a sense sacrilege, and after his death his supporters built up a picture of him as saint and martyr. The other side, the Lancastrians, who supported the claims of Henry IV and his successors, saw Richard as a weak and foolish king who voluntarily abdicated because he recognized his own unfitness to carry out his royal duties. Shakespeare combines both pictures with complete dramatic consistency. And in the ritual note which pervades the play he pictures a phase of English civilization very different from the breezy background of power politics we see in the *Henry IV* plays. The deposition scene is a careful inversion of the coronation ritual, and Bolingbroke's impatience with Richard's histrionics is also the modern man's impatience with the stylized forms of medieval life. The self-indulgent lyricism of many of Richard's own speeches reflects the predominantly lyrical interest that seems to have been a feature of Shakespeare's dramatic art in this phase of his development (we see it also in *Romeo and Juliet*, written at about the same time), but it also helps to build Richard's character and to differentiate it from that of his more realistic and practical supplanter.

Henry IV Part I and Part II (1597–98) show Shakespeare combining the political with the comic in a new and striking manner. The central theme is the education of Prince Hal, Henry IV's son and later Henry V, and this is worked out with many echoes of the older moralities. But the figure who represents Riot is so much more than a character in a morality play that the whole tone and character of the two plays are altered by his presence. Falstaff is no conventional Vice, but a comic figure of immense proportions who embodies in his speech and action an amoral gusto in living at the same time as he stands for a way of life which the prince must repudiate before he can be king. Shakespeare uses the Percy rebellion in Part I in order to put Falstaff in some degree in his proper moral place: the colossus of the Boar's Head tavern, so richly amusing in his comic vitality in his habitual environment, becomes less satisfactory as a human being when he is found using his authority as an officer to line his own pockets and impair the strength of the king's forces or, on the battlefield against determined rebels, faking a heroic action for himself. The way for the final and inevitable rejection of Falstaff by his former boon companion now become king is prepared throughout the latter section of Part I and the earlier section of Part II. Much ink has been spilt on the rejection of Falstaff: the simple fact is that he is (and is meant to be) engaging but not admirable, that he belongs to the amoral world of the Boar's Head, not to the moral world of the dedicated Christian ruler. He enters the latter world only to be ejected from it, and though we are properly sorry for him we must realize that the amoral becomes the immoral in this new context, and must be removed from it.

This is to consider the two Henry IV plays as a single dramatic unit, and there are convincing arguments for and against this view. It is perhaps simplest to take the common-sense position that Shakespeare wrote the first part as a play complete in itself, but when he continued it in the second he adjusted his continuation to a comprehensive and consistent view of the meaning of the whole action of both parts. In Part I the three levels of the action—the high political, surrounding Henry IV; the low comic, surrounding Falstaff; and the plausible, even attractive, but politically immoral world of Hotspur and his fellow rebels—each has its appropriate language and its place in the total politico-moral pattern. Hotspur's heroic egotism and Falstaff's unheroic egotism are both contrasted with the attitude of heroic unselfishness which is the implied ideal attitude for the ruler. In Part II, the country justices, Shallow and Silence, represent yet another level, and in a sense a deeper one: they represent the England which remains unchanged throughout all the political struggles of ambitious men to achieve control of the state, the world of inefficient innocence, unconsciously comic (unlike Falstaff, who is consciously so), foolish and pretentious, yet impressively and averagely human. The juxtaposition of different moral and social levels in both parts helps to give the play its richness and brilliance. Statesmen, rebels, roisterers; the King and his sons and advisers; Falstaff with Peto and Bardolph and Mistress Quickly and Doll Tearsheet; Percy and his friends; Shallow and Silence—each group has its place in the unfolding action (or series of actions), each reveals something about England, about the relation between moral character and human behavior, about the nature of man. The Henry IV plays can be seen as part of the general pattern of Shakespeare's picture of English history from Richard II to the Tudor; but they are, much more significantly, entertaining, stimulating, and esthetically satisfying plays whose subject, like the subject of all great drama, is human nature. And Falstaff remains, greater even than the plays which contain him, the richest comic creation in English literature.

Henry V (1598–99) concludes the historical series. It is narrower in scope and interest than the Henry IV plays, concentrating, according to tradition, on Henry as ideal warrior and man of action with a conventional piety and a gift for military rhetoric that impressed Shakespeare's contemporaries more than they impress us. The witty and aloof prince of the Henry IV plays has become a copybook model for a conquering prince, a much narrower concept than that of the Renaissance gentleman. Henry V has none of the tortured idealism of Brutus or the intellectual and moral complexity of Hamlet; his kind of success comes to simpler and in some respects less attractive characters. A brisk, well-constructed, happily varied play, *Henry V* is good theater and contains some admirable rhetorical verse. But it is the narrowest and occasionally the stuffiest of all of Shakespeare's maturer plays, and one for which the modern reader or audience has to make a special effort to align his sensibility with that of the Elizabethans.

King John (ca. 1596–97) stands somewhat apart from Shakespeare's other history plays, where he deals with the cycle of English history from the deposition of Richard II to the founding of the Tudor dynasty by Henry VII in 1485. Its relation to an older play, entitled *The Troublesome Reign of King John,* published in two parts in 1591, remains problematical: there is clearly some connection, and perhaps the *Troublesome Reign* is a "bad quarto" of an earlier version of Shakespeare's play as we have it. The older play covers the whole of King John's reign, portraying him as a champion of English ecclesiastical independence against intolerable papal claims to supremacy; its tone is strongly anti-Catholic. In Shakespeare's *King John* the anti-Catholic tone has been significantly moderated and John himself (though not the simple villain of later historians) is far from a hero. The character of the Bastard Faulconbridge; the dramatic conflicts between Queen Eleanor, King John's mother, and Constance, mother of Arthur, John's nephew; Pandulph, the Papal legate, succeeding by his cunning rhetorical argument in persuading King Philip of France to turn against John with whom he has recently sworn amity; the pathetic scene between Hubert and young Prince Arthur—these are some of the elements in the play which show Shakespeare bursting the bounds of the older chronicle form, not to concentrate on the psychological and moral problems of an individual character, as he did in *Richard III* and *Richard II,* but to give free rein to a curiosity and an exuberance which make the play lively and fascinating in spite of its structural deficiencies. The political interest which emerges so strongly in the Henry IV plays is visible here—the concern with the ethics of rebellion and the unity of England and the character of the good ruler—but the play's true appeal lies elsewhere: in the Bastard's vividly presented quality of the forthright Englishman, in the vitality and variety of the whole. Altogether, *King John* is a most interesting and promising transitional play, which occupies an important though lonely place in the Shakespeare canon.

In the years when he was experimenting with different kinds of history plays and perfecting his romantic comedy Shakespeare was also thinking about tragedy. *Richard III* was tragedy of a kind, but Shakespeare was soon dissatisfied with this kind of play and never wrote another like it. About the same time that he wrote *Richard II* (1595–96) he also produced *Romeo and Juliet*, a play of star-crossed lovers based on an Italian story which had already been handled in English (via the French) both in prose and in verse. Shakespeare's immediate source was the verse rendering, Arthur Brooke's poem *The Tragical History of Romeus and Juliet*, though he produces a quite different effect by speeding up the action and by giving the characters new life and motivation. It is, however, as Shakespeare tells it, a tragedy of circumstances rather than of character, brilliantly rendered in passionate lyrical-dramatic terms. Romeo and Juliet themselves are the quintessence of young love; the speed and ardor of their mutual adoration are symbolic of the recklessly dedicated love that is the mark of first real passion (how different from the maturer and more sophisticated love of Antony and Cleopatra!), which banishes alike sentimentality and false modesty to burn brightly and honestly until fate brings all to an untimely close. We first see Romeo as the conventional, sentimental lover of Rosaline, sighing histrionically, though not forgetting to ask, "Where shall we dine?" His first sight of Juliet, daughter of the Capulets with whom his own family of Montague is engaged in deadly feud, banishes all that nonsense and makes a man of him. When his lively and mocking friend Mercutio sees Romeo again for the first time since he and Juliet have declared their mutual love, he is struck by his liveliness and wit: "Why, is not this better now than groaning for love? Now art thou sociable; now art thou Romeo. . . ." Throughout the play Shakespeare, by a variety of devices, sets the love of Romeo and Juliet against other views of love: to Capulet, it is a matter of a suitable family alliance; to the Nurse, a matter of physical, sexual satisfaction; to Paris, Capulet's chosen husband for his daughter, a matter of good breeding and decorum.

The norm of the play's expression is both lyrical and declamatory. When Romeo, disguised, first meets Juliet in the home of his family enemy, they share the speaking of a sonnet together, and with its last line comes their first kiss. Juliet's surging speech as she impatiently awaits her bridegroom's arrival for the one night fate is to allow them to spend together is a formal epithalamium as well as an expression of physical passion so honest and frank that it shocked Victorian editors (Shakespeare makes no attempt to conceal the physical element in ideal romantic love). And the lovers' reluctant recognition of the dawn which brings to an end their first and last night of love is in the form of a traditional "aubade" or dawn poem. At the same time, each character has his own idiom which rings true to his personality. And the characters themselves are clearly conceived and brilliantly presented. The Nurse, that well-meaning but gross figure whose failure to understand that love is more than mere sex finally leaves Juliet to face her fate alone, is one of Shakespeare's great comic creations; Mercutio, the witty, mocking gallant, is the ideal Renaissance bachelor, and almost steals the show before his death— resulting from his getting mixed up in the Montague-Capulet feud— takes him out of the way and at the same time helps to precipitate the tragedy. Capulet, Friar Lawrence, Tybalt, Benvolio, and the others play their parts as less fully realized but clearly presented and deftly handled characters whose speech and actions are always both appropriate to themselves and helpful to the working out of the play. The picture of the two ideal young lovers discovering their love only to be trapped by circumstance into premature death is not profound tragedy; it has no meaning other than to present the glory of true love and the fatuity and futility of those hatreds and conventions that destroy it. But it is sheer bad luck rather than either the fatal feud or Capulet's sudden impulse to marry off his daughter to Paris immediately that finally brings on the tragedy. Life is not indicted; true love remains a glory, and the lovers die without disillusionment. Ophelia and Desdemona, who die bewildered, ignorant of the cause of their own destruction and of their hero's cruelty, are part of a sadder world and products of a profounder imagination.

During the next few years Shakespeare produced histories and comedies, and when he turns to tragedy again, in *Julius Caesar* (1599–1600), he is seeking a profounder way of finding individual human tragedy in history than he did in either *Richard III* or *Richard II*. The source of the play, as of all Shakespeare's Roman plays, is Sir Thomas North's *Lives of the Noble Grecians and Romans*, translated from the Greek of Plutarch via the French of Jacques Amyot. In Plutarch's lives of Caesar, Brutus, and Mark Antony, Shakespeare read history through biography and went on to show dramatically some of the paradoxical ways in which private character influences and is influenced by public affairs. In a sense, the theme of the play is the relation between private and public virtue: they are not identical, as Brutus thought, and the humanitarian idealist does not necessarily make the best politician or even the best patriot. In *Richard II* Shakespeare showed how qualities which, in a private person, though far from admirable might yet have a certain charm, were fatal in a ruler. In *Julius Caesar* he probes much more subtly into this problem, and shows the liberal idealist bringing about the very opposite result to that which he intended. Brutus, like Hamlet and in some degree like Othello, is destroyed largely by his own virtues. In Brutus, nobility of character implies political innocence; in Hamlet, intelligence and sensitivity produce inability to face the world as it is; in Othello integrity and forthrightness produce credulity and, through credulity, tragic mistrust of the one person whom above all he should have trusted. Each of these characters may well have acted better if he had been a less good man. A more worldly Brutus, a less morally sensitive Hamlet, a tougher and more cunning Othello, would have done less harm in the world. This goes far deeper than simply the relation between private and public virtue. It includes, among other problems, that of the relation between innocence and virtue, or at least between innocence of character and effectiveness of moral action. It is an old problem: Milton was to treat it, in his own way, in *Paradise Lost*, where "our credulous mother, Eve" allowed herself to be fooled by Satan into tasting of the forbidden tree. Eve's real fault was lack of sophistication; she was unsuspicious of what Satan, in his serpent disguise, told her; she was a "sucker" and swallowed his story. But would she have been more virtuous to be suspicious? Is it morally wrong to be a "sucker"—as Eve was with respect to the serpent, as Othello was with respect to Iago, as Brutus was with respect to such political sophisticates as Antony, as Hamlet was— we might almost say—with respect to life?

A man destroyed by his own virtues is a truly tragic theme, and one familiar enough in the modern world where the tragedy of the liberal intellectual is a commonplace. But of course this is not the only theme of *Julius Caesar*. Cassius is the co-hero, and, skilled politician though he is, with little scruple in playing on Brutus' finer feelings, he admires Brutus and cannot help allowing Brutus to achieve moral ascendancy over him, once the murder of Caesar is accomplished. The coarser nature is dominated by the finer—to the destruction of both of them and of the ideal to which they had sacrificed everything. In the quarrel scene it is Cassius who first gives way, and it is under the influence of this moral domination by Brutus that, against his better judgment, Cassius allows Brutus to have his way in his ill-advised plan of seeking immediate battle at Philippi. Nowhere is the Epicurean Cassius more like the stoic Brutus than when he commits suicide because he is ashamed of having lived "so long, /To see my best friend ta'en before my face." And that suicide, rather than military defeat, seals the doom of the republican forces. Cassius is not as unlike Brutus as he thinks. Both are made fools of by Antony—Brutus, of course, especially, for it was Brutus who, against Cassius' advice, insisted on Antony's being given permission to speak. If Cassius is shrewder and more practical than Brutus he is basically an idealist too, an intellectual, whom Caesar had come to suspect because "he thinks too much." If he appears a cunning man of action beside Brutus, he is almost equally a babe in the wood when seen beside Antony, the man without innocence, the man who knows how to unite his personal affections with his political ambitions. (Though it is an unstable equilibrium and, as Shakespeare shows us later in *Antony and Cleopatra,* it cannot be maintained throughout a lifetime.)

Julius Caesar is thus a political tragedy, exploring the relation between private and public virtue, between personal morality and political efficiency, between innocence and action. A well-knit, lean play, with no superfluous fat or subsidiary levels of action (though we must remember that the text we have may represent a shortened acting version), it is one of the most clean-cut and straightforward of Shakespeare's tragedies. The blank verse is fluent and businesslike, rising where necessary to a noble eloquence and falling to a quieter colloquial movement where the action demands it. The moments of quiet in the play—Brutus with Portia, Brutus with his sleepy page, Lucius—are beautifully managed and add that note of controlled pathos which emphasizes the personal tragedy of the public figure. And at the end victorious efficiency pays its tribute to defeated innocence. "This was the noblest Roman of them all." The words are Antony's, referring to Brutus, and they represent his "real" opinion, as they do Cassius'—and Shakespeare's. The failures are, in an important sense, the better men. Henry V is a mechanical figure beside Brutus or Hamlet.

Hamlet (1600–01), the most popular and the most discussed of Shakespeare's tragedies, is both more complex in theme and more subtle in treatment than *Julius Caesar.* The existence of three separate texts—a "bad quarto" (1603), which is apparently a garbled reconstruction, largely from memory, of Shakespeare's play put together by a player who doubled the parts of Marcellus and the Second Player; the "good" quarto of 1604 which represents Shakespeare's full text; and the Folio text of 1623, a cut acting version, with nevertheless some passages not in the 1604 quarto—has deflected a great deal of critical attention to purely textual matters, while the relation of the play to a lost earlier *Hamlet,* probably by Kyd, has also led to much speculation. The story itself is an ancient one, originating in Scandinavia as the tale of Amleth, a prince who pretended madness in order to fool his usurping uncle and regain his throne. Late in the twelfth century it was told—already an old story, that had come down through oral tradition—by the Danish historian Saxo Grammaticus in his Latin *Historia Danica*. In Saxo's version we find important elements which remain in Shakespeare's play and which critics have long argued about. Amleth's madness, in Saxo, is assumed so that his usurping uncle would regard him as a completely mindless lunatic not worth killing: its purpose is sheer self-preservation. The usurping uncle sends agents to try to find out whether Amleth's idiocy is genuine—and one of these agents is a girl, the original of Ophelia, while another, the original of Polonius, hides himself in the straw of Amleth's mother's room to overhear a conversation between mother and son, and is discovered and killed by Amleth. Amleth in the end achieves his revenge, slays his wicked uncle, and becomes king. This story—a tale of revenge from the heroic age—underwent some modifications in later versions, and then, apparently in the late 1580's, a dramatist who is generally taken to have been Kyd dramatized it as a Senecan revenge play in the Elizabethan mode, incorporating some of the devices that had been so successful in *The Spanish Tragedy*. Here for the first time we get the ghost—a Senecan device—crying for revenge, and here, too, the original murder is done secretly by poisoning, not openly as in Saxo, so that the wicked uncle is not publicly known as wicked and the ghost is required to reveal the truth to Hamlet. This makes it unnecessary for Hamlet to feign madness in order to save his life, as he does in Saxo, but Kyd was a great hand at madness and kept this element in the story (indeed, he added to it by making the Ophelia character go mad also) though the motivation for it is now much less clear. He also, true to the Senecan fashion, killed off the hero and the other major characters in the end, and introduced Laertes, the fencing match, and the poisoned rapier and drink. We know something of this lost *Hamlet* largely from a degraded version of it which exists in German, and our knowledge is important, because it enables us to see Shakespeare's play as a reworking of a melodramatic Senecan revenge play into a profound poetic tragedy.

Shakespeare's task was to impose a new, tragic meaning on this traditional story, by his arrangement and presentation of the action, by the kind of life and motivation he gave to the characters, and by the overtones of meaning and suggestion set up by his poetic handling of the characters' language. Though T. S. Eliot has questioned the success with which he transformed the old material into a con-

sistent work of dramatic art, the experience of generations of playgoers and readers is sufficient proof that Shakespeare has given it
profound and disturbing new dramatic life. In the character of
Hamlet he takes the Brutus type and by giving him increased complexity and sensitivity within the story's traditional atmosphere of
ambition, murder, and revenge gives the play a wholly new dimension. This is the tragedy of moral sensitivity in a wicked world, the
tragedy of the idealist come suddenly face to face with reality, the
tragedy of imagination betraying its owner. Or so the play has been
read by many. Hamlet, his innocent world shattered by the marriage
of his adored mother to the uncle who has succeeded his hero-
worshiped father to the throne which in any case rightly belongs to
Hamlet himself, is in a bad enough mental state before the ghost
reveals that his "uncle-father" has more than incest (for marriage
with a sister-in-law was technically incest), ambition, and drunkenness to answer for: he is also guilty of fratricide. Old-fashioned
revenge in the heroic tradition is not going to restore his lost world
or bring back to health an imagination increasingly "tainted" by
disgust and horror at sex, Court life, and politics. Surrounded by the
suspicious Claudius, the bewildered Ophelia, the lost Queen, the
worldly busybody Polonius (to whose coolly self-interested support
Claudius owed the throne), and the spies and opportunists of the
Court, Hamlet can do nothing but brood and indulge his festering
imagination. He can confide in nobody—not even fully in Horatio,
his one trustworthy friend. His madness is partly real hysteria, partly
an attempt to fence off curiosity about his real state of mind and
intentions. It serves only to increase suspicion, while his reckless
baiting of Claudius, which he seems unable to resist, plays into the
usurper's hands. No one can help him. In Ophelia he sees only tainted
womanhood—tainted because of his mother's sin; in Horatio, the
happy extrovert, "the man who is not passion's slave," whom he can
admire but not imitate. Occasionally we get glimpses of the old Hamlet, gentle, accomplished, princely; occasionally, when the event
presses and his sudden temper is roused, he can break away into
violent action, as in his slaying of Polonius—which again plays right
into the King's hands. When he tests the truth of the ghost's story
by putting on the play within the play, his baiting of the King and
the way he presents the play ("one Lucianus, *nephew* to the king")
allow the Court to think that his trouble is thwarted ambition and
that he is threatening to get rid of the King and succeed to the
throne himself (as the old Amleth did), and determines Claudius to
get rid of him immediately. His one clear chance to kill Claudius he
will not take, making the excuse that the villain is praying and he

would prefer to slay him when he is engaged in some activity which will ensure his immediate descent to Hell; and he goes on to the famous scene in his mother's bedroom where he rubs her face in the dirt in a desperate attempt to make her see and feel how she has shattered his world and betrayed everything that was decent in the Hamlet family. He escapes Claudius' plot by a mixture of luck, courage, and contrivance, and comes back to find Ophelia dead and Laertes incensed against him, meeting his doom at last by Laertes' poisoned rapier, but not before he has finally, in a surge of contemptuous anger, killed Claudius. In the end, all the principal characters are dead—Polonius, Ophelia, the Queen, Claudius, and Hamlet—and Fortinbras, the man of action, the soldier who believes in such crude sentimentalities as military glory, the Henry V type, succeeds to the throne.

Does Shakespeare give proper dramatic shape and conviction to it all? That the play is tremendously effective on the stage there can be no doubt. From the tense, quiet opening, with the sentries apprehensive and jittery, to Fortinbras' final elegy on Hamlet, scene succeeds scene with mounting dramatic interest, moments of tension are adroitly followed by more relaxed interludes, characters create themselves by speech and action with astonishing vividness and humanity, and the struggle between Hamlet and his destiny is played out. Is Hamlet consistent? Are his actions properly motivated? Do his soliloquies sometimes reveal their author's distresses and speculations rather than Hamlet's? Is there not some disproportion between Hamlet's behavior and the situation that calls it forth? We can answer all these questions unfavorably to Shakespeare— Hamlet is not always consistent, the motives for his actions are sometimes in doubt, sometimes in the soliloquies Shakespeare rather than Hamlet seems to be speaking, there is not always a close and easily demonstrable connection between the situation and Hamlet's response to it—but this does not mean that Shakespeare has bungled the problem of giving satisfying dramatic shape to the old story. The element of mystery in Hamlet's motivation helps to enlarge the dimensions of the play. Personality is not a cut-and-dried affair which can be explained by a simple cause-and-effect relationship. If there are elements in the original story that Shakespeare feels obliged to use even though they do not appear to be directly connected with his conception of the action and the characters, it is to his credit as an artist that he uses them to help suggest the mystery of personality rather than as mere mechanical appendages to the action. We may be told that Hamlet's rash killing of Polonius and his contemptuous treatment of the corpse derives from elements in the old story that

Shakespeare felt he had to include, but the important fact is that in Shakespeare's play these things are dramatically compelling and esthetically satisfying to those who know nothing of the sources of the plot. It is a mistake to confuse the dramatically and artistically successful with the psychologically explicable. Hamlet may remain in part a mystery, but that mystery is bound up with the mystery of life. And the play has the dimensions of life together with the formality and completeness of art.

Scholarship can concentrate on Shakespeare's treatment of his sources, on the way in which Elizabethan dramatic conventions helped to determine his treatment of any given point, or on the degree in which a knowledge of the Elizabethan view of the world explains Hamlet's attitude to the ghost or Polonius' behavior at Court. All this knowledge is helpful, but it must not be allowed to obscure the fact that in his handling of an older story, his use of contemporary dramatic conventions, and in his Elizabethan habit of mind Shakespeare operates as a successful dramatist, creates a moral world that challenges and illuminates, builds up a pattern of tragic action that does arouse "pity and fear" to leave us in the end "in calm of mind, all passion spent." That Shakespeare does this so brilliantly in *Hamlet* is partly due to his having discovered by now a method of enabling his principal characters, at selected moments in the play, to render their state of mind to the audience or the reader. The Shakespearean soliloquy, which reaches its maturity in *Hamlet*, is not merely an expansion of the conventional "aside" or a simple speaking aloud of a coherent stream of thought. It is a poetic rendering of a character's complete mental and emotional state at a critical point in his development, drawing on all the resources of imagery and rhythmic movement for its total expression. For this is poetic drama, not "realistic" drama, and the recurrence of related images, the rise and fall of certain rhythms, the sounding of certain overtones of meaning and suggestion, are as important in building up the total significance of the play as the mere sequence of events or paraphrasable content of the speeches.

Containing something of the larger dimensions of life within the limiting formality of art, *Hamlet*, perhaps more than any other of Shakespeare's tragedies, lends itself to a variety of interpretations. Hamlet is both the ideal Renaissance prince and the conventional malcontent, the traditional avenger and the sensitive idealist in a brutal world, and other things besides. And, in lesser degree, the same multiple description can be given of the other characters. The play is not, however, simply a series of portraits; the action is what gives it shape and primary meaning, and it is a mistake to remove the characters from the action and speculate about them as though they are characters in a psychologist's case-book (though the fact that critics have been tempted to do this is surely a tribute to Shakespeare's dramatic skill). Of the many meanings that can be extracted from the action of *Hamlet*, perhaps the most tragic, and the one which fits in best with what appears to be Shakespeare's view of the essential tragedy of human life at this time, is that here is a presentation of the paradox of guilt and justice. Justice demands appropriate action where a crime has been committed, but in fact no action is ever appropriate. The tragedy of *Hamlet*, as in some degree of *Othello*, is that moral outrage demands action when no action can be of any use. In a sense, we can say that the ghost was at fault in appearing to Hamlet in the first place and setting him—for what might be called purely selfish reasons—a task which, even if accomplished, could do no possible good. When Hamlet's whole nature was outraged by his mother's behavior and then by the news of his father's murder, he naturally felt that something must be done. But what? What could be done that would make any difference—any difference at all to the things that really mattered? Would a dagger through Claudius' ribs restore Hamlet's shattered universe? Would it restore his earlier idealized image of his mother or remove the "blister" that had been set on his innocent love? This is a tragedy of moral frustration. What are you going to do about past crimes which have shattered your preconceptions about the nature of life? There is nothing you can ever do about the past, except forget it. And yet, of course, Hamlet could not forget. Revenge is no real help—what sort of action, then, *is* of help? None that is directed toward undoing the past: only purposive action directed toward the future can ever help. And that is at least one explanation of Hamlet's long delay in carrying out the ghost's command: he wanted action that would undo the past, and no action could do that, revenge least of all, for that would only re-enact the past.

The punishment can never fit the crime, for it can never undo it. We may think we may be able to find appropriate action, as Lear thought:

> I will have such revenges on you both
> That all the world shall—I will do such things—
> What they are yet, I know not; but they shall be
> The terrors of the earth;

but in fact we never do, and it is impossible that we ever should. Lear's frustration at feeling a deep moral indignation which can have no "objective correlative" in action is, in part, the cause of his madness, as it is of Hamlet's moods and Othello's self-torture (for in *Othello* there is no action that can take care of the supposed fact of Desdemona's infidelity). Only when he gives up the whole idea of action does Lear recover and achieve redemption. The morally outraged man, the finer and more sensitive he is, will feel all the more need for action, the need to do something about his shocking revelation; and his frustration at finding no adequate action produces tragedy. Even the ghost in *Hamlet* learns at last—perhaps learns sooner than Hamlet himself—the futility of trying to undo the past by physical action. He declines from the armed warrior whom we first see to become on his last appearance a pathetic domestic figure ("enter the ghost in his night gown") only interested in trying to make contact with his morally lost wife and in saving her from Hamlet's morbid rage. This remarkable scene—the only one in which we see the Hamlet family together, father, mother, and son—has a strange kind of pathos, with the Queen unable because of her guilt to see her husband's spirit so that the ghost, after a vain effort to re-establish the family unit, as it were, departs in silence forever. On the other side is the Polonius family, all destroyed, too, through involvement in Hamlet's tragedy—innocent involvement on Ophelia's part, almost innocent on Laertes', and only relatively guilty on the part of Polonius. We last see *them* together fairly early in the play, when Laertes is being seen off by his devoted father and sister—also a touching domestic tableau, with its own meaning in the play. The tragedy of Hamlet concerns more than the wreck of a noble spirit, and the longer Hamlet dwells on the past and searches for a way of undoing it, the more innocent—as well as guilty—people become involved in it. And so interpretation can go on, for the meaning of *Hamlet* echoes on indefinitely.

Othello (1603–04), the second of Shakespeare's great tragedies, is a more closely packed and concentrated play. Exploring again some of the paradoxes of good and evil and the irony of evil being bred out of innocence, Shakespeare here concentrates on a domestic issue and produces the most relentless and the saddest of his tragedies. Iago, the "realist," the man who thinks he knows how to get on in the world, who relishes his power to manipulate people like puppets, is more than a mere device to get the plot started, as some modern critics see him, or than the embodiment of "motiveless malignity" that Coleridge saw; he is both the disgruntled professional soldier and the hard-boiled cynic who feels personally outraged when a simple-minded hero like Othello gets ahead in the world and he, who knows the world so much better, fails to get on. Othello himself, the romantic Moor with his background of "antres vast and deserts idle," can fight for Venice and save her from her enemies but knows that he does not really know these people, and that knowledge makes him Iago's prey. The story of a jealous ensign inventing slanders to make his Moorish captain believe that his devoted white wife has been faithless to him and then helping him to slay her comes from the Italian writer Cinthio's collection of stories, the *Hecatommithi*, and as Cinthio tells it is a crude enough tale, far from promising material for a tragedy. Shakespeare makes it into a tragedy by his arrangement and patterning of the details, by his characterization, by the symbolic use of detail, and by the language in which he makes the characters express themselves. The opening, with the whispering at street corners flaring suddenly into Othello's confrontation with his unrecognized enemies and his noble defense of his marriage before the Senate, is a little play in itself, and one with a happy ending. Othello's simple dignity carries all before it:

> Keep up your bright swords, for the dew will rust them.

And the habit of command:

> Hold your hands,
> Both you of my inclining and the rest.
> Were it my cue to fight, I should have known it
> Without a prompter.

And the superb combination of respect and self-assurance:

> Most potent, grave, and reverend signiors,
> My very noble and approv'd good masters,
> That I have ta'en away this old man's daughter,
> It is most true; true, I have married her:
> The very head and front of my offending
> Hath this extent, no more . . .

It is this self-assurance that Iago sets out to destroy. Iago the puppet-master, who enjoys life most when he can manipulate the lives of others from behind the scenes, sets himself to manipulate this commanding Moor. And because he is a Moor, and noble, and so deeply in love with Desdemona that he can scarcely believe his good fortune, and inexperienced and therefore self-distrustful in domestic matters (especially where Venetians are concerned), Iago succeeds in destroying him. That Iago destroys Desdemona too is (in Shakespeare's play but not in his source) incidental: he has no malice against her; he is out to destroy successful innocence, which to him ought to be a contradiction in terms, and he can only get at that through Desdemona. He wants nothing out of it all except the destruction of Othello: he makes this heroic figure dance to his piping, makes a puppet out of him—and what happens after that, he scarcely thinks about. If he had thought, he would have known that sooner or later the truth would have come to light; but he never looked beyond his immediate aim.

What makes it all possible is Othello's incredulity in the face of his own supreme happiness—a kind of modesty, which makes him vulnerable to Iago's suggestion that he does not in fact enjoy the happiness he has thought was his.

> It gives me wonder great as my content
> To see you here before me. O my soul's joy!
> If after every tempest come such calms,
> May the winds blow till they have waken'd death! . . .
>   If it were now to die
> 'Twere now to be most happy for, I fear,
> My soul hath her content so absolute
> That not another comfort like to this
> Succeeds in unknown fate.

Desdemona does not share his sense of insecurity, and replies:

>   The heavens forbid
> But that our loves and comforts should increase,
> Even as our days do grow.

She has defied her own father and chosen Othello and takes her happiness as a right. And when Othello, inflamed by Iago's cunning and plausible lies, turns on her, she is hurt and bewildered, but does not lose her faith. She goes to her death not knowing what it is all about, and that is what makes the play almost unbearably painful; only the fact that in spite of everything her faith in Othello and in herself for choosing him remains, prevents her tragedy from being altogether too painful to read or witness—and even so, it only just prevents it.

Othello is not a study in jealousy—for that, as Coleridge pointed out, we must go to Leontes in *The Winter's Tale.* Iago has to work desperately hard to catch Othello in his trap, and even then he is helped by coincidence before he can succeed. It is not jealousy, but anguish that this beautiful and innocent-seeming creature, whom he loved, could be so horribly guilty, that so torments him. All reason and order and beauty are shattered: "chaos is come again." A soldier, a man who was used to meeting a situation with the appropriate action, he here confronted a situation so monstrous, so destructive of reason, that nothing could be done about it. Something had to be done, but nothing could be done. Othello was not a philosopher like Hamlet who could at least mark time by introspection and speculation while pondering the problem of the irrevocability of performed evil. The man of action must do something—but what? "Othello's occupation's gone," his world is shattered, here was the outrage of irreversible evil. Something had to be done—and the only action that seemed at all relevant and proper in the circumstances was to kill Desdemona. He did not kill her in jealous rage. He made no move himself to kill his supposed rival Cassio. He killed Desdemona for the sake of his moral universe, as the only action somehow appropriate to the situation. "It is the cause, it is the cause, my soul." And when the truth is finally known, though it cannot make life tolerable for Othello, it at least restores his moral universe and he can resume his former dignity of bearing before performing the now inevitable act of self-slaughter.

King Lear (1605–06), which Swinburne called "the most elemental and primeval" of Shakespeare's plays, is in sharp contrast to the concentrated domestic tragedy of *Othello*. The main story goes far back into ancient British mythology; Lear himself is originally the old Celtic sea-god, and the folk tale of the king and his three daughters was attached to this character by Geoffrey of Monmouth in the twelfth century. The story as Geoffrey told it was repeated several times in English literature before Shakespeare (by Holinshed and Spenser among others), and there was an older play on the subject which Shakespeare used as one of his sources. With the main story Shakespeare combined the tale of Gloucester and his two sons —the substance of which he found in Sidney's *Arcadia*—to achieve an extraordinary double-plotted tragedy where the main action is echoed and commented on, as it were, by the subplot. And, as though instinctively recognizing the mythological and folklore elements in the original story, Shakespeare fills his play with archetypal images and ideas which combine and reverberate to produce a large cosmic view of man's fate at the same time as the individual tragedies of Lear and his daughters, and Gloucester and his sons, are played out. *King Lear* is thus the largest in conception and implication of all Shakespeare's tragedies; it is poetic drama heightened to a grand symbolic level without losing that uncanny insight into ordinary human psychology that continues to astonish us in Shakespeare. The play is thus a happy hunting ground for those who are interested in discovering the symbolic pattern of imagery in Shakespeare, for in his handling of images of nature, of sex, of astronomy, of order, in the paradoxical counterpointing of symbols of light and dark, of sight and blindness, of knowledge and ignorance, of good and evil, Shakespeare brings his highest poetic and dramatic powers to bear. It is an immense play, immense in power and meaning and in the weight of tragic knowledge which it conveys. Both poetically and dramatically it goes as far as poetic drama can go.

The tragedy in *Lear* is Shakespeare's own: the old play ends happily. Indeed, though Shakespeare got his crude raw material from the old play and from other sources, he has reworked it so completely that his play is in every sense that matters a wholly original work of the imagination. The simple folk characters become fraught with moral and psychological meaning. Lear, the passionate old king who seeks to indulge his vanity by arranging for public protestations of the daughters' love, pretending that this is to determine how much of his kingdom he is to give to each, provokes his youngest and best-loved daughter, whose share he had already decided to be the largest and whose victory in the love protestations he took completely for granted, to a stubborn understatement. She is her father's daughter, and the palpably exaggerated speeches of her sisters, together with the whole idea of assessing love by extravagance of assertion, arouse her pride. Her father's anger, the product of frustrated vanity, produces her banishment and leaves the two evil sisters with the power. In his powerful presentation of this opening situation Shakespeare sets going the themes of true and false vision, of self-knowledge and self-blindness, that are to be handled with so many variations throughout the play. Kent's protests against Lear's act of supreme folly brings only the cry "Out of my sight!" to which Kent replies, "See better, Lear, and let me still remain /The true blank of thine eye." Already Shakespeare has found means of introducing Gloucester and his bastard son Edmund, who is determined to revenge the unjust shame of his bastardy by acting as he was begot, "naturally," as though kindness and justice and the affection that binds families together were unnatural inventions of human "art." But Lear's banishment of his best-loved daughter is unnatural in the opposite sense, just as Goneril and Regan's behavior to their father afterward is unnatural. But what *is* natural, and what are the principles that govern human affairs? Every important character has his own answer to this question, and the action of the play itself provides a larger answer than any individual can arrive at. Lear himself, being king, being used all his life to pomp and circumstance, to the trappings of rank and the automatic protestations of loyalty and devotion to which his position entitles him, has never had the opportunity of seeing things "naturally," of understanding himself or others. Only when Goneril and Regan have combined to strip him of the signs of rank he had reserved for himself in giving away his kingdom, does Lear begin to see the difference between what man needs as a biological organism and what he wants to sustain his human dignity:

> O, reason not the need! Our basest beggars
> Are in the poorest thing superfluous.
> Allow not nature more than nature needs,
> Man's life is cheap as beast's. . . .

(Here is a different "nature" again, life in its simple biological aspect.) Lear achieves self-knowledge through suffering: he learns for the first time in his life to see "naturally" as a man rather than artificially as a king; but the conditions of his education are too hard and he learns at the cost of his reason and, in large measure, of his personality.

Only the Fool realizes from the beginning that, having given way his kingly power, his artificial personality, Lear can no longer count on the artificial relationships which it produced:

> *Lear.* Dost thou call me fool, boy?
> *Fool.* All thy other titles thou hast given
>   away; that thou wast born with.

The Fool is a remarkable transformation of a stock Elizabethan dramatic character into a species of chorus, whose wry commentary on Lear's actions between his "giving all to his daughters" and his succumbing to madness helps to add a new ironic dimension to the play. The king is foolish, the Fool is wise; like Yeats' Crazy Jane, Lear's Fool explores the paradoxes of pretention and reality, but he is also a dramatic character himself, whose destiny is pathetic rather than tragic. In Act I, scene 4, the banished Kent (returned in disguise to serve his ungrateful master), the Fool, and Lear, engage in a conversation that is both realistic (it is in prose, except for the Fool's snatches of song) and stylized, almost, as Granville-Barker points out, ritualistic; Lear, now first beginning to realize faintly the consequences of his folly; the Fool, heartbroken and reckless, flashing bitter home truths at his brooding master; Kent listening and waiting, to see how he can be of service to the doomed old man. When the truth about his daughters' intentions is finally apprehended by Lear, incredulity gives way to epic anger, and anger to a desperate attempt to come to terms with this unthinkable new knowledge; and he finally goes out into the storm to face "nature" at its most uncompromising, to realize elemental facts about life from which he had hitherto been completely shut away, and at last to lose his reason under this rough schooling.

Meanwhile, Shakespeare has gone ahead with the Gloucester story and presented Edmund's plot against his noble but simple-minded brother Edgar, who is driven to flee into the countryside disguised as a mad beggar. Here, as in his other tragedies, Shakespeare raises the question of the relation between innocence and moral effectiveness: it is Edgar's naïve credulity which produces his own plight and his father Gloucester's cruel treatment. Edmund calls Edgar

> a brother noble
> Whose nature is so far from doing harms
> That he suspects none.

It is Eve and the serpent again.

It was a bold stroke of Shakespeare's to bring together Edgar, feigning madness, Lear, now going truly mad, and the Fool, but he succeeds in keeping the different levels of folly distinct, and, more than that, each contributes its own strand of meaning to the complex symbolic statement about life that the play makes. Lear begins by being solely concerned with the injustice he has received at the hands of his two daughters, accepting the storm because it is "natural" and not malicious and seeing in Edgar's plight confirmation of his own fate. A concern for impersonal justice succeeds his earlier immediate concern for revenge, and gradually, as his madness grows, a new kind of moral insight emerges to end in the recognition that there is no division into the just and the unjust: "None does offend, none." This comes near the recognition that we all share in everybody else's guilt, which is one of the underlying themes of *Measure for Measure*. The artifice of rank can produce an apparent division into judge and criminal, but with the "natural" vision of madness this is seen to be a false picture. This is more than the movement from vengeance to compassion for the sinner, which it is often taken to be; the statement that "none does offend" follows a fierce picture of universal lechery and deceit which shows the same kind of bitter disgust with sex that some of Hamlet's speeches show. It is because all are equally guilty that none does offend. The road to true humility runs through these bitter insights.

Gloucester, the moral simpleton who pays a terrible penalty for his simplicity and finds a new dignity in suffering, sees better blind than he had seen when he had his eyesight, just as Lear sees the world more clearly after he has gone mad. But of course it is not as simple as that. The moving scene where Lear, recovered from his madness to find Cordelia bending over him, fully achieves his new character of the humble and ambitionless private man also shows us a Lear who had lost the pride and dignity which, moral pitfalls though they were, gave stature to his personality. Pride is both a good and a bad quality, and Shakespeare was to treat the problem more particularly in *Coriolanus*. But he is much concerned with it in the great tragedies. Lear is not redeemed until he loses his pride, but the redeemed Lear is but the pale shade of a man. Yet when Hamlet regains his pride ("It is I, Hamlet the Dane") he recovers our sympathy. And Cleopatra redeems herself when she acquires pride. Macbeth has ambition and courage, but no pride, and none of Shakespeare's true villains has pride. (Othello has it, but not Iago, and it is perhaps partly true to say that Othello's *pride* is hurt when he thinks he has discovered Desdemona's infidelity.)

Lear is full of such moral ambiguities; it says more about man than any other of Shakespeare's plays. The ambiguity of the moral world is never so effectively illustrated as by the rapid and apparently effortless way in which Shakespeare can turn out fierce disapproval of Lear into profound sympathy for him. In this teeming tragedy, with its cunning alternation of prose and verse, its paradoxical play with reason and madness and innumerable other pairs of apparent contraries, Shakespeare challenges all the categories with which men comfort themselves into a delusion that they know the moral universe they live in. Perhaps the ultimate statement made by tragedy is that the moral universe is more complicated and more self-contradictory than we can allow ourselves to think in our daily lives.

In *Macbeth* (1606) Shakespeare took two different stories from Holinshed's *Chronicles of Scotland* (Donwald's murder of King Duff and the career of Macbeth) and worked this somewhat primitive material into a profound dramatic presentation of the progress of evil within a human personality. The shortest of the tragedies (though the text as we have it may have been cut), it is given power and scope by the poetic expansion of meaning through imagery as well as by the persuasive and moving projection of character. Shakespeare here solves the problem of the hero-villain in a more subtle and impressive fashion than he did in *Richard III*. Macbeth is first presented as a true heroic figure, loyal and brave, in whom the witches' prophecy precipitates a phase of consciousness that had hitherto lain submerged below his acknowledged thought. (It does not matter whether we take the witches as real or symbolic: the psychological meaning is the same.) Lady Macbeth, the most devoted of wives, steels herself to encourage her husband to win a crown whose meaning for both of them is mystical rather than clearly apprehended in terms of power and glory. She speaks of the crown as

> . . . the golden round
> Which fate and metaphysical aid doth seem
> To have thee crown'd withal.

and neither she nor Macbeth ever dwells on any specific advantage
it will bring them. The crown is the symbol of the ultimate earthly
ambition, of something beyond the grasp of ordinary man, as it was
for Tamburlaine

> . . . the ripest fruit of all,
> That perfect bliss and sole felicity,
> The sweet fruition of an earthly crown.

They both shrink from the deed that is to bring them this symbolic
reward, and Lady Macbeth, who makes the greater initial effort and
seems more unscrupulous at the beginning, collapses most completely in the end. They are both aware of the unnatural quality of
their act—indeed, contrasts between the "natural" and the "unnatural" are as frequent in the poetic imagery of *Macbeth* as they are in
Lear, though somewhat differently used, and when the deed is done
they know that they are committed to a way of life that is at war
with nature. No sooner is the murder committed than Macbeth feels
that he has lost forever the great natural means of refreshment
and renewal:

> Methought, I heard a voice cry, "Sleep no more!
> Macbeth does murder Sleep,"—the innocent Sleep;
> Sleep, that knits up the ravell'd sleave of care,
> The death of each day's life, sore labour's bath,
> Balm of hurt minds, great Nature's second course,
> Chief nourisher in life's feast.

And Lady Macbeth professes to believe that the difference between
the temporary death of sleep and true death is illusory:

> The sleeping and the dead
> Are but as pictures; 'tis the eye of childhood
> That fears a painted devil.

But appearance and reality are willfully confused at one's peril, as
Macbeth's hallucinations and his wife's sleepwalking are later to
show.

Macbeth's disillusion begins almost immediately after the com-
mission of the crime. Hallucination begins at once:

> What hands are here? Ha! They pluck out mine eyes,

and hands and eyes—doing, seeing, contradicting and confusing and terrifying each other—persist throughout the imagery of the play. His question that follows at once—

> Will all great Neptune's ocean wash this blood
> Clean from my hand?—

is echoed later by Lady Macbeth's

> What, will these hands ne'er be clean?

in the sleepwalking scene. She faces it out bravely enough at first: "A little water clears us of this deed," but the note is already one of desperate encouragement to her husband rather than of real confidence. And when the knock at the gate comes immediately afterward, Macbeth wishes the deed undone:

> Wake Duncan with thy knocking: I would thou couldst!

It all turns to dust and ashes, with no interval for enjoyment of the crown so dearly won. Lady Macbeth plays the perfect wife, encouraging and cheering her husband, for as long as she can (except for Brutus and Portia, the Macbeths are the most happily married couple in Shakespeare), but as he is driven by the logic of his position to ever more crimes, to become at last the obsessed nihilist, she cannot keep up in body or spirit and takes her own life at last. By this time Shakespeare has modulated Macbeth from haunted villain to a man rendered heroic by sheer lack of hope, a man who faces the total lack of meaning in his life with fatalistic determination. There is a sort of dignity in this, witnessed by the moving expression of the nothingness he finds in life that is provoked by the news of his wife's death. This is a very different kind of tragedy from *Julius Caesar* or *Othello*, where innocence can help to produce evil; the Macbeths are never innocent, but they are ignorant, deluded, self-deceived about what they really want in life and about the meaning of it all. In the end Macbeth is not so much damned as reduced to moral nothingness, in the midst of which he can keep on acting only by an almost superhuman exertion of will power. Thus the villain is a hero in a sense, and though Macbeth is destroyed by the evil he does, he does not let down the human species in his manner of facing that destruction.

Macbeth is no moral monster; he is a sensitive and able man driven by an obsession with an unexamined ambition to do what he knows to be evil and what at first his whole nature shrinks from. Of course he becomes bloodier as he proceeds, for that is the nature of crime, but the real tragedy lies in his discovery of the meaninglessness of his ambition almost as soon as it is achieved and his condemnation to carry on and pay over and over again the price for what he knows is worthless. He is left with nothing at all but physical courage. But this is a drastic oversimplification of the tragic theme. As in *King Lear*, Shakespeare in *Macbeth* creates a whole symphony of meaning by the patterns of recurring images in the play and overtones of suggestion of the nature of good and evil, of problems of choice and responsibility, of the relation of human behavior to the natural order, of appearance and reality, and many other things besides.

Antony and Cleopatra (1607) is the most spacious of Shakespeare's tragedies, and in a sense the most relaxed. In *Hamlet* and *Othello* and *Lear* the tone and the imagery often suggest that the dramatist is putting into dramatic terms some personal obsession or emotional disturbance of his own; in *Macbeth* we are more at a distance and the tragedy does not appear to be one in which the author's personal emotional history is involved. In *Antony and Cleopatra* we feel this to an even greater degree. Shakespeare is clearly at the height of his powers; his confident mastery of dramatic structure is as obvious as his positively negligent control of language. The poetry of the play is abundant and magnificently handled, serving always to increase the area of relevant dramatic meaning. The movement to and fro between Rome and Egypt (with Athens in between), the simple yet cunning way in which the Elizabethan platform stage is exploited to enable the action to flow with uninterrupted movement (an effect spoiled by the modern division of the play into scenes separated by a dropped curtain), the devices Shakespeare uses to suggest that the whole Roman world is involved in Antony's struggle between Roman loyalty and Egyptian magic, the evocative suggestions of the old Antony (whom we saw in *Julius Caesar*) contrasting with the Antony we now see, "the nemesis of the sensual man," as Granville-Barker has put it—these among other features of the play sufficiently demonstrate the author's superb craftsmanship. From the very beginning the contrast between the Roman and the Egyptian view is emphasized: the Roman soldier watched the Egyptian pageantry in Cleopatra's palace:

> Nay, but this dotage of our general's
> O'erflows the measure. . . .

The lovers' passion is dotage to Roman eyes, but Antony is still "*our* general." And a moment later we see the other side. "The triple pillar of the world transformed /Into a strumpet's fool," in the Roman view, is then shown as he appears in his own and the strumpet's eyes.

> *Cleopatra.* If it be love indeed, tell me how much.
> *Antony.* There's beggary in the love that can be reckoned.

But then the summons from Rome comes: Antony learns that his wife Fulvia is dead and war threatens, and he who has said

> Let Rome in Tiber melt and the wide arch
> Of the rang'd empire fall! Here is my space.
> Kingdoms are clay; . . .

is struck by "a Roman thought" and mutters to himself:

> These strong Egyptian fetters I must break
> Or lose myself in dotage.—

echoing Philo's word "dotage" that we heard in the first line of the play. Cleopatra tries all her tricks to keep him in Egypt, but, when she sees he is determined to go, puts on her noblest bearing to become, no longer the shrew or the temperamental lover, his protecting goddess of Victory:

> Upon your sword
> Sit laurel victory, and smooth success
> Be strew'd before your feet!

We hear the lewd chatter of the Egyptian court, with Cleopatra trying to while away the time in her lover's absence, in scenes adroitly interspersed with those which show the wary reconciliation of Octavius Caesar and Antony, sealed by Antony's marriage to Octavia, Caesar's sister. The Roman empire (not yet formally an empire) holds; its enemies are cowed by the reunion of Antony and Octavius, and a cynical truce with the rebels is celebrated by the drunken scene in Pompey's galley, where the three rulers of the Roman world get drunk and the well-meaning Lepidus, the ineffectual third in the triumvirate, has to be carried out. Enobarbus, Antony's hard-boiled follower, suggests a song and dance, and joins the hands of Antony, Octavius, and the ill-fated Sextus Pompeius as, tired and surfeited, they sing "Come, thou monarch of the vine"— a scene which can be compared with that in *Othello* when Iago "fastens a cup of wine" on Cassio and strikes up a forced merriment with the song, "And let me the canakin clink."

But, in spite of Octavia, we know that Antony will go back to Egypt, and Enobarbus knows it too. "You shall find the band that seems to tie their friendship together will be the very strangler of their amity. Octavia is of a holy, cold, and still conversation," he tells Menas as they are chatting after the great reconciliation. And

we have already heard Antony, seizing the lame excuse of a sooth-
sayer's prophecy, saying:

> I will to Egypt;
> And though I make this marriage for my peace,
> I' th' East my pleasure lies.

The struggle is not a tragic one. Octavius Caesar is a cold fish and
his sister a conscientious Puritan: the sensual man belongs in
Alexandria.

Up to this point the interest of the play lies in the rapid alternation
of different points of view and different kinds of character, until a
full picture of the whole Roman position is built up. Shakespeare was
never more brilliantly at ease in the creation of character. The slightest minor figure has his own accent. Lepidus, the poor third member
of the triumvirate, hero-worshiping Antony and awed by Caesar;
Sextus Pompeius, the would-be rebel who has not the courage of his
own ambitions; Enobarbus telling the wide-eyed Agrippa and Mae-
cenas all about the wonders of Egypt, like a modern businessman
returned from a trip to France telling the boys back home what Paris
night life is really like (and including in his account the great description of Cleopatra when she first met Antony—most appropriately introduced here)—in these and other scenes and characters a
shrewd and humorous knowledge of human nature manifests itself
in language continually shifting in tone and scope in accordance
with the dramatic and poetic needs of the moment.

So Antony returns to Cleopatra and the breach between him and
Octavius Caesar is made final. The second movement of the play
shows the aging roué and the temperamental sensualist facing the
vengeance of the cold and confident Octavius. There is never any
doubt as to who will win; the interest here lies in the changes and
passions that the varying fortunes of war produce in Cleopatra and
in less degree in Antony. Antony, influenced by Cleopatra's foolish
exhibitionism, weakly decides to fight by sea instead of on land, and
when Cleopatra (against Enobarbus' advice) joins the fleet with her
flagship, only to flee when the battle begins and draw Antony after,
the stage is set for an explosion of passionate self-contempt on
Antony's part which shows at last that he has lost his grip. He gives
way to self-pity and sentimental speeches to his servants, and for
once Cleopatra has nothing to say. A temporary improvement of his
fortunes brings back the old Antony again, but it is a brief Indian
summer. In the sea fight that follows, the Egyptian fleet surrenders
and Antony believes that Cleopatra has deliberately betrayed him.
His impotent rage frightens her into sending him a false message of

her suicide, and then at last Antony—his accent moving ever into richer poetry—knows that the end has come; in following Cleopatra to the grave he is reconciling Rome and Egypt, for suicide is the Roman way out. When he dies at last in Cleopatra's arms he boasts that he does

> not basely die,
> Not cowardly put off my helmet to
> My countryman—a Roman by a Roman
> Valiantly vanquish'd.

Cleopatra's lament over him first begins to raise this passion between a middle-aged sensualist and a royal prostitute to a higher level. She realizes that the world for her is destroyed—

> O, wither'd is the garland of the war,
> The soldier's pole is fall'n. Young boys and girls
> Are level now with men. The odds is gone,
> And there is nothing left remarkable
> Beneath the visiting moon—

and at the same time that she is, after all, but a mortal woman with ordinary human passions:

> No more but e'en a woman, and commanded
> By such poor passion as the maid that milks
> And does the meanest chares.

Her problem now is how to come to terms with what remains of life.

Shakespeare does not hurry, however, to elevate Cleopatra to tragic stature. The final movement of the play is Cleopatra against Octavius Caesar: she tries every way of finding out what Caesar (in spite of his polite protestations) means to do with her, and humiliates herself in the process. But at last she learns from Dolabella (whom she has twisted round her finger with a word) that Caesar's intention is to take her to Rome and exhibit her there; then and only then does she find the courage to follow Antony in the Roman way. And this is the measure of Shakespeare's genius, that he spares neither Antony nor Cleopatra anything; he bungles his own death; she, after his death and her great lament, becomes for a while a low trickster apparently only interested in saving what she has left. Only when the game is finally up does she admit that without Antony life is impossible; but in that admission and in the splendid poetic gesture of her final suicide, she is redeemed at last into tragedy. She finds true pride, and dignity, and the quiet humor that sees over the other side of death without panic or self-pity. Yet she does not lose her original character. Her dying speech is as sensual as all her other speeches, and almost her final thought is that she must die before Charmian in case Charmian gets to the next world before she does and kisses Antony first. As everything is hushed into the final pageantry, with the crowned and royally robed queen awaiting death from the asp at her breast, the language becomes ritualistic while losing nothing of its sensuality:

> Charmian. O Eastern star!
> Cleopatra.   Peace, peace!
> Dost thou not see my baby at my breast,
> That sucks the nurse asleep?
> Charmian.   O, break! O, break!
> Cleopatra. As sweet as balm, as soft as air, as
> gentle—O Antony! . . .

The final pageant, the dead queen flanked by her two dead hand-maidens, meets Caesar's gaze as he enters, and the play ends with the Romans held by the strange and moving spectacle.

Clearly, this is tragedy of a very special kind, tragedy in a very different sense from that of *Hamlet* or *King Lear*. The theme is not the conflict between love and duty that Dryden made of it in his *All for Love*. True, Shakespeare makes clear that the fate of the civilized world is involved in Antony's decisions, but the conflict between public duty and private passion is not his major interest, nor is he chiefly concerned with the conflict between the Roman and Egyptian ways of life, though this, too, is an element in the play and one of the themes suggested by the pattern of its imagery. Cleopatra is shown as shrewish, hysterical, sadistic, dishonest, and cowardly, as well as beautiful, queenly, and heroic. Antony is selfish and fatuous as well as generous and noble. Are they great lovers or merely great sensualists? They are both experienced in the ways of sexual pleasure and often talk as though that is all that love involves. Yet this is far from being a disillusioned or a cynical play. We are continually fascinated by the richness and variety of character and the way in which history is bound up with psychology. There is little pity or fear in the play, but rather a lively human curiosity throughout. And the poetry keeps enlarging the moment, showing experience as ever live-lier and richer. We watch fascinated as Antony, most Roman when most enslaved by Egypt, goes to his self-inflicted death, and then follow Cleopatra's twistings and turnings with ever increasing inter-est and wonder. We make no new moral judgment on either, because that is decided at the beginning and is never in question: they are both behaving badly, and their sophisticated passion does not excuse them. But there is a wonder in it all, and Cleopatra in her death finds, as it were, the objective correlative of that wonder. The sensual life ends in a blaze of ritual pageantry: it has its own amoral nobility.

Hamlet, Othello, Lear, and *Macbeth* were apparently written between 1600 and 1606, the phase of Shakespeare's career generally known as his great "tragic period." It has been held that the note of personal disillusion, sex nausea, and bitterness which some have seen in these plays, and which came to a climax in the savage misanthropy of *Timon of Athens* (written sometime between 1605 and 1608), not really a tragedy at all but a picture of human ingratitude and hypocrisy turning the world of men into a world of beasts, lacking all order and health, indicates that Shakespeare was going through a desperately disillusioned period in his own life at this time, of which *Timon* marks the climax and which later (after, it has even been suggested, a nervous breakdown) gave way to a new serenity, reflected in the last plays. This is possible, though it is dangerous to correlate too closely literal biography and the life of the imagination. Whatever biographical inferences we may draw, the fact remains that Shakespeare looked on the dark side of life during these years, and the comedies which he wrote during this period (except for *The Merry Wives of Windsor,* an uninspired professional farce written to order, which in any case may be as early as 1597) have a very different atmosphere from those written immediately earlier. *Troilus and Cressida* (ca. 1602), *All's Well that Ends Well* (1602–04), and *Measure for Measure* (1604) have been called "problem plays" or "bitter comedies," because, though not technically tragedies and, in the case of the last two, having a "happy" ending, they have nothing of the golden cheerfulness of the "middle comedies" and show human behavior as (to put it mildly) gross and unedifying. That Shakespeare's state of mind during these years was such that, when asked by his company for a comedy, he could produce only this kind of "bitter comedy," is a view which was once popular, but more recent critics have refused to see these plays as hybrids produced by the working of a tragic imagination on comic material and have adduced many arguments to show that each has its own unity and its own impressive pattern of meaning and that the concept of "problem play" is irrelevant and misleading. It is true that careful and continued reading of each of these plays produces an increasing impression of their literary value, and *Troilus and Cressida* and *Measure for Measure* have both been hailed as masterpieces of the very highest order by modern scholar-critics, instead of as the interesting failures which their predecessors had judged them to be. Nevertheless, the reader (or spectator) who takes these plays together will certainly find something different and puzzling about their tone, and the academic snobbery which denies the validity of this impression to explain away all difficulties in terms of Elizabethan sensibility or Shakespeare's sources runs counter to the critical judgment of three hundred and fifty years. (The preface to the second of the two 1609 quartos of *Troilus and Cressida* suggests that the first audiences found the play puzzling.)

Troilus and Cressida takes two themes—the story of Troilus and Cressida as developed in medieval and subsequent literature and the background theme of the siege of Troy, also familiar in medieval and later writing—and treats them in a spirit of restless disillusion. Much in the background is taken for granted: Troilus is already in love with Cressida when the play opens, and Cressida's coyness is brief and superficial; the whole Troy story and the place in it of the various Greek and Trojan characters is assumed, so that to those who do not know the Troy story as it appeared in medieval and early Renaissance literature the play appears extremely allusive and sometimes even sketchy. The title theme does not dominate the play. At least as much interest is centered on the difference between the Greek and the Trojan attitude (the Greek, represented by Ulysses, being realistic and "modern," the Trojan, represented by Hector and by Troilus himself, being old-fashioned and "romantic"), and on character conflicts such as those between Ajax, Achilles, and Ulysses on the Greek side and Hector, Troilus, and Pandarus on the Trojan. On the Trojan side, Hector admits that it is unjust and unnatural to hold Helen, yet he refuses to surrender her to the Greeks and so end the war because his muddled notions of honor demand that the struggle be carried on. On the Greek side, Ulysses gives his famous speech on order and demonstrates how the Greeks' failure to take Troy up till now results from a lack of proper order and subordination in their behavior. The romantic rhetoric of the Trojan council of war contrasts with the opportunist rhetoric (reminiscent sometimes of *Henry V*) of the Greek. And Thersites, the licensed fool, covers everything with his scabrous comment, reducing all human actions to their lowest animal level. Pride is exposed, chivalry degraded, prudence mocked, and ideal passion rewarded with casual faithlessness. The boorish Ajax scores over Achilles; the wise Ulysses constructs a brilliant plan for bringing the sulky Achilles back into the fight, only to have it proved wholly unnecessary when the death of Patroclus achieves the same end in a moment; Achilles treacherously slays Hector when he finds him resting with his armor doffed; and Troilus, the prudent Ulysses by his side, watches with tortured incredulity while his beloved Cressida, the very night after she has left him, gives herself to Diomede. Shakespeare uses chivalric devices (the personal challenge, and its consequences) to bring the two camps together, so that passionate Trojan and worldly-wise Greek can watch the betrayal side by side—while, from the other side of the stage, the foul-mouthed Thersites observes and comments on both watchers and watched, both Cressida and Diomede on the one hand and Ulysses and Troilus on the other. The play ends with Hector slain and his corpse ignominiously treated, Troilus in a frenzy of revenge against all Greeks, Cressida Diomede's mistress, and the repudiated Pandarus (who has the last word) reduced to a bawdy "trader in the flesh."

Troilus and Cressida may well have been written in the first instance for performance at one of the Inns of Court, which may account for the peculiar kind of sophistication found so often in the play. It may also have been influenced by a new fashion of dramatic satire introduced by Ben Jonson and John Marston. And in the treatment of Cressida, Shakespeare was following the tradition as it had developed after Chaucer, just as his presentation of the Trojan war derives in large part from Lydgate's *Troy Book* and Caxton's *Recuyell of the Histories of Troy*. But the flavor of the play as a whole remains strange. Shakespeare presents an unfinished story—a story much more familiar to his contemporaries than that of Hamlet or Lear—whose end was already known to the Elizabethan audience. They knew what the fate of Troy finally was, and what happened at last to Achilles, Troilus, and Cressida. It is as though Shakespeare has deliberately arrested time, to show the plans and expectations of men in a double perspective, first in the context of the moment and then in the larger context of past, present, and future. And indeed time is much referred to in the play. When Trojans and Greeks meet in chivalric courtesy, Ulysses prophesies the fall of Troy and Hector replies:

> I must not believe you.
> There they stand yet, and modestly I think
> The fall of every Phrygian stone will cost
> A drop of Grecian blood. The end crowns all,
> And that old common arbitrator, Time,
> Will one day end it.

Ulysses replies to this: "So to him we leave it." The disposition of human affairs is left to Time. Meanwhile, men behave as their beliefs or their passions or their apparent self-interest demand. Ulysses' speech to Achilles—

> Time hath, my Lord, a wallet at his back,
> Wherein he puts alms for Oblivion,
> A great-siz'd monster of ingratitudes—

makes the point that a man is judged by his present behavior, not his past reputation:

> O, let not virtue seek
> Remuneration for the thing it was;
> For beauty, wit,
> High birth, vigour of bone, desert in service,
> Love, friendship, charity, are subjects all
> To envious and calumniating Time.

But Ulysses' shrewd opportunism is no safeguard. The future reveals the true meaning of the present in its own fashion; Cressida in Calchas' tent with Diomede is the final gloss on Cressida protesting eternal love to Troilus, and Troilus' speech at the spectacle expresses his anguished recognition of the fact that both present and past are equally true. Time tests all ideals and finds us all out in the end. *Troilus and Cressida* ends without a climax or a resolution: the true end, as Shakespeare's audience well knew, lay in the death of Troilus, the degeneration of Cressida, and the sack of Troy.

All's Well that Ends Well (which may be a reworking of an earlier play) is a "problem play" in a very different sense. In spite of its element of formlessness (which seems deliberate), *Troilus and Cressida* is a mature and interesting play, the product of a powerful imagination and an astringent wit. But *All's Well* is a somewhat mechanical handling of a folk theme which Shakespeare found in the story of Giletta of Narbon as translated in William Painter's *Palace of Pleasure* from Boccaccio's *Decameron*. There are indeed two folk themes: the story of Helena's curing the King and her reward in obtaining a husband of her choice, and the story of the deserted wife winning back her husband by substituting herself, unknown to him, in the bed of his mistress and so fulfilling seemingly impossible conditions. Neither theme is interesting or credible to the modern mind, and our difficulty with the play lies, not, as perhaps in *Troilus* and certainly in *Timon*, in the bitterness of spirit with which Shakespeare handles his material, but in his inability to present it dramatically with sufficient poetic and imaginative force to create a level of probability that can convince us. There are interesting poetic moments and some fine touches in the play, and the character of Parolles (an inglorious Falstaff, with only the shabbiness and the nastiness apparent) has its possibilities, though only superficially exploited; but the main action moves stiffly, and the atmosphere remains that of an early comedy such as *The Two Gentlemen of Verona*. Bertram, the physically courageous but morally weak hero who repudiates the gifted wife who has chosen him, remains a cad until the end, in spite of the machinery of redemption which Shakespeare appears to have prepared for him, while Diana (the lady whom Bertram thinks he is with the night he sleeps with his own wife) and her mother exist simply to speak the words that carry forward the story to its required end. We tend to think that it is the morality of the play that is offensive and "bitter"; but the morality is the folk morality which Shakespeare had successfully embodied in earlier comedies: the failure here is a failure of the imagination. Whatever the reason, the story did not light up for Shakespeare in terms of his art, and it remains a cold and baffling play.

Measure for Measure, the final comedy in this group, is at once the most interesting and the most challenging. The plot, found both as a tragedy and as a prose tale in the work of the Italian writer Cinthio, and thence used by the English George Whetstone, also in both a play and a prose tale, in a version somewhat nearer to Shakespeare's, contains in itself a multiplicity of overtones which in part account for the disturbing nature of the play as Shakespeare wrote it. The basic theme is indeed older than either Whetstone or Cinthio: the story of the judge or ruler who offers to save the girl's lover or husband or brother if she will yield herself to him and who, after the girl has yielded, deliberately breaks his promise, goes back into the mists of folklore. In pre-Shakespearean versions the girl does yield to the ruler, but Shakespeare, by means of a device he had already used in *All's Well*—the secret substitution of one girl for another in the bed of the seducer—keeps his heroine chaste throughout; further, he follows Whetstone (and not Cinthio) in saving the girl's brother and having the ruler only imagine that he has been put to death. There are many themes involved in this apparently simple story. In the first place there is the ironical theme of the judge himself guilty of what he has others punished for. (Claudio, the brother in *Measure for Measure*, is sentenced to death for premarital intercourse with his fiancée.) *Quis custodiet ipsos custodes?* Who shall guard the state's guardians, and what happens when the judge is more guilty than the man he condemns? This is bound up with a theme not unrelated to the deep-seated Oedipus motif—the ruler, in an honest attempt to uncover guilt, reveals that he is himself the guilty one. This is the detective story where the detective, conscientiously following the clues, proves himself to be the criminal. Such a notion has both its comic and its tragic side. The uncovering of the hypocritical judge as the true villain can easily be made the subject of pure comedy, and this, as Dr. Hanns Sachs pointed out, was done in Heinrich von Kleist's comedy *Der zerbrochene Krug* (The Broken Jug), in which a judge is forced by circumstances to conduct a careful cross-examination which proves himself to have been the criminal in the case under investigation. Finally, there is the Christian element in the story, which Shakespeare emphasizes in his title. (Cf. Luke, Chapter vi: "Judge not, and ye shall not be judged; condemn not, and ye shall not be condemned: forgive, and ye shall be forgiven. . . . For with the same measure that ye mete withal it shall be measured to you again.") In *Measure for Measure* everybody is in some degree guilty, and it is only after the much injured heroine has pleaded for mercy for the man who has injured her that it is revealed that the injury was in intention only. All are guilty, and mercy rather than justice saves the day.

Shakespeare further complicated the story by having a disguised duke, the real ruler, watch over all the proceedings unknown to the actors. The Duke, before leaving the country on a temporary absence, gives over his rule to Angelo, hoping that Angelo, a sternly puritanical character, will have the firmness to revive laws which the Duke himself has been too kindhearted to enforce, with resulting increase of sexual immorality among all classes. Angelo begins by sentencing to death young Claudio for intercourse with his fiancée and refusing to listen to any pleas for mercy. Claudio's sister Isabella, passionately chaste and about to enter a nunnery, pleads with Angelo for her brother's life, and Angelo, suddenly smitten with lust for Isabella, agrees to save him if she yield herself to him for one night. She of course refuses, but the Duke disguised as a friar persuades her to agree to a plot whereby Mariana, formerly betrothed to Angelo but later deserted by him when her dowry was not forthcoming, is substituted for Isabella without Angelo's being aware of the substitution. After spending some hours secretly at night with the supposed Isabella, Angelo goes back on his word and orders Claudio to be immediately executed, but the disguised Duke arranges for the head of a man who has died in prison to be brought to Angelo as Claudio's, and Claudio is spared. Finally, in a carefully contrived denouement, Angelo is exposed and, after a plea for his forgiveness made by Isabella while she still thinks Claudio has been executed, forgiven. Behind this main action runs a stream of sordid low life, with bawds, brothels, and much talk of venereal disease.

The play puzzles largely because of the different and sometimes mutually conflicting themes bound up in the story as Shakespeare develops it. The "gulling" of the hypocrite (in the manner of Ben Jonson's comedies) is one way of treating Angelo, but he is at the same time presented as a genuinely puritanical character who suddenly discovers, to his dismay and even horror, that he is as much subject to sensual temptation as ordinary men—he might even be said to be a man who has sublimated his tendencies toward sadistic sensuality in the practice of stern justice, but who, on being faced with a beautiful woman pleading for mercy for a brother condemned to death, regresses into the sensualist and sadist. Similarly, Isabella is both a stern, otherworldly character who fiercely abuses her brother for a momentary lapse in his desire to have death rather than have his sister lose her chastity and who at the same time cheerfully plays the procuress with Mariana, and a symbol of radiant purity who, at the end of the play, embodies its Christian moral of mercy before strict justice. The gulling of the hypocrite, the testing of the puritan, the judge discovered to be the criminal, the discovery that all are guilty and none has the right to judge, and that mercy rather than justice is the proper "measure for measure"—here is, indeed, an intermingling of tragic and comic themes. No wonder that *Measure for Measure* has elements of Jonsonian comedy, Sophoclean irony, and Christian morality. That Shakespeare should have chosen such a theme is doubtless some evidence of his state of mind at the time he wrote it; but it is worth noting that *Measure for Measure* is not a "bitter comedy" simply because he was asked to write a comedy when he was in the middle of a "tragic period," but a serious play between tragedy and comedy whose complications and difficulties arise from the implications of its plot. And there is no point in complaining that no character seems wholly sympathetic, that even virtue is made to appear uncongenial, if one realizes that a basic theme in the play is precisely that none are guiltless and that in judging one another we have no right to condemn but only to forgive. This is in a sense a deeply pessimistic position, but the notion that man's duty is to be merciful to his neighbor because all men are in some degree evil was not original with Shakespeare. *Measure for Measure* is Shakespeare's most comprehensive treatment of the notion of original sin, with which he was much concerned at this stage of his career.

Coriolanus, probably written between *Antony and Cleopatra* and *Cymbeline*, the latter being the first of Shakespeare's final group of plays, stands somewhat alone. It is in a sense a political play, dealing with the fortunes of a hero whose aristocratic pride provoked popular ill-will, but it is not political in the way that *Julius Caesar* is political: in *Julius Caesar* Shakespeare explores the tragic implications of private virtue operating without the requisite political shrewdness in a public context. The tragedy of Coriolanus is not that of Brutus, and the play in which he is the hero has none of the wider implications and overtones of *Julius Caesar*. Coriolanus, egotistical, aristocratic, contemptuous of the people, is opposed by the tribunes for his antipopular attitude and, in spite of his great military services to Rome, is exiled after the tribunes have maneuvered to make him lose his temper and display his "treasonable" attitude to the people. His virtues are immense personal courage and a certain boyish arrogance which is not without charm; his defects of character lie in complete lack of self-knowledge, his total inability to handle people (even soldiers, for though he is a magnificent fighter he has not the qualities of a great military leader), and lack of any kind of imaginative understanding of other people. It is partly this lack of understanding which leads him to treat the people with such contempt, for to him they are not human beings but an aggregate of foulsmelling changeableness.

There is immense irony in Coriolanus' objection to the variability of the people—

> Hang ye! Trust ye?
> With every minute you do change a mind,
> And call him noble that was now your hate—

in the light of his own subsequent behavior. Enraged at his banishment, he joins his country's enemies and leads a Volscian army against Rome. His action here is that of a man with no awareness of his own nature or the basis of his own principles, and when he is finally prevailed upon by his mother to spare Rome (which means ultimately his own death at the hands of the Volscians) it is because he is overcome by an unfamiliar emotion which is all the more powerful because of its unfamiliarity. His revenge on Rome is instinctive and irrational, and it destroys the basis of his own personality, which has hitherto been a fierce pride in his own aristocratic patriotism and an almost religious feeling for his own class. Though his mother, who had brought him up in the military virtues and in disdain of the common people, learns through hard experience another point of view (in her final speech to her son she pleads that he should act not as the warrior but in the more blessed role of peacemaker), Coriolanus does not develop at all. His enraged reversal of his natural role involves him in a much more profound instability of purpose than anything he had charged the common people with, and with the resulting emptying of his personality he can respond to his mother's plea, which temporarily fills the vacuum, as it were, but he cannot advance to any understanding of the superiority of the peacemaker to the warrior or to any redemption through suffering. He meets his death the same boyish, bewildered, instinctive character he is at the beginning, and it is through this immaturity, almost, in a sense, this inno-cence, that Shakespeare preserves throughout the play sufficient sympathy for him to enable his fall to be seen as tragic at all.

Coriolanus is thus one of the most limited in scope of Shake-speare's mature plays. The design is more rigid, the verse is more compact and workmanlike, the implications are more strictly con-trolled, than in any of the great tragedies. The design has not the flexibility which allows him in *Hamlet* or *King Lear* to ring in through overtone and suggestion the most far-reaching comments on the human situation, and even in *Macbeth*, the most compact of the great tragedies, the human context is richer. It is not surprising that after this Shakespeare moves on to a different kind of play alto-gether: *Coriolanus* suggests that he had done what he could with tragedy and was now looking at the dramatic possibilities of the tragic situation with less excitement. From now on he moves not only toward new themes but toward new dramatic conventions.

Shakespeare's final group of plays, the so-called "romances," have certain characteristics in common and seem to reflect a new attitude both to life and to his art. *Pericles, Cymbeline, The Winter's Tale,* and *The Tempest* all deal in one way or another with evil and inno-cence, guilt and atonement, uncorrupted youth undoing original sin and starting life afresh. Mythology, folklore, and magic find their way into these plays to a greater degree than in any other of Shake-speare's mature work, so that it can hardly be claimed (as some critics have asserted) that they represent a new faith in the essential good-ness of man: the remoteness of the setting and the introduction of the magical element indicate a different level of probability from that found in *Hamlet* or *Othello,* a symbolic world where (unlike the real world) innocence can triumph and the gods enable the evil past to be undone. In *Pericles,* Marina and her mother, both assumed to be dead, are found in the end alive and innocent; in *Cymbeline,* Imogen similarly comes alive again; in *The Winter's Tale* the statue of Hermione proves in the end to be the living Hermione, long thought dead; and in *The Tempest,* Alonso and his company are miraculously redeemed from drowning to find repentance and new virtue. The dramaturgy in these plays is relaxed, almost casual, with masque elements and other spectacular devices introduced to em-phasize the note of symbol and ritual. Shakespeare has done with probing directly the tragic paradoxes of human nature, and he now reaches out to a larger poetic symbolism through which the moral patterns and possibilities of human life can be presented with the calm beauty of one who is no longer tortured by his own involve-ment.

Pericles, of uncertain date and probably of composite authorship, is the least satisfactory of these plays. The text we have (a corrupt Quarto: *Pericles* does not appear in the First Folio) seems to consist of several layers, indicating revision, and some parts are very crude. The story, too, deriving from a widely dispersed tale of Greek origin, told by John Gower in his *Confessio Amantis* (and the use of Gower, rather crudely, as chorus, indicates plainly enough that he was the source), is too crowded with incident to be easily rendered dramatically. Antiochus, king of Antioch, has incestuous relations with his own daughter; Pericles, prince of Tyre, discovers this, thereby arousing Antiochus' anger. To avoid the effects of Antiochus' wrath, Pericles flees from his own kingdom of Tyre and after succoring starving Tarsus sets sail again, is shipwrecked, lands at Pentapolis, where he marries Thaisa, the King's daughter, then sets off by sea again for Tyre. But he is again shipwrecked; during the storm Thaisa gives birth to a daughter, Marina, before apparently dying, and her body is committed to the sea in a chest. The chest is washed up at Ephesus, where Cerimon restores the apparently dead Thaisa to life and she becomes a priestess of Diana. Meanwhile Pericles and Marina arrive at Tarsus, where Pericles stays a year before returning to Tyre, leaving Marina in the care of Cleon, governor of Tarsus and his wife Dionyza. But Dionyza grows jealous of Marina, who outshines her own daughter, and plans her murder; before she can be murdered, however, she is carried off by pirates to Mytilene, where she is sold to a brothel, but her angelic innocence converts the customers to virtue and she retains her chastity. Pericles is told ·by Cleon and Dionyza that his daughter is dead, and he devotes himself to grief. But fate brings his ship to Mytilene where he finds Marina in a moving scene of mutual discovery. Finally, under Diana's guidance, he proceeds to Ephesus, where he finds his wife, long supposed dead.

To get all of this complicated story across requires the use of choruses and dumb shows, employed clumsily enough. But the main theme centers on Marina, lost and found again, subjected to the corrupting influence of the brothel yet preserving always her shining innocence. And the sea, on which Marina was born and into which Thaisa disappears to be cast up later alive, dominates the play, a symbol of purification, of "death by water" which precedes resurrection. T. S. Eliot's poem "Marina" distils the essential meaning:

> What seas what shores what grey rocks and what islands
> What water lapping the bow
> And scent of pine and the woodthrush singing through the fog
> What images return
> O my daughter.

Pericles is a symbolic play, a religious play, dealing with death and resurrection, with ritual purification and the redemptive power of innocence. Uneven and botched up in places as it is, it has its Shakespearean moments of grave beauty; and though by itself—so uncertain is the text and the authorship—it could tell us little about the direction in which the later Shakespeare's imagination was moving, taken with the following three plays it helps to build up a picture of a Shakespeare who has turned away from what (with all the necessary qualifications) might be called the psychological realism of the great tragedies to a new, more symbolic, kind of play in which he could come to terms with the problem of evil in a different manner.

Cymbeline, The Winter's Tale, and *The Tempest* all appear to have been written (in this order) between 1609 and 1612. In *Cymbeline* Shakespeare took a story from the *Decameron* (of a husband, making a wager on his wife's virtue, tricked by his friend into believing that the friend has succeeded in seducing her) and the setting from that part of Holinshed which deals with the ancient British kingdom. He got some details from various parts of Holinshed and other elements in the plot from other sources, including folklore, and wove them all together into a story almost as complicated as *Pericles*. An element of fairy tale runs right through the play. Imogen, the princess who marries against her parents' wishes; Cymbeline's Queen, the wicked stepmother; the potion which brings apparent death but really only sends the drinker into a prolonged swoon; the "Snow White" theme of the apparently dead girl being covered with flowers by her simple companions—these are familiar enough elements in any folk literature. The evil Cloten, son of the wicked stepmother by an earlier husband, is also a folk character, though Shakespeare gives him a fully individualized personality. Imogen herself is pure Shakespeare, idealized yet real, one of those spirited heroines whom he created so happily in his "middle comedies" and who here is subjected to much more grievous trials than anything which befell Rosalind or Viola. For the theme of this play, as of *Pericles*, is innocence triumphant, emerging victorious from the darkest possible circumstances. Her own banished husband turned against her by the vile trick of Iachimo; the wicked Cloten pursuing her; misfortune and evil dogging her footsteps wherever she goes; she yet takes her destiny into her own hands and, having survived the shock of hearing that her husband has ordered her to be murdered and the counter shock of seeing what she thinks is the dead body of her husband, survives to win her husband back in the final scene of explanation and reconciliation.

Evil mounts to an ugly climax in the play before the countermovement sets in, and Shakespeare leaves us in no doubt of its reality.
Iachimo, the subtle Italian, is as nasty a case of small-minded pride
and perverted ingenuity as one can find in literature, and Cloten is a
sadistic boor. Only the Queen, the wicked stepmother, with her
stagy asides and her poison potions, remains a purely fairy tale character, and her final suicide is as unreal as the rest of her actions. This
is a tragicomedy, a play in which all the terror of tragedy is given
full vent before the tide is allowed to turn. Those who maintain that
Shakespeare now felt in a kindly mood toward life have surely paid
too little attention to Cloten or to the tortured speech Posthumus
makes when he thinks his wife has betrayed him, a speech full of the
sex nausea we find in *Hamlet* and *Lear*. Tragicomedy was the fashion now, the Blackfriars audiences wanted all the thrills of tragedy
with the happy ending of comedy, and they wanted, too, the
masque-like devices, the music and pageantry, which Shakespeare,
yielding to public taste, now freely gave them. It may be that this is
the only explanation one needs for these final romances or tragicomedies: Shakespeare, the professional playwright, was changing
his style in response to public demand. Yet one cannot be satisfied
with this explanation. The themes of these final plays are too similar
and the ritual of forgiveness runs too persistently through them all,
for this not to be a reflection in some way of Shakespeare's mind at
this time. The point is, however, that it was not an easy forgiveness
resulting from a new optimistic belief that vice is always defeated by
virtue. Evil in all its horror is imparted directly in these plays. Salvation comes by magic or coincidence, and the ritual of pardon is performed in the serenity of a brave new world in which we cannot
literally believe. Even so, in *Cymbeline*, the grosser villains are disposed of first. Cloten has his head cut off by Guilderius with cheerful matter-of-factness and the Queen conveniently ends her own life.
Those who are pardoned are those whose acts, in spite of themselves,
turn out to have brought forth nothing but good. As in *Measure for
Measure*, time has brought good results out of evil intentions, and no
one standing on the stage in the remarkable last act of *Cymbeline*
has managed to achieve any lasting evil. That is their good luck, or
rather the playwright's magical manipulation of events. And so, as
Cymbeline says, "Pardon's the word to all."

Cymbeline (like *Pericles*, though to a smaller extent) has its moments of dramatic awkwardness and crudity, which make one wonder whether the text as we have it is Shakespeare's throughout. But
The Winter's Tale presents no such problem. The source of this play
is Robert Greene's prose pastoral romance, *Pandosto, or The Tri-*

umph of Time, and in working the essential features of this story into a play Shakespeare produced the greatest of his tragi-comedies. *The Winter's Tale* is notorious for flouting the "unity of time" as well as of place with supreme confidence. The first three acts take place in Sicily, and form almost a complete play in themselves. Leontes grows causelessly jealous of his wife, Hermione, imagining that she is having an affair with his friend Polixenes, king of Bohemia; Polixenes, warned in time, flees for home, and Hermione is brought to trial and accused of adultery with him. The obsessed Leontes insists on believing her guilt, even when the Oracle of Apollo has declared her innocence, but news of the Queen's death in prison shocks him to his senses, and we leave him a sadder and wiser man. Meanwhile Hermione's infant daughter, born in prison and suspected by Leontes of being Polixenes' bastard, has been ordered by Leontes to be put to death, but Antigonus, on whom the charge is laid, carries the baby off to sea, to leave her on the seacoast of Bohemia before being himself pursued and eaten by a bear. This last piece of action is a simple device to provide a bridge to the next part of the play and at the same time get rid of the inconvenient Antigonus. Apart from this, the first three acts constitute a brilliant tragic play. The sudden growth of causeless jealousy in Leontes is presented with remarkable psychological insight and an assured poetic diction which combines colloquial overtones with an almost casual richness of poetic suggestion. Hermione faces her accuser with tragic dignity. Paulina, her faithful attendant and wife of Antigonus, stands up for her lady before the obsessed Leontes and is the only one who dares tell him home truths to his face. Mamillius, the young son of Hermione and Leontes, is introduced in the best child scene in Shakespeare, before his death is reported as a result of his mother's imprisonment. At the end, Mamillius dead, Hermione dead and her infant daughter on the way to destruction, the consequences of Leontes' wicked jealousy appear to have worked themselves out. He knows better now, but it is too late to do anything about it.

Part of the essential tragedy of *Hamlet* and *Othello* is that one can never undo the past; evil once done is done, and there is no way of restoring the lost world of innocence. But in these last plays Shakespeare finds a way of at least partially undoing evil. It is done by trickery, one might say—Hermione is not really dead, but hidden by Paulina; the infant daughter is saved and brought up as a shepherdess—but it is a symbolic trickery, whose function is to suggest, once again, a ritual of redemption. Act IV takes us to Bohemia sixteen years later, and it is a new world, where even roguery is innocent. The lost princess is now Perdita, a shepherd's supposed daughter, and—true to the logic of fairy tale—she bears in her face and manners the hereditary stamp of her royal birth, so that she attracts Prince Florizel, Polixenes' son, and the two fall in love. Autolycus, the rogue, is the most engaging of all Shakespeare's minor villains (if villain he can be called). Bohemia is fairyland, real enough in its pastoral atmosphere, its sheep-shearing feast and flowered countryside, but fairyland none the less, where time keeps innocence until the opportunity has come for sending it back to do its redeeming work in the real world. The freshness and beauty of the Florizel and Perdita scenes have been noted by everyone who has ever discussed the play: the idyllic pastoral note is sounded here more splendidly and movingly than anywhere else in English literature, yet the psychology—the psychology of young love—is real, and the countryside the real English countryside. When Polixenes breaks in on this idyll to discover Florizel's identity and abuse both Florizel and Perdita for daring to fall in love so out of their degree, his vile temper and cruel threats do not seriously disturb us: fathers are expected to be angry in such circumstances, and Polixenes' anger, though mean-spirited and selfish, has not the tragic overtones of Leontes' jealousy. Besides, Perdita knows that

> The self-same sun that shines upon his court
> Hides not his visage from our cottage, but
> Looks on all alike.

So the couple flee to Sicily, where Leontes receives them kindly until Polixenes arrives in pursuit and reveals his son's disobedience; but the final discovery of Perdita's identity turns all to happiness.

This, significantly, is not the end of the play, and the climax of reconciliation between the young lovers and their parents is not presented, only related in the conversation between several gentlemen. The climax is reserved for the discovery by Leontes that Hermione is still alive. Paulina introduces her as a newly finished statue of the dead queen, but the statue turns out to be the living queen, kept in seclusion all these sixteen years. But is the past really undone? For sixteen years Hermione has deliberately allowed her husband to think her dead, and she returns to life now to greet her daughter. The text gives her no greeting to her husband; her first words are to ask a blessing on her daughter. And there is no return to life for Mamillius. The curse is not fully lifted from the older generation: what Leontes has done he has done, and it cannot after all be undone. The younger generation can do better; they bring new innocence and new hope; and Hermione returns from the grave to give her blessing to them. She says to Perdita

> . . . thou shalt hear that I,
>
> Knowing by Paulina that the oracle
> Gave hope thou wast in being, have preserv'd
> Myself to see the issue.

She says nothing about being happy to live with Leontes again: all her thought is for her daughter. And the play ends with Leontes trying in his pattering speech to act the part of the leader of this group who have eyes for one another rather than for him.

The Tempest treats the theme of forgiveness and the younger generation most explicitly of all, and at the same time most symbolically. Prospero's island—Shakespeare's imagination had been turned in that direction by news of a shipwrecked crew surviving nine months in the Bermudas—is not subject to the normal laws of human destiny, for Prospero controls all with his magic and he can set the stage for the desired solution. In a sense this compact and familiar story is less Christian than any of Shakespeare's earlier treatments of guilt and justice. *Measure for Measure* leaves us with a final sense of identity with the guilty: all are guilty, and we forgive each other for that reason. But Prospero has no real kinship with the other characters; he stands outside the action and stage-manages it, with Ariel's help. The ritual of forgiveness is conducted by a priest who is not himself in need of pardon. That is perhaps why many readers and spectators of *The Tempest* have found Prospero a pompous bore, with his prosy expositions of earlier events to both Miranda and Ariel and his easy loss of temper with inattention or weakness. Though he may not be, as was once held, Shakespeare himself taking his farewell of the stage, he is certainly in a sense the creator of the other characters in the play, controlling them from above, a godlike figure who renounces his godhead only at the end of the play when, the action satisfactorily concluded, he breaks his magic staff to take his place among common humanity. He is in some respects like the Duke in *Measure for Measure*, for both manipulate the other characters in a godlike way; but the Duke is involved in his world more than Prospero is, and symbolizes that involvement by marrying Isabella at the end.

Miranda is youth and innocence, and her union with Ferdinand has the same symbolic meaning as that of Florizel and Perdita. Trinculo and Stephano represent gross animality, mankind at its lowest, and the spirits that serve them are not like Ariel, but alcoholic spirits which destroy the judgment—and it is the alcohol that attracts Caliban:

> That's a brave god, and bears celestial liquor.
> I will kneel to him.

Ariel is the wise man's spirit, representing the scientist's control over nature. The other characters represent different degrees of good and evil at the human level—except for Caliban, who remains a somewhat puzzling character. He is the conquered savage who has rejected the education of his master and is punished by slavery for that rejection. "I pitied thee," Prospero tells him,

> Took pains to make thee speak, taught thee each hour
> One thing or other: when thou didst not, savage,
> Know thine own meaning, but wouldst gabble like
> A thing most brutish, I endow'd thy purposes
> With words that made them known. But thy vile race,
> Though thou didst learn, had that in't which good natures
> Could not abide to be with; therefore was thou
> Deserv'dly confin'd into this rock, who hadst
> Deserv'd more than a prison.

And Caliban replies:

> You taught me language, and my profit on't
> Is, I know how to curse.

Yet the island was Caliban's, "by Sycorax my mother," and Prospero took it from him by force. Prospero, as the superior order of being, would have, on the Elizabethan view, the right to dominate the inferior, so Shakespeare does not seem to be posing an ethical problem here. Caliban, savage son of a witch, the denier of civilization, who refuses to fit into Prospero's scheme of things and is punished for his refusal, is in a strange way both evil and innocent. He is, in his own way, a child of nature; he loves music; he is credulous, and easily fooled by human art. There is perhaps more to be said for him than for the human villains whose treachery to each other constitutes a deeper evil than does Caliban's crude villainy: *corruptio optimi pessima*.

The action takes place throughout on the island, washed by the purifying sea. It is shipwreck which saves Alonso and Antonio from their wickedness; as in *Pericles*, death by water proves to be redemption. It is shipwreck, too, that brings Ferdinand to Miranda, and having done that, brings to her gaze other representatives of the outside world, causing her to exclaim:

> O wonder!
> How many goodly creatures are there here!
> How beauteous mankind is! O brave new world,
> That has such people in't!

She is deceived: it is not a brave new world but a shabby old one. Her innocence is ignorance; she takes the motley assortment of schemers and traitors to be angels; and one is left wondering how she will cope with the realities of the everyday world when she has left the island for Italy. One remembers that it was Othello's ignorance of the "civilized" way of life which led him to trust Iago.

So in the end Shakespeare avoids tragedy by shifting his action to a magic island in which all can be controlled by a benevolent will: *The Tempest* is a magical play, full of grave beauty and rich poetry, a play out of this world, a wish-fulfillment play in which virtue has all the power and innocence meets its appropriate destiny. This is the Garden of Eden, with God, as Prospero, personally in charge to prevent the Devil from prevailing; Miranda is a prelapsarian character who, as the play ends, is about to leave the shelter of Paradise to test her virtue in the wicked world. When Eve, "our credulous mother," left Paradise she had already been tempted and had fallen, and she and Adam went out into the world disillusioned and knowledgeable. But credulous Miranda goes out unfallen into the world, whither Shakespeare refuses to follow her. His last gesture is to avert his eyes from the workaday world at the same time as he sends his characters back into it. There they may become figures in other plays—tragedies no less than comedies, since they will now be unprotected by Prospero's magic.

Shakespeare's last word can hardly be Prospero's

> We are such stuff
> As dreams are made on, and our little life
> Is rounded with a sleep,

for if that is all that life is, it is a strange thing to spend one's career interpreting it dramatically. No; life is worth something after all. The characters in *The Tempest* leave the magical island of redemption to go back into civilization with all its imperfections and temptations; and this is a good thing, for man belongs with his kind, and there is a glory even in the tragic paradoxes of the human situation. In the epilogue Prospero asks to be released, by the applause of the audience, from "this bare island," and the adjective is significant. "Let me not," he says

> Since I have my dukedom got
> And pardon'd the deceiver, dwell
> In this bare island by your spell; . . .

The magic world is but a "bare island" after all, compared with the ordinary world of men. Just as, in *Paradise Lost* "all th' Eastern side of Paradise, so late their happy seat" appeared to Adam and Eve as flaming and terrible when they looked back for a moment before going down into the world that was all before them, so Prospero's Eden becomes uninhabitable at the end. Perhaps Shakespeare's last word, like Milton's, was that man cannot live in Paradise.

Shakespeare spent the last seven years or so of his life at Stratford, in New Place, the large house he had bought there in 1597. After an active life as man of the theater, playwright, and man of property, he seems to have retired in some degree from the London theatrical world. His company, the King's men (earlier the Lord Chamberlain's men), had now both the Globe as a "public" theater and the "private" theater of Blackfriars, in both of which Shakespeare's last plays were acted. Beaumont and Fletcher, two promising younger playwrights, were now writing for the company, having already established themselves with their courtly and sentimental plays at the Blackfriars. Shakespeare wrote his last group of magical romances from Stratford; his imagination had moved away from the everyday human scene to dwell in a more symbolic world. Twice, in 1612–13, he gave his younger colleague John Fletcher a hand with a play, the first time with *Henry VIII*, the larger part of which has, on somewhat dubious internal evidence, been attributed to Fletcher, and the second with *The Two Noble Kinsmen*, where Fletcher seems to have worked over Shakespearean scenes and fitted them into the finished play. *Henry VIII* is a lively dramatic rendering of the high points of that King's reign, with some fine dramatic moments and some great spectacles, emphasizing at the end the Tudor succession and the glories of Queen Elizabeth's reign to come. Henry's repudiation of his first wife, Katherine of Aragon and his love for Anne Boleyn; the proud Wolsey at the height of his power provoking his own fall; the trial of Katherine; the rise of Cranmer and Cromwell; the birth of Elizabeth—these are treated in sequence, with little dramatic unity but considerable dramatic verve. Most of the better scenes in the play appear to be Fletcher's, though the character of Queen Katherine—the most sustained success in the play—is probably Shakespeare's own throughout. *The Two Noble Kinsmen* is a dramatization of the story told by Chaucer in his *Knight's Tale;* it was first published in 1634 as the joint work of Fletcher and Shakespeare, and recent scholarship is still busy trying to distinguish the contribution of each. In conception and tone the play is Fletcher's.

In the last few years of his life Shakespeare appears to have written nothing at all. The reasons can only be conjectured. It may be that his imagination had transcended the limits of dramatic expression and he now felt that language was too weak an instrument. Cer-

tainly in his later plays he used language with a poetic force and
subtlety which indicated that he was prepared to beat more meanings out of verse expression than ordinary logical use of words allows.
Especially from *Antony and Cleopatra* on do we find a daring lack of
metaphorical consistency in favor of a fiercer and richer kind of
meaning:

> > > > > > > > The hearts
> > That spaniel'd me at heels, to whom I gave
> > Their wishes, do discandy, and melt their sweets
> > On blossoming Caesar.

Or consider the curious elliptical construction of these lines from *The
Winter's Tale:*

> > > I am question'd by my fears, of what may chance
> > > Or breed upon our absence; that may blow
> > > No sneaping winds at home, to make us say
> > > "This is put forth too truly."

Not that Shakespeare's later poetry is always complex and packed;
he achieves some of his greatest effect by a magical simplicity:

> > > Finish, good lady; the bright day is done,
> > > And we are for the dark.

We must not forget that Shakespeare was more than a brilliant
dramatist and man of the theater: he was also the greatest poet the
English language has yet produced, and any adequate account of his
achievement would have to include a discussion of his poetry. From
the "sugared" style of

> > > But soft! what light through yonder window breaks?
> > > It is the east, and Juliet is the sun, . . .

to the bold syntax and packed thought of

> > > > > > > Was this taken
> > By any understanding pate but thine?
> > For thy conceit is soaking, will draw in
> > More than the common blocks: not noted, is't,
> > But of the finer natures? by some severals
> > Of head-piece extraordinary? lower messes
> > Perchance are to this business purblind? say, . . .

Shakespeare's poetic usage covers an enormous range. The later
poetry, with its flexible rhythms, startling vocabulary, and syntactical

audacity achieves a quality and depth of expression that seem to exhaust the utmost possibilities of language. Scholars, seeking for methods of dating uncertain plays, have discovered that in the later plays there is a large number of "weak" endings (an extra light syllable added to the iambic pentameter line), a trick that Shakespeare may have picked up from Fletcher, with whom it was a regular practice. But, however useful for purposes of dating plays, this extra light syllable is the least part of the flexible richness of Shakespeare's style. It is a style whose packed elliptical treasury of meaning and suggestion achieves blinding clarity on the very threshold of total obscurity. Nothing more was left to be done with language.

Shakespeare began his literary career as a poet, and he never ceased to be fascinated by the poetic possibilities of image, conceit, metaphor, and symbol. The lyrical music of *A Midsummer Night's Dream*, *Richard II*, and *Romeo and Juliet* succeeded the Marlovian rhetoric of *Richard III* and gave way to the richer orchestration of *As You Like It* and *Twelfth Night*, which in turn is deepened and further enriched in the great tragedies, to emerge with its most potent magic in *Antony and Cleopatra*. The movement is from conceit to a more original and exploratory use of language, from metaphor to symbol. At the end, in *The Tempest*, after the brilliant audacities of the immediately preceding plays, he returns to a more formal Elizabethan utterance, which gives us the grave beauty of Prospero's great speech in which he renounces his magic: "Ye elves of hills, brooks, standing lakes and groves, . . ."

Shakespeare's use of prose, for comic, ironic, mad, or simply realistic scenes, and the different uses to which he puts prose in different phases of his career, are also worth attention. Most of all, one must realize what Shakespeare did to the vocabulary at his disposal. He inherited a language that was in the process of expansion by translation and borrowing, a language flexible enough to enable him to cast his own stamp on it, to manipulate it, enlarge it, wrest it to his purpose, with remarkable freedom. Spenser was behind him, and Marlowe and Lyly, and the Elizabethan song writers and Petrarchan sonneteers, and Ovid and Mantuan and Italian poets and short story writers, and translations from the classics and from the Bible. He was conscious, as other writers of his time and later were, of the advantages to be derived from combining and counterpointing the Anglo-Saxon and the Latin elements in English. Above all, as for all truly great poets, language was for him not only expressive but cognitive and exploratory; for him, the nature of reality could be probed by the very fact of rendering it in poetic speech. This great poetic gift was put at the service of an equally great dramatic gift. He had the true objectivity of the artist, the supreme craftsmanship of the man of the theater, a humane curiosity about man and his nature, an extraordinary ability to conceive and create character, and an unrivaled mastery of the English language. That was William Shakespeare: he remains the unchallenged champion in the whole field of English literature.

CHAPTER TEN

Drama from Jonson to the
Closing of the Theaters

As for Jonson, . . . I think him the most learned and judicious
writer which any theatre ever had. . . . He was deeply conversant
in the Ancients, both Greek and Latin, and he borrowed boldly from
them. . . . If I would compare him with Shakespeare, I must acknowledge him the more correct poet, but Shakespeare the greater
wit. Shakespeare was the Homer, or father of our dramatic poets;
Jonson was the Virgil, the pattern of elaborate writing; I admire him,
but I love Shakespeare." So wrote Dryden, in his *Essay of Dramatic
Poesy* (1668), expressing a view which was not only common to his
age but which also corresponds in some degree to what all subsequent critics have felt about the difference between Shakespeare
and Ben Jonson. Shakespeare, with a largeness of vision and flexibility of technique, worked with the popular dramatic tradition of his
time and produced an English poetic drama which owed nothing to
any external doctrine of correctness but which developed, out of the
pressure of its own vitality, its own kind of form and unity. Jonson,
more learned and deeply concerned with classical precedent, ap-
proached his art from a quite different point of view. With him the
formula came first, and the classical model was the source of the
formula. He knew in advance what the function of comedy was, and
what sort of humor was proper to it. He knew the rules of dramatic
structure and he understood what propriety was, from the same
sources. When he wrote plays based on Roman history, he knew
what Roman historians to quote from and what phases of Roman
life to refer to. Pedantic, imitative, and supremely self-confident in
his learned art, he is the one great example in English of the Renaissance Humanist (in the narrowest sense of that term) turned dramatist and poet.

If he were only that, he would be remembered more as a literary curiosity than as a great literary figure. But he was also a rugged Englishman with a sardonic relish for the varied and colorful London life of his day; he had a boisterous and even a cruel sense of humor which manifested itself in his best comedies with a bizarre brilliance; he showed enormous vigor and impressive originality even when most closely following classical models or applying rules derived from classical theory or practice; and he had in addition a quality which is not often associated with those already mentioned—a delicate artfulness in the handling of word and image in lyrical verse which enabled him to produce such well remembered examples of perfect verbal patterning as "Drink to me only with thine eyes," "Slow, slow fresh fount," and "Queen and huntress, chaste and fair." The contrast between Jonson and Shakespeare is not therefore the simple one between the Renaissance Humanist obsessed by classical rule and precedent and the "natural genius" inventing his own kind of art with the help of a popular tradition. Jonson's sardonic view of human nature owed nothing to classical sources, while his lyrical gift, however much it may have been stimulated by classical epigram and the Greek Anthology, reflected an important facet of his personality. No English writer was more highly idiosyncratic than Jonson, and his picturesque and violent life—which included (after bricklaying and soldiering) the slaying of an actor in a duel and consequent imprisonment and branding, a temporary conversion to Roman Catholicism, a fierce literary quarrel with his fellow dramatists Marston and Dekker, a journey to Scotland on foot, a career as principal purveyor of masques to King James I's court, and a bitter feud with Inigo Jones, the architect and stage designer who had provided the sets for his masques—is sufficient testimony to his individuality and self-confidence. In the latter part of his career he was the leader of an important literary group and indeed something of a literary dictator, the first significant example of that species in English literature. His life, which ran from 1573 until 1637, not only spanned the flowering time of that literary era which we loosely call Elizabethan, but reached well into the reign of Charles I and into a very different cultural atmosphere from that which prevailed at the end of the sixteenth century, when Spenser was working on his *Faerie Queene* and Shakespeare was developing his true powers.

That Jonson was eclipsed as a dramatist by Shakespeare is clear enough to later eyes, but to the critics and playgoers of the seventeenth century it was not so clear. Jonson had a claim on literary men that Shakespeare had not; he bullied them into admiration by the force of his literary claims and the supreme confidence he showed in pressing them. It was a long time before a critical theory developed which was adequate to cope with the richness and subtlety of Shakespeare's plays and the incredible wealth of his genius; but from the beginning Jonson could be proved good by the available critical apparatus. Dryden, in *An Essay of Dramatic Poesy*, provides a model analysis of a play, and the play is Jonson's *Epicœne, or the Silent Woman*. "I will take the pattern of a perfect play from Ben Jonson, who was a careful and learned observer of the dramatic laws." Shakespeare could not be so analyzed; he drew on the images of Nature "not laboriously, but luckily"; "he needed not the spectacles of books to read Nature; he looked inwards, and found her there." Jonson was thus the more respected in the seventeenth century because his plays were more amenable to criticism.

Jonson's first important and successful play was *Every Man in his Humour* (1598),[1] a comedy of intrigue owing much to Roman comedy but highly original in tone and manner. He wanted to present a satiric picture of his own age, to write with cool irony of contemporary human foibles, as he considered Plautus and Terence had done. (But he thought of himself also as an English Juvenal.) He considered himself a realist, and in the Prologue he attacked both the themes and the conventions of contemporary drama and contrasted his own aim. He will not "serve the ill customs of the age" and refuses

> To make a child, now swaddled, to proceed
> Man, and then shoot up, in one beard, and weed,
> Past threescore years: or, with three rusty swords
> And help of some few foot-and-half-foot words,
> Fight over York and Lancaster's long jars,
> And in the tiring house bring wounds to scars.
> He rather prays, you will be pleased to see
> One such today as other plays should be,
> Where neither chorus wafts you o'er the seas,
> Nor creaking throne comes down, the boys to please,
> Nor nimble squib is seen, to make afeard
> The gentlewomen, nor rolled bullet heard
> To say, it thunders, nor tempestuous drum
> Rumbles, to tell you when the storm doth come;
> But deeds and language such as men do use,
> And persons such as comedy would choose
> When she would show an image of the times
> And sport with human follies, not with crimes.

[1] The dates given for Jonson's plays are those of their first performance. None of the plays was published singly in Jonson's lifetime, but he brought out a collected volume in 1616, reprinted with a second volume in 1640. Plays of other dramatists are also dated by their first performance when it is known.

This is the language of a conscious reformer of the stage, who sees himself doing something both artistically better and morally worthier than his contemporaries are producing. He was to be more correct in structure, more contemporary in theme, and more improving in effect. The function of comedy was the reproving of human foibles by holding them up to ridicule, and he adapted the old explanation of human character by the four humors to develop a "comedy of humours," a comedy, that is, in which each character is seen to be dominated, and even obsessed, by one particular quirk. He explained his view in the "induction" to his next comedy, *Every Man Out Of His Humour:*

> Why, humour, as 'tis *ens*, we thus define it $\qquad$ [*ens:* an
> To be a quality of air or water, $\qquad\qquad\qquad\qquad$ existing
> And in itself holds these two properties, $\qquad\qquad$ thing.]
> Moisture and fluxure; as, for demonstration,
> Pour water on this floor, 'twill wet and run;
> Likewise the air, forced through a horn or trumpet,
> Flows instantly away, and leaves behind
> A kind of dew; and hence we do conclude
> That whatsoe'er hath fluxure and humidity,
> As wanting power to contain itself,
> Is humour. So in every human body
> The choler, melancholy, phlegm and blood,
> By reason that they flow continually
> In some one part, and are not continent,
> Receive the name of Humours. Now thus far
> It may by metaphor apply itself
> Unto the general disposition,
> As when some one peculiar quality
> Doth so possess a man that it doth draw
> All his affects, his spirits and his powers,
> In their confluctions, all to run one way:
> This may be truly said to be a humour.

He goes on to say that those who "affect a humour" merely by some trick of costume, and boast of these petty and affected humors, are apes who ought to be scourged:

> . . . I will scourge those apes
> And to these courteous eyes oppose a mirror,
> As large as is the stage whereon we act,
> Where they shall see the time's deformity
> Anatomized in every nerve and sinew
> With constant courage, and contempt of fear.

Jonson's insistence on the humors was at cross purposes with his realistic intention, though he never seems to have realized this. A "humorous" character is bound to be a caricature, never presented as a fully realized human being but only as the fop, the blusterer, the jealous husband, the anxious father, the uncouth country cousin aping city manners, the hypocritical Puritan, or some similar type. Jonson lacked tenderness, and he lacked, too, that ability to enjoy the essential humanity of his immoral characters, as Shakespeare so clearly did with Falstaff. He was never faced with the problem that in some degree has troubled so many of the greatest dramatists and novelists—the problem of preserving a moral pattern while at the same time showing such a thorough awareness of the humanity of his evil characters that (to know all being to forgive all) moral disapproval is almost dissolved in psychological understanding. The comedy of humors inevitably avoids that problem. Comedy becomes satire, character becomes oddity, evil becomes culpable folly. There is humor enough (in the modern sense) in Jonson's comedy; he presents his obsessed characters with wit, liveliness of comic extravagance, and cleverly manipulated absurdity (of which one of the most effective examples is the scene in *The Poetaster* where Crispinus, who represents John Marston, is given an emetic which forces him to vomit up his long Latinate words), and at times comedy in his hands degenerates into farce; it is however splendid farce, which deals not with ridiculous situations merely, but with ridiculous situations as they arise from ridiculous elements in human nature. It is Dickensian in some respects, but when Dickens laughs the overtones are humanitarian. Jonson's laughter is sterner, and underlying it is his own enormous self-confidence, which at times rises to arrogance.

Every Man In His Humour was first set in Italy but the scene was soon changed to London, whose life and manners were always Jonson's real interest. The action of the play is designed to exhibit the fatuities, the follies, the obsessions, the pretentions, and the absurdities of the different characters; the foolish and boastful are "gulled" and exposed; plots and disguises help to forward the intrigue, and the play ends in reconciliation and mirth. Much of the dialogue is in prose, a vigorous and basically colloquial prose which bears the impress of the idiosyncrasy of the speaker. The blank verse, which is largely confined to expository passages and scenes where the tension is fairly relaxed, is firm and workmanlike, with again colloquial overtones. *Every Man Out of His Humour* (1599) concentrates with greater single-mindedness on the illustration of ridiculous "humours." The satiric note is dominant throughout; the characters (who in the folio edition of Jonson's *Works*, 1616, are each described in an introductory note somewhat in the manner of the "character writers" of the period) are given names indicating their particular foible: Carlo Buffone, "a public, scurrilous and profane jester"; Fastidius Brisk, "a neat, spruce, affecting courtier, one that wears clothes well, and in fashion; practiseth by his glass how to salute"; Sordido, "a wretched hob-nailed chuff, whose recreation is reading of almanacs, and felicity, foul weather"; Fungoso, "the son of Sordido, and a student; one that has revelled in his time, and follows the fashion afar off, like a spy"; Sogliardo, "an essential clown, brother to Sordido, yet so enamoured of the name of a gentleman, that he will have it, though he buys it"; and so on. Jonson himself is introduced as Asper, explaining and commenting on the action in conversation with his friends Cordatus and Mitis. The latter two act as a sort of Chorus. The play is more episodic than its predecessor, and incidents are contrived to illustrate the follies and idiosyncracies of the different characters with little regard to the development of the main action, although everything is tied up at the end with considerable ingenuity. Every one is finally shaken out of his absurd humor by suitable punishment or exposure. In spite of the Italian names this, too, is a London play full of the atmosphere of contemporary London.

Cynthia's Revels was first acted in 1600 by the boys of the Queen's Chapel, and it is full of that special kind of virtuosity which Elizabethan child actors could display so brilliantly. A satire on contemporary gallantry using mythological characters does not represent a very happy convention; the plot is overelaborate and confused; masques are introduced, with music and dancing; and altogether one has the impression that Jonson has let his ingenuity run away with him. The play shows many kinds of skill—it includes some cleverly mannered prose, some carefully chiseled blank verse, and the perfectly wrought lyric, "Slow, slow fresh fount"—but they do not contribute to a dramatic unity. (It is worth noting that Jonson, for all his concern with classical rule and precedent, often has less artistic unity in his plays than Shakespeare. The reason is easy to see: Shakespeare developed the unity appropriate to his original art form, while Jonson often imposed an external unity on his material.) It was typical of Jonson that he should have concluded the play with an Epilogue in which he aggressively asserted:

> By God, 'tis good, and if you like't, you may.

By this time Jonson was involved in that quarrel with Marston and others which is known as the War of the Theatres, and his play

The Poetaster (1601) was a vindication of his position against his enemies. The scene is set in Augustan Rome. We see Horace (Jonson) moving with dignity in the literary world of Rome, friend of Virgil and of Augustus Caesar though pursued by the envy of fools and knaves. Ovid, Propertius, Tibullus, among others, are introduced, and there is much learned reference to Latin literature. Ovid's famous encounter with a bore which he records in Book 1 of his *Sermones* is turned into an encounter with Crispinus (Marston) in an amusing street scene. The whole play has more life and vigor than one would expect from such exhibitionist use of classical reading, but the satire is very limited in scope and the author's patent self-glorification sometimes irritates. The effortless identification of himself with one of the principal figures in the Golden Age of Latin literature and of his enemies with Roman impostors and poetasters who yapped at the heels of the great Augustans illustrates both the way in which his imagination dwelt in the Rome of his studies and the importance which he attached to literature and its practitioners, symbolized most effectively by Virgil and his contemporaries. In this respect Jonson's attitude to life and letters was that of the true Renaissance classical Humanist.

Fortunately, Jonson turned aside from those literary controversies which so confined his satirical talent, to enrich and develop his own species of satiric comedy. *Volpone, or the Fox* (1605) is the first and the greatest of a series of comedies which show Jonson's characteristic mixture of savagery and humor, of moral feeling and grim relish of the monstrous absurdities of which human nature is capable, disciplined with a new sharpness and given new depth and scope. Taking a hint from the *captatores,* legacy hunters of Rome, described by Petronius and others, Jonson contrived the story of a cunning rich man who feigned a mortal illness so that his wealthy neighbors would court his favor in the hope of being named his heir. Volpone is childless, and thus of obvious interest to the legacy hunters. His servant Mosca cunningly plays on their hopes and fears, promising each that Volpone is on the point of naming him as his heir and urging him to speed the process by a further proof of regard and friendship. Thus each is induced to bring gifts to the supposedly dying Volpone in the expectation of receiving them back together with all of Volpone's property when he dies. But Jonson does more than exploit the irony of this situation. The eager legacy hunters, falling over themselves in their haste to prove their devotion to Volpone, are played with cunningly by Mosca to the point where they become not only willing but anxious to do much more than merely give Volpone gifts. One disinherits his son in order to name

Volpone his heir, thus proving his friendship, while another, normally extravagantly jealous of his pretty wife, is induced to persuade her to give herself to the dying man in the confident hope that this supreme gift will clinch Volpone's choice of him as his heir. In the end everyone is overreached; Mosca overreaches his master, and both finally overreach themselves so that their villainies are exposed and punished. The scene is set in Renaissance Italy, accepted by the English imagination of this time as the proper home of vice, but the satire is general and deeply misanthropic. The working out of the plot is extremely ingenious; the mounting pace of the trickery and the villainy raises a horrified interest which never flags, and the progressive exposure of the depths to which lust for wealth can degrade the human character is made with an obsessive fierceness that shows Jonson at the height of his satiric powers. The tone is set at once by Volpone's opening words as he pays his daily worship to his wealth:

> Good morning to the day; and next, my gold!—
> Open the shrine, that I may see my saint.

The blank verse moves with speed and vigor; less subtle and flexible than the mature Shakespeare's, it does combine strength with a conversational movement. In the extravagance of imagery with which Volpone and Mosca express their ambitions and designs, Jonson not only suggests the obsessive nature of their drive for wealth and power but also, through the infatuated exaggeration of the tone, provides an implicit criticism of this attitude. The characters are deliberately restricted in scope in the interests of the satiric purpose. There are moments when the play moves close to tragedy, and the scene where Celia, Corvino's wife, expresses her horror when she discovers that her husband intends to force her to Volpone's bed shows Jonson moving closer to what one might call Elizabethan romantic tragedy than he ever moved again. It is in this scene that Volpone, now revealed as a cunning old lecher as well as a sadistic miser, sings to his shrinking victim the song, "Come, my Celia, let us prove, /While we can, the sports of love," which has in its context much grimmer overtones than can be imagined when it is read or sung separately.

Volpone was followed by Epicœne, or The Silent Woman in 1609, The Alchemist in 1610, and Bartholomew Fair in 1614. Epicœne, though much admired by Dryden and analyzed in his Essay of Dramatic Poesy as a perfectly constructed comedy, is the slightest of these mature comedies and is more concerned with the "gulling" of fools and hypocrites than with the satiric exploration of vice. The principal character, Morose, has the "humour" of being unable to stand noise, and lives surrounded by silence; he marries a young girl, supposed to be perpetually silent, in order to disinherit his nephew. But the girl turns out to be an incessant talker and the nephew finally agrees to arrange a divorce in return for a satisfactory financial settlement. In the end it is revealed that the girl is a boy in disguise; the whole thing has been a plot by the nephew to gull his uncle. A bare summary of the plot, however, tells little about the qualities of the play, which is full of odd characters and fantastic humor—a Jonsonian holiday in which the author gives full play to his characteristic blend of learning and realism, of boisterous humor and contrived grotesquerie. The play is in prose throughout, and thus lacks that criticism through obsessive imagery that is found in Jonson's greatest comedies. *The Alchemist* is more in the vein of *Volpone,* though it lacks the latter's misanthropic fierceness. It is a satiric comedy, dealing with a pretended alchemist whose victims include a great variety of characters all of whom are attracted by the hope of easy gold. This situation enables Jonson to display a great variety of human weakness and hypocrisy. As in *Volpone,* a principal theme is the way in which greed can make people gullible. In the absence of his master Lovewit, Face brings Subtle, the quack alchemist, to his master's house and there he proceeds to raise money from the gullible greedy, who include Drugger, a tobacco merchant, Dapper, a lawyer's clerk, the ambitious and sensual Sir Epicure Mammon, and two Puritan Brethren of Amsterdam whose conversation and behavior give Jonson the opportunity to ridicule Puritan hypocrisy and absurdity. Each character has his own characteristic extravagance of language as well as the mental fatuity which makes him a preordained dupe; it is a brilliant portrait gallery. Again like *Volpone,* the plot is cunningly developed and the action moves fast until the unexpected return of Lovewit puts an end to the activities of Face and Subtle. But Lovewit does not represent impartial justice or the moral norm; Face confesses to him and is pardoned, for Lovewit loves a jest, and only the unfortunate Subtle and Doll Common, the third in the trio of tricksters, meet some kind of retribution in the end. Jonson continually varies the system of mirrors, as it were, which he uses to reflect his moral position. In *Volpone,* the principal characters, Volpone and Mosca, batten on the greed of others, exposing to the full their selfishness and avarice; but this battening and this exposure arise from greed, selfishness, and avarice even greater than that of the victims. Similarly, in *The Alchemist,* Face and Subtle are motivated by greed in playing on the greed of others. But here there is

no simple poetic justice at the end; Lovewit's return does not destroy
Face, for the master cannot resist the situation Face presents him
with, and the play ends with Lovewit in possession of the money
and goods which the gulled fortune-seekers had deposited with
Face. This wry twist in the end provides a further comment on
society. But Jonson's true criticism of his characters, here as in most
of his mature comedies, lies in the verse he makes them speak; the
obsessive extravagance with which they express their ambitions
makes clear, by the very fact that it *is* obsessive extravagance, that
here is a wide deviation from the true moral and social norm. A
well-known example of this is a speech of Sir Epicure Mammon:

> I will have all my beds blown up, not stuft:
> Down is too hard: and then, mine oval room
> Filled with such pictures as Tiberius took
> From Elephantis, and dull Aretine
> But coldly imitated. Then, my glasses
> Cut in more subtle angles, to disperse
> And multiply the figures, as I walk
> Naked between my succubae. My mists
> I'll have of perfume, vapoured 'bout the room,
> To lose ourselves in; and my baths, like pits
> To fall into; from whence we will come forth,
> And roll us dry in gossamer and roses.

Bartholomew Fair is the most expansive of Jonson's mature satiric
comedies and the most English in atmosphere. The plot here is
less important than the speech and action of the individual characters and the roistering atmosphere of the Fair at which most of the
play is set. The humors and follies of the complacent Littlewit and
his wife Win; of the Puritan Zeal-of-the-Land Busy anxious (for
pecuniary reasons) to marry Win's mother, the widowed Dame
Purecraft; of Justice Overdo, who gets himself into trouble by appearing at the Fair in disguise in order to discover what villainies
really go on there; of Bartholomew Cokes of Harrow on the Hill,
whose fatuous complacency makes him an easy victim of the professional pickpocket Ezekiel Edgeworth and his accomplice Nightingale the ballad seller—these are revealed against the noise and
bustle of the Fair, where Ursula the pig-woman, Joan Trash the
gingerbread woman, and many others carry on their raucous business. The play is full of life and color, and if the structure is less
artful than that of his other mature comedies, this is compensated
for by the boisterous high spirits and the zestful rendering of
London life that Jonson here gives us. The satirical note is sounded
clearly enough, but (unlike *Volpone* and even *The Alchemist*) satire

is subordinated to comedy and the main interest of the characters (even Zeal-of-the-Land Busy, who is shown as alternately stupidly fanatical and grossly hypocritical) lies in the rich humor of their folly. Here indeed, Jonson "sports with human follies not with crimes," and the play ends with everyone chastened by experience but not otherwise punished.

Jonson also produced two tragedies on Roman themes, *Sejanus* (1603) and *Catiline* (1611), moved probably by Shakespeare's success with *Julius Caesar*. But his approach was very different from Shakespeare's. Not only did he choose much less well-known incidents from Roman history, but he drew on the original Latin sources—Tacitus, Suetonius, Juvenal, Seneca, and Dion Cassius in the case of *Sejanus*—and introduced numerous details from these works. He even cited in his preface the actual editions of the Latin authors that he had used. Nevertheless, he allowed himself some liberty in shaping the tragic pattern of the action. In *Sejanus,* he did not keep to the classical unity of time, though his preface shows that he had some qualms of conscience about this. There he conceded that he had not observed "the strict laws of time" or employed the classical chorus, but pleaded that he had "discharged the other offices of a tragic writer . . . in truth of argument, dignity of persons, gravity and height of elocution, fulness and frequency of sentence [i.e. moral sayings]." The play does move with dignity and achieves a certain tragic force in the ironic way in which the hero's intriguing ambition and final reversal of fortune are handled. Though the characters are not probed beyond their more obvious qualities which help to motivate the plot, Jonson succeeds in giving dramatic force to his picture of a police state in which the most unscrupulous and egotistical planning cannot yield any permanent power, for everyone is spying on everybody else and the Emperor himself spins his secret web at a distance. The climactic scene where Tiberius' letter about Sejanus is read to the Senate shows Jonson's special kind of dramatic irony at its most successful: the Senate, anxious to follow the Emperor's line, is deliberately baffled by his ambiguous and shifting references to Sejanus, and does not know whether to hail him or denounce him; until, at the end, the meaning is made clear and denunciation follows. *Catiline* is a more "regular" play, complete with ghost and chorus. The story of Catiline's conspiracy is told with conspicuous use of classical sources; the usual vein of savage satire runs through the play, and the attempt to provide motivation for Catiline's action (he becomes indirectly involved with jealous women and one of them worms the story out of one of the conspirators) provides an ironic commentary on the relation between the lower human passions and the shaping of political history, but the characters are not developed nor are their motives explored with any real dramatic subtlety. *Catiline* lacks the ironic vigor of *Sejanus*.

Of Jonson's later comedies—*The Devil is an Ass* (1616), *The Staple of News* (1625), *The New Inn* (1629), *The Magnetic Lady* (1632), and *A Tale of a Tub* (1633)—all that need be said is that they show him playing variations, with differing degrees of success, on his favorite satiric-comic themes; though each has its bright moments, and even some splendid passages, none is of the quality of his best mature comedies and there is little reason to dispute the conventional view that these later works show Jonson in decline. An exception must, however, be made for the unfinished pastoral drama, *The Sad Shepherd, or, A Tale of Robin Hood*, which shows an attractive vein of poetic fancy, combining the pastoral with the realistic.

That Jonson possessed this kind of poetic fancy is made abundantly clear by his masques, of which he wrote a large number throughout his career. The purpose of the masque was entertainment at Court or at a great house. Spectacle and movement were an important part of it, and the arts of the stage designer and the composer were often as important in its production as that of the poet. The origin of the masque is a matter for the anthropologist; it is connected with mumming and with seasonal revels on Twelfth Night, May Day, and similar occasions. From a fairly early period in England we find the custom of masked visitors arriving at a party to dance, present gifts, and mingle with the guests; eventually the masque, in its more stylized Italian form, became a regular part of festivities accompanying coronations, state visits of foreign princes, and royal or noble marriages. These masques drew on classical mythology for their characters and themes, which were treated with deliberate fancifulness. Throughout the reigns of Henry VIII, Elizabeth, James I, and Charles I the court masque flourished. Jonson was a principal purveyor of masques to James I and his queen. His saturnine wit and misanthropic irony disappeared when he turned to the production of these courtly entertainments, in which he showed a very different side of his genius—a delicate fancy, a lyrical grace, and a lively sportiveness. His lines may lack fluidity, but they have the other virtue of a finely chiseled shape. This is perhaps a two-dimensional art, lacking all complexity and that infinite reverberation of meaning which marks the greatest poetry. There is no echoing profundity in such lines as

> Beauties, have you seen this toy
> Called Love, a little boy
> Almost naked, wanton, blind,
> Cruel now, and then as kind?
> If he be amongst ye, say:
> He is Venus' runaway;

or in

> Stay, my sweet singer,
> The touch of thy finger
> A little, and linger
> For me, that am bringer
> Of bounds to the border,
> The rule and recorder
> And mouth of your order,
> As priest of the game
> And prelate of the same.

But they represent excellent workmanship, and they take their place very effectively in the masques of which they are part. In the "antimasque" (which Jonson introduced), with its deliberate change of tone from the masque proper, he could show something of his other side and add many different kinds of contrasting notes, from the comically realistic to the gruesome and the grotesque. Jonson's long career of collaboration with the architect and designer Inigo Jones (which ended with their quarrel in 1630) meant that his masques were produced with particular visual effectiveness.

Finally, one must mention *Eastward Hoe* (1605), a play written jointly by Jonson, Marston, and Chapman, though we cannot be certain about the limits of the contribution of each. This attractive comedy displays qualities which none of its three authors shows in his independent work. The Jonsonian comedy in it has a lightness of touch not typical of Jonson, and Chapman's reflective psychology and Marston's melodramatic bitterness are both subdued to a brighter, gayer mood. The plot is a bourgeois morality, dealing with a city goldsmith's two apprentices, one virtuous and one vicious, and their respective fates, which are balanced by the fates of the goldsmith's two daughters, the younger sweet and modest and the elder foolish and worldly. The bad apprentice lands in jail but is saved from the gallows by timely repentance; the virtuous apprentice ends by marrying his master's younger daughter and eventually, as deputy-alderman, mercifully judging his erring former colleague. The foolish elder daughter is duped by an unscrupulous adventurer and after being humbled by misfortune is reduced to seeking mercy from the sister and father she had previously scorned. The lively realism of the action, the glimpses of middle-class London life and manners, the strong character drawing, the good-natured humor, combine to give *Eastward Hoe* unusual charm. Whether its morality is intended seriously, or, as seems probable, it is really a subtle burlesque of tradesmen's morality, it stands apart from the work of its joint authors as a more genial kind of play than any of them ever managed to produce alone.

Shakespeare and Jonson are the two giants among Elizabethan and early Jacobean playwrights; but there were many others who wrote with success both for the public and the private theater, sometimes individually, sometimes in cooperation, sometimes anonymously. Writing for the theater was the obvious way for a literary man whom destiny had placed on the lower slopes on Fortune's Hill (to use a common Elizabethan figure) to secure public acclaim and economic satisfaction. In some respects the drama in the late sixteenth and early seventeenth centuries can be compared to the novel in the nineteenth and twentieth centuries, and a theatrical success might be compared to a modern best seller. But there are important differences. Though plays were printed, generally in cheap quarto editions, and were often eagerly read by the literate, it was as acted plays that they made their impact and achieved popularity. The audience, though varied in its class composition, was not large enough to make long runs possible, so that there was a continuous demand for new plays. Old plays were rehashed, new plays on themes that had proved popular rushed out, and every possible variation played on the kinds of tragic and comic situation that appealed to the Elizabethan and Jacobean imagination. Dramatists drew for their plots on Italian *novelle*, on classical history and on recent English and European history, on old plays, stories, legends, and on any source that provided or suggested a plot in which injured men sought revenge, ambitious men overreached themselves, characters displayed heroic dignity in holding out for a while against the encroachment of inevitable doom, passion led men—and women—into strange jungles of horror or self-deception or pathos or all three, obsessed or foolish men demonstrated their folly and were duly gulled by their superiors in wit—indeed, anything that provided the opportunity for the dramatic display of emotional and physical violence and a presentation of the absurdities and the wonders of which passionate man is capable. Some dramatists, like George Chapman, infused an ethical and philosophical spirit into their plays; some, like John Marston, became intoxicated by exuberant language and produced some quite extraordinary fustian; some, like

Cyril Tourneur (if he really is the author of the anonymous *Revenger's Tragedy*) played variations—sometimes strangely impressive ones—on the old revenge theme; some, like John Webster and, rather differently, John Ford, explored the individual moment of passion with haunting poetic brilliance. Others explored in comedy conflicts between the social classes—especially between citizens and courtiers—and pointed the way toward that counterpointing of gullible bourgeois respectability and amoral aristocratic sophistication which is the theme of so much Restoration comedy. Others again churned out routine stuff in reasonably competent blank verse, presenting again and again the kinds of situation which had proved themselves most popular. Many plays of the period have not survived. Printed copies of plays were regarded as ephemeral light literature unworthy of the attention of any librarian: the first librarian of the Bodleian Library, Oxford (which was opened in 1602) was instructed by Sir Thomas Bodley to reject plays and similar "baggage books" for fear of scandal. One must remember, too, that in spite of the enormous popularity of the drama during this period, Puritan hostility toward the playhouse increased rather than diminished, and when the Puritans finally gained control of the government they closed the theaters. The closing of the theaters in 1642 brought this greatest of all periods in the history of English drama to an end; but it is arguable that the form of poetic drama developed by the Elizabethans had by this time completely run its course and that, quite apart from the closing of the theaters, there was no further road that way. The next phase of English drama, which appeared after the Restoration, produced a very different kind of dramatic literature.

It is impossible for the historian of English literature to do justice to a dominant literary form such as poetic drama between 1580 and 1640 and the novel in the nineteenth century and after; to do so would mean taking up so much space that there would be no room for anything else. If Shakespeare and Ben Jonson had not existed, the literary historian would devote pages to Chapman and Middleton and Webster and Ford and Beaumont and Fletcher without any disproportion; each of these is more interesting and produced plays of greater intrinsic value than any playwright of the eighteenth century and perhaps even of the nineteenth. But in the light of the peak achievements of their period, they must remain minor figures, paying the penalty of the period's dramatic richness.

George Chapman (ca. 1559–1634) has been generally known, ever since Keats wrote his famous sonnet, as a translator of Homer; but his somber ethical imagination (which is reflected in the way he handles the Homeric heroes) produced five tragedies which show the Elizabethan interest in Stoic philosophy in an original and impressive form. *Bussy d'Ambois* (1604) is a study of an old soldier (like Othello) lost and betrayed in a peacetime world of courtly intrigue: but the traitor is as much his own passion, which takes him completely by surprise in welling up in affection for a married lady of the Court, as the sophisticated characters who resent his blunt martial manner. Chapman's dramatic verse has its own dark and crowded intensity; it is sometimes congested and not always dramatic, but it bears the stamp of a brooding, original mind. Sometimes we feel that Chapman has not properly come to terms with the theater, or adequately reconciled his ideas about man's behavior and destiny with his sense of character in action. His great men try to achieve a Stoic calm; sometimes, like Bussy d'Ambois, they are surprised and betrayed by passion; sometimes, like Clermont d'Ambois in *The Revenge of Bussy d'Ambois* (ca. 1610), he does achieve a Senecan detachment, but the spectacle of a Stoic character philosophizing and debating with himself against a somewhat perfunctory background of traditional revenge-play properties is an odd one (though in *Hamlet*, Shakespeare manages it without oddness), and suggests that Chapman was searching for a kind of intellectual drama which the conventions of the Elizabethan stage denied him. In both these plays, Chapman derived his plot from recent French history. He did this also in *The Conspiracy and Tragedy of Charles, Duke of Byron* (1608), a tragedy in two parts where again a man of potentially heroic stature is destroyed by his own passions, on which his enemies find it easy to play. *Chabot, Admiral of France* (ca. 1613) and *Caesar and Pompey* (printed 1631) explore different aspects of stoical virtue. The loyal and noble Chabot is bayed by his barking enemies, and stands stiffly honest until his innocence establishes itself, but not before his sense of injustice has eaten into his heart, to produce his eventual death. In *Caesar and Pompey* the interest centers on the exemplary Stoic calm of Cato, and the achievement of such calm, after much vacillation, by Pompey.

Chapman's attempt to produce a philosophical drama within the conventions of the Elizabethan theater, while not wholly successful in dramatic terms, produced some of the most interesting and individual plays of the period. His comedies, deriving both from the intrigue of Latin comedy and the "humours" of Ben Jonson, are less individual, but at least one, *All Fools*, in its deftly constructed plot (from Terence) and kindliness of tone, is still capable of affording civilized pleasure.

John Marston (d. 1634) is a very different sort of dramatist. Having begun as a writer of coarse and violent verse satires, which display a certain ingenious pedantry in their lavish vocabulary of abuse, he turned to drama, where he shows the same extravagant language in melodramatic tragedies of love and revenge and cynical comedies which combine bitter exposure of human folly and ambition with wild farce. *Antonio and Mellida* (1599) and *Antonio's Revenge* are, like so many Elizabethan and Jacobean plays, set in Italy, which was now seen as a land of political violence and psychological extravagance, where the claims of rank and power could be set against those of proud poverty in startling patterns of cunning intrigue and twisting passion. The first of these twin plays deals with the intercomplications of private passion and political malice in a plot made up of elements from many different stock Elizabethan dramatic situations; the second, similarly drawing on stock situations, shows stoical characters dedicated to revenge, and so involved in that conflict between self-control and passion which we have seen was of such interest to Chapman. The conflict is resolved in a peculiar kind of philosophical rant which is nevertheless quite unlike Chapman's philosophical speeches. In the midst of the rant and the general extravagance of vocabulary, a strange kind of poetic excitement occasionally breaks through, showing that Marston is more than a writer of melodramatic fustian. *The Malcontent* (printed 1604), the story of a supplanted Duke who returns to his dukedom in disguise and vents his bitterness by cynically assisting his supplanter, comes to an unexpectedly happy ending when the usurping Duke gives the dukedom back to the Malcontent who then contemptuously pardons everybody. As not infrequently happens in Marston's plays, the motivation sometimes becomes obscure, and we are allowed to forget the reasons for the Malcontent's behavior in the virtuosity of his cynicism. The manipulation of passion, as well as the handling of the more purely comic scenes and the minor complications of the plot, show a fundamental uncertainty between diagnosis and rhetoric and between an interest in Jonsonian "humours" and an interest in moral situations. But *The Malcontent* is a remarkable performance, none the less. Of Marston's other comedies, *The Dutch Courtesan* is the most interesting. It is a complex and sordid story of love, lust, and conspiracy, with a subplot concerning the gulling of a stupid and miserly citizen by a sprightly trickster. As in *The Malcontent*, the happy ending of the main plot does violence to its predominant tone.

Marston is the Crispinus of Ben Jonson's *Poetaster*, and Jonson's picture of him vomiting up his strange, invented words has its justification. The animosity between Marston and Jonson is part of a somewhat tedious chapter in Elizabethan stage history known as the War of the Theaters. Dekker was also involved in this quarrel and also both attacked and was attacked by Jonson. Dekker is the Demetrius of *The Poetaster* and he in turn ridiculed Jonson in his play *Satiromastix, or the Untrussing of the Humorous Poet* (1601). Other plays by all these dramatists also contributed to the controversy, in which Marston showed himself the most ill-tempered. But Marston became reconciled to Jonson later, at least temporarily; he collaborated with him, as well as with Chapman, in *Eastward Hoe,* and dedicated *The Malcontent* to him in 1604.

Thomas Heywood (ca. 1570–1641) was a professional man of the theater and miscellaneous writer who produced many more plays than the twenty-three or so that survive as his and had a hand in very many others. He himself claimed to have "had either an entire hand or at least a main finger in two hundred and twenty plays," and there is no reason to suppose that he was not telling the truth. The theater of his day demanded constant new material, and Heywood was professionally equipped to provide it. He wrote on historical and patriotic themes; he glorified the London citizenry and prentices in plays which showed him appealing to urban middle-class feeling; he had a vein of somewhat ribald comedy which he worked into his most serious plays with little or no sense of construction or appropriateness; and, in *A Woman Killed with Kindness* (1603) and *The English Traveller* (ca. 1627), produced two impressive examples of the kind of play that has been called "domestic tragedy," plays, that is to say, that deal with the tragic results of passion or lust in ordinary family situations, in an atmosphere of sentimental morality.

Charles Lamb's well-known description of Heywood as a "prose Shakespeare" has some justification if it means that he dealt with many of the themes that Shakespeare handled without any of Shakespeare's poetic power or dramatic cunning but with fluency and facility and with a keen eye for the pathetic. His language is pedestrian, but it rises to occasional heights in moments of simple emphasis on pity or passion or regret. *A Woman Killed with Kindness* is the story of a happy marriage broken when the wife is seduced by the husband's friend; the husband, on discovering his wife's infidelity, has his moment of rage and horror, but controls himself with an effort and decides to punish his wife only by sending her away to live with her servants in one of his manors. The sinning wife realizes and acknowledges her sin at the moment of discovery, and dies repentant and brokenhearted, having summoned her husband to her bedside, where he assures her of his forgiveness. *The*

English Traveller deals with a similar theme, though the plot has a curious complication: the hero is chastely in love with a woman happily married to an old man; she returns his love, and they agree to marry on the old man's death. Both have an affection for the old man and repudiate any desire to hasten his death. The hero's friend seduces the wife, whose sin is discovered, and she dies almost immediately, repentant and self-reproachful. There is (as so often in Heywood) a completely irrelevant comic subplot, but the main story is developed with skill and considerable power. A certain delicacy of feeling, the author's combination of compassionate heart with inquiring mind, and a quiet but confident moral tone, give these plays their distinctive character. Heywood can be boisterous enough elsewhere, as in his early play celebrating the heroic exploits of four prentices, *The Four Prentices of London*, which Beaumont made fun of in 1608 in his *The Knight of the Burning Pestle*.

Thomas Dekker (ca. 1570–1641) was another versatile professional who turned his hand to a variety of kinds of writing, including prose pamphlets which show a remarkable knowledge of London low life. Again, only a small proportion of his plays survive. Apparently of humble origin and self-educated, he gives in all his work the impression of an untrained talent making the most of itself with whatever material comes to hand. Like so many other dramatists of his day, he collaborated with others whenever he got the opportunity, and it is not always possible to determine the extent of even his existing work. Of the comedies written by Dekker alone, *Old Fortunatus* (1599) and *The Shoemaker's Holiday* show his characteristic combination of a romantic imagination with an eye for realistic detail. *The Shoemaker's Holiday* (1599) retains its popularity as a lively, boisterous comedy of London life, taking its plot from Thomas Deloney's prose story of Simon Eyre, the London shoemaker who rose to become Lord Mayor and virtually the patron saint of prentices. The play brings together urban realism with a happy folk element. Dekker had a genuine poetic talent, a real gift for delineating character and a sentimentally optimistic view of human nature, and the combination produces his characteristic note. *Old Fortunatus*, published in 1600, is a morality play, based on German legend: Old Fortunatus is offered a gift by Fortune; he chooses an unexhaustible purse rather than a wiser gift, and the choice eventually produces his own death and that of his two sons. It is an ill-organized and uneven play; but its impressive opening scene contains some of Dekker's finest dramatic poetry.

Perhaps Dekker's greatest achievement is *The Honest Whore*, a play in two parts in the first of which (1604) Middleton is thought to have had a hand. But the second part, which is the more interesting and original, is all Dekker's own. The first part tells the story of Bellafront, the prostitute who redeems herself and is finally married to her original seducer. The second shows her being pressed to resume her former life both by her debauched and ruined husband and by the very man who had instigated her conversion, but she stands firm, watched over (unknown to herself) by her father, Orlando Friscobaldo, who turns out to be the *deus ex machina* of the play. In spite of a crude and implausible subplot, *The Honest Whore* (Part II, ca. 1605) is a remarkable and original play; indeed both these plays show a new kind of moral imagination closely linked to an almost Dickensian sense of character. Orlando Friscobaldo is one of the few characters in Elizabethan and Jacobean drama outside Shakespeare who, besides playing an integral part in the moral pattern of the play, is also a convincing and memorable character in his own right, remembered after the details of the play are forgotten. Dekker resembles Heywood in his fluency and his feeling for middle-class urban life; but he has both a vein of poetry and a sense of character that Heywood lacks. The "citizen comedy" produced by these and other dramatists of the period is a reminder that, although Puritan opposition to the stage was centered in London, the London citizenry as a whole were eager theater goers and developed a taste for seeing themselves glorified on the stage.

Other dramatists of the period turned to the revenge theme. After the subtilizing and deepening of the revenge play in *Hamlet* there would seem to be little enough left to do in this line, but some of the Jacobean dramatists took it up again and sought further variations. Cyril Tourneur (ca. 1575–1626) in *The Atheist's Tragedy* (ca. 1608) and *The Revenger's Tragedy*, especially in the latter (if this play, published anonymously in 1607, really is by Tourneur), explored the corrupting power of revenge, constructing a kind of tragedy whose chief interest lies in the spectacle of injured innocence turning monstrous in the endeavor to avenge its wrongs. *The Revenger's Tragedy* has echoes from Hamlet, as in the opening scene, with Vendice standing aside to meditate bitterly on a skull while the wicked and lecherous Duke with his equally lecherous wife and son pass across the stage, but the tone is quite un-Shakespearean. The plots, the disguises, the moments of calculated frightfulness, the melodramatic ingenuity of the Duke's murder, illustrate the avenger's mounting hysteria, his insane self-confidence, his utterly obsessive concern with his revenge and with that only, his savoring of the actual moment of revenge by gloatingly revealing himself and his motives to the dying victim—all this produces an atmosphere of contrived horror which, while splendid in its way, is too deliberately artful to enable the reader or spectator to lose himself in the dramatic situation. At the end of the play, Vendice and his brother Hippolito, who started off as injured innocents, have become monstrous connoisseurs of cruelty who have ceased to have any contact with the ordinary world. With the Duke and his son dead, Antonio, who takes over the government, wonders "how the old duke came murdered," and the two brothers admit their responsibility with a lunatic cheerfulness:

Hippolito: 'Twas all done for the best, my lord.
Vendice: All for your grace's good. We may be bold to speak it now.
             'Twas somewhat witty carried, though we say it—
             'Twas we two murdered him.

And Vendice is astonished when the new duke orders them to execution. His single-minded pursuit of revenge has destroyed his sanity and humanity. *The Atheist's Tragedy* (ca. 1608) is a more general study of corruption of personality through ambition and lust, but it has the same lingering over the contrived grisly episode. The blank verse in both plays combines a conversational quality with a somber power; the movement is conversational but the imagery is often exotic or deliberately shocking. The most effective lines (and we remember Tourneur, as we do Webster, for specific passages rather than for complete plays) are, however, simple and forthright in diction as well as movement, and owe their effectiveness to their terrible simplicity, as in Castiza's speech to her mother when the latter has agreed that Castiza should be the duke's mistress:

> Mother, come from that poisonous woman there.

Simplicity of diction combined with an exotic touch in the imagery is found in many of Vendice's speeches, as in the often quoted:

> And now methinks I could e'en chide myself
> For doating on her beauty, though her death
> Shall be revenged after no common action.
> Does the silkworm expend her yellow labours
> For thee? For thee does she undo herself?
> Are lordships sold to maintain ladyships,
> For the poor benefit of a bewildering minute?
> Why does yon fellow falsify highways,
> And put his life between the judge's lips,
> To refine such a thing—keeps horse and men
> To beat their valours for her?

John Webster (ca. 1580–1625) is a greater poet than Tourneur but he has less control over dramatic structure. Ambition, covetousness, and lust are the motivating factors in the cunningly cruel behavior of his villains, and sometimes we have the impression that motive is really unimportant and the interest of the plays lies in the virtuosity with which cruelty is manifested or the nobility with which even a vicious character confronts his doom when there is no alternative. *The White Devil* (ca. 1610) and *The Duchess of Malfi* (ca. 1614) are far and away his best plays, and they are both episodic in structure, allowing the author to arrest the dramatic movement while he exploits with brilliant poetic effect the terror or grandeur or pathos of the moment. The moral lines are less clearly drawn than in Tourneur. Vittoria Corombona, the heroine of *The White Devil*, is also the villain, or at least one of the villains. She is false to her husband and becomes the mistress of the Duke of Brachiano, who for her sake murders both her husband and his own duchess. She is not, however, fully implicated in the Duke's guilt, while those who bring her to trial and condemn her for her adultery are themselves corrupt and ambitious men. The true villain is Vittoria's brother Flamineo, the Duke's pander, but even he achieves dignity in dying:

> I am i' the way to study a long silence:
> To prate were idle. I remember nothing.
> There's nothing of so infinite vexation
> As a man's own thoughts.

The ramifications of the plot defy summary, and the play resolves itself into memorable scenes: Vittoria's trial, where she dominates the proceedings by her superb dignity; Cornelia's lament over her murdered son (an episode which has nothing to do with the action of the play but which Webster dwells on because it provides him with an opportunity of building up an atmosphere of wild pathos); Flamineo's final duel of wits with his sister, concluding in the death of both and Vittoria's dying cry:

> My soul, like to a ship in a black storm,
> Is driven, I know not whither.

The ambitions and lusts which drive the characters in Webster's plays are beyond ordinary human compass; there is something Faustian about them—they are after they know not what. They kill and betray and contrive for reasons which, though connected with some kind of self-interest, are deliberately left vague. And surrounding all is the corruption of Court life, which helps to breed these ambitions and poisons the virtue in everybody. Vittoria's last words curse the Court:

> O, happy they that never saw the court,
> Nor ever knew great men but by report.

Thus, traditional satire of Court life, the theme of the Machiavellian man and the cruelties and luxuries of Italy, the revenge theme, and the notion that in moments of ultimate crisis even evil characters can redeem themselves by a stoic dignity—all these threads are woven together by Webster and given color and strength by the morbid splendor of his verse.

The Duchess of Malfi is structurally a much simpler play and its plot can be briefly summarized: the young widowed duchess is forbidden by her brothers to remarry but secretly marries her own steward, and when this is discovered the brothers prepare cunning horrors for her and then have her killed. As usual with Webster, the motivation is obscure. Early in the play it appears that considerations of honor have led the brothers to forbid their sister's remarriage, while, at the end, one of them confesses that he had hoped to inherit her wealth if she remained a widow. But this does not matter. The interest and value of the play lie in the individual episodes. The piling up of horrors for the Duchess by Bosola, the brothers' instrument, trembles occasionally on the brink of the ridiculous, but Webster never allows a scene to fall over the edge. Even the masque of madmen—the imprisoned duchess is surrounded by lunatics released from a madhouse, and one of them howls a dismal dirge—stops short of the ridiculous because Webster keeps our eyes fixed on the stoical duchess who, made to sup her fill of horrors, retains the dignity to say

> I am Duchess of Malfi still.

Before her execution every conceivable emblem of death, every kind of morbid horror, is brought to her; in Charles Lamb's words, "she has lived among horrors till she is become 'native and endowed unto that element.' She speaks the dialect of despair, her tongue has a snatch of Tartarus and the souls in bale." At the end she is no longer terrified by the prospect of rough strangulation:

> What would it pleasure me to have my throat cut
> With diamonds? or to be shot to death with pearls?
> I know death hath ten thousand several doors
> For men to take their exits; any way, for Heaven sake,
> So I were out of your whispering.

When Ferdinand, her brother, sees his sister dead, he has a fit of remorse:

> Cover her face; mine eyes dazzle: she died young.

There are more stratagems and horrors before the play comes to an end with the violent death of both brothers and of Bosola.

In the Court atmosphere of ambition, jealousy, deceit, lust, and sadism this strange and terrible tale unfolds itself, with Webster using every opportunity to pull out all the stops and arrest the action in a sense of perverse poetic beauty. Webster's art, like Tourneur's, is decadent, if by decadence we mean the desperate search for effect indulged in by those who work in a literary tradition after it has been fully exploited by a consummate genius. Perhaps after Shakespeare only this kind of brilliant sensationalism was left; but it is brilliant, and it does yield a genuine comment on life in its own strange way.

Thomas Middleton (ca. 1570–1627) is in some respects more in the tradition of Dekker and Heywood. Like them, he dealt in his comedies with London life, though he neither glorified nor romanticized it; instead, he drew on it for characters, sometimes almost Jonsonian in their humors, whose follies and trickeries are presented with high-spirited enjoyment. Tricksters and dupes recur in his comedies, and often they change places in the end, the trickster himself being caught out. There is something of the Latin comedy of intrigue here, too, but the plays have a boisterous realism of their own. The very titles suggest the atmosphere—*A Trick to Catch the Old One, A Mad World, my Masters, A Chaste Maid in Cheapside*. The last of these, not published until 1630 though first acted some twenty years earlier, is a rollicking comedy of folly and intrigue, with a romantic love plot taking its place on equal terms with a number of other plots which expose the stupidities, vanities, and humors of different characters. Villains overreach themselves, simpletons are gulled, different kinds of fatuity bring their appropiate rewards, cool self-interest generally pays off, and all this is presented by means of a breathless plot in which different characters are brought into contact with each other in rapid succession for the sole purpose of giving each the opportunity to precipitate his proper fate. This is typical of Middleton's comedy, which is witty, sometimes farcical, generally good-natured, and full of life. In his late comedy, *A Game at Chess* (1624), he treated a topical political theme allegorically and, though its anti-Spanish tone (it was produced just after the breaking off of negotiations with Spain for marrying Prince Charles to the Infanta) won it enormous popularity at the time, its allegorical ingenuity, and the extraordinary skill with which the characters are associated with the movement of the black and the white pieces in a chess game, have preserved it only as an exercising ground for scholars.

Like so many other dramatists of the period, Middleton collaborated with other playwrights, his most successful collaborations being with William Rowley. The one tragedy that he wrote by himself, *Women Beware Women* (probably 1612), is a powerful and somber work, written in an assured, flexible blank verse which can effectively mingle the cadences of conversation with the note of strong tragic feeling. The main plot concerns the degeneration of Bianca, wife of Leantio, after the Duke of Florence has seduced her in her husband's absence: but the play is far from a simple study in degeneration. Leantio is a merchant's agent who has "stolen" an aristocratic wife from Venice; from the beginning he hardly credits his own good fortune, and on presenting his wife to his mother expresses the hope that nothing will be done to make Bianca dissatisfied with her comparatively humble lot. Leantio's devotion to his wife cannot prevail over the claims of business, which call him from home, and in his absence the Duke, who sees Bianca at her window as he passes by in procession, falls in love with her. The scene where the mother plays at chess with Livia (who acts as procuress for the Duke) while in another room the Duke effects his seduction of Bianca is one of the great moments in Jacobean drama; but it is not, like many of Webster's scenes, an isolated moment where the play is halted while the dramatist displays his virtuosity. The action moves on with grim logic. Leantio returns, happily anticipating a blissful reunion with his wife, to find Bianca cool and ironical. When a messenger comes to invite Bianca to the Duke's, Bianca mocks her husband's fears and defies his advice (he is by this time in no position to command) not to go. Bianca grows in wantonness and hardness and Leantio in misery. He forces himself to hate his unfaithful wife and accepts the proffered love of Livia almost indifferently. There is a subplot, more closely connected with the main plot than in most Elizabethan and Jacobean tragedy outside Shakespeare, in which Isabella marries a loutish young man in order to cover her affair with Hippolito, her uncle. Having developed both the plots to a culmination of grim irony, Middleton seems to have been somewhat at a loss; in the end he kills everybody off in one of those general slaughters at an entertainment (in which murderous plans go awry and destroy the planners) so dear to the dramatist of the period. In spite of this perfunctory ending, *Women Beware Women* remains a remarkable and arresting tragedy.

Middleton's other great tragedy he wrote in collaboration with Rowley. This is *The Changeling* (1632), also an ironic story of degradation. Beatrice-Joanna, in order to escape marriage to a man she dislikes, hires De Flores, who loves her but whom she utterly despises, to murder him. She thinks she can use his devotion to serve her own ends, but finds that once he has committed the murder she is completely at his mercy and must become his mistress. The scene where De Flores comes to Beatrice to announce that his mission is accomplished, and she gradually and incredulously learns his true price for the deed, is done with psychological cunning and great dramatic irony. Even when she at last learns what he is proposing, she cannot see how she has sacrificed all claim to moral stature and is now completely in his power, physically and morally:

> Why, 'tis impossible thou canst be so wicked,
> Or shelter such a cunning cruelty,
> To make his death the murderer of my honour!
> Thy language is so bold and vicious,
> I cannot see which way I can forgive it
> With any modesty.

But at last she learns where she stands, and she becomes De Flores' mistress, achieving even a kind of masochistic satisfaction in her role. Meanwhile the way is open—ostensibly—for her to marry the man for whose love she had had her other suitor murdered. Her involvement with De Flores, and the fact that her husband would discover that he had not married a maid, compel her to further subterfuges and crimes, until inevitable discovery brings about her death, immediately before which she realizes to the full the true nature of the moral trap she had set for herself. She dies addressing her father in words that T. S. Eliot was to echo in "Gerontion":

> O, come not near me, sir, I shall defile you!
> I that am of your blood was taken from you
> For your better health; look no more upon't,
> But cast it to the ground regardlessly,
> Let the common sewer take it from distinction. . . .

The subplot (from which the play derives its title) deals with a man's disguising himself as a "changeling" or half-wit in order to make love to the wife of the keeper of the lunatic asylum. Its relation to the main plot is not of the closest, though there are some ironical parallels and contrasts which may be seen as heightening the total tragic effect. The asylum keeper's wife retains her moral control in the midst of insanity, in contrast to Beatrice, who surrenders to the madness of passion.

Other plays are ascribed to Middleton and Rowley, including an interesting version of romantic tragicomedy in *The Spanish Gypsy* (1621–22), but none approaches the stature of *The Changeling*. The quietly assured blank verse, with its supple rhythms and blending of the colloquial and the passionate, the searching tragic irony (for example, in the way Beatrice is first the superior, then the victim, and finally the emotional dependent of De Flores, and the relation of this progress to the moral meaning of the play) and the psychological penetration, are qualities of tragedy of a high order. These qualities are sufficiently akin to those displayed by *Women Beware Women* to justify us in believing them Middleton's rather than Rowley's (though Rowley seems to have had a similar kind of talent to Middleton's in tragedy). Finally, it is worth noting that in Middleton's plays, both comedies and tragedies, there is no moral disorder: he never exploits moral corruption for purely sensational purposes, or suggests (as Ford seems to do) that passion is its own justification. There is a firm moral order underlying his plays, and he lets us see it clearly in moments of crisis as well as in the general way in which the plot unfolds.

In the plays of Francis Beaumont (ca. 1584–1616) and John Fletcher (1579–1625) the Jacobean drama gives up any serious attempt to grapple with moral problems to indulge in the skillful professional exploitation of titillating, pathetic, or emotionally extravagant situations. The comedies which Fletcher wrote alone have none of the moral vigor and poetic strength of Ben Jonson at his best; they are smooth, even slick, productions, the verse tripping loosely along with extra syllables at the end of the blank verse line, the plots full of tricks and surprises, the settings generally some never-never land of romantic extravagance where heroic gesture replaces a moral code. This description applies in some degree to all the plays of this popular couple, who collaborated on over fifty in the second decade of the seventeenth century. In these plays they introduced a new kind of tragicomedy, where passion and honor whirl the action into every kind of confusion, before the casting off of a disguise or the revelation of some concealed relationship or some such device brings about the resolution. The tragic element looks forward to the heroic play of the Restoration, just as the preference of social poise to moral adjustment in so many of their comedies looks forward to Restoration comedy.

Philaster (ca. 1610) opens the series of Beaumont and Fletcher tragicomedies, and it is one of the best examples of this sort of play. Philaster, the popular heir to the throne of Sicily, has been ousted by a usurper, whose daughter Arethusa he loves and who loves him. He occasionally engages in threatening remarks about the usurping King, but, largely because of his love for the King's daughter, goes no further. After Philaster and Arethusa, meeting secretly, have confessed their mutual love, Philaster tells her that he will send his page

Bellario to wait on her and bear messages between them. This Bellario (whom the reader or audience guesses almost at once to be a girl in disguise, although nobody in the play realizes it until the end) is devoted to Philaster, who thus describes to Arethusa how he comes to have him as a page:

> Hunting the buck,
> I found him sitting by a fountain's side,
> Of which he borrowed some to quench his thirst,
> And paid the nymph again as much in tears.
> A garland lay him by, made by himself
> Of many several flowers bred in the vale,
> Stuck in that mystic order that the rareness
> Delighted me: but ever when he turned
> His tender eyes upon 'em, he would weep,
> As if he meant to make them grow again.
> Seeing such pretty helpless innocence
> Dwell in his face, I asked him all his story:
> He told me that his parents gentle died,
> Leaving him to the mercy of the fields,
> Which gave him roots; and of the crystal springs,
> Which did not stop their courses; and the sun,
> Which still, he thanked him, yielded him his light.
> Then he took up his garland and did show
> What every flower, as country-people hold,
> Did signify, and how all, ordered thus,
> Expressed his grief, and, to my thoughts, did read
> The prettiest lecture of his country-art
> That could be wished: so that methought I could
> Have studied it. I gladly entertained
> Him, who was glad to follow; and have got
> The trustiest, loving'st, and the gentlest boy
> That ever master kept.

Meanwhile Arethusa is being courted, with her father's approval, by the empty, boastful Spanish prince Pharamond, who, when Arethusa refuses to allow him to anticipate his marriage rights, comforts himself with a loose lady of the Court. They are discovered together at night, but the lady, by accusing Arethusa of keeping Bellario for her private lust, successfully blackmails the King, and Pharamond is restored to his favor. Arethusa, accused by her father of improper behavior with Bellario and charged with the same offense by Philaster himself, is rendered desperate; and after a fine tangle of events, in the course of which Philaster, Arethusa, and Bellario find themselves together in a wood under circumstances that throw further suspicion on the latter two, producing rage, passion of various kinds, explanations, and mutual but frustrated suicide attempts by Philaster and Arethusa, the truth is at last revealed, Arethusa vindicated, Bellario shown to be a girl who had forsaken her home for love of Philaster, Pharamond exposed and expelled, and Philaster restored to his kingdom. The play contains several set speeches of the kind already quoted (for example, the speech in which Bellario explains his conduct in the last act), and the tone throughout is reminiscent of Sidney's *Arcadia* except that the high Sidneian code has been reduced to something much less coherent and magnanimous. There is, of course, a superficial similarity between this sort of thing and Shakespeare's last plays; but the similarity is one of machinery rather than of tone or poetic richness.

Philaster is a "pretty" play, and it contains much pretty poetry. The same can be said of *A King and No King* (1611) which plays with a pretty prurience on the theme of incest, only to reveal at the end that the supposedly incestuous pair are not really brother and sister at all, so all is well. Beaumont and Fletcher's tragedies are similar in tone to their tragicomedies, distinguished only by a different manipulation of the conclusion. *The Maid's Tragedy,* for example (ca. 1611), perhaps the best of them, deals with a husband who discovers on his wedding night that his wife, Evadne, is the King's mistress and the marriage is to be one in name only, a cover for Evadne's affair with the King. His first reaction, apart from his frustration, is to express regret that the villain responsible for this mockery of a marriage is the King:

> In that sacred word
> "The King," there lies a terror: what frail man
> Dares lift his hand against it? Let the gods
> Speak to him when they please: till when, let us
> Suffer and wait.

His second is to torture himself with thoughts of his reputation: if only his shame is not found out:

> Methinks I am not wronged;
> Nor is it aught, if from the censuring world
> I can but hide it. Reputation,
> Thou art a word, no more!—But thou hast shown
> An impudence so high, that to the world
> I fear thou wilt betray or shame thyself.

There is a grimly comic scene when the bride and groom are welcomed the next morning with good-natured jests about loss of virginity and the wars of love, to which each responds in the way that will avert suspicion of the truth. Evadne in due course has her conscience awakened by her brother, who persuades her to murder the King when he lies in bed ready to receive her. Her husband, however, does not receive her back with open arms when he learns this, and in despair she stabs herself. The husband meanwhile has had his own troubles. Aspatia, who had been betrothed to him before he married Evadne and still loves him, seeks him out disguised as a man and provokes him to a fight in which she is slain. Evadne's brother explains everything to Lysippus, the murdered king's brother, who concludes the play by explaining that

> on lustful kings
> Unlooked-for sudden deaths from Heaven are sent;
> But cursed is he that is their instrument.

The play has some powerful and gripping moments (e.g. when, in Act IV, scene 1, Evadne finally expresses her remorse and repentance to her much-wronged and bewildered husband) and many of the passionate speeches show considerable poetic cunning. Yet, like so much of Beaumont and Fletcher, it has a certain hollowness at the core. The poetry is not integrated into the play, giving depth and richness to the dramatic situation by the subtle deployment of imagery, but is used more exhibitionistically for purposes of mere display or to give a general sense of moral confusion. These dramatists, Fletcher in particular, have been praised for the beauty of their verse, and it is true that in a play such as Fletcher's *The Faithful Shepherdess* (1608–09) there is a stylized pastoral charm which has considerable appeal; but neither of them was able to use dramatic verse consistently in that exploratory manner which is the mark of the greatest poetic dramatists. They were highly skilled professional playwrights who knew what was wanted in both the public and the private theater of their day and knew also how to tickle the somewhat jaded palates of King James I's morally shabby Court.

Beaumont's *The Knight of the Burning Pestle* (1608) must be exempted from all the generalizations above. It is a brilliant satirical comedy, mocking the popularity of Spanish romances and similar chivalric works among London prentices and their masters as well as burlesquing such urban heroics as are found in Thomas Heywood's *The Four Prentices of London*. The device of a play within a play is used with particularly happy effect, and the comments of the watching citizen and his wife on the action in which their apprentice Ralph is taking part are not only highly amusing in themselves but also achieve a cumulative effect which amounts almost to the presentation of a counterplay side by side with the main action. The aristocratic Beaumont is of course quite unsympathetic to the claims of the citizens, but this lack of sympathy, far from harming the play, purges his work for once of its besetting sentimentality and allows his wit full play.

Fletcher collaborated with other playwrights besides Beaumont, notably with Philip Massinger (1583–1640), whose early years as a dramatist were spent as Fletcher's assistant. Massinger also collaborated with other playwrights. Of the plays that he wrote alone, of which ten survive (though some nineteen surviving plays have been attributed to him), the two comedies *A New Way to Pay Old Debts* (printed 1633) and *The City Madam* (1632) are the liveliest and most successful. The former, whose plot owes something to Middleton's *A Trick to Catch the Old One* (ca. 1605), is the comedy of the overreaching of an overreacher. Sir Giles Overreach, the heartless extortioner whose financial and legal cunning has succeeded in ruining many members of the landed gentry to his own benefit, is himself caught in a trap baited with his own ambition; the preparing and the springing of the trap is presented with considerable life and color, though sometimes by means of devices which could be more fruitfully used in a Dickens novel than in a dramatic work. The characters —Wellborn, the reformed prodigal; Allworth, the good young gentleman; Greedy, the gluttonous and unscrupulous justice of the peace; Order, Amble, Furnace, and Watchall, servants to the good lady Allworth; Marall, Overreach's man who betrays his master in order to curry favor with Wellborn when he thinks Wellborn's fortunes are in the ascendant again, but does not reap the expected reward; Tapwell and Froth, the contemptible alehouse keeper and his wife—these are in the tradition of the Jonsonian comedy of humors, with hints from Fletcher. But if Massinger's comedy is Jonsonian, the differences between his comedies and Jonson's are significant. *Volpone,* the play of Jonson's which we are reminded of most in reading *A New Way,* has more than the simple moral feeling (selfishness and cruelty bring their inevitable punishment) or the crude class feeling (impoverished noblemen are still noblemen, naturally superior to rich merchants, and the attempt by upstarts to enter the ranks of the gentry is to be ridiculed and condemned) that we find in Massinger. The moral passion in Jonson is both deeper and subtler than Massinger's, and it is conveyed by the movement and imagery of the actual verse spoken by his villains, so that the moral order which is implicitly set against Volpone's code is suggested to the reader by the very language Volpone uses in professing his villainies. When Massinger tries to achieve this sort of effect, he produces simply the villain who declares his own villainy in naïve melodramatic terms; he seems to have had no notion of the possibility of building up an implicit moral order through imagery. Further, the undoing of villains in Massinger is achieved by mechanical contrivance; we do not feel that the splendid villainy of Sir Giles Overreach —and it is a splendid villainy as Massinger portrays it—is effectively challenged and destroyed by what happens to him, as we do with Volpone; he is undone because his opponents, who happen to be on the side of virtue, are even more ingenious than he is. One gets, of course, a certain warm satisfaction out of this kind of play, but it is a satisfaction of a fairly simple kind. Massinger's blank verse, though it lacks the Jonsonian overtones, has an adroit flexibility, a craftsmanlike welding of conversational rhythms with more formal elements, that pleases the ear.

Massinger's class feeling comes out strongly in *The City Madam* (1632), where the monstrous social pretensions of Lady Frugal (wife of Sir John Frugal, a London merchant) are mocked and suitably punished. Here again the moral pattern is simple, and villainy (which includes social pretension) is exposed and reformed by mere ingenious contrivance. The chief villain, Luke Frugal, brother of Sir John and left by him in charge of his family and fortune while Sir John is supposed to be away, has not quite the consistency or the dramatic probability of Sir Giles Overreach, though there is a similar power shown in his portrayal. If the moral feeling in Massinger is coarser than in Jonson, it is at least real in its simple way, as it is not in many of his contemporaries or in his successors in Restoration drama; and if Massinger's social attitude reflects that of the audiences of the private theaters, a crude hostility to bourgeois pretension on the part of the nobility, it still has some trace of the Elizabethan conception of hierarchy and order, however vulgarized, which is not to be found in Restoration comedy, where aristocracy is a matter of sophistication of speech and manners only.

Massinger's tragedies have been much admired, but T. S. Eliot's description of them as "dreary" is true of most of them. He could construct a good plot, he could manipulate blank verse with dexterity, he could rise to occasional heights of real eloquence. *The Roman Actor* (1626), which has some suggestions of Jonson's *Sejanus*, contains some scenes of power and originality; *The Duke of Milan* (printed 1623) has an ingeniously wrought action; *The Maid of Honour* (ca. 1621) is a romantic study of female virtue in a context of conflicting honor and passion which suggests Fletcher; and some of the tragedies of which he is joint author—*The Fatal Dowry* (printed 1632) with Nathan Field, *The Virgin Martyr* (1620) with Dekker—show both power and ingenuity. But the tragic vision in

Massinger, as in so many Jacobean playwrights, is eclectic and even dissipated; his world of comedy is both more credible and more coherent.

John Ford (1586–ca. 1639), after learning his trade as a dramatist in collaboration with Thomas Dekker and William Rowley, developed an interest in the psychology of frustrated and of illicit love, which produced a number of plays written between 1627 and 1633, of which the most interesting are *The Broken Heart* (ca. 1629) and *'Tis Pity She's a Whore* (ca. 1624). His almost clinical curiosity about the aberrations of the love passion is combined with that taste for the melodramatic incident and the extravagantly contrived tableau which is characteristic of so much Jacobean drama. His blank verse has a strong, somber quality, and is at its best when used to project a mood of distraught melancholy. *The Broken Heart* combines, in a crowded plot, a strange variety of themes involving love, revenge, despair, and regret. It is perhaps a sign of decadence in drama that the dramatist is unable to construct an impressive tragedy out of such essentially simple situations as those which lie at the heart of *Othello* and *Macbeth;* neither Ford nor any of his contemporary Jacobean dramatists were able to reach the profounder areas of tragic meaning through the symbolic overtones of their poetic language and the brilliant balance and manipulation of incident and character. The distractions of frustrated or immoral passion, with the extravagant speech and action to which they lead, provide both the line of the plot and the scope of the tragedy: language merely presents the action in appropriately doomed accents. In *The Broken Heart* the center of interest, and of the reader's or spectator's sympathy, keeps shifting disturbingly. Orgilus is in love with Penthea, whose brother Ithocles has forcibly married her to Bassanes, a jealous nobleman. Thus at the beginning of the play Orgilus is the wronged hero, Penthea the unfortunate heroine condemned to a loveless marriage, and Bassanes an incongruously comic figure who tortures himself and his wife with groundless jealousy. Orgilus, supposed to be out of the country, finds a way of visiting Penthea in disguise and pleads that their earlier betrothal constitutes a true marriage which would justify their secret love-making. Penthea, though returning Orgilus' love, and torn between love and wifely duty, repudiates his reasoning, but at the eventual cost of her own reason: she ends by starving herself to death. Meanwhile Ithocles has fallen in love with the Princess Calantha, the King's daughter (the scene is set in Sparta), and, tutored by his own passion, repents his earlier treatment of his sister. The spotlight shifts to him, and he becomes for the time being a sympathetic figure. Calantha looks with favor on him, and it looks for a while as though she and Ithocles at least face a happy ending. But Orgilus is still out for revenge against Ithocles, and murders him in the same scene which shows the death of Penthea. Soon afterward, the King dies. The Princess Calantha is dancing at the wedding celebrations of Euphranea (Orgilus' sister) and Prophilus when one by one messengers arrive to whisper to her the news of, first, the death of her father, secondly, the death of Penthea, and finally, the murder of Ithocles. She continues dancing with apparent gaiety—a scene which drew extravagant admiration from Charles Lamb but which is too artificially contrived to be wholly convincing dramatically—and then, her father's death having made her Queen, solemnly metes out justice. In the final scene she dies of a broken heart while kissing the cold lips of Ithocles, and the dirge which she has previously prepared for the occasion is sung as she expires. Thus the play, which starts out by concentrating on Orgilus and Penthea, shifts its main interest in turn to Ithocles and to Calantha. While there are some impressive pictures of a divided mind—notably in the speech of Penthea repudiating Orgilus' suggestion—and the whole play goes to a strangely effective melancholy music, the isolation and extravagance of the set pieces ("Sirs, the song!" cries the Prince of Argos, a rejected lover of the Princess, when she announces that she is dying) make the whole play a curiously artificial production.

'Tis Pity She's a Whore is more straightforward in its main action, though it is cumbered with some dubious comic scenes and an unnecessary number of minor machinations leading to death by violence. Its chief concern is with the incestuous love of a brother and sister. The physical passion of Giovanni for his sister Annabella is presented with an almost gloating precision. The play opens abruptly with Giovanni's unavailing attempt to persuade a friar of the lawfulness of such love, and moves on to a remarkable scene in which, after some preliminary fencing, brother and sister declare their mutual passion and surrender to it with triumphant abandon. Annabella's subsequent pregnancy makes it necessary for her to marry one of her many suitors, a nobleman called Soranzo, whose servant Vasques, acting with an inadequately motivated zeal, ferrets out the truth about the incest and plans on his master's behalf an appropriate revenge on both brother and sister. The revenge, as so often in this kind of drama, takes place at a party. Annabella, repentant, receives her brother in her room before the festivities begin and puts aside his renewed declarations of physical passion with talk of repentance and grace. He stabs her, to prevent her further defilement by her husband and in the end is killed himself by Vasques' hired assassins. The atmosphere of Italian violence in which the play moves is only loosely related to the main action in which the fact of incest is presented with that curious mixture of romantic fatalism and clinical exploration which is characteristic of Ford. The moral pattern of the play is obscure. Annabella dies repentant, but from the beginning she has been the weaker character; Giovanni dies exulting in his passion, proud of having put his sister out of Soranzo's reach, and confident of seeing her again in another world. Critics have debated whether Ford is a deliberate immoralist or merely the disinterested psychological inquirer. Perhaps the simplest explanation of the theme and atmosphere of the play is that, at this late stage in the movement of Elizabethan and Jacobean drama, the theme of normal love between the sexes had been so thoroughly explored that the only way to contrive a tragedy with a new interest was to concentrate on incest. Drama, it might be said, becomes decadent when it is content to exploit the moment without any probing of cause or consequence, or when it seeks eccentric causes for common emotions, or when it uses human emotion for the simple purpose of making our flesh creep. These three categories are all found in Jacobean drama; Ford's best plays seem to come in some degree into the second.

James Shirley (1596–1666) was in full career as a dramatist when the closing of the theaters by the Puritans in 1642 put an end for the time being to the publicly acted drama in England. He was a competent professional, and wrote tragedies of Italianate intrigue and villainy or of dark passion, tragicomedies in the Fletcher tradition, and comedies of manners which in some degree point forward to the comedy of the Restoration. His best tragedy is probably *The Cardinal* (1641), a lively mixture of ambition, passion, love, and murder, reminiscent sometimes of *The Duchess of Malfi*, but never quite attaining Webster's brilliant fixing of the tragic moment. Fluent, versatile, always competent but rarely brilliant, Shirley suggests the relaxed professional rather than the original genius. His tragic world is made up of the orts and fragments of Elizabethan and Jacobean tragedy; his world of comedy (as his most popular comedy, *The Lady of Pleasure*, reveals) is moving rapidly away from the Jonsonian order toward the witty surface and unanchored sophistication of the Restoration, though it never quite gets there.

Richard Brome (d.ca. 1652) is another dramatist who manipulated Jonsonian themes. The minor dramatists of the reign of Charles I played further variations on what were by now familiar subjects.

Such new notes as were now sounded emphasized the retreat of the drama from contemporary popular life, the victory of the private over the public theater, which the closing of the theaters throughout the Commonwealth period further emphasized. The cavalier lyrist Sir John Suckling (1609–42), the clever and short-lived Thomas Randolph (1605–35), and William Cartwright (b. 1611) are among those whose plays reflect new courtly influences from France and Spain. Sir William Davenant (1606–68) experimented pallidly with new techniques for the stylization of passion and was among those who reflected a new court interest in the theories of Platonic love. This Caroline version of Platonism combined with the Fletcherian interest in honor produced the recipe which was to be important in the heroic play of the Restoration. French romances—those of d'Urfé and Mademoiselle de Scudéry—also played their part here. The modulation of the heroic world of Sir Philip Sidney into the world of Caroline gallantry shows a moral decay suggestive of the decline of a whole phase of civilization. The themes and attitudes that were to emerge in the Restoration theater were being prepared behind the scenes under the Commonwealth.

Whether a literary form, such as the poetic drama or the prose novel, has an inevitable cycle comparable to that of a human being is arguable: a great deal depends on the whole texture of the civilization within which the form flourishes. It is tempting to suppose that English poetic drama passed through a natural process of development, maturity, and decline, between, say, Marlowe and Shirley. That it passed through such a process can hardly be denied (though we must remember that in talking in such terms about literature we are talking metaphorically, not literally), but it can be doubted whether the process can usefully be considered "natural." The relation between the public and the private theater, the conditions of employment for actors and playwrights, the relation between art and entertainment, the varying atmosphere of the Court, shifts in the state of the national consciousness, the special qualities of individual genius—these and other factors in the contemporary situation had their different kinds of influence on the course of English drama during the Elizabethan, Jacobean, and Caroline periods. One fact is as clear as it is in the last analysis incapable of full explanation: English poetic drama during these years reached heights it never attained before or since. The literary historian, having discussed the drama of this age, will never again have to devote so much attention to drama (either in prose or poetry). In the Restoration drama the heroic world of the Elizabethans appears quite separated from its deep moral base, and the result is a literature that is witty or rhetorical but never truly great. And in that final fling of the Cavaliers, the last, distorted echoes of an aristocratic sensibility are heard. After that, it is to the middle classes, and their characteristic literary creation the prose novel, that the literary historian turns if he wants to follow the record of the English moral imagination as it worked through narrative art.

CHAPTER ELEVEN

Poetry after Spenser:

the Jonsonian and the

Metaphysical Traditions

IN SPENSER, as we have seen, the patriotic impulse which affected the Elizabethan imagination in so many different ways was only one of many strands which he wove together in his great poetic synthesis. Other Elizabethan poets exhibit this impulse, and the interest in English history which so often accompanied it, singly and more naïvely. William Warner (ca. 1558–1609) produced in his *Albion's England* a versified history of England in monotonous "fourteeners," a work which enjoyed great popularity in its day, and which was enlarged in subsequent editions from the four books of the original edition of 1586 to six books in 1589, nine in 1592, and sixteen in 1606, when the story was carried down to the reign of James I. It is a sobering thought that the Elizabethans, in the richest period of their great poetic flowering, were still enthusiastic over verse like this:

Which her foredooms seemed to effect in her that her succeeded,
In Queen Anne Bullen, who, for she in Lutherism proceeded,
Was hated of the Papists and envied because preferred,
And through the King's too light belief (for kings have sometimes erred)
She lost her head, and might have said, some thought, ere she did die,
That for the pleasure of a prince go many things awry.
So died the gracious mother of our now most glorious Queen,
Whose zeal in reverent Foxe his works authentical is seen.
The King's four other queens (for why he died a sexamus)
Shall pass, though Jane did bear a son to him, a king to us,
Edward the sixth, and of the same we shall deliver thus.

This is in the didactic tradition of Lydgate's *Fall of Princes* and of the *Mirror for Magistrates*, as well as of Elizabethan patriotic historical verse; the combination was rarely fortunate. Samuel Daniel (1562–1619), whom we have already noticed as a sonneteer and who was also a versatile lyrist who could produce both artfully phrased and happily cadenced short poems and longer poems of compliment and reflection in a style which Coleridge called "the natural ground of prose and verse," was seduced by the historical-didactic muse with not altogether happy results. His *The Complaint of Rosamond* (1592), a poem of almost a thousand lines in rhyme royal, is one of those gloomy pseudo-autobiographical pieces whose popularity in the sixteenth century remains a mystery: its opening lines set the tone:

> Out from the horror of infernal deeps
> My poor afflicted ghost comes here to plain it, . . .

His *Civil Wars,* of which the first four books appeared in 1595 and which was enlarged in subsequent editions but never completed, makes some attempt to present epically the same phase of English history on which Shakespeare concentrated in his history plays, and from a similar point of view. The eight-line stanzas (*ottava rima*) in which the story is carried forward move with a certain sturdiness and occasionally with eloquence; Daniel does achieve intermittently a sense of scope and design, as well as a style capable of rising to an occasion without obvious strain; but the attempt to create an epic out of relatively recent history is probably misguided: he finds it impossible to subdue his material to an epic shape.

Michael Drayton (1563–1631), a versatile poet whose sonnets we have noted and who in the course of his long poetic career tried his hand at most of the Elizabethan modes (including drama, but nearly all his plays are lost), succumbed to the didactic-historical temptation with his *Mortimeriados* of 1596, which became after much alteration the *Barons' Wars* of 1603. This account in *ottava rima* of "the lamentable civil wars of Edward the Second and the Barons" is dull and episodic, in spite of its occasional moments of passionate dialogue. Of Drayton's other historical poetry, the most interesting is that contained in *England's Heroical Epistles* (1597), modeled on the *Heroides* of Ovid: these are written in flexible heroic couplets, in a style which blends a variety of Elizabethan poetic idioms with something learned from Ovid himself, and the result often has both grace and power. But Drayton's concern with his native country found its most elaborate expression in his vast and elaborate geographical poem, *Polyolbion* (1612, 1622), "a Chorographical Description of Tracts, Rivers, Mountains, Forests, and other Parts of this Renowned Isle of Great Britain, with Intermixture of the most Remarkable Stories, Antiquities, Wonders, Rarities, Pleasures, and Commodities of the same." Descriptive, topographical, anecdotal, celebratory, this panoramic work in twelve-syllable couplets is a storehouse of lovingly recorded information about the regions of England and their legends. If it cannot be read through with pleasure today it can at least be profitably looked into as a remarkable manifestation of that special kind of interest in England bred by Elizabethan patriotic feeling (and Drayton remained Elizabethan in feeling and attitude even when writing under the Stuarts). Spenser had a similar interest, and subsumed it in the larger synthesis of the *Faerie Queene;* Drayton, like so many of Spenser's contemporaries and successors, found no adequate poetic form through which to express at length his patriotic topographical excitement. In the early seventeenth century the threads which Spenser had woven together —pastoral, patriotic, didactic, allegorical—come apart, and are found separately in those poets who came under his influence.

Of Drayton's other work, mention might be made of his early pastorals, contained in *Idea: The Shepherd's Garland,* 1593, whose eighth eclogue is an interesting pseudo-Chaucerian pastoral ballad; his two vigorous patriotic odes, "To the Virginian voyage" and "To the Cambro-Britons and their harp, his Ballad of Agincourt"; the rather coyly self-conscious fairy piece *Nymphidia; The Shepherd's Sirena,* a deftly modulated pastoral narrative in alternately rhyming iambic lines of seven syllables with an inset shepherds' song that has a delicately chiming stanza and chorus, in the purest Elizabethan tradition (though it appeared first in 1627); and *The Muses' Elizium,* his last work, published in 1630, in which, belatedly, the Elizabethan pastoral imagination finds one of its purest and happiest expressions.

The didactic muse of the Elizabethans was not, of course, always associated with patriotic or historical themes. The age produced a considerable variety of educational and philosophical verse, some of which, like Daniel's *Musophilus* (1599), a dialogue between a lover of the Muses and his worldly opponent, Philocosmus, has the grave eloquence appropriate to the poetry of intellectual discussion, while much is crudely versified instruction of no poetic value. The same year in which Daniel brought out his *Musophilus* saw the publication of another unusually interesting didactic poem, the *Nosce Teipsum* of Sir John Davies (1569–1626). This long poem in quatrains discusses the vanity of human knowledge and the importance of cultivating the individual soul: the verse moves with considerable ease, and gives both dignity and elegance to the theme, but it remains verse rather than poetry. Davies' earlier poem, *Orchestra* (1596), "a poem of dancing" in rhyme royal, presents the dance as the principle of order and pattern in the universe. A certain mild dramatic force is given to the poem by making it an argument between Antinous, chief of Penelope's suitors in Ulysses' absence, and Penelope: Antinous tries to persuade her to dance on the grounds that dancing is the basis of the cosmic order. The poem is interesting for its picture of the Elizabethan view of universal order (which can be related on the one hand to the concept of subordination and "degree" summarized in Ulysses' famous speech on that subject in Shakespeare's *Troilus and Cressida* and on the other to Milton's view of the divine harmony and the music of the spheres, as well as to other neo-Platonic notions of life as dance, that of W. B. Yeats, for example); the stanzas are modulated with considerable skill, and the poem moves with grace and liveliness. It is one of the most successful philosophical poems in English. Davies belongs, with Fulke Greville and George Chapman, to that small group of interesting Elizabethan minds who found original and often effective ways of giving poetic expression to their philosophical reflections.

The Elizabethan didactic impulse also found expression in satire. Horace and Juvenal were the chief models, the former suggesting a line of wit that was to run on to Dryden and Pope, the latter suggesting a more violent satire of direct abuse. The notion prevailed among the majority of Elizabethan satirists that satire should be rough, obscure, and violent: they wrongly derived the term from "satyr." Thomas Lodge's *A Fig for Momus* (1595) contains relatively mild satires, more Horatian than Juvenalian in tone, expressed with considerable neatness. John Donne's satires, written in the 1590's, are violent and vivid, often deliberately rough in their handling of iambic couplets and indiscriminating in their attribution of vices to the victims. Joseph Hall's *Virgidemiarum* (1597) moves between Donne's violence and the milder Horatian manner of Lodge; his themes are for the most part not the major vices but literary fashions of the day and petty meannesses and stupidities, although he professes to be anxious to "check the misordered world and lawless times." He, too, uses the rhymed iambic couplet, which now comes to be regarded as the appropriate verse form for satire. John Marston's *Scourge of Villainy*, also published in 1597, is satire of the rough kind; its almost melodramatic violence, exhibitionist striking of attitudes, and mock-heroic exaggeration gives Marston's satiric verse a flavor all its own, but it is too fitful to arouse sustained interest. Sir John Harington's *Metamorphosis of Ajax*, published in 1596, stands somewhat apart from these other Elizabethan satires. The tone of his work is clever undergraduate mock-heroic rather than satirical. Harington was also an accomplished writer of epigram, a form much cultivated by the Elizabethans. It was under the influence of the Latin epigrammatist Martial that English epigram in the Elizabethan age really grew up: Harington and Sir John Davies were two of its most successful practitioners, and the publication of their epigrams was followed by a spate of collections of epigrams in the first two decades of the seventeenth century. The Elizabethan epigram was generally a miniature satire, and provided exercise in pithy and concise expression of which English verse still stood in need. The most accomplished follower of Martial in English at this period, consummate master of epigram both satirical and commemorative, was Ben Jonson. His satirical epigrams are not obviously above those of Davies and Harington, but his epitaphs and verses of compliment and commemoration are superior to anything else done in the epigrammatic style at that time. His epitaph on the child actor Salomon Pavey is justly famous, as is the poem "On My First Son":

> Farewell, thou child of my right hand, and joy;
> My sin was too much hope of thee, lov'd boy.
> Seven years tho'wert lent to me, and I thee pay,
> Exacted by thy fate, on the just day.
> O, could I lose all father now. For why
> Will man lament the state he should envy,
> To have so soon scap'd world's and flesh's rage,
> And, if no other misery, yet age?
> Rest in soft peace, and, ask'd, say here doth lie
> Ben Jonson his best piece of poetry.
> For whose sake henceforth all his vows be such
> As what he loves may never like too much.

The Elizabethan age is popularly regarded as the great age of the singing lyric, the mellifluous poem which enchants the ear even before it appeals to the mind or the emotions. We have seen how in the earlier part of Queen Elizabeth's reign experiment with lyric measures often yielded mechanical doggerel, and we have noted, too, that many of the most successful Tudor lyrics inherit their cadences and stanza forms from the medieval lyric. But by the last years of the sixteenth century the exercising of the English language in a variety of lyric measures produced a spate of finely controlled, musically sounding lyrics, more than enough to justify the view that the Elizabethan age is the age par excellence of that kind of poetry. These lyrics are found in songbooks, in plays, and in collections of various kinds. One can only pick out a few examples. Thomas

Lodge's "Love in my bosom like a bee," from his prose romance *Rosalind*, 1590; George Peele's "His golden locks time hath to silver turned," from his *Polyhymnia*, 1590; Nicholas Breton's "Pastoral" ("Flora hath been all about") from *The Passionate Shepherd*, 1604; Thomas Nashe's "Adieu, farewell earth's bliss," with its famous third stanza:

> Beauty is but a flower
> Which wrinkles will devour:
> Brightness falls from the air,
> Queens have died young and fair,
> Dust hath closed Helen's eye.
> I am sick, I must die.
> Lord, have mercy on us!

from his comedy, *Summer's Last Will and Testament;* Thomas Dekker's "Art thou poor, yet hast thou golden slumbers, /O sweet content?" from his *Pleasant Comedy of Patient Grissill* (printed 1603), and the well-known "Golden slumbers kiss your eyes" from the same play; "Weep you no more, sad fountains," from John Dowland's *Third and Last book of Songs or Airs,* 1603—these are random selections from a rich mass of material which includes songs with music as well as spoken lyrics and which continues without a break into the middle of the seventeenth century. Nor must we forget the lyrics in the plays of Shakespeare and Ben Jonson and the incidental songs in Sidney's *Arcadia.* Shakespeare was a master of the mature Elizabethan mellifluous style, among many others, and in his narrative poems, as well as in his strange and powerful symbolic poem *The Phoenix and the Turtle,* used it with extraordinary richness. *The Phoenix and the Turtle,* with its short-lined quatrains and its combination of finely tempered verse with mystical overtones, shows Elizabethan "golden" poetry hammered out to a new fineness: this poem in many ways represents the high point of the Elizabethan lyric style. But the control, the serenity, the mastery of tempo and of modulation of tone, remained an achievement of the Elizabethan Age, a power over language which the Elizabethans achieved, which is illustrated in a great variety of ways, from narrative poems to madrigals, in the late sixteenth and early seventeenth centuries.

A lyric poet of the period who deserves more particular mention is Thomas Campion (1567–1619), composer as well as lyrist, whose experiments in combining the arts of poetry and music produced some happy subtleties in the handling of English verse rhythms. Using both classical and popular material, Campion produced a large variety of lyrical verse which, although written to be sung to specific airs, many of which Campion composed himself, conveys in its own movement and cadence sufficient verbal melody to please the ear when read apart from the music. In the address to the reader which prefaces the first *Book of Airs* (published in 1601 and edited by Philip Rosseter, who composed the music and perhaps the words for Part II of the volume), Campion wrote: "What Epigrams are in Poetry, the same are Airs in music, then in their chief perfection when they are short and well seasoned." The music gave Campion a greater freedom, or a greater subtlety, in the handling of meters, and his fine ear enabled him to use this opportunity to the full, as we find in the flexibility of such a stanza as

> Follow thy fair sun, unhappy shadow,
> Though thou be black as night,
> And she made all of light,
> Yet follow thy fair sun, unhappy shadow.

Or this:

> Will you now so timely depart,
>   And not return again?
> Your sight lends such life to my heart
>   That to depart is pain.
> Fear yields no delay,
>   Secureness helpeth pleasure:
> Then, till the time gives safer stay,
>   O farewell, my life's treasure.

Many of his best lyrics are, however, more simply regular, as "When to her lute Corina sings," "Follow your saint, follow with accents sweet" (where there is an occasional interesting variation of the basic metrical scheme), and "When thou must home to shades of underground."

Campion produced several other books of airs, as well as some masques, some technical discussions of music, and a critical tract, *Observations in the Art of English Poesie* (1602) where he attacked rhyme (in spite of the fact that he practiced it so skillfully himself) and argued for a flexible, rhymeless, quantitative English verse. His arguments were answered the following year by Samuel Daniel in *A Defence of Rhyme*, which defends rhyme on the grounds of its universality and antiquity. This ends the Renaissance controversy about rhyme and quantitative meters in England. Campion's arguments are ingenious and strongly urged, and they seem to arise in some measure from his thinking of musical rhythms in connection with verse (as later Gerard Manley Hopkins' arguments for "sprung rhythm" were to suggest a view of verse rhythms more like musical bars than the conventional metrical feet). Only once, however, is he wholly successful in practicing the rhymeless art of English poesy which he recommends in his *Observations:* this is in a poem which he gives in his discussion as one example of a classical verse form in English. The handling of vowel music and the cunning modulation of the flow of the verse in this poem more than make up for the lack of rhyme:

> Rose-cheeked Laura, come.
> Sing thou smoothly with thy beauty's
> Silent music, either other
>> Sweetly gracing.
>
> Lovely forms do flow
> From concent divinely framéd;
> Heav'n is music, and thy beauty's
>> Birth is heavenly.
>
> These dull notes we sing
> Discords need for helps to grace them;
> Only beauty purely loving
>> Knows no discord,
>
> But still moves delight,
> Like clear spring renewed by flowing,
> Ever perfect, ever in them-
>> Selves eternal.

The Elizabethan age in poetry flowed naturally into the Jacobean, and 1603, the year in which King James VI of Scotland became also King James I of England, is not a significant date in literary history. Yet there were important changes which followed James's accession. Some historians have contrasted the disillusioned years of his reign with the spacious days of great Elizabeth; the contrast could equally be made between the atmosphere of the latter years of Elizabeth's reign and that of its heyday. But changes in the atmosphere of the Court and in Court patronage were significant in an age when the arts still looked to the Court and where poets hoped for appointments that depended on the royal favor. Even so, to the literary historian the death of Spenser in 1599 is a more important date than the death of Elizabeth in 1603. Spenser, the greatest nondramatic poet of his age, drew together most of the important trends in Elizabethan thought to achieve in the *Faerie Queene,* incomplete and perhaps incapable of ever having been completed as it is, one of the most remarkable poetic syntheses in English. The poetic map of England immediately after Spenser is most clearly described in terms of the ways in which the Spenserian tradition was continued and ways of revolting against it. No single poet had the stature to continue the

Spenserian tradition as Spenser had developed it; the various elements, pastoral, allegorical, patriotic, topographical, "faerie," were handled separately, as we have seen. Aspects of the Spenserian tradition are carried on by Drayton; by George Wither (1588–1667), whose pastoral poetry has a certain grace and charm, though his satiric and didactic verse has less interest; by Wither's friend William Browne (ca. 1591–ca. 1643) whose *Britannia's Pastorals* (1613, Book II 1616) show a mixture of romantic idealization of the rustic life and realistic description, a limited and tenuous continuation of one side of Spenser; and by even more minor pastoral poets whose work is found in songbooks and other collections of the early seventeenth century.

The most interesting inheritors of the moral and allegorical side of Spenser are the brothers Giles (1585–1623) and Phineas (1582–1650) Fletcher. Giles Fletcher's *Christ's Victory and Triumph,* published in 1610 (Part I: *Christ's Victory in Heaven;* Part II: *Christ's Victory on Earth;* Part III: *Christ's Triumph Over Death;* Part IV: *Christ's Triumph After Death*), has a baroque vigor that is sometimes startling. The eight-line stanza concludes with an alexandrine which often has a Spenserian ring; there are Spenserian words such as "elamping," "ydraded," "embrandèd"; and the allegory is often Spenserian, as in the description of Mercy and Repentance in Part I. The verse is well managed and vigorous:

> There is a place beyond that flaming hill,
> From whence the stars their thin appearance shed;
> A place beyond all place, where never ill
> Nor impure thought was ever harbourèd;
> But saintly heroes are for ever said
>   To keep an everlasting sabbath's rest,
>   Still wishing that, of what they're still possessed,
> Enjoying but one joy, —but one of all joys blest.

The pictorial quality is rather different from Spenser's ("A star comes dancing up the orient," "And little angels, holding hands, danced all around"), and there is a fondness for punning which is sometimes more metaphysical than Spenserian ("Or maker of the man, or manner of his making," "Depraved of son should he deprived be"). Sometimes, however, the verse is almost pure Spenser:

> He was the son of blackest Acheron,
> Where many frozen souls do chattering lie,
> And rules the burning waves of Phlegethon,
> Where many more in flaming sulphur fry,
> At once compelled to live and forced to die; . . .

Or this:

> Like as a ship, in which no balance lies,
> Without a pilot, on the sleeping waves,
> Fairly along with wind and water flies,
> And painted masts with silken sails embraves,
> That Neptune's self the bagging vessel saves,
> To laugh awhile at her so proud array;
> Her waving streamers loosely she lets play,
> And flagging colours shine as bright as smiling day.

Some of the set descriptive pieces (that of Despair in Part II, for example) show considerable virtuosity, and the sensual and erotic picture of the temptation of Christ shows how the Spenserian school always tended to think of temptation in terms of sex. The description of Vain-glory's garden in Part II is reminiscent of Spenser's Bower of Bliss; but in Fletcher the erotic strain is often inadequately assimilated into the texture of the poetry. The straining for effect often results in a sort of incongruity which is common in this kind of poetry:

> Where all are rich, and yet no gold they owe   [owe: own]
> They all are kings, and yet no subject know,
> All full, and yet no time on food they do bestow.
>
> (Part IV)

There are some striking and memorable phases, e.g.,

> Swelter in quiet waves of immortality

which stayed in the memory of Milton, a great admirer of the Fletchers, whose influence is seen in his early work. We cannot help thinking of Milton's "Nativity Ode" when reading this, from Part IV:

> . . . for heaven's smiling brow
> Half insolent for joy began to show:
> The early sun came lively dancing out,
> And the brag lambs ran wantonly about,
> That heaven and earth might seem in triumph both to shout.

Phineas Fletcher is less interesting, and certainly less accomplished as a poet. *The Purple Island* (1633), though it has a conventional pastoral opening, is a tedious allegory of the human body, the island corresponding in all its geographical features to the parts of the body, described in the greatest anatomical detail. The body as a castle fortified against the besieging enemy was a common medieval allegorical theme: here, with its profusion of pseudoscientific detail, it becomes insufferably tedious, allegory petering out in mere classification. *The Piscatorie Eclogues,* which appeared in the same volume, show smoothness of versification and a rather tired conventionality. *The Locusts, or Apollyonists,* published in 1627, is an expanded English version of the original Latin version, *Locustae vel Pietas Jesuitica;* it is a violent anti-Catholic poem, attacking the Jesuits, the Pope, Rome, the Greek Orthodox Church of Russia, and the doctrine of purgatory and other Catholic beliefs and practices. Book V describes the Gunpowder Plot (seen as planned in Rome, with Devils and Cardinals plotting together), and the poem concludes with praise to God for His delivery of England from Catholics and Devils. The poem contains some allegorizing in the Sackville tradition and some of its descriptions may have given hints to Milton; but for the most part its spluttering violence is unimpressive. *Sicelides, a Piscatory,* "as it hath been acted in King's College, in Cambridge," is worth mentioning chiefly as an oddity. A play written mostly in couplets, with a Sicilian setting, including among its characters Cyclops as well as two humorous "foolish" fishers to provide supposedly comic relief, with a plot in which love, female guile, supposed death, and disguise all play their parts, *Sicelides* serves to show that in a "piscatory" anything can happen.

A didactic poet of a rather different kind is John Davies of Hereford (ca. 1565–1618), whose dull verse disquisitions, *Mirum in Modum* (1602), *Microcosmos* (1603), and others show that verse was still considered the appropriate form for moral, religious, and psychological discussion. Davies (who is to be distinguished from the other John Davies discussed on page 348 was a determined writer of every kind of nondramatic poetry known to his age. Some of his epigrams have a certain coarse vigor.

Before we leave this group of didactic and religious poets, something must be said about Joseph Sylvester's (1563–1618) translation of *La Semaine, ou Création du Monde* by the French Protestant poet Guillaume de Salluste du Bartas (1544–90). This translation, entitled *Divine Weeks and Works,* appeared in 1605, and introduced an almost metaphysical violence of imagery, a deliberately incongruous use of simile and metaphor (the line "and periwig with wool the bald-pate woods" is still quoted), which helps to explain the quality of much of the imagery used in religious poetry immediately afterward. Its religious content appealed to a large section of the public of the time, who were interested more in its edifying subject matter than in its unwieldy form or baroque style, but the style inevitably had its influence. "Sylvester's Du Bartas" became the Protestant poem par excellence of its time. The young Milton read it with eagerness, and it left its traces throughout his work.

The religious poetry of Francis Quarles (1592–1644) was equally popular in the next generation. His *Emblems* (1635) popularized in England a species of writing which already had a long history in Europe. The emblem is a symbolic picture with a text and a verse exposition. It naturally tends toward an epigrammatic style: Quarles's favorite form was to cite the scriptural text, elaborate it in a fairly discursive moral or descriptive poem, add a couple of texts from one of the Church Fathers, and conclude with a four-line moral epigram. The result is poetry which is ingenious rather than inspired. Quarles has been called "something of an inferior Herbert," and it is true that he has Herbert's simple moral earnestness and a similar kind of ingenuity while lacking both Herbert's deeper devotional feeling and his ability to sublimate ingenuity to a level of poetic expression which combines passion with calmness.

The interesting if unequal work of the Catholic poet Robert Southwell (1561–95) stands rather apart from the other English religious poetry of the period. Some of his lyrics use the old "fourteeners," either broken up or in a single line, and the lilt can be very monotonous; at the same time he can combine a deliberate preciosity of language (partly Italian in inspiration) with an intense religious passion in a way that occasionally suggests Crashaw. His best known lyric, the Christmas poem "The Burning Babe," was admired by Ben Jonson and has been much praised since, and though its lilt is cumbersome and its language not always happy, it does achieve a certain visionary power.

All these poets, except perhaps Southwell, can be associated in some way with the Spenserian tradition, or at least they show what happened to the chief Spenserian themes and forms immediately after Spenser. There were also other—and stronger—elements at work in English poetry of the early seventeenth century. Ben Jonson and John Donne, each in his own way, represented in some degree a revolt against or at least a turning away from the Spenserian tradition, and the result was decisive for the future of English poetry. Jonson, with his sense of decorum, clarity, proportion, and classical form, brought to lyric poetry both a craftsmanship and a tone which owed much to the classical poets of Rome—Catullus, Martial, Horace —and at the same time never seemed far removed from colloquial English and from the tough realism of the common-sense approach. We have already noted the virtues of his lapidary verses and said something of the precise beauty of his best love lyrics. He wrote, in a great variety of measures, poems of compliment to friends and patrons, autobiographical poems about his own circumstances, different kinds of odes which included the first examples of the true

Pindaric form in English, devotional poems, epistles, elegies, "occasional" poems of many kinds, as well as songs and epigrams. Echoes of Greek and Roman poets sound throughout his work with many different notes. Who would guess at first reading that the formal elegance and limpid clarity of the well-known "Drink to me only with thine eyes" results from a cunning concatenation of passages taken from the *Epistolae Eroticae* of the late Greek prose writer Philostratus? In spite of all he learned from the classics, however, there is something highly personal, even idiosyncratic, in the tone of much of his poetry, which indicates how perfectly he was able to subsume his classical inspiration in his own temperament. If the Roman satirists suggested the terms of his outbursts of moral indignation, his moral tone is nevertheless his own, and we cannot mistake the Jonsonian air of

> Not to know vice at all, and keep true state,
>   Is virtue, and not Fate.
> Next to that virtue, is to know vice well,
>   And her black spite expel.
> Which to effect (since no breast is so sure
>   Or safe, but she'll procure
> Some way of entrance) we must plant a guard
>   Of thoughts to watch and ward . . .

or of

> It is not growing like a tree
> In bulk, doth make man better be;
> Or standing long an oak, three hundred year,
> To fall a log at last, dry, bald, and sere.
> A lily of a day
> Is fairer far in May,
> Although it fall and die that night;
> It was the plant and flower of light.
> In small proportions we just beauties see,
> And in short measures life may perfect be.

Or of this, from the "Ode to himself":

> And since our dainty age
>   Cannot endure reproof,
> Make not thyself a page
> To that strumpet the stage,
>   But sing high and aloof,
> Safe from the wolf's black jaw and the dull ass's hoof.

There is a relaxed, personal note in Jonson's longer verse epistles which, however, never threatens his sense of form. And always there is a sense of the essential strength and vigor of the English language; there is a virility about all Jonson's verse, but again it is a virility which often coexists with the utmost delicacy and grace.

This is to use the English poetic language differently from the way Spenser employed it. The high ornamental strain of what might be called the Petrarchan tradition in English poetry came to a climax in *The Faerie Queene*, where it was combined with other strains. But Jonson's view of the diction of *The Faerie Queene* was that "Spenser writ no language," and he deliberately moved away from the Spenserian mode toward one that was both more classical and more personal. That Jonson is the father of the "Cavalier" strain in English poetry which ran through the seventeenth century, and Donne the father of the "metaphysical" strain which ran parallel with it, and that both were different ways of reacting against the Spenserian tradition which could go no further after *The Faerie Queene*, used to be the standard interpretation of the seventeenth-century poetic scene. Like all such generalizations, it has a considerable element of truth without being wholly true. Modern scholarship has established that the Donne tradition has its roots in a tradition of rhetoric and symbolism which goes far back in European literature and is not as distinct from the Petrarchan conventions as used to be thought. Further, while the differences between Jonson and Donne are clear, their respective followers often combined the influence of the two poets, which came together more often and more easily than could be expected of essentially opposed poetic styles. Some of Jonson's more discursive, personal pieces, with their highly individual tone and their strong colloquial movement counterpointing the formal run of the verse, can be—and have been—mistaken for poems of Donne. This is not to say that Jonson and Donne wrote the same kind of poetry, or even that the "Sons of Ben" (as Jonson's followers called themselves) were also squarely in the Donne tradition; but it does mean that the fact that there were common elements in the styles of the two poets (for all their many and obvious differences) made it easier for their followers to combine elements from the style of each. Against the highly stylized artfulness of Spenser, Jonson set classical cogency and symmetry and Donne set a poetry which combined violence of personal passion with intellectual ingenuity and an imagery both starkly realistic and startlingly cunning. Both objected to the mere sweetness of the latter phases of the Petrarchan tradition as well as to the "no language" of Spenser, and for both the personality of the poet rather than the demands of a "poetic" subject and attitude determined, in the last analysis, the choice of tone and image.

In so far as the metaphysical school of poetry (the term was first used for Donne and his followers by Dr. Johnson in his discussion of Cowley in *Lives of the English Poets:* "The metaphysical poets were men of learning, and to show learning was their whole endeavour") has as its aim the introduction of a more strenuous intellectual strain into poetry, one may agree with those scholars who see George Chapman (ca. 1559–1634) as its first member. Chapman's poetry brings to the treatment of love and other themes a stern philosophical note, both Stoic and Christian, and his verse can be intellectually strenuous and sometimes obscure. *Ovid's Banquet of Sense* (1595) includes that most un-Petrarchan sonnet sequence, "A Coronet for his Mistress Philosophy," and *The Shadow of Night,* published the previous year, contains some deliberately murky writing. But the distinguishing quality of metaphysical poetry as practiced by Donne and his successors is not simply philosophical subtlety or intellectual rigor (qualities often found in the moral and didactic poetry discussed earlier in this chapter) but a peculiar blend of thought and passion, of the colloquial with the ingenious, of realistic violence and meditative refinement. If philosophy is found in Chapman and others, ingenuity is found in abundance in the Petrarchan "conceits" of conventional Elizabethan love poetry, and those who consider ingenuity of metaphor peculiar to metaphysical poetry do not seem to realize that they will find precisely this quality in almost any Elizabethan sonnet-sequence. Further, one must make distinctions among the metaphysical poets themselves, who are less like each other than has often been supposed. Donne stands apart, both chronologically and temperamentally, from the other poets to whom the term "metaphysical" is generally applied.

John Donne (1572–1631) was born and brought up a Roman Catholic, and though he later argued himself into the Anglican position and ended his life as Dean of St. Paul's, his training as a Catholic in an age of religious polemic, together with the scholastic element that was still part of the university education of his day, helped to determine the set of his mind. In his youth he combined the gaiety and sophistication of a city spark with omnivorous reading, which helps to account for the tone of curious wit in much of his early poetry. This poetry, which was not published during his lifetime but was known to a select circle through circulation in manuscript, consists of five satires, twenty "elegies" (if they are all Donne's), and the *Songs and Sonets.* The satires, written in deliberately rough couplets, have a colloquial vigor combined with a strain of ingenious ratiocination:

> Judges are Gods; he who made and said them so
> Meant not that men should be forc'd to them to go
> By means of Angels; when supplications
> We send to God, to Dominations,
> Powers, Cherubims, and all heaven's Courts, if we
> Should pay fees as here, daily bread would be
> Scarce to kings; so 'tis. Would it not anger
> A Stoic, a coward, yea a Martyr
> To see a Pursuivant come in, and call
> All his clothes, copes; books, primers; and all
> His plats, challices; and mistake them away,
> And ask a fee for coming?

They give us some vivid glimpses of the London of the period, as well as of Donne's self-arguments about religion:

> On a huge hill
> Cragged and steep, Truth stands, and he that will
> Reach her, about must and about must go,
> And what the hill's suddenness resists, win so;
> Yet strive so, that before age, death's twilight,
> Thy Soul rest, for none can work in that night.

The elegies are poems about love, written also in iambic pentameter couplets, dealing with the theme in a great variety of ways. Some are cynical, dealing with the paradoxes and fatuities of lust at work. Some celebrate a clandestine love with an uncomfortable realism. One, "The Autumnal," is a poem of grave compliment to an older woman apparently of high rank, opening with the well-known lines

> No Spring nor Summer beauty hath such grace
> As I have seen in one Autumnal face.

Some are simply exercises in wit. One, the seventeenth, celebrates variety in love. The nineteenth is a clever and lively piece of provocative bawdry, a description of his going to bed with his mistress. But the twelfth and sixteenth are strangely powerful love poems, addressed presumably to his wife (whom he secretly and imprudently married in 1601, at great cost to his career) when he had to leave her to go on a mission abroad. The passionate movement of the sixteenth, the variations in tempo corresponding to the rise and fall of the emotion, show clearly that Donne is here transmuting the naked experience directly into poetry in a way quite foreign to the Petrarchan tradition:

> By our first strange and fatal interview,
> By all desires which thereof did ensue,
> By our long starving hopes, by that remorse

> Which my words' masculine persuasive force
> Begot in thee, and by the memory
> Of hurts, which spies and rivals threaten'd me,
> I calmly beg: but by thy father's wrath,
> By all pains which want and divorcement hath,
> I conjure thee, and all the oaths which I
> And thou have sworn to seal joint constancy
> Here I unswear, and overswear them thus,
> Thou shalt not love by ways so dangerous.
> Temper, O fair Love, love's impetuous rage:
> Be my true mistress still, not my feign'd page. . . .

He is dissuading his wife from her rash plan to follow him abroad disguised as his page. After this initial passionate appeal, he lists the dangers with damning urgency:

> Men of France, changeable camelions,
> Spittles of diseases, shops of fashions,
> Love's fuellers, and the rightest company
> Of players, which upon the world's stage be,
> Will quickly know thee, and no less, alas!
> Th' indifferent Italian, as we pass
> His warm land, well content to think thee page,
> Will hunt thee with such lust and hideous rage
> As Lot's fair guests were vexed.

The conclusion is equally powerful, but in a different way:

> When I am gone, dream me some happiness,
> Nor let thy looks our long-hid love confess,
> Nor praise nor dispraise me, nor bless nor curse
> Openly love's force, nor in bed fright thy nurse
> With midnight's startings, crying out, "Oh, oh,
> Nurse, O my love is slain, I saw him go
> O'er the white Alps alone; I saw him I,
> Assail'd, fight, taken, stabb'd, bleed, fall, and die."
> Augur me better chance, except dread Jove
> Think it enough for me to'have had thy love.

The *Songs and Sonets* are, however, by far the most interesting poems. They are love poems, written at different times in different moods, and addressed to different persons. Some show the same cynical strain that is found in many of the Elegies, expressed often with ingenious violence and metrical cunning:

> Go and catch a falling star,
>   Get with child a mandrake root,
>   Tell me where all past years are,

> Or who cleft the Devil's foot;
> Teach me to hear Mermaids singing,
> Or to keep off envy's stinging,
>   And find
>   What wind
> Serves to advance an honest mind.
>
> If thou beest born to strange sights,
>   Things invisible to see,
> Ride ten thousand days and nights
>   Till age snow white hairs on thee;
> Thou, when thou return'st, wilt tell me
> All strange wonders that befell thee,
>   And swear
>   Nowhere
> Lives a woman true, and fair.

The conclusion has a characteristic turn:

> Tho' she were true when you met her,
> And last till you write your letter,
>   Yet she
>   Will be
> False, ere I come, to two, or three.

The opening of these poems shock the reader into attention, sometimes by a question:

> Now thou hast lov'd me one whole day,
> Tomorrow, when thou leav'st, what wilt thou say?
> Wilt thou then antedate some new made vow?
>   Or say that now
> We are not just those persons which we were?

First the shock, then the ingenious development of the thought: this is Donne's characteristic method.

This method Donne employs equally in those poems among the *Songs and Sonets* which seems to be addressed not to casual mistresses but to someone truly and passionately loved, some perhaps to Anne More, who became his wife. Here indeed is that union of passion and ratiocination which critics have seen as Donne's chief quality. Again there is often the opening question, and then the development of the original thought in terms of ideas derived from scholastic philosophy or from new scientific notions:

> I wonder by my troth what thou and I
> Did, till we lov'd? Were we not weaned till then,
> But suck'd on country pleasures childishly?

Or snorted we in the seven sleepers' den?
'Twas so; but this, all pleasures fancies be.
If ever any beauty I did see
Which I desir'd and got, 'twas but a dream of thee.

And now good morrow to our waking souls,
Which watch not one another out of fear;
For love all love of other sights controls
And makes one little room an everywhere.
Let sea-discoverers to new worlds have gone,
Let maps to other, worlds on worlds have shown:
Let us possess one world—each hath one, and is one. . . .

The opening, both conversational and startling, projects the reader
into the poem in a way that is quite new in English poetry; once in
the poem, the reader is held by the complex development of the
thought which, twisted this way and that, serves to embody rather
than to cool the passion. It is true that often these love poems do not
quite maintain the magnificence of their opening: we have the feeling that the emotion itself has carved out the stanza form at the beginning and subsequent stanzas have to be shaped with more deliberation to the form so carved out. But on the whole it is surprising
how often the ingenuity echoes in its own way the tremulousness of
passion. These poems abound in memorable openings:

For Godsake hold your tongue and let me love, . . .

If yet I have not all thy love,
Dear, I shall never have it all.

Twice or thrice had I loved thee
Before I knew thy face or name, . . .

Busy old fool, unruly sun,
Why dost thou thus
Through windows and through curtains call on us—

which last is a thoroughly new rendering of the old *aubade* which
goes back to early Provençal poetry.

There are other kinds of love poems in *Songs and Sonets* besides
the cynical and the genuinely passionate. Some, like "A Valediction,
of weeping" and "Sweetest love I do not go" sound a gentler note of
protective tenderness, but again combined with intellectual cunning. Some, such as "Twickenham Garden," show a more conventional strain of exaggerated compliment, picturing the author as the
afflicted lover who is hurt almost to death by the cruelty of his beloved; these, Grierson suggested, might have been written as poems
of compliment to ladies of high rank. "A Nocturnal upon Saint Lucy's

Day" builds up by every kind of philosophic ingenuity a picture of the poet as reduced to a state of absolute nothingness by the death of the lady who is the subject of the poem:

> Study me then, you who shall lovers be
> At the next world, that is, at the next Spring;
>   For I am every dead thing
>   In whom love wrought new alchemy.
>   For his art did express
> A quintessence even from nothingness,
> From dull privations and lean emptiness.
> He ruin'd me, and I am re-begot
> Of absence, darkness, death; things which are not.

Others again are merely ingenious, sometimes in satiric vein. In all, the *Songs and Sonets* alone are enough to substantiate Donne's claim to be considered an original poetic genius of a high order.

Something of the religious tensions within Donne is indicated by the strange poem, *The Progress of the Soul*, in fifty-two ten-line stanzas, in which his original intention appears to have been to trace the progress of the soul of the apple which Eve pulled (i.e., the soul of heresy) from its original appearance in Eden through all the great heretics of history, ending with Queen Elizabeth. He had almost certainly abandoned Roman Catholicism for the Church of England by the time he wrote this, but it shows clear Catholic sympathies. The original plan was modified, and the poem as we have it (not published in Donne's lifetime) carries the soul only as far as Adam's daughter Themech, "sister and wife to Cain, that first did plow." This leads to a reflection on the paradox that human progress often springs from the works of bad men, with the conclusion that moral values are relative.

> Who ere thou beest that read'st this sullen writ,
> Which just so much courts thee as thou dost it,
> Let me arrest thy thoughts: wonder with me
> Why plowing, building, ruling and the rest
> Or most of those arts whence our lives are blest
> By cursed Cain's race invented be,
> And blest Seth vext us with Astronomy.
> There's nothing simply good nor ill alone;
> Of every quality comparison
> The only measure is, and judge, opinion.

The poem is a "sullen writ" indeed, satirical, extravagant, pessimistic, its tone determined perhaps by the general disillusion with Queen Elizabeth which was abroad during her final years, especially after the execution of the Earl of Essex in February, 1601. The poem is dated August, 1601.

Donne's epigrams, and his letters of compliment to possible patrons (letters made necessary by the jolt to his career caused by his imprudent marriage), are less interesting, though two of his verse *Letters to Several Personages,* "The Storm" and "The Calm," are sharply etched pictures of the effect of these different conditions at sea on the spirits of the men aboard. The two *Anniversaries,* written as funeral elegies on the fifteen-year-old daughter of Sir Robert Drury (a girl whom he had never met) are elaborately worked out poetic arguments about the decline of the world since the death of the girl, and the discomforts of earthly life. The first, entitled "An Anatomy of the World," written and published in 1611, broods with many ingenious illustrations over the world's decay and disorder; the second, entitled "Of the Progress of the Soul" and not to be confused with the earlier poem of the same title, appeared the following year and deals in a similar way with "the incommodities of the soul in this life and her exaltation in the next." It is the latter poem which contains the often quoted metaphysical description of a blush:

> her pure and eloquent blood
> Spoke in her cheeks, and so distinctly wrought
> That one might almost say, her body thought.

The *First Anniversary* has the even better-known lines about the conflict between new thought and old values:

> And new philosophy calls all in doubt,
> The element of fire is quite put out;
> The sun is lost, and th'earth, and no man's wit
> Can well direct him where to look for it.
> And freely men confess that this world's spent,
> When in the planets and the firmament
> They seek so many new; they see that this
> Is crumbled out again to his atomies.
> 'Tis all in pieces, all coherence gone; . . .

Donne's *Divine Poems,* most though not all of which were written in the last phase of his life, when the witty and worldly "Jack Donne" of Lincoln's Inn had given way to the grave divine, explore traditional devotional attitudes with a new subtlety as well as a startling directness. In the best of these poems the paradoxes of art reflect with anguished intensity the paradoxes involved in man's relation with God. They were written after his wife's death, when Donne had put the worldly and the sensuous life completely behind him and was probing with fierce anxiety for the right relationship with eternity. Nothing could be further from the community hymn, written to reflect these aspects of religion which are common to a whole society and which therefore can be enunciated in general terms by a congregation in unison, than these strenuous religious poems:

> Batter my heart, three person'd God; for you
> As yet but knock, breathe, shine, and seek to mend. . . .

Even the puns convey the urgency:

> I have a sin of fear that when I have spun
> My last thread, I shall perish on the shore:
> Swear by Thyself that at my death Thy Son
> Shall shine as he shines now, and heretofore;
> And, having done that, Thou hast done:
> I fear no more.

There is still the question as to which is the true Church:

> Show me, dear Christ, thy spouse so bright and clear.

Sometimes, as in the longer poem in couplets, "Good Friday: Riding Westward" (a relatively early religious poem, dated 1613, four years before the death of his wife), the ingenuity of the thought is more striking than the passionate complex of thought and feeling: in this poem the main point is that he is going west, but his thoughts turn east, where Christ was crucified, and he explores the possibilities of this paradox. But even here the conclusion is grave and passionate:

> O think me worth thine anger, punish me,
> Burn off my rusts and my deformity,
> Restore thine image so much by thy grace
> That thou mayst know me, and I'll turn my face.

The nineteen *Holy Sonnets*[1] contain the core of Donne's religious poetry, and most of its finest examples. Here are not only "Batter my heart" but "Death be not proud," "At the round earth's imagin'd corners blow," and "What if this present were the world's last night?" Exactly the same combination of passion and argument as is found in the *Songs and Sonets* can be found in these poems (though perhaps the most obviously metaphysical of all Donne's religious poems is not any of the "Holy Sonnets" but the "Hymn to God my God in my sickness"). The passion here is, however, more complex; it is

---

[1] Donne's spelling, "sonets" in the title *Songs and Sonets* and "sonnets" in *Holy Sonnets*, has been followed because the "sonets" are not sonnets in the modern sense, whereas the "sonnets" are. The different spellings used by Donne are, however, probably accidental.

that mixture of hope and anguish that characterizes the religious man searching for the right relationship with God, aware both of his own unworthiness and of God's infinite greatness. There are, too, many traditional devices of Christian devotional literature exploited in these poems, though in Donne's own way. Donne's religious style is perhaps less absolutely novel than his secular style: the metaphysical mode thrives on paradox, and there have always been paradoxes at the heart of religious experience.

Donne's influence was felt both by secular and by religious poets. The finest of the religious "metaphysicals" was George Herbert (1593–1633), an Anglican poet who postponed taking up his religious vocation for many years, during which he faced the worldly temptations of both academic and public life, resisting them in the end (after, it must be admitted, his hopes of advancement had been frustrated) to become, during the last three years of his short life, the sweetly pious rector of Bemerton celebrated by Isaac Walton's biography. His collection of religious poems, *The Temple: Sacred Poems and Private Ejaculations*, published in 1633, show him both expressing his own sense of the conflict between the claims of worldly wit and sophistication and those of true Christian devotion, and also exploring, with a combination of colloquial ease and emblematic cunning, the significance of the main symbols and beliefs of Protestant Christianity. (Historically, Herbert's religious appeal has been both to High Anglicans and dissenters; his theology was in fact more Calvinist than was for long realized, but Calvinism had its place in the Church of England before the Civil War exacerbated theological as well as political feeling on both sides, and Herbert was firmly committed to the forms of worship of the established Church of his country.) Whether Herbert's poetry is "metaphysical" in the sense that Donne's is can be debated: recent critical opinion has tended to minimize the common elements in the poetry of those who have traditionally been regarded as the "metaphysical poets" of the seventeenth century. Affinities can be shown between Herbert's style and that of Sidney on the one hand and Wyatt on the other (but it must be remembered that the colloquial passion of Wyatt is often echoed by Donne), and it has also been argued that Herbert's manner of exploring analogies between emblematic objects (such as the human body or parts of the church building and its furniture) and religious truths is less like the individual argument of Donne's poetry than it is related to the use of the "hieroglyph" in Christian art throughout the Renaissance or, indeed, to a much older Christian tradition of exegesis through emblematic and metaphorical interpretation. But we have only to put Herbert's poetry beside

Quarles' to see the difference between a simple emblematic poetry and a poetry which uses the highest resources of art to shock the reader into new kinds of knowledge and of self-realization. There can be little doubt that Herbert learned from Donne (who was a great friend of his mother and whose poems he saw in manuscript) and that his combination of a simple and direct tone with ingenuity of argument and compelling intensity of feeling is "metaphysical" in the Donne sense. On the other hand, Herbert's poetry could never be mistaken for Donne's; its accent is wholly its own; the sensibility at work is quite un-Donnelike; and the combination of religious autobiography with presentation in due order of the great Christian themes, each associated with its proper season of the Christian year, is clearly the work of one who set his pastoral duties to his flock above the exploration of his own relationship with God—and this cannot be said of Donne's religious poetry. Herbert is artful enough in his own way—sometimes more artful than Donne in his—and he frequently uses musical devices and analogies to a greater extent than any other of the metaphysical poets.

In an early sonnet Herbert had asked

> Doth Poetry
> Wear Venus' livery? only serve her turn?
> Why are not sonnets made of thee, and lays
> Upon thy altar burnt? Cannot thy love
> Heighten a spirit to sound out thy praise
> As well as any she?

—where "thee" is of course God. He wished to bring all the resources of poetry into God's service. Yet, as a pastor, his duty was to teach Christian truths simply rather than explore his own religious emotions subtly:

> Who says that fictions only and false hair
> Become a verse? Is there in truth no beauty?
> Is all good structure in a winding stair? . . .
>
> I envy no man's nightingale or spring;
> Nor let them punish me with loss of rhyme
> Who plainly say, *My God, My King*.

If, in spite of this affirmation, Herbert's poetry is not plain in the sense that a community hymn is plain, that is largely because he draws not only on experiences which he considers common to all Christians but also on knowledge (of the Bible, of Anglican worship, of Christian doctrine, of ways of thought and feeling common to his age), and, weaving together the facts of religious experience with emblematically presented items from this knowledge, he produces poetry which arrests attention by its opening statement of its theme and maintains interest and excitement by the unexpected way it uses traditional Christian material in working the theme out. The combination of shock and repose in Herbert's poetry is something difficult to parallel in English literature. There is conflict in the poetry, yet there is calm trust; disturbed speculation yet simple faith; ingenious language—"Love enchanting language, sugar-cane, /Honey of roses . . ."—and the gentle simplicity of a wise and compassionate preacher. How these elements come together could only be demonstrated by careful analysis of individual poems; it must suffice here to refer to some of the poems which best illustrate the combination: "Redemption," "Church-Monuments" (where the sense of dissolution into dust is emblematically marked in the structure of the poem by the dissolving flow of the stanzas, which fall into each other as sand falls down an hourglass), "The Church-Floor," "Virtue," "The Bunch of Grapes," "Love Unknown," and "The Collar."

Herbert explores many ways of rendering in the shape and texture of a poem the theme which is its subject. Not only does he occasionally use "pattern poetry," as in "Easter Wings" where the two stanzas are in the shape of wings, the sense expanding and contracting as the line lengthens and shortens; but he loses no opportunity of reflecting the nature of the subject and the ebb and flow of the emotion in the run of the rhymes, the varying line-lengths, and the shifts in the tempo of the verse. He used a remarkable variety of stanza forms, constantly creating new ones to meet the needs of a new subject. He can work the simplest and commonest objects into his expression of total meaning, for he was filled with the sense of multiple analogies existing (as a result of God's design) between man, nature, and art. In "Denial" the second and fifth lines of each stanza remain unrhymed while the poet is describing his separation from God, but in anticipating his reconciliation the rhyme is "mended":

> . . . Therefore my soul lay out of sight,
>   Untun'd, unstrung:
> My feeble spirit, unable to look right,
>   Like a nipt blossom, hung
>   Discontented.
>
> O cheer and tune my heartless breast,
>   Defer no time;
> That so thy favours granting my request,
>   They and my mind may chime,
>   And mend my rhyme.

In "The Collar" he begins with a characteristic colloquial violence,

> I struck the board, and cried, "No more.
>   I will abroad. . . ."

The rebellion against God's beneficent discipline waxes ever more violent, reflected with great precision in the movement of the verse, until the sudden change at the close:

> But as I raved and grew more fierce and wild
>   At every word,
> Methought I heard one calling, *Child:*
>   And I replied, *My Lord.*

There is no search, as sometimes in Donne, for the true religion; Herbert knows very well which form of Christianity is the right one; the struggle in his poetry is between the world and complete surrender to God, and even then it is often an exemplary struggle rather than a simple autobiographical confession—i.e., it is expressed so as to serve as a guide for all Christians. Perhaps no religious poet in English has so effectively combined the strongly individual with the general and exemplary. The "metaphysical" mode, as well as traditions of Christian devotional literature, helped him to do this, but the art and the sensibility are his own. The gentle charm of his prose work, *A Priest to the Temple: or the Country Parson, his Character and Rule of Holy Life*, reflects only one side of his character—the side which Walton and posterity have preferred to dwell on. His poetry shows a craftsmanship geared so perfectly both to the sensibility at work and to the theme being presented that one is tempted to see in it the perfect blending of art and religion.

Richard Crashaw (1612/13–1649), a Catholic convert who spent the latter part of his life as an exile on the continent, is generally considered with Herbert among the religious metaphysicals, though his poetry displays a sensibility and a technique equally different from Donne and from Herbert. The title of his *Steps to the Temple*, published in 1646, is a clear reference to Herbert's *Temple*, which he admired, but he had none of Herbert's quietly controlled cunning in developing a Christian theme at the same time personally and publicly; his pressing of all the senses into the service of the expression of religious passion, his use of erotic and other images of physical appetite in a deliberately paradoxical religious sense, his relish of extravagant paradox involving the secular and the divine, tears and ecstasy, the sensuous and the spiritual, show not so much the union of passion and thought which is characteristic of Donne as the deliberate search for startling and paradoxical expression which will shock and excite the reader. When Donne shocks, it is by the stark reality of the self which he reveals—his wit reflects an inner tension; and Herbert, for all his ingenuity, subdues his material beneath a quiet surface. Crashaw, with a lushness of religious experience which is typical of one aspect of the Counter Reformation throughout Europe, explores with an almost feverish enthusiasm every way of presenting the spiritual world in sensuous terms. His earliest work was a volume of Latin epigrams, *Epigrammata Sacra*, 1634, which show in pious ingenuities the kind of trick he was to exploit more elaborately in his later poems. The epigrams include the famous one on the water changed into wine, with its final line, *Nympha pudica Deum vidit, et erubuit,* which a contemporary translation (perhaps Crashaw's own) rendered: "The conscious water saw its God and blushed." This is typical of Crashaw's baroque manner, and he could be very much more elaborate than that.

Crashaw's Nativity hymn "sung as by the shepherds" concentrates with a warm passion on the babe in the cradle, and adjectives like "sweet," "balmy," "rosy," "curled," "new-bloomed" are characteristic, as, in another way, are the lines

> The babe whose birth embraves this morn,
> Made his own bed e're he was born.

"Saint Mary Magdalene, or The Weeper" is accompanied in the original volume by an emblem of a bleeding heart with the face of a weeping woman, and the following couplet:

> Lo, where a wounded heart with bleeding eyes conspire,
> Is she a flaming fountain, or a weeping fire?

In the poem he plays about with the idea of Mary Magdalene's tears, which are pearls, dew, medicine, wine, spring showers, among many other things. The imagery is pursued with an almost intoxicated ingenuity:

> O cheeks! beds of chaste loves
> By your own showers seasonably dashed;
> Eyes! nests of milky doves
> In your own wells decently washed;
> O wit of love! that thus could place
> Fountain and garden in one place.

It is this poem too, that has the well-known extravagant lines (describing the Magdalene's eyes):

> Two walking baths, two weeping motions,
> Portable and compendious oceans.

The "Hymn to the Name and Honour of the Admirable Saint Teresa"
shows Crashaw at his most concentrated and intense. The subject
obviously kindled a real passion in him, and the strength and power
of the octosyllabic couplets in which he presents his contemplation
of the child going to voluntary martyrdom are beyond anything
else in his poetry. True, the tremulous simplicity of

> Farewell house, and farewell home!
> She's for the Moors and martyrdom

may sound ludicrous in some ears, though to others it has a moving
gravity. It is a matter both of religious doctrine and of sensibility if
not simply of "taste." But often the power is recognizable in spite
of everything:

> Scarce has she blood enough to make
> A guilty sword blush for her sake;
> Yet has she a heart dares hope to prove
> How much less strong is Death than Love.

Crashaw's heavily "conceited" style and his deliberate mingling
of sensuous and spiritual imagery reflects a movement that was
European in scope and more influential in Italy and Spain than in
England. The movement is known as "secentismo" with reference
to seventeenth-century Italian literature, and secentismo in Italy
is related to Gongorism (from the poet L. de Góngora y Argote) in
Spain. The style was popularized in Italy by G. B. Marino's long
poem, L'Adone, and the imagery of Crashaw's "Weeper" in particular
derives from Marino and his followers (hence the term "Marinism"
applied to Crashaw). Whether one considers the whole movement
a disease or a laudable extension of the scope of figurative language
depends perhaps on individual taste and sensibility. Like baroque
in art, the style can sometimes "surprise by a fine excess" but it also
drops easily into overluxuriance and vulgarity.

Henry Vaughan (1622–95) regarded himself as a disciple of
George Herbert. The preface to his collection of religious poems,
Silex Scintillans, published in 1655, condemns the "willingly-studied
and wilfully-published vanities" of "those ingenious persons which in
the late notion are termed wits," repudiates his own earlier secular
love poetry as of this kind, and attributes the "diversion of this foul
overflowing stream" to "the blessed man, Mr. George Herbert, whose
holy life gained many pious converts (of whom I am the least)."

Personal misfortune, the civil troubles of the time, and the influence of his mystical brother Thomas, all helped to turn Vaughan to a poetry of religious contemplation which contains many verbal echoes of Herbert; yet, though Vaughan clearly owes so much to Herbert and to the Donne tradition, his most characteristic poems have an individuality of tone that distinguishes them sharply from any other metaphysical poetry. Vaughan is conscious of a veil which separates time from eternity, man from God, and is constantly seeking for ways to penetrate it. The world of Nature and of things is not for him, as for Herbert, a collection of hieroglyphs of the Christian story but rather a world of creatures and objects whose existence, being on a more primitive level than man's, brings them into closer touch with spiritual reality.

> I would I were a stone, or tree,
>   Or flower by pedigree,
> Or some poor high-way herb, or spring
>   To flow, or bird to sing!
> Then should I (tied to one sure state)
>   All day expect my date;
> But I am sadly loose, and stray
>   A giddy blast each way;
> O let me not thus range!
>   Thou canst not change.

Childhood, too, is closer to God than the adult state, and in such a poem as "The Retreat" Vaughan tries to recapture the innocence of infancy:

> Happy, those early days, when I
> Shin'd in my angel infancy,
> Before I understood this place
> Appointed for my second race,
> Or taught my soul to fancy ought
> But a white, celestial thought, . . .
> When on some gilded cloud or flower
> My gazing soul would dwell an hour,
> And in those weaker glories spy
> Some shadows of eternity. . . .
> O how I long to travel back
> And tread again that ancient track! . . .

The mundane world was relieved by occasional private glimpses of eternity, but it was a sad fate on the whole to be cut off behind the temporal curtain. Vaughan would think of those who had penetrated it—

> They are all gone into the world of light,
>   And I alone sit lingering here;
> Their very memory is fair and bright,
>   And my sad thoughts doth clear—

and wish that he too, while still in this world, could see beyond
the veil or else be translated at once into eternity:

> Either disperse these mists, which blot and fill
>   My perspective still as they pass,   [perspective:
> Or else remove me hence unto that hill   telescope.]
>   Where I shall need no glass.

His attitude to childhood in "The Retreat" has been compared to
Wordsworth's in the "Immortality Ode," and his poem "The Waterfall"—which moves from an affectionate address to the loved water
to a meditation on its mystical significance—has been considered
Wordsworthian in its attitude to Nature; but the similarity is superficial in either case, especially the second. If Wordsworth might
have written

> Dear stream! dear bank, where often I
> Have sat and pleased my pensive eye

so might James Thomson, and neither Thomson nor Wordsworth
would have continued thus:

> O useful element and clear!
> My sacred wash and cleanser here,
> My first consigner unto those
> Fountains of life, where the Lamb goes!
> What sublime truths, and wholesome themes,
> Lodge in thy mystical, deep streams! . . .

There was a genuine mystical strain in Vaughan's thought, and
sometimes as in "The World," with its arresting opening—

> I saw Eternity the other night
> Like a great Ring of pure and endless light,
>   All calm as it was bright—

it is the mystic's matter-of-factness in talking of his strange otherworldly insights that gives his poetry its most impressive quality.
Much of Vaughan's poetry is conventionally ingenious in its expression of religious feeling; the minority of striking poems, which
include "The Waterfall," "And do they so?," "Man," "The Night,"
"The Retreat," "The World," and "They are all gone into a world
of light," do not always succeed in sustaining throughout the whole

composition the note of mystic passion which is sometimes struck so magnificently. Vaughan's technique, one might almost say, was not quite up to his insights. His verse rang out with most power and beauty when his own quietist and mystical vision was at its most intense; when the moment of vision faded and he was left to develop his theme with mere verbal ingenuity, the quality of the poetry at once dropped.

The poetry of Thomas Traherne (ca. 1634–74) and the most interesting of his prose remained unknown until it was discovered in manuscripts at the end of the last century. His prose *Centuries of Meditations* gives the clearest and most impressive view of his quest for innocence and joy, for the incorruptible world with all its glories which can be had for the seeking. Even more than Vaughan, Traherne is dependent on his vision; for him expression is forced by the vision, and he never attains Vaughan's occasional control and calm beauty, still less the formal perfection of Herbert. Traherne's characteristic mood was a joyful primitivism; the child's unschooled appreciation of all about him was the type of the proper attitude, and his best known poem, "Wonder," expresses this:

> How like an angel came I down!
> How bright are all things here!
> When first among his works I did appear,
> Oh, how their glory did me crown!

The idealization of childhood, when, as he put it in his poem "Eden," "A learned and happy ignorance /Divided me /From all the vanity, From all the sloth, care, sorrow, that advance /The madness and the misery /Of men," suggests sometimes Vaughan, sometimes Blake, sometimes Wordsworth; and perhaps all three poets, for all their important differences, were in touch with a common mystical strain in English thought. It is at least significant that James Joyce, in the third episode of *Ulysses*, when Stephen Dedalus is meditating on the mystery of birth, the links between the generations, and the descent of all mankind from the symbolic and mystical first human pair, Adam and Eve, should quote from a description in the third of Traherne's *Centuries of Meditations:*

The corn was orient and immortal wheat, which never should be reaped, nor was ever sown. I thought it had stood from everlasting to everlasting. The dust and stones of the street were as precious as gold: the gates were at first the end of the world. . . . Boys and girls tumbling in the street, and playing, were moving jewels. I knew not that they were born or should die; but all things abided eternally as they were in their proper places.

These, then, are the principal seventeenth-century religious poets who, in varying degrees, show, or have been thought to show, the influence of Donne. In addition to these "religious metaphysicals" there are also secular poets in the metaphysical tradition. But before we discuss these, let us turn back and consider the parallel tradition, that of the "Sons of Ben." Few if any of those poets who thought of Ben Jonson as their master were not also influenced to some extent by Donne, but in most of them the lyric strain is recognizably Jonsonian.

Robert Herrick (1591–1674) had a sensibility much less masculine than Jonson's, but, like Jonson, he turned to the classical lyric for inspiration and was concerned to achieve elegance and precision of form. His combination of classical paganism with English folk themes gave a special note to his celebrations of country festivities and seasonal customs; by temperament a hedonist, by profession (for much of his life) a country parson, by literary taste both an epigrammatist and a writer of formal lyrics of description, compliment, elegy, and love, Herrick produced his own synthesis of classical, Christian, and English which is like nothing else in seventeenth-century English literature. His *Hesperides*, published in 1648 together with his religious poems, *Noble Numbers*, opens with "The Argument of his Book" which lists the themes with which he is going to treat:

> I sing of brooks, of blossoms, birds, and bowers,
> Of April, May, of June, and July flowers;
> I sing of may-poles, hock-carts, wassails, wakes,
> Of bridegrooms, brides, and of their bridal cakes;
> I write of youth, of love, and have access
> By these to sing of cleanly wantonness; . . .
> I write of groves, of twilight, and I sing
> The court of Mab, and of the Fairy King;
> I write of Hell; I sing, and ever shall,
> Of Heaven, and hope to have it after all.

The Christian theme is something of an afterthought; he hopes to have heaven "after all" and meanwhile cheerfully offers his readers a volume containing over a thousand secular poems mostly hedonist in attitude and pagan in tone, together with a much smaller group of religious poems which show a simple confidence in his own ultimate salvation.

Though on first going to his country vicarage in 1629 (he was ejected by the Puritans in 1647 but returned after the Restoration) he appeared to languish for the city, where he had enjoyed the

company of Jonson and other wits in such gatherings as he celebrated in his ode for Ben Jonson—

> Where we such clusters had
> As made us nobly wild, not mad;
> And yet each verse of thine
> Outdid the meat, outdid the frolic wine—

he turned readily to the celebration of rustic content in Horatian
mood:

> Here, here I live with what my board
> Can with the smallest cost afford.
> Though ne'er so mean the viands be,
> They well content my Prue and me.
> Or pea, or bean, or wort, or beet,
> Whatever comes, content makes sweet.

The Horatian theme is enriched by strains from Catullus, Tibullus,
Ausonius, Anacreon, and other Latin and Greek (but mostly Latin)
lyrics. He plays all sorts of variations on the *"carpe diem"* theme:

> Gather ye rosebuds while ye may,
> Old time is still a-flying,
> And this same flower that smiles today,
> Tomorrow will be dying.

He celebrates love, as a delight rather than as a passion, and has
numerous short poems of compliment to Julia or some other clas-
sically-named mistress in which a degree of metaphysical ingenuity
sometimes mingles with the classical grace and formality:

> Whenas in silks my Julia goes,
> Then, then, methinks, how sweetly flows
> The liquefaction of her clothes.

The noun "liquefaction" has both a suggestiveness and precision
here, which is almost metaphysical, as has the term "Protestant" in
his well known "To Anthea, who may command him anything":

> Bid me to live, and I will live
> Thy Protestant to be, ...

Poems of seasonal celebration sometimes contain also an amatory or
complimentary theme, as in "Corinna's Going a-Maying," and sometimes he celebrates the countryside and what it affords in the strains
of Marlowe's "Come live with me and be my love":

> Live, live with me, and thou shalt see
> The pleasures I'll prepare for thee:

> What sweets the country can afford
> Shall bless thy bed and bless thy board.

Most of all he is aware of the rituals that mark the different points in the rustic year:

> At shearing-times, and yearly wakes,
> When Themilis his pastime makes,
> There thou shalt be, and be the wit,
> Nay more, the feast, and grace of it.
> On holy days when virgins meet
> To dance the hays with nimble feet,
> Thou shalt come forth, and then appear
> The queen of roses for that year.

"The Hock-Cart, or Harvest Home" celebrates the harvest festival in sturdy octosyllabic couplets replete with images drawn from farming activity and country cheer. Some of his poems celebrating or inviting to social feasting are reminiscent, both in movement and imagery, of Jonson's poems in similar vein; often, however, similarities between Jonson and Herrick are noted only to reveal significant differences—as in Jonson's "Still to be neat, still to be dressed," and Herrick's "Delight in Disorder," where there is a cunningly implied sense of wantonness in the details of Herrick's poem which is lacking in the graver statement of Jonson's.

Herrick's success in Romanizing his celebration of English country rituals is a belated Renaissance manifestation in English literature. While sometimes, as in "Oberon's Feast," he deals playfully with pure English folklore, on numerous other occasions he combines the Roman with the English. "A Hymn to the Lares" refers to the wassail bowl and "North-down ale," and conversely his numerous short poems describing the "ceremonies" for various Christian festivals ("Ceremonies for Christmas," "Ceremonies for Candlemas Eve," etc.) often have the air of describing a Roman ritual.

In dealing with such obvious country subjects as flowers Herrick often uses conceits which are not Petrarchan but which are hardly metaphysical. "How roses came red" or "How violets came blue" give a playfully ingenious mythological interpretation of the phenomenon he is describing, but the effect is one of ingenuousness rather than ingenuity. More interesting are those flower poems where he associates the short life of the flower with the transience of human affairs: this theme gives him some of his most attractive lyrics:

> Fair daffodils, we weep to see
>   You haste away so soon;
> As yet the early-rising sun

> Has not attained his noon.
>   Stay, stay
> Until the hasting day
>   Has run
> But to the even-song;
> And, having prayed together, we
>   Will go with you along.
>
> We have short time to stay as you;
>   We have as short a Spring,
> As quick a growth to meet decay
>   As you, or anything.
>   We die
> As your hours do, and dry
>   Away
> Like to the summer's rain,
> Or as the pearls of morning's dew
>   Ne'er to be found again.

Some critics have professed to see a metaphysical strain in Herrick's *Noble Numbers*. It is true that occasionally there is a note somewhat reminiscent of Herbert though without Herbert's metrical variety:

> Can I not sin, but thou wilt be
> My private protonotary?
> Can I not woo thee to pass by
> A short and sweet iniquity?
> I'll cast a mist and cloud upon
> My delicate transgression, . . .

But the conventional view that Herrick's religious poetry expresses an almost childish faith, a naïve trustfulness that in the end God will see him through, is nearer the truth. These are mostly short poems, giving thanks for a life of modest content ("A Thanksgiving to God for his House") or expressing in deliberately childlike terms his confidence in the Christian creed ("His Creed"), or asking in advance for divine help when it will be most needed ("His Litany to the Holy Spirit"), or playing with little conceits about God and immortality. Herrick's religious poems have grace and clarity of expression; but for the most part they are curiously complacent in attitude and show none of the conflicts or deeper perceptions that we find in the "religious metaphysicals."

Thomas Carew (1594/5–1640) both praised Ben Jonson for his successful spoliation of the ancient classics—

> Nor think it theft, if the rich spoils so torn
> From conquered authors, be as trophies worn—

and paid tribute to Donne as the poet who "ruled as he thought fit /The universal monarchy of wit":

> The Muses' garden with pedantic weeds
> O'er spread, was purg'd by thee, the lazy seeds
> Of servile imitation thrown away,
> And fresh invention planted.

In combining the classical influence of Jonson with the metaphysical influence of Donne, Carew produced a mixture especially suited to the atmosphere of the Court of Charles I. As Sir Herbert Grierson expressed it, "in Carew's poems and Vandyke's pictures the artistic taste of Charles's Court is vividly reflected, a dignified voluptuousness, an exquisite elegance, if in some of the higher qualities of man and artist Carew is as inferior to Wyatt or Spenser as Vandyke is to Holbein." This is true Cavalier poetry, polished, gay, and witty. Without the formal precision of Jonson, the adroit Roman paganizing of Herrick, or the gentlemanly ease of his younger contemporary, Sir John Suckling, Carew has his own kind of urbanity. The gallantry of his love poems does not always conceal a cynicism at the core, but the control, the restrained touch of stylization in all his best work, shows a sense of style in living that truly reflects the Cavalier spirit of the time and is not unattractive. Occasionally, as in the well-known song, "Ask me no more where Jove bestows," he combines Jonson's lapidary elegance with a stately singing note as well as a touch of metaphysical ingenuity, and the combination is perfectly achieved. Sometimes he echoes Donne in the frank psychological curiosity with which he explores an emotional or a sensual situation (as in "To a Lady that desired I would love her" and, in a different way, "A Rapture"), but he has a tendency to laugh off the implications of his conceits with an elegant shrug, lacking Donne's ability to carry through to the end the fusion of passion and wit. It is "wit" in Carew, too—almost in the modern sense—rather than thought. There are many echoes of Donne in his poems, but the exhibitionist quality in his conceits often derives as much from Marino as from Donne. Carew's songs were meant to be sung, and lose something when merely read. His longer poems often run into mere showiness. But he had an artistic conscience; even his showiness is carefully modulated, and he always knew what he was doing.

Another heir to both Jonson and Donne is Sir John Suckling (1609–42), though both streams are shallower now. Lively, gay, very much the worldly courtier, Suckling looks to the cynical strain in Donne's early love poems and to the lighter of Jonson's lyrics. His poem, "Oh, for some honest lover's ghost" is an altogether more superficial performance than Donne's "I long to talk with some old lover's ghost." His "Hast thou seen the down i' the air" is a flippant parody (turned to satire) of Jonson's exquisite song of compliment, "Have you seen but the white lily grow." He is at his best where he combines a colloquial ease with a neatly patterned song-stanza, as in the well-known "Why so pale and wan, fond lover?" or "I prithee send me back my heart" or "Out upon it I have loved /Three whole days together." "A Session of the Poets" is a lively trotting poem in thirty four-line stanzas with a deliberately crude accentual meter, describing himself and his fellow poets competing for the laurel, only to see it given in the end by Apollo to an alderman on the grounds that "it was the best sign /Of good store of wit to have good store of coin." The poem is interesting in giving Suckling's views of his contemporaries. Carew's "muse was hard-bound, and th' issue of 's brain." Suckling describes himself as an amateur who "loved not the muses so well as his sport." The description is accurate enough: Suckling's poetry shows the Cavalier at play.

The true Cavalier poet is, however, Richard Lovelace (1618–58), whose gallantry has in it a truer strain of chivalry than Suckling's, a strain that links him with Sidney and Sir Walter Ralegh and the older tradition of Renaissance courtesy. The royalist ideal was indeed grounded in that older tradition, as we can see in Lovelace and, most clearly, in the few but noble lyrical utterances of the Scottish royalist, James Graham, Marquis of Montrose. Lovelace's "To Althea from Prison" uses imagery that is as much Petrarchan as metaphysical, but the poem brings a new kind of idealism into the English lyric of the period. The same can be said of "To Lucasta, Going to the Wars," which has the lapidary quality of Jonson at his best as well as a simple gravity of tone that we cannot find in Suckling. More metaphysical in imagery, if classical in inspiration, is the interesting poem, "The Grasshopper," where a description of the heedless grasshopper is adroitly turned into a celebration of friendship. There is something of the strength of Wyatt in Lovelace at his best, as well as echoes of the Sidneian and Spenserian association of ideal love and beauty with honor and the good life. The seventeenth-century royalist ideal was perhaps anachronistic, and a somewhat faded neo-Platonism often lay behind it; but Lovelace at least gave it effective expression.

Of the minor Cavalier poets, mention may be made of Sidney

Godolphin (1610–43), the majority of whose poems remained in manuscript until the twentieth century. He, too, has the graver note which we sometimes find in Lovelace (in Suckling's "Session of the Poets" Apollo advises Godolphin "not to write so strong"), together with a restrained metaphysical touch which adds just the right note of subtlety to the quiet clarity of his style. The influence of Donne and Jonson combine here most happily.

Richard Corbet, bishop of Oxford and Norwich (1582–1635), is a minor lyrist of the period whose character and poems reflect a robust joy of life which was to become one element in Cavalier opposition to the Puritans. His one famous poem, "A Proper new ballad, intituled The Faries' Farewell, or God a mercy Will," gives lively expression to the sense that the Puritan spirit had killed the happy superstitions of Old England:

> Farewell, rewards and fairies,
>   Good housewives now may say,
> For now foul sluts in dairies
>   Do fare as well as they.
> And though they sweep their hearths no less
>   Than maids were wont to do,
> Yet who of late for cleanliness
>   Finds sixpence in her shoe?
>
> Lament, lament, old abbeys,
>   The fairies lost command;
> They did but change priests' babies,
>   But some have changed your land,
> And all your children sprung from thence
>   Are now grown Puritans;
> Who live as changelings ever since,
>   For love of your demains.

"There never was a merry world since the fairies left dancing and the parson left conjuring," said John Selden in the middle of the century, and this remark, together with Corbet's poem, shows that there was much more than political or theological opinions involved in the Civil War and also helps to explain why the large majority of those interested in the arts and letters (Milton was the great exception) were on the royalist side.

Sir William Davenant's dramatic work and his "heroic poem" *Gondibert* are discussed in Chapter 15, but it can be noted here that his lyric poetry is in the Cavalier tradition, combining in its way Jonsonian and metaphysical influences. The song, "The lark now leaves his wat'ry nest," is built on a conceit that is almost metaphysical in its ingenuity, but it lacks that exploratory power of the true metaphysical style. This is typical of the way the Cavalier poets modified the metaphysical conceit so as to bring it closer to the Petrarchan manner against which it had originally revolted. But Jonson and the Roman lyrical poets gave them a classical sense of form and the spirit of the age provided a gayer tone, so that the result is very different from the typical Petrarchan love poem of the Elizabethan age.

We have discussed the religious poets who in differing degrees were influenced by Donne, and the secular poets who considered themselves "Sons of Ben" even if they also show something of Donne's influence. There were also secular metaphysical poets, who continued the Donne tradition not in religious poetry but in poetry of love, compliment, elegy, or meditation. Lord Herbert of Cherbury (1583–1648), better known for his philosophical and historical writings in Latin and English and his spirited autobiography, learned from Donne to employ a precise intellectual imagery in his poetry, but he lacks Donne's immediacy and variety; the thought dominates the passion. The poetry of Henry King (1592–1669) shows Donne's influence clearly (as well as, occasionally, Jonson's grace and neatness) and in one poem, "The Exequy," an elegy on the death of his young wife, he produced a minor masterpiece which fuses passion and argument in the finest metaphysical style. John Cleveland (1613–58) was one of those in whose hands the metaphysical style turned to mere ingenuity of metaphor and simile, but a poem like "Mark Anthony" shows a mixture of metaphysical ingenuity and lusty vulgarity that was to affect poets of the Restoration, and his satirical poetry, with its strong royalist viewpoint and lively verbal tricks, was to provide suggestions for Samuel Butler's *Hudibras*.

Cleveland was extremely popular in his own day, but no less so than Abraham Cowley (1618–67), with whose poetry the metaphysical style finally works itself out. Cowley was a copious and versatile poet. Speaking of his collection of poems, *The Mistress*, published in 1647, Dr. Johnson remarked that it had "no power of seduction. Her beauty and absence, her kindness and cruelty, her disdain and inconstancy, produce no correspondence of emotion. His poetical account of the virtues of plants, and colours of flowers, is not perused with more sluggish frigidity. The compositions are such as might have been written for penance by a hermit, or for hire by a philosophical rhymer who had only heard of another sex." The modern critic is not disposed to quarrel violently with Johnson's judgment, even though he does not share Johnson's view of the metaphysical style in general. But Cowley does strike fire sometimes, and in his more Horatian moods he can be happily cogent. A thoughtful poet, he reflects in his work some of the major philo-

sophical currents of his time, and it is not his fault if the newer
streams of thought were sometimes shallow. He was a good classicist,
and his imitations of Pindar set the style for the eighteenth-century
Pindaric ode. His unfinished religious epic *Davideis* (in heroic
couplets) is one of the several English abortions of this kind: a biblical epic professedly imitative of Virgil in style, attempting to combine neoclassic notions of the epic with Christian repudiation of
pagan machinery, trying to follow classical precedent in the presentation of the material yet showing the influence of Crashaw's translation of the first book of Marino's *Sospetto d'Herode* and of
Sylvester's Du Bartas—the poem was a mixture of heterogeneous
motives from the start. It emphasizes, however, the transitional nature of Cowley's poetry: he looked forward to eighteenth-century
neoclassical as well as backward to the metaphysicals. His prose
essays are models of quiet clarity bringing the familiar autobiographical note confidently and easily into English prose. His poetry,
however, is important chiefly for illustrating the progressive restric-
tion of the poet's intellectual and emotional world as the seventeenth
century moved toward its final quarter. The "dissociation of sensibility" which T. S. Eliot saw as a phenomenon of the English poetic
mind throughout the eighteenth and nineteenth centuries is already
present in Cowley. The metaphysical style is not really suited to his
temperament or his vision of the world, and it is significant and
appropriate that Johnson began his *Lives of the Poets* with a discussion of Cowley and of metaphysical poetry as a preparation for dealing with the poetry of his own century. In giving Cowley the headmaster's nod of dismissal before summoning the younger boys who
are to be promoted on their merits to the leading positions in the
school, Johnson was making a historical judgment with which the
modern reader, whatever his opinion of the new regime, will not
wish substantially to disagree.

Andrew Marvell (1621-78), however, gives us pause. His best
poetry combines true metaphysical wit with perfect classical grace
and poise to a greater degree than any other poet of the century.
But this was not the road that English poetry was to take. Marvell
—whose best poems were written in the early 1650's and were not
published in his lifetime—stood alone, like Milton, creating his
own synthesis out of the clashing elements swirling about him. The
posthumous volume of his poems which appeared in 1681 appealed
to a taste that was already out of fashion, and Marvell's own later
work shows him developing a satirical strain (already evident, but
far from dominant, in his early poetry) which exhibited a much
more restricted kind of wit than that displayed in his finest poems;
Marvell's political satires look back to Cleveland's and forward to

Dryden's. His best and most characteristic poems are those in which an adventurous wit is perfectly subdued to the quiet texture of his verse to produce a poetry at once contemplative and exciting, gravely formal and mysteriously suggestive. A precise and loving observation of nature, an ethical gravity, and an ability to put intellectual play to serious use are qualities found together in, for example, "On a Drop of Dew," which begins with the most accurate description of a dewdrop on a rose and maneuvers the picture into a symbol of the soul's relation to earth and Heaven. The wit is integral to the poem, and bound up both with its accuracy of observation and its moral feeling. "The Nymph Complaining for the Death of her Faun" is on the surface a simple poem in gently moving octosyllabic couplets, but, in the words of Eliot, "Marvell takes a slight affair, the feeling of a girl for her pet, and gives it a connexion with that inexhaustible and terrible nebula of emotion which surrounds all our exact and practical passions and mingles with them." The poem, like all of Marvell's best, is so carefully wrought that quotation cannot suggest its true quality, but an extract may give some idea of its movement:

> Thenceforth I set myself to play
> My solitary time away
> With this; and very well content,
> Could so mine idle life have spent.
> For it was full of sport; and light
> Of foot and heart; and did invite
> Me to its game: it seemed to bless
> Its self in me. How could I less
> Than love it? O I cannot be
> Unkind t' a beast that loveth me.

"To his Coy Mistress," with its wonderful manipulation of images of exaggeration—

> Had we but world enough, and time,
> This coyness, Lady, were no crime.
> We would sit down, and think which way
> To walk, and pass our long love's day.
> Thou by the Indian Ganges' side
> Should'st rubies find; I by the tide
> Of Humber would complain. I would
> Love you ten years before the Flood,
> And you should if you please refuse
> Till the conversion of the Jews—

shows not only a truly serious use of sprightly wit but also, in its threefold movement, a sense of form which provides a wholly new dimension. The second section of the poem suddenly deepens and extends the significance of the earlier wit:

> But at my back I always hear
> Time's wingéd chariot hurrying near,
> And yonder all before us lie
> Deserts of vast Eternity.
> Thy beauty shall no more be found,
> Nor, in thy marble vault, shall sound
> My echoing song: then worms shall try
> That long preserv'd virginity,
> And your quaint honour turn to dust
> And into ashes all my lust.
> The grave's a fine and private place,
> But none I think do there embrace.

The third movement conquers time by intensity of present passion:

> . . . Let us roll all our strength, and all
> Our sweetness up into one ball,
> And tear our pleasures with rough strife
> Through the iron gates of life.
> Thus, though we cannot make our sun
> Stand still, yet we will make him run.

The "Gather ye rosebuds" theme is here given new subtlety and suggestiveness by the handling of the wit and the ordering of the images.

Equally remarkable is "The Definition of Love"—

> My love is of a birth as rare
> As 'tis for object strange and high:
> It was begotten by despair
> Upon impossibility—,

"The Picture of T.C. in a Prospect of Flowers," a poem which combines delicate charm with a slowly emergent gravity, and "The Garden," which, by a finely ordered imagery and a cunning progression of thought, distills cumulatively the essence of lonely garden felicity as symbol of the unfallen life in Eden. The "Horatian Ode upon Cromwell's Return from Ireland" is another poem in which the manipulation of variety and order in the images and the carefully controlled modulation of the thought results in a unity of remarkable richness and power. Horatian in its clarity and strength, and showing other classical influences as well, it is nevertheless wholly original in its controlled variations of tone. The picture of Cromwell coming

> . . . from his private gardens, where
> He liv'd reservéd and austere

to act as the minister of fate in casting "the kingdom old /Into another mould" gives way to one of Charles at his execution:

> He nothing common did or mean
> Upon that memorable scene,
>   But with his keener eye
>   The axe's edge did try.

And this in turn yields to a further picture of Cromwell the conqueror, to end with the disquieting warning that

> The same arts that did gain
> A pow'r must it maintain.

Both Cromwell and King Charles are seen in a context of divine justice and order working themselves out, and this enables Marvell to be fair to them both. A similar position is taken in his longer poem in heroic couplets, "The First Anniversary of the Government under O. C.," though here the praise of Cromwell is louder and clearer.

Marvell's poems are very unequal. His long poem in eight-line stanzas "Upon Appleton House" (Lord Fairfax's seat, where Marvell lived for some years) is too discursive to respond to the poet's attempt at ordering, and the imagery is at times merely ingenious, but there are some admirable stanzas. The "Mower" poems show his love of nature put, as so often, at the service of a moral theme. The well-known "Bermudas" is quite perfect of its kind: with its rich and various imagery, musical beauty of movement, and simple gravity of feeling, it strikes "an holy and a cheerful note" to a degree rarely equaled in English poetry. His satirical verse in heroic couplets, whether the earlier "Tom May's Death," "Flecknoe," or "The Character of Holland" or the later series written after the Restoration, of which the longest is "The Last Instructions to a Painter," cannot begin to compare with his best lyrical poetry. They show a strain of cheap and boisterous cruelty and an exhibitionist wit which are quite unlike the Marvell of the other poems. Marvell was here following the new fashions of the times. It is significant that in "The Last Instructions to a Painter" Marvell was following a popular fashion of verse comment on contemporary affairs in the form of advice to a painter on what to paint and how to paint it. Much more attractive are Marvell's prose writings in defense of religious toleration.

Marvell, like Milton, was a Christian Humanist, and though he is generally regarded as a Puritan poet, his own career illustrates perfectly the dilemma of a sensitive and serious temperament caught up in a civil conflict which he deplored. Unlike Milton, Marvell could never commit himself wholeheartedly to the Commonwealth cause; he accepted it, largely because

> 'Tis Madness to resist or blame
> The force of angry Heaven's flame,

and he was friendly with many of the Parliamentary leaders. In 1657 he was appointed assistant to Milton in the Latin Secretaryship. But looking back afterward, he said that "upon considering all, I think the cause was too good to have been fought for. Men 'ought to have trusted God—they ought to have trusted the King with the whole matter." In his best poetry as in his character he combined the best of Cavalier wit and courtesy with the quiet gravity of a humane Puritan. But the combination was too individual and too subtle to provide a pattern for future poets.

CHAPTER TWELVE

Milton

JOHN MILTON (1608–74) stands by himself, a lonely and dedicated figure, in seventeenth-century English literature; yet no man was more profoundly affected by the events of his time. The great debate on religion and politics which divided the English nation in the middle of the seventeenth century helped to determine the course of Milton's career and the shape of his literary ambitions. The origins of the conflict were complex; James I and his son Charles I lacked the adroitness and flexibility of Queen Elizabeth in responding to the demands of an increasingly self-conscious Parliament, nor did they see in the steady rise of the commercial classes, with their economic individualism and Puritan morality, an inevitable historical process which demanded some modification of the aristocratic and paternalist view of the monarchy held by the Stuarts; and in the end Charles' lack of tact in handling Parliament, his clumsy devices for providing himself with money in the absence of Parliamentary votes of supply, his insistence on uniformity of worship and standardization of the liturgy, and his lack of realization of the state of mind of a large number of his subjects in both England and Scotland, provoked a civil conflict which ended in Charles' trial and execution in 1649 and in England's unprecedented seventeen-year experiment in non-monarchical government. On the whole, artists and men of letters were on the royalist side during the Civil War; the Court party stood for the graces of life, and royal patronage was still an important factor in a successful artistic or literary career. But many writers were torn between personal loyalty and interest on the one hand and moral or political principle on the other, and took sides with reluctance. The core of parliamentary support came from London burghers as well as from other urban centers and from the south and east of the country generally, while the Church of England, the larger part of the nobility and gentry, and the country folk of the north, west, and Midlands, supported the King. There were, of course, exceptions and anomalies. There were high-minded Puritan aristocrats who supported Parliament, and pockets of royalism in Puritan parts of the country. The antiroyalist side was far from homogeneous; political, religious, and economic motives prevailed in different proportions with different people, and on the left wing there was a host of radical sects, utopian prophets, religious idealists, and apocalyptic enthusiasts of all kinds. On the royalist side there were many who had been critical of Charles' behavior but who shuddered at the thought of bearing arms against the King; while there were others who supported the rebellion on constitutional grounds but boggled at the King's execution. The upheaval in political thinking —and political thinking at this time involved religious thinking— produced by the Civil War was tremendous; pamphlets, tracts, sermons, and proposals came from the printing presses in huge quantities, with innumerable persons (as Milton was to put it in his *Areopagitica*) "disputing, reasoning, reading, inventing, discoursing, even to a rarity and admiration, things not before discoursed or written of." For a poet like Milton, convinced of his own genius and determined to put it at the service of his country, this atmosphere was both dangerous and fascinating. Christian and Humanist, Protestant patriot and heir of the golden ages of Greece and Rome, he faced what appeared to him to be the birth-pangs of a new and regenerate England with high excitement and idealistic optimism. It was this excitement and this optimism which led him to commit himself so completely to the parliamentary side in the Civil War; and that commitment was decisive for his middle and later poetic career.

"I was born in London of an honest family; . . . My father destined me from a child to the pursuits of literature; and my appetite for knowledge was so voracious, that, from twelve years of age, I hardly ever left my studies, or went to bed before midnight." So Milton tells us in his *Second Defence of the English People,* and his stress on his early literary interests, pursued with his father's encouragement, is significant. He was given a Christian Humanist education from the start. At St. Paul's School, which he attended from 1615 or 1620 to 1625, he found a curriculum originally framed according to the Humanist ideals of Erasmus and Colet and still maintaining many of the characteristics of Renaissance Humanist scholarship. He studied Latin, Greek, and Hebrew (in addition to being tutored in Hebrew at home by Thomas Young, a Presbyterian divine), and got a thorough grounding in classical rhetoric, which he was taught to apply to the analysis of Latin and Greek prose and verse. The view of rhetoric as a noble skill necessary for the citizen who is to take a proper part in public affairs—the view of Isocrates and Cicero, not that of Aristotle, for whom it was the art of persuasion, morally neutral in itself, not yet that of Plato, for whom it was a dangerous and superficial art liable to mislead and corrupt—was the one which Milton learned at school; and this helps to explain why later as a literary man he deemed it his duty to engage in public affairs and also why, after his disillusionment over the possibility of a regenerate England resulting from the defeat of Charles, he became more and more suspicious of rhetoric, showing its abuse, and the abuse of democratic debate, in the speeches of Satan and his followers in *Paradise Lost*, and in *Paradise Regained* giving all the rhetoric to Satan, the tempter, while putting into the mouth of Jesus language deliberately stripped of all rhetorical ornament.

When Milton came to Christ's College, Cambridge, in 1625, he was already a dedicated spirit, eager to prepare himself to become a great poet. He was shocked to find scholastic disputation on trivial subjects still being used as a means of education—St. Paul's was ahead of Cambridge in its educational theories—and voiced his disagreement in his own Latin oratorical exercises. In the first of these Latin "prolusions," delivered in College before an audience of his fellow undergraduates, he referred to the unfriendliness of the majority of the audience and the small minority of his supporters, while in the third, delivered in the Public Schools, he attacked the scholastic philosophy and the barren disputes to which it gave rise, asking rhetorically what pleasure there could be in the quarrelings of crabbed old men, and describing his difficulty in getting through the long pages of verbose quibbling which he had been forced to read. "Divine Poetry," Rhetoric, and History were set against the "useless and boring controverseries and verbal wranglings [which] have no power to stir the soul." Geography, too, is recommended as an alternative subject; how much better it would be, he told his fellow students, if instead of wasting time on useless philosophical disputation they toured the whole earth with the help of a map and saw the places made famous by history and literature. Milton in this prolusion often talks in strains strongly reminiscent of Francis Bacon, whose attack in *The Advancement of Learning* on the barrenness and mere verbalism of scholastic philosophy had obviously impressed him. The second prolusion discusses the Pythagorean and Platonic notion of the music of the spheres, a notion which haunted Milton throughout his life, appealing both to his love of music and his sense of order and hierarchy, as well as to his passionate belief in purity and chastity (by which he did not mean celibacy), for only the pure and chaste could ever hope to hear that divine harmony. The fact that Milton was known in Cambridge as "The Lady of Christ's"

indicates the conspicuousness of his high idealism and his aloofness
from the horseplay and the immoralities that were not uncommon
among the undergraduates of the time.

The young Milton began his poetic career with verse paraphrases
of Psalms and Ovidian Latin elegies—the Christian and the Humanist
each producing his own kind of verse. One of the main problems of
his career was to be the possibility of the fusion of these two strains
and the nature of the context within which they might be fused; but
it is significant that he began by keeping them separate. There seems
little enough connection between his version of Psalm 136, written
in 1624—

> Let us with a gladsome mind
> Praise the Lord, for he is kind,
> For his mercies aye endure,
> Ever faithful, ever sure—

and a set of elegiac verses written probably in the same year:

> . . . Ecce novo campos Zephyritis gramine vestit
> Fertilis, et vitreo rore madescit humus.

> See, the bountiful daughter of Zephyr dresses the fields in new grass,
> and the earth is moist with glistering dew.

The Latin verses show a luxuriance, a relish of nature and, a little
later, of female beauty which find no place in his early English verse.
His first formal poem of any length in English is probably the "Ode
on the Death of a Fair Infant Dying of a Cough" (which Milton
dates "Anno Aetatis 17," but which appears to have been written in
his twentieth year, in 1628), and here he does use both classical
mythology and Christian ideas. The poem is an exercise, skillful
enough in some of its parts, but inadequately integrated. The first
part has Ovidian reminiscences as well as some Spenserian touches:

> For since grim Aquilo his charioteer
> By boist'rous rape th' Athenian damsel got,
> He thought it touched his deity full near,
> If likewise he some fair one wedded not;
> Thereby to wipe away th' infamous blot
> Of long uncoupled bed and childless eld,
> Which 'mongst the wanton gods a foul reproach was held.

Later, a more individual note is heard, a note that was to sound more
clearly in "Lycidas":

> Yet art thou not inglorious in thy fate;
> For so Apollo, with unweeting hand,

> Whilom did slay his dearly-loved mate,
> Young Hyacinth, born on Eurotas' strand,
> Young Hyacinth, the pride of Spartan land;
>   But then transformed him to a purple flower:
> Alack, that so to change thee Winter had no power.

The infant, he continues, cannot be dead: she must be in some happy sphere above. Perhaps she was a fallen star, now reinstated by Jove? Or was she Astraea, "that just Maid who once before /Forsook the hated earth," now revisiting us? Or Mercy, or Truth? The speculations are ingenious, but inorganic. In the end, he tells the mother (who was his own elder sister: the infant was his niece) to cease lamenting:

> Think what a present thou to God hast sent,
> And render him with patience what he lent;
>   This if thou do, he will an offspring give
> That till the world's last end shall make thy name to live.

The concluding consolation is perfunctory, just as the classical mythologizing is decorative rather than functional. At the same time, the poem shows considerable technical virtuosity.

Milton's quarrel with the Cambridge curriculum apparently led to a difference with his tutor and a brief rustication from the University in his second year. During the period of rustication, at home in his father's house in London, he wrote the first of his Latin "Elegies" (not, of course, elegies in the modern sense: the title refers to the verse form, not the content) to his old school-friend, Charles Diodati. The fluency and sureness of Milton's elegiac Latin verse show a remarkable mastery of the language; it shows, too, that Milton was steeped in Ovid, whose style he could reproduce with uncanny skill. He pretends in this poem to be happier by the Thames than he could be by the sedgy Cam. He describes his present life as altogether pleasant, reading, visiting the theater, or walking in the country in the spring sunshine, enjoying the beauties of nature and of handsome girls:

> Nos quoque lucus habet vicina consitus ulmo,
>   Atque suburbani nobilis umbra loci.
> Saepius hic, blandas spirantia sidera flammas,
>   Virgineos videas praeteriisse choros.
> Ah quoties dignae stupui miracula formae
>   Quae possit senium vel reparare Iovis!
> Ah quoties vidi superantia lumina gemmas,
>   Atque faces quotquot volvit uterque polus;
> Collaqueque bis vivi Pelopis quae brachia vincant,

Quaeque fluit puro nectare tincta via,
Et decus eximium frontis, tremulosque capillos,
Aurea quae fallax retia tendit Amor; . . .

And I also visit the grove where the elms stand close together, and the noble shade of a place just outside the city. Here you may often see maidens go dancing by, stars breathing gentle flames. Ah, how often have I been struck dumb by the miracle of a beautiful form which might even make old Jove young again! Ah, how often have I seen eyes brighter than gems and all the stars that either pole moves round, necks which excel the arms of the twice-living Pelops and the Way which flows coloured with pure nectar, a brow of superb beauty, waving tresses that are golden nets flung by deceiving Love. . . .

This section of the poem ends with an eloquent description of "Alma Venus," Venus the life-giver, deserting her traditional haunts to come to London. The poem is worth dwelling on because it reveals a side of Milton which the reader of his English poems only rarely sees; yet its existence was important for Milton's poetic career.

Milton was seventeen when he wrote the verse letter to Diodati. He was writing a lot of Latin elegiac verse at this time. It was in 1626, too, that he wrote the Latin poem "On the Death of the Beadle of Cambridge University," an ingenious and skillful exercise in mythologizing, and the more serious and formal Latin elegies on the deaths of the Bishop of Winchester (Lancelot Andrewes) and the Bishop of Ely. (No sign yet of the antiepiscopal violence which Milton was to show later.) Another Latin poem of the same year, in hexameters this time, was "In Quintum Novembris." ("On the Fifth of November"), a mock heroic poem on Guy Fawkes' Gunpowder Plot in which Milton's delight in coining epic phrases, in conjuring up an atmosphere of darkness and horror, and in rousing Satanic speeches is clearly seen. The careful investigator of *Paradise Lost* would do well to study Satan's speech and the description of the "place wrapped eternally in the darkness of night" ("locus aeterna septus caligine noctis") in this Latin poem.

Among Milton's other Latin poetry written at Cambridge is the Fourth Elegy, written in 1627, addressed to his old tutor Thomas Young, in which he appears to be showing off his skill; a poem in hexameters denying that Nature is subject to old age; and the Seventh Elegy, on spring and love, which begins with an invocation to Venus and a dialogue between the poet and Cupid, and which contains some of his most sensual poetry, ending with a conventional picture of himself as Cupid's victim. It is interesting to note that when he published these elegies in the 1645 volume of his poetry he appended to the seventh and last an apology for the wantonness and levity which had led him astray: but he did not suppress any

of the poems. The finest of all Milton's Latin poems is the Fifth Elegy
—written probably in 1628; Milton apparently did not number his
Elegies chronologically—"In Adventum Veris" ("On the Coming of
Spring"), where, in a rich Ovidian verse, he describes the revival
of nature, of his own poetic inspiration, and of love and joy and
passion. The poem breathes sensuous enjoyment and optimism; its
mythology is consistently Greek, its feeling pagan. "In Adventum
Veris" is the fullest and finest expression of a side of Milton he
rarely allows us to see again.

If Milton's Latin Elegies show his ability to manipulate in verse
a classical paganism, his Latin "Prolusions" give some insight into
his intellectual position during his years at Cambridge. He took
his stand against the notion that Nature was decaying, and he championed the idea that knowledge could and should move forward
in continuous progress. He was clearly on the optimistic side in the
debate on the Decline of the World which was a central theme in
the seventeenth century.[1] It was also in one of the prolusions that
he first committed himself to the choice of his native English as his
main poetic language in the future. In July, 1628, he wrote a "Vacation Exercise" in Latin, as an end-of-term entertainment, and after
the Latin fooling was over—Milton amused himself by playing with
some Aristotelian and Scholastic notions—he appended a personal
statement in English:

> Hail, native language, that by sinews weak
> Didst move my first endeavouring tongue to speak.

With that naïve and rather engaging egotism that remained a
characteristic of his throughout his life, he proceeded to tell his
fellow students that he had high ambitions as a poet in the English
language:

> Yet I had rather, if I were to choose,
> Thy service in some graver subject use,
> Such as may make thee search thy coffers round,
> Before thou clothe my fancy in fit sound:
> Such where the deep transported mind may soar
> Above the wheeling poles, and at Heav'ns door
> Look in, and see each blissful deity
> How he before the thunderous throne doth lie,
> Listening to what unshorn Apollo sings. . . .
> Then sing of secret things that came to pass
> When Beldam Nature in her cradle was;
> And last of kings and queens and heroes old,

[1] See Chapter 13, p. 489-90.

> Such as the wise Demodocus once told
> In solemn songs at King Alcinous' feast,
> While sad Ulysses' soul and all the rest
> Are held with his melodious harmony
> In willing chains, and sweet captivity.

He proposed to write grave poetry about the gods, about the creation of the world, and about human heroes. As for style, he wished his native language to bring him

> Not those new-fangled toys, and trimming slight
> Which takes our late fantastics with delight;
> But cull those richest robes and gay'st attire,
> Which deepest spirits and choicest wits desire.

It is doubtful whether Milton was specifically referring here to Donne and the metaphysical style; he was probably repudiating the meretricious ingenuity of some of his fellow students.

Milton was also an accomplished writer of Italian verse, and he wrote a number of Italian sonnets, probably in 1628, which, like his Latin poems, show a side of him that he hesitated to reveal in English. These poems show him as the lover, in Petrarchan style, of a foreign lady—apparently called Emilia. The expression is highly stylized, but there is a grace and a charm about much of the expression, notably in the sonnet that begins

> Qual in colle aspro, al imbrunir di sera
>   L'avvezza giovinetta pastorella
>   Va bagnando l'herbetta strana e bella
>   Che mal si spande a disusata spera
> Fuor di sua natia alma primavera, . . .

> As, on a rugged hill, when twilight darkens,
>   The young shepherdess, familiar with the place,
>   Keeps watering a strange and beautiful little plant
>   Which feebly spreads its leaves in the unfamiliar clime,
> Far from its native fostering springtime. . . .

One of the Italian sonnets is addressed to Diodati, telling him "con maraviglia" of his conversion to love—love not of a conventional golden-haired, red-cheeked girl, but of a "pellegrina bellezza," a foreign beauty, with lovely black eyes, the ability to speak more than one language, and an enchanting gift of song. Another gives a portrait of himself, whom he describes as gentle, candid, and steadfast, unyielding except to the arrows of Love. One of the Italian poems is a *canzone*, in which he defends his writing in Italian on the grounds that that is the language of Love. It is interesting that he imagines men and girls teasing him for writing in foreign language by assuring him that his proper language is English, in which already "the immortal guerdon of eternal leaves is putting forth its shoots to crown your locks." He was still in training to be a major English poet.

In 1629, while still at Cambridge, Milton wrote his first wholly successful English poem. This was "On the Morning of Christ's Nativity." In his Sixth Elegy—a Latin letter addressed to Charles Diodati in December, 1629—he announced that he was "singing of the heaven-born King, harbinger of peace, and of the happy centuries promised in the holy books," and the poem appears to have been intended as the first of a series in a high religious vein, celebrating different occasions of the Christian year. It consists of an introduction and hymn, both done with a combination of deliberate quaintness in imagery and conceits and a studied simplicity of feeling which produced a remarkable effect. Tillyard has compared the poem to a fifteenth-century Italian painting of the Nativity, with its combination of brilliant coloring and naïve juxtaposition of realistic and symbolic detail. It has indeed a remarkable pictorial quality, but it also has an interesting musical quality both in the handling of the language and in the form of the whole. In structure it suggests an "introduction and trio" in seventeenth-century music, with the former (in rhyme royal) more heavily orchestrated than the latter (the hymn, in an eight-lined stanza mingling short and long lines). There is a sense of movement in the poem, too: the poem states in the fourth and last stanza of the introduction that he is bringing his ode as an offering to the infant Christ—

> O run, prevent them   [i.e., come before the Wise Men]
> with thy humble ode,
> And lay it lowly at his blessed feet—

and by the end of the poem the guiding star has stopped over the birthplace, the journey of the Magi is over, and the gifts have been delivered. But the real theme of the poem is the rout of pagan gods and superstitions by the divine Babe, who figures as a classical hero rather than as the suffering servant. The note of celebration is struck in the opening line:

> This is the month, and this the happy morn,

while the first stanza of the hymn illustrates the deliberately baroque quality of the imagery:

> It was the Winter wild,
> While the Heav'n-born child,

> All meanly wrapt in the rude manger lies;
> Nature in awe to him
> Had dofft her gaudy trim,
>   With her great Master so to sympathize:
> It was no season then for her
> To wanton with the sun, her lusty paramour.

Milton goes on to give a picture of peace descending on the world at the nativity: the fourth stanza of the hymn banishes images of war and the fifth brings the poem to a temporary stop with its careful building up of a sense of hush:

> But peaceful was the night
> Wherein the Prince of light
>   His reign of peace upon the earth began:
> The winds, with wonder whist,
> Smoothly the waters kiss't,
>   Whispering new joys to the mild Ocean,
> Who now hath quite forgot to rave,
> While Birds of Calm sit brooding on the charméd wave.

The shepherds on the lawn who "sat simply chatting in a rustic row" are gradually made aware of the arrival of the "mighty Pan." The Music of the Spheres (a favorite notion of Milton's) assails their ears, and the glittering ranks of angels, guarding the divine order of the universe of which the musical harmony is the audible symbol, appear to their sight. With the picture of the divine music ringing out, the poem rises to its highest point ("Ring out ye crystal spheres") before gradually dying away to its close. For an ecstatic moment Milton's imagination would like to believe that the age of gold has been brought back to earth, and he gives an eloquent picture of its imminent arrival:

> And speckl'd vanity
> Will sicken soon and die,
>   And leprous sin will melt from earthly mould,
> And Hell itself will pass away,
> And leave her dolorous mansions to the peering day.
>
> Yea, Truth and Justice then
> Will down return to men,
>   Th' enamel'd arras of the rainbow wearing,
> And Mercy set between
> Thron'd in celestial sheen,
>   With radiant feet the tissued clouds down steering,
> And Heav'n as at some festival
> Will open wide the gates of her high palace hall.

Milton checks this fancy with reluctance: this is not yet to be, and he goes on to give a most cunningly developed picture of the old order being routed by the new; the oracle of Apollo is now dumb, the local classical divinities pass mourning from their haunted springs and dales, "the Lars and Lemures moan with midnight plaint," the pagan gods of ancient Palestine flee away, and

> The brutish gods of Nile as fast,
> Isis and Orus and the Dog Anubis haste.

The infant Christ, like the infant Hercules strangling snakes in his cradle, "can in his swaddling bands control the damned crew." The ode then moves to a picture of the Babe being laid to rest guarded by the hierarchic orders of angels:

> And all about the courtly stable
> Bright harness'd angels sit in order serviceable.

This image of rank, order, courtliness, and stability gives Milton's conception of a harmonious universe, and on this note the poem ends.

Milton never wrote another poem quite in this style. His ode on the Passion, written soon afterward in an endeavor to continue the religious series, was left unfinished after eight labored stanzas; "this subject the author finding to be above the years he had when he wrote it, and nothing satisfied with what was begun, left it unfinished," as Milton noted later when he included the poem in the 1645 volume. Christ's passion was not a congenial subject to Milton; he preferred the heroic to the crucified Christ, his own temperament combining with the Protestant tradition to reject any mystical agonizing over the cross in favor of celebrating the divine hero who combats error and evil and by strength of will is able to resist all temptation. As we shall see, Paradise for Milton was regained not by Christ crucified but by Christ, "a second Adam in the wilderness," reenacting Adam's temptation and this time resisting instead of falling as Adam did. The Passion was not therefore a subject to which Milton's genius rose, and he rightly stopped the poem midway after experimenting unsuccessfully with a number of over-elaborate devices for expressing grief.

In his Latin elegiacs addressed to Diodati in December, 1629, Milton had mentioned that he was composing, as well as his "Nativity Ode," something simpler to be played on his native reed, and this may refer to the cheerful fragment "On May Morning":

> Now the bright morning star, day's harbinger,
> Comes dancing from the East, and leads with her
> The flowery May, who from her green lap throws
> The yellow cowslip and the pale primrose.

Or perhaps the reference is to "L'Allegro" and "Il Penseroso," which are now thought to have been written at Cambridge, probably late in his residence there. These two companion poems are skillful exercises in creating a mood by appropriate imagery and tone. "L'Allegro" opens with a mock-violent dismissal of "loathéd Melancholy" in a crashing of chords, after which the smoothly tripping solo instrument takes up the main theme. The happily modulated lines in which Milton describes a day in the life of the cheerful man show appropriate mythological and pastoral imagery developed in order to build up a mood of contented living. It is a carefully stylized picture, with the description of Euphrosyne, mirthful daughter of the west wind and the dawn, of a vine-covered rustic cottage, of milkmaids singing, mowers whetting their scythes, and shepherds making love under the hawthorn. The poem is full of light and movement. Its structure is chronological, beginning with "the dappled dawn" rising to the accompaniment of the lark's song, and going through a day of cheerful pastoral activities until sunset turns l'Allegro's thought to tournaments, pageants, poetry, and music. Milton exploits classical mythology, English folklore, and medieval romance in the course of this variegated poem. A sense of the dignity and orderliness of agricultural labor, which was to emerge again and again in Milton's poetry, gives a certain weight of significance to the pastoral imagery, which remains nevertheless lighthearted in tone:

> While the plowman near at hand
> Whistles o'er the furrowed land,
> And the milkmaid singeth blithe,
> And the mower whets his scythe,
> And every shepherd tells his tale
> Under the hawthorn in the dale.

There is a happy stylization here, a stylization even more deliberately cultivated in such an image as

> Hard by a cottage chimney smokes
> From betwixt two aged oaks,

with its careful symmetry. This is a very formal art; every activity has its proper symbols, which link the poem up at all points with a complex tradition in both art and life. In "Il Penseroso" the images are organized to present a mood of contemplation and grave intellectual activity. The coloring of this poem is darker than that of "L'Allegro": moonlight, dark woods, the song of the nightingale are appropriate symbols here. The sound of the far-off curfew, the glowing embers of a dying fire half-lighting a gloomy room, the midnight lamp of the lonely student in the tower—these images are as stylized as their counterparts in "L'Allegro," and distill a mood in the same way. Though the verse form of the two poems is the same, the pace of "Il Penseroso" is slower. Music is a pleasure to both l'Allegro and il Penseroso, but in the latter it is associated with religion and study.

> But let my due feet never fail
> To walk the studious cloisters pale,
> And love the high embowéd roof,
> With antique pillars massy proof,
> And storied windows richly dight
> Casting a dim religious light.
> There let the pealing organ blow
> To the full-voic'd choir below
> In service high and anthems clear. . . .

There is an Anglican (if not a Catholic) feeling here: Milton had not yet become suspicious of cloisters and stained glass windows and the Anglican service.

Milton took his B.A. at Cambridge in 1629 and his M.A. in 1632, then retired to his father's house in Horton, Buckinghamshire, to continue the task of preparing himself to be a great poet. Before he left Cambridge he had written, in addition to the poems already discussed, two "conceited" epitaphs (very much in style at the time) on the university carrier, an epitaph on the Marchioness of Winchester in the simpler style of Ben Jonson at his most lapidary, a sonnet on the nightingale showing a skillful blend of Italian, classical, and other influences, the more "metaphysical" sonnet in praise of Shakespeare which appears in the Second Folio of 1632, and, soon after his twenty-third birthday—in December, 1631—the sonnet "How soon hath Time, the subtle thief of youth," in which he reflects on his slowly developing maturity. Milton refused to allow himself to be hurried in his task of self-preparation. In a letter to a friend, of which two drafts are extant and with which he sent this sonnet, he replies to his friend's admonishments about his not entering on a profession. The friend appears to have suggested "that too much love of learning is in fault, and that I have given up my self to dream away my years in the arms of studious retirement like Endymion with the Moon." Milton replies that it is not "a poor regardless and unprofitable sin of curiosity" that holds him back (for how could that prevail against "a desire of honour and repute and immortal fame"?), nor "the endless delight of speculation, but this very consideration of that great commandment" (about using one's talent) that leads to his not pressing forward; such a consideration "keeps off, with a sacred reverence and religious advisement how best to undergo—not taking thought of being late, so it give advantage to be more fit."

At Horton, where his father had retired, Milton—to quote his own account in the Latin *Second Defence*—"enjoyed an interval of uninterrupted leisure, which I entirely devoted to the perusal of the Greek and Latin classics; though I occasionally visited the metropolis, either for the sake of purchasing books, or of learning something new in mathematics or in music, in which I, at that time, found a source of pleasure or amusement." He was also reading the Christian Fathers and a great deal of history, and probably much else besides. His poetic achievement was to be based on a solid foundation of knowledge. His actual poetic output during his nearly six years at Horton was small: "On Time" (if this was not written towards the end of his period in Cambridge), "Upon the Circumcision," "At a Solemn Music," *Arcades* (possibly earlier), *Comus*, and "Lycidas," together with a translation of Psalm 114 into Greek hexameters, and a verse letter in Latin hexameters to his father. "On Time" shows Milton experimenting most successfully with the verse paragraph, probably with the Italian *canzone* in mind. The manipulation of the varying line lengths, expanding or contracting to respond to the shifts of emphasis and interest until the final soaring upward in triumph of Eternity over Time—

Triumphing over Death and Chance and thee O Time—

is handled with great skill. "Upon the Circumcision" tries to apply a similar technique to an uncongenial theme, and the result is unhappy: once again, Milton was uncomfortable in handling the theme of Christ's suffering. "At a Solemn Music" repeats the success of "On Time" in a poem of very similar structure. As Time and Eternity are set against each other in the latter poem, with Eternity soaring out in the climax, so in the latter earthly music and the divine Music of the Spheres answer each other, with the heavenly music sounding out in the end in triumphant chorus. These two short poems, in which the form is molded by the thought and emotion, show Milton already developing an architectonic power and a sure control over verse movement. They show him leaving behind the influence of Giles Fletcher's *Christ's Victory and Triumph* and Sylvester's transla-

tion of Du Bartas' *Divine Weeks*, which had been so strong in his
early religious poetry, to forge a style of his own.

Arcades shows Milton in a new role, as is made clear by the subtitle, "Part of an Entertainment presented to the Countess Dowager
of Derby at Harefield by some noble persons of her family, who
appear on the scene in pastoral habit. . . ." Milton was probably
invited to contribute to this noble entertainment by the musician
Henry Lawes, who wrote the music for *Arcades*, as for *Comus*. Milton's model was the Jonsonian masque, but there is an Elizabethan
freshness about the songs, and a controlled grace about the aristocratic compliment which is the purpose of the whole entertainment,
that are not quite Jonsonian. It is a simple enough affair. The "noble
persons of her family" in pastoral habit move across the lawn toward
the Countess' country house singing the first song:

> Look nymphs, and shepherds look,
> What sudden blaze of majesty
> Is that which we from hence descry,
> Too divine to be mistook:
>   This, this is she
> To whom our vows and wishes bend;
> Here our solemn search hath end.

After three more such stanzas, the Genius of the Wood (a part played
by Lawes) approaches and addresses the members of the Countess'
family in courtly tones:

> Stay gentle swains, for though in this disguise
> I see bright honour sparkle through your eyes. . . .

With considerable delicacy Milton moves this speech from compliment to the Countess to a discussion of his favorite Music of the
Spheres and back to the Countess again. The Genius of the Wood
describes his beneficent work on the Countess' estate, and then goes
on to talk of his other activities:

> But else in deep of night, when drowsiness
> Hath lock'd up mortal sense, then listen I
> To the celestial Sirens' harmony,
> That sit upon the nine enfolded spheres
> And sing to those that hold the vital shears
> And turn the adamantine spindle round
> On which the fate of gods and men is wound.
> Such sweet compulsion doth in music lie,
> To lull the daughters of Necessity
> And keep unsteady Nature to her law

> And the low world in measur'd motion draw
> After the heavenly tune, which none can hear
> Of human mold with gross unpurged ear;
> And yet such music worthiest were to blaze
> The peerless height of her immortal praise,
> Whose lustre leads us. . . .

A second song follows, the delicate, lightly dancing

> O'er the smooth enamell'd green
> Where no print of step hath been,
>   Follow me as I sing,
>   And touch the warbled string. . . .

—which has overtones both of Puck and of Ariel. The final song, with its strangely moving opening

> Nymphs and shepherds dance no more

brings the entertainment to a close, concluding with a final compliment to the Countess:

> Such a rural Queen
> All Arcadia hath not seen.

This is an aristocratic art, Elizabethan in feeling, courtly in tone, yet always essentially simple in manner. These songs give us some basis for speculating about what Milton might have developed into had he been a contemporary of Sidney and Spenser in fact as he was in many ways in spirit. One does not readily think of Milton as a courtly poet, or as writing from halfway up Fortune's Hill with his eye on the summit; but *Arcades* does show him for once in this role.

Milton's next aristocratic entertainment, "A Mask presented at Ludlow Castle" (generally called *Comus*, but that was not Milton's title), is a more elaborate affair. That Milton should have been commissioned to write this masque indicates that he had come to be regarded with favor by the kind of aristocratic artistic circles in which Henry Lawes was so well established. The Dowager Countess of Derby, for whom he wrote *Arcades*, lived at Harefield, only a few miles from where Milton was living at Horton, and the Earl of Bridgewater, for whose inauguration as Lord President of Wales *Comus* was written, was the Countess' stepson. So we can see how the young poet came to be invited to collaborate with Lawes in producing a masque for the Ludlow Castle entertainment. But history and his own temperament were against Milton's exploiting further his aristocratic connections and their accompanying possibilities of patronage. The issues that were to produce the Civil War were already dividing the nation: Charles I was in the midst of his sustained and ultimately unsuccessful attempt to govern without Parliament and impose his view of Church and State on the country. At the same time, something in Milton's own character led him to base his courtly entertainment on his passionately held doctrine of the mystical virtues of chastity, an odd theme for a celebratory masque at an earl's castle, and one which must have caused some eyebrow-raising at the first performance, in spite of the masque's undoubted popularity.

Comus was first published anonymously in 1637: nothing else by Milton (except the Shakespeare sonnet) had yet been published. It appeared with a dedication to the son of the Earl of Bridgewater by Henry Lawes, which includes an interesting indication of the masque's popularity: "Although not openly acknowledged by the author, yet it is a legitimate offspring, so lovely and so much desired that the copying of it has tired my pen to give my several friends satisfaction, and brought me to a necessity of producing it to the public view." The reason why Milton did not "openly acknowledge" the work is suggested by the quotation from Virgil's *Eclogues* which he chose as epigraph:

> Eheu quid volui mihi! floribus austrum
> Perditus. . . .

> Alas, what wretchedness have I brought upon myself!
> I have let loose the south wind upon my flowers . . .

He had written the masque because he had been requested to do so, but he did not feel himself to be really ready. So in "Lycidas," wrung from him in 1637 by "bitter constraint and sad occasion dear," he began by explaining that for a second time he had been compelled by events to pluck the as yet unripe fruit of his art:

> Yet once more, O ye laurels, and once more
> Ye myrtles brown, with ivy never sere,
> I come to pluck your berries harsh and crude,
> And with forc'd fingers rude
> Shatter your leaves before the mellowing year.

In September, 1637—two months before completing "Lycidas" and a month and a half after the drowning of Edward King, which was the occasion of the poem—he wrote in a Latin letter to Charles Diodati: "Do you ask me what I am thinking of? With God's help, of immortal fame! And what am I doing? Growing my wings and preparing for flight; but as yet my Pegasus rises on very tender pinions."

This picture of careful self-preparation to write great poetry is unmatched in the history of English literature. It shows, among other things, that Milton had the high ideal of poetry first formulated in the Renaissance: his Humanism and his Christianity combined to produce and define his poetic ambition.

Comus is in the Elizabethan masque tradition, one of the last English works of its kind. Book X of the *Odyssey*, Platonic and neo-Platonic philosophy, Spenser's description of the Bower of Bliss in Book II of the *Faerie Queene*, William Browne's *Inner Temple Masque* (treating of Circe and Ulysses), Jonson's *Pleasure Reconciled to Virtue* (a masque where Comus figures as a glutton), Peele's *Old Wives Tale*, Fletcher's *The Faithful Shepherdess*, each suggested something to Milton, and it is worth listing these varied influences if only to illustrate Milton's remarkable ability to synthesize effortlessly the results of wide reading. *Comus* opens with the attendant spirit (played by Lawes) speaking, in the calm recitative of formal blank verse, the introductory expository speech:

> Before the starry threshold of Jove's court
> My mansion is, where those immortal shapes
> Of bright aerial spirits live insphered
> In regions mild of calm and serene air,
> Above the smoke and stir of this dim spot
> Which men call Earth, . . .

He speaks of the tutelary deities of the region (managing to pay a compliment to the Earl of Bridgewater while doing so), tells of the peer's daughter and two sons coming "through the perplex'd paths of this drear wood" to greet their father, and warns of Comus the enchanter, son of Bacchus and Circe, who lies in wait to trap the unwary into his "sensual sty." He departs, and Comus enters with his rout of monsters (men and women transformed into beasts). Comus' speech, sharply distinct from the earlier formal blank verse, moves trippingly, almost tipsily, in its tones of revelry:

> The star that bids the shepherd fold,
> Now the top of heav'n doth hold;
> And the gilded car of day
> His glowing axle doth allay
> In the steep Atlantic stream, . . .
> Meanwhile, welcome joy and feast,
> Midnight shout and revelry,
> Tipsy dance and jollity. . . .
> Now to the moon in wavering morrice move,
> And on the tawny sands and shelves
> Trip the pert fairies and the dapper elves.

> By dimpled brook and fountain brim
> The wood-nymphs, deck'd with daisies trim,
> Their merry wakes and pastimes keep:
> What hath night to do with sleep?

The lilt to this sounds innocent enough (though the ear accustomed
to Milton's cadences will note the occasional drunken lurch); but one
of the themes of the masque is the distinction between guilty and
innocent mirth, and after some thirty-five lines the tone changes, to
make clear that we are here dealing with the former variety:

> Come, let us our rites begin,
> 'Tis only daylight that makes sin,
> Which these dun shades will ne'er report.
> Hail, goddess of nocturnal sport,
> Dark-veil'd Cotytto, t' whom the secret flame
> Of midnight torches burns; . . .

A dance by Comus and his company follows, broken off by the entry
of the Lady, who has become separated from her brothers and is lost
in the wood. Comus falls into a more formal speech—

> Break off, break off, I feel the different pace
> Of some chaste footing near about this ground—

and lays his plans. The Lady enters, and in flexible verse with conversational overtones explains her plight:

>   . . . I should be loth
> To meet the rudeness and swill'd insolence
> Of such late wassailers; yet O where else
> Shall I inform my unacquainted feet
> In the blind mazes of this tangl'd wood?

As she dwells on her situation, the verse becomes slower and more
stately:

> They left me then, when the gray-hooded Ev'n
> Like a sad votarist in palmer's weed
> Rose from the hindmost wheels of Phoebus' wain.

But she senses the presence of Comus, and the movement of the
verse changes again:

> What might this be? A thousand fantasies
> Begin to throng into my memory
> Of calling shapes, and beck'ning shadows dire,
> And airy tongues, that syllable men's names
> On sands and shores and desert wildernesses.

She recalls her virtue and her chastity, and announces in somewhat stilted verse her confidence in them, then sings a song, in the hope of attracting her brothers' attention. The song is about Echo and Narcissus, a perfect piece of mythological delicacy, with the final two lines swelling out to a profounder meaning:

> Sweet Echo, sweetest nymph that liv'st unseen
> Within thy airy shell
> By slow Meander's margent green,
> And in the violet embroider'd vale
> Where the love-lorn nightingale
> Nightly to thee her sad song mourneth well:
> Canst thou not tell me of a gentle pair
> That likest thy Narcissus are?
> O if thou have
> Hid them in some flow'ry cave,
> Tell me but where
> Sweet Queen of Parley, Daughter of the Sphere.
> So mayst thou be translated to the skies,
> And give resounding grace to all Heav'n's harmonies.

Comus is ravished by the song, which moves him to an eloquent expression of admiration:

> But such a sacred and home-felt delight,
> Such sober certainty of waking bliss,
> I never heard till now.

He hails the Lady in tones reminiscent of Caliban's attitude to Miranda, and the ensuing dialogue shows him playing skillfully the role of guide and comforter to the Lady. He knows the wood, and will help her find her brothers, whom he saw recently:

> Two such I saw, what time the labour'd ox
> In his loose traces from the furrow came,
> And the swink't hedger at his supper sat.

If he is adroit enough to convince the Lady, it is no wonder that he also convinces the reader, who finds in this part of the masque some of the most charming verse, expressive of quiet joy in the English countryside and satisfaction in agricultural labor well done (which we know to have been Milton's own attitude), put into Comus' mouth. We have echoes of Puck:

> I know each lane and every alley green,
> Dingle or bushy dell of this wild wood

and of the Spenserian pastoralists. The Lady, not surprisingly, agrees to follow Comus, and as they depart the two brothers enter, searching for their sister. "Unmuffle, ye faint stars," the elder brother cries, in tones that might have been used by Romeo or some other of Shakespeare's early heroes, but as the dialogue between the brothers develops, and the elder preaches to the younger Milton's grand doctrine of the mystical virtue of chastity that always preserves from harm, something of the dramatic life goes out of the verse. The statement of the doctrine is eloquent enough, but didactically rather than dramatically.

The attendant spirit, disguised as the shepherd Thyrsis, then enters and tells of Comus, his nature and his threat, in a fine set piece of descriptive verse. The younger brother is appalled at the threat to his sister, but the elder reaffirms the young Milton's view that virtue always guarantees the safety of its possessor:

> Virtue may be assail'd, but never hurt,
> Surpris'd by unjust force, but not enthrall'd

—a view which his later contemplation of the nature of temptation led him to modify. Thyrsis explains about the magic herb which will undo Comus' enchantments, and they depart, the scene changing to Comus' palace, where the Lady is now confronted with Comus in his true colors. This is the most dramatic scene in the masque, and the give and take between Comus and the Lady is done with great spirit. The claims of sensual pleasure are pressed by Comus with a persuasive charm—this is the misuse of rhetoric which Milton was to show more profoundly in the speeches of Satan and his followers in *Paradise Lost*. Again we have the slightly tipsy lilt to the speech (faintly reminiscent of Eve's "distempered" speech on returning to Adam after eating the fatal apple):

> Why are you vext, Lady? Why do you frown?
> Here dwell no frowns nor anger; from these gates
> Sorrow flies far. . . .

To the Lady's lively reply Comus returns an even more skillful speech, denouncing "lean and sallow abstinence" and painting a seductive picture of Nature's bounty, meant to be used. He goes on:

> If all the world
> Should in a pet of temperance feed on pulse,
> Drink the clear stream and nothing wear but frieze,
> Th' all-giver would be unthank'd, would be unprais'd, . . .
> And we should serve him as a grudging master,
> As a penurious niggard of his wealth,

And live like Nature's bastards, not her sons,
Who would be quite surcharg'd with her own weight,
And strangl'd with her waste fertility; . . .

The picture of Nature choked by her own unused abundance that
Comus goes on to paint is brilliantly done, and shows Milton's gift
for dramatic verse. For a man of his temperament, and his strongly
held personal views, it is remarkable how he is able to get inside
Comus' character (as later he is to get inside Satan's) and put some of
his most persuasive verse into Comus' mouth. This is—perhaps it
need hardly be said—a deliberately dramatic device, with Comus as
with Satan, and to argue that because it is successful Satan is the
"real" hero of *Paradise Lost* is as absurd as to argue that Comus is
the real hero of Milton's masque—both views show a basic misunderstanding of the nature of Milton's art.

We need not follow the plot through. The Lady is rescued, Sabrina is hailed, in another charming song, to come and release her
from the chair to which she is magically bound, and *Comus* ends
with a cluster of songs and dances in true masque style. It is characteristic of Milton that after the dance—*innocent* mirth this time, but
perhaps the distinction is not as clear as Milton intended—the attendant spirit, in his song, proclaims that "enough is as good as a feast"—

Back shepherds, back, enough your play,
Till next sunshine holiday; . . .

The epilogue, spoken by the spirit, suggests Ariel again:

To the ocean now I fly,
And those happy climes that lie
Where day never shuts his eye,

but it ends with a Miltonic moral:

Love virtue, she alone is free,
She can teach ye how to climb
Higher than the sphery chime;
Or, if virtue feeble were,
Heav'n itself would stoop to her.

Comus is a remarkable performance. Its freshness, variety, sureness of touch, and mastery of different tones show how far Milton
had gone in developing high technical skill. Its variety is perhaps
excessive; the different styles—including a not very successful imitation of the Greek *stichomythia* in some of the dialogue—are not always adequately subdued to the total design. But we must remember
that this is a masque, meant to be sung and acted, and without the

music and the somewhat stylized dramatic action it loses a great deal.

"Lycidas" first appeared (signed simply J. M.) in 1638, in a collection of elegies (mostly Latin) on Edward King, a fellow student of Milton's at Cambridge, who had been drowned in the Irish Sea. The sudden cutting off of a man of great promise, destined for the Church, forced Milton to face the general question of premature death in talented and dedicated young men. It is not that, as has been claimed, "Lycidas" is about John Milton rather than Edward King. But the elegy is about Lycidas and not King—by expanding the individual King into a symbolic pastoral character, standing for the young man of promise in any context, Milton makes his death more significant and the problems faced by it more disturbing. How can one face the fact that, in a world where the wicked prosper and the most incompetent people survive to get high posts of leadership, the young man who dedicates himself to a life of ideal service to his country may be cut off before he has had an opportunity of completing his training and rendering his service? As a dedicated man himself, Milton saw the implications of King's death. By adopting the traditional form of the pastoral elegy Milton was able to bring together his concepts of priesthood and of bardship in the single symbolic figure of the good shepherd who pipes and tends his flock. Further, for Milton pastoral and agricultural activity always symbolized the most elemental aspects of human endeavor; there was for him something profoundly satisfying in contemplating the annual round of the seasons, each with its appropriate rural tasks (and this makes it difficult for him in *Paradise Lost* to accept agricultural labor as a curse imposed as a result of the Fall), so that the pastoral convention is not for him an otiose tradition, but a living art form with a genuine contemporary significance.

Classical, Christian, and personal elements are fused in "Lycidas" to make an elegy both highly formal and highly individual. The famous outburst against the Anglican clergy (Milton had begun by now to take sides in the religious quarrels of his time) is not simply a personal aside; if the theme of the poem is the premature death of the dedicated poet-priest, then surely it is relevant to consider the unhappy fact that unworthy poet-priests survive to mislead the people while worthy ones die young; yet the tone is highly personal. One can find a precedent in classical or Renaissance usage for everything Milton does in "Lycidas"; yet it remains a unique poem, with a quality and a flavor all its own. The poem moves from a slow and eloquent statement of the occasion of the poem to a reminiscence of his student days with King expressed in moving and elemental pastoral terms, thence to sad reflection on the inability of guardian angels to protect their own:

> What could the Muse herself that Orpheus bore,
> The Muse herself, for her enchanting son,
> Whom universal nature did lament
> When by the rout that made the hideous roar
> His gory visage down the stream was sent
> Down the swift Hebrus to the Lesbian shore?

Even Calliope, the muse of epic poetry, could not protect her son Orpheus against the fury of the Thracian bacchanals—a thought to which Milton returns again and again in his poetry. He then goes on to wonder whether after all it might not have been better to enjoy himself while he could instead of living an austere, dedicated life, in the hope of one day becoming a great poet:

> Alas! What boots it with uncessant care
> To tend the homely, slighted shepherd's trade,
> And strictly meditate the thankless muse?
> Were it not better done, as others use,
> To sport with Amaryllis in the shade,
> Or with the tangles of Neaera's hair?

The grave eloquence of the question marks its seriousness. The answer, given by Phoebus, that fame is the spur, and fame is not to be gained in earth but in heaven, is not a true resolution of the question, and the poem moves to a new start with the interrogation of those who might have been expected to protect Lycidas. The note of elegy sounds with ever more plangency as the sense of the inevitability of the fatal accident rises; Cambridge deplores her lost son, and St. Peter laments that such a one as Lycidas should have been taken when so many bad shepherds flourish. Disgust and anger, entering the very fabric of the verse, replace elegy here, but disgust and anger will not bring back Lycidas, and the poet returns to contemplate the dead shepherd, desperately covering his body with flowers to smother his grief and frustration, and then—in a magnificent and characteristically Miltonic surge of the verse—calling on the guardian angel of England to look homeward and see her plight. Geographical imagery here, giving the whole sense of the Celtic southwest corner of England and its place in British history and mythology, is handled with great skill, and artfully put at the service of the emotion, which is both elegiac and patriotic. The ending is a double one: first, the Christian consolation of Lycidas' place in Heaven, then the return to the poet piping his sad song but determined now that it is over to face the morrow with determination. The solution to the problem posed by the poem is to turn to the task that lies to hand so long as one can:

> Thus sang the uncouth swain to th' oaks and rills,
> While the still morn went out with sandals gray.
> He touch'd the tender stops of various quills,
> With eager thought warbling his Doric lay:
> And now the sun had stretch'd out all the hills,
> And now was dropt into the Western bay.
> At last he rose, and twitch'd his mantle blue:
> Tomorrow to fresh woods and pastures new.

It is a conclusion both classical, Christian, and Miltonic. In the sober morning light the poet turns to fresh woods and pastures new. One meets grief by the assertion of purpose—a very different conclusion from Keats' answer to a very similar question, "when I have fears that I may cease to be, before my pen has gleaned my teeming brain." Keats' solution was not to "work for the night is coming," but to

> . . . stand alone, and think
> Till love and fame to nothingness do sink.

Of course the greatness of "Lycidas" does not lie simply in the movement of the thought and the emotion. The handling of the verse paragraphs, the placing of the rhymes, the varying of the line lengths, and all the devices Milton employs in order to combine the ceremonial with the personal without rending the fabric of the poem, show a mature poet at work. He may have thought his art unripe; but in fact this kind of poetic art could mature no further. He could only go further as a poet by turning to a different kind of poetry. And by the time he did that, he, and his world, had changed significantly.

Milton's period of leisured self-preparation for poetry at Horton came to an end in 1638, when he embarked on a fifteen-month period of European travel, most of it spent in Italy. Professor Hanford has called Milton's Italian journey "one of the great *Wanderjahre* of literary history, a moment of contact between cultures comparable with the Italian journeys of Erasmus and of Goethe," and the description is apt enough, for Milton went abroad in a spirit of high purpose, to visit distinguished men of letters, absorb the atmosphere of Mediterranean culture, and establish, as it were, the European context of his ambitions as native English poet. He spent two months in Florence, where he demonstrated his skill as a Latin poet before one of the important literary societies there—one of the "private academies," as Milton called them, in which Italy at that time abounded, where literary men met for readings and conversation. "No time," wrote Milton of his Florentine stay in the *Second Defence*, "will ever abolish the agreeable recollections which I cherish of Jacob Gaddi, Carolo Dati, Frescobaldo, Coltellino, Bonomatthei, Clementillo, Francini, and many others. From Florence I went to Sienna, thence to Rome, where, after I had spent about two months in viewing the antiquities of that famous city . . . I continued my route to Naples. There I was introduced . . . to John Baptista Manso, Marquis of Villa, a nobleman of distinguished rank and authority, to whom Torquato Tasso, the illustrious poet, inscribed his book on friendship." Milton had a wonderful time in Italy, taking an active part in the cultural life of the cities he visited and making many friends. His friendship with Manso produced a set of complimentary verses in Latin hexameters entitled "Mansus," where he paid tribute to Tasso's patron and ended, characteristically, by talking about himself, expressing the wish that it would be his lot to find such a friend if he embarked on epic accounts of "our native kings," and of the wars of Arthur against the Saxons. Manso was also one of those Italians who addressed Latin complimentary verses to Milton, included in the prefatory matter to the 1645 edition of Milton's poems. The Italian visit produced a revival of Milton's Latin versifying; these included a poem to the Roman poet Giovanni Salzilli and several short tributes in hexameters to the Neapolitan singer, Leonora Baroni.

Although Milton spoke out freely on religious matters in Italy—he tells us in the *Second Defence* that on his departure Manso "gravely apologized for not having shown me more civility, which he said he had been restrained from doing, because I had spoken with so little reserve on matters of religion"—this did not prevent him from enjoying himself and making friends and admirers.

"When I was preparing to pass over into Sicily and Greece,"—to quote again from Milton's account in the *Second Defence*—"the melancholy intelligence I received of the civil commotions in England made me alter my purpose; for I thought it base to be travelling for amusement abroad, while my fellow-citizens were fighting for liberty at home." But he took his time about returning. He visited Rome again (where he estabished contact with the important musical circles there), and Florence, thence to Bologna, Ferrara, Venice (where he spent a month and shipped home the books he had collected in Italy), Verona, Milan, and along Lake Leman to Geneva, where he met the distinguished Protestant scholar and theologian Giovanni Diodati, uncle of his friend Charles Diodati. He finally reached England at the beginning of August, 1639, in that uneasy period between the settlement of the so-called First Bishops' War and the outbreak of the Second in 1640. Milton settled down in London, undertaking the education of his two orphaned nephews, Edward and John Philips, and later taking in also some other pupils. He pondered on education, and at the same time (not immediately seeing it as his duty to offer his services to the antiroyalist cause) meditated on topics for an epic and on plans for a drama on the subject of the Fall. His self-preparation as a poet was still continuing.

King Charles had summoned the Short Parliament in 1640 in the hope of getting a money vote, but Parliament insisted on redress of grievances first, and Charles dissolved Parliament in disgust after three weeks. The Second Bishops' War ended in October after the defeat of Charles' army by a Scottish force, and Charles had to summon Parliament again. This, the Long Parliament, turned at once to the punishment of those who had advised the King in his absolute course—notably the Earl of Strafford and Archbishop Laud—and then proceeded to legislate for the regularizing of parliamentary procedure and the curbing of the royal authority. The Long Parliament had a narrow Puritan majority, who introduced a bill for the abolition of episcopacy and the reorganizing of the Church. This "root and branch bill" aroused the strong opposition of the substantial minority who wished to see a moderate episcopacy and a certain amount of toleration in church matters (in other words, to revert to the position of the Church of England before Laud had imposed his uniform ceremonial and method of worship). The two sides engaged in a fierce pamphlet war, and it was into this war that Milton entered with an anonymous pamphlet supporting his old tutor Thomas Young. Bishop Hall had published, in December, 1640, a moderate enough defense of a limited episcopacy, under the title, *A Humble Remonstrance to the High Court of Parliament*. Young and a group of his fellow ministers wrote a reply (the authors' combined initials formed the word "Smectymnuus," under which name the pamphlet appeared), and this reply was in turn answered both by Hall and by James Ussher, Archbishop of Armagh. Milton joined in on Hall's side, his first pamphlet *Of Reformation in England and the Causes that have hitherto hindered it*, appearing just before the replies to Smectymnuus by Hall and Ussher and not directly referring to the controversy; but Milton's subsequent antiepiscopal pamphlets enter more directly into the controversy, and are concerned to refute Hall and Ussher. Milton produced five pamphlets in all on this subject, between April, 1641, and March, 1642, and their titles indicate the continuous dingdong nature of the argument. The second was *Of*

Prelatical Episcopacy, and whether it may be deduced from the Apostolical Times, by virtue of those Testimonies which are alleged to that purpose in some late treatises; one whereof goes under the name of James, Archbishop of Armagh. Then *Animadversions upon the Remonstrant's Defence against Smectymnuus* in July, 1641, and *The Reason of Church Government Urged against Prelaty* in February, 1642. In the same month as the latter appeared a pamphlet on the other side, whose title is also instructive: *A Modest Confutation of a Slanderous and Scurrilous Libel entitled Animadversions upon the Remonstrant's Defence against Smectymnuus.* And in March came Milton's *An Apology against a Pamphlet called a Modest Confutation of the Animadversions upon the Remonstrant against Smectymnuus.*

The main thought in Milton's antiprelatical pamphlets was that the English Reformation had not been completed in Tudor times, and now was the time to complete it. He has the true Protestant view of the Reformation, rejoicing to recall "how the bright and blissful Reformation (by divine power) struck through the black and settled night of ignorance and antichristian tyranny." He asks himself, in his first pamphlet, "how it should come to pass that England (having had this grace and honour from God, to be the first that should set up a standard for the recovery of lost truth, and blow the first evangelic trumpet to the nations, holding up, as from a hill, the new lamp of saving light to all Christians) should now be last and most unsettled in the enjoyment of that peace, whereof she taught the way to others." He replies by interpreting the ecclesiastical history of England from the time of Henry VIII, and distinguishing three "hinderers of reformation"—antiquarians (whom he distinguishes from "useful and laudable" antiquaries), libertines, and politicians. *Of Reformation in England* is a vigorously argued pamphlet, marshaling evidence from history and literature (he cites Dante, Petrarch, Chaucer, and Ariosto, as well as ecclesiastical writers) and pressing its points forcefully and with a certain dignity in a prose whose long sentences are managed with considerable rhetorical skill. *Of Prelatical Episcopacy* turns to the arguments of the other side, and refutes them point by point in what to the modern reader is tedious detail, though here, as in the former pamphlet, there comes through clearly Milton's view of the lamentable gap between the simple Gospel injunctions and the elaborate paraphernalia of ecclesiastical systems. Milton is particularly anxious to deny (as his opponents were anxious to maintain) that modern episcopacy could be deduced from the practice of apostolic times. "The pure and living precept of God's word only" is the proper guide for Christians. "But if any shall strive to set up his ephod and teraphim of antiquity against the brightness and perfection of the gospel; let him fear lest he and his Baal be turned into Bosheth." *Animadversions* deals in a more satirical way with Hall, whose arguments he sets out and replies to in question-and-answer form, often turning the argument *ad hominem* in what Milton considered a sportive manner. *The Reason of Church Government* (the first to appear with the author's name) is an elaborately reasoned defense of the presbyterian form of church government against the episcopal; there is no sportiveness here, only an earnest and scholarly argument. *An Apology* shows how the debate had deteriorated into personalities. Milton had himself been personally attacked by this time, and he replied in kind, showing his characteristic ability to identify himself with a cause and to regard autobiography as defense of the cause. This pamphlet is full of picturesque abuse, and parts are in a style of colloquial flippancy which, while popular in controversial literature of the time, does not wear well. This manner, with the progress of the debate forced upon Milton, led to a pettiness and lack of generosity that are found all too often in Milton's controversial prose.

There is something else, however, which is found in these antiprelatical pamphlets which is purely Miltonic and which throws much light on Milton's state of mind at this time. He was still the dedicated poet, though the necessities of the time might take him temporarily into other kinds of writing. On his return from Italy he had been full of poetic plans, and was desolated to find that his friend Charles Diodati, to whom he had looked forward to talking of his Italian triumphs and his literary intentions, had died the previous year. In the Latin elegy on Diodati—an eloquent and skillful pastoral elegy—he cannot resist saying something of the plans for an epic he had hoped to discuss with his friend. After repeating the refrain

> Ite domum impasti, domino iam non vacat, agni,
> Go home unfed, my lambs, your master now has no time for you,

he proceeds:

> Ipse ego Dardanias Rutupina per aequora puppes
> Dicam, et Pandrasidos regnum vetus Inogeniae,
> Brennumque Arviragumque duces, priscumque Belinum,
> Et tandem Armoricos Britonum sub lege colonos;
> Tum gravidam Arturo fatali fraude Iogernen,
> Mendaces vultus, assumptaque Gorlois arma,
> Merlini dolus. O, mihi tum si vita supersit,
> Tu procul annosa pendebis, fistula, pinu
> Multum oblita mihi, aut patriis mutata camenis

Brittonicum strides! Quid enim? omnia non licet uni
Non sperasse uni licet omnia. . . .

For my part, I shall tell of the Dardanian ships in the Rutupian sea, and of
the ancient kingdom of Inogen, daughter of Pandrasus, and of the chiefs, Bren-
nus and Arviragus, and old Belinus, and of the Armorican settlers who at last
came under British law; then of Igraine pregnant with Arthur by a fatal trick,
the features of Gorlois and his arms falsely assumed by Merlin's trickery. O
then, my pipe, if further life remains to me, you shall hang far away on some
old pine tree, wholly forgotten by me, or else sound forth in harsher tones a
British theme to your native muses. What then? One man cannot do everything, nor can one man hope for everything.

These were themes from early British history, and he intended to
choose among them for his epic. With the kindling of his imagination
at the prospect of a new and regenerate England arising out of the
completion of the Reformation for which he was pleading in his
antiprelatical pamphlets, he thought of himself more and more as
the poet of that brave new world, waiting for the completion of
God's deliverance to utter forth his mighty harmonies. He thinks now
more of divine than of secular subjects. But he does still think of
poetry, and his poetic ambitions are higher than ever. Who else but
Milton could end a pamphlet on church government as Milton ended
Of Reformation in England, with a passionate outburst expressing
his faith in a reformed and greater England of which he will be the
poet?

O how much more glorious will those former deliverances appear, when
we shall know them not only to have saved us from greatest miseries past, but
to have reserved us for greatest happiness to come! Hitherto thou hast but
freed us, and that not fully, from the unjust and tyrannous claim of thy foes;
now unite us entirely, and appropriate us to thyself, tie us everlastingly in
willing homage to the prerogative of thy eternal throne. . . .

Then, amidst the hymns and hallelujahs of saints, some one may perhaps
be heard offering at high strains in new and lofty measures to sing and celebrate thy divine mercies and marvellous judgments in this land throughout all
ages; whereby this great and warlike nation, instructed and inured to the fer-
vent and continual practice of truth and righteousness, and casting far from
her the rags of her old vices, may press on hard to that high and happy emulation to be found the soberest, wisest, and most Christian people at that day,
when thou, the eternal and shortly expected King, shalt open the clouds to
judge the several kingdoms of the world, and distribute national honours and
rewards to religious and just commonwealths, shalt put an end to all earthly
tyrannies, proclaiming thy universal and mild monarchy through heaven and
earth; where they undoubtedly, that by their labours, counsels, and prayers,
have been earnest for the common good of religion and their country, shall receive above the inferior orders of the blessed, the regal addition of princi-

palities, legions, and thrones into their glorious titles, and in supereminence of beatific vision, progressing the dateless and irrevoluble circle of eternity, shall clasp inseparable hands with joy and bliss in overmeasure for ever.

This is a remarkable outburst to find in a pamphlet on episcopacy. It is the true voice of the young Milton, but it is also the voice of his times, combining with the immense ambition of the poet the utopian optimism of the Puritan reformer. We must remember this tone of boundless optimism when we come to assess the nature of Milton's disillusion at the failure of the Commonwealth and the restoration of Charles II.

The personal note emerges in the most unexpected places in his prose pamphlets. In the *Animadversions* he turns suddenly from a contemptuous dismissal of one of the Remonstrant's arguments to contemplate with almost mystical fervor the coming heaven on earth. The prose is tremulous with excitement as he addresses God:

O perfect and accomplish thy glorious acts! for men may leave their works unfinished, but thou are a God, thy nature is perfection: shouldst thou bring us thus far onward from Egypt to destroy us in this wilderness, though we deserve, yet thy great name would suffer in the rejoicing of thine enemies, and the deluded hope of all thy servants. When thou hast settled peace in the church and righteous judgment in the kingdom, then shall all thy saints address their voices of joy and triumph to thee, standing on the shore of that Red Sea into which our enemies had almost driven us. And he that now for haste snatches up a plain ungarnished present as a thank-offering to thee, which could not be deferred in regard of thy so many late deliverances wrought for us one upon another, may then perhaps take up a harp, and sing thee an elaborate song to generations. . . . Come forth out of thy royal chambers, O Prince of all the kings of the earth! put on the invisible robes of thy imperial majesty, take up that unlimited sceptre which thy Almighty Father hath bequeathed thee; for now the voice of thy bride calls thee, and all creatures sigh to be renewed.

After this it is not surprising that in the *Apology for Smectymnuus*, after rebutting charges of unchastity made against him by his opponents, he goes on to elaborate his theory of chastity, explaining how he came to hold it, and the Platonic and Christian authorities for it, concluding significantly: "Nor did I slumber over that place [in the Bible] expressing such high rewards of ever accompanying the Lamb with those celestial songs to others inapprehensible, but not to those who were not defiled with women, which doubtless means fornication; for marriage must not be called a defilement."

Even in the serious and scholarly argument of *The Reason of Church Government* Milton manages to become autobiographical, beginning the second book by. expressing regret that the advance-

ment of knowledge should require controversy, which was not really
his task. "But when God commands to take the trumpet and blow a
dolorous or a jarring blast, it lies not in man's will what he shall say
or what he shall conceal." He explains that his "sharp but saving
words" are, unfortunately, necessary. "I should not," he goes on,
"choose this manner of writing, wherein knowing myself inferior to
myself, led by the genial power of nature to another task, I have the
use, as I may account it, but of my left hand." At this point, while
admitting that "I shall be foolish in saying more to this purpose," he
cannot resist the urge to go on and talk about his career and ambitions, mentioning the praise his poems had received in Italy, his determination "to fix all the industry and art I could unite to the
adorning of my native tongue," and the kinds of poetry he contemplated writing:

> Time serves not now, and perhaps I might seem too profuse to give any
> certain account of what the mind at home in the spacious circuits of her mus-
> ing hath liberty to propose to herself, though of highest hopes and hardest at-
> tempting; whether that epic form whereof the two poems of Homer and those
> other two of Virgil and Tasso are a diffuse, and the book of Job a brief, model:
> or whether the rules of Aristotle herein are strictly to be kept, or nature to be
> followed, which in them that know art and use judgement, is no transgression
> but an enriching of art: and lastly, what king or knight before the conquest
> might be chosen in whom to lay the pattern of a Christian hero. . . .

After epic, he goes on to consider tragedy, wondering "whether
those dramatic constitutions, wherein Sophocles and Euripides reign,
shall be found more doctrinal and exemplary to a nation." There are
dramatic models in Scripture, too, "a divine pastoral drama in the
Song of Solomon" and "the majestic image of a high and stately
tragedy" in the Apocalypse of St. John. Finally, he considers the possibilities of the lyric, either in the Greek style of Pindar or Callim-
achus or in the style of the Hebrew poetry of the Old Testament.
Milton concludes this autobiographical digression by explaining that
he was originally intended for the Church, "till coming to some maturity of years and perceiving what tyranny had invaded the church,
that he who would take orders must subscribe slave and take an oath
withal, which, unless he took with a conscience that would retch, he
must either straight perjure or split his faith; I thought it better to
prefer a blameless silence before the sacred office of speaking,
bought and begun with servitude and forswearing. Howsoever, thus
church-outed by the prelates, hence may appear the right I have to
meddle in these matters, as before the necessity and constraint appeared." It is clear already that Milton was not going to find it easy
to go along with any major Christian sect. Though he had thrown in

his lot with the Presbyterians, a few years later he was to complain in a sonnet of "the new forcers of conscience under the Long Parliament," and he moved ever closer to the Independents and to Cromwell, who supported them, finding himself eventually among the small Cromwellian group committed to the execution of the King.

It was Milton's precipitate marriage, probably in the spring of 1642, that helped to move him toward a more independent and liberal position in ecclesiastical as in other matters. After years of dedicated chastity, he suddenly turned all his passionate idealistic thought about a perfect mate onto a flighty young girl of royalist family, imagining that her dumbness in his presence was a sign of modest thoughtfulness and looking forward to an intellectual as well as a physical companionship which he felt he had fully earned. Both were rapidly disillusioned; and Mary Powell soon returned to her parents' home on a visit from which she did not return until a reconciliation was patched up in the summer of 1645. The emotional shock to Milton was enormous and, with his usual gift for deriving general conclusions from a personal situation, he immediately set himself to discover and to proclaim publicly the legal and other problems involved, and their solution. Marriage was meant to be a perfect companionship, spiritual, intellectual, and physical, and if through well-meaning misjudgment it turned out to be something very different, release should be made possible. This was the position he argued in *The Doctrine and Discipline of Divorce*, published in August, 1643. It was because his ideal of marriage was so high, not because he took a low view of it, that he pleaded for easiness of divorce. The personal note rings out with sad naïveté in Chapter III.

The soberest and best governed men are least practised in these affairs; and who knows not that the bashful muteness of a virgin may ofttimes hide all the unliveliness and natural sloth which is really unfit for conversation? Nor is there that freedom of access granted or presumed as may suffice to a perfect discerning till too late; and where any indisposition is suspected, what more usual than the persuasion of friends that acquaintance, as it increases, will amend all? And lastly, it is not strange though many who have spent their youth chastely, are in some things not so quick-sighted, while they haste too eagerly to light the nuptial torch, nor is it, therefore, that for a modest error a man should forfeit so great a happiness, and no charitable means to release him, since they who have lived most loosely, by reason of their bold accustoming prove most successful in their matches, because their wild affections, unsettling at will, have been as so many divorces to teach them experience. Whereas the sober man honouring the appearance of modesty, and hoping well of every social virtue under that veil, may easily chance to meet, if not with a body impenetrable, yet often with a mind to all other due conversation inaccessible, and to all the more estimable and superior purposes of matrimony useless and almost lifeless;

and what a solace, what a fit help such a consort would be through the whole life of a man, is less pain to conjecture than to have experience.

It is the virtuous man, with no experience of women, who is most likely to make a fatal error of judgment in marriage, while the rakes, having sown their wild oats, have learned from experience and choose more wisely when they come to marry. Alas, what boots it with uncessant care. . . .

Milton's defense of divorce naturally provoked much opposition, which led him to write, in 1644 and 1645, three further pamphlets in more controversial vein, one citing the opinions of an earlier divine who had favored divorce, another reinforcing his arguments with a great play of scriptural texts, and a third replying, with a wealth of sportive abuse, to an opponent who had attacked his first divorce pamphlet. Meanwhile Parliament, now dominated by the Presbyterian party, who were anxious to silence opposition views, had passed an act requiring all books to be licensed by an official censor. Milton and his printer ignored this, and an inquiry was ordered. Though nothing further developed, Milton's blood was up; once again, personal situation and general principle combined to produce a passionately held conviction. The result was *Areopagitica* in 1644, a classic defense of liberty of the press, where Milton's highly individualistic temper led him to put forward arguments which, while familiar to nineteenth-century liberal thought, were new and strange indeed in the seventeenth century. Truth will prevail over error only in open conflict; and in any case (an unexpected argument from a passionate Puritan Christian) truth is not in its single wholeness capable of being grasped by men, each of whom may only discover a single, and different, fragment:

> Truth indeed came once into the world with her divine Master, and was a perfect shape most glorious to look on; but when he ascended, and his apostles after him were laid asleep, then straight rose a wicked race of deceivers, who . . . took the virgin Truth, hewed her lovely form into a thousand pieces, and scattered them to the four winds. From that time ever since, the sad friends of Truth, such as durst appear, imitating the careful search that Isis made for the mangled body of Osiris, went up and down gathering limb by limb still as they could find them. We have not yet found them all, Lords and Commons, nor ever shall do, till her Master's second coming.

Truth is strong, but not single:

> For who knows not that Truth is strong, next to the Almighty. She needs no policies, nor stratagems, nor licensings to make her victorious—those are the shifts and defences that error uses against her power. Give her but room, and do not bind her when she sleeps, for then she speaks not true, ...

Yet it is not impossible that she may have more shapes than one. What else is all that rank of things indifferent, wherein Truth may be on this side, or on the other, without being unlike herself?

There is the indignity, too, of being subject to the ferula like a schoolboy. "When a man writes to the world, he summons up all his reason and deliberation to assist him; he searches, meditates, is industrious, and likely consults and confers with his judicious friends, after all which he has done he takes himself to be informed in what he writes, as well as any writ before him." Who is any parliamentary censor to challenge John Milton? In any case, controversy strengthens truth, and to believe things merely on authority is no real belief. Good can only be known by evil, truth by falsehood, virtue by trial against the temptations of the world. "To sequester out of the world into Atlantic and Utopian polities, which never can be drawn into use, will not mend our condition; but to ordain wisely as in this world of evil, in the midst whereof God hath placed us unavoidably." Or again: "I cannot praise a fugitive and cloistered virtue unexercised and unbreathed, that never sallies out and sees her adversary, but slinks out of the race, where that immortal garland is to be run for, not without dust and heat." There is a note of patriotism, too, in the pamphlet, and of expectation of great things to happen shortly in England. "Lords and Commons of England," he exclaims, "consider what nation it is whereof ye are . . ." The roar of debate going on in the country is a sign of health and vigor: some wonderful dispensation will soon be vouchsafed.

Now once again by all concurrence of signs, and by the general instinct of holy and devout men, as they daily and solemnly express their thoughts, God is decreeing to begin some new and great period in his Church, even to the reforming of reformation itself. What does he then but reveal himself to his servants, and, as his manner is, first to his Englishmen.

Areopagitica is a noble and eloquent plea, overwhelmingly optimistic in tone even though one of the premises of the argument is the inaccessibility of total truth to men as a result of the Fall. Much of it would seem to come more appropriately from the pen of a John Stuart Mill than that of a seventeenth-century Puritan. That Milton could write this classic piece of liberal pamphleteering is one of many indications of the complex nature of his Christian Humanist mentality.

In 1644, between his first and second divorce pamphlets, Milton published his little treatise *Of Education*, in the form of a letter to Samuel Hartlib, whose known interest in educational reform and in the ideas of John Comenius made him an obvious recipient of such a communication. Milton is here concerned with the training of an elite in regional academies containing about a hundred and thirty pupils and a staff of about twenty. His educational ideal is a Christian Humanist one; he defined the end of learning as "to repair the ruins of our first parents by regaining to know God aright, and out of that knowledge to love him, to imitate him, to be like him," and shortly afterwards declares, in the true spirit of Renaissance Humanism, "I call . . . a complete and generous education that which fits a man to perform justly, skilfully, and magnanimously all the offices, both private and public, of peace and war." He opposes early emphasis on such "abstract" studies as rhetoric and logic, insisting on a great variety of substantial reading in Latin and Greek, from the point of view of the usefulness of their content (including agriculture, geometry, astronomy, geography, medicine, and natural history) and not merely of their stylistic elegance. Thence the students proceed to classical writers on ethics and economics, "and either now or before this, they may have easily learned at any odd hour the Italian tongue." Politics comes next, and then (Hebrew together with "the Chaldee and the Syrian dialect" now having been learned) biblical studies and church history, and only after that come "choice histories, heroic poems, and Attic tragedies," and rhetoric and logic follow at a still later stage. Regular exercise, walks in the country, fencing, and recreation "with the solemn and divine harmonies of music" are also prescribed. The curriculum is of course impossibly large by modern standards, but it must be remembered that Milton is concerned (though he never explicitly says so) with training a ruling class of specially gifted people. It is interesting that Milton should see his pupils as gaining scientific and practical knowledge through reading appropriate Latin and Greek works; unlike some nineteenth-century English defenders of the classics, he saw classical culture not only as a source of "sweetness and light" but also as a means of instruction in the material things of civilization. The specifically Christian side of his program takes up less space; but that was because there was such universal agreement on its importance that he did not have to dilate on it.

Looking back afterward on his earlier writings, Milton wrote in the *Second Defence* that he came to write on marriage, education, and freedom of the press by a simple logical process:

When the bishops could no longer resist the multitude of their assailants, I had leisure to turn my thoughts to . . . the promotion of real and substantial liberty, which is rather to be sought from within than from without, and whose existence depends not so much on the terror of the sword as on sobriety of conduct and the integrity of life. When, therefore, I perceived that there were three species of liberty which are essential to the happiness of social life—religious, domestic, and civil; and as I had already written concerning the first, and the magistrates were strenuously active in obtaining the third, I determined to turn my attention to the second, or the domestic species. As this seemed to involve three material questions, the conditions of the conjugal tie, the education of the children, and the free publication of the thoughts, I made them objects of distinct consideration.

One cannot help thinking, however, that this is rationalization after the event and that it was Milton's personal circumstances and interests that impelled him to write on these subjects at this time.

Meanwhile, Milton was moving steadily away from the Presbyterians, whom he came to regard as narrow and intolerant, toward the Independents, who eventually gained control of Parliament and began to think more and more in terms of a republic. Between 1646 and 1648 Charles was defeated and imprisoned, escaped to renew the Civil War, and was finally defeated again. Milton was writing no pamphlets at this time; he wrote a few sonnets reflecting his views of various contemporary events, continued teaching his nephews and others, published a volume of his minor poems, worked on a history of Britain, continued to meditate on his future epic, and watched with interest the tide of affairs. Charles was brought to trial on January 20, 1649, and executed ten days later. The execution was the work of a determined minority who were resolved to end the *mystique* of kingship once and for all. It is probable that Milton by this time had moved very close to the position of this minority. At any rate, barely a fortnight after the execution there appeared the first of his third series of pamphlets, concerned with constitutional questions and the rights of the people against tyrants: this was *The Tenure of Kings and Magistrates*, designed to prove—in the words of its subtitle—"that it is lawful, and hath been held so through all ages, for any who have the power, to call to account a tyrant, or wicked king, and after due conviction, to depose, and put him to death, if the ordinary magistrates have neglected or denied to do it. And that they who of late so much blame deposing, are the men that did it themselves." It is a carefully reasoned argument, based on both historical precedents and general moral principles, in favor of the revocability of the supreme civil power. "Since the king or magistrate holds his authority of the people, both originally and naturally for their good in the first place, and not his own, then may the people, as oft as they shall judge it for the best, either choose him or reject him, retain him or depose him, though no tyrant, merely by the liberty and right of freeborn men to be governed as seems to them best." Milton was going behind Stuart theories of divine right and Tudor theories of absolutism to a liberal political tradition common to medieval and Renaissance thought, and at the same time looking forward in some degree to John Locke's *Second Treatise on Civil Government*. From now on Milton's identification with the group that brought about Charles' execution and the setting up of the Commonwealth was complete. The result was that he became the official apologist of the regicides before Europe as well as an important servant of the new government. In March, 1649, he was appointed Latin Secretary to the Council of State (the post was also called Secretary for Foreign Tongues). He had postponed writing his greatest poetry until he was sure that his period of self-preparation was complete, and now history had caught him up and he had to postpone it further.

In addition to conducting the Government's foreign correspondence in Latin, Milton was now required to defend its policy publicly. The execution of Charles had shocked Europe, and in England there was still a great deal of personal feeling for the dead King, a feeling exploited by the publication in February, 1649, of *Eikon Basilike*, "the true portraiture of his Sacred Majesty in his solitudes and sufferings" in the form of a record of his supposed self-communings during his last years (though actually invented by Bishop Gauden). Milton undertook to destroy the effect of this dangerously popular work, with its sentimental, idealizing picture of the King, and in *Eikonoklastes* ("the Image-breaker"), published in October, 1649, he produced a stinging attack on the royal character as revealed in *Eikon Basilike*. Though he begins with some generosity—"To descant on the misfortunes of a person fallen from so high a dignity, who hath also paid his final debt both to nature and his faults, is neither of itself a thing commendable, nor the intention of this discourse"—the work soon becomes insistently carping in tone, ingeniously pressing every point that can be made against the King's character and behavior, tracing his actions in political and ecclesiastical matters in considerable detail. His purpose is to destroy the image of the saint and martyr built up by Bishop Gauden and replace it by that of a vain and hypocritical tyrant. In the very first chapter he seizes with glee on the fact that Charles had "so little care of truth in his last words, or honour to himself, or to his friends, or sense of his afflictions, or of that sad hour that was upon him, as immediately before his death to pop into the hand of that grave bishop who attended him, for a special relique of his saintly exercises, a prayer stolen word for word from the mouth of a heathen fiction praying to a heathen god; and that in no serious book, but the vain amatorious poem of Sir Philip Sidney's Arcadia; a book in that kind full of worth and wit, but among religious thoughts and duties not to be named; nor to be read at any time without good caution, much less in time of trouble and affliction to be a Christian's prayer-book." That Milton was the first to recognize this plagiarism testifies to his own intimate knowledge of *Arcadia*, a work which in other circumstances he would have been glad to praise.

The next stage of Milton's official pamphleteering for the Commonwealth involved a European rather than a purely English audience. The French scholar Claude Saumaise, generally known as Salmasius and now living in Holland, had been commissioned by the exiled Charles II to write a public attack in Latin on those who were responsible for the execution of Charles I, and the result was his *Defensio Regia pro Carolo I.* This appeal to Europe by a distinguished scholar was dangerous for the Commonwealth Government, and Milton replied with a long Latin reply, *Ioannis Miltoni Angli pro Populo Anglicano Defensio contra Claudii anonymi, alias Salmasii, Defensionem Regiam.* This *Defence of the English People* is a detailed and scornful reply to Salmasius, mingling legal, historical, and moral arguments with fierce personal attacks on the character, scholarship, and grammar of Salmasius. The defense seems to have been effective; Salmasius, now living at the court of Queen Christina of Sweden, left in disgrace and died soon afterward. But other champions took up the fight against the regicides. A powerful anonymous work appeared in 1652, with the rhetorical title, *Regii Sanguinis Clamor ad Coelum, adversus Parricidas Anglicanos,* "The Cry of the King's Blood to Heaven against the English Parricides." To this Milton replied with *Joannis Miltoni Angli pro Populo Anglicano Defensio,* the *Second Defence of the English People,* which appeared in May, 1654. This, too, contains much personal abuse, directed against Alexander More, whom Milton wrongly took to be author of the *Regii Sanguinis Clamor;* Milton had received personal abuse in the *Clamor* and gave at least as good as he got. But there is also a note of high patriotic eloquence in the work, and, in addition, those revealing autobiographical passages in which he countered abuse by talking of his own education and ambitions. He talks of his youth, his friendships, his studies, his Italian visit, his feelings when the Civil War broke out, in a long passage which is of the first importance for the student of Milton's mind. He explains and defends his entry into controversial pamphleteering.

I saw a way was opening for the establishment of real liberty; that the foundation was laying for the deliverance of man from the yoke of slavery and superstition; that the principles of religion, which were the first objects of our care, would exert a salutary influence on the manners and constitution of the republic; and as I had from my youth studied the distinctions between religious and civil rights, I perceived that if ever I wished to be of use, I ought at least not to be wanting to my country, to the church, and to so many of my fellow-Christians, in a crisis of so much danger; I therefore determined to relinquish the other pursuits in which I was engaged, and to transfer the whole force of my talents and my industry to this one important object.

Milton's identification of himself with the cause he championed was never more clear.

The personalities into which the controversial habits of the age pushed Milton led him at last to a work devoted wholly to a defense of himself. More, not unnaturally resenting Milton's violent attack on himself for a work which he had not written, replied with a fierce attack on Milton, in which he particularly sneered at his crude vanity in taking it upon himself to lay down the law to Cromwell (who became Lord Protector in 1653). Milton's reply, *Joannis Miltoni pro se Defensio contra Alexandrum Morum*, "John Milton's Defence of Himself against Alexander More," appeared in 1655: it is personal and abusive and of little interest to the modern reader. It is interesting, however, that Milton shows himself sensitive to More's charge that he employed "language of unwashed foulness, words naked and indelicate," and he replied not only by returning the charge ("No shade could veil your filthiness, not even that notable fig-tree") but also by citing illustrious precedents for the use of plain, naked words —Sallust, Herodotus, Seneca, Plutarch, "the gravest of authors." Further, if it is to be considered indecent to speak frankly about "subjects abundantly gross," "how often will you have to charge with indecency and obscenity Erasmus, . . . Thomas More, . . . the ancient fathers of the church, Clemens Alexandrinus, Arnobius, Lactantius, Eusebius, when they uncover and cast derision upon the obscene mysteries of the old religions!"

After this there was a pause in Milton's pamphleteering until after Cromwell's death in 1658, when he addressed himself to the question of the relation between the civil and the ecclesiastical power in a pamphlet entitled *A Treatise of Civil Power in Ecclesiastical Causes*. Milton had never been satisfied with any sort of church establishment, his highly individualistic temperament reinforcing the Protestant conception of every man with his Bible constructing his own path to God (though C. S. Lewis has shown that the insistence on spiritual leaders and followers was also a Protestant characteristic in the sixteenth and seventeenth centuries). "Seeing, therefore, that no man, no synod, no session of men, though called the church, can judge definitely the sense of scripture to another man's conscience, which is well known to be a general maxim of the Protestant religion; it follows plainly, that he who holds in religion that belief, or those opinions, which to his conscience and utmost understanding appear with most evidence or probability in the scripture, though to others he seem erroneous, can no more be justly censured for a heretic than his censurers." It is the same argument that he had urged in *Areopagitica;* man can only embrace the truth as he sees it. (He does not, however, push his principles so far as to wish toleration for those whose view of the truth forbids them to accept scripture as a divinely authoritative work at all; he was Milton after all, not John Stuart Mill.) The *Treatise* was addressed to Parliament in the vain hope of producing a practical effect. A second pamphlet on the same subject, *Considerations touching the likeliest means to remove Hirelings out of the Church,* appeared in 1659, after Cromwell's son, Richard Cromwell, had given up the attempt to carry on his father's position and the Rump Parliament (what remained of the Long Parliament after the dismissal of the Presbyterians in "Pride's Purge" in 1648) was recalled by the army to consider the position. Hopeful as ever, Milton saw in this turn of events a chance of moving nearer his ideal commonwealth, and sketched out a plan for an almost unsalaried clergy drawn only from those truly eager for spiritual service, instead of a class of ecclesiastics representing "a distinct order in the commonwealth, bred up for divines in babbling schools, and fed at the public cost, good for nothing else but what was good for nothing."

With the political situation fluid again, and the question of what form of government England should have again under discussion, Milton with an almost pathetic hopefulness published his *Ready and Easy Way to Establish a Free Commonwealth.* And yet the optimism is somewhat forced, as the note of premonition in the introduction shows: ". . . If their absolute determination be to enthrall us, before so long a Lent of servitude, they may permit us a little shroving time first, wherein to speak freely, and take our leaves of liberty." But the optimism rises as he continues: "Now is the opportunity, now the very season, wherein we may obtain a free commonwealth, and establish it for ever in the land, without difficulty or much delay." And later: ". . . few words will save us, well considered; few and easy things, now seasonably done." There is a new tone of almost desperate pleading in parts of this brief tract, in which he recommends to favor his favorite scheme of a single Parliament "in perpetuity of membership for life," a stable oligarchy of the best men chosen by a properly qualified electorate. The pamphlet aroused interest and produced replies, and a second, enlarged edition appeared on the very eve of the Restoration, by which time any possibility of a new republican form of government had vanished. The conclusion of the second edition has a nostalgic eloquence, as though Milton really knew that history had overtaken him:

What I have spoken, is the language of that which is not called amiss "The good old Cause;" if it seem strange to any, it will not seem more strange, I hope, than convincing to backsliders. Thus much I should perhaps have said, though I was sure I should have spoken to trees and stones; and had none to cry to, but with the prophet, "O earth, earth, earth!" to tell the very soil itself, what her perverse inhabitants are deaf to. Nay, though what I have spoke should happen (which thou suffer not, who didst create mankind free! nor thou next, who didst redeem us from being servants of men!) to be the last words of our expiring liberty. . . .

The Restoration of Charles II brought all Milton's political hopes to an end, destroying at the same time his vision of a reformed and regenerate England which had sustained him for so long. Further political pamphleteering was now useless. Only in 1673, two years before his death, he turned again to pamphleteering to argue in *Of True Religion, Heresy, Toleration, and the growth of Popery*, in favor of toleration of all creeds based on honest interpretation of God's word, however mutually different, and against that one species of Christianity that imposes a man-made tradition on all.

Meanwhile, he had gone blind, the left eye beginning to go in 1644 and total blindness developing by 1652. His enemies saw God's judgment in this, but Milton accepted his affliction with dignity and fortitude, comparing himself, in the *Second Defence*, to "those wise and ancient bards whose misfortunes the gods are said to have compensated by superior endowments." The record of Milton's adjustment to the fact of his blindness is plain in his writings. First, the famous sonnet on his blindness, "When I consider how my light is spent," showing momentary rebellion turning to trust in God's purpose for him —"They also serve who only stand and wait." (So, in *Paradise Regained*, Jesus meditates on his Father's purpose for him, and concludes that he must trustfully await its manifestation.) Then the dignified passage in the *Second Defence*, comparing himself to blind heroes and sages of old. Then the lines at the beginning of Book III of *Paradise Lost*:

. . . nor sometimes forget
Those other two equall'd with me in fate,
So were I equall'd with them in renown,
Blind Thamyris and blind Maeonides,
And Tiresias and Phineus, prophets old.
Then feed on thoughts, that voluntary move

Harmonious numbers; as the wakeful bird
Sings darkling, and in shadiest covert hid
Tunes her nocturnal note. Thus with the year
Seasons return, but not to me returns
Day, or the sweet approach of ev'n or morn,
Or sight of vernal bloom, or summer's rose,
Or flocks or herds or human face divine;
But cloud instead, and ever-during dark
Surrounds me, from the cheerful ways of men
Cut off, and for the book of knowledge fair
Presented with a universal blank
Of Nature's works, to me expunged and ras'd,
And wisdom at one entrance quite shut out.
So much the rather thou, celestial light,
Shine inward, and the mind through all her powers
Irradiate; there plant eyes; all mist from hence
Purge and disperse, that I may see and tell
Of things invisible to mortal sight.

And then in the beginning of Book VII:

Standing on earth, not rapt above the pole,
More safe I sing with mortal voice, unchang'd
To hoarse or mute, though fall'n on evil days,
On evil days though fall'n, and evil tongues;
In darkness, and with dangers compast round,
And solitude; yet not alone, while thou
Visit'st my slumbers nightly, or when morn
Purples the East: still govern thou my song,
Urania, and fit audience find, though few.

And in the end he makes a tragic hero of the blind Samson.

Milton wrote sonnets intermittently throughout his life, some of them mere exercises, but most reflecting his attitude to contemporary events and often showing him in undress, as it were. He used the sonnet form with an originality and a variety which mark him out as one of the great sonneteers of England; but he did not go back to the Elizabethan sonneteering tradition, which was dead by Milton's time. He went to Italy independently, adopting the Petrarchan (not the "Shakespearean") form and in doing so giving a new vitality to the English sonnet. He seems to have been influenced by the Italian sonneteer Giovanni della Casa in his shaping of the sonnet as a continuous verse paragraph, with the thought cutting across the rhyme divisions and the division into *octave* and *sestet*. His early sonnet "O Nightingale" is an accomplished exercise; his reflections on his late maturing in "How soon hath Time, the subtle thief of youth," shows him using the sonnet form to produce a personal utterance that combines dignity of tone, flexibility of movement, and mastery of structure. During the Civil War he wrote sonnets of an "occasional" nature, such as "When the assault was intended to the city," with its quiet formality, or the sonnets of compliment to friends, "Lady that in the prime of earliest youth," or those to the Lady Margaret Ley and to Mr. Henry Lawes (whose friend he remained although Lawes was a devoted Royalist). "I did but prompt the age to quit their clogs" gives his vigorous reaction to the reception of his divorce pamphlets, while "On the New Forcers of Conscience under the Long Parliament" (a *sonetto caudato*, or "tailed" sonnet with a coda or tail of six extra satiric lines) shows Milton's kind of ironic humor:

> Men whose life, learning, faith and pure intent
> Would have been held in high esteem with Paul
> Must now be nam'd and printed heretics
> By shallow Edwards and Scotch what d'ye call:
> But we do hope to find out all your tricks,
> Your plots and packing worse than those of Trent,
> That so the Parliament
> May with their wholesome and preventive shears
> Clip your phylacteries, though baulk your ears,
> And succour our just fears,
> When they shall read this clearly in your charge:
> New Presbyter is but Old Priest writ large.

A similar rough sportiveness is found in his sonnet "On the Detraction which followed on my writing certain Treatises," with its deliberately humorous rhymes. The sonnets of compliment to Fairfax and Cromwell reflect his admiration of these antiroyalist heroes; that to Cromwell is an appeal to him not to accept the proposed limitation of freedom to preach. "Peace hath her victories /No less renown'd than war," he eloquently reminds him:

> Help us to save free conscience from the paw
> Of hireling wolves whose gospel is their maw.

The indignant eloquence of "On the Late Massacre in Piemont" has a fine Miltonic ring and shows how flexibly Milton could use the sonnet form, while the charming "Lawrence, of virtuous father virtuous son" gives a glimpse of a Milton who rarely appears in the poems: it is an invitation to dinner ("of Attic taste, with wine, whence we may rise /To hear the lute well touch'd, or artful voice /Warble immortal notes and Tuscan air") to a young friend. Of the two sonnets to his friend Cyriack Skinner, one is a pleasantly modulated appeal to relax:

> For other things mild Heav'n a time ordains,
> And disapproves that care, though wise in show,
> That with superfluous burden loads the day,
> And when God sends a cheerful hour, refrains.

The same year (1655) he wrote to Skinner of his blindness in the sonnet, "Cyriack, this three year's day these eyes." The conclusion is in the vein of the *Second Defence:*

> What supports me, dost thou ask?
> The conscience, friend, to have lost them overplied
> In liberty's defence, my noble task,
> Of which all Europe talks from side to side.
> This thought might lead me through the world's vain masque
> Content though blind, had I no better guide.

Finally, there is "Methought I saw my late espoused saint," a simply eloquent and moving sonnet about his dead second wife, who died in February, 1658.

The Italian sonnet had not originally been used only to write of love, though English sonneteers before Milton, developing only one aspect of the Petrarchan tradition, had assumed so. Milton knew Tasso's "heroical sonnets" of compliment and praise, and took the hint in his sonnets to Fairfax, Cromwell, and Sir Henry Vane. For originality, variety, and craftsmanship Milton's sonnets are unique in the language.

Two other works of Milton must be mentioned before we go on to discuss his last and greatest poetry. These are his *History of Britain*, begun in the 1640's and published in 1670, and the Latin work *De Doctrina Christiana* ("Of Christian Doctrine"), worked on at different periods of his life. The latter work, not published until 1825, is an elaborate presentation of Milton's own interpretation of Christianity, of great interest as providing the logical and theological basis on which *Paradise Lost* was to be reared (though the principles of the *De Doctrina* are never as clear in *Paradise Lost* as one might expect them to be after reading the former work). The *History*, which never gets further than the Roman conquest, shows Milton's interest in the early history of his country, which he at one time explored thoroughly for possible epic themes. He used his sources with critical care, and went to the original authorities whenever he could. He cannot help moralizing the story as he goes, for to his mind his nation's story was full of warnings and useful lessons; but the work remains in its way an impressive original rendering of the history of a difficult period. The long paragraphs and rather hurried style make

MILTON 435

it difficult for modern readers to read comfortably, with the result
that it is less well known than other early histories which have some
claim on our attention.

Milton meditated many subjects, from both British and biblical
history, before he finally decided on the Fall as the theme for his
great epic. There exists a manuscript of his in which he jotted down
a great variety of subjects both for epic and for plays. A list of
twenty-eight incidents from Roman, British, and early English history begins with "Venutius, husband of Cartismandua" and ends
with "Edward Confessors divorsing and imprisoning his noble wife
Editha, Godwins daughter"; the list includes the suggestion that "A
Heroicall Poem may be founded somewhere in Alfreds reigne, especially at his issuing out of Edelsingsey on the Danes; whose actions
are wel like those of Ulysses." The biblical themes include "Abram
from Morea, or Isack redeemd," "Baptistes" ("beginning from the
morning of Herods birth day"), "Sodom" ("the scene before Lots
gate"), "Herod massacring, or Rachel weeping," "Christ Bound,"
"Christ Crucified," "Christ Risen," and "Lazarus." The biblical subjects are presented mostly as subjects for tragedies. There are two
lists of biblical *dramatis personae*, one including Michael, Heavenly
Love, Lucifer, Adam, Eve, Conscience, Death, Faith, Hope, and
Charity, with a Chorus of Angels, and Labour, Sickness, Discontent,
Ignorance and others as "mutes." The other includes Moses, Justice,
Mercy, Wisdom, Lucifer, Adam, Eve, and others. There is a summary
of the action of *Paradise Lost* in five acts, with Moses speaking a prologue, and brief notes on over fifty other biblical subjects. There is
an elaborate summary of the action of a play called *Adam Unpara-
diz'd*. But, though he may well have begun *Paradise Lost* as a drama,
Milton cannot have worked long at it before deciding that the epic
was the appropriate form for a great poetic work on a theme of such
universal implications. How much of *Paradise Lost* he had written
before the collapse of all his political hopes with the Restoration, we
cannot say. Some parts would appear to have been written between
the writing of the *Second Defence* and his last pamphlets just before
the Restoration, while much of the latter part of the poem must have
been written after the period of confusion and danger which Milton
went through in 1660. Professor Hanford suggests that the second
half of *Paradise Lost* was written between Milton's third marriage
in February, 1663, and his giving his young friend and pupil Thomas
Ellwood the completed manuscript to read in September, 1665. It
was published in 1667.

At long last, Milton had written that poem "doctrinal to a nation"
that he had been determined to write from his earliest years. It was
inevitably a very different poem from the one whose Platonic idea

haunted him in his Cambridge and Horton days, and different, too, from the poem he would have written had he not lived to see the wreck of all his hopes for a regenerate England. In the invocation at the beginning of Book VII he notes the change in his circumstances while denying that there has been any change in his voice:

> More safe I sing with mortal voice, unchang'd
> To hoarse or mute, though fall'n on evil days;

Unchanged to hoarse or mute, certainly, but changed in subtler ways. *Paradise Lost* was a richer, profounder, and maturer epic because of what Milton had gone through before he completed it. A decorative poetic treatment of the Christian story of the Fall was no novelty in European literature. A younger Milton might have added another, and probably the most workmanlike as well as the most deeply felt, to the number of naïve poems of this kind, modeling himself on Sylvester's translation of Du Bartas whose superficial influence is so clearly seen in *Paradise Lost* as we have it but whose tone and texture is so utterly different from Milton's poem. Milton's *Paradise Lost* is a poetic rendering of the story of the Fall in such a way as to illuminate some of the central paradoxes of the human situation and illustrate the tragic ambiguity of man as a moral being.

Paradise Lost was a heroic poem, but its theme was to be far above the themes of conventional heroic poems. To narrate the story of the Fall of Man was

> sad task, yet argument
> Not less but more heroic than the wrath
> Of stern Achilles on his foe pursued
> Thrice fugitive about Troy wall, or rage
> Of Turnus for Lavinia disespous'd,
> Or Neptune's ire, or Juno's, . . . ;
> If answerable style I can obtain
> Of my celestial patroness, who deigns
> Her nightly visitation unimplor'd,
> And dictates to me slumb'ring, or inspires
> Easy my unpremeditated verse:
> Since first this subject for heroic song
> Pleas'd me, long choosing and beginning late,
> Not sedulous by nature to indite
> Wars, hitherto the only argument
> Heroic deem'd, . . .

The "answerable style" demanded a verse which allowed of both a dignity and a flexibility, an ability to rise to the most sublime heights and at the same time to indicate through changes in movement shifts in moral attitude, differences in cosmic status, and the relationship between the four great theaters of action—Heaven, Eden, Hell, and (by suggestion and implication only, yet most strongly and significantly), the ordinary, familiar postlapsarian world. The popular view that Milton in *Paradise Lost* had but one voice, and that an organ one, is wholly unjustified. No epic poet was a master of such a variety of styles as Milton, and the variety with which he could use "English heroic verse without rime" (as he calls it in his preliminary note on the "measure," in which he somewhat unnecessarily attacks rhyme and sees himself as recovering ancient liberty to English heroic poetry) can be seen at once if we put, say, Satan's first speech in Book I, rallying his fallen host, beside the trancelike, nightmare tone of Eve's description of her dream to Adam in Book V, and then turn to God's gentle teasing of Adam about his desire for a mate in Book VIII or the tipsy lilt of Eve's speech when, returning to Adam from the fatal tree, she makes her apology for being late in a rush of words "with countenance blithe." Or we might consider the description of ideal nature in the first account of Eden in Book IV, the primal courtesy of Adam and Eve's mutual talk before the Fall, the simplicity and freshness of Eve's speech in Book IV beginning "Sweet is the breath of morn," in some respects quite different from yet in others similar to the gentle penitential tone of her speech in Book X, "Forsake me not thus, Adam," in which the moral recovery of the pair begins. As for Milton's epic similes, often considered as merely elaborate poetic exercises, these have an important function in the poem as providing the only link between cosmic scenery of the epic and the world of ordinary men in their day-to-day activities throughout all of history and geography.

Milton's statement of his theme at the beginning of Book I not only follows epic precedent in making such an opening statement; it also, in a remarkably sustained verse paragraph, indicates the ambitious and comprehensive nature of his task and establishes his status as an epic poet on a higher moral plane than the Latin and Greek classics.

> Of Man's first disobedience, and the fruit
> Of that forbidden tree, whose mortal taste
> Brought death unto the world, and all our woe,
> With loss of Eden, till one greater Man
> Restore us and regain that blissful seat,
> Sing Heav'nly Muse, that on the secret top
> Of Oreb or of Sinai didst inspire
> That shepherd, who first taught the chosen seed
> In the beginning how the Heav'ns and Earth

Rose out of chaos: or if Sion Hill
Delight thee more, and Siloa's brook that flow'd
Fast by the oracle of God, I thence
Invoke thy aid to my advent'rous song,
That with no middle flight intends to soar
Above th' Aonian Mount, while it pursues
Things unattempted yet in prose or rhyme.
And chiefly thou, O Spirit, that dost prefer
Before all temples th' upright heart and pure,
Instruct me, for thou know'st; thou from the first
Wast present and with mighty wings outspread
Dove-like satst brooding on the vast abyss
And mad'st it pregnant. What in me is dark
Illumine, what is low raise and support;
That to the height of this great argument
I may assert eternal providence
And justify the ways of God to men.

The placing of the pauses, the rise and fall of the emotion, the high emotional charge in which the poet's sense of dedication and of communion with the great biblical figures of the Old Testament is communicated, the supplicatory cadence of the appeal to have his darkness illumined and his mind elevated, and the powerful simplicity of the concluding statement of his purpose—all this represents poetic art of a high order. Milton had experimented much with the verse paragraph in his earlier poems, and in *Paradise Lost* he was able to handle it with a variety and a structural cunning that go beyond anything else of the kind in English poetry. Classical echoes mingle with stark English simplicities and with overtones of meaning deriving from Milton's awareness of the precise meaning of relevant words in the Hebrew Bible. ("Dove-like satst brooding o'er the vast abyss," for example, is Milton's rendering of the precise meaning of the word in Genesis 1:2 translated by the Authorized Version as "moved"— "And the Spirit of God moved upon the face of the water"—but explained by both Jewish and Christian commentators as implying brooding and hatching. "This is that gentle heat that brooded on the waters, and in six days hatched the world," wrote Sir Thomas Browne in *Religio Medici*.) It is worth noting that Milton wrote of "the ways of God to men," not something like "designs of Deity to all mankind"; nothing could be more simply and effectively put than the statement of his purpose.

Paradise Lost shows Milton as Christian Humanist using all the resources of the European literary tradition that had come down to him —biblical, classical, medieval, Renaissance. Imagery from classical fable and medieval romance, allusion to myths, legends, and stories of all kinds, geographical imagery deriving from Milton's own fascination with books of travel and echoes of the Elizabethan excitement at the new discoveries, biblical history and doctrine, Jewish and Christian learning—all these and more are found in this great synthesis of all that the Western mind was stored with by the middle of the seventeenth century. Like *The Faerie Queene*, Milton's epic is a great synthesizing poem, but Milton's synthesis is more successful than Spenser's because he places his different kinds of knowledge—biblical, classical, medieval, modern—in a logical hierarchy, and never mingles, as Spenser often does, classical myth and biblical story on equal terms. If all the resources of classical mythology are employed in order to build up an overwhelming picture of the beauty of Eden before the Fall, that is because Milton is saying that here, and here only, were all the yearnings of men for ideal gardens fully realized—

> Hesperian fables true,
> If true, here only, . . .

The description of Eden in Book IV is indeed one of the finest examples of Milton's use of pagan classical imagery for a clearly defined Christian purpose.

> The birds their choir apply; airs, vernal airs,
> Breathing the smell of field and grove, attune
> The trembling leaves, while universal Pan
> Knit with the Graces and the Hours in dance
> Led on th' eternal Spring. Not that fair field
> Of Enna, where Proserpin gath'ring flow'rs,
> Herself a fairer flow'r, by gloomy Dis
> Was gather'd, which cost Ceres all that pain
> To seek her through the world; nor that sweet grove
> Of Daphne by Orontes, and th' inspir'd
> Castalian spring, might with this paradise
> Of Eden strive; . . .

There is a tremulous glory in this description of ideal nature fully realized, and repetitions such as "airs, vernal airs," and "gath'ring flow'rs, herself a fairer flow'r" help to give the proper emotional quality to the verse. The classical imagery is neither purely decorative nor as solidly grounded in reality as the biblical groundwork of the story: Milton uses myth for what it is, the imaginative projection of all man's deepest hopes and fears. Matthew Arnold cited the lines about Proserpin and Ceres as a touchstone of great poetry, but did not pause to inquire why. It is in the combined suggestion of infinite beauty and of foreboding and loss that Milton manages to capture precisely the sad sense of transience which accompanies all postlapsarian response to beauty, and thus even while describing a prelapsarian scene he introduces overtones of the Fall. And more than that—these overtones emphasize a paradox that lies at the very heart of *Paradise Lost*, namely, that only after one has lost something ideally lovely can its true worth be known; the Fall is necessary so that we may pursue the ideal, in the teeth of all the obstacles that now confront us, with a deeper sense of its desirability.

Critics have objected to Milton's use of the apostrophe in such words as "gath'ring flow'rs" as though this were something monstrously artificial, instead of his indication that he meant the words to be spoken as they are pronounced in ordinary speech, not with the artificial "poetic" articulation of syllables not normally sounded. He writes "gather'd" and not "gathered," because some poets wrote the latter form intending the word to be pronounced "gatheréd."

Book I shows us the fallen angels in Hell beginning to recover from their defeat and prostration. The high-sounding rhetorical verse in which Milton describes and which he puts into the mouths of these great and perverted creatures indicated both that Milton had grown suspicious of rhetoric (perhaps because of his disillusion with the Long Parliament debates) and that he was aware that evil had its own attractiveness, which he was careful not to minimize. The speeches of Satan and his followers in Books I and II are magnificent in their way, "Miltonic" in the popular sense of the word; they represent the attractiveness of plausible evil. If evil was never attractive there would be no problem for man. It is because high-sounding rhetoric can so easily "make the worse appear the better reason" and that man so easily thrills to grandiose rantings about honor and revenge uttered with all the mock passion and the theatrical trimmings of a Nuremberg rally, that Satan is so great a danger. To see Satan as a hero because Milton goes out of his way to show the superficial seductiveness of this kind of evil is to show an extraordinary naïveté. The descriptions of Satan's regal state at the beginning of Book II is a magnificent evocation of all the barbaric splendor which the Greeks (and Milton with them) so shuddered at in the Persians. As for the supposed nobility of Satan, it does not take a very close reading of his speeches to see that a self-frustrating spite is his dominant emotion and that it is just when he uses the most impressive heroic terms that his language most lacks meaning. Of course, there are traces of true heroism in him. Milton was making the point that *corruptio optimi pessima*, the corruption of the best becomes the worst, as well as the subtler point that every great human virtue has its moral dangers and can appeal for the wrong reasons.

The scenes in Heaven, in Book III and elsewhere, are by common consent the least effective parts of the poem. Milton was here too detailed in his anthropomorphism. The nonsensical charge that he lacked a specific visual imagery (as though specific visual imagery was always essential to great poetry) is quite beside the point here, for the trouble is that there is too much of it. If he had been content, as he was in the magnificent description of Eden, to use large general terms highly charged with the appropriate emotion as a result of their cadence and tone and of the whole poetic movement of the context, he would have done better. Abstract images of light and joy could have rendered God more effectively than literal descriptions and earnest defensive arguments put into His mouth. Another reason for the relative ineffectiveness of these parts of the poem is that God continually gives the *logical* (not the poetic) answer to all the doubts we feel about the fairness of allowing an innocent couple to be so cunningly tempted and then drastically punishing them and their descendants. We cannot help taking God's arguments as arguments, and arguing back as we read. And as the arguments are far from invulnerable, the poem suffers. The purely logical case for God —that He made man with free will and therefore, even though God knew before the creation of man that man would fall, man's Fall was man's own fault and properly punished; and that the Christian scheme of redemption (even though, on Milton's own showing, it would save only a tiny minority of men in human history) was the product of pure mercy and love, an undeserved blessing which showed God repaying good for evil—is full of fallacies as Milton and Milton's God argue it. Indeed, so inadequate is this presentation of the purely formal case for God that Milton's picture in Book III of God insisting that after the Fall *someone* must be punished, Adam or anybody else who might be found, if justice is to be satisfied, strikes one as unchristian and positively evil:

> He with his whole posterity must die,
> Die he or Justice must; unless for him
> Some other able, and as willing, pay
> The rigid satisfaction, death for death.

This picture of a judge telling the court after a murderer has been found guilty that in order that justice must be done somebody, the guilty man or some member of the jury or the public, must be hanged—it doesn't matter who so long as there is a hanging—is very far from the Christian doctrine of atonement. Clearly, Milton's heart was not fully in this sort of justification of the ways of God to men, whatever he might have consciously thought. His poetic instinct was

better than his logical powers, and the true justification of the ways of
God to men lies in the way in which it emerges as the poem develops
that virtue can only be achieved by struggle, that the Fall was inevitable because a passive and ignorant virtue, without the challenge of
an imperfect world, cannot release the true potentialities of human
greatness. Of course, the cost of making such a release possible was
enormous; but that was part of the nature of things as well as part of
la condition humaine.

The poem recovers magnificently with Satan's arrival in Eden in
Book IV, and it is a fine symbolism which makes us see Eden, in
all its unfallen glory, first through Satan's eyes. Milton takes his time in
bringing his camera to focus on Adam and Eve. He moves round the
garden first, showing the varied glories in imagery at once general
("ambrosial fruit of vegetable gold") and highly evocative before
showing us—again with Satan acting as the camera eye—to the
noble, naked dignity of our first parents. Nothing could be more
simply passionate than the summing up of this great description:

> So hand in hand they pass'd, the loveliest pair
> That ever since in love's embraces met, . . .

Adam's reception of Raphael in Book V gives Milton the opportunity to emphasize the beauty of prelapsarian simplicity:

> Meanwhile our primitive great sire to meet
> His god-like guest walks forth, without more train
> Accompani'd than with his own complete
> Perfections; in himself was all his state,
> More solemn than the tedious pomp that waits
> On princes, when their rich retinue long
> Of horses led, and grooms besmear'd with gold
> Dazzles the crowd and sets them all agape.

Here the familiar postlapsarian world is brought in by a simple contrast, but Milton has many subtler ways of doing it. Milton seems
to be fascinated by innocent nakedness; he emphasizes the pair's
nakedness, especially Eve's, again and again:

> . . . Meanwhile at table Eve
> Minister'd naked, and their flowing cups
> With pleasant liquors crown'd. . . .

He had already, at their very first appearance, given his picture of
innocent sexuality and emphasized that here, and neither in perpetual celibacy nor in the barren artificialities of the courtly love tradition, lay the true use of sex. There is indeed an oblique war carried

out by Milton throughout *Paradise Lost* against conventional notions of heroism (which turn out to be diabolical) and against conventional attitudes to sex, both courtly and Puritan. Again and again there is an implicit contrast made between the Garden of the Rose tradition and the Garden of Eden and between the heroic gestures of romance and the true heroism of the virtuous man.

Of course, as innumerable editors have pointed out, Milton uses all the epic devices he could find in classical epic. But the significance of his use of these devices is not that, knowing he was writing an epic, he used appropriate epic devices. It is that he found a way of making most of these devices work poetically in expanding the meaning of the paraphrasable content of the poem. Further, these epic devices represent but a small proportion of the different means he uses—in imagery, vocabulary, cadence, paragraphing, shifts of tone, etc.—to give poetic effectiveness to his story. Far too much critical attention has been spent on pointing out parallels between *Paradise Lost* and earlier epics, instead of emphasizing the highly individual way in which Milton uses his epic machinery.

Raphael's account of the war in Heaven, which occupies part of Book V and all of Book VI, is poetically the least original part of *Paradise Lost*. There is an inherent difficulty in a situation where one of the protagonists is Almighty God, all knowing and all powerful, who can bring anything to pass merely by willing it. Military conflict seems otiose, and God's deliberations on what to do ("Nearly it now concerns us to be sure /Of our omnipotence") appear absurd. In the same way the posting of angelic guards round Eden to prevent Satan's entry, when God has already told the angels that Satan will enter and successfully tempt Adam and Eve, is mere gesturing. Even the building up of Abdiel into a hero as the only one of the angels in Satan's group to defy him to his face seems pointless: what was Abdiel doing among Satan's host anyway? The nearer Milton approaches the defiances and conflicts of classical epic the less convincing *Paradise Lost* is. Angelologists like C. S. Lewis can argue that the wounds suffered by the angels in the conflict are perfectly consistent with Milton's conception of their natures, but that is beside the point. The whole physical conflict, which falls between allegory and history, is misconceived. There are memorable descriptive passages in this part of the poem, but they do not possess the rich suggestive power of other parts. Raphael's account of the creation in Book VII is more poetically effective, with Milton drawing ingeniously on imagery from Genesis, the Psalms, Proverbs, Job, and Plato. But here too the poem is marking time; its true progress is halted. We return to the true Miltonic poetic texture in the scene in

Book VIII where Adam tells Raphael of his own experiences after his creation.

Book IX is one of the great books. From the self-tormenting spitefulness of Satan we move to the sweetly courteous difference of opinion between Adam and Eve about the propriety of Eve's gardening alone in another part of Eden that morning, for a change. We are left to assume, though this is never stated, that this suggestion was put into Eve's mind by Satan when he lay by her ear in the form of a toad as she slept the previous night. But neither she nor Adam is yet fallen, and the quiet grace of their discourse illustrates at its best a quality which Milton always tried to bring into his verse when describing the behavior and conversation of the pair before the Fall. (The faults of his style in such passages are more a Wordsworthian oversimplicity than a "Miltonic" heaviness, as in "No fear lest dinner cool.") When Adam consents to let Eve go, knowing that "thy stay, not free, absents thee more," we feel that Eve, having, woman-fashion, won her point, does not really want to act on it and only goes because she feels her previous insistence makes it necessary that she should. They part reluctantly, and as Eve slowly slides her hand out of her husband's Milton uses the richest resources of classical mythology to dwell for the last time on her innocence and beauty. It is a slow and moving passage, as though Milton is reluctant to have them part. Eve promises to be back "by noon amid the bow'r, /And all things in best order to invite /Noontide repast." She will be back to make lunch, in fact. But that lunch was never made or eaten. At noon Eve was standing beneath the forbidden tree, the arguments of the cunning serpent reinforced by her own appetite; and the noontide repast that both she and her husband eventually ate was the fatal apple. Milton's lingering on this final moment when prelapsarian man and woman stood hand in hand for the last time produces its own haunting emotion. We are made to realize fully that Eve, for all her promises, will never return again—not *this* Eve, not the unfallen bride with her innocent display of her naked beauty; the woman who tripped back to Adam with a branch of the forbidden tree to give to him was a very different person.

The temptation scene itself shows the skilled orator taking advantage of simplicity. Eve is "our credulous mother," and she is fooled by the cunning serpent, whose final effort is significantly compared by Milton to the speech of "some orator renown'd /In Athens or free Rome." If she had known more she would have been more suspicious of this plausible eloquence; but she could not know more without eating of the forbidden Tree of Knowledge; and so the paradox is emphasized. Her sin was disobedience, it is true; but what caused her to commit this sin was credulity. She was taken in by cunning lies, never having met with lies or cunning before. Is credulity sinful and suspicion a virtue? It is the problem of Othello's trusting Iago. There is no solution; only a moral paradox at the heart of the matter.

Eve falls through credulity; Adam falls because he does not realize that the duty of an unfallen man who wants to help a fallen beloved is not to share her sin, and so render them both helpless, but to intercede for her while he is yet sinless. In a cunning parody of the courtly love tradition, Milton has Adam eat the apple as (in Eve's delighted words) a "glorious trial of exceeding love." And so they both become irresponsible and fatuous. Eve had changed as soon as she had eaten the apple, bowing to the tree in drunken worship, and spilling out her story to Adam in the most brilliant of all "Sorry I'm late, but—" speeches in English poetry. Now sex becomes guilty, shame follows self-consciousness, the pair bicker with sullen regret (how different the tone of their speech here from its earlier tone!), and Book IX ends in disillusion and bitterness. Book X charts the change that begins to take place on earth and in Hell as a result of the Fall, but its most interesting passages are those showing us the gradual process of recovery on the part of Adam and Eve. Adam's bitter repudiation of Eve—"Out of my sight, thou serpent!" —is followed by Eve's beautifully modulated penitential speech which we have already noted. And so at last they come to prayer and repentance.

The final part of *Paradise Lost* (which was, incidentally, first published in ten books and then rearranged in twelve) shows Michael displaying or narrating the future history of the world to Adam. It is a miserable story, from Cain's committing the first murder to the final picture of the world going on "to good malignant, to bad men benign, /Under her own weight groaning, till the day /Appear of respiration to the just /And vengeance to the wicked." The story of Christ's passion and triumph, which breaks the dismal chronicle with a momentary gleam of light and elicits in Adam his great hail to the "fortunate fall"—

> O goodness infinite, goodness immense,
> That all this good of evil shall produce,
> And evil turn to good—

is not, as Michael reveals the story, the culmination but only an incident in the long story, and is in some respects a less cheering incident than the quiet beauty of the picture of the earth returning to normal after the flood, never again to be so overwhelmed:

> . . . but when he brings
> His triple-coloured bow, whereon to look
> And call to mind his cov'nant: day and night,
> Seed-time and harvest, heat and hoary frost
> Shall hold their course, till fire purge all things new,
> Both Heav'n and Earth, wherein the just shall dwell.

This, with its sense of satisfaction in the procession of the seasons and man doing his daily agricultural labor, everything in its due time, gets us close to the heart of the poem.

In the end Milton and Adam turn from grandiose public hopes to the "paradise within," content with the prospect of "with good /Still overcoming evil, and by small /Accomplishing great things." Adam and Eve leave their former Paradise with quiet confidence, to face a world of work and endeavor and mutual help. Milton could not praise a fugitive and cloistered virtue, could not conceive of a life of pure meditation, could not imagine life in Eden lasting. At the same time he had lost his earlier confidence that Heaven on Earth could be restored by a regenerate, fully reformed England. Public virtue became for him almost a contradiction in terms, and only private virtue was real. The arts of public virtue, notably rhetoric, were suspect. In *Paradise Regained* he was to make this point even clearer, for Satan tempts Christ there to the public life, which he rejects, with all its accompanying splendors. This was not a wholly new view of Milton's, for, together with the public ambitions of his early years, he had felt also the necessity of submitting himself quietly and patiently to God's purpose for him—as Christ does in *Paradise Regained*. The sonnets on his twenty-third birthday and on his blindness should not be forgotten when we come to consider how far the turn to the "paradise within" represented a radical change in Milton as a result of the failure of his political hopes for England. On the other hand, the change, though it should not be exaggerated, cannot be denied. We have only to put the line

> Peace to corrupt no less than war to waste

from Book XI of *Paradise Lost* beside the line from his sonnet to Cromwell

> Peace hath her victories
> No less renown'd than war . . . .

to see a startling result of that change. Another result was the relegation of the "Miltonic" style to the Devil's side. The high rhetorical manner, invocations such as

Power and Dominions, Deities of Heav'n

and exhortations such as

Awake, arise, or be for ever fall'n

belonged to Satan's speech, to the public manner, to evil; God, angels, and men when they were not imitating Satan, spoke in a quieter and more carefully modulated tone. Those who think that *Paradise Lost* is a silly poem redeemed only by its organ tones— a poem to be read for its sound and not its sense—are taking Satan's view as Milton saw it.

All great works of literature contain more than their ostensible subject: starting from a particular set of beliefs, a story such as the biblical story of the Fall or a journey through the underworld, the true poet, in presenting his material, keeps reaching out at every point to touch aspects of the human situation which are real and recognizable whatever our beliefs may be. But through turns of phrase, handling of imagery, simultaneous exploitation of the musical and the semantic aspects of words and of all the evocations and suggestions that can be obtained from allusions to the great mythological imaginings of mankind, the poet turns his story and his creed into a unique means of shedding light on man. The combined knowledge of man's nobility and his weakness, the sense of man's looking back or forward to a golden age coupled with the knowledge that, partly because of the very characteristics of man as man, such a golden age can be envisioned but never realized, the sense that man's life is governed by chance and linked always with the movements of the day to night and back to day, with the passing of the seasons, with resolutions that fluctuate and moods that alter, but a sense, too, that only a determination to do what can be done at the moment of decision can ever achieve anything—all this and a thousand more such archetypal ideas are carried alive and passionately into the mind of the reader by *Paradise Lost*. The poem has its barren patches, and the arguments about free will in Heaven may leave us unconvinced. But as a poem the subject of *Paradise Lost* is less the logical justification of the ways of God to men than the essential and tragic ambiguity of the human animal. Expanding his meaning by every kind of poetic device to include almost all that Western man had thought and felt, pivoting the action on a scene which, as Milton describes it, illuminates immediately the paradox of man's ambition (at once good because noble and bad because arrogant) and human love (both bad because selfish and because passion clouds the judgment and good because unselfish and self-sacrificing), link-

ing the grandiose action at every point to suggestions of man in his
daily elemental activities in fields, cities, and on the ocean, developing all the implications of man's perennial desire for a better world
with the continuous awareness of man's tendency to trip himself up
and turn his very virtues into snares—achieving all this in spite of the
plot, or at least by expanding the plot into something infinitely more
than its summarizable meaning, by placing an image where it will
speak most richly and by linking up units to each other so that the
chorus of implication grows ever richer, reverberates ever more
widely, Milton, operating as a poet rather than as a theologian or
moralist, in spite of himself probes more deeply into man's fate than
his formal scheme would seem to allow. Work was a punishment for
the Fall, but images of daily work well done are used throughout the
poem to establish a note of satisfaction and recovery. Perpetual
spring gave way after the Fall to the procession of the seasons, yet
it is the procession of the seasons itself that gives meaning and dignity to human life as Milton reveals it by the pattern of image and
suggestion in his poem. And in the end, Paradise, the ideal world of
innocent idleness, has become uninhabitable. As they look back on
it for the last time, the angels guarding it seem dreadful figures from
another world. It is a great and memorable ending:

> . . . for now too nigh
> Th' archangel stood, and from the other hill
> To their fix'd stations all in bright array
> The cherubim descended, on the ground
> Gliding meteorous, as ev'ning mist
> Ris'n from a river o'er the marish glides
> And gathers ground fast at the labourer's heel
> Homeward returning. High in front advanc'd,
> The brandish'd sword of God before them blaz'd
> Fierce as a comet, which with torrid heat
> And vapour as the Libyan air adust
> Began to parch that temperate clime; whereat
> In either hand the hast'ning angel caught
> Our ling'ring parents, and to th' eastern gate
> Led them direct, and down the cliff as fast
> To the subjected plain,—then disappear'd.
> They looking back, all th' eastern side beheld
> Of Paradise, so late their happy seat,
> Wav'd over by that flaming brand, the gate
> With dreadful faces throng'd and fiery arms.
> Some natural tears they dropp'd, but wip'd them soon;
> The world was all before them, where to choose
> Their place of rest, and Providence their guide.

They hand in hand with wand'ring steps and slow
Through Eden took their solitary way.

The image of the laborer returning homeward in the evening sets the emotional tone of this concluding passage: always for Milton, daily agricultural labor duly accomplished was a highly charged symbol of satisfaction in human achievement. Eden becomes hot and frightening. Below, the "subjected plain" awaits them— subjected in the literal Latin sense of lying below them and in the other sense of awaiting their conquest of it. The simple phrase, "so late their happy seat," renews the elegiac tone with memories of lost felicity. But natural tears give way to the pioneering spirit of hope. "The world was all before them." And so they go forth, hand in hand yet in a sense solitary; they know now that, while mutual love and help sweeten all human toil, complete communion between individuals is impossible, for love and comradeship are bound up with self-interest. All is here said that can be said about man's capacity to hope in spite of despair, about loneliness and companionship, about the healing effects of time and the possibility of combining bewilderment with a sense of purpose, man as both elegist and pioneer. The style, with its quiet gravity, is more characteristically Miltonic than the Milton-Satan style which most people think is the invariable style of *Paradise Lost*. The manipulation of the pauses alone shows the highest art.

Paradise Regained and *Samson Agonistes* were published together in 1671, the former apparently written after the publication of *Paradise Lost*. There is no clear evidence as to when *Samson* was written, but theme and versification together with the date of publication suggest that it was one of his latest works if not his final achievement, though some scholars have suggested an earlier date. Both works had clearly been long maturing in Milton's mind. *Paradise Regained* is a much more limited poem than *Paradise Lost*, dealing only with one specific aspect of Christian story in four books. Milton is here treating of the temptation of Christ in the wilderness as what might be called a ritual re-enaction of the original Fall, only this time with temptation withstood instead of succumbed to. Taking the order of the temptations from the account in Luke, not in Matthew (where the order is different) Milton, following a well-established Christian tradition, sees in it an undoing of the Fall. Christ faces the wiles of Satan *quasi homo*, as Man not as God (and Milton always preferred to see Christ as heroic man rather than as God incarnate), and his triumph is therefore redemptive for mankind. As God tells His angels:

He [Satan] now shall know I can produce a man
Of female seed far abler to resist
All his solicitations, . . .
That all the angels and ethereal powers,
They now, and men hereafter, may discern
From what consummate virtue I have chose
This perfect man, by merit call'd my son,
To earn salvation for the sons of men.

Satan's motive in tempting Christ—and again Milton is here following a well-established tradition—is both to find out if he is really the prophesied Messiah and to tempt him to destroy his perfection and messianic claims by committing specific sins. Satan is here a rather seedy character compared with the fallen angel of *Paradise Lost;* his address to his fellows in Book I, announcing his determination to find out who this man is, is a sullen and shabby affair, the rhetoric sounding hollow, as though Satan did not believe himself in the possibility of his own success. The interest soon shifts to the mind of Christ, whom we see communing with himself after his forty days in the wilderness without food, wondering what God has in store for him, and determined to await patiently the revelation of His purpose. Satan's first appearance to him, in the likeness of "an aged man in rural weeds," produces a quiet dialogue in which the cunning persuasiveness of the supposed innocent old pauper as he suggests that by turning stones into bread Christ would both save himself from starvation "and us relieve with food," is met by a firmly quiet, slightly contemptuous reply which is characteristic of Christ's speech to Satan throughout the poem. His first remark is simply

Who brought me hither
Will bring me hence, no other guide I seek.

When Satan's suggestion becomes more specific, Christ calmly points out that God supported Moses on the mount and Elijah in the wilderness: "Why dost thou then suggest to me distrust?" Christ also states that he knows Satan's identity—which, we cannot help feeling, gives him a quite unfair advantage over Eve, who did not know who spoke through the serpent. Christ's calm refusal to do anything which might suggest distrust of God—and it must be emphasized that the temptation to turn stones into bread is not, as Milton presents it, a temptation to gluttony, but a temptation to distrust—produces a change in Satan's style, which becomes steadily more persuasive and rhetorical. That rhetoric, the art of persuasion, is here on the side of evil is abundantly clear. Christ's language is quiet, precise, even homely, the language of private not public discussion. Satan, having been recognized, proceeds to build himself up as at once heroic and pitiful, a character worthy of respect and at the same time deserving of compassion, and flattery is added to this cunning mixture of boasting and self-pity. It is a remarkable speech, ending with deliberate art on an elegiac note:

> This wounds me most (what can it less) that man,
> Man fall'n shall be restor'd, I never more.

Christ is not fooled:

> To whom our Saviour sternly thus replied.
> Deservedly thou griev'st, compos'd of lies
> From the beginning, . . .

He goes on to taunt Satan with having been the deceiver of man through the oracles of the pagan world; but "God hath now sent his living Oracle /Into the world." Satan counters this hopelessly with the argument that he loves virtue though he does not follow it, adding that God allows sinners to approach his altar, and therefore Christ should give access to him. Christ replies tersely:

> Thy coming hither, though I know thy scope,
> I bid not or forbid; do as thou find'st
> Permission from above; thou canst not more.

So the first temptation ends, Satan temporarily disappears, and Jesus is left alone in the wilderness:

> for now began
> Night with her sullen wing to double-shade
> The desert; fowls in their clay nests were couch'd;
> And now wild beasts came forth the woods to roam.

The quiet desolation of the scene is significant. The hero is alone in the waste land. Satan tempts him to take easy ways out, later trying to persuade him to exchange his lonely private life for the glories and satisfactions of a successful public career. But all temptations to public life are refused, and Jesus remains a private man at the end of the poem.

Book II gives us a glimpse of the disciples wondering what has happened to their master, then moves to Satan reporting to his devils his lack of success and repudiating contemptuously Belial's fatuous advice to "set women in his eye" in favor of further temptations "of worth, of honour, glory, and popular praise." We then turn to Jesus, communing with himself again, wondering what is to happen to him. Satan returns, this time in courtly garments, and brings on a

magnificent banquet, a temptation to luxury and sensuality, but the
Saviour's quiet contempt persists. "And with my hunger what hast
thou to do? /Thy pompous delicacies I contemn." Satan turns to
argue Christ's lack of power and authority. How can he save the
world without these? "Money brings honour, friends, conquest, and
realms"—

> They whom I favour thrive in wealth amain,
> While virtue, valour, wisdom sit in want.
>   To whom thus Jesus patiently replied:
> Yet wealth without these three is impotent. . . .

Significantly, Jesus goes on to cite examples from both biblical and
classical history of heroes who, their work over, returned to private
life. As for power, "he who reigns within himself, and rules /Passions,
desires, and fears, is more a king."

In Book III Satan, with increasing cunning and all kinds of verbal
trickery, makes more explicit the contrast between private and
public life:

> These God-like virtues wherefore dost thou hide?
> Affecting private life, or more obscure
> In savage wilderness, wherefore deprive
> All earth her wonder at thy acts, thyself
> The fame and glory, glory the reward
> That sole excites to high attempts the flame
> Of most erected spirits, . . . ?

This is coming more shrewdly home: Milton in "Lycidas" had recognized that "Fame is the spur . . ." But Jesus replies with cold contempt that the praise of the rabble is not worth having. (An un-
Christlike argument, surely, but one that reflects Milton's own
disillusion with public opinion in England.) Conventional glory is
won by meaningless and destructive wars. Patience and temperance
are the true virtues, and Job and Socrates are cited. This leads Satan
to press the moral aspect of the conquest of the evil by the good:
would not the deliverance of Israel from the Roman yoke be a good
thing? (Even as Milton had thought the deliverance of England
from episcopacy and Charles I would be a good thing.) The argument
here is pressed closely: a righteous war against the heathen is
urged. But again Jesus replies coldly: "All things are best fulfill'd
in their due time." ("They also serve who only stand and wait," in
fact.) He will continue "Suffering, abstaining, quietly expecting
/Without distrust or doubt." Satan presses his point with a magnificent
picture, both historical and geographical, of the power-pattern in

the Middle East and Mediterranean, with a ringing use of place names reminiscent for the first time of *Paradise Lost*, and offers his help and advice to Jesus in regaining David's throne. But again Jesus answers coldly, repudiating with quiet contempt "much ostentation vain of fleshly arm." As for the people of Israel, they serve for their sins, and will be called back to God in His own time.

Book IV shows Satan employing all "the persuasive rhetoric /That sleek'd his tongue" to build up a magnificent picture of the civilization of Greece and Rome. Here we have the grand style of *Paradise Lost*. A brilliant evocation of the whole world of Roman civilization, with a sense of the color and movement and variety of the whole Roman world, is followed by an equally brilliant evocation of the wisdom of Greece. To the first, offered by Satan in exchange for Jesus' homage, Jesus replies (becoming ever more contemptuous of the now desperate Satan): "I never lik'd thy talk, thy offers less." To the second he replies with more careful arguments. The wisdom of the Greeks is not dismissed with contempt. There is a note of genuine compassion when he says of the Greek philosophers

> Alas! what can they teach, and not mislead,
> Ignorant of themselves, of God much more, . . .

And though Greek philosophy has its virtues, they are pale beside the Hebrew prophets. "Sion's songs" are better than Greek literature (which is not to say that Greek literature is bad). The biblical prophets "with our Law, best form a king." Satan, frustrated and furious, carries Jesus back to the wilderness and tries, ridiculously, to frighten him with a night of storm and "hellish furies." The next morning he replies quietly to Satan's attempt to frighten him: "Me worse than wet thou find'st not." Enraged and desperate, Satan brings Jesus to a pinnacle of the temple, on which he sets him, hoping that he will call on angels to support him and thus both reveal his identity and at the same time lose it by invoking divine aid for his personal safety, or else fall and be destroyed. But neither of these things happens: Jesus stands unaided; Satan is confounded. An angelic choir hails Jesus' triumph over temptation and Jesus himself

> Home to his mother's house private return'd.

The identification of the private life with virtue and the public with evil could not be more emphatic. This is how Milton's own experience had led him to interpret the story of the temptation in the wilderness.

The Book of Job as well as Spenser's *Faerie Queene* (Book II, Canto VIII) and Giles Fletcher's *Christ's Victory and Triumph* gave suggestions to Milton for *Paradise Regained*, and of course he drew on established Christian tradition. But the "brief epic" is nevertheless remarkably original in treatment, in its presentation of the conflict between public ambition and quiet trust. If the character of Jesus suffers somewhat as a consequence—he seems an oddly cold and stoical character, with none of the warmer virtues—it must be remembered that in this poem he is opposing the false charm of rhetoric and resisting the temptation to exchange the "Paradise within" for grandiose public action.

In *Samson Agonistes* Milton dramatized the bare story from Judges in the form of a classical tragedy in which Aeschylus' *Prometheus Bound* and Sophocles' *Oedipus at Colonus* served as models. His introduction explains that tragedy is "the gravest, moralest, and most profitable of all other poems." Aristotle's theory that tragedy has "the power by raising pity and fear, or terror, to purge the mind of those and such like passions" is cited, and every effort is made to prove that tragedy is of the highest seriousness. He explains that he has followed the ancient model, both in plot and in verse form, and that "according to ancient rule and best example" the action is kept "within the space of 24 hours." A Greek tragedy on a biblical theme is perhaps Milton's final way of reconciling his Christianity with his Humanism.

The tragedy is in the form of a series of dialogues between Samson and the various people who visit him, one at a time, with intervening monologues by Samson, comments by the chorus, and the final reported account of Samson's death in pulling down the heathen temple on the Philistines. In the course of the action Samson gradually (and not always in a continuous forward movement) recovers a proper state of mind, which combines penitence, recognition of the nature of his earlier fault and the justice of his present fate, and a confident submission to whatever destiny God has in store for him. The temptations which face him, a blind prisoner of the heathen Philistines, are despair on the one hand and a belief in his ability to decide his own destiny (instead of waiting on God's revelation of His purpose) on the other. In the end, God's purpose is revealed, and he goes to participate in the Philistine festival knowing that that is what God wishes him to do. His death in destroying his enemies was the destiny prepared for him.

The theme of the play is the process of Samson's recovery, and each of the characters who visit him—his father Manoa, his wife Dalila, the Philistine giant Harapha, and the Philistine officer—represent different temptations, in resisting which he proceeds further toward recovery. We see him first lamenting his present state, "Eyeless in Gaza at the mill with slaves," and contrasting it, with bitter self-reproach, with his former career as a dedicated servant of God and a hero of his people. The verse moves from a firm and flexible blank verse to a more complex lyric measure where cunningly varied line lengths and deliberately varied metrical feet respond to the movement of the emotion:

> O dark, dark, dark, amid the blaze of noon,
> Irrecoverably dark, total eclipse
> Without all hope of day!
> O first created beam, and thou great word,
> "Let there be light, and light was over all,"
> Why am I thus bereav'd thy prime decree?
> The sun to me is dark
> And silent as the moon,
> When she deserts the night,
> Hid in her vacant interlunar cave. . . .

The Chorus, in a similar varied measure, comments on Samson's state and contrasts it with his former heroic exploits for his people. Samson, in discussion with the chorus, tells some of his story and distinguishes (rightly, in Milton's view) between his own wrongdoing, for which he takes the blame, and the follies and sins of omission of Israel's governors, which are really responsible for the present state of his people. The Chorus, in a well-known interlude, debate the question of God's justice with a passionate to-and-fro movement which indicates the emotional earnestness with which Milton posed the question. Manoa, Samson's first visitor, then comes to rub salt into Samson's wounds (though not consciously) by saying "I told you so" about his marriage to a Philistine woman. Samson responds with a mixture of self-reproach and self-respect. Manoa, whose bustling confidence that he can make everything come out well in the end reminds one a little of Oceanus in *Prometheus Bound*, looks forward to a happy ending, but such talk depresses Samson and he becomes more and more hopeless, verging on the sin of despair. Manoa leaves to try and arrange Samson's ransom, leaving Samson to give passionate expression to his hopelessness and the Chorus to ponder the baffling ways of God, who raises a man up from earliest youth to a high destiny, only to dash him down again in middle life.

The entry of Dalila, announced by the Chorus in terms which make clear that she is decked out in all her finery, brings a new temptation. She explains that she betrayed Samson for love of him, not expecting the Philistines to blind and imprison him, but hoping they would simply cut his hair to remove his great strength and leave him to her uxorious care. She is not lying: she is proffering to Samson a dangerous kind of love, and wants him back.

> Mine and Love's prisoner, not the Philistines'.

This is not Milton's concept of marriage, and when Dalila actually suggests that a blind Samson is better off than a seeing one, as being more completely under her loving protection, we see clearly that Milton is attacking here a variant of the courtly love tradition (with the man as "love's prisoner") which he attacked in other ways in *Paradise Lost*. It is a real temptation, because sex is involved, and the savagery with which Samson forbids Dalila to approach him indicates his fear of succumbing if once he allows physical contact between them. His repudiation of her stings her into a spiteful declaration of her determination to seek appreciation from the Philistines, and she goes, leaving the Chorus to ponder the strange power of physical love. Harapha then comes to taunt Samson, who answers his bravado with calm and confident words:

> All these indignities, for such they are
> From thine, these evils I deserve and more,
> Acknowledge them from God inflicted on me
> Justly, yet despair not of his final pardon
> Whose ear is ever open.

He vindicates his earlier career with dignity, and in the end chases Harapha from the scene by merely making a pretended motion toward him. The Chorus hail Samson's reviving spirits, and note that patience is the true exercise of saints.

The Philistine officer now enters and summons Samson to give an exhibition for the Philistine lords at their feast of Dagon. Samson returns a contemptuous negative, but then, contemplating his growing hair and returning strength, suddenly begins to feel "some rousing motions in me," indicating a divine impulse to go with the messenger after all. He leaves in high dignity, telling the Chorus:

> Happ'n what may, of me expect to hear
> Nothing dishonourable, impure, unworthy
> Our God, our law, my nation, or myself;
> The last of me or no I cannot warrant.

Manoa returns, confident that he can secure his son's release, looking forward to a completely restored Samson, with eyesight as well as strength given back. His optimistic speculations are interrupted by a shout from the temple of Dagon, and he exchanges apprehensive speculation with the Chorus. The announcement by a messenger, in a set speech in the true Greek dramatic tradition, of Samson's end brings comment by the Chorus (who are careful to point out that Samson died "self-kill'd /Not willingly"—he was not guilty of the sin

of suicide) and a final realization by Manoa that the end is heroic
and fitting:

> Come, come, no time for lamentation now,
> Nor much more cause: Samson hath quit himself
> Like Samson, and heroicly hath finish'd
> A life heroic, . . .
> Nothing is here for tears, nothing to wail
> Or knock the breast, no weakness, no contempt,
> Dispraise, or blame, nothing but well and fair,
> And what may quiet us in a death so noble.

The Chorus echo this thought:

> All is best, though we oft doubt,
> What th' unsearchable dispose
> Of highest wisdom brings about,
> And ever best found in the close.
> Oft he seems to hide his face,
> But unexpectedly returns
> And to his faithful champion hath in place
> Bore witness gloriously; whence Gaza mourns
> And all that band them to resist
> His uncontrollable intent.
> His servants he, with new acquist
> Of true experience from this great event,
> With peace and consolation hath dismiss'd,
> And calm of mind, all passion spent.

Samson Agonistes is the only successful Greek tragedy in English,
but its inner substance is not really Greek; the theme of a fallen
hero's achievement of a new and subtler kind of heroism is not
Sophoclean, but Christian in a very Miltonic way. The autobiographical overtones in the play are obvious and have often been
commented on. Whether *Samson* was Milton's final work or not, it
can be taken as his last word on his own situation. This passionately
individual Christian Humanist poet, so powerfully enmeshed in the
history of his own time, with his great sense of poetic mission, his
deflection into public service, reaching the full flower of his poetic
achievement in the midst of a civilization in which he had completely
lost faith, presents a fascinating and moving picture. He was the
greatest English nondramatic poet and the last English poet to take
and use as his poetic heritage everything that Western civilization,
with its twin origins in Hebrew and classical thought, had so far
achieved.

CHAPTER THIRTEEN

Prose in the Sixteenth and Seventeenth Centuries

THE INTELLECTUAL CONFLICTS and shifting tides of opinion in the sixteenth and seventeenth centuries are more directly shown in the prose of the period than in its poetry. Pamphleteering of all kinds, polemical religious argument, political, educational, and literary theorizing, flourish now as never before, with the result that the literary historian has to deal with a mass of miscellaneous prose most of which can hardly be called strictly "literature," yet which, in addition to providing an occasional work of real literary merit, provides an interesting view of the state of English prose style and the various ways in which English prose was being exercised and developed. Besides this large quantity of miscellaneous prose writing, there are devotional works, sermons, translations of many different kinds, histories, biographies, accounts of contemporary events, and prose fiction (both translation of Italian *novelle* and original work). Two forces are seen at work in most of this varied prose writing: first, the breakthrough of colloquial speech, with its vigor and raciness, into the written word, and secondly, the attempt to mold a consciously artistic English prose style. The two forces are, surprisingly enough, often found in conjunction, with colloquial vigor and overelaborate parallels or antitheses alternating in the same work. No permanent resolution was achieved in the sixteenth or early seventeenth centuries, in spite of the occasional prose triumphs of the age. Though an impersonal devotional prose developed, descending from the devotional prose of Rolle and Hilton in the fourteenth century, and a biblical prose was wrought by the English translators of the Bible from Tyndale to the translators of the Authorized Version of 1611, it remains true that nearly all prose writers of the Elizabethan and immediately subsequent period wrote a highly idiosyncratic prose: there was, except for prayer and biblical translation, no common tradition of prose style on which individual writers could play their own variations, as eighteenth-century writers had from Addison on; every prose writer had first to solve the problem of creating his own style.

We can see colloquial prose disciplining itself into effective written speech in such documents as the fifteenth-century *Paston Letters*, family letters which, while wholly informal and unliterary, nevertheless have style—the style of fluent, educated speech, only slightly less discursive than actual speech would be. It is, however, a naïve prose, unsuited for any heavier burden than that of exchange of family news. Similarly naïve is the narrative prose of the English translation of the *Gesta Romanorum*, a collection of tales compiled in Latin in the late thirteenth century and translated into English in the middle and later fifteenth century. These popular stories of adventure and magic were put into an English whose style suggests that of the oral teller of tales. The same can be said of the very popular collection of saints' lives known as the *Golden Legend*, originally compiled in Latin by Jacobus de Voragine and translated into English in the second quarter of the fifteenth century, and of the English versions of the *Travels of Sir John Mandeville*. A more artful prose was demanded by the religious controversies which began in England over a century before the Reformation. The pre-Reformation Lollard movement, coinciding as it did with an extension of the ability to read among laymen, produced theological controversy in the vernacular on both sides: hitherto those who were not themselves clerics had for the most part received, and been content to receive, their religious education through preaching and oral instruction, but now both attackers and defenders of the ecclesiastical *status quo* began to appeal to the people in vernacular literature. The most distinguished fifteenth-century prose work resulting from the religious controversies provoked by the Lollards was Reginald Pecock's *The Repressor of Over Much Blaming of the Clergy*, written in the middle of the century. This humane and reasonable defender of the Catholic position against the Lollards— his sweet reasonableness with heretics led to his own prosecution as a heretic in the end—was concerned to find a way of putting into English, theological and other abstract concepts which had not hitherto been expressed in that language. The result is a work full of strange invented words and odd inversions; but though the style is often awkward and even puzzling, it remains a remarkable single-handed attempt to enlarge the potentialities of English prose for serious discourse, and it has an impressive dignity for all its oddness.

Various experiments in the handling of a utilitarian English prose were made in the fifteenth century; among them are treatises on medicine, hunting, hawking, and political theory, mostly translated from the French or Latin. The finest literary prose of the century was that of Malory's Arthurian stories, already discussed in Chapter 5. Malory's prose, magnificent though it is for its purpose, had no significant influence on the future course of English prose narrative; it is rather the final achievement of medieval prose narrative than the first beginnings of a modern style. William Caxton, who printed Malory and gave his collection of Arthurian stories the title *Morte Darthur* by which it has been known for centuries, was himself a prolific translator as well as a pioneer printer. His translated *Recuyell of the Histories of Troye*, published at Bruges in 1475, is the first printed book in English. Caxton's importance as a printer is paramount; after his return to England in 1476 following a long stay abroad, first as merchant and then as printer, he printed much of the best of older English literature available to him, including Chaucer, Gower, and Malory, together with prose romances, translations of Latin classics (including works or parts of works by Cicero, Virgil, Ovid, and Boethius), and numerous works of piety, morality, and information. But Caxton is also important as a translator and a writer of English prose, if only for the vast quantity of translated material that he produced and made available. His translations tend to be dominated by the originals; he had not a strong enough sense of English style to be able to turn a foreign language into clear idiomatic English possessing a firm sentence structure of its own; he often paired a French and an English word together as if uncertain which was the proper one to use and hoping that at least one of them would achieve the desired effect; and he frequently got lost in long sentences. But he struggled tirelessly with the English language, trying to find an "English not over rude, ne curious, but in such terms as shall be understanden by God's grace," and he thus takes his place as one of the important exercisers of English prose in one of the most interesting transitional periods of its history.

Humanism and Protestantism, whose impact on English life and thought at the end of the fifteenth and the beginning of the sixteenth century has been briefly described in Chapter 5, made their own contributions to the development of English prose. Sir Thomas More, whose Latin *Utopia*, published in 1516, marks his chief literary contribution as a Humanist, made his contribution to English prose mainly in his religious works. His polemical writings against the reformers begin with the *Dialogue* "of images, praying to saints, other things touching the pestilent sect of Luther and Tyndale," published in 1528, and continue with a series of belligerent attacks on Tyndale against whom he defended the orthodox Roman Catholic position. The original *Dialogue* is by far the liveliest of these, for its dramatic form (it consists of a series of conversations between himself and a messenger, with brisk interruptions and interludes of cheerful anecdote) gives More the opportunity to display his humor and the verve of his colloquial style. His other controversial religious works are strange mixtures of pedantry, piety, robust humor, scurrility, and railing. Rhetorical tricks of denunciation are found side by side with passages of earnest analysis on the one hand and of rollicking vulgarity on the other. The intrusion of colloquial vitality into his most serious prose discussions is a constant feature of More's work. From the point of view of the development of English prose, the colloquial element was important as helping to keep alive in written English the invigorating element of good speech, though More never found a style which for any length of time successfully domiciled happily together the vernacular vigor and more formal qualities. His style reflected the paradox (or so it has seemed to some) of a man who was both saint and humorist.

More interesting and far more appealing than his attacks on Tyndale is his *Dialogue of Comfort against Tribulation,* written when he was in the Tower of London awaiting death. Cast in the form of a conversation between two Hungarian gentlemen anticipating possible martyrdom if the Turkish advance continues, it discusses with searching honesty the fears and hopes of a Christian in prospect of "shameful and painful death." It is the most personal of his works and reveals most clearly the nobility as well as the charm and humor of his character. Even in dealing with a subject of this immense gravity he introduces his illustrative anecdotes, his jests, and what in a later age would have been called music-hall stories, and for once the reader accepts the mingling of grave and gay as the appropriate reflection of the mind of a resolute Christian determined that even while awaiting martyrdom he will not lose sight of the humor of daily life and will take comfort from the more innocent of human follies, including his own.

William Tyndale (d. 1536), More's opponent in his religious controversies, is more distinguished as the great pioneer of English Bible translation than as a religious pamphleteer and theological writer. His prose writings on religious questions possess a speed and vigor which More's style lacks; he has a way of conveying to the reader an almost gay conviction of his own rightness, by the rapid accumulation of arresting short clauses; yet he has not More's humor, though his writings reflect an ebullience of character that we do not detect in More, for all the latter's fondness for the humorous anecdote. The theological points on which More and Tyndale differed so strongly are bound up with the whole pattern of religious controversy of the age, and that is more a subject for the historian of religious thought than for the literary historian. One point of difference is illustrated by the story told by the Protestant martyrologist John Foxe in his *Acts and Monuments:* Foxe tells how, in discussion with a "learned man" who was praising the Pope's law above God's, "Master Tyndall . . . answered him, I defy the Pope and all his laws, and said, if God spare my life ere many years I will cause a boy that driveth the plough shall know more of the Scripture than thou dost." Tyndale's attitude toward the Pope and the ecclesiastical hierarchy in general, and his view of the Bible and its authority in Christian life, were essentially that of the Lollards in an earlier generation. The Bible was the supreme authority in religious affairs and the King was equally the supreme authority in civil matters. Tyndale held, too, that it was the individual's state of mind, rather than his actions, which earned him salvation; that is, in theological terms, he set faith above good works. But no easy summary can do justice either to Tyndale's views or to More's. They were both involved in that great controversy over the nature of Christian discipline and authority, the relation between faith and works, the true vehicle of the Christian tradition, and (to use the title of one of Tyndale's works) "the obedience of a Christian man," which raged throughout the sixteenth century and later and wrought so much change in the European scene. As Professor C. S. Lewis has pointed out, both were at their best when arguing for positions which were really common ground between them.

The sermon was a literary form more apt for the development of a formal prose than the controversial religious pamphlet. The Middle Ages had developed its own traditions and styles of preaching (as the lay reader can gather from Chaucer's *Pardoner's Tale*), and the medieval homiletic tradition did not dry up suddenly at the Renaissance but continued to influence, in varying ways, the preacher's methods and devices. Nevertheless, new styles and new kinds of sophistication came into English preaching in the sixteenth and seventeenth centuries. The sermons of Dean Colet combined powerful rhetoric with high idealism in a notable manner; Bishop Fisher introduced humanistic variations into an essentially medieval homiletic style, rising on occasion to a grave and gentle eloquence; Hugh Latimer (ca. 1490–1555) was a great popular preacher who knew how to make effective use of the most casual and anecdotal material, preserving an appearance of impromptu speaking which greatly added to the immediacy of the effect. The Elizabethan settlement, completed with the establishment of the thirty-nine articles in 1571, produced the Church of England, Catholic in profession but national in character, repudiating the authority of the Pope but episcopal in organization, a national Catholic Church stripped of the abuses of Rome but resisting the demands of the Puritans for extreme simplicity and severity in worship, for the abolition of episcopacy, and for granting spiritual authority to individuals who claimed it on the grounds of grace vouchsafed to them and of preaching ability. The settlement provided a wide roof under which different shades of opinion could shelter together, as later divisions into "high" and "low" Church (both within the Church of England) were to testify; but it left out both Roman Catholics and the more extreme Puritans. The Puritans, to whom preaching the Word was a sacred obligation, would have had a greater effect on English preaching if they had not eventually been forbidden to preach by the repressive legislation introduced in support of the establishment by Archbishop Whitgift. Fortunately, the Church of England produced early in its history a succession of learned and able ecclesiastics who brought preaching in England in the late sixteenth and early seventeenth centuries to a new level of literary art. The Puritan preachers, who re-emerged under the Commonwealth and later strongly influenced the style of nonconformist preaching, are important in the history of the spoken sermon; but the great Anglican preachers are of more concern to the literary historian.

The term "Puritan" has been used with many shades of meaning. Those who accepted Calvin's theology and also demanded that his system of church government be set up in England on the grounds that it was the one proper system to be discovered from the text of the New Testament and was therefore compulsory for all true Christians, represented the hard core of the party. But there were Calvinists prominent in the Church of England well into the seventeenth century; the active controversy between Puritan and Anglican in Queen Elizabeth's reign centered on the method of church government. The Church of England was committed to episcopacy, and the Puritans were equally committed to opposing the whole notion of an episcopal hierarchy. It must be remembered that Henry VIII's reformation did not affect the theology, the hierarchy, or the ritual of the Church in England; it merely removed the Pope's authority at the top of the hierarchy and substituted that of the King. The short reign of his son, Edward VI, gave free play to more purely

Protestant forces, but with the accession of Edward's sister Mary, in 1554, England was reconciled with Rome and those vocal Protestants who did not escape to Geneva were vigorously persecuted. The exiles returned on the accession of Elizabeth in 1558, considerably embittered by the Marian persecutions, much more uncompromising in their Calvinist views, and hopeful that with a Protestant queen now on the throne they could look forward to the implementation in England of the Calvinist form of church government. But Elizabeth deliberately avoided both extremes in the religious controversies she found prevailing on her accession; she sensed the nation's combination of conservatism and nationalism in religious matters in spite of the brilliance and passion of the Puritan propagandists, and her settlement was Protestant, national, and antipapist without being anti-Catholic. She retained the bishops—whether as necessary machinery for implementing her own authority over the Church, in the spirit of her successor James' remark, "No Bishop, no King," or for more disinterested reasons, need not concern us. The result was a spate of Puritan criticism of the bishops, both as individuals and as an institution.

The bishops eventually set up machinery to silence their critics, controlling both the press and the pulpit, but no sooner was the machinery completed when the anonymous pamphleteer who called himself Martin Marprelate began to issue his series of spirited attacks on the bishops. These pamphlets, which appeared in 1588 and 1589, have tremendous vigor; popular in style, colloquial in speech, full of witty taunts, vulgar jeers, and all the humorous rhetorical tricks of an expert street-corner orator, they introduced a new manner into religious pamphleteering. Though Martin Marprelate was never discovered, his printers were caught, and that put an end to the pamphlets, but not before they had so disturbed the bishops that they hired writers to attack Martin in his own style. One of these anti-Martinist pamphlets was by Lyly, others were for long erroneously attributed to Nashe; some of them succeed in capturing Martin's exuberant vitality of style. Nashe may have written the pamphlet called *An Almond for a Parrot*, which shows his characteristic command of racy invective and picturesque exaggeration. At any rate, Nashe's undisputed prose writings, which include satirical pamphlets and a picaresque novel, show these qualities to a most remarkable degree. The Elizabethan satirical pamphlet, as practiced by Nashe, Lodge, and others, thus owes something to the style developed by Elizabethan religious controversy.

If religious and other controversies helped to stimulate the development of a polemical prose style, a more profound shaping of English prose was going on at the same time by means of the discipline of translation. The earliest and one of the most significant of the great Elizabethan translations was Thomas North's *Lives of the Noble Grecians and Romans* (1579), translated from Plutarch via the French of Amyot. North's Plutarch provided the Elizabethans in large measure with their view of the ancient world; he provided the personalities, the political and domestic details, the "properties," not only for Shakespeare in his Roman plays but also for the educated Englishmen of the time. His style is vigorous, idiomatic and flexible, and it is significant that Shakespeare sometimes follows him almost verbatim. Sir Thomas Hoby's translation, published in 1561, of the greatest of all the "courtesy books," Castiglione's *Il Cortegiano*, "The Courtier," made available to Englishmen a notable exposition of the high Renaissance ideal of the gentleman—an ideal combining the two medieval alternatives, the active and the contemplative life, the whole seasoned with a passionate neo-Platonic sense of a graduated ascent from earthly to divine beauty. Hoby's style is uneven and not really able to cope consistently with the happy eloquence of the original Italian; but Castiglione's picture of an ideal Court done with such liveliness and enthusiasm, with dramatic dialogue and incidental short stories, does communicate itself in Hoby's translations for all its occasional uncertainties. Hoby was influenced in some degree by Sir John Cheke's view that English should be used in its native purity, uncorrupted by borrowings from other languages; but Cheke went to extremes in his advocacy of "pure and unmixed" English—his spelling reform and his ardent Saxonism can be seen in his curious translation of Matthew and part of Mark—while Hoby only intermittently seeks for the Anglo-Saxon equivalent of a word of Romance or Latin origin.

The Italian *novella*—"trifling tale," as Sir Thomas Hoby translates the word, but that perhaps only indicates his own fundamental seriousness of mind—so important as providing plots for Elizabethan drama, also attracted English translators. William Painter's *Palace of Pleasure*, published in 1566 with a second volume in 1567, contains a large variety of such stories, many taken not directly from the Italian but from the rather more verbose French versions in Belleforest's *Histoires Tragiques*. The authors include Boccaccio, Bandello, Cinthio, and Margaret of Navarre, as well as Livy, Herodotus, and Plutarch. Geoffrey Fenton's *Tragical Discourses*, published in 1567, contains Italian *novelle* elaborated and moralized. George Pettie's *Petite Palace of Pettie his Pleasures*, 1576, tells a dozen stories from classical sources (mostly Ovid and Livy) in an elaborate rhetorical style in which we first see sustained that characteristic Elizabethan attempt to achieve a literary prose through a careful use of parallels, antitheses, balanced similes, and the other devices associated with euphuism. Lyly's *Euphues*, briefly discussed in Chapter 7, develops this style, which is modified somewhat in the sequel, *Euphues and his England;* in the prose dialogue of his plays Lyly advances to a true courtly prose with a charm and delicacy of its own.

The noblest achievement of sixteenth-century English prose translation was, however, done on the Bible. The Wycliffite versions had been renderings from the Latin of the Vulgate; they had, moreover, been made before printing came to England, and could not therefore have the circulation that the printed Bible could have. The sixteenth-century movement was both Protestant and Humanist in impulse—the former in that it sprang from the desire to make available to the ordinary reader the one original source of Christianity, and the latter in its determination to translate from the original Hebrew and Greek. The combination of the two impulses is symbolized by the fact that William Tyndale, pioneer translator of the Bible into English from the original languages, published in 1529 a translation of Erasmus' *Exhortation to the Diligent Study of Scripture* in which the great Humanist uttered words that were heartily echoed by the Protestant translator:

> I would that all women should read the Gospel and Paul's Epistles, and I would to God they were translated into the tongues of all men, so that they might not only be read and known of the Scots and Irishmen but also of the Turks and Saracens. . . . I would to God the plowman would sing a text of the Scripture at his plowbeam and that the weaver at his loom with this would drive away the tediousness of time. I would the wayfaring man with this pastime would expel the weariness of his journey. And to be short I would that all the communication of the Christian should be of the Scripture, for in a manner such are we ourselves as our daily tales are.

This, of course, was not orthodox Catholic doctrine. The medieval Church took the view that ordinary folk should not read the Bible themselves, but should have appropriate portions of the Vulgate interpreted to them by properly trained experts. The demand for a vernacular Bible was a feature of many medieval heresies, and was sternly resisted by the Church. As the criticism of the Church that was eventually to bring about the Reformation spread in England as elsewhere, the demand for Bible translation also grew. The Church shifted its ground somewhat in the face of this growing demand and began to object to the Wycliffite translations because they were erroneous rather than because they made the Bible readily accessible to the public. Sir Thomas More, discussing Bible translation in 1528, made it clear that in his view the Church could only have condemned the Wycliffite versions if they were textually corrupt and contained heretical notes, and he accordingly assumed that these versions did in fact have these faults. More's main objections to Tyndale's translation were its heretical glosses and its untraditional terms.

Official opinion against vernacular Bible translation was, however, slow in changing, and Tyndale did his work secretly abroad. The first edition of his New Testament was seized at the printer's in Cologne in 1525, before the printing was complete, and Tyndale moved to Worms, where he brought out two editions of the work in the same year. He then turned his attention to the Old Testament, having acquired a very respectable knowledge of Hebrew, and published his version of the Pentateuch in 1531. A version of the Book of Jonah appeared the following year, and in 1534 he brought out a revised edition of his New Testament, to which was added a translation of select passages from the Old Testament Prophets. Further revisions of the New Testament appeared in later years. Tyndale's New Testament circulated widely, though surreptitiously. The translation was officially condemned by the ecclesiastical authorities in England as well as in a royal proclamation of 1530 which, however, significantly affirmed the royal intention of providing for an authorized translation when the time was ripe. Attempts were made to trap Tyndale into coming to England. He was eventually betrayed in 1535, and burned at the stake at Vilvorde the following year.

Tyndale was a strongly Protestant translator who deliberately rendered (to Thomas More's horror) *ecclesia* as "congregation" not "church," *charis* as "favor" not "grace," and so on, because he wished to avoid the Roman Catholic implications of the established terms. And because he rendered the New Testament from the Greek (Erasmus' edition, with help from his Latin version) and the parts of the Old Testament he translated from the Hebrew, instead of following the traditional Roman Catholic view that the Vulgate was the true Christian text, he was bound to introduce certain novelties into men's conception of the Bible. Further, he shared with Luther the view that a biblical rendering should respect the language of the common man and be clear and straightforward, and this led him to an occasional phrasing which sounds too brightly popular to ears accustomed to the statelier prose of the Authorized Version. But his simplicity gives his prose, for all its occasional oddness to modern ears, a special charm, and though later translators added a more liturgical note to Tyndale's honest clarity, they retained the basic simplicity, which remains the norm of narrative prose in the Authorized Version. Tyndale had a true gift of phrase, and introduced many words, phrases, and cadences which remain unchanged in the Authorized Version. The English language was richer for his biblical endeavors, and the line of Bible translation which led unbroken to the Authorized Version had been begun. As far as the New Testament went, all subsequent English renderings to 1611 and beyond were in effect revisions of Tyndale or of his revisers, and his translation of the Pentateuch and other parts of the Old Testament gave Protestant Christianity a rich store of words and phrases (including "scapegoat," "mercy seat," "long-suffering" and many more) which became a permanent part of the English language.

In 1535—five years after Henry VIII's proclamation condemning Tyndale's translation yet affirming the royal intention of eventually providing for an authorized translation—the first complete English Bible appeared, the work of Miles Coverdale, a man inspired by the same ideals as Tyndale but milder and more compromising in character. This was not the authorized version for which the English bishops were preparing, but Coverdale assumed that his work (which was probably printed at Zurich) would be acceptable to the King, to whom it was dedicated. A later edition of Coverdale's Bible, published in 1537, bore the legend: "Set forth with the King's most gracious license." The main battle had been won, and the 1537 quarto edition of Coverdale's Bible was in a sense the first "authorized version" of the Bible in English. (Since the King was by now "supreme head" of the Church as well as of the State, his "license" implied a twofold authorization.) Coverdale had not Tyndale's scholarship in Hebrew and Greek, and his translation was admittedly derived from later Latin and German versions. He mentions "five sundry interpreters" whose work he drew on, and these were fairly certainly the Zurich Swiss-German Bible of 1524–29 (by Zwingli and Leo Juda), Luther's German Bible, Pagninus' Latin Bible of 1528, the Vulgate, and Tyndale's New Testament and Pentateuch. For the Old Testament, except the Pentateuch, the Zurich Bible is his primary source, with occasional renderings of Pagninus and Luther preferred to those of the Zurich version. The basis of his Pentateuch is Tyndale's, and Tyndale also influenced Coverdale's rendering of Jonah. Coverdale's New Testament is a revision of Tyndale largely by the Zurich text. When his other authorities left him in genuine doubt, he fell back on the Vulgate.

Lacking Tyndale's original scholarship, Coverdale was free to choose renderings and phrasings that pleased his ear rather than satisfied a demand for strict scholarly accuracy. He possessed a fluency which sometimes produced a fine flowing cadence and at other times led him into diffuse paraphrase. His fluency had a permanent effect on the style of the English Bible, for it was he more than any other single translator whose sense of rhythm produced that musical quality which is particularly evident in the Authorized Version of 1611. His influence did not work only through "Coverdale's Bible" of 1535 and its later editions, for Coverdale put his services at the disposal of later official translators and his revisions of phrasing in subsequent versions helped significantly to mold the style of the Authorized Version. In 1537 appeared a composite version, known as "Matthew's Bible," made up of Tyndale's translation of as much of the Old Testament as he had translated, Coverdale's translation of the remainder of the Old Testament, and Tyndale's New Testament (the professed translator Matthew, whether a real or a fictitious person, being introduced to cover up the Government's inconsistency in now allowing parts of a translation they had earlier vehemently condemned). This version, like the edition of Coverdale's Bible of the same year, was "set forth with the King's most gracious license," and it was strongly supported by the bishops. More important, it was the basis for the series of revisions that culminated in the King James, or Authorized Version of 1611. Its imperfections were freely admitted by the bishops, even though Archbishop Cranmer promoted it as strongly as he could, and the Great Bible, a revision of Matthew's Bible made by Coverdale at the instance of the King's minister Thomas Cromwell, was published in April, 1540. In this version (which shows, in the Old Testament, the influence of Sebastian Münster's Latin translation) Coverdale introduced many of the felicities of phrasing that have remained in the English Bible.

The Great Bible ran into many editions, but there were continuous suggestions of a further major revision. On the death of Edward VI the progress of English Bible translation was temporarily halted. The Catholic Queen Mary on her accession stopped abruptly the printing of vernacular Bibles in England. Many of the Protestants most interested in Bible translation went into exile, and it was at the colony of these exiles at Geneva that the next English translation of the Bible was made. This, known as the "Geneva Bible," published at Geneva in 1560, was a thorough revision of the text of the Great Bible after the original Hebrew of the Old Testament and in the New Testament a revision of Tyndale after the original Greek and Beza's Latin New Testament of 1556. The Geneva translators had the help of such other versions and aids to translation as had recently appeared on the Continent, and they made full use of it. Their version was the most accurate and scholarly English translation that had yet been made, and though it is not officially in the direct line of succes-

sion of the Authorized Version, it was in fact heavily drawn upon
by the King James translators. On the whole, the Geneva translators
sacrificed style to accuracy, and there is a pedantic flavor about the
work, particularly noticeable in the spelling of Old Testament proper
names, which follows the Hebrew exactly. The Geneva Bible is the
first English Bible to break up the Old Testament text into numbered
verses, a perhaps unfortunate practice which has persisted until the
"Bible designed to be read as literature" of our own day. The Puritan
habit of text-quoting must have been largely responsible for this
desire to have each verse numbered for ease of reference. The pro-
fuse marginal notes were another feature of the translation displeas-
ing to modern eyes as it was to Elizabethan Anglicans.

The accession of Queen Elizabeth in 1558 marked a reversion to a
middle-of-the-road Protestant policy. The Great Bible was again regarded as the official version and ordered to be set up in churches
(the Geneva Bible, being the work of more extreme Protestants who
were considerably to the "left" of Elizabeth's position, was not officially recognized). In 1568 the Great Bible was superseded by a further revision made by a company of bishops and hence known as the
"Bishops' Bible." This version was not, however, altogether successful. A combination of the work of different revisers working with
little common policy or discipline, it is patchy and uneven, and in
accuracy considerably behind the Geneva Bible, which continued to
be the most popular translation in England until after 1611. Finally,
when James I ascended the throne in 1603 he appointed a company
of learned men consisting of the most competent Hebrew and Greek
scholars available (excluding, however, those who were antagonistic
to the Anglican Church) to prepare a great new revision. This work,
begun in 1604 and completed in 1611, after meticulous and carefully
coordinated labor, has remained *the* English Bible ever since. It was
as accurate a translation of the available Hebrew and Greek texts as
the combined scholarship of the age could make; but, more than that,
the company of translators who worked on it were sufficiently sensitive to the demands of a biblical prose in keeping with the finest
stylistic achievements of Tyndale and Coverdale that again and
again they seemed to be able to strike the right note with unerring
felicity. True, the style of the Authorized Version was in some degree
archaic by now, and the revisers were thus deliberately perpetuating
a biblical style which was something apart from contemporary English prose, a style that had been forged in almost a century's experimentation. The Authorized Version, it must be remembered, was not
a new translation, but a revision, ostensibly of the Bishops' Bible but
in fact making as much use of the Geneva Bible. It was the culmina-

tion of the successive versions of which Tyndale's was the first. And though archaic in its time, it had a great influence on the rhythms and the vocabulary of later English prose, especially in the seventeenth and the nineteenth centuries.

There were other biblical versions produced during this period which were not in the line of succession of the Authorized Version. There was, for example, the Bible translated by Richard Taverner, published in 1538, which was an independent revision of Matthew's Bible which received no official recognition. Sir John Cheke's rendering of Matthew and part of Mark, which remained unpublished until 1843, is interesting for its determined attempt to provide genuine English equivalents of ecclesiastical terms from the Greek and Latin; thus "parable" becomes "biword," "proselyte" becomes "freshman," "crucified" becomes "crossed." But the most important English Bible outside the main tradition of the Protestant translations of the sixteenth and early seventeenth centuries was the Roman Catholic translation from the Vulgate, of which the New Testament appeared at Rheims in 1582 and the Old Testament at Douai (Douay) in 1609–10. The moving spirit in the preparation of this version was Cardinal Allen, president of the English College at Rheims—the college had moved from Douai to Rheims in 1578 on account of the expulsion order against English residents issued by the magistrates in that year —and a distinguished Bible scholar. Writing in Latin to a friend in September, 1578, Allen explained how the Catholic preachers were at a disadvantage compared with the Protestant, who were familiar with the English Bible and did not therefore need to translate extempore from the Vulgate when preaching to a popular audience. The Catholic preacher, he said, was liable to stumble in his English renderings, which would make a bad impression on his hearers. Although it were perhaps better that no translation into *barbaras linguas* were made, yet the disadvantages the Catholic cause suffered by not having an English version while the Protestants had were sufficient to overrule the traditional objections to vernacular versions. The result was a scholarly rendering of the Latin Vulgate text. The emphasis was on accuracy rather than on stylistic grace, and though the Rheims and Douay Bible is a notable English translation it has not the independent literary merit, nor has it had the influence, of the Authorized Version.

The Book of Common Prayer of 1549, the work of Archbishop Cranmer and others, happily combines the earlier tradition of liturgical prose with the new tradition of Protestant biblical translation. Its style derives in large measure from the stately Latin liturgical prose of the medieval service book used in the diocese of Salisbury,

known as the *Use of Sarum*, as well as from the devotional Books of
Hours, originally in Latin but occasionally in English, in the fourteenth and fifteenth centuries and (with significant doctrinal differences) after the Reformation. The version of the Psalms and other
biblical passages in *The Book of Common Prayer* was that of the
Great Bible of 1540—i.e., Coverdale's revision of Matthew's Bible.
The combination of Latin and English, medieval and modern, liturgical, devotional, and biblical styles was not only remarkably effective from the literary point of view; it also symbolized and exhibited
that unique combination of the traditional and the reforming which
was such a significant aspect of the English Reformation. *The Book
of Common Prayer*, which was confirmed as the official Church of
England prayer book under the Elizabethan settlement, remains eloquent testimony to the English genius for preserving continuity
amid change.

Humanism and the Reformation meet in English Bible translation,
the former providing the philological tools, the latter the religious
impulse. Meanwhile, both humanistic and religious prose continued
independently. Sir Thomas Elyot (ca. 1490–1546) produced in 1531
The Book of the Governor, an English contribution (though deriving
from Erasmus, the Italian Patrizzi, and other European sources) to
the abundant Renaissance literature of instruction for members of
the ruling class, of which, as we have seen, Castiglione's *Il Cortegiano* is the most impressive. Elyot's book shows a profound belief in
the importance of order or "degree," and it stresses equally practical,
intellectual, and esthetic education. His prose is consciously artful,
but not excessively tricked out with any of the euphuistic devices by
means of which writers later in the century tried to give literary
dignity to their style. He combines stateliness and clarity; he uses
anecdote and allusion adroitly, but with no great liveliness; and the
result is workmanlike without being exciting. Elyot's later work includes miscellaneous translations and popularizations of medical, political, and educational subjects, and the first significant Latin-Eng-
lish dictionary. Roger Ascham (1515–68) is an attractive Protestant
Humanist whose *Toxophilus* (1545) is a patriotic treatise on archery
as an English national sport done with liveliness and charm; it is cast
in dialogue form, but the appeal of the work derives less from the
exploitation of the dramatic possibilities of the dialogue than from
the personal observation and the lovingly described detail in the
pictures of English life. His educational treatise, *The Schoolmaster*,
published after his death in 1570, is concerned first with the practical
details of teaching, advocating gentleness and patience instead of the
rod, and, secondly, with the method of teaching Latin. His attitude

is narrowly Humanist; he advocates the imitation of select classical authors for the proper molding of style and shows the characteristic Humanist contempt for medieval romances. For all his charm and gentleness, especially evident in the discussion of teaching methods, he shows the narrowness of the Protestant Humanist: "In our forefathers' time, when Papistry, as a standing pool, covered and overflowed all England, few books were read in our tongue, saving certain books of Chivalry, as they said, for pastime and pleasure, which, as some say, were made in monasteries by idle monks or wanton canons, as one for example, *Morte Arthure,* the whole pleasure of which book standeth in two special points, in open manslaughter and bold bawdry." Ascham also attacks rhyme, and inveighs against the immorality of the Italianate Englishman and "the enchantments of Circe, brought out of Italy to mar men's manners in England." Ascham's prose style has a plain vigor; it is not, however, the plainness of colloquial speech that he affects, but a studied plainness deriving from his belief in the native strength of the English language (he was like Sir John Cheke, though less extreme, in his preference for words of English origin) and a deliberate balancing of sentences and alternation of long sentences with short. Cheke, whom we have already mentioned as a purist in his vocabulary and author of an odd translation from the New Testament, was a notable Greek scholar and teacher; he produced in 1549 a prose pamphlet entitled *The Hurt of Sedition* which sets forward with great force the Tudor position with regard to rebellion (and so helps to explain, for example, Shakespeare's attitude in *Henry IV Part I* and elsewhere) and does not show his Saxonism as his biblical translation does, employing a style of no great individuality or distinction. Thomas Wilson (ca. 1525–81) is another English Humanist, whose most important work is *The Art of Rhetoric,* published in 1553 and in a revised and enlarged edition in 1560. This can reasonably be called the first modern handbook of English composition, though its sources are to be found in Quintilian and Cicero. He anticipates euphuism in his advocacy of similes drawn from natural (or unnatural) history and in his advice on the pairing and balancing of clauses; yet he is no advocate of artificiality, condemning "inkhorn terms" and recommending a style without affectation and excessive Latinisms. His own style can be unduly rhetorical at times, but, like so many Elizabethan prose writers, he has the gift of enlivening discussion with anecdote.

History and biography were also fields in which Elizabethan prose exercised itself. Edward Hall (ca. 1499–1547) produced in his *Union of the two Noble and Illustre Families of Lancaster and York* an account of English history from Henry IV to Henry VIII from what might be called the official Tudor viewpoint; he showed the pattern as developing from trouble through tragedy to Tudor redemption, thus fixing what has been called the "Tudor myth," which some critics have seen as so important a clue to the understanding of Shakespeare's history plays. Hall's style was condemned by Ascham as "indenture English" (i.e., coupling together words of similar meaning in pairs, for emphasis and rhetorical effect: "all regions which by division and dissension [are] vexed, molested and troubled [are] by union and agreement relieved, pacified and enriched"), but at his best Hall can use this device to give gravity and even dramatic power to his writing. He is a rhetorical writer who balances his sentences with deliberate and sometimes excessive art. He is also a historian who sees a grand moral pattern in history and spares no effort to bring out in relief the high points of his story. Sir Thomas More had done something similar on a smaller scale in his Latin *History of Richard III* (written 1513–14 but not published until 1565) which was translated into English and appeared in the collected folio edition of More's English works in 1557.

Raphael Holinshed's *Chronicles*, of which the first edition appeared in 1577 and the enlarged second edition (the one which Shakespeare used) in 1587, is a compilation of English, Scottish, and Irish history deriving from a variety of earlier sources (including Hall, and Sir Thomas More's *Richard III*). The original plan was an ambitious "universal cosmography" projected by the London printer Reginald Wolfe, but the completed work was much less comprehensive. It did, however, include geographical as well as historical accounts of the countries dealt with. The *Description of England* included in the *Chronicle* is by William Harrison, who writes in a cheerful, rapid, anecdotal style, pleasingly garrulous, and gives much valuable information about the England of his day. The *Description of Scotland* is translated by Harrison from the Scots version (by John Bellenden, 1536) of the Latin history of Scotland by the Scottish Humanist Hector Boece, published in 1527. Holinshed had other collaborators, and the total result is a somewhat discursive work, with the history lacking the sharp outlines of Hall, but clearly told, with a feeling for the lively incident and high patriotic tone.

Tudor patriotism encouraged the chronicler and the historian, and at the same time the Renaissance view of history as a "mirror for magistrates," a source of moral lessons for the ruler of a state, helped to increase the vogue for history. Patriotism also encouraged antiquarian study, which begins to become important at this period, with Archbishop Parker, John Stow, John Speed, John Leland, and William Camden. Each of these made important contributions to the

study of English antiquities. Parker, with the help of his assistant
John Joscelyn, pioneered in the study of Anglo-Saxon, one of his
motives being to show the national nature of the English Church
even in Anglo-Saxon times and so demonstrate the historical continuity of the Church of England. Leland, realizing that the dissolution of the monasteries and the dispersal of their libraries might destroy forever important literary documents, embarked on (to cite the
title of one of his major works) "a laborious journey and search for
England's antiquities" and also produced a Latin list of British authors and their works which represents the true beginning of English
literary scholarship. Leland's cataloguing work of British authors was
continued by the violently Protestant John Bale and the violently
Catholic John Pits. Stow, with Parker's help, edited a number of
medieval English chronicles; he also edited Chaucer, and produced
a *Summary of English Chronicles* in 1565, *The Chronicles of England*
in 1580 (entitled *Annals* in later editions) and, his most important
work, *A Survey of London* in 1598. Speed (like Stow, originally a
tailor by trade) was antiquary, historian, and cartographer, but
it is as a cartographer that he is most important. Camden's *Britannia,*
easily the greatest antiquarian work of the period, was published
originally in Latin in 1586 and appeared in English in 1610.

At the other extreme from the local topographical work of antiquaries is the grandiosely conceived world history, of which the most
impressive example in English is Ralegh's *The History of the World,*
published unfinished in 1614. Ralegh's work is a remarkable mingling
of the medieval and the Renaissance—and perhaps can be used as
evidence by those who maintain that the Renaissance marked no real
change in human thought. Based (as far as historical information
goes) entirely on secondary sources, it is an attempt to see a provi-
dential pattern working through world history—history which begins
with the Creation, accepts the biblical record of events implicitly,
yet shows a shrewd critical mind at work in dealing with postbiblical
events and in commenting on men and affairs. There is a certain
majesty in the grand moral pattern which Ralegh sees unfolding in
the events he describes, and the moral eloquence of the style provides the proper tone for this sort of history, with its somber sense of
the brevity of individual life and the vanity of human plans. The
medieval *ubi sunt* theme is here, and Ralegh has the medieval sense
of human affairs as a pageant directed and watched by God; but he
has a sense of the heroic too, an admiration for skill and magnanimity
wherever found, and a feeling for parallels and contrasts between
past and present. He did not get beyond 168 B.C.

The sixteenth century saw the rise of a new interest in biography as well as in history. Sometimes, as in More's work on Richard III, the impulse is historical and the biography becomes a species of history, but another motive sometimes manifested itself. This was the desire to commemorate and celebrate a distinguished figure, not as in a medieval saint's life, where the narrative tended to be typical and exemplary, but out of personal admiration, affection, or curiosity. The Humanists, both in England and abroad, developed a tradition of writing eulogistic biographies of their fellows (deceased or still living). These are often in Latin, such as the group of biographies of Humanists (including Colet, Linacre, Fisher, More, and Latimer) brought out by George Lily in 1548. The most distinguished representative in English of this *genre* in the sixteenth century is William Roper's life of his father-in-law, Sir Thomas More. This is written with an affectionate gravity, in a prose style which, in spite of its long and somewhat cumbersome sentences, succeeds in conveying the writer's personal attitude and interest; the dialogue, where the sentences are shorter and the voices strangely authentic, is particularly successful.

John Foxe's *Acts and Monuments,* published in English in 1563 after the publication of an original Latin version at Basel in 1559, is biography of a different sort. Foxe's aim was to write the story of Christian martyrs of all times, and he added in successive editions detailed accounts, from the Protestant point of view, of the persecution of Protestants under Mary. Foxe's work is not all original, for he includes narratives of others in various degrees of abridgement. The effect of the work is cumulative; in spite of a cumbersome English style, the succession of detailed incidents in the portion dealing with the Marian persecutions does succeed in creating a lively impression of the dedicated heroism of the martyrs and the senseless malice of their persecutors. The book (known, since an edition of 1776, as *The Book of Martyrs*) was an immensely influential piece of Protestant hagiography. Foxe's anti-Catholic bias is, of course, strong; but he never consciously distorts his material, much of which was drawn from the accounts of eyewitnesses which he obtained after his return from exile on the accession of Queen Elizabeth. Further, he was a genuinely humane man who disapproved of cruelty whichever side practiced it; it is this humanity which provides the note of passion in his account of individual sufferings, rather than exultation at the thought of proving the wickedness of his religious opponents.

Among the Protestant writers in the brief reign of the Catholic Mary may be mentioned John Ponet or Poynet, whose *Short Treatise of Politique Power,* written in exile and published anonymously abroad in 1556, the year of his death, attacked with eloquence and spirit the whole conception of Tudor monarchy. There were not many writers of the time who questioned the view that the ruler, as God's vicegerent, cannot be lawfully attacked by his subjects; Ponet attacked it with vigor, undercutting the whole position of those who saw disobedience to the ruler as disobedience to God and who held that only God and never his subjects could punish an erring ruler, by an appeal to natural law as understood in medieval political thought. And that reminds us that the Tudor despotism was a Renaissance invention; the position maintained, for example, by Sir John Cheke in *The Hurt of Sedition* was strictly modern; Ponet, though antipapal, was more medieval in his political thought than some Protestant Humanists, which illustrates some of the difficulties of writing intellectual history.

Among the miscellaneous themes to which Elizabethan pamphleteers devoted their attention, the denunciation of real or fancied evils was a favorite. Stephen Gosson's *School of Abuse,* published in 1579, is chiefly remembered for having provoked Sidney's *Defence of Poesie* in reply. Gosson's work is not in its own right an important piece of criticism; it is a routine denunciation of contemporary literature and the theater; but it is of some interest as an exercise in rhetorical invective. The subtitle—"containing a pleasant invective against Poets, Pipers, Players, Jesters and such like Caterpillars of a Commonwealth"—shows something of his exhibitionist style. His balanced sentences, alliteration, and other stylistic devices show the artful rhetorician as much as the indignant moralist:

> Oh what a wonderful change is this! Our wrestling at arms is turned to wallowing in ladies' laps, our courage to cowardice, our running to riot, our bows into bowls, and our darts to dishes. We have robbed Greece of gluttony, Italy of wantonness, Spain of pride, France of deceit, and Dutchland of quaffing. Compare London to Rome, and England to Italy, you shall find the theatres of the one, the abuses of the other, to be rife among us. . . . In our assemblies at plays in London, you shall see such heaving and shoving, such itching and shouldering, to sit by women; such care for their garments, that they be not trod on; such eyes to their laps, that no chips light in them; such pillows to their backs, that they take no hurt; such masking in their ears, I know not what; . . . such ticking, such toying, such smiling, such winking, and such manning them home, when the sports are ended, that it is a right comedy to mark their behaviour, to watch their conceits, as the cat's for the mouse, . . .

Other pamphleteers also attacked the abuses of the time, more often from a general conservative viewpoint than from an extreme Puritan position; bewailing the lost virtues of Old England, denouncing new fashions and follies, as Philip Stubbes, in his *Anatomy of Abuses* (1583), attacked the wearing of starched ruffs by women. ("The women there use great ruffs and neckerchers of holland, lawn, cambric, and such cloth, as the greatest thread shall not be so big as the least hair that is; and lest they should fall down, they are smeared and starched in the devil's liquor, I mean starch . . .") George Whetstone's *Touchstone for the Time* (1584) similarly denounces the "many perilous mischiefs bred in the bowels of the city of London." And there were many other similar pamphlets.

Gosson was answered (as well as by Sidney) by Thomas Lodge in his privately printed and suppressed pamphlet, *Honest Excuses*. Lodge was better at attack than defense, however, and his *Alarm against Usurers* (1584) and *Wit's Mercury* (1596) contain—especially the latter—some lively pictures of contemporary abuses in a style where a rhetorical euphuism struggles with a robust realistic humor, the realistic humor winning in the end. The best of all the Elizabethans in this vein, however, is Thomas Nashe, whose *Anatomy of Absurdity* ("containing a brief confutation of the slender imputed praises to feminine perfection, with a short description of the several practices of youth and sundry follies of our licentious times; no less pleasant to be read, than profitable to be remembered, especially of those who live more licentiously, or addicted to a more nice stoical austerity"), published in 1589, shows him employing every kind of verbal and rhythmic device to arrest the attention of the reader. Nashe's characteristic mixture of roaring colloquialism and fancy rhetoric is more successful than might be imagined, especially in his later work, such as *Pierce Penniless, his Supplication to the Devil*, an extraordinary combination of character portraits of types, anecdote, abuse, preaching, fiction, and sheer high spirits. Nashe became involved in a fierce pamphlet war with Gabriel Harvey, whom he abuses fiercely in *Pierce Penniless* and elsewhere. His *Lenten Stuff* shows Nashe's roistering exhibitionist style to best advantage; it is a mock-heroic celebration of the red herring, in which the most fantastic Latinisms take their place in a style which is nevertheless colloquial and popular in tone. He finds the origin of the herring in the metamorphosis of Hero, after she and Leander had come to their tragic end:

To recount *ab ovo*, or from the church-book of his birth, how the herring first came to be a fish, and then how he came to be king of fishes, and graduationately how from white to red be changed, would require so massy a tome as Holinshed; but in half a pennyworth of paper I will epitomize them. Let me see, hath anybody in Yarmouth heard of Leander and Hero, of whom divine Musaeus sung, and a diviner Muse than him, Kit Marlowe?

Two faithful lovers they were, as every apprentice in Paul's churchyard will tell you for your love, and sell you for your money; the one dwelt at Abydos in Asia, which was Leander; the other, which was Hero, his Mistress or Delia, at Sestos in Europe, and she was a pretty pinckany and Venus priest; and but an arm of the sea divided them; it divided them and it divided them not, for over that arm of the sea could be made a long arm. In their parents the most division rested, and their towns that like Yarmouth and Leystoffe [Lowestoft] were still at wrig wrag and sucked from their mothers' teats serpentine hatred against each other. Which drove Leander when he durst not deal above board, or be seen aboard any ship, to sail to his lady dear, to play the didopper and ducking water spaniel to swim to her, nor that in the day, but by owl-light.

Leander, after he is drowned, is changed into a ling (the fish), and Hero to a herring. The detailed invention with which the story is told shows a most fertile vein of fantasy, as well as a Rabelaisian wit. Here, for example, is the account of what happens to Hero's nurse after her metamorphosis:

The nurse or mother Mampudding, that was a cowering on the back side while these things were a tragedizing, led by the scritch or outcry to the prospect of this sorrowful heigho, as soon as, through the revalled button-holes of her blear eyes, she had sucked in and received such a revelation of Doomsday, and that she saw her mistress mounted a cockhorse and hoisted away to hell or heaven on the backs of those rough headed ruffians, down she sunk to the earth, as dead as a door nail, and never mumped crust after. Whereof their supernalities (having a drop or two of pity left after the huge hogshead of tears they spent for Hero and Leander) seemed to be something sorry, though they could not weep for it, and because they would be sure to have medicine that should make them weep at all times, to that kind of grain they turned her which we call mustard-seed, as well as she was a shrewish snappish bawd, that would bite off a man's nose with an answer and had rheumatic sore eyes that ran always, as that she might accompany Hero and Leander after death as in her lifetime; and hence it is that mustard bites a man so by the nose, and makes him weep and water his plants when he tasteth it; and that Hero and Leander, the red herring and ling, never come to the board without mustard, their waiting maid; and if you mark it, mustard looks of the tanned winscot hue of such a withered wrinkle-faced beldam as she was that was altered thereto. . . .

Whippet, turn to a new lesson, and strike we up "John for the King," or tell how the herring scrambled up to be King of all fishes. So it fell upon a time and tide, though not upon a holiday, a falconer bringing forth certain hawks out of Ireland—

and off Nashe goes to another piece of absurd invention, told in the same extraordinary style. There is nothing like this in English again until we come to some parts of Joyce's *Ulysses*, though Sir Thomas Urquart's translation of Rabelais, done in the middle of the seventeenth century, has something of Nashe's linguistic gusto and inventiveness. Nashe is one of the great individual prose stylists in English.

Nashe's rambling narrative, *The Unfortunate Traveller, or The Life of Jack Wilton* (1594), is a picaresque tale of adventure, perhaps suggested by the Spanish *Lazarillo de Tormes*. The picaresque or "rogue" novel was a suitable form for prose narrative in the infancy of the novel, for it did not demand any real integration of plot, but, by taking its hero on a series of adventures in different places, enabled the author to engage in a great variety of miscellaneous descriptive writing. *The Unfortunate Traveller* has been called the first English historical novel (the hero, who tells his story in the first person, was supposed to have lived much earlier in the century, and Nashe introduced some pseudohistorical episodes), but it is not really important as a contribution to the development of English prose fiction. Its basis is episodic narrative linked by memory and coincidence; and though Nashe had an eye for detail and the writing has a vivid pictorial quality as though everything is seen in brilliant sunlight, its discursiveness and complete formal irresponsibility make it very much less than a novel. It contains some remarkable individual stories, and is written in a style considerably simpler, with shorter sentences, than that of *Lenten Stuff*. It has its place in the history of English fiction, but as an interesting individual experiment rather than an "influence."

Robert Greene, like Nashe, was dramatist, pamphleteer, and writer of prose fiction. His *Groatsworth of Wit bought with a Million of Repentance* (1592, best known for its early reference to Shakespeare) is an autobiographical pamphlet written with verve but with no great distinction of style. Greene wrote a number of pamphlets, moving from a moderately euphuistic style to a more racy and colloquial one. His "conny catching" pamphlets, which have the ostensible object of putting the reader on his guard against the rogues and tricksters of London, reveal his extensive knowledge of London's underworld, and he tells his stories of swindles and immoralities with all the zest of a good crime reporter. Indeed, there is something of the journalist in the Greene of these later pamphlets, though his earlier work shows the more pretentious man of letters. His earlier writing includes romantic prose tales deriving in both style and kind of subject from Lyly's *Euphues*, which had many imitators in the 1580's. But in his romances, too, there is a progressive shedding of excessive rhetoric; the later ones, *Pandosto* (1588) and *Menaphon* (1589), being clearer in narrative outline and less prone to rhetorical digressions and elaborate soliloquies than the earlier. Thomas Lodge was another who combined pamphleteering with the writing of prose tales deriving from Greek romance. His *Rosalind* (1590), like Greene's *Pandosto,* was used by Shakespeare. The style of Lodge's prose romances is formal and rhetorical, influenced by Lyly (whose *Euphues* is discussed in Chapter 7), but at his best Lodge's narrative prose has a flow and a control that makes it much more satisfactory to the ear than many examples of the euphuistic style; the artificiality is there, but it is subdued to the narrative, which moves with conspicuous ease.

Perhaps the Elizabethan writer of prose fiction who is of most historical interest is Thomas Deloney, whose three tales (or groups of tales), *Jack of Newbury, The Gentle Craft,* and *Thomas of Reading,* all written in the 1590's, show him as the storyteller of the bourgeois craftsman. *Jack of Newbury,* for example, deals with the weavers: the hero is a heroic weaver who rises to become a famous and wealthy clothier employing large numbers of people. *The Gentle Craft* deals with the shoemakers, and contains the tale which Dekker used as the plot of his *Shoemakers' Holiday.* Deloney portrays and appeals to the new middle classes of the time, revealing the bourgeois society which arose after the medieval craft guilds had been replaced by the domestic system of manufacture. His style is somewhat pedestrian, but straightforward and competent, and the dialogue is particularly good. The details of the lives and activities of hardworking craftsmen, kind employers, and disguised noblemen posing as apprentices not only throw interesting light on the Elizabethan social scene: they also show the first faint outline of the mature English novel, which was to develop as the special contribution to literature of the middle classes, for long concerned with the relationship between social classes, the possibilities of advancement from one class to another, and in general with the relation between gentility and morality.

It is sometimes difficult to distinguish Elizabethan fiction from Elizabethan reporting. Dekker's graphic picture of London smitten by plague, *The Wonderful Year* (1603), is a piece of reporting, but it shows the macabre imagination of some of the late Elizabethan and Jacobean playwrights. This, for example, is hardly straight journalism:

What an unmatchable torment were it for a man to be barred up every night in a vast silent charnel-house, hung to make it more hideous with lamps dimly and slowly burning, in hollow and glimmering corners; where all the pavement should instead of green rushes be strewed with blasted rosemary, withered hyacinths, fatal cypresses and yew, thickly mingled with heaps of

dead men's bones; the bare ribs of a father that begat him lying there, here
the chapless hollow scull of a mother that bore him, round about him a thousand corpses, some standing bolt upright in their knotted winding sheets,
others half mouldered in rotten coffins, that should suddenly yawn wide open,
filling his nostrils with noisome stench and his eyes with the sight of nothing
but crawling worms. And to keep such a poor wretch waking, he should hear
no noise but toads creaking, screech-owls howling, mandrakes shrieking . . .

Dekker also followed Greene and Nashe in producing accounts of
the London underworld, as in *The Seven Deadly Sins of London*,
News from Hell brought by the Devil's Carrier, *The Belman of London*, and *Lanthorne and Candlelight*, all published between 1606
and 1608. *The Gull's Hornbook* (1609) gives a lively picture of varieties of fools and rogues in London with an irony that is humorous
rather than biting.

Nothing better illustrates the range of the Elizabethan imagination, even when ostensibly merely reporting contemporary events,
than to set side by side the accounts of London low life just discussed
with Richard Hakluyt's final version of his great book of voyages, *The
Principal Navigations, Voyages, Traffiques and Discoveries of the
English Nation*, which appeared in three volumes between 1598 and
1600. Hakluyt was a compiler and editor, and he brought together
accounts by many different hands of all the great English voyages of
discovery and adventure that he could lay hands on. His motive was
both scientific and patriotic; he wished to bring together all the
available knowledge about distant lands and the sea routes to them,
and to testify to the glory and enterprise of English seamen. The collection includes Sir Walter Ralegh's exciting and haunting *Discovery
of Guiana* and his *Report of the Fight about the Azores* (from which
Tennyson got the material for his famous ballad of the *Revenge*),
both of which had been previously published independently; Edward Hare's account of Sir Humphrey Gilbert's last voyage, pedestrian in style but epic in content; accounts of voyages by Drake and
Hawkins; and hundreds of others, some told in a vivid, heroic style,
others more flatly. Much of what we know of the great Elizabethan
voyagers and their adventures comes from Hakluyt's collection. None
of the other collections of accounts of voyages has the appeal of
Hakluyt's. Samuel Purchas, an ambitious geographer who took all
history as well as geography for his province, produced in *Purchas
his Pilgrimage* (1613) an encyclopedic survey of the world and its
peoples past and present, and in 1625, in four large folio volumes,
Hakluytus Posthumus, or Purchas his Pilgrims, which drew on his
earlier work and on Hakluyt's unpublished papers in an attempt to
provide a complete "history of the world in sea voyages and land

travel by Englishmen and others." The work is not, however, a coherent unity, nor does it have the attractiveness of Hakluyt.

We have already mentioned the religious controversies between
Puritans and Anglicans, to which the Marprelate pamphlets are one
of the liveliest contributions from the Puritan, anti-episcopal side. The
story of Elizabethan religious prose is not, however, confined to the
record of this kind of popular controversy; the argument was also
conducted on a high philosophical and theological level by scholars
and thinkers who brought to bear much heavier artillery than lively
abuse. The details of this more formal controversy are not strictly
the concern of the literary historian. But since it lies behind, and indeed produced, Richard Hooker's great Anglican prose work, *Of the
Laws of Ecclesiastical Polity*, some reference must be made to it.
Hooker gave the final Anglican answer to the Puritan position which
had been maintained most forcefully by Thomas Cartwright in three
replies to John Whitgift's pro-episcopal answer to certain Puritan
works (this gives some idea of the house-that-Jack-built chain of
events, reminiscent of Milton's early career as a prose pamphleteer).
Cartwright's position cannot be easily summarized, but in general it
is not unfair to say that he was arguing for a theocracy: church discipline is also civil discipline, which it commands, and the Christian
ruler, working through the same kind of church officers that Calvin
instituted at Geneva, applies the "Word of God" as revealed in the
Bible and interpreted by God's duly "called" Presbyterian ministers.
The ecclesiastical discipline, which Cartwright and those who
thought as he did wished to see imposed, touched every aspect of
human activity and recognized no distinction between religious and
civil or even between matters essential and matters indifferent: the
religious authorities claimed control over everything, and the state
was in fact subordinate to the church.

Richard Hooker (1554–1600) published the first four books of his
Ecclesiastical Polity in 1594 and the fifth in 1597. The other three
were published posthumously, and there was for long some doubt as
to their authenticity, but this is now accepted, though it is clear they
are not in their final form. The work as a whole is a masterpiece of
exposition which involves legal and philosophical as well as theological argument. Hooker had none of Cartwright's tendency to see the
world in two opposed colors, one divine and therefore alone proper,
the other merely human and therefore evil. He sees reason, the law
of nature, as coming from God, as providing a light by which men
can achieve worthy things. Scriptural law does not govern the whole
of life; there are numerous matters not dealt with by Scripture to be
considered and weighed by reasonable Christian men and agreed

upon in the light of their reason. Further, times change, and what is the most effective way of achieving the Church's purpose at one time may not be so at another. The whole question of episcopacy is discussed not only with reference to the question of the apostolic succession, but also with regard to history, tradition, and convenience. He has a feeling for tradition and at the same time realizes that different circumstances require different procedures; he has a sense of the community of all Christians, together with keen concern for the position and function of an English national Church; he sees scriptural injunction as requiring to be supplemented by reasonable inference and common counsel; he sees the civil ruler as legal head of the English Church, but he assumes that the ruler, with the advice of the properly established civil and ecclesiastical bodies (i.e., Parliament and Convocation), will proceed according to the laws of the Church, which in fact he makes into law by implementing, and would never for a moment consider him to be above those laws (he is no supporter of the new, extreme notions of Tudor despotism). Above all, Hooker has a flexibility of mind which enables him to wind into his argument with cumulative reasonableness. No summary can do justice to the majestic ordering of his case, moving from a general discussion of law in Book 1, to a consideration of the scope of scriptural or divine law in Book 2, to the place of the national Church within the State in Book 3, to the Church's control of her own position free of both Rome and Geneva in Book 4, and so on. On the whole, the first two books lay down the general principles, and the later books discuss their application. At the bottom of all Hooker's argument lies his sense of the divine, creative, ordering, and multiple nature of law, "whose seat is the bosom of God, whose voice the harmony of the world." He is basically opposed to the monolithic position of Cartwright, although, of course, it would be wildly anachronistic to seek in his work any trace of the modern liberal position with regard to universal toleration of all creeds. He is immensely erudite without being exhibitionist; never flustered, never merely doctrinaire. His argument has gaps, and few modern readers would find it wholly acceptable; but it remains a remarkable single-handed attempt to produce a complete intellectual explanation and vindication of the theory and practice of the English Church as established under Elizabeth. Hooker's prose is that of a scholar and thinker; there is no showing off, no stylistic gymnastics, but always a careful functional use of language. His sentences are often long, but rarely cumbersome, for the movement of clauses mirrors the movement of his mind. It is a ratiocinative prose, as much a lawyer's as a philosopher's perhaps, but calm, dignified, and always molded by its subject. There are occasional flashes of lively popular language, and a subdued, somewhat quizzical sense of humor, quite different from the flashier wit of the writers of the Elizabethan underworld. *Of the Laws of Ecclesiastical Polity* is one of the very few English classics of its kind.

While churchmen debated the theory and practice of church government, the secular mind of Francis Bacon (1561–1626) was meditating an ambitious scheme for laying anew the foundations of human knowledge on which could be reared an ever-increasing understanding and control of nature. To this scheme he gave the general name of the Great Instauration (or Renewal). Reacting against scholastic philosophy and against all a priori thinking and systems of thought derived deductively from premises laid down by authority, the Great Instauration, basing knowledge on observation, would restore a truer relationship between the observing mind and observed nature and so make scientific progress possible. For Bacon, "the furthest end of knowledge" was not theoretical insight but "the relief of man's estate"; it was to be for "the benefit and use of man." The sequence was to be from observation to understanding to practical application. Bacon proposed to himself six stages in the realization of his scheme, beginning with the classification of existing knowledge, with a precise mapping of all gaps and deficiencies, and proceeding through the development of a new, inductive, logical method (the New Organon) and the collection of basic data to provide lists of examples of the new method in operation, thence to a preliminary report of the achievements of the method, and finally to a full-dress presentation of the new philosophy and method and its results in explaining the natural phenomena of the universe. The sixth and final stage could not of course be reached by any single individual: it represented the eventual aim of human knowledge. Of the other five stages, the first is represented by Bacon's *Advancement of Learning* (1605, with an enlarged Latin version in 1623); the second by the unfinished Latin work, *Novum Organum,* which appeared together with a general statement of the aims and plan of the Great Instauration (*Magna Instauratio*) in 1620; and the others only by fragments.

Bacon was not the first to propose an inductive scientific theory, or to attack scholasticism; nor did his writings achieve a philosophic revolution of the kind which Descartes brought about a generation later. Further, he was not in touch with the actual achievements of contemporary science, was ignorant of and sometimes hostile to new advances in astronomy and medicine and curiously uninfluenced by the revival of Greek science and Platonic mathematics which were so important for the scientific achievements of the Renaissance.

Nevertheless he spoke with prophetic eloquence of the new conception of knowledge and its function, popularizing a point of view which was to become increasingly significant later in the century. His diagnosis of much of the accepted philosophy of his time as mere verbal jugglery had something of the same effect as the work of the more popular of the logical positivists and semanticists of the 1930's: "For the wit and mind of man, if it work upon matter, which is the contemplation of the creatures of God, worketh according to the stuff and is limited thereby; but if it work upon itself as the spider worketh his web, then it is endless, and brings forth indeed cobwebs of learning, admirable for the fineness of thread and work but of no substance or profit."

The Advancement of Learning is in two books: the first states and answers arguments that have been brought forward against learning and the second providing a detailed classification of all the kinds of knowledge, with the deficiencies noted. The argument against learning comes from theologians, from politicians, and from the habits and studies of learned men themselves. The first he answers in their own terms; the second he answers by an appeal to history and experience; and in tackling the third he admits that here are "three vanities in studies" which have been responsible for attacks on learning in general. These "vanities" or "distempers" of learning are in ascending order of gravity, fantastic and exhibitionist styles of writing, the kind of logic chopping which degenerates into mere verbalism, and "delight in deceiving and aptness to be deceived; imposture and credulity." The greatest error of all, however, is "mistaking or misplacing the last or furthest end of knowledge"—which is control over nature for the benefit of man. Book I concludes with positive arguments to prove the dignity of learning, both "divine proofs" and "human proofs." Bacon, it should be noted, conceded the study of divinity to the divines, distinguishing between God's word, as revealed by Him and studied by His ministers, and God's work, the natural world, the province of scientific inquiry; but though the separation between theology and philosophy had been made before (e.g., by William of Ockham), Bacon makes the separation to protect science from religion (to use modern terms) not, as Ockham had done, to protect faith from reason. Thomistic philosophy did not make this separation, subsuming philosophy in theology, but later scholastic thought did sometimes recognize a "twofold truth." Such a division was found useful by seventeenth-century thinkers such as Bacon and Hobbes in providing a clear field for secular thought.

Book II of *The Advancement of Learning* is a brilliant piece of classification, full of the witty definitions and apt and lively phrases so characteristic of Bacon's vigorous expository style; but in spite of this the modern reader will find this sort of detailed schematization somewhat tedious. Among the many interesting definitions, that of poetry might be singled out, for it is curiously Freudian: "it [poetry] doth raise and erect the mind, by submitting the shows of things to the desires of the mind; whereas reason doth buckle and bow the mind unto the nature of things." (The dwindling number of those who profess to believe that Bacon wrote Shakespeare's plays might reflect on this definition of poetry and consider whether it could possibly be made to apply to *Hamlet* or *Othello*.)

The *Novum Organum* contains the famous account of "the four classes of idols which beset men's minds," a fine example of the imaginative wit which Bacon so often displayed in making his points. The Idols of the Tribe (deriving from the limitations of human nature), the Idols of the Cave (deriving from personal character and idiosyncrasies), the Idols of the Marketplace (popular superstitions and confusions), and the Idols of the Theatre ("because in my judgment all the received systems are but so many stage-plays representing worlds of their own creation after an unreal and scenic fashion"), all militate against the proper use of observation and reason. Again, this reminds us of a modern semanticist analyzing the sources of verbal confusion or of a psychologist explaining the origins of irrational prejudice. Bacon was not himself a great scientist or a great philosopher; he was a master of prose exposition whose colorful and memorable phrases helped to popularize a new view of science.

The New Atlantis, published incomplete in 1627, is a slight work; it describes how a group of seafarers come upon an unknown island in the South Sea, where they are hospitably entertained and told of the high state of morality and civilization prevailing there, notably of the wonders of Salomon's House, a research institution in the description of which Bacon illustrates his own ideas of how research should be carried on. It all seems rather naïve in an age when scientific research is as highly developed and as much taken for granted as it is now; but it is interesting as providing further evidence of Bacon's desire to popularize his views of the importance of experimental science, that "commerce between the mind of man and the nature of things, which is more precious than anything on earth" as he called it in his *Magna Instauratio*.

Bacon's *Essays*—beginning with a volume of ten essays, written in a pungent aphoristic style, in 1597, with expansions and additions and a progressively more discursive style in the volumes of 1612 and 1625, the last containing fifty-eight essays—consist of reflections on human affairs by a practical psychologist who wishes to base his ethical prescriptions on a sound knowledge of human nature. The essay as a literary form had been invented by Montaigne shortly before Bacon adopted it; but Montaigne, with his rambling curiosity about himself and his genial and sceptical humanism, represented a different side of Renaissance thought. The easy flow of Montaigne's prose represented a relaxed self-consciousness far removed from the impersonal wisdom affected by Bacon, whose early essays read almost like a series of proverbs. It is the aphoristic element in his style that makes so many of his sentences—particularly his opening sentences—memorable and quotable. "What is truth? said jesting Pilate; and would not stay for an answer." "Men fear death as children fear to go in the dark; and as that natural fear in children is increased with tales, so is the other." "Revenge is a kind of wild justice . . ." "He that hath wife and children hath given hostages to fortune." "A man that hath no virtue in himself ever envieth virtue in others." The essays deal as much with public as with private life, discussing "great place," nobility, "seditions and troubles," empire, and "the true greatness of kingdoms and estates," as well as truth, death, parents and children, marriage, envy, love, and "wisdom for a man's self." He speaks as a man of the world, illustrating his generalizations by references to history (often classical history) and his own experience. Realistic in politics, shrewd but not coldly calculating in practical affairs, Christian in a general theistic way with more than a touch of Stoicism, occasionally rising to a somber eloquence in discussing time and change and death or led into the display of a personal enthusiasm as in the essay on gardens, Bacon in his essays is an impressive if hardly an endearing character. There is a moderately Machiavellian side to his thought: "The best composition and temperature is, to have openness in fame and opinion; secrecy in habit; dissimulation in seasonable use; and a power to feign, if there be no remedy." He is reconciled to human nature: "Why should I be angry with a man for loving himself better than me?" He knows how to relax with a variety of delights, but it is significant that he ends his essay on "masques and triumphs" with the sentence: "But enough of these toys." Montaigne in one way, Bacon in another, are very far from the medieval mind; and they are far, too, from some of the more passionate movements of their own time. It is hardly extravagant to suggest that Bacon lives in the same world as Benjamin Franklin, not in that of the author of *Piers Plowman,* or in that of Spenser or Milton or George Herbert.

Bacon's *History of Henry VII* (1622) is a conscientious study of that king's policy in the light of which he is able to give an integrated picture of the events of his reign. The work shows Bacon's interest in statecraft, his political and legal knowledge, his command of an effective narrative and expository style, and a historico-psychological imagination which enabled him to put imaginary speeches into the mouths of his characters in the manner of classical historians. Others of Bacon's works, more or less fragmentary contributions to the six-fold plan of the Great Instauration, were published in various collections of his literary remains after his death.

If Bacon separated God's word and God's work in order to be able to concentrate freely on the latter, Sir Thomas Browne (1605–82) divided his attention between the two, investigating the facts of nature with a Baconian empiricism (though with a religious excitement at the ingenuity of the Creator thus revealed, which Bacon wholly lacked) and at the same time glorying in his acceptance by faith of religious mysteries on which his imagination loved to dwell. Browne was both Baconian experimentalist and Christian mystic, author both of *Pseudodoxia Epidemica* (generally known as *Vulgar Errors*), an exposure of erroneous notions about nature held by the credulous, and of *Religio Medici*, a discursive statement of his religious faith with a deliberate emphasis on wonder and mystery. The impact of the "new philosophy" in the seventeenth century naturally differed according to the temperament of the individual. Browne had a "unified sensibility" in the sense that he could move freely between mystery and experiment and saw no conflict between the duty of the man of science and that of the man of religion. This is related to his genial autobiographical manner of discussion and his interest in what might be called philosophy as play; if in discussing one kind of truth you are also aware of another kind, you will not be too intense in your method of presenting either.

The relation—sometimes the conflict—between science and religion becomes henceforth an important aspect of English thought. Although seventeenth-century theological controversy for the most part ignored the new science, its effects were indirectly visible in the great debate between those who believed optimistically in inevitable progress and those who held that the world was steadily declining. The classic statement of the pessimistic position was Godfrey Goodman's massive work, *The Fall of Man, or the Corruption of Nature Proved by the Light of our Natural Reason*, published in 1616. This was answered by George Hakewill's *Apology of the Power and Providence of God in the Government of the World*, published in 1627, with enlarged editions in 1630 and 1635. The argument as to whether the world had steadily declined from an original Golden

Age or was steadily progressing and improving represents two poles of human thought which are perhaps always with us; but the seventeenth century saw the conflict brought into focus with particular clarity. It was this debate which underlay the conflict between Ancients and Moderns which developed later in the century; whether the classical literature of the Greeks and Romans represented a summit of human literary achievement which later ages could never quite reach, or whether modern refinement and ingenuity could surpass the achievements of the ancient world, was an argument which flowed from the larger debate on the decline of the world. The narrowing of the issue in this way reflects a contraction of the intellectual universe of the late seventeenth and early eighteenth centuries as compared with that of the earlier seventeenth century. The comfortable deistic solution of the science-religion conflict, making God the First Cause who retired from the universe after the creation, the divine watchmaker who made and wound up the watch before leaving it to be admired and investigated by the pious and the curious, was the eighteenth-century systematization of a position implicit in Bacon. Scientific progress then becomes increasingly successful in discovering how the watch was made and how it works, while literary progress is measured by the degree to which writers equal or perhaps even excel the great achievements of the classical world.

Sir Thomas Browne remained at the still center of the controversies of his day, cultivating an inclusive tolerance which enabled him to reconcile almost anything with almost anything else. *Religio Medici*—which circulated for some time in manuscript, and appeared in two unauthorized editions in 1642, before the appearance of the authorized edition in 1643—might almost be called an exercise in inclusiveness of thought and feeling. The very title—"the religion of a doctor"—emphasizes a reconciliation of traditional opposites, the numinous and the scientific; for, as Browne points out in the very first sentence, the world does not generally consider doctors to have any religion at all. His favorite image is the circle, his favorite concept the microcosm. The prose of *Religio Medici* is so richly harmonized that one might almost say that its meaning is conveyed vertically rather than horizontally. Browne's constant endeavor is to break down distinctions and include all things in a single context. In sentence after sentence he reaches out to embrace apparent contradictions and bring them together; each sentence—or at least each paragraph—is thus a microcosm of the book as a whole. Consider, for example, his discussion of the relation between Protestants and Catholics:

We have reformed from them, not against them; for (omitting those Improperations and Terms of Scurrility betwixt us, which only difference our Affections, and not our Cause,) there is between us one common Name and Appellation, one Faith and necessary body of Principles common to us both; and therefore I am not scrupulous to converse and live with them, to enter their Churches in defect of ours, and either pray with them, or for them.

Here we have the whole of *Religio Medici* in little: reformation does not imply disagreement; any admission of difference is softly tucked away within brackets; and at the end there is the cunning suggestion that praying *for* somebody (which would really indicate that we are concerned for him because he is not of our faith) amounts to the same thing as praying *with* him (which indicates that we *are* of the same faith). The actual statement of the case—an appeal for toleration—is reinforced by stylistic devices and by every kind of quasi-logical suggestion that can be derived from language.

Religio Medici begins with a definition of the author's brand of Christianity, a definition which gradually expands to include, by a "general charity to Humanity," virtually all faiths professed by men. Though a member of the Church of England ("there is no Church whose every part so squares unto my Conscience; whose Articles seem so consonant unto reason, and as it were framed to my particular Devotion, as this whereof I hold my Belief, the Church of England"), Browne "could never divide myself from any man upon the difference of an opinion, or be angry with his judgment for not agreeing with me in that from which perhaps within a few days I should dissent my self." By various quasi-logical and autobiographical devices he brings all humanity into the circle of his own faith. Faith and reason are at first distinguished:

As for those wingy Mysteries in Divinity, and airy subtleties in Religion, which have unhing'd the brains of better heads, they never stretched the *Pia Mater* of mine. Methinks there be not impossibilities enough in Religion for an active faith; the deepest Mysteries ours contains have not only been illustrated, but maintained, by Syllogism and the rule of Reason. I love to lose myself in a mystery, to pursue my Reason to an *O Altitudo!* . . . I can answer all the Objections of Satan and my rebellious reason with the odd resolution I learned of Tertullian, *Certum est, quia impossibile est.* I desire to exercise my faith in the difficultest point; for to credit ordinary and visible objects is not faith, but persuasion.

But though faith and reason are thus opposed, they are eventually reunited, if not logically at least symbolically, by being discussed in terms of each other and by the inclusion of both in a third term, such as God's Wisdom, which created the world to be "studied and contemplated by Man: 'tis the Debt of our Reason we owe unto God, and the homage we pay for not being Beasts." God's work and God's word are distinguished, but again only to be reunited: Nature is the Art of God. This being so, "there are no Grotesques in Nature." Every created thing is beautiful and wonderful in its way. Man himself is a little world. "We carry with us the wonders we seek without us: there is all Africa and her prodigies in us, we are that bold and adventurous piece of Nature, which he that studies wisely learns in a compendium what others labour at in a divided piece and endless volume." God's work is also a book, like His word. "Thus there are two Books from whence I collect my Divinity; besides that written one of God, another of His servant Nature, that universal and public Manuscript, that lies expans'd unto the Eyes of all; . . ."

Religio Medici continues with the adducing of examples showing the inclusive attitude at work. Both the miraculous and the scientific explanations of the same phenomenon are accepted; atheism is explained away as never having really existed; pagan gods are included in the Christian scheme; soul and body, life and death, are so defined as to include each other. Martyrdom is deprecated as symbolizing an exclusive rather than an inclusive attitude. And even when Browne has reluctantly to concede that salvation is granted by God only to Christians, he adds significantly: "yet those who do confine the Church of God, either to particular Nations, Churches, or Families, have made it far narrower than our Saviour ever meant it." Part II of the work is, logically enough, a discussion of charity, the state of mind which favors maximum inclusion. It is essentially an autobiographical illustration of his own charitable and tolerant disposition: "Methinks there is no man bad, and the worst, best." He can exclude nobody from his charity, and, as "every man is a Microcosm, and carries the whole World about him," his own tolerance takes on universal dimensions. The work concludes with the author's submission to the will of God.

Browne's style, with its coupling of Anglo-Saxon and Latin words and its sentences composed of an arrangement of fairly short clauses rising and falling in a carefully contrived cadence, is in many respects a reflection of his sensibility. "Do but extract from the corpulency of bodies, or resolve things beyond their first matter, and you discover the habitation of Angels, which if I call the ubiquitary and omnipresent Essence of God, I hope I shall not offend Divinity: for before the Creation of the World God was really all things." The Latinisms here are introduced with a deliberate relish; they reflect that savoring of words and attitudes which is part of Browne's literary character. But it is worth noting that this sentence works up to a crucial statement which is itself expressed (except for the one word "Creation") in words of Anglo-Saxon origin: "for before the Creation of the world God was really all things." Browne's stylistic artifice is perhaps more obvious in *Hydriotaphia* (*Urn Burial*) and *The Garden of Cyrus*, published together in 1658. In the former, the digging up of some old sepulchral urns "in a field of old Walsingham" provokes Browne to eloquent meditation on burial customs of the past and on the mysteries and solemnities of mortality. The opening sentence of the Epistle Dedicatory sets the tone of the work:

When the Funeral pyre was out, and the last valediction over, men took a lasting adieu of their interred Friends, little expecting the curiosity of future ages should comment upon their ashes, and, having no old experiences of the duration of their Reliques, held no opinion of such after-considerations.

Historical curiosity, philosophical speculation, mystic contemplation, and the suggestiveness and sonority of a rich and carefully manipulated vocabulary, combine to make *Hydriotaphia* a remarkable piece of virtuosity. The antiquarian, the Platonic mystic, the Christian moralist, and the artist all contribute to the total effect, but the artist is generally in the ascendant. "We whose generations are ordained in this setting part of time, are providentially taken off from such imaginations; and being necessitated to eye the remaining particle of futurity, are naturally constituted unto thoughts of the next world, and cannot excusably decline the consideration of that duration, which maketh Pyramids pillars of snow, and all that's past a moment." The artifice here is patent, as it is in the well-known passage beginning "What Song the Syrens sang, . . ." which includes the remarkable sentence: "But to subsist in bones, and be but Pyramidally extant, is a fallacy in duration." *The Garden of Cyrus*, in its riot of speculation concerning the quincunx pattern in heaven and earth, combines a scientific air with a poetic tone in a strange and fascinating way. Sometimes, the vocabulary is almost a parody of the scientific: "The *Reticulum* by these crossed cells makes a further digestion in the dry and exuccous part of the Aliment received from the first Ventricle." But more characteristic is the famous paragraph which begins the concluding movement of the work:

But the Quincunx of Heaven runs low, and 'tis time to close the five ports of knowledge; we are unwilling to spin out our awaking thoughts into the phantasms of sleep, which often continueth præcogitations; making Cables of

Cobwebs, and Wildernesses of handsome Groves. Beside Hippocrates hath spoke so little, and the Oneirocritical Masters have left such frigid Interpretations from plants, that there is little encouragement to dream of Paradise itself. Nor will the sweetest delight of Gardens afford much comfort in sleep; wherein the dullness of that sense shakes hands with delectable odours; and though in the Bed of Cleopatra, can hardly with any delight raise up the ghost of a Rose.

No more fascinating evidence exists of the coexistence in the seventeenth century of new scientific ideas and old notions of authority, and of the "hydroptic thirst" for all knowledge, ancient and modern, than the vast encyclopedic treatise by Robert Burton (1577–1640), *The Anatomy of Melancholy*, published in 1621, with several revised editions between 1624 and 1651. This work, now regarded as a rich anthology of curious notions, picturesque anecdotes, and varied quotations from both ancients and moderns, was intended as a scientific examination of the various distempers of the mind to which Burton gives the generic name "melancholy"— a medical and psychological work in which all known knowledge on the subject would be presented. If it has long been valued as a source of quaint or suggestive quotations or as a work to be dipped into and relished for its oddity, this is because the comprehensiveness of Burton's aim, the transitional nature of the age he lived in, and his own mixture of sympathy, curiosity, erudition, superstition, and common sense, gives his work a texture and a flavor that can be found neither in the medieval world nor in the modern scientific world after the foundation of the Royal Society. The organization of the book into discussions of the symptoms, causes, and cure of different kinds of melancholy is logical enough, but no central principles provide coherence to the whole. Unbounded curiosity about man and a humane and sensible concern for his welfare are perhaps Burton's chief qualities; they are sufficient to give a tone but not to provide a method or a principle of integration to his work. The elaborate and detailed synopses to each "partition" of the work testify to Burton's methodological intentions, but the digressions and the illustrative anecdotes remain the most memorable parts of his book. The long section on "heroical or love melancholy," with its powers, causes, symptoms, and cures, is the richest part of the book to modern eyes and its quizzical yet sympathetic tone, its profusion of information with a refusal to come down on any side of a controversy, is characteristic of Burton. We must not forget, however, that Burton was an Anglican priest by profession, and when he discusses religious melancholy, as he does in his final section, he mingles religious consolation with the humanist advice to avoid extremes and extravagances. "Thy soul is eclipsed for a time, I yield, as the sun is shadowed by a cloud; no doubt but those gracious beams of God's mercy will shine upon thee again, as they have formerly done: those embers of faith, hope and repentance, now burned in ashes, will flame out afresh, and be fully revived." This is a somewhat different Burton from the writer who, discoursing of the "prognostics" of love melancholy, remarks:

Go to Bedlam for examples. It is so well known in every village, how many have either died for love, or voluntarily made away themselves, that I need not much labour to prove it; *Nec modus aut requies nisi mors reperitur amoris* [love knows no limit or escape save death]: death is the common catastrophe to such persons.

> *Mori mihi contingat, non enim alia*
> *Liberatio ab aerumnis fuerit ullo pacto istis.*
>
> [Would I were dead, for nought, God knows,
> But death can rid me of these woes.]

But quotation can give no conception of the variety and multiplicity of Burton's extraordinary work, in which religion and science intermingle, medicine and psychology are set against a cosmic background, and ironic observations of the human comedy are made the excuse for a display of an almost irresponsible erudition. Burton's prose style is flexible and varied; he can be colloquial, pedantic, picturesque, or epigrammatic. The perpetual interlarding of his English with Latin quotations produces a strange mosaic effect. Perhaps it can be said that Burton had no style; there is too much variety and digression. *The Anatomy of Melancholy* is, however, a remarkable work, a significant symptom of the times and a *tour de force* without parallel in English literature.

That the seventeenth century is a watershed in the history of English thought is sufficiently proved by the fact that it saw the publication of work by Bacon, Browne, Burton, and Hobbes. Thomas Hobbes (1588–1679), materialist, rationalist, and empirical psychologist, broke completely with tradition and endeavored to work out a new science of man by the application of "natural reason" to the understanding of "bodies." "The word *body*, in the most general acceptation, signifieth that which filleth, or occupieth, some certain room, or imagined place; and dependeth not on the imagination, but is a real part of what we call the *universe*. For the universe, being the aggregate of all bodies, there is no real part thereof that is not also body . . ." Causality was reducible to motion, the ultimate ef-

fective principle in a reality that was made up of "bodies." Hobbes'
Leviathan (1651) attempts, with ruthless logic, to deduce a complete
political theory from his view of man which is in turn based on a
view of the human passions which in its turn is derived from his
materialist view of sensation. There are empirical elements in
Hobbes' psychology as well as elements deductively inferred from
his general view of body and motion. On the whole, however, the
Leviathan is a closely reasoned and brilliantly phrased argument
in which Hobbes builds up from his analysis of man, a theory of
the state as essentially an instrument for preventing perpetual conflict between men. Its aim is security, freedom from the perpetual
risk of sudden death—at almost any price. For men, Hobbes maintains, are naturally prone to strive for ever increasing power. "I put
for a general inclination of all mankind a perpetual and restless
desire of power after power, that ceaseth only in death." Thus, without a civil power to control them, they would live in perpetual civil
war, and human life would be "solitary, poor, nasty, brutish and
short." To avoid such a state, men have made an implicit contract
with each other to surrender their natural rights to do as they
think fit, on condition that everyone else does the same, and to set
up some individual or group as guarantor and enforcer of that
contract. The individual or group—who is not a party to the contract—thus becomes the representative of all, and only by obedience
to him can man have any chance of a decent life. Disorder, social
and political chaos, with the attendant chance of sudden death, is
for Hobbes the ultimate basis of all good political action, just as
vanity, each individual's restless desire for increasing power, is the
main principle of disorder and conflict. Life is sweet at any price,
and while there is no supreme good for Hobbes, there *is* a supreme
evil, the prospect of sudden death. The best way of organizing a
commonwealth, for Hobbes, is the way which, at whatever cost,
minimizes that prospect. As for religion, that was to be decided by
the ruler as a purely civil matter.

Hobbes's was an individual contribution which had no great influence on English political or ethical thought. Popularly regarded
as an arch-atheist and archmaterialist, as well as the defender of
absolutism, he could play no part in shaping the future of English
thought, which, with characteristic compromise, moved in the direction of Deism and constitutional monarchy. Locke, not Hobbes,
was to be the great philosopher of the eighteenth century, as New-
ton (who proved the existence of a designing creator by showing how
the universe was mathematically ordered) was to be its scientist. But
the boldness and individuality of Hobbes's thought, and the pictur-

esque liveliness of his language, made him a significant, though an isolated, figure in his day. He was a symptom, too: one could not imagine his work appearing in an earlier age, and it would have been surprising (though not impossible) in a later. Bacon tried to break down medieval thought; Hobbes was filling a vacuum left by its decay.

For all the signs of modernity and secularism in seventeenth-century philosophical prose, the dominant interest of the age was religion, and there were many more books devoted to religious subjects—collections of sermons, devotional and theological works, works of exposition, exhortation, and controversy—published between 1600 and 1660 than works of any other kind. Sermons, both spoken and written, enjoyed a popularity which the modern reader finds hard to understand. Puritans and Anglicans alike stressed the importance of preaching, which in the Elizabethan period was often highly controversial (Puritan preaching being often suspect as dangerous to the Elizabethan settlement) but which in the reigns of James I and Charles I was generally more hortatory or expository. Many skills were involved, including those of rhetoric, logic, and theological and linguistic scholarship, and they were employed in a great variety of ways. The range of styles and manners was enormous, from the rousing of the emotions by passionate and grotesque imagery to the most closely reasoned *explication de texte*. The Middle Ages had developed its own *artes praedicandi* and medieval techniques are often found still flourishing in the seventeenth-century sermon. A popular tradition of sturdy and colorful exhortation and an erudite tradition of subtle commentary existed side by side, with every kind of gradation in between and every kind of permutation and combination of the two. Of the scores of notable preachers of the period, we might single out for mention three great Anglicans—Lancelot Andrewes, whose fame has been revived in our own time by T. S. Eliot, John Donne, and Jeremy Taylor.

Lancelot Andrewes (1555–1626), whose sermons were published individually or in groups before the posthumous *XCVI Sermons* appeared in 1629, has a packed, intense style, in which an argument is developed with subtle insistence and sometimes an almost hypnotic iteration. The cumulative effect of his short, condensed sentences, with their probing for the precise meaning of a biblical text, can be very powerful, though his thought is not easy to follow and the rhetorical ingenuity manifested in the plays on words can be excessive. Donne's sermons (of which six were published individually during his lifetime and three collections were published posthumously, in 1640, 1649, and 1660) have a more obvious appeal, at least to the modern reader, with their mixture of the colloquial, the intellectual, and the mystical. Like those of Andrewes—and indeed like nearly all the sermons of the time—they are carefully worked out arguments, whose structure from a citation of the text to its amplification, illustration, and application, can only be appreciated by a careful reading of the whole; but his shifts in tone, his awareness of the claims and distractions of the everyday world in the midst of his religious ecstasies, his ability to break out into great passages of rhapsody or elegy or sheer power, often lead him to break the bound of the formal organization of his sermon. His own personality enters into his preaching in unexpected ways and places, and the mixture of intellectual and emotional elements can produce, as in his poetry, a strange and powerful utterance. It may be, as Eliot has said, that "about Donne there hangs the shadow of the impure motive," that he "lacked spiritual discipline" compared with Andrewes; but the result is often to make his preaching more individual and more interesting. Donne's prose style tends to fall into long sentences made up of linked short clauses, arranged in parallel rather than in series, as it were; neatness in subordination of clauses in the total pattern of the sentence was an achievement of the next age. Both Andrewes and Donne also produced devotional works, which bring the reader into more intimate contact with their religious meditations. Andrewes' devotional manual, originally written in Greek, appeared in an English translation in 1647 as *Private Devotions;* it is sometimes known by the Latin title of *Preces Privatae.* Donne's *Devotions upon Emergent Occasions* (1624), a record of his religious meditations during a long and serious illness, is simpler in style than his sermons, and has a vivid personal quality in its tone and idiom.

There were plain preachers in the first half of the seventeenth century as well as those who employed a highly colored rhetorical or metaphysical style, and it was the style of plain preaching that was to come to the fore after the Restoration. But the most impressive as well as in many ways most distinctively Anglican sermons and devotional works of the period were not of the plain school. The most conscious stylist of them all was Jeremy Taylor (1613–67), whose early *Liberty of Prophesying* (1647), a thoughtful and moving plea for toleration, is written in a simpler style, cogent in its earnest lucidity, than his later work. *Holy Living* (1650), a devotional manual concerned with the conduct of Christian life in all its phases, both personal and social, is a kind of work which had been fairly common in the Middle Ages but which had not been produced in England since the Reformation. The prose has a fuller eloquence than that of *The Liberty of Prophesying*, but it has not the richer luxuriance of *Holy Dying* (1651), a work in the medieval tradition of the *ars moriendi*, drawing on a long tradition of religious thought and feeling about death and the contempt of this world, but with its elaborate rhetorical style drawing new music out of these old themes. Combining classical and Christian sources, making use of details of contemporary life as well as of biblical and classical history and literature, employing a strong visual imagination to find concrete illustrations for general ideas, Taylor succeeds in giving new weight and harmony to some of the great traditional themes of his religion. His sentences, like those of so many prose writers of the period, consist of clauses arranged in extended sequence, with parallel clauses modifying or answering or emphasizing each other. Taylor cultivated a similar style for his sermons, of which several collections were published in his lifetime.

Of preachers and devotional writers on the Puritan side, mention might be made of Thomas Adams (whose date of birth is unknown and who died in or soon after 1653), a great preacher who knew how to use allegorical and other devices in order to stir the conscience of London audiences, and Richard Baxter (1615–91) whose numerous tracts and exhortations, as well as his long autobiographical work, *Reliquiae Baxterianae*, long remained popular. His two best known works, *The Saints' Everlasting Rest* and *Call to the Unconverted* (1657), manuals of practical religion, took an important place in the Evangelical tradition in both England and America. A very different character from these was the Anglican Thomas Fuller (1608–61), biographer, historian, antiquary, preacher, essayist, and divine, an attractive and versatile writer whose *Holy State* (1642), a book of practical conduct, is an eclectic work in which common sense, Christian feeling, belief in a social hierarchy, and a taste for the illustrative anecdote and character sketch, combine to produce a series of essays and sketches rather than a wholly unified work. Fuller was (among other things) a wit, a realist, and a *raconteur*. His *History of the Worthies of England* is a collection of English biographies arranged by counties in their alphabetical order, a remarkable storehouse of information, anecdotes, and miscellaneous facts and stories of all kinds. Information about the "natural commodities," manufactures, buildings, and proverbs of each county are given, before he proceeds to give biographical notes on the "worthies." Fuller got his information from earlier antiquaries (such as Camden, Speed, and Stow) as well as from his own researches: he traveled over the country interrogating those who had known any "worthies," consulting local records and examining places and buildings. His other works include *The Church History of Britain*, published in 1655 together with *The History of the University of Cambridge*, in both of which the antiquarian and anecdotalist combine with the recorder of his own times.

Fuller's biographies are the work of a lively and discursive antiquarian; those of Izaak Walton (1593–1683) are different both in tone and intention. His *Lives* of John Donne, Henry Wotton, Richard Hooker, George Herbert, and Bishop Robert Sanderson, first published separately between 1658 and 1678, represent a characteristically gentle combination of realistic biography and idealizing hagiography. His portrait of Donne—whom he knew only in the final phase of his career, the pious Dean of St. Paul's—concentrates on his character as a divine, seeing in his entering on holy orders a parallel with the life of St. Augustine: "Now the English Church had gained a second St. Austin; for I think none was so like him before his conversion, none so like St. Ambrose after it! and if his youth had the infirmities of the one, his age had the excellencies of the other; the learning and holiness of both." His facts are not always correct—he makes some serious errors particularly in his life of Hooker, whom he never knew—but the simple charm of his narrative, with its graceful style and gentle tone of honest admiration, makes his biographies classics of their kind. "Charm" also is the obvious term to apply to that wholly delightful book, *The Compleat Angler* (1653), one of the great pastoral works in English, in which a fishing manual is transformed by the infusion of the author's personal feeling, his love of rural peace, of song, of clean and well-cared-for country inns, and of his fellow men, into an enchanting picture of human contentment in a realistic and not a Utopian setting. The form of the work is a series of conversations between Piscator, the angler, and other characters whom he meets in the course of his five days' fishing expedition. Piscator instructs the others in fishing, and they discourse, fish, and sing together, dining in the evening at a convenient inn, where the hostess is neat and courteous, and innocent mirth, with singing over a cup of barley wine, is enjoyed by all. The subtitle of the work, "The Contemplative Man's Recreation," provides a clue to its atmosphere. Beneath the simple account of a week's fishing, talking, and making innocently merry is a sense of the ideal fisherman as the type of Christian gentleness and humility: ". . . he found that the hearts of such men, by nature, were fitted for contemplation and quietness; men of mild, and sweet, and peaceable spirits, as indeed most Anglers are: these men our blessed Saviour, who is observed to love to plant grace in good natures, though indeed nothing be too hard for him, yet these men he chose to call from their irreprovable employment of fishing, and gave them grace to be his disciples, and to follow him, and do wonders."

Finally, something remains to be said about the seventeenth-century prose form known as the "Character." This was defined by Sir Thomas Overbury, one of its practitioners, as "a picture (real or personal) quaintly drawn in various colours, all of them brightened by one shadowing." It is essentially a portrait of a type rather than an individual, often done with an almost exhibitionist wit. The form derives from the Greek natural philosopher Theophrastus, whose *Characters* begin with a brief description of a vice (such as dissimulation, flattery, loquacity, superstition, and so on) and then go on to describe the typical possessor of that vice. ("Distrustfulness is a disposition to suspect all men of dishonesty. The Distrustful Man is this sort of man. When he has sent one of his slaves to buy provisions he sends another one after the first to find out exactly what they cost. In travelling he carries his own money and sits down every few hundred yards to count it." etc.) All Theophrastus' *Characters* deal with vices: if he also wrote characters of virtues they have not survived. The first collection of characters in English was Joseph Hall's *Characters of Virtues and Vices*, published in 1608. Hall is much less succinct in expression than Theophrastus; his sketches are longer and he is less the witty observer of men than the Christian moralist seeking to improve his readers by warning or example. As he says in his Proem to Book I (which deals with virtues): "Virtue is not loved enough; because she is not seen: and Vice loseth much detestation; because her ugliness is secret. . . . What need we more, than to discover the two to the world? This work shall save the labour of exhorting and dissuasion." Hall is livelier in Book II (the vices) than with virtues, where the tones of the preacher sometimes suggest themselves. He has his own kind of wit, as the conclusion of his character of the busybody shows: "He knows not why, but his custom is to go a little about and to leave the cross still on the right hand. One event is enough to make a rule: out of these rules he concludes fashions, proper to himself; and nothing can turn him out of his course. If he have done his task, he is safe: it matters not with what affection. Finally, if God would let him be the carver of his own obedience he could not have a better subject: as he is, he cannot have a worse."

Characters or Witty Descriptions of the Properties of Sundry Persons (1614), by Sir Thomas Overbury and others, shows the Character becoming a more deliberate exercise of wit. "A good woman is a comfort, like a man. She lacks nothing but heat. Thence is her sweetness of disposition, which meets his stoutness more pleasingly; so wool meets iron easier than iron, and turns resisting into embracing." "A Puritan is a diseased piece of Apocrypha: bind him to the Bible, and he corrupts the whole text: ignorance and fat feed are his founders; his nurses, railing, rabies, and round breeches: his life is but a borrowed blast of wind; for between two religions, as between two doors, he is ever whistling." These Characters are less concerned with general moral issues than with giving pictures of types common in England at the time, and they are thus of great interest to the social historian. The picture of the Amorist throws some light on Hamlet: "Is a man blasted or planet-strooken, and is the dog that leads blind Cupid; . . . He is never without verses and musk comfits, and sighs to the hazard of his buttons; . . . He is untrussed, unbutton'd and ungartered, not out of carelessness, but care. . . ."

The fashion was now in full swing, and Overbury's collection was followed by John Earle's *Microcosmography* (1628–29), the work of a careful artist whose characters combined effective wit with genuine moral feeling. Earle is less of an exhibitionist than many of the character writers of the period; his wit is put at the service of a kindly curiosity about his fellow men, as in his well-known sketch of "A Child":

A Child is a man in a small letter, yet the best copy of Adam before he tasted of Eve or the apple; and he is happy whose small practice in the world can only write his character. He is nature's fresh picture newly drawn in oil, which time, and much handling, dims and defaces. His soul is yet a white paper unscribbled with observations of the world, wherewith, at length, it becomes a blurred notebook. He is purely happy, because he knows no evil, nor hath made means by sin to be acquainted with misery. He arrives not at the mischief of being wise, nor endures evils to come, by foreseeing them. He kisses and loves all, and, when the smart of the rod is past, smiles on his beater. . . . We laugh at his foolish sports, but his game is our earnest; and his drums, rattles and hobby-horses, but the emblems and mocking of man's business.

Some of the titles of Earle's characters show his range: "A Young Raw Preacher," "A Mere Dull Physician," "A Mere Formal Man," "A Young Gentleman of the University," "A She Precise Hypocrite," "The Common Singing-Men in Cathedral Churches."

Later Character writers tended to move from the general picture to the individual portrait. Samuel Butler (whose Characters were written in the late 1660's but not published until 1759) was concerned with contemporary follies and eccentricities, and all his sketches are sharply satirical. But after him the character becomes more individualized, and by the time Addison and Steele make use of the form in their *Tatler* and *Spectator* essays it has become the individual character portrait, ready to join the other streams that flowed into the English novel.

CHAPTER FOURTEEN

Scottish Literature to 1700

How far Scottish literature can be properly said to be the concern of the historian of English literature is a debatable question. Before the Union of the Scottish and English Parliaments in 1707, and to an even greater extent before the Union of the Crowns in 1603, Scotland was an independent kingdom with a vigorous culture of its own and in many respects a closer cultural relationship with the European continent (particularly France) than England had. But the northern kingdom was smaller and poorer than the southern, which made frequent attempts to dominate its neighbor, sometimes successful; lowland Scotland and northern England were geographically and linguistically more closely akin than northern England and southern England; and Scotland was comparatively slow in developing as a unified nation. These three facts make it sometimes difficult to define the identity of Scottish literature even before 1603, while after 1603 the increasing number of Scottish writers who wrote in English for English readers makes the difficulty even greater—great enough, indeed, to make it very much a matter of arbitrary choice whether someone like Drummond of Hawthornden, or James Thomson (author of *The Seasons*), or Tobias Smollett is considered in an English or a Scottish context. But in the Middle Ages, when Scots was a literary language with both a national tradition and a European perspective, the fact of an identifiable Scottish literature and Scottish literary tradition is unquestionable.

Even in the medieval period, however, the situation is complicated, though in a different way. In the Anglo-Saxon or Old English period of English literature the language spoken in what is now Scotland was either one of three Celtic languages, or Norse, or the same language that was spoken and written in northern England as far south as the Humber. Much of Lowland Scotland during this period was linguistically part of Northumbria. The borders between England and Scotland were continually shifting, and the mélange of

Scots, Picts, Strathclyde Britons, Norsemen, and Anglo-Saxons which (with a sprinkling of Normans) was to make the Scottish people was still in the formative process. Gregory Smith has pointed out that the fragment of *The Dream of the Rood* carved in runes on the Ruthwell Cross in Dumfriesshire (probably about the year 800) might have been carved, so far as the language is concerned, in Edinburgh or in York. At this period, Scotland was (in the words of a modern Scottish historian) "partly a piece of England, speaking English, partly a Norwegian colony, speaking Norse, and the rest three independent kingdoms, speaking three separate Celtic languages." Gradually the kings of Scotland won the eastern Lowlands from Northumbria and the north and the west from Norway, and the languages of Scotland shook down into two—"Scots" (which the medieval Scots called "Inglis"), originally identical with the Anglian speech of northern England, and the Celtic language we know as Scottish Gaelic. The former was spoken and written in the Lowlands, the latter in central, western, and northern Scotland. Early Scots is thus a form of English written in Scotland by Scotsmen. But by the fifteenth century, when the phase of the language which we call Middle Scots develops, Scots has become a highly complex literary speech, used by all the Scottish writers in non-Gaelic Scotland in the golden century which produced, in the so-called "Scottish Chaucerians," Scotland's greatest poets. Scotland's struggle for independence against the English kings Edward I and Edward II at the end of the thirteenth and beginning of the fourteenth centuries had helped to mold a heterogeneous group of people into a nation and to give it a strong national feeling; while the genius of the early Stuart kings in the fifteenth century encouraged the production of a national culture. Between about 1430 and 1513, when the disastrous Battle of Flodden undid at a blow so much of the first four Stuarts' work, Scottish literature, using Middle Scots as its literary language, showed a poise, a maturity, and a national character to a degree never afterward equaled, even though the literary language survived for another century and even though in the eighteenth century a deliberate attempt was made by a handful of writers, notably Robert Fergusson and Robert Burns, to revive a native Scottish literature by drawing on the spoken Scots vernacular.

The Scottish literature we are concerned with here is that written in Early and Middle Scots; Scottish Gaelic literature belongs to the Celtic world and has no place in a history of this kind. (At the risk of confusing the reader, it must be repeated that Middle Scots was called "Inglis" by those who wrote in it, and "Scottis" was the name they gave to Gaelic.) Much medieval Scottish literature has not survived: many tales, romances, and popular poems exist as titles only, listed in *The Complaint of Scotland* (1549), while Dunbar's "Lament for the Makars," probably written about 1500, mentions many poets whose works have not come down to us. The earliest name in Scottish literature is Thomas the Rhymer, or Thomas of Ercildoune, who is supposed to have lived in the thirteenth century and to have written a romance, *Sir Tristrem;* the existing northern romance of that title (mentioned in Chapter 2) used to be attributed to Thomas. But he is altogether too shadowy a figure to be able to move clearly from the world of mythology into that of history. As we have noted, early Scots represents the same form of Middle English that was spoken in the northern half of England, and any romance written in the northern form of Middle English before the fifteenth century might as easily have been written in Scotland as in England. No separate discussion of Scottish metrical romances is therefore necessary, even though diligent Scottish historians have found a distinctively Scottish tone in some of them. They belong to the general medieval cycles of romance, and their language is a northern form of English. Even John Barbour (ca. 1320–95), whose historical metrical romance *Bruce* deals in a patriotic spirit with recent Scottish history, is not yet writing in a language or a tradition distinctively Scottish. But Barbour's feeling and manner are distinctively Scottish. Though his form is that of the romance, he is writing history, of the trials and achievements of a Scottish hero who won through against overwhelming odds, regaining his country's independence from England. The spirit is more heroic than romantic, suggesting more the *chansons de geste* than the later courtly French romances. Barbour writes to preserve the memory of great deeds:

> I wald fain set my will
> Gif my wit micht suffice theretil,
> To put in writ a soothfast story
> That it last aye furth in memory,
> Sa that na time of length it let,
> Na gar it wholly be forget.   [gar: make, cause]

Barbour tells his story with vigor and precision, and his accounts of combats are done with carefully selected details. The patriotic note is sounded throughout, and the theme of freedom occasionally breaks to the surface as in the famous outburst:

> A! fredome is a noble thing.
> Fredome maiss man to have liking:
> Fredome all solace to man givis:
> He livis at ease that freely livis. . . .

The *Bruce* makes a very respectable beginning to a national literature.

Andrew Wyntoun's *Oryginale Chronykil of Scotland*, written about 1400, is versified history (in Barbour's octosyllables) of no great literary interest, but Blind Harry's *Wallace*, celebrating the earlier hero of the Scottish War of Independence, is a romance which has none of Barbour's claims to historical accuracy. Blind Harry is only a name, traditionally associated with the *Wallace*. The poem, in decasyllabic couplets, was written in the latter part of the fifteenth century; it treats Wallace as a popular hero, and the narrative is full of life and variety, though metrically somewhat plodding. This is an unsophisticated art, and its appeal lies in the very naïveté with which character is described and the story unfolded. It long retained popularity in Scotland, and an early eighteenth-century version in later Scots was avidly read, with violently patriotic enthusiasm, by the young Robert Burns.

The achievement and prestige of Chaucer naturally had its influence on the Scottish writers of the fifteenth century, but it is an influence that has often been overestimated. Of the so-called "Scottish Chaucerians"—King James I (if he really was the author of *The Kingis Quair*), Robert Henryson, William Dunbar, Gavin Douglas—only the first can be properly called Chaucerian; the others, while of course they learned from Chaucer, worked in a European context with differing degrees of individual genius. *The Kingis Quair* ("The King's Book") is the story, told in the first person, of how James I of Scotland, when a prisoner in England, saw and fell in love with Lady Jane Beaufort, who later became his wife. Born in 1394, James was captured at sea by the English in 1406 and kept as a virtual prisoner in England until 1423, when he married Jane Beaufort, niece of the powerful Duke of Exeter and of his equally powerful brother the Bishop of Winchester, and returned to Scotland as a result of a Scottish-English settlement. *The Kingis Quair* is attributed to James in the only extant manuscript of the poem, dating from the late fifteenth century and thus written some seventy years after the poem was presumably composed, but whether it is actually by him is doubtful. The mingling of Scottish and English forms in the language of *The Kingis Quair* may represent the language of a Scot who spent seventeen years of his life in England, but it may even more plausibly be taken to be language of a Scottish poet who was consciously imitating Chaucer. The poem, in rhyme royal stanzas (hence the adjective "royal"), opens with a picture of the poet sleepless in bed, taking up Boethius to read and led by his reading to reflect on the uncertainties of fortune. He thinks

how, unlike Boethius (who fell from high to low estate), he himself found fortune first his foe and then his friend. (This makes clear
that the poem, whether by James or not, must have been written
after James had been freed from his imprisonment, for he is referring to the change from his years of imprisonment to his later
state as a free man and a successful lover.) As he muses, dawn comes,
and he hears the matins bell ring; the bell seems to say to him: "Tell
on, man, what thee befell." So he proceeds to tell his story. First he
gives an account of how he sees the beautiful Jane Beaufort from
his prison window and immediately falls in love with her: there are
clear reminiscences here of the imprisoned knights falling in love
with Emily in Chaucer's *Knight's Tale*. Then he has a vision in
which his spirit is transported above to "the glad empire of blissful
Venus." He has an interview with Venus, in which he seeks her
aid; she sends him to Minerva, who gives encouraging advice, and
then his spirit descends again to a pleasant river bank "enbroudin
all with fresche flouris gay" where he beholds a great variety of
animals and eventually finds Fortune and her wheel. Fortune instructs him how to climb, and then he awakes. The poem ends with
expressions of thankfulness for his present happiness.

The Kingis Quair is a conventional poem in a medieval mode which
was common throughout Europe. Its style and language owe something to Chaucer and to Lydgate (though the author mentions only
Chaucer and Gower as "my maisteris dere" in his concluding stanza).
But in spite of the use of common conventions and the echoes of
other writers, the poem has a freshness and an individuality that set
it apart from the majority of medieval dream allegories in the Rose
tradition. Whether or not this is an autobiographical poem written
by King James, the personal touch is real and vivid, and the use of
this poetic form to tell a story of individual courtship gives a new
turn to the courtly love tradition. Though *The Kingis Quair* was not
the first poem to link courtly love with marriage, it was the first to do
so in this concrete and detailed way. The sense of agitation that overcomes him on seeing the lady from his window is conveyed in a
stanza at once stylized and realistic:

> And in my hede I drewe ryght hastily.
> > And eftsones I lent it forth ageyne,
> And sawe hir walk, that verray womanly,
> > With no wight mo bot onely women tueyne.
> > Than gan I studye in myself and seyne,
> > 'A! suete, ar ye a wardly crëatúre,
> > Or hevinly thing in likeness of natúre?'

The fluctuations of emotion are conveyed with a wry vigor; the usual references to classical gods and goddesses have a certain sprightliness; the descriptions of flowers and animals and fishes in the scene by the river are both formal and vivid:

> That full of lytill fischis by the brym,
>   Now here, now there, with bakkis blewe as lede,
> Lap and playit, and in a rout can swim   [can: did]
>   So prattily, and dressit tham to sprede   [dressit: addressed]
>   Thair curall fynnis, as the ruby rede,   [curall: coral]
> That in the sonne on thair scalis bryght
> As gesserant ay glitterit in my sight.   [gesserant: shining mail]

The list of heraldic animals, with its "There saw I" formula deriving originally from Statius, has its unexpected touches, such as the line that reads:

> The lytill squerell, full of besyness.

The Kingis Quair has neither Chaucer's metrical cunning nor his complex of ironic and sympathetic attitudes; it is perhaps basically a literary exercise by an amateur; but in its handling of detail in describing both inward states and external scenes it is curiously appealing.

Robert Henryson is the first Middle Scots poet with the range and artistry to achieve major stature. Little is known of his life; he was schoolmaster at Dunfermline, and was born in the first half of the fifteenth century, and he was dead by 1508, when Dunbar's "Lament for the Makars," which refers to him as dead, was first printed. Henryson's *Fables* (most, but not all, out of Aesop) are narrative poems done with humor and verve and a flexible handling of the rhyme royal stanza. The humor is not Chaucer's; it is based more on the accurate placing of realistic detail; but Henryson does use Chaucer's trick of giving pretentious language to animals, with ironic effect, as in the tale of the town mouse and the country mouse, where the town mouse sniffs disdainfully at her sister's rustic fare:

> 'My fair sister' (quod scho), 'have me excusit.
> This rude dyat and I can not accord.
> To tender meit my stomok is ay usit,
> For quhylis I fair alsweill as ony Lord.   [quhylis: at times]
> Thir wydderit peis, and nuttis, or thay be bord, [wydderit: withered]
>
> Wil brek my teith, and mak my wame fful sklender,
> Quhilk was before usit to meities tender.'   [quhilk: which]

The country mouse visits the town mouse's rich home, and the two sisters enjoy a splendid feast in the pantry, though the country mouse cannot help asking suspiciously:

> 'Ye, dame' (quod scho), 'how lang will this lest?'

They eat and drink and sing "haill yule, haill!" until their festivities are interrupted by the entry into the pantry of the steward, on which

> They taryit not to wesche, as I suppose.   [wesche: wash]

The country mouse has scarcely recovered from her shock and terror, when Gib the cat enters, and she escapes from him with difficulty. And so she leaves, flinging a last word to her urban sister:

> Almichtie God, keip me fra sic ane ffeist!

All this is more than "pawky" Scottish humor: there is a counter-pointing of formal and colloquial elements which marks the mature artist and an ease in handling of the verse which is far removed from the mechanical doggerel so common among English poets in the century after Chaucer.

"The Cock and the Fox" tells the same story as Chaucer tells in his Nun's Priest's tale, and again the tone and style are Henryson's own, though of course he owes something to Chaucer. The fox talks to the cock of the cock's father:

> Off craftie crawing he micht beir the Croun,
> For he wad on his tais stand and craw.   [tais: toes]
> This was na le; I stude beside and saw.   [na le: no lie]

The force and precision of "I stude beside and saw" are typical of Henryson's narrative style. Or consider this stanza from "The Fox and the Wolf," where the Fox is making his confession to Friar Wolf:

> 'Art thow contrite, and sorie in thy Spreit
> For thy trespas?' 'Na, Schir, I can not duid: [duid: do it]
> Me think that hennis ar sa honie sweit,
> And Lambes flesche that new are lettin bluid;
> For to repent my mynd can not concluid,
> Bot off this thing, that I haif slane sa few.'
> 'Weill' (quoth the Wolff), 'in faith, thow art ane schrew.'

Some of the material in these thirteen *Fables* comes from the medieval Reynard cycle and the majority of the stories themselves come from Aesop, probably the Latin version of the Englishman Walter (Gualterus Anglicus). But the handling throughout is artful and original. Henryson appends a "Moralitas" to the end of each

fable, where the simple didacticism (as well as the genuine piety) of
the schoolmaster replaces the humorous vivacity of the storyteller:
the fables themselves, however, are complete without these dull
appendages.

Henryson's most sustained and serious work is his narrative poem,
The Testament of Cresseid, which continues Chaucer's story to tell
of Cressida's end. Here he handles rhyme royal with much greater
weight than in the *Fables;* the verse moves with impressive gravity
against a clearly visualized realistic background, and there rises as
the story proceeds a deep note of compassion, always characteristic of
Henryson, very different from Chaucer's quizzical irony. The poem
opens with a description of the poet trying to keep himself warm on
a winter evening: it is a powerful and precise picture, reminding us
that the Scottish medieval poets were the first in Europe to move
away from the idealized Mediterranean setting of so much European
literature and treat realistically of nature as they knew it. Indeed,
Henryson accepts his own country, its manners, climate, and social
customs, as a natural background for his poetry to a degree unique
among medieval poets. *The Testament of Cresseid* opens with no
formal rose garden, but with a vivid winter scene:

> The Northin wind had purifyit the Air
> And sched the mistie cloudis fra the sky,
> The froist freisit, the blastis bitterly
> Fra Pole Artick come quhisling loud and schill,
> And causit me remufe agains my will.

The poet sits at home huddled over a fire, and cheers himself up with
a drink and a book:

> I mend the fyre and beikit me about,   [beikit: warmed]
> Than tuik ane drink my spreitis to comfort,   [spreitis: spirits]
> And armit me weill fra the cauld thairout;
> To cut the winter nicht and mak it schort,
> I tuik ane Quair, and left all uther sport,
> Writtin be worthie Chaucer glorious,
> Of fair Creisseid, and worthie Troylus.

And so he goes on to tell the sequel of the story Chaucer told. It is
done with gravity and tenderness, with sharp realistic touches and a
quiet eloquence. Cressida, smitten with leprosy, leaves her father to
enter the leper house:

> Quhen thay togidder murnit had full lang,   [murnit: mourned]
> Quod Cresseid: "Father, I wald not be kend.   [kend: known]
> Thairfor in secreit wyse ye let me gang

> Into yone Hospitall at the tounis end.
> And thidder sum meit for Cheritie me send
> To leif upon, for all mirth in this eird   [leif: live]
> Is fra me gane, sic is my wickit weird."   [weird: destiny; sic: such]

She goes out, with her cup and clapper, and on entering the hospital she lay "in ane dark Corner of the Hous allone" and made her lament. The lament is a formal complaint, effectively using the *ubi sunt* theme. The climax of the poem is handled with a beautiful restraint. Cressida goes out to beg with the other lepers, and Troilus, at the head of a company of Trojan knights, rides by.

> Than upon him scho kest up baith hir Ene,
> And with ane blenk it come into his thocht   [blenk: look]
> That he sumtime hir face befoir had sene.
> But scho was in sic plye he knew hir nocht,   [plye: plight]
> Yit than hir luik into his mynd it brocht
> The sweit visage and amorous blenking
> Of fair Cresseid sumtyme his awin darling.

He gives alms to the lepers and Cressida, when she discovers who he is, falls into a swoon. On recovering, she prepares for death, bequeathing her body to worms, her cup and clapper and money to her fellow lepers, and the ring she had got from Troilus back to him again. When, on her death, Troilus receives his legacy, his heart nearly bursts for sorrow, and he says:

> "I can no moir;   [moir: more]
> Scho was untrew, and wo is me thairfore."   [scho: she]

> Sum said he maid ane Tomb of Merbell gray,
> And wrait her name and superscriptioun,   [wrait: wrote]
> And laid it on hir grave quhair that scho lay,
> In goldin Letteris, conteining this ressoun:
> "Lo, fair Ladyis, Crisseid, of Troyis toun,
> Sumtyme countit the flour of Womanheid,
> Under this stane, lait Lipper, lyis deid."

The superb restraint of this ending marks perhaps Henryson's finest achievement as an artist.

Something of the same quiet gravity is seen in Henryson's *Orpheus and Eurydice*, especially in the complaint of Orpheus, with its musical refrain

> Quhair art thou gone, my love Euridices.

Robene and Makyne is a lively pastoral ballad of great charm, suggesting the old French *pastourelle*. Among his other poems, *The*

Bludy Serk (Shirt), a religious allegory done with vividness and power, is the most impressive. Henryson has not Chaucer's range or complexity, but within his own fairly wide limits he is a literary artist of great skill and integrity.

William Dunbar (ca. 1460–ca. 1520) is a very different poetic character. A brilliant and versatile craftsman, in whose hands Middle Scots became a virtuoso instrument, he was also a man of powerful original personality who imposed his own character, with a vigor that is sometimes startling, on everything he wrote. He of course knew the work of Chaucer and Gower and Lydgate, paying tribute to the first as "rose of rethoris [eloquent writers] all" and referring to the "sugurit lippis and tongis aureate" of the other two; but he is no disciple of any of them. The vitality and originality of his work is in startling contrast to the plodding dullness of so much fifteenth-century English poetry. In his verse we see with an almost Hogarthian vividness the life of late fifteenth-century Edinburgh—the court of James IV and his Queen at Holyrood, the jostling for benefices among the clergy, the activities of merchants and lawyers, all the teeming activities of nobility, churchmen, and citizenry. Dunbar's portraits of Edinburgh life are unique in medieval literature, not only for their variety and brilliance of detail, or for the verbal craftsmanship and manipulation of innumerable stanza forms which they display, but also for their complex counterpointing of secular and religious, of the relish of surface color combined with the somber underlying sense of the transience of all earthly things and the ultimate relation of everything to the Passion of Christ. A Court poet and a rollicking abuser of the Court, a highly personal poet who draws on his own shifting moods and experiences to find themes for his verses and at the same time a poet with a profound sense of the conventions of medieval literature, a poet very much of his own time and country who nevertheless draws heavily on Latin and French elements to construct a poetic language which is almost an international medium and yet powerfully Scottish, a Goliardic poet full of rollicking wit and sometimes of outrageous obscenity and a devotional poet whose richly echoing religious poems chime hauntingly across the centuries —these are some of the paradoxes of Dunbar's character. If he lacks Henryson's gentleness and quietly ironic sympathy, he has a range and a virtuosity beyond Henryson's.

In his most formal poetry Dunbar employed an "aureate" Scots drawing directly on Latin for the weightier part of its vocabulary (Latin was of course the scholarly language of Europe and one of the literary languages of Scotland at this time). In set pieces like "The Thrissil and the Rois" (written to celebrate the marriage of James IV

of Scotland to Margaret Tudor of England in 1503) he employs the
medieval Rose tradition—the May morning, the dream, and the rest
of it—with an accent of his own. "The Goldyn Targe," in some respects his most ambitious poem, is a dream allegory in which the
aureation of the language achieves a very special effect:

> Ryght as the stern of day begouth to schyne   [stern: star]
> Quhen gone to bed war Vesper and Lucyne,   [begouth: began]
>   I rais and by a rosere did me rest;   [rosere: rose garden]
> Up sprang the goldyn candill matutyne,
> With clere depurit bemes cristallyne,   [depurit: purified]
>   Glading the mery foulis in thair nest;
>   Or Phebus was in purpur cape revest   [or: before]
> Up raise the lark, in hevyns menstrale fyne
> In May, in till a morrow myrthfullest.

The Latin words here slow down the pace of the verse and provide
an apt gravity for this serious didactic poem. But the effect is quite
different from that obtained by aureation in his religious lyrics, as in
"Ane Ballat of our Lady":

> Hale, sterne supernel Hale, in eterne,
>   In Godis sicht to schyne!
> Lucerne in derne for to discerne   [lucerne in derne: lamp
>   Be glory and grace devyne;   in darkness; be: by]
> Hodiern, modern, sempitern,
>   Angelicall regyne!   [queen of angels]
> Our tern infern for to dispern
>   Helpe, rialest rosyne.
>   *Ave Maria, gracia plena!*
> Haile, fresche floure femynyne!
> Yerne us, guberne, virgin matern [yerne: move; guberne: govern]
>   Of reuth baith rute and ryne.   [both root and stream of pity]

It is a remarkable achievement to have constructed a Scots language
in which a Latin line can take its place naturally. But this is more
than a cleverly chiming use of words. The note of ritual celebration
and the note of appeal, of beseeching, are sounded simultaneously.
The macaronic tradition in medieval religious poetry is here given a
new meaning and purpose.

The same poet can write begging letters to the king (with a variety
of refrains—"my painful purse so prickles me," "your Grace beseech
I of remeid," "excess of thought does me mischief," and many
others); or purely "occasional" poems like that on his headache or the
"Meditatioun in Wynter" with its fine evocation of a medieval northern winter:

> In to thir dirk and drublie dayis,   [drublie: wet]
> Qhhone sabill all the hevin arrayis   [when sable covers all
>   With mystie vapouris, cluddis, and skyis,   the heavens]
>   Nature all curage me denyis
> Off sangis, ballattis, and of playis. . . .

He can reflect wryly on the difficulty of knowing how to conduct himself in a censorious world:

> How sould I rewill me or in quhat wys,   [rewill: rule]
> I wad sum wyse man wald devys;
> Sen I can leif in no degre,   [leif: live]
> Bot sum my maneris will dispys.
> Lord God, how sould I governe me?

The poem continues for ten stanzas, each with the same refrain ("Lord God, how sould I governe me?"), the poet mocking (or half-mocking) himself as well as the society he lives in. Dunbar is a great master of the refrain, using it for every purpose from low humor to sublimity, and often combining self-mockery with serious irony.

His poems addressed to the King show an attitude both familiar and respectful: many of them are petitions (for most of his life Dunbar sought in vain for ecclesiastical preferment) in which general moral advice is combined with personal reproof or specific requests, with every variety of humor, irony, or mock humility. Many of these petitionary poems have titles suggesting that they are concerned with general moral problems—"Of Discretion in Asking," "Of Discretion in Geving," "None May Assure in this Warld"—and it is fascinating to watch how Dunbar counterpoints the general and the particular. He can write a humorous "Welcome to the Lord Treasurer," a self-deprecating "Petition of the Gray Horse, Auld Dunbar," a general "Complaint to the King," a charmingly complimentary poem of new year greeting to the King, a brilliantly rollicking account "Of a Dance in the Quenis Chalmir," a complaint addressed to the Queen against James Dog, the keeper of her wardrobe, with the refrain "Madame, ye haff a dangerous Dog!" followed by another poem about the same James Dog when he had got from him what he wanted, with the refrain this time "He is na Dog; he is a Lam." He satirizes every kind of abuse at Court, at the law-courts, and among the shopkeepers in poems packed with life and color. His "Dance of the Sevin Deidly Synnis," in a fast moving twelve-line stanza, is both brilliantly pictorial and full of movement, one of the most impressive and original renderings of this common medieval theme. His vivid account of the war between the soutars (shoemakers) and the tailors, in a similar stanza, has the same speed and vivid handling of detail;

it is followed by an "amends" to the tailors and soutars for the satire on them in a much simpler stanza beginning

> Betuix twell houris and ellevin,
> I dremed ane angell came fra Hevin
> With plesand stevin sayand on hie,   [stevin: voice;
> Teylouris and Sowtaris, blist be ye.   sayand: saying]

The refrain, "Taylors and Soutars blest be ye" runs with grave irony throughout the ten stanzas of the poem. Dunbar could use the medieval dream convention for every purpose from stately compliment to private feuding. His roistering "flyting" (poetic warfare—a tradition in Scots poetry) with Kennedy, with its rich and varied vocabulary of abuse and its rapid movement geared cunningly to an elaborate eight-line stanza, is a masterpiece of its kind.

At first sight, one is inclined to divide Dunbar's poems into the ceremonious and the familiar, but, though it is easy to distinguish the two extremes, many of his most characteristic poems combine both notes with remarkable skill, and in that combination lies much of their appeal. He can play his own variations on every kind of traditional form—e.g., in his long narrative poem, *The Tua Mariit Wemen and the Wedo* ("The Two Married Women and the Widow") he adopts the structure of the French *chanson d'aventure* and the tone (in some degree) of the *chanson de mal mariée* to give a lusty, realistic picture of female immorality—a kind of comic parody of courtly love poetry where the love involved is mere animal lust. In this poem Dunbar uses the old alliterative verse form:

> Apon the Midsummer evin, mirriest of nichtis,
> I muvit furth allane, neir as midnicht was past,
> Besyd ane gudlie grein garth, full of gay flouris,
> Hegeit, of ane huge hicht, with hawthorne treis; . . .

In over five hundred lines of robust dialogue between the three characters Dunbar paints a picture of female animality and unscrupulousness which might have been suggested in some degree by Chaucer's Wife of Bath, but which is quite different in tone. It is typical of Dunbar that he should open the poem with a ceremonious description of the traditional midsummer evening: it is only when he proceeds to give an account of the overheard conversation of the three women that we begin to realize how far the poet is taking us from the medieval rose garden.

Dunbar's best known poem is his "Lament for the Makars" (Poets) with its haunting Latin refrain, *Timor mortis conturbat me*. But he has many poems which show the same kind of musical gravity. Of these perhaps the most powerful is his poem on the Resurrection of Christ, with its refrain *Surrexit Dominus de sepulchro:*

> Done is a battell on the dragon blak,
> Our campioun Chryst confountet hes his force;
> The yettis of hell ar brokin with a crak,   [yettis: gates]
> The signe triumphall rasit is of the croce,
> The divillis trymmillis with hiddous voce,   [divillis trymmillis: the devils
> The saulis are borrowit and to the blis can go,   tremble; borrowit:
> Chryst with his blud our ransonis dois indoce: released]
> *Surrexit Dominus de sepulchro.*

Here the imagery of chivalry is put to religious purposes ("the dragon black" is of course Satan) and the note of chivalric adventure combines with that of Christian awe and liturgical sonority to produce poetry of remarkably rich texture.

Dunbar was a great metrist, and used an extraordinary variety of stanza forms, some of which seem to be original with him. Latin hymns, Goliardic verse, the Church service (which he sometimes parodies), the various stanza forms of Provençal poetry, are only some of the many influences—Latin, English, continental—which helped to shape his richly various poetry. The influences are all assimilated into his own highly idiosyncratic personality. The lack of tenderness in his verse has put off those who expect all Scottish poetry to be like Burns at his most sentimental or at least like the gentle Henryson. But Dunbar has a good claim to be considered the finest artist among them all. It is significant that modern Scottish poets, wishing to free themselves from the sentimentalities of a debased Burns tradition, should have raised the cry: "Back to Dunbar."

Gavin Douglas (ca. 1475–1522) lived to see the confidence and vivacity of the reign of James IV give way to the depression and confusion that followed the disastrous battle of Flodden in 1513 when the King himself together with the flower of Scottish chivalry was slain fighting against the English. His poetic career belongs to the pre-Flodden period, and shows him combining medieval convention, new modes from the Italian Renaissance, metrical and verbal virtuosity, and (at times) a sharply original sensibility. *The Palice of Honour* is an elaborate dream allegory written in a tricky nine-line stanza with an exuberance of poetic properties and an exhibitionist verbal dexterity which mark the poem as a show piece. He employs aureation as Dunbar did, and his coined words help him in the difficult task of finding rhymes (which are restricted to two in each nine-line stanza). The variety of effects obtainable from a poetic diction which ranged from elaborate Latinate terms to vigorous colloquial Scots enabled Douglas to change his tone more frequently than we find in most medieval dream allegories, and contrasts between the stately and the vigorous, the richly enameled and the grotesque, musical chiming and a deliberately harsh emphatic speech, are to be found frequently. The work concludes with a "ballad of honour" in three stanzas in which the first has two internal rhymes to the line, the second three, and the third four:

> Haill, rois maist chois til clois thy fois greit micht!
> Haill, stone quhilk schone upon the throne of licht!
> Vertew, quhais trew sweit dew ouirthrew al vice, . . .[1]

King Hart is a much less elaborate allegory in a simpler eight-line stanza, dealing with the heart's (or soul's) adventures with Dame Pleasance and others: in the end, Age knocks at the gate, Youthheid and others flee, and King Hart prepares for death. It is a vigorous handling of a common medieval theme.

Douglas' most remarkable achievement was his translation of Virgil's *Aeneid* into Middle Scots rhyming couplets. This is not only a pioneer work—the earliest rendering of Virgil into any branch of the English language—but also a remarkable production in its own right. Though the impulse to render Virgil into his native literary language represents a kind of interest which it is legitimate enough to consider as part of the complex of movements we call the Renaissance (in fact, Douglas tells us that he was moved to try his hand at a genuine translation because of his annoyance with Caxton's fake version), it is because he renders Virgil so vividly in terms of the life and color of the medieval world he knew that Douglas succeeds so well. There is a precision and a vitality about Douglas's version which, if it does not give us the Tennysonian Virgil with its heavy emphasis on the "*lacrimae rerum*" side which has become the fashion since the nineteenth century, does give us a genuine epic Virgil full of strength and movement and emotional conviction. It is the epic rather than the elegiac Virgil that he gives us. Neither Scots nor English is as compact a language as Latin; expansion is inevitable, particularly in a verse rendering; and, on the whole, Douglas expands with tact and skill. The freshness and ease of movement of Douglas' rendering cannot be readily illustrated by a short extract, but here (in a slightly simplified spelling) is a passage from Book I describing Aeneas before Dido:

[1] The reader will read Middle Scots more easily if he remembers that "i" is used to lengthen the preceding vowel, as in *rois*, and "qu" or "quh" is the English "wh."

Up stude Enee, in clear licht shining fair,
Like til ane god in body and in face,
For his mother grantit her son sic grace;
His crisp hairis were plesand on to see
His favour gudly, full of fresh beautie,
Like till ane younker with twa laughand ene;
Als gracious for to behold, I wene,
As ivoire bone by craft of hand weill dicht,
Or as we see the burnist silver bricht,
Or yet the white polist marble stane shine,
When they bene circulit about with gold sa fine.
Or ever they wist, before them all in hy,
Unto the queen thus said he reverently: . . .

Equally if not more remarkable are Douglas' Prologues to the individual books, especially those to Books VII, XII, and XIII, which
give pictures respectively of winter, spring, and summer of a kind
that are not easily—if at all—paralleled in medieval literature. The
loving particularization of detail, the sense of atmosphere and landscape, with which he describes the Scottish scene at different times
of the year show both a quality of observation and a kind of *Einfühlung* that are not generally considered medieval qualities and
which are not indeed found elsewhere in European literature for
two and a half centuries. The Middle Ages did well enough with
spring—and Douglas' picture of May at the beginning of Book XII
is for this reason his least original—but for a picture of a northern
winter landscape rendered with a combination of faithful observation and moral feeling we can only turn to Douglas:

Sour bitter bubbis, and the showris snell   [bubbis: blasts]
Seemit on the sward ane similitude of hell,   [snell: keen]
Reducing to our mind, in every steid,
Ghostly shadowis of eild and grisly deid,
Thick drumly skuggis derknit so the heaven;   [drumly: turbid; skuggis:
Dim skyis oft furth warpit fearful levin,   shadows; levin: lightning]
Flaggis of fire, and mony felloun flaw,   [flaw: blast]
Sharp soppis of sleet, and of the snipand snaw.   [snipand: biting]
The dowie ditches were all donk and wait,
The low valley flodderit all with spate,
The plain streetis and every hie way
Full of flushis, dubbis, mire and clay.   [flushis, dubbis: puddles]

The effect of the description is largely cumulative, and it needs to be
quoted at length. He describes the bare moors and hillsides with

"herbis, flouris, and grasses wallowit away," the naked woods, the plight of the birds, the "puir laboureris and busy husbandmen" who "went wet and weary draglit in the fen," the sheep huddling under banks, and the domestic animals kept "by manis governance, on harvest and on simmeris purveyance." The picture concludes with an account of the East wind:

> Wide where with force so Eolus shoutis schill   [schill: shrill]
> In this congealit season sharp and chill,
> The caller air penetrative and pure   [caller: fresh]
> Dasing the blood in every creäture,
> Made seek warm stovis and bien firis hot,
> In double garment clad and wylie-coat   [wylie-coat: waistcoat]
> With michty drink, and meatis comfortive,
> Agane the stormy winter for to strive.

This is from the Prologue to Book VII; the description of a June day in the Prologue to Book XIII is equally fine. It is in descriptions like these that the full force of the native element in the Scots vocabulary can be brought out. Incidentally, Douglas was the first to call his language "Scottis" rather than "Inglis." In describing the problems of translation in his Prologue to Book I he explains:

> And yet forsooth I set my busy pain,
> As that I couth, to make it braid and plain,
> Kepand na Sudroun bot our own langáge,
> And speakis as I lernit when I was page.
> Nor yet sa clean all Sudroun I refuse
> Bot some word I pronounce as nychbour dois.
> Like as in Latin bene Greek termis some,
> So me behuvit whilom, or than be dumb,
> Some bastard Latin, French, or Inglis use,
> Where scant were Scottis; I had na other choiss.

Douglas was an assured poet, confident of his craft, blending personal experience and literary convention with conscious artistry. His allegorical work tends to be either overloaded with tricks of the trade or, conversely, pedestrian in movement if not in diction; but his *Aeneid*, with the Prologues, represents a degree of poetic art of which no poet south of the Border was capable in the century and a quarter after Chaucer.

Sir David Lindsay (ca. 1486–1555) was for more than two centuries after his death the most popular Scottish poet in Scotland, but the reason was theological rather than literary: as Allan Ramsay was to put it:

> Sir David's satires helped our nation
> To carry on the Reformation,

> And gave the scarlet dame a box
> Mair snell than all the pelts of Knox.   [snell: sharp]

The traditional view of him as an early Protestant helping by his satirical verses to expose the abuses of the Catholic Church has obscured his real interest as a Court poet deeply concerned with the state of the kingdom and projecting that concern in a great variety of ways in his poetry. Scotland after the disastrous battle of Flodden was in a state calculated to arouse concern; during the minority of the infant King James V the country was rent with divisions between pro-French and pro-English parties, and the glories of James IV's reign seemed very far away indeed. Lindsay's first poem, *The Dreme*, is a dream allegory in which the plight of John the Common Weill (John Commonwealth) is exposed in that character's vivid complaint of the state of the realm:

> Allace, quod he, thow seis how it dois stand
> With me, and quhow I am disherisit
> Of all my grace, and mon pass of Scotland,   [mon pass of:
> And go, afore qhuare I was cherisit.   must leave]
> Remane I heir, I am bot perysit.   [perysit: laid waste]
> For there is few to me that takis tent   [takis tent: pay heed]
> That garris me go so raggit, rewin and rent.   [garris: makes]

He casts his eye over all the regions of Scotland and finds injustice and violence, "unthrift, sweirnes [sloth], falset, povertie, and stryfe," everywhere. The picture of a corrupted Scotland is set in a larger vision of the earth, the planets, heaven and hell, but it is the vivid detail of the descriptions of contemporary Scotland that remains in the mind, and such passages as the introductory account of the poet's January walk by the sea preceding his falling asleep and dreaming. The Complaint of John the Common Weill comes at the end of the poem, as the climax of the dream, after which the poet, awakened by the salute of guns from a newly arrived ship, takes up his pen to write of his vision and advise the young king "to rewle thy realme in unitie and peace."

Lindsay had been the King's companion and attendant when James was a small child, and as a result the relation between the two was intimate, which gives a curiously personal tone to those poems in which the poet addresses his royal master. In *The Complaynt of Schir David Lyndsay*, a spirited and attractive address to the King in easily moving octosyllabic couplets, he reminds him of their former relationship:

> I tak the Queenis Grace, thy mother,
> My lord Chanclare, and mony other, . .
> I tak thame all to beir witnys . . .

How as ane Chapman beris his pak,
I bure thy grace upon my bak,
And, sumtymes, strydlingis on my nek,
Dansand with mony bend and bek.
The first sillabis that thow did mute
Was *pa, Da Lyn:* upon the lute
Than playt I twenty spryngis, perqueir, [perqueir: by heart]
Qhhilk was gret piete for to heir.

The poem goes on to attack the King's bad advisers, but Lindsay's real purpose is to ask for money: this is a begging letter, like so many of Dunbar's poems, but its tone is more intimate than Dunbar's, full of an affectionate humor which is very different from Dunbar's wilder variety. Another poem in a similar vein is a complaint put into the mouth of Bagsche, "the Kingis auld hound"; and he has other minor satirical poems and "flytings."

The Testament of the Papyngo is a more elaborate "complaint," in the form of the last words of the King's parrot. It is a highly colored poem in rhyme royal, attacking the laziness, greed, and hypocrisy of the clergy (who are birds, as are all the characters of the poem) and showing that panoramic vision of Scottish history and circumstances so characteristic of Lindsay. The moral indignation is not consistently integrated into the fabric of the poem, but there are moments of fine satiric invention and a memorable incidental elegy on James IV. An even more comprehensive didactic work is *Ane Dialog Betwuix Experience and ane Courteour*, in jogging octosyllabic couplets (with some incidental stanzaic variations), which relates the present woes of Scotland to the whole past, present, and future of the country with surprisingly little poetic life. Or at least what poetic life there is in the poem is smothered by its tedious length.

Lindsay's masterpieces are his enormously long moral-allegorical play, *Ane Satire of the Thrie Estaitis* and that lively, realistic, humorous, deftly manipulated verse tale, *The Historie of ane nobil and wailyeand squyer William Meldrum* (generally known as *Squire Meldrum*). The former is an astonishingly successful handling of an unpromising form, and herald of a Scottish drama which history was to frustrate. It was first performed in 1540 (but not with any of the texts that have survived), and was revived, in an abbreviated version, with immense success at the Edinburgh Festival in 1948. It is more than an attack on the abuses of the Church for which it was so long remembered: it is a picture of man in his moral and psychological condition and in his social and economic environment presented through allegorical figures who are at the same time lively characters behaving with a forceful individuality of a kind that illuminates rather than obscures their allegorical function. Very roughly, the plot is about Rex Humanitas (King Humanity) who, going back on his promise to amend his ways and rule well and justly, is seduced by Lady Sensuality; Flattery, Falsehood, and Deceit join the King's company, each taking new hypocritical names (Flattery, for example, calls himself Devotion). Verity reproves the King and others; Chastity laments that she is cast out; Diligence and Solace consider what can be done. The entry of Divine Correction results in the departure of Sensuality and the King's receiving Good Counsel, Verity, and Chastity. Good Counsel advises the King on his duty as a ruler, and Diligence summons the Three Estates. There follows an "interlude" concerning a Poor Man and a Pardoner, the latter a richly comic figure and at the same time an embodiment of the evils associated with his kind. Then comes the second part of the main play. But a continuation of the summary would be pointless: it sounds like a typical medieval morality, except for its length and the number of characters. The interest of *Ane Satire* lies not in its plot but in the magnificently realized detail of speech and action with which it is carried forward. Neither summary nor quotation can do justice to the verve, the color, the combination of genuine *saeva indignatio* at human vice with a relish for the follies and foibles of mankind, which characterize this work. In the second part, John the Common Weal is a central figure, and Lindsay uses him to present with pity and dignity the claims of the "common man." The play is as full of compassion as it is of humor, as full of detailed social and psychological observation as of moral generalizations. The rhyming couplets (varying from octosyllables to decasyllables) give way on occasion to other verse forms; but everything *moves*, and though the plot is too diffuse for the play to hang together as a tightly knit unity, and the verse too simple to achieve anything like the overtones of poetic statement that Elizabethan poetic drama is capable of, the projection of a vision of man, in terms which allow both the liveliest humor and the deepest moral feeling, is achieved.

For *Squire Meldrum* one can make no such claim; it is an altogether less ambitious work—based on the lives of an almost contemporary couple—done with complete success. It represents the medieval romance brought down to earth, as it were, with traditional chivalric and modern realistic elements neatly counterpointed. The modern reader may peruse its sprightly octosyllables with Butler's *Hudibras* in his mind—somehow, it is difficult to resist thinking of

Hudibras when reading *Squire Meldrum*—but in fact its tone is wholly different, not mocking or satirical, but humorous in an interested and friendly way. Altogether, it is a rather unexpected poem to find at the end of Scottish medieval literature.

Of anonymous medieval Scottish poetry outside the ballads, the most characteristic are poems which show the conventional situations of the European lyrical forms sharpened and localized by a colorful realism, such as "The Wowing of Jok and Jynny" and two accounts of popular festivities, "Christis Kirk on the Grene" and "Peblis to the Play." These last two poems have been attributed both to James I and James V, more plausibly to the latter, and they represent a tradition which has never really died out in Scottish literature, though it has suffered some strange mutations.

The Reformation came to Scotland more violently than it came to England and it disrupted the national culture to a far greater degree. A sign of the times was that remarkable collection of poems known as the *Gude and Godlie Ballatis*, of which the earliest surviving edition belongs to 1567, but which had very probably appeared in earlier editions in the 1540's. This is a Protestant work, Lutheran in tone, divided into four sections, of which the first is a Catechism, both in prose and in verse, the second a group of sixteen "spiritual sangis," the third "certaine ballatis of the Scripture," and the fourth "The Psalmes of David with uthir new Pleasand Ballatis." Some of the poems in the collection are translations of Lutheran hymns, and there are traces of Danish and Swedish as well as French influence. The tone of some of the verses in the first part is reminiscent of modern Negro spirituals:

> Moyses upon the mount Sinay,
> With the great God spak face for face,
> Fastand and prayand but delay,   [but: without]
> The tyme of fourtie dayis space.
> O God be mercyfull to us.

The "spiritual sangis" contain poems based on medieval hymns and carols (e.g., "To us is borne a bairne of bliss" and "In dulci jubilo") as well as hymns of Lutheran origin ("Faithful in Christ, use your riches richt") and others which sound a more individual note, for example:

> Richt soirly musing in my mynde,
> For pitie soir my hart is pynde,   [pynde: pained]
> Quhen I remember on Christ sa kynde,
>   that savit me:
> Nane culd saif from Thyle till Ynde,
>   bot only He.

But by far the most interesting section is that containing the "new Plesand Ballatis," which have been, significantly, "changit out of prophane ballatis in godlie sangis for avoydance of sin and harlatrie." Here popular songs have been made over into religious poems, sometimes successfully, sometimes with ludicrous results. It is not difficult to see what has happened in this song:

> Johne, cum kis me now,
> Johne, cum kis me now;
> Johne, cum kis me by and by
> And mak no moir adow.

> The Lord thy God I am,
> That Johne dois thee call;
> Johne representit man,
> By grace celestiall.

Sometimes the transformation of a secular song into a religious poem is remarkably successful:

> All my Lufe, leif me not,
>> Leif me not, leif me not;
> All my Lufe, leif me not,
>> Thus myne alone:
> With ane burding on my bak,   [burding: burden]
> I may not beir it I am sa waik;
> Lufe, this burding from me tak,
>> Or ellis I am gone.

The antipapal note is sometimes sounded, and when this is combined with the rollicking chorus of the original popular song, the result is curious:

> The Paip, that pagane full of pryde,   [Paip: Pope]
>> He hes us blindit lang;
> For quhair the blind the blind dois gyde,
>> Na wonder baith ga wrang:
> Lyke prince and king he led the ring
>> Of all iniquitie:
> Hay trix, tryme go trix,
>> Under the grene wod-tree.

The best are often the simplest, such as

> Go, hart, unto the Lamp of licht,
>> Go, hart, do service and honoúr;
> Go, hart, and serve him day and nicht,
>> Go, hart unto thy Savioúr.

And the simple substitution of God or Christ for the name of the lover can change a love lyric into a religious poem of considerable appeal:

> All my hart, ay this is my sang,
> With doubill mirth and joy amang;
> Sa blyith as byrd my God to sang:
> Christ hes my hart ay.

It is clear that the Reformers, for all their zeal against the drama and against popular entertainments and their suspicion of most secular imaginative literature, had ears and voices of their own.

The question of religion in Scotland was not to be settled until the end of the seventeenth century, and between 1560 and 1689 the country was frequently torn apart by civil and religious conflict. The death of James V in 1542, after a second disastrous defeat of a Scottish army by the English, left Scotland with an infant Queen and quarreling religious and political parties. A Parliament summoned without the proper royal authority in 1560 implemented John Knox's views and established the reformed faith in Scotland. The following year young Mary Queen of Scots, who had been brought up in France, arrived in Scotland to begin her troubled and tragic reign. Her arrival was celebrated by Alexander Scott in a poem entitled "Ane New Yeir Gift to the Quene Mary, Quhen scho come first hame." After welcoming the Queen, Scott proceeds to give her lengthy advice about reverencing the "true kirk" (Scott was a reformer, though a moderate one), founding her reign on the four cardinal virtues of wisdom, justice, fortitude, and temperance, punishing wicked and unchaste pastors, righting the wrong of the poor, and making all the estates of the realm attend to their proper business, to end with an elaborately chiming alliterative stanza of compliment and greeting:

> Fresch, fulgent, flurist, fragrant flour formois,[Flurist: flourishing;
> Lantern to lufe, of ladeis lamp and lot,   formois: beautiful]
> Cherie maist chaist, cheif charbucle and chois;
> Smaill sweit smaragde, smelling but smit of smot: [smaragde:
>   emerald: but smit of smot: without trace of stain]
> Noblest natour, nurice to nurtour; note
> This dull indyte, dulce dowble dasy deir,
> Send be thy sempill servand Sanderris Scott: [send be: sent by]
> Greting grit god to grant thy grace gude yeir.

This aureate and artful language is in the tradition of the fifteenth-century Scottish poets, though its virtuosity is more deliberately precious than that of Henryson or even Dunbar. We know little about Alexander Scott's life: most of his poetry is found in the Bannatyne Manuscript (the collection made by George Bannatyne in 1568, which preserves so much medieval Scottish poetry), and so must have been written before 1568. He is a musical and craftsman-like lyrist who wrote songs for Court airs and verses in accepted lyric stanzas, a poet who obviously leans rather heavily on the tradition in which he is writing, taking from it rather more than he gives to it; but he *is* in a tradition, and this gives his art both grace and confidence. He can sing to May in the medieval mode:

> O lusty May, with flora quene,
> The balmy dropis frome Phebus schene,   [schene: beautiful]

or musically lament his parting from his love:

> Departe, departe, departe,
> Allace! I most departe,
> From hir that hes my hart,
> With hairt full soir,
> Againis my will indeid,
> And can find no remeid,
> I wait the panis of deid
> Can do no moir.

Many of his love poems are delicately wrought, revealing not only a cunning ear but also a personal feeling both deep and gentle. He can also be vigorously satirical (as in "Ane ballat maid to the derisioun and scorne of wantoun wemen") and amusingly mock-heroic, as in the lively "Iusting and debait up at the Drum, Betuix W^a Adamsone and Johnie Sym."

Scott was a Court poet, and it must be remembered that Scotland continued to have a Court until Mary's son, James VI, went south in 1603 to become James I of England. Some of the other Court poets of the first half of the sixteenth century may be represented among the anonymous lyrics of the Bannatyne manuscript. James VI took a scholar's interest in poetry: one of his tutors was George Buchanan, known throughout Europe as a poet and dramatist in Latin. James wrote an essay on the technique of writing Scottish poetry, he translated some French and other poetry, and he produced passable verses himself. The chief poet of his Court was his friend William Montgomerie (ca. 1545–ca. 1611), whose remarkable long poem *The Cherry and the Slae* is one of the latest and most original handlings of the medieval Rose tradition. The complex musical stanza in which this poem is written was to be revived in the eighteenth century with interesting results. Here is the first of the poem's 114 stanzas:

> About ane bank, quhair birdis on bewis   [bewis: boughs]
> Ten thousand tymis thair notis renewis

> Ilke houre into the day: [ilke: every]
> The Merle and Mavis micht be sene,   [Merle, Mavis:
> The Progne and the Phelomene,   blackbird, thrush]
> Quhilk caussit me to stay:
> I lay and leynit me to ane bus,   [bus: bush]
> To heir the birdis beir,   [beir: song]
> Thair mirth was sa melodius,
> Throw nature of the yeir:
>   Sum singing, sum springing,
>   With wingis into the sky:
>   So trimlie, and nimlie,
>   Thir birdis they flew me by.

The poem, in its elaborate and leisurely way, seems to have as its central theme an argument as to whether the poet should pursue the perfect and perhaps unattainable cherry or be content with the more ordinary sloe, but the arguments, moralizings, and "pithy" apothegms of abstract characters such as Hope, Experience, Courage, and Reason take the poem far from this simple debate between two possible objects of love, though where precisely they take it is not easy to discover. The fascinating stanza in which the poem is written is first found in a poem entitled "The Bankis of Helicon," which may also be by Montgomerie, who may have invented the stanza on this occasion (it goes to a tune of the same name). King James, in his *Reulis and Cautelis to be observit and eschewit in Scottis Poesie*, discussed "all kyndis of cuttit and brokin verse, whairof new formes are daylie inventit according to the Poetes pleasure," and Montgomerie was apparently one of those who "inventit" them according to his pleasure.

Another elaborate and musical stanza is that employed by Montgomerie in his poem "The Solsequium" (marigold):

> Like as the dumb solsequium, with care ourcome
>   Dois sorrow, when the sun goes out of sicht,
> Hings doun his head, and droops as dead, nor will not spread,
>   Bot locks his leaves through languor all the nicht,
>   Till foolish Phaeton rise
>   With whip in hand,
>   To purge the crystal skyis
>   And licht the land.
> Birds in their bour waitis for that hour
>   And to their prince ane glaid good-morrow givis;
> Fra then, that flour list not till lour,
>   Bot laughis on Phoebus loosing out his leavis.
> So stands with me, except I be where I may see
>   My lamp of licht, my lady and my luve; . . .

The stanza conveys a musical gravity which fits perfectly with the poem's mood. Montgomerie also wrote sonnets, metrical versions of psalms, and love lyrics in a variety of stanza forms. He engaged in a "flyting," too, the "Flyting of Montgomerie and Polwart," which has the comic exuberance of its kind. Such graceful love songs as "Sweet hairt, rejoice in mind" are rather like Alexander Scott's in the same vein. Montgomerie was a Court poet and song writer, and much of his best work consists of song lyrics written in a European courtly tradition. Scots poetry was still very much in the orbit of European culture.

Of the other Scottish poets of the period, John Stewart of Baldynnis (ca. 1550–ca. 1605) is an interesting craftsman who produced an abridged version of *Orlando Furioso* in decasyllabic quatrains and a considerable amount of technically interesting verse, including the charming "Of Ane Symmer House"; William Fowler (1562–1612), a versatile poet whose best work is contained in his sequence of sonnets called *The Tarantula of Love*—some of these have a quiet gravity and control that is impressive; and Mark Alexander Boyd (1563–1601), a shadowy figure who wrote in Latin, Greek, and French and produced one remarkable sonnet in Scots, "Fra bank to bank, fra wood to wood I rin." These were all writers of Court verse, untouched by the fiercer moods of the Presbyterians. But there were Presbyterian poets who did more than produce metrical versions of the Psalms. Alexander Hume (ca. 1560–1609), Presbyterian minister, deliberately set out to write a more serious kind of poetry than the Court poets were capable of. "In princes' Courts," he wrote in the preface to his *Hymns or Sacred Songs* (1599), "in the houses of greate men, and at the assemblies of yong gentilmen and yong damosels, the chief pastime is to sing prophane sonnets, and vaine ballads of love, or to rehearse some fabulous faits of Palmerine, Amadis, or such like raveries." The serious and devotional lyrics he wrote in his somewhat Anglicized Scots are of no great interest today; but once he succeeded in writing a well-nigh perfect poem, a limpid, beautifully modulated picture, in a simple four-line stanza, of a summer's day from dawn to dusk, entitled "Of the Day Estivall."

The Union of the Crowns in 1603 brought a change in the Scottish literary landscape. The migration of James to England, as well, of course, as the prestige and achievement of Elizabethan English poetry, encouraged the Scottish poet to try the English literary language, and the group of Scots poets at the English Court in the early part of the seventeenth century—Sir Robert Aytoun, Sir David Murray, Sir Robert Ker, Sir William Alexander—wrote exercises, sometimes skillful, sometimes stiff, in which, the whole man not being able to operate, mere convention tended to take control. William Drummond of Hawthornden (1585–1649) stayed at home, a quiet scholarly man who admired Sidney and knew, as well as the English poets, Ronsard and Tasso and Marino, not to mention Virgil and Petrarch. His love poetry is elegantly conventional in an English and not a Scottish way; sometimes, in personal elegiac or religious verse, he strikes out something more individual and complex, but in general one is inclined to agree with Ben Jonson's charge that he "smelled too much of the schools." James Graham, Marquis of Montrose (1612–50), in character and reputation something of a Scottish Philip Sidney, gave his literary and political loyalties to the English Cavalier tradition which at this time had no true equivalent in Scotland. The Court poet in Scotland had now no native center to turn to, with the result that Scottish Court poetry and music came to be transcribed and collected by individual gentlemen for their own nostalgic pleasure instead of being actively created and published. So a man like Montrose, loyal to his King and his Court, naturally turned to the Cavalier tradition in England. He wrote only a handful of poems, some of which seem to have been achieved by sheer strength of character; it is significant that, in his very last poem, written on the eve of his execution, the force of the expression demands one Scots word, "airth" (direction), on which the whole poem pivots.

Lacking the Court as a cultural center, turning more and more to England for literary inspiration, it would seem that the Scottish writer had now no choice but to accept English as his literary language, even if that involved splitting his personality in some degree (for Scots was still the *spoken* language of non-Gaelic Scotland). But the situation does not develop as simply as that. Some time in the middle of the turbulent seventeenth century there appeared a new kind of Scots poem, "The Life and Death of the Piper of Kilbarchan, or the Epitaph of Habbie Simson," by Robert Sempill of Beltrees (ca. 1595–ca. 1668). This vulgar, vigorous, rollicking poem, written for amusement by a member of the landed gentry, is not written in a literary language but in a Scots vernacular. For Scots has now become a vernacular, drawing on popular speech rather than on an artistic tradition. Sempill writes jocularly, amusingly, almost patronizingly. Here is his opening stanza:

> Kilbarchan now may say alas!
> For she hath lost both game and grace,
> Both *Trixie* and *The Maiden Trace;*   [names of tunes]
> But what remead?   [remead: remedy]

For no man can supply his place:
Hab Simson's dead.

If we put this beside a stanza by Alexander Scott or Montgomerie (not to say of Dunbar or Henryson) we see at once a difference of weight: though Scott and Sempill both use images drawn from popular speech, Scott's language is more highly charged, it has more gravity and greater reverberation. "Habbie Simson" is sprightly popular verse written for amusement by an amateur, and written in a language which by this time few educated people felt to be suitable for the highest kind of art. True, it draws on a tradition of poetry of popular revelry which earlier had produced such poems as "Christis Kirk on the Grene" and "Peblis to the Play," but it is frivolous rather than truly humorous because it does not grow out of that tradition but uses it with what almost might be called condescension. This is not to say that "Habbie Simson" is not an important poem; it is indeed important historically, both for drawing attention to the possibilities of folk humor as a way of bringing the vernacular back into current poetry and for suggesting the mock elegy as a poetic form, and for reviving an old stanza form which was to play such an important part in eighteenth-century Scottish poetry; but it lacks a dimension. The Scottish vernacular came more and more to be associated with rusticity, and Scots dialect verse, written more or less phonetically in a mood of patriotic primitivism or of music-hall humor, replaced poetry written in a full Scottish literary language in which the whole man could speak. Between Sempill of Beltrees and Burns, Scottish vernacular poetry had to learn how to be the product of the whole man, how to achieve scope and density—in short, how to recover the lost dimension.

The difference between a vernacular and a literary language is that in the latter case there is a literary tradition, arising out of the different forms of the spoken language and transcending them, which reflects back on the spoken language and gives it a steady relationship to the national culture. Once the literary tradition is broken, once there is no literary language growing out of the spoken language (however different from it it may be, and however many artificial elements may have been added), the spoken language is bound to disintegrate into a series of regional dialects. So, after the Norman Conquest of England, the central literary position of West Saxon was lost, since French replaced Anglo-Saxon as the literary language, and Middle English fell into a series of regional dialects. Only after the re-establishment of English as the literary language of England did a linguistic norm emerge and, while differences between spoken dialects persisted, the language was pulled together by the integrating force of a literary tradition. Similarly in Scotland, Middle Scots, in virtue of its literary tradition, had been a language and not a vernacular; Scots became a mere vernacular only after the literary language of most of its serious writers had ceased to be Scots. How to use the *vernacular* as a *language* in serious literature was the problem faced by the eighteenth-century Scottish poets. The problem was never permanently solved, for English remained the main language of serious expression; it was solved occasionally and temporarily, partly by happy accident, partly by the intervention of genius.

Of the ballads, one of the acknowledged glories of Scottish literature, we have spoken in an earlier chapter. Something must be said, however, of Scottish literary prose. There is not a great deal, for it developed late (as it does in any culture) and succumbed to English relatively early. Latin was the language of Scottish historians and moralists well into the fifteenth century and later. A treatise on *The Craft of Deyng* (dying), attributed to the mid-fifteenth century, is the first known piece of Scots prose that has any claim to be considered literary; it has an attractive simplicity and directness. Other Scots prose of this century seems to consist entirely of translations, such as Gilbert Hay's competent rendering of three French works on knighthood, warfare, and government and John Gau's *Richt Vay to the Kingdom of Heuine* (1533), a Protestant work from the German (via the Dutch) published in Sweden. Murdoch Nisbet based his Scots version of the New Testament on Wyclif, probably about 1530; it is of more philological than literary interest. John Bellenden (b. 1495) translated Livy and Hector Boece's Latin *History of Scotland* in the 1530's; his prose is workmanlike and unadorned. But by far the most interesting Scots prose work of the sixteenth century is *The Complaynt of Scotland*, of doubtful authorship, published apparently in Paris in 1549. It is based on a French work, *Le Quadrilogue invectif* by Alain Chartier, and the author applies to Scotland, Chartier's description of the unhappy state of his country. *The Complaynt* is dedicated to the Queen Mother, Marie of Guise, in a heavily loaded "aureate" style, which has, however, a certain stateliness and dignity. This is the most artful Scots literary prose yet to have appeared. In a prologue addressed to the reader, which follows the dedication, the author explains that he is going to proceed in a simpler language, "domestic Scottis langage, maist intelligibil for the vulgare pepil," though he explains that "it is necessair at sum tyme til myxt oure langage with part of termis drewyn fra Lateen, be rason that oure Scottis tong is nocht sa copeus as is the Lateen tong." The main part of the complaint—long and detailed—does use a simpler Scots than the aureate dedication. But the complaint is interrupted by a "Monolog Recreatif." This is a curious and most interesting section. It opens with an account of the author setting out for a walk on a summer evening; the sunset is described in meticulous detail, then night comes, and passes, and the sun rises. There follows an extraordinary description—highly mannered, yet with a certain vivid realism—of the various beasts and birds and the different noises they make on waking. Other scenes follow, and eventually we follow the author away from the seashore (where he has spent some time) inland to a company of shepherds, with whom he gets into conversation. This is a pastoral set piece. One of the shepherds discourses at length on the advantages of the rustic life, citing innumerable authorities, but at last he is interrupted in the full tide of an account of the horrible corruption of cities by his wife, who says: "My weil belovit husband, I pray thee to decist fra that tideus melancolic orison . . ." She proposes that they tell stories instead, and the proposal meets with general approval. So they tell tales and dance and sing, and the names of their tales, songs and dances are listed in a long catalogue which is one of our main sources of knowledge of the lost literature of Scotland. The author then enters a meadow, falls asleep, and continues the main burden of his complaint by means of a vision.

Lindsay of Pitscottie's *Historie and Cronicles of Scotland* (1575) is a continuation of Boece's Latin history in Scots, done with considerable liveliness and full of memorable anecdotes. By this time the Reformation had turned more and more Scotsmen's eyes away from their old ally France and toward Protestant England. The Geneva Bible was in use among many Scottish Protestants, and partly under its influence and partly as a result of a deliberate attempt to address a wider audience, Scottish prose came to adopt more and more English forms. John Knox's vigorous polemical prose shows this movement. His *History of the Reformation*, written in the 1560's but not published until 1644, uses a deliberately Anglicized Scots. The result of this was for a while that Catholic writers clung to Scots and Protestant writers used a more Anglicized written language. Ninian Winzet challenged Knox vigorously in an extremely forceful colloquial Scots prose. The ultimate victory of the Reformation in Scotland, however, together with many other factors, social, educational, and economic, altered this picture. Though the Church of Scotland (like the lawyers of Scotland) asserted its independence of England by using a forthright spoken Scots, written prose came more and more to be English, and by the middle of the seventeenth century a Scottish literary prose hardly existed. It was to be revived again only in the dialogue of certain Scottish novels; but the Scottish novel was born too late for it to provide a means for the continuation of a full Scots literary prose.

A Selected List of Mandarin Classics

While every effort is made to keep prices low, it is sometimes necessary to increase prices at short notice. Mandarin Paperbacks reserves the right to show new retail prices on covers which may differ from those previously advertised in the text or elsewhere.

The prices shown below were correct at the time of going to press.

☐	7493 1392 7	**The Good Companions**	J. B. Priestley	£7.99
☐	7493 1391 9	**Angel Pavement**	J. B. Priestley	£6.99
☐	7493 1393 5	**Lost Empires**	J. B. Priestley	£5.99
☐	7493 0658 0	**A Question of Upbringing**	Anthony Powell	£3.99
☐	7493 0656 4	**A Buyer's Market**	Anthony Powell	£3.99
☐	7493 1200 9	**What's Become of Waring?**	Anthony Powell	£5.99
☐	7493 0343 3	**The Moon and Sixpence**	Somerset Maugham	£5.99
☐	7493 0422 7	**Cakes and Ale**	Somerset Maugham	£5.99
☐	7493 0344 1	**Of Human Bondage**	Somerset Maugham	£7.99
☐	7493 0134 1	**To Kill a Mockingbird**	Harper Lee	£4.99
☐	7493 0461 8	**The Balkan Trilogy**	Olivia Manning	£9.99
☐	7493 0562 2	**School for Love**	Olivia Manning	£4.50
☐	7493 1198 3	**The Doves of Venus**	Olivia Manning	£4.99
☐	7493 1199 1	**A Romantic Hero**	Olivia Manning	£4.99
☐	7493 2052 4	**Of Mice and Men**	John Steinbeck	£4.99
☐	7493 1780 9	**The Grapes of Wrath**	John Steinbeck	£6.99
☐	7493 2047 8	**East of Eden**	John Steinbeck	£6.99

All these books are available at your bookshop or newsagent, or can be ordered direct from the address below. Just tick the titles you want and fill in the form below.

Cash Sales Department, PO Box 5, Rushden, Northants NN10 6YX.
Fax: 01933 414047 : Phone: 01933 414000.

Please send cheque, payable to 'Reed Book Services Ltd.', or postal order for purchase price quoted and allow the following for postage and packing:

£1.00 for the first book, 50p for the second; **FREE POSTAGE AND PACKING FOR THREE BOOKS OR MORE PER ORDER.**

NAME (Block letters) ....

ADDRESS ....

....

☐ I enclose my remittance for ....

☐ I wish to pay by Access/Visa Card Number

Expiry Date

Signature ....

Please quote our reference: MAND